Crime Solvability Factors

Richard Timothy Coupe ·
Barak Ariel · Katrin Mueller-Johnson
Editors

Crime Solvability Factors

Police Resources and Crime Detection

Springer

Editors
Richard Timothy Coupe
Institute of Criminology
University of Cambridge
Cambridge, UK

Katrin Mueller-Johnson
Institute of Criminology
University of Cambridge
Cambridge, UK

Barak Ariel
Institute of Criminology
University of Cambridge
Cambridge, UK

Institute of Criminology, Faculty of Law
The Hebrew University
Mount Scopus, Jerusalem, Israel

ISBN 978-3-030-17159-9 ISBN 978-3-030-17160-5 (eBook)
https://doi.org/10.1007/978-3-030-17160-5

This Springer imprint is published by the registered company Springer Nature Switzerland AG
The registered company address is: Gewerbestrasse 11, 6330 Cham, Switzerland

Contents

Contributors

Barak Ariel Institute of Criminology, University of Cambridge, Cambridge, England, UK;
Institute of Criminology, Faculty of Law, The Hebrew University of Jerusalem, Rehovot, Israel;
Institute of Criminology, Faculty of Law, The Hebrew University, Mount Scopus, Jerusalem, Israel

Richard Timothy Coupe Institute of Criminology, University of Cambridge, Cambridge, England, UK

Patrick Gerard Donnellan Greater Manchester Police, Manchester, UK

Colin Duffy iNet Telecom Ltd. (Voipfone), London, UK

Anthony Jones Metropolitan Police, Westminster, UK

Bronwyn Killmier Formerly of South Australia Police, Adelaide, SA, Australia

Katrin Mueller-Johnson Institute of Criminology, University of Cambridge, Cambridge, England, UK

Denis O'Connor Institute of Criminology, University of Cambridge, Cambridge, England, UK

Tom Olphin Institute of Criminology, University of Cambridge, Cambridge, England, UK

Colin Paine Thames Valley Police, London, UK

Rebecca Riggs Metropolitan Police, London, UK

Paul Robb Institute of Criminology, University of Cambridge, Cambridge, UK

Simon Rose Metropolitan Police Service, London, UK;
Institute of Criminology, University of Cambridge, Cambridge, England, UK

Stephanie Sharp British Transport Police, London, UK

Introduction

Richard Timothy Coupe, Barak Ariel and Katrin Mueller-Johnson

Effective and efficient crime investigation and detection complement preventive approaches in containing criminal activity. A good record on detecting crime is important for maintaining public confidence in policing services, since victims and other citizens expect culprits to be brought to justice. Policing provides deterrence through the offender's fear of being caught (von Hirsch et al. 1999)—the same threat that underlies prevention via guardianship or guardianship objects, much of which is aligned with routine activity theory (Cohen and Felson 1979). Even with existing levels of crime investigation and detection in combination with preventive approaches, crimes of all types—property, violent and sexual—persist in substantial quantities in many developed countries, not least in Australia and the UK, where most of the evidence presented in this volume originates. Preventive approaches appear unlikely to be capable of combating offending alone without effective police capacity to detect crime. Cost-effective crime investigation and detection is not merely important; it is an indispensable part of any crime reduction strategy, both directly in terms of the arrest and rehabilitation of criminals and indirectly through deterrence and enhancing perceptions of police professionalism and legitimacy.

Successful crime detection requires an understanding of which offences it is possible and not possible to solve so that investigative resources may be used to good purpose and wasted effort reduced to a minimum. Whether crimes can be detected and how easily they may be detected depends on offence solvability—how easily they may be solved and whether it is possible to solve them. Crimes possess characteristics that make them more or less solvable (Eck 1983; Brandl and Frank 1994; Greenwood and Petersilia 1975), so that cost-effective detection requires informed decisions about which cases ought to be prioritised and which investigative activities ought to have police resources allocated to them. Hence, crime detection depends on

R. T. Coupe (✉) · B. Ariel · K. Mueller-Johnson
Institute of Criminology, University of Cambridge, Cambridge, England, UK
e-mail: rtc23@cam.ac.uk

B. Ariel
Institute of Criminology, Faculty of Law, The Hebrew University of Jerusalem, Rehovot, Israel

R. T. Coupe et al. (eds.), *Crime Solvability Factors*,
https://doi.org/10.1007/978-3-030-17160-5_1

offence solvability and properly resourced investigations (Coupe 2016). Realising the potential for solving crimes depends on providing sufficient resources to meet the investigative requirements of those crimes that can be solved. Investigative requirements reflect incident solvability characteristics, and resources 'unlock' the evidence linked to solvability that results in incident detection (Coupe 2016). The alignment of resources with incident solvability therefore enables cost-effective crime detection. This volume considers the issues of which characteristics of different types of crime help predict the cases that may be detected, which investigative activities are most likely to result in positive outcomes and, hence, the prioritisation of cases for investigative effort.

The principal aim of research into crime solvability is to determine the incident characteristics that are associated with arrest, charge, detection, or case clearance, all of which indicate that an offender has been identified and caught. In predicting which incidents are most and least likely to be detected, solvability factors help inform case screening and resource allocation decisions. Currently, crime screening to select subsets of promising cases for activities at crime scenes and detectives' further investigations is based principally on officer experience (Robb et al. 2015; Robinson and Tilley 2009). Practical experience also guides decisions about whether or not a rapid patrol response would be beneficial (Coupe and Blake 2005). The findings presented in these chapters indicate that police officers' decisions about which cases to investigate and which particular activities to resource would be more accurate and cost-effective if informed by scientific measurement. At present, there are few published solvability studies, particularly those measuring how the resourcing of offences of varying solvability affects detection outcomes.

This book aims to address these shortcomings by presenting findings from a variety of applied solvability studies with high-quality police data linking offence solvability factors to detection outcomes. Its purpose is to help practitioners appreciate the benefits of complementing experience with a scientifically measured approach to investigating and solving different types of crime. It also promises to improve scholarship in incident solvability, a little-studied aspect of criminology. By examining the solvability characteristics of different offences and the ways in which they relate to detection outcomes, the following chapters provide insights into how resources should be applied to police activities for solving property, violent and sexual offences, how solvability and detections might be improved, and the ways in which solvability varies across jurisdictions.

In examining the solvability factors for property and violent crime, the volume's chapters examine the potential for detecting different types of offence, the solvability factors around which officers build investigations, and the factors that are key to solving different crimes. One aim of solvability research is to inform 'first officers' and detectives about cost-effective crime screening and related resource allocation decisions. The volume includes chapters on the solvability and detection of property offences (Chapters "Population-Level Analysis of Residential Burglaries"–"Detecting and Combating Internet Telephony Fraud") and violent, sexual and faith hate crimes (Chapters "Targeting Factors that Predict Clearance of Non-domestic Assaults"–"Reporting, Detection and Solvability of Sex Offences on

Railways"). There are chapters ("Homicide Resources, Solvability and Detection", "Investigative Activities, Resources and Burglary Detection" and "The Organisation and Deployment of Patrol Resources: Cost-Effective On-Scene Arrest at Burglaries") that consider incident solvability and the measured use of resources in different investigative stages, including patrol response, so that their relative effects on detection outcomes may be understood. The volume includes studies of less serious, high-volume crimes, such as pickpocketing (Chapter "Pickpocketing on Railways"), as well as more serious offences, including homicide (Chapter "Homicide Resources, Solvability and Detection"). A number of studies cover the solvability and detection of crimes, including offences with a variety of seriousness, such as faith hate crime (Chapter "Solvability Factors and Investigative Strategy for Faith Hate Crime: Anti-semitic and Islamophobic Assault, Criminal Damage and Public Order Offences in London"), non-domestic assaults (Chapter "Targeting Factors that Predict Clearance of Non-domestic Assaults") and sexual offences (Chapter "Reporting, Detection and Solvability of Sex Offences on Railways"). Offence solvability can change or be changed with the development of new technologies; thus, some chapters describe empirical studies of the potential to improve incident solvability by using offender–offence profiling approaches (Chapter "Offender–Offence Profiling: Improving Burglary Solvability and Detection") and by predicting repeat victimisation and harnessing security devices to entrap offenders (Chapters "Boosting Offence Solvability and Detections: Solving Residential Burglaries by Predicting Single and Multiple Repeats" and "Improving Offence Solvability and Detection Rates at Non-residential Burglary: Predicting Single and Multiple Repeat Incidence"). Chapter "Detecting and Combating Internet Telephony Fraud", on telephone fraud, illustrates the difficulties in combating electronic internet-based offending in circumstances where there is initial reliance on electronic clues and physical separation of offenders from victims or victims' property.

Change in Detection Rates

Detection rates have dropped since the mid-1990s despite a decline in total crime incidence (Blumstein and Wallman 2000), which might have been expected to improve officer resources per offence. While accurate recording has played a role in this, more activities have been criminalised, and there have been shifts in crime types and increases in the reporting of certain offences. The criminalisation of certain types of pornography and racial and faith hate crime, and the elevated reporting of domestic violence and sexual offences, can consume officer resources—the more so that the police feel obliged, often rightly, to investigate them, given either their immediacy or because of the reputational risks of failing to address them. Racial and faith hate crime incidence has risen as these offences are viewed more seriously and continuing migration to global cities situates more ethnically disparate and sometimes antagonistic groups in close proximity (Stavisky 2018). Where victims may designate offences as involving racial or faith hatred, as in England and Wales, increases in such offences have been particularly marked. Non-crime events may also take a high priority, so that, for instance, dealing with missing persons can account for 19% of one English police force's patrol officer time (Doyle 2018).

Greater offender mobility across both local and national jurisdictions appears likely to have contributed to the drop in detections. Fewer offences committed by offenders who are more mobile are solved (Lamme and Bernasco 2013), while foreign offenders committing burglary or stealing vehicles and immediately exporting stolen goods to other countries, such as Eastern European criminals operating in Scandinavia, are less easily apprehended. Similarly, in order to avoid arrest, offenders may flee to countries from which extradition can be difficult.

The rapid increase in cybercrime may not always be counted in detection figures. If it is, detection rates plummet, since cyber-offences in countries like the UK now almost match in numbers all traditional crimes and can have exceptionally low detection rates, estimated at 1 in every 600 cases in England and Wales. Most fraud cases are perpetrated electronically, and only 4% of these are solved (Robbins 2018). There is an insufficient supply of officers with the technical knowledge required to investigate these offences, and too few resources are allocated to combating them. Moreover, many electronic Web-based offences are perpetrated internationally. With offenders and victims in different national jurisdictions, poor cooperation between police forces and an absence of agreed extradition arrangements hamper investigation and detection. The issues faced under these circumstances will be examined in Chapter "Detecting and Combating Internet Telephony Fraud", which deals with Internet telephony fraud.

Reduced resourcing of UK police services since 2015 is also implicated in the sharply reduced detection rates for offences like burglary and robbery during the last few years—as low as half of the 2013 levels (Blakely 2018). The current state of detection levels and scarce resources highlights the benefits of more measured examination of how different types of crime are prioritised and screened for investigation. Solvability is a key issue in determining which cases ought to be prioritised for investigation. It hardly makes sense to allocate significant resources to investigating cases that almost certainly cannot be solved and others that can only be detected at great expense—the more so if they can be viewed as less serious, such as certain public order offences. Unless a case is very serious, such as a homicide or rape, which the police must try to solve so as to meet their own professional integrity and society's expectations of them, it is rational to focus scarce resources only on the incidents it is possible to solve. The majority of offenders are versatile (Blumstein et al. 1988), so that an approach based on solvability factors can exploit the higher solvability of certain types of crime to improve detection rates more cost-effectively: catching a versatile offender by investigating a more easily detected crime may make more sense than pouring resources into complex investigations from which arrests are very unlikely to result. Most offenders are also prolific, and the probability they will be arrested increases the more offences they commit (Ahlberg and Knutsson 1990). Together, offender versatility and prolificacy provide larger numbers of more diverse criminal opportunities for investigation and arrest. It appears that—for the higher-volume, less serious offences that dominate criminal activity—it will be a better strategy to apply scarce investigative resources to solvable offences and seek to arrest offenders responsible for difficult-to-detect or undetectable offences at other crimes they commit that are more solvable, especially if more cost-effectively solvable. This is the principle behind the 'triage' method used in medicine to prioritise cases for treatment.

'Triaging' Cases

'Triage' is the medical process of using the severity of patients' conditions to determine their treatment priority. It is thought to have originated from the medical work of the surgeon-in-chief of the Napoleonic army in Italy, Baron Larrey (Willmott 1814). Triaging involves rationing scarce treatment resources to prioritise those whose lives are likely to be saved by immediate care over those who are either unlikely to live or likely to live irrespective of the care provided. The idea of triage may be adapted for managing investigative decisions for crime cases of varying solvability. Cases that are highly likely to be solved would be accorded the highest investigative priority, with medium solvability cases that are likely to demand higher resource inputs for clearance being accorded lower priority. Less serious cases that are unlikely to be detected, or can be detected only with significant use of resources, would not be investigated. As with medical triage, due to intentionally withholding treatment or downgrading selected cases, investigative triage has ethical implications. Every victim might expect the police to investigate his or her case, even if this may result in an overall decline in the number of offenders brought to book or the squandering of resources. It would be difficult to neglect to investigate the relatively small numbers of very serious violent or sexual offences, such as homicide or rape, nor is it likely that any police service would either wish to do so or in fact customarily do so in current practice. Similarly, cases involving the theft of substantial sums of money ought to be investigated, with the offenders arrested and, if possible, the losses recovered. Investigative inclusion criteria should also consider victim effects, since smaller losses may have more serious implications for the less affluent than larger ones for the better off (Barnard 2015). Even for less serious offences, the maintenance of known or visible deterrence is also needed. Not investigating shop theft cases—as is the case in England and Wales, where the theft of goods of less than £200 or Internet fraud incidents where losses do not exceed £600 are not investigated—is liable to weaken deterrence and encourage offending, particularly below these investigative thresholds.

Despite these exceptions, a focus on cases that it is possible to solve would promise to deliver outcomes that maximise detections while relying on offenders responsible for difficult- or impossible-to-solve incidents to commit more solvable crimes in future that lead to their arrest. Just as it is difficult to justify undertaking medical operations that surgeons know will not extend or save a patient's life, it would be wasteful and pointless to undertake investigations that could never make a positive contribution to detection. There is little to be gained by diligently searching for forensic samples that officers are virtually certain do not or cannot exist, trying to track down non-existent eyewitnesses or continually questioning people who could not possibly have witnessed a crime. While difficult-to-solve serious offences must be kept open to potential investigation, and, to maintain deterrence, sufficient less serious cases must be investigated through to arrest, under conditions of scarce resources, effort is better directed at property and violent assault cases of high solvability rather than squandering officer time on equivalent low-solvability cases that officers are virtually guaranteed to fail to detect.

Much current policing practice involves this very approach but without the measured statistical predictors of detection, which this volume argues will result in achieving improved detection rates more cost-effectively. Reliance on experience alone will undoubtedly result in the investigation of more cases where no promising leads emerge, while some solvable cases that could be detected will be missed. In contrast, a scientific approach to solvability and detection is pragmatic since it enables screening decisions to be placed on a firmer, measured basis. There will always be some uncertainty about which cases it is possible and not possible to solve and, if solvable, the ease with which this will be undertaken. All crime screening systems involve these uncertainties and are necessarily imperfect. However, the analysis of solvability factors promises to make crime screening systems far less imperfect by narrowing uncertainties about case solvability and screening. As a result, officer effort saved by investigating fewer unsolvable cases can be diverted to solvable ones that would otherwise not be investigated or cases that would otherwise receive too few investigative resources to unlock the available evidence that helps secure a conviction. Solvable cases which possess promising characteristics for detection and unpromising low-solvability ones at which effort is fruitlessly directed can be identified by examining how the police have fared with clearing previous comparable cases. By studying the range of investigative approaches employed for different types of crime, solvability factors—the characteristics of cases that mean they can or cannot be detected and that identify those more and less likely to be detected—can be established. Chapter "Targeting Factors that Predict Clearance of Non-domestic Assaults", on non-domestic assaults, and Chapter "Pickpocketing on Railways", on theft on railways, compare the success of statistical and experience-based approaches to case screening, investigation and detection. That officers' reliance on practical experience may have resulted in missed investigations that might have produced the evidence items needed to solve them helps to gauge the benefits of statistical prediction.

The Importance of Detecting Crime

Solving crime has an enduring importance for police services through deterring offending, dispensing justice and helping maintain public confidence in policing. Arrest enables offenders to be subjected to justice, enabling either rehabilitative intervention or custodial sentencing. There are greater rehabilitative benefits to be derived from community sentencing compared with short-term imprisonment (Wermink et al. 2010), irrespective of gender (Mears et al. 2012): imprisonment does not reduce subsequent offending (Nagin et al. 2009; Weatherburn 2010), but, instead, increases it (Bales and Piquero 2012), while worsening rehabilitation (Killias et al. 2000), particularly for less serious and younger offenders (Petrosino et al. 2010). There is also evidence of inter-generational transmission effects from imprisonment, both for sons (Murray et al. 2012; van de Rakt et al. 2012) and mothers (Wildeman et al. 2012).

Nevertheless, falls in offending due to incapacitation are unlikely to be inconsequential. Apart from criminals whose offending does indeed fall following incarceration, comparisons of custodial and community sentencing do not always consider falls in offending while incarcerated. Longer-term removal of imprisoned offenders from the community curtails, if not eliminates, their offending while incarcerated and these offending reductions offset reductions attributable to giving community rather than custodial sentences. By denying offenders the freedom to commit crime, incarceration is estimated as being responsible for almost a third of the US crime drop in the 1990s (Spelman 2006). Irrespective of the long-term effects on criminal careers, crime detection serves to protect the public by incarcerating dangerous sexual and violent offenders. Both custodial and non-custodial interventions in offending careers necessarily depend on crime detection and the arrest of offenders. It seems certain that the failure to solve the crimes committed by never, rarely or far less often arrested offenders will result in delayed or zero intervention in criminal careers. This would lead to a loss of offending reductions due to incarceration and the rehabilitative benefits of community sentencing, and leave unsupervised criminals in the community, free to commit crimes.

Moreover, it appears likely that detections help contain crime since the deterrent effects on offending of the fear of being arrested outweigh those due to the threat of custodial sentencing or sentencing severity (von Hirsch et al. 1999), though this is likely to vary according to the type of crime and characteristics of criminals. Fear of arrest may be less affected, therefore, by high levels of attrition that result in low conviction rates (Morgan and Newburn 1998). Offenders' perceptions, however, are key to offending behaviour, and failure to solve crimes is likely to embolden offenders to commit further offences. It is also liable to damage regard for the police by both offenders and non-offenders. Crime surges during riots partly reflect criminal opportunism (Lewis et al. 2011) and the looting and damaging of property for fun (Hope 2012) indicating that 'normative compliance' (Bottoms 2001) alone is insufficient to contain citizens with criminal dispositions under all circumstances. It is apparent that, when deterrence derived from policing activities is inoperative, normative compliance does not hold for certain subsets of the population, suggesting that those with criminal tendencies are held in check by other means, notably a policing presence or the perception that the formal guardianship provided by officers poses a threat. New York's recently improved control of homicides, for instance, reflects the threat and reality of interception by rapid patrols responding to real-time 'reporting' of gunshots using the NYPD's Domain Awareness System: information from CCTV cameras, automatic number plate readers, chemical and radiation sensors, emergency calls, and microphones that 'recognise' gunshots is sent directly to the mobile electronic devices of the jurisdiction's 35,000 officers (de Quetteville 2018). Chicago's algorithmically driven 'ShotSpotter' system, based on gunfire detection technology and an extensive network of cameras, uses predictive software that enables police to be alerted about gunshots within 30 s so that patrol responses often precede witnesses' 911 alerts by several minutes (Blakely 2018).

Normative compliance, therefore, frames crime control within societies like the UK, where 35% of males have a criminal conviction by the age of 35 (Morgan and Newburn 1998). It is evident, however, that policing also helps contain criminal behaviour via the threat of arrest, since for those criminally disposed, weaker normative compliance is supplemented by policing deterrence. This particularly concerns high-volume property crimes, which can be more 'lightly' policed when resources are scarce, yet frequently involve violence: a fifth of UK burglaries, for instance, are aggravated by violence (Budd 1999). Youths carrying knives, knife crime incidence and middle-class adult drug use run the risk of undermining existing behavioural norms unless they are deterred via a number of means, including the arrest of offenders. Arrests for committing criminal acts assist in cementing normative compliance and help combat the development of new norms. As such, detecting crimes is one of policing's principal contributions to the maintenance of society's values regarding the rule of law.

Professional competence is important in shaping confidence in the police (Bradford et al. 2009), and detecting crimes is an indispensable part of the public's view of police professionalism. Even if the police demonstrate success in clearing cases, however, this may have only asymmetric effects on society's view of them, preventing a drop in regard if successful but damaging police reputation if unsuccessful (Skogan 2006).

Technical Change and Cyber-Offences

The principal approaches to the investigation and detection of most crimes tend to endure. In one sense, they cannot change, because investigation inevitably responds to the inherent characteristics of offences that determine solvability, and officers follow the evidence, the sources and characteristics of which do not change for the majority of offender–victim contact offences. Most evidence derives from crime scenes, and these will therefore remain the primary source of the evidence that results in crime clearance. Technological changes can improve the recovery of such evidence, enhancing the importance of different activities or types of personnel skills. Novel or improved forensic methods, for instance, can raise the potential for resourcing specialists and immediate on-scene activities to take advantage of these developments.

The surge in electronic crimes using the Internet downgrades these traditional evidence sources, given the separation of offender and victim, who are frequently located in different national jurisdictions covered by different police forces—not a feature of most other types of offending. Policing is—predictably—habituated to approaches to investigation and detection based on victim–offender contact crimes, since other forms of offending were previously less common, though evident in financial crimes. Crime scenes that have not been visited by offenders are increasing in number as electronic offences that involve no direct physical contact between the offender and the victim or the victim's property become rife in step with the proliferation of devices connected to the Web. With victims and offenders spatially, if not temporally, separated, a crime scene in the sense of a place where the victim has their property stolen or is injured by an offender no longer exists. There are, therefore, fewer clues as to the offender's identity, although there may be electronic clues that link offenders to victims, such as IP address information. Even with electronic fraud perpetrated from another national jurisdiction, money needs to be withdrawn from the banking system eventually, so that conventional approaches to investigation may be successful if applied in real time. The speed with which money transfers can be effected makes tracking and intercepting the cybercriminal difficult even in the same national jurisdiction, let alone in cases where offences are perpetrated from other countries, where authorisation and cost hurdles hamper timely investigation and sometimes even prohibit it altogether. Chapter "Detecting and Combating Internet Telephony Fraud" airs these challenges and considers how telephonic cyber-offences may be combated.

Crime Types and Investigative Activities in Different Stages

Most crimes concern the theft of property or involve less serious violent offences. Crime investigation and detection is predominantly reactive (Tilley et al. 2007), with the police responding to calls for assistance. They result from a failure to prevent offending. Only a small proportion is solved using proactive policing activities (Tilley et al. 2007). Offence characteristics influence solvability, and this frames resource inputs into different reactive investigative activities. Investigations are reactive in that they follow crime incidence and are a response to offence characteristics, which influence solvability and the potential to 'unlock' evidence. Investigations occur in two principal stages (Fig. 1). The first comprises the initial patrol response and investigations at the scene with first officers questioning eyewitnesses and specialist officers collecting forensic evidence. These activities result in 'intermediate outputs' that include arrests at the scene and suspect, vehicle and forensic evidence (Fig. 1) that drive further investigations. Many cases are filed 'undetected' if there is little or no useful evidence and if they are not serious violent or sexual offences. Some incidents where there is an arrest do not require any further evidence, but, as Chapter "Investigative Activities, Resources and Burglary Detection" shows, these constitute a minority of cases.

The second stage involves further investigations of selected cases by detectives using evidence outputs from earlier activities at the scene to produce investigative outcomes, resulting in either detected or undetected cases. These include surveillance, matching known offenders to suspect descriptions, tracing stolen property,

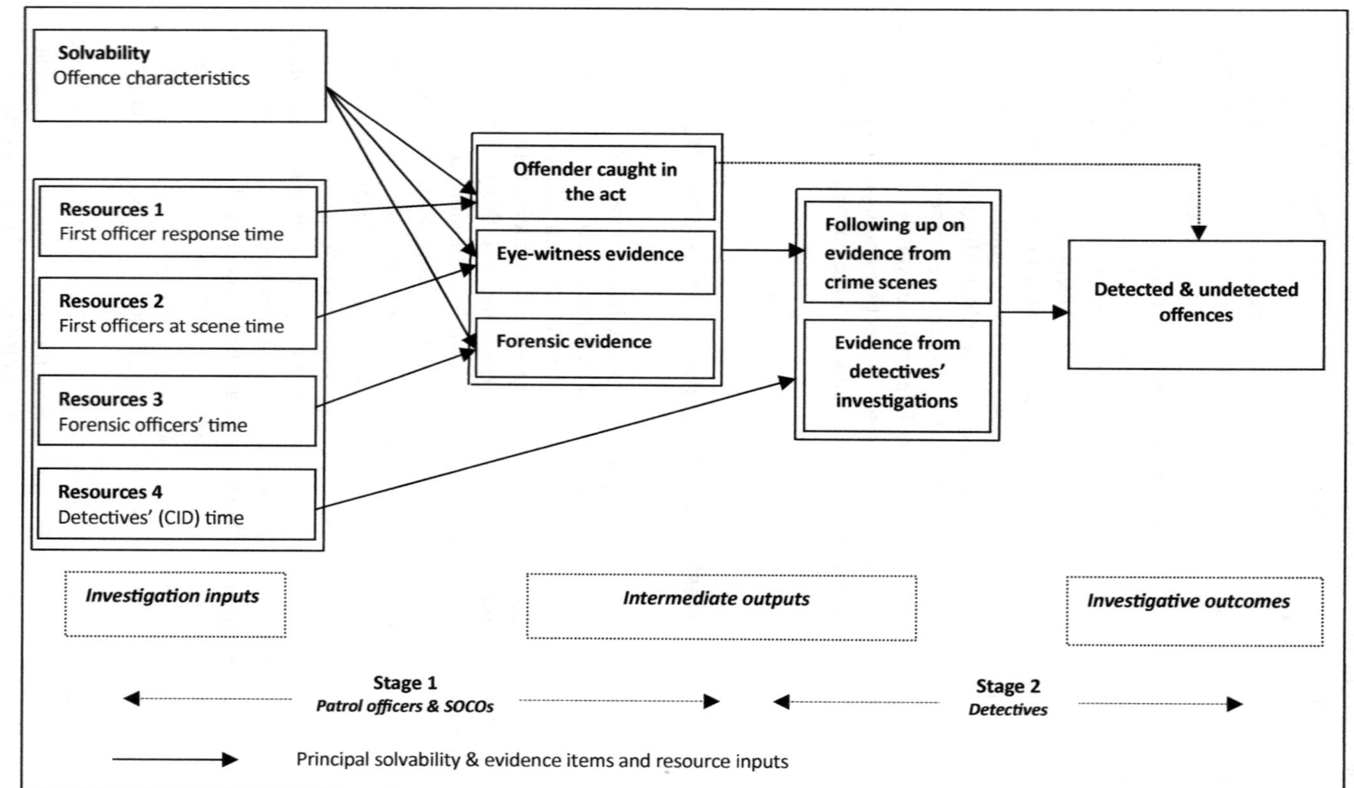

Fig. 1 Role of resources and solvability in burglary investigation (From Coupe 2016)

collating the results of forensic tests, checking vehicle registrations and consulting registered informants. Further investigation of incidents without strong first-stage evidence is more common for serious offences such as homicide, rape, assaults that result in life-changing injury, and high-value property and financial crime. Even for these offences, evidence from the scene commonly plays a significant, if not the dominant, role in investigations. Practising officers refer to the initial period following a homicide report as the 'golden hour'.

Since detectives follow the evidence collected by first officers in order to solve offences, most solvability factors are linked to initial incident characteristics. This is illustrated below in the studies on burglary (Chapters "Population-Level Analysis of Residential Burglaries" and "Assessing Solvability Factors in Greater Manchester, England: The Case of Residential Burglaries"), metal theft on railways (Chapter "Metal Theft Solvability and Detection"), pickpocketing (Chapter "Pickpocketing on Railways") and non-domestic assault (Chapter "Targeting Factors that Predict Clearance of Non-domestic Assaults"). However, there is also a need for solvability factors to guide case screening for particular investigative activities carried out by first officers and detectives, since not every solvable case is detected in the same way, and some cases benefit from certain types of investigations, while others do not. Examples of this are identifying the subset of cases where questioning eyewitnesses at non-residential burglary scenes will likely prove fruitful (Chapter "Solvability Indicators for 'First Officers': Targeting Eyewitness Questioning at Non-residential Burglaries") or screening residential burglary cases for particular sorts of further investigations (Chapter "Investigative Activities, Resources and Burglary Detection"). Similarly, not every report of an in-progress burglary presents opportunities to catch offenders red-handed, and Chapter "The Organisation and Deployment of Patrol Resources: Cost-Effective On-Scene Arrest at Burglaries" presents empirically based guidance as to which incidents will benefit most from a rapid response and how this may be cost-effectively achieved by prioritisation of incidents using solvability indicators.

Organisation of Contents

This volume comprises six main sections with 19 chapters, 14 of which use original data from police services in the UK to carry out solvability analyses and provide practical advice on case screening, investigation and detection. The second chapter critically evaluates existing research into crime solvability and detection and studies of the resourcing of police investigative activities in order to highlight the gaps in knowledge that this volume aims to resolve. Chapters "Population-Level Analysis of Residential Burglaries"–"Detecting and Combating Internet Telephony Fraud" comprise studies that identify the solvability factors for property offences (residential and non-residential burglary), pickpocket offences, metal theft on railway property and Internet telephony fraud. Some of these studies estimate the gains from statistical prediction and case screening compared with using practical experience alone. Chapters

"Detecting and Combating Internet Telephony Fraud"–"Reporting, Detection and Solvability of Sex Offences on Railways" examine incident solvability for violent, sexual and hate offences and consider non-domestic assaults, faith hate crime and sex offending on railways. Chapters "Offender–Offence Profiling: Improving Burglary Solvability and Detection", "Boosting Offence Solvability and Detections: Solving Residential Burglaries by Predicting Single and Multiple Repeats" and "Improving Offence Solvability and Detection Rates at Non-residential Burglary: Predicting Single and Multiple Repeat Incidence" research ways of improving incident solvability and detection outcomes. There is a study based on South Australian Police data that assesses the scope for using offender–offence profiling to predict the identities of subsets of offenders likely to be responsible for specific groups of residential burglaries. There are also two studies that examine the benefits of predicting repeat domestic and non-domestic burglary incidence in order to entrap offenders. Unlike the other chapters, which support reactive investigation, a predictive-entrapment approach to arrest is proactive. Chapters "Homicide Resources, Solvability and Detection", "Investigative Activities, Resources and Burglary Detection" and "The Organisation and Deployment of Patrol Resources: Cost-Effective On-Scene Arrest at Burglaries" measure the role of resources together with incident solvability in determining detection outcomes. Chapter "Homicide Resources, Solvability and Detection" examines how homicides are resourced, investigated and detected. Every UK homicide is thoroughly investigated so that solvability factors are based on detection outcomes—as for other offences considered in the volume—but other solvability indicators, such as the number of investigative actions per case, are also investigated, so that solvability is framed in terms of investigative strategy or the types of investigative activities that need to be undertaken for different types of homicide cases. With nine-tenths of cases detected, the chapter measures solvability and investigative effort under conditions of full or near-full investigative funding. Chapter "Investigative Activities, Resources and Burglary Detection" examines officer time resource inputs in different investigative stages into incidents of varying solvability in order to provide insights into how positive detection outcomes may be best achieved cost-effectively, while Chapter "The Organisation and Deployment of Patrol Resources: Cost-Effective On-Scene Arrest at Burglaries" uses data on burglary solvability and patrol resources to identify which 'in-progress' incidents can benefit more from higher resource inputs. Chapter "Resources, Solvability and Detection: A Theoretical Model" considers the theoretical lessons that can be drawn, presenting a resource–solvability theory of detection that outlines the origins of incident solvability in jurisdictional environments with distinctive offender profiles and showing how resource inputs into investigative activities interact with case solvability to produce detection outcomes of varying cost-effectiveness. Implications are drawn for policing and about the need for and potential of further scholarship.

References

Ahlberg, J., & Knutsson, J. (1990). The risk of detection. *Journal of Quantitative Criminology, 6*(1), 117–130.

Bales, W. D., & Piquero, A. R. (2012). Assessing the impact of imprisonment on recidivism. *Journal of Experimental Criminology, 8,* 71–101.

Barnard, P. (2015). *Online vehicle sales fraud—Can police target prevention messages more efficiently and effectively?* (MSt thesis). University of Cambridge.

Blakely, R. (2018, January 08). US murder rate plunges after police algorithm predicts crime. *The Times.*

Blumstein, A., Cohen, J., Das, S., & Miotra, D. (1988). Specialization and seriousness during adult criminal careers. *Journal of Quantitative Criminology, 4*(4), 303–345.

Blumstein, A., & Wallman, J. (2000). *The crime drop in America.* Cambridge: Cambridge University Press.

Bottoms, A. (2001). Compliance and community penalties. In A. Bottoms, L. Gelsthorpe, & S. Rex (Eds.), *Community penalties: Changes and challenges.* Willan: Cullompton.

Bradford, B., Jackson, J., & Stanko, E. (2009). Contact and confidence: Revisiting the impact of public encounters with the police. *Policing & Society: An International Journal of Research and Policy, 19*(1), 20–46.

Brandl, S. G., & Frank, J. (1994). The relationship between evidence, detective effort, and the disposition of burglary and robbery investigations. *American Journal of Police, 13*(3), 149–168.

Budd, T. (1999). *Burglary of domestic dwellings: Findings from the British Crime Survey* (Home Office Statistical Bulletin 4/99). London: Home Office.

Cohen, L. E., & Felson, M. (1979). Social change and crime rate trends: A routine activity approach. *American Sociological Review, 44*(4), 588–608.

Coupe, R. T. (2016). Evaluating the effects of resources and solvability on burglary detection. *Policing and Society: An International Journal of Research and Policy, 26*(5), 563–587.

Coupe, R. T., & Blake, L. (2005). The effects of patrol workloads and response strength on burglary emergencies. *Journal of Criminal Justice, 33*(3), 239–255.

de Quetteville, H. (2018, June 07). There's a weapon that police could deploy against violent crime—But they're not using it. *The Telegraph.* https://www.telegraph.co.uk/news/2018/06/07/weapon-police-could-deploy-against-violent-crime-not-using/.

Doyle, R. (2018). Personal communication from a serving officer from the Devon & Cornwall Police Service concerning the patrol resources used to deal with missing persons.

Eck, J. E. (1983). *Solving crimes: The investigation of burglary and robbery.* Washington, DC: Police Executive Research Forum.

Greenwood, P. W., & Petersilia, J. (1975). *The criminal investigation process: Volume I: Summary and policy implications.* Santa Monica, CA: The RAND Corporation.

Hope, T. (2012). Riots, pure and simple? *Criminal Justice Matters, 87*(1), 2–4.

Killias, M., Aebi, M., & Ribeaud, D. (2000) Does community service rehabilitate better than short-term imprisonment? Results of a controlled experiment. *The Howard Journal, 39*(1), 40–57.

Lamme, M., & Bernasco, W. (2013). Are mobile offenders less likely to be caught? The influence of the geographical dispersion of serial offenders' crime locations on their probability of arrest. *European Journal of Criminology, 10*(2), 168–186.

Lewis, P., Newburn, T.,Taylor, M., Mcgillivray, C., Greenhill, A., Frayman, H., & Proctor, R. (2011). Reading the riots: investigating England's summer of disorder. Reading the riots, The London School of Economics and Political Science and The Guardian, London: UK. http://eprints.lse.ac.uk/46297/1/Reading%20the%20riots%28published%29.pdf

Mears, D. P., Cochran, J. C., & Bales, W. D. (2012). Gender differences in the effects of prison on recidivism. *Journal of Criminal Justice, 40,* 370–378.

Morgan, R., & Newburn, T. (1998). *The future of policing.* Oxford: OUP.

Murray, J., Loeber, R., & Pardini, D. (2012). Parental involvement in the criminal justice system and the development of youth theft, marijuana use, depression and poor academic performance. *Criminology, 50*(1), 255–302.

Nagin, D. S., Cullen, F. T., & Jonson, C. L. (2009). Imprisonment and reoffending. In M. Tonry (Ed.), *Crime and justice: A review of research* (Vol. 38). Chicago: University of Chicago Press.

Petrosino, A., Petrosino, C. T., & Guckenburg, S. (2010). *Formal system processing of juveniles: Effects on delinquency*. Oslo, Norway: The Campbell Collaboration. www.campbellcollaboration.org.

Robb, P., Coupe, R. T., & Ariel, B. (2015). 'Solvability' and detection of metal theft on railway property. *European Journal on Criminal Policy and Research, 21*(4), 463–484.

Robbins, J. (2018). *Exclusive: More than 96% of reported fraud cases go unsolved*. https://www.which.co.uk/news/2018/09/exclusive-more-than-96-of-reported-fraud-cases-go-unsolved/.

Robinson, A., & Tilley, N. (2009). Factors influencing police performance in the investigation of volume crimes in England and Wales. *Police Practice and Research: An International Journal, 10*(3), 209–223.

Skogan, W. G. (2006) Asymmetry in the impact of encounters with the police. *Policing & Society, 16*(2), 99–126.

Spelman, W. (2006). The limited importance of prison expansion. In A. Blumstein & J. Wallman (Eds.), *The crime drop in America*. Cambridge: Cambridge University Press.

Stavisky. (2018). *The role of ethnic communities and ethnic identities in explaining relationships with, and attitudes towards, the police in the London borough of Hackney* (Doctoral thesis). University of Cambridge.

Tilley, N., Robinson, A., & Burrows, J. (2007). The investigation of high volume crime. In T. Newburn, T. Williamson, & A. Wright (Eds.), *Handbook of criminal investigation* (pp. 226–254). London: Willan Publishing.

van de Rakt, M., Murray, J., & Nieuwbeerta, P. (2012). The long-term effects of paternal imprisonment on criminal trajectories of children. *Journal of Research in Crime and Delinquency, 49*(1), 81–108.

von Hirsch, A., Bottoms, A. E., Bumey, E., & Wikstrom, P. O. (1999). *Criminal deterrence and sentence severity: An analysis of recent research*. Oxford: Hart Publishing.

Weatherburn, D. (2010). The effect of prison on adult re-offending. *Crime and Justice Bulletin* (New South Wales, Bureau of Crime, Statistics, and Research) Number 143.

Wermink, H., Blokland, A., Nieuwbeerta, P., Nagin, D., & Tollenaar, N. (2010). Comparing the effects of community service and short-term imprisonment on recidivism: A matched samples approach. *Journal of Experimental Criminology, 6*, 325–349.

Wildeman, C., Schnittker, J., & Turney, K. (2012). Despair by association? The mental health of mothers with children by recently incarcerated fathers. *American Sociological Review, 77*(2), 216–243.

Willmott, R. H. (1814). *Memoirs of military surgery* (Vols. 1–3). Baltimore: Cushing.

Existing Research on Solvability

Tom Olphin and Richard Timothy Coupe

Introduction

Research into the solvability of crime appears to have begun when Isaacs (1967) examined 1905 crimes and found that, of the 349 cases where the victim named a suspect, 86% were solved, but that 88% of the 1556 cases without named suspects remained unsolved. Greenwood (1970) also found that cases with named suspects were more likely to feature arrests than cases where only a description or other evidence was available. These studies brought about an understanding that the types of evidence available to investigators affect the likelihood that a case will be solved.

This early research was built upon by the RAND Corporation (Greenwood et al. 1975), who examined case assignment files to demonstrate how detectives used their time and conducted an analysis of solved crimes to identify the methods by which they were solved. They found that most solved cases involved either an arrest at the scene (around 22%), identification of an offender at the time of reporting (around 44%) or actions they described as being 'routine' for investigators (around 34%), such as showing mugshot albums to witnesses. From this, they concluded that 'case solutions reflect activities of patrol officers, members of the public and routine clerical processing more than investigative techniques' (Chaiken et al. 1976, p. 1) and that the information the victim provides to the initial responding officer is the most important factor (Greenwood and Petersilia 1975). Whilst these findings were based on a methodology with a low response rate and small sample size, other researchers have found that most detections are due to actions taken by the attending officer at the scene (Coupe and Griffiths 1996; Brandl and Frank 1994) and that general follow-up

T. Olphin (✉) · R. T. Coupe
Institute of Criminology, University of Cambridge, Cambridge, England, UK
e-mail: to288@cam.ac.uk

R. T. Coupe et al. (eds.), *Crime Solvability Factors*,
https://doi.org/10.1007/978-3-030-17160-5_2

investigations by detectives are ineffective in non-homicide investigations (Weisburd and Eck 2004). Much more recently, Telep and Weisburd (2011) argued that there is still insufficient evidence in relation to the efficacy of detectives, and other authors have found that the clearance of crimes is not as simple as the RAND authors would suggest, with Webbink et al. (2017) finding that, where crime suspects were shown in television programmes, the larger the viewership, the greater the probability of solving the crime. This would most certainly be considered part of the secondary investigation.

Eck (1983) examined burglary and robbery offences to test three hypotheses in relation to the mechanism by which crimes are solved. The first, the circumstance-result hypothesis, was drawn from the findings of the RAND study and the theory that most cleared cases would be solved regardless of the amount of effort expended as part of the secondary investigation. The second—drawn from the findings of Folk (1971), who stated that investigative effort determined the outcomes of cases, regardless of leads—Eck labelled the effort-result hypothesis. Eck then presented a third hypothesis: the triage hypothesis.

The hypothesis proposes three types of cases. The first are those that practically solve themselves and require little to no detective work. Second came the suggestion of a new group of cases that offer leads and are solvable, but whose solution relies on investigative work. The third category is composed of cases that may never be solved, and which certainly cannot be solved using a reasonable level of resourcing. The triage hypothesis presented a set of cases that, if the investigative effort were concentrated, may have improved chances of being solved.

Eck (1983) recognized that some information found during the initial investigation was predictive of whether an arrest would be made. However, this finding also applied to the presence of actions performed by detectives following on from the initial investigation. This supported the triage hypothesis whilst providing evidence against both other hypotheses. Whilst it is unlikely that the groupings of cases are quite as clean as suggested by Eck (1983)—with some cases that would be deemed unsolvable being solved and some apparent self-solvers remaining undetected (Coupe 2016)—Eck's triage hypothesis provides an explanation for crime solvability that fits with most available evidence and provides scope for improvements in investigative effectiveness.

The technology available to investigators has improved dramatically since 1983, and Bradbury and Feist (2005) note that investigative factors such as the availability of analysable forensic evidence may have changed the proportions of these groups by moving cases from being unsolvable to being solvable with reasonable effort. Eck's triage hypothesis suggests that, if the group of cases that are solvable with effort can be identified and focused upon, clearance rates should improve. This provides solvability researchers with an opportunity to steer policing effort towards those cases where the additional effort will have the most meaningful impact.

Identification of Solvability Factors

Solvability factors are items of information, including leads, that are components of the crime or are available for investigators to act upon and, when examined together, determine the likelihood of solving a crime.

Coupe (2014) discussed two types of studies examining solvability factors. Solvability studies examining multiple factors have mainly considered burglary and robbery, whilst studies of clearance and detection have considered the effects of various factors on other crime types such as assault, rape and homicide (Ousey and Lee 2010; Paré et al. 2007; Roberts 2008; Wellford and Cronin 1999). Both types demonstrate that there are characteristics of investigations that are differentially present in solved and unsolved cases.

In addition to the two types that have previously been identified, we would also argue for a third relevant type: that of case attrition analysis, which has mostly been conducted in relation to sexual offences. It is understood that this differs due to the requirement that the case reaches a successful conclusion in court, but the methods of assessing the valuable factors are much the same.

How Is Solvability Determined?

In order to identify those factors that are more prevalent in solved cases, researchers need to identify how they define whether a crime is solved or not. It could be argued a successful conviction is the most definitive criterion for determining whether a crime has been solved. However, as Williams and Sumrall (1982) pointed out, there are numerous factors aside from evidence in the case that can influence conviction. To avoid the loss of cases due to factors that are out of police control, it therefore appears most sensible to identify cases as solved when a prosecutor would be satisfied that there is sufficient evidence to charge a person with the crime.

Arrest has been employed in the USA in the same way as detection is used in the UK, as both require a prosecutor to approve the outcome. This is a good example of how solvability research will necessarily differ between countries: in the UK, the arrest could not be used as a measure of solvability, as it simply requires an officer to have reasonable grounds to suspect that the person to be arrested has committed an offence.

Measurement of the imposition of a sanction on an offender (sanction detection) has been used by numerous UK studies (Burrows et al. 2005; Donnellan 2011; Paine 2012), but this may miss cases where sanctions are not imposed despite the evidential threshold being met. Other researchers have argued that clearance by non-sanction detection may be open to 'manipulation' (Bloch and Bell 1976, p. 7) and 'bias' (Greenwood 1970, p. 5). The UK Home Office (2011, p. 15) have since applied rules to non-sanction detections, with the result that these are now restricted to cases where the evidential standard required for charging is met but where either the police or the Crown Prosecution Service (CPS) determines that sanctions should not be imposed.

As of April 2014, offences in the UK are recorded as solved by the Home Office if they have positive outcomes. This includes all outcomes—whether sanction or non-sanction—where the evidential standard for charging has been met and is the current mechanism for recording crime clearance in the UK. This currently appears to provide the most accurate, and complete, outcome measure available to solvability researchers.

High-Volume and Acquisitive Crimes

To date, the majority of solvability studies have examined volume or acquisitive crimes—a category of crimes that includes theft, burglary, robbery and criminal damage. Consistent with the findings of the RAND Corporation (Greenwood et al. 1975), both on-scene capture of suspects and suspect identity information have consistently been found to be more prevalent in solved than in unsolved cases (Burrows et al. 2005; Coupe and Griffiths 1996; Eck 1979, 1983; Paine 2012; Stevens and Stipak 1982). This finding has been consistent across a range of crime types, including non-residential burglary (Coupe and Kaur 2005), robbery (Newiss 2002) and vehicle crime (Burrows et al. 2005). Pelfrey and Hanna (2011), developing Greenwood's (1970) early work, found not only that a name was beneficial but that the likelihood of clearance improved with each additional level of suspect information, with a full identification being optimal, followed by a name and description, then a full description and finally a name with no description.

Paine and Ariel's (2013) findings that footprints, fingerprints and DNA were important in the prediction of burglary solvability which are consistent with the results of some other authors (Bond 2007), whilst others (Burrows et al. 2005; Coupe and Griffiths 1996) have disputed their value. Antrobus and Pilotto (2016), using a randomly controlled trial, showed that more burglaries in Queensland can be detected with longer forensic visits to crime scenes, boosting cases solved with fingerprint evidence from 3 to 7% and with DNA from 2 to 4%. Despite findings and policy documents that highlight the value of forensic evidence (Association of Chief Police Officers [ACPO] 1996; Bradbury and Feist 2005), Robinson and Tilley (2009) demonstrated that the use of forensic techniques was inconsistent. Different sorts of forensic evidence may be solvability factors for the detection of crimes perpetrated by different types of offender: fingerprint evidence results in the arrest of younger residential burglars in Adelaide, whereas older burglars are more frequently caught out by DNA specimens (Killmier 2014).

Other factors that have been found to relate to increased solvability for volume offences are the offence being witnessed (Donnellan 2011; Paine 2012), the availability of CCTV (Robb et al. 2015), offence commission during daylight hours (Coupe and Blake 2006; Coupe and Girling 2001), the availability of resources (Coupe and Griffiths 2000) and reporting early in the commission of the offence (Coupe and

Blake 2005). Speed of response may be linked to solvability (Blake and Coupe 2001; Clawson and Chang 1977), but this may only be the case if the crimes are reported immediately (Bieck and Kessler 1977) or if patrols arrive at the crime scene within five minutes of the offence being reported (Spelman and Brown 1981).

In relation to arson, Hopkins (2009) found that endangerment of life, forensic scene attendance, witness statements and response time—each of which relates to the seriousness of the offence—all appear linked to solvability. He went so far as to comment (Hopkins 2009, p. 88) that, 'after these opportunities are lost, there often appears to be little potential in pursuing an investigation as the effort required to obtain a detection begins to outweigh the rewards'.

Lockwood (2014) found that, when a burglary occurred in an area with higher levels of broken-window-style police enforcement, it was more likely to be cleared by arrest; his results also indicated that residential burglaries were no more likely to be solved than non-residential burglaries—a finding at odds with Pelfrey and Hanna (2011), who found that business burglaries were in fact more often solved.

Although investigating stolen property makes only a small contribution to burglary detection, particularly residential burglary (Coupe and Griffiths 1996; Donnellan 2011; Paine 2012), Robb et al. (2014) found that proactive policing methods involving checks at scrap metal dealers' premises were associated with increased solvability for metal theft offences. Theft of exceptionally heavy items, such as railway track, was also associated with higher rates of detection, given the conspicuousness of the heavy lifting equipment and vehicles needed at the crime scene (Robb et al. 2014).

Offender behaviour can also affect solvability. Tillyer and Tillyer (2015) demonstrated that committing robberies in groups may be dangerous for offenders, as the likelihood of arrest for robbery increased significantly as the number of co-offenders increased. Other distinctive offender characteristics, such as versatility involving violent offending and higher prolificacy (Ahlberg and Knutsson 1990), both of which boost the odds of being arrested, or offending at a greater distance from home, which diminishes them (Lamme and Bernasco 2013), do not feature as solvability factors. Unlike the number of offenders, which is often reported by eyewitnesses, these offender characteristics are, for the most part, unknown when crimes are reported. Attempts to identify distinctive modi operandi for high-volume crimes have, in general, proved unsuccessful and few, if any, solvability studies have cited them as factors improving detection outcomes.

The variety of factors that have been found to be connected to offence solvability demonstrates the value of large data sets with a wide range of variables when attempting to predict whether cases will be cleared.

Violent Crimes

Greenberg et al. (1977) found it difficult to identify solvability factors for violent offences. Since then, few studies have examined the solvability of non-lethal violent crime, and even fewer have utilized samples large enough to identify factors with low prevalence. However, it has been suggested (Skogan and Antunes 1979) that violent offenders are more likely to be described or identified, which in turn assists the investigation.

Roberts (2008) used logistic regression to examine the effect of the incident and contextual characteristics on arrest for non-lethal violence and found that, for robbery and aggravated assault, incidents with multiple victims or with concomitant offences were more likely to be cleared. Consistent with other research (D'Alessio and Stolzenberg 2003), victim injury was associated with higher solvability.

Connecting a known offender to a violent crime has also been associated with greater likelihood of clearance (Eitle et al. 2005; Peterson et al. 2010), and Tilley et al. (2007) concluded that eyewitness reports that provide suspect information or facilitate the offender being caught nearby are the most indicative factor in relation to whether a violent offence will be solved. This is consistent with Baskin and Sommers' (2012) findings that victim and witness accounts were significantly linked with solvability. Eitle et al. (2005) also found that offences that occurred in dwellings were more likely to be solved. However, this may be linked to the offenders being known. There is some conflict over the benefit of forensic evidence in relation to the clearance of violent offences. Baskin and Sommers (2012) found no link, whilst Peterson et al. (2010, 2013) demonstrated clear associations between the collection and analysis of physical evidence and arrest of suspects—a result that may well be linked to the statistical power that was available in these studies.

A number of factors have been observed to be associated with a reduced likelihood of clearance of violent crime. Roberts (2008) showed the use of a firearm in the commission of the offence and time elapsed since the offence to be less commonly found in correspondence with solved crimes. Incidents between strangers are also associated with lower clearance levels for robbery and assault (D'Alessio and Stolzenberg 2003; Snyder 1999). For kidnapping offences (Tillyer et al. 2015), the likelihood of arrest is higher in non-stranger offences. Where offences were committed by strangers, the co-occurrence of other crimes and similar factors that may help provide additional evidence was associated with a higher risk of arrest.

As can be seen in Chapter "Targeting Factors that Predict Clearance of Non-domestic Assaults", Olphin (2015) built upon the work of these researchers by conducting an in-depth analysis of 29,105 non-domestic violent crimes. This research identified 25 solvability factors and 13 case-limiting factors. The sample size used in this research provided a benchmark for other studies of solvability and allowed factors affecting violent crime solvability to be identified where others had struggled. This also evidenced the importance of analysing a sufficiently large sample to identify factors that do not occur frequently and may help explain why previous authors have disagreed on the importance of forensic information as a solvability factor.

Homicide

Whilst not technically solvability analyses, a large amount of work in the arena of homicide clearance has been conducted, which can be drawn upon to identify potential factors that would be of use for other solvability research. As Gottfredson and Hindelang (1979) argued, the most serious offences often elicit a greater response from police and the legal system. This is consistent with the detection rates in England and Wales for murder being much higher than for assault. However, the inability of the police to solve all homicides and the presence of factors linked to the clearance of murder indicate the likelihood that solvability factors can be identified for all crime types.

Roberts (2007) examined 1579 murders and identified factors that were more likely to be associated with cleared cases. As with a number of other studies, Roberts found that crimes with a female victim (Regoeczi et al. 2000) or with a younger victim (Addington 2006; Litwin 2004; Mouzos and Muller 2001; Puckett and Lundman 2003; Regoeczi et al. 2000; Roberts 2014; Wolfgang 1958) were associated with greater solvability. The latter finding may be due to children being more likely to have a guardian with them or to be hurt by someone they know (Cardarelli and Cavanagh 1992). Victims involved in drug- or gang-related activity were more likely to be associated with solved cases, a finding that is consistent with Litwin and Xu (2007) but not with Lee (2005). Roberts (2007) also demonstrated that witnesses and physical evidence were key indicators of solvability, along with offenders who were under the influence, non-stranger offenders, contact-type weapons and concomitant serious offences, although the presence of concomitant offences has been argued to act in the opposite direction by others (Litwin 2004; Riedel and Rinehart 1996; Wellford and Cronin 1999). Use of firearms in the offence was found to limit solvability, possibly due to reduced evidence transfer between offender and victim (Geberth 1996).

Similar to Alderden and Lavery (2007) and Jiao (2007), many studies of homicide have used logistic regression to examine links between cases' identified characteristics and their clearance. The use of contact weapons such as knives consistently indicates increased solvability (Addington 2006; Mouzos and Muller 2001; Puckett and Lundman 2003). As with Roberts (2007), firearm usage is associated with lower solvability in some studies (Litwin 2004; Ousey and Lee 2010), though not in others (Riedel and Rinehart 1996; Wellford and Cronin 1999). The victim–offender relationship is an important factor (Brown and Keppel 2012; Lee 2005; Litwin and Xu 2007; Roberts 2014), which may link to findings that homicides inside dwellings are more solvable (Litwin 2004; Regoeczi et al. 2008; Wellford and Cronin 1999) and that crimes by offenders who are strangers are associated with lower clearance rates (Lee 2005; Mouzos and Muller 2001; Ousey and Lee 2010). Lee (2005) also found cases with more than one victim or that elicited interest from *The New York Times* to be more likely to be cleared.

Ponce et al. (2007) found solvability factors for homicide to include evidence of overkill, which may indicate familiarity and rage, a non-isolated or public body recovery site, evidence of head or facial wounding, the victim being stabbed, the offence occurring during the day and the victim not being a gang member. Rydberg and Pizarro (2014) demonstrated that homicides where victims engaged in deviant lifestyles were associated with increased time before clearance by arrest. As with other crimes, eyewitness testimony appears a key in whether homicides are cleared (Corwin 1997; Geberth 1996; Riedel and Rinehart 1996; Wellford and Cronin 1999). This may help explain Alderden and Lavery's (2007) finding that late-night (00.00 to 05.59) homicides were less likely to be solved, and Wellford and Cronin's (1999) discovery that crimes occurring in good weather conditions showed higher solvability. The presence of physical evidence has been linked to an increased likelihood of clearance in homicide (Briody 2004), child abduction homicide (Brown and Keppel 2012) and cold cases (Davis et al. 2014). However, as with other crime types, some studies have failed to show this, potentially due to low sample size (Peterson et al. 2010) or inferior DNA testing capability for old crimes (Baskin and Sommers 2010). Balemba et al. (2014) found that the type of offence is important for sexual homicide, but this may relate to the amount of evidence recovered. For sexual homicide, Beauregard and Martineau (2014) found that the forensic awareness of the offender may affect the length of time needed to find the body and therefore delay the apprehension of the offender, but does not appear to impact upon detection overall.

The argument made by Greenwood et al. (1975) that the skill of detectives was unimportant conflicts with the findings of Marché (1994) and Puckett and Lundman (2003), who found that investigator experience appears to aid detection of homicides, especially those with low solvability. Similar to findings from other crime types (Burrows and Tarling 1982; Tilley and Burrows 2005), high officer workload (Roberts 2014) and lower numbers of detectives per case (Wellford and Cronin 1999) have been argued to correspond with a lower likelihood of clearing cases. Keel et al. (2009) also found self-reported caps and approval requirements on overtime to be associated with lower homicide clearance rates. These findings demonstrate that it is possible to identify solvability factors for even the most serious of offences and that failure to use these factors to guide the allocation of investigative resources may result in fewer crimes being solved.

Sexual Offences

For sexual offence cases, as with homicide, it has been necessary to draw from case attrition analyses due to a lack of other solvability research. Case attrition studies use successful prosecution as the outcome measure and examine the association between factors and attrition of the case. Hohl and Stanko (2015) conducted an analysis of sexual offence case attrition in London, finding that case attrition was more likely if police or prosecutors perceive there to be evidence against the truthfulness of the allegation, if police records show a previous false allegation, if there are inconsistencies in the victim's account or if evidence or police opinion cast doubt on the allegation. These findings demonstrate the extent to which the British criminal justice system still contains an element of personal bias and judgement when it comes to progressing or dropping cases. Other researchers have also found connections between case attrition and previous sexual intercourse or a previous relationship between the victim and the offender (Brown et al. 2007), and a lack of threats, violence or other serious coercion may also inhibit case completion (Fitzgerald 2006; Ingemann-Hansen et al. 2008). Hester (2006) demonstrates that it is not just sexual offences that suffer from dramatic attrition: under 4% of domestic violence incidents in their sample reached a successful criminal justice conclusion.

Brown et al. (2007) also found that the initial meeting being in private may inhibit case completion, but that cases are more likely to proceed if the victim and offender are strangers, the rape occurs in a public space, there is evidence of non-consent such as violence, use of a weapon or witness evidence to this effect, and if corroboration is available to substantiate the allegation. Fitzgerald (2006) found that cases were less likely to progress if the victim were a young child, if more than ten years elapsed between offence commission and reporting and—contrary to previous research—if the offender were a stranger.

Parkinson et al. (2002) examined attrition in child sexual offence cases and found that reasons for not proceeding to trial included parents wishing to protect children, the crime not being reported to police, influence or threats by the perpetrator or other family members and the child being either too young or too distressed.

Menaker et al. (2016) found that forensic evidence, whilst by no means a magic bullet for solving crimes, could help expedite cases and, when available alongside other evidence, assisted case completion. Investigators believed that forensic evidence was more useful in adult sexual offences, as child sexual offences generally did not have forensic opportunities due to the nature of the assault (touch or indecency rather than rape) or because of a time delay before the offence was reported. Fallik and Wells (2015) addressed the issue of sexual assault kits not being submitted by assessing the benefits of submitting previously untested kits for analysis. This is described as having minimal impact. However, in a number of cases, this did lead to the identification of evidence that would have been useful had the kit been analysed earlier. Randol and Sanders (2015) found that, despite the apparent value of forensic evidence in stranger rape cases, there were barriers to the effective use of forensics, including resource constraints, backlogs at state crime laboratories, a lack of knowledge about the crime laboratory's processes and priorities and misconceptions about the efficacy of CODIS as a tool to identify unknown offenders.

Resourcing, Solvability and Detection

Resources include buildings, police employees and equipment. Police staff resources include warranted officers and support staff, including crime analysts and forensic specialists. These are often measured in terms of personnel numbers or staffing time but may also take account of experience and specialist knowledge. Equipment ranges from vehicles and helicopters to forensic materials and electronic devices. Staffing accounts for 75% or more of policing costs in countries like the UK, the USA and

Australia. Investigative activities are actions or events that use resources to produce evidence and detection outcomes.

Few studies of solvability and crime detection have included measures of police resources. Although the number of different activities has been used as a measure of resource use or effort (e.g. Eck 1983), the quantity of resources used often differs markedly for the same activities, with different amounts of time being spent questioning suspects or witnesses (Brandl and Frank 1994) and large variations in the numbers of patrol officers or units responding to what, at first sight, are similar incidents (Coupe and Blake 2005).

Officer numbers have been commonly used to measure resources. Supply of officers and crime demand are the inputs into the 'workload-detection' model (e.g. Tilley and Burrows 2005), in which changes in inputs modify detection outcomes. The finding (Tilley and Burrows 2005) that every additional ten property offences (burglaries, thefts of and from vehicles) per officer lowered detection rates by 1.5% also confirms that police resources in relation to crime demand are important determinants of whether or not crimes are solved.

With regard to first officers attending crime scenes, deploying officers as single-crewed rather than double-crewed units improved patrol supply, promising to markedly improve on- and near-scene arrests (Blake and Coupe 2001), a finding which led to the Police Reform Act of 2002 proposal that officers in England and Wales should be deployed in single-crewed units wherever possible. Lighter demands placed on beat patrol resources enabled stronger patrol responses by more units, and most on-scene arrests occurred when these coincided with highly solvable incidents, providing direct confirmation of the twin roles of solvability and resources (Coupe and Blake 2005). Better-resourced and speedier first responses also resulted in more murders being solved (Wellford and Cronin 1999).

In follow-up burglary and robbery investigations using suspect evidence, detectives spent more time on cases with moderate than weak evidence and the least time on cases with strong suspect evidence, whilst twice the time was spent on cases where an arrest was made (Brandl and Frank 1994); most cases, excluded from the analysis, had such weak evidence that police screened them out prior to further investigation. The assignment of more detectives to cases resulted in more murders being solved (Wellford and Cronin 1999), whilst the investigative demands of homicides varied according to whether they were 'self-solving' homicides or 'who-dun-it' cases, which commonly required far greater resources and involved teams of 10–50 officers (Innes 2002).

Forensic resources are also important for detecting crime (Tilley and Ford 1996; Bradbury and Feist 2005). Forensic tasks involve specialist staff resources for collecting and processing specimens, and technical equipment and knowledge are involved in forensic analysis techniques. These are applied to imprint, body or chemical materials (Newburn 2007) or equipment left by criminals at the scene, such as different types of vehicles.

Studies that use individual offence data to examine the relationship between resources and detection have invariably concluded that effort or resources have a strong effect on case detection, whereas aggregated data studies differ, with resources associated with detection in the UK but not in North America.

Besides studies using the individual offence as the unit of analysis, there have been aggregated data studies of the relationship between police resources, crime demand and detections. Strong associations emerged between the number of officers per offence and case detection rates for the 43 police forces (Audit Commission 1993) and 278 basic command units (BCUs) (Burrows and Tilley 2005) in England and Wales. Although Chaiken (1975) and Wellford and Cronin (1999) also found higher investigative workloads to depress case clearance, other North American studies have pointed towards weaker links between measures of resource levels and case clearance (Roberts 2008; Ousey and Lee 2010).

It is possible that workload effects in North American research may have been masked by controlling for correlated variables. These include crime type and 'community size' (Paré et al. 2007), 'rural/urban force' (Cordner 1989), logged population size and number of 'event history incidents' (Roberts 2008) since larger cities have more crimes and poorer resources per crime (Cordner 1989; Klinger 1997), more of which are allocated to non-patrol policing (Langworthy and Hindelang 1979) and, compared with small forces, to administration (Ostrom et al. 1978). Wellford and Cronin's (1999) study, in contrast, included only large cities so that other differences, such as those between rural and urban forces or population size, did not statistically affect the measurement of the links between resources and crimes. If marked contrasts between the police forces and jurisdictions included in the same aggregated data studies in North American have affected findings with variables that confound workload effects, then resources may, in fact, have as notable an effect at the jurisdictional level in North America as in the UK. Even if this is not the case, incorporating solvability into the workload-detection model may strengthen the relationship between resources, crime demand and detections.

There is scant evidence concerning the effects on incident detection of resources compared with case solvability. It is likely that incident solvability, whilst inherent in the characteristics of cases, also depends on the investigative resources applied to cases. The interaction between solvability and resources will be considered in the section of the volume on resources, particularly Chapter "Investigative Activities, Resources and Burglary Detection", in which findings on burglary solvability and resourcing are used to critically re-evaluate Eck's (1979, 1983) research. Furthermore, there is little, if any, evidence on the effects of different types of the police officer—whether more senior and more experienced, with uniform as well as detective skills, and whether from a local force compared with a specialist crime unit—on detection outcomes. Chapter "Solvability Factors and Investigative Strategy for Faith Hate Crime: Anti-semitic and Islamophobic Assault, Criminal Damage and Public Order Offences in London" on faith hate offences, for instance, examines the effects of officer seniority and the use of local London borough police officers compared with specialist squads on detection outcomes, whereas in Chapter "Homicide Resources, Solvability and Detection", single- and double-crewing, the benefits or otherwise of using dogs, the benefits of officers with superior local knowledge acting as first responders and the effects of more and less powerful police response vehicles are examined.

Issues Faced by Solvability Researchers

Crime and investigations data recording systems in police agencies are not usually designed with research in mind. This complicates matters for researchers, as there is a trade-off between power and the identification of potentially important variables. As was discussed in the section on violence above, the volume of cases used in solvability analysis can determine whether less prevalent factors are identified. By prevalence, we mean the rate of occurrence of the factor in the population. This can be quite small, such as when examining the types of items that are stolen; more power would allow a more in-depth examination of whether the types of item stolen relate to solvability. As has been suggested above, lack of power appears to result in variables not being identified; stating that factors are not relevant when in fact the research simply lacked the power to identify it would be a dramatic weakness.

Thus, adding more cases allows researchers to identify more factors, yet there are downsides to this as well. The time constraints of reviewing free-text reports or statements do not allow for the identification of non-electronically recorded variables in large data sets. This results in some variables being inaccessible to large-scale, powerful research, with factors such as the use of intelligence or proactive tactics usually being inaccessible in electronic records. In terms of suspect information, it might also be beneficial to be able to examine the availability of different levels of information, as this is such a powerful factor, so that suspects who are named can be differentiated from vaguely described suspects.

Equally, there can be a dearth of records on the investigative activities undertaken and the resources allocated to them, hampering the linking of these to detection outcomes. As a result, research benefits from supplementing police records by examining non-electronically recorded information and free-text reports and collecting data on the different resources used and the details of investigative activities, not merely on whether an activity is undertaken. It may be that research involving smaller samples may also be needed to provide insights and advance understanding based on a comprehensive solvability study. Only rarely do current systems record investigative detail. One such example is the UK Ministry of Justice's HOLMES database for recording the investigations of major crimes such as homicides, data from which will be analysed in Chapter "Homicide Resources, Solvability and Detection".

It might be possible to combine the two methods by selecting a subsample of records from the overall data set for more detailed examination. This would facilitate the assessment of data accuracy and identification of additional factors, as well as providing an understanding of the mechanisms by which factors link to solvability, rather than just an overview of the links that exist. This would also allow for an examination of the integrity of the data and for some degree of analysis in relation to the data accuracy of the policing agency—something that could dramatically affect the validity of any model.

It is also imperative that researchers gain as much insight as possible into the meaning of the data that are used; by way of example, Olphin (2015) discovered that the field on the crime system where CCTV was recorded as present was in fact asking whether the officer thought there might be CCTV. This is a very different matter and does not therefore answer the question of whether having CCTV available in fact aids the solvability of crime.

To date, the generalisability of models has also not been determined. Whilst there are similarities between factors identified by different research teams, there are also major differences, which mean that it would be very beneficial to build models in numerous different policing areas, with different population and environmental characteristics, and compare each model to the others.

Solving More Crimes (and Other Outcomes)

Despite the difficulties faced by solvability researchers, there are numerous potential benefits that policing agencies could reap from well-conducted solvability research. Merely identifying the factors that are more prevalent in solved cases than unsolved ones allows emphasis to be placed on the gathering of those types of evidence, whether proactively by deploying additional evidence-gathering tools in high-crime areas, or reactively by reallocating resources so more time is spent on attempts to gather certain types of evidence than others.

This then allows policing agencies to make well-evidenced decisions in relation to the amount of resources allocated to the initial evidence-gathering process. Roman et al. (2009) demonstrated how this can be expanded in their assessment of the cost-effectiveness of using DNA to solve property crimes. During a randomized controlled trial, they added DNA processing to the treatment group and were able to identify that there were additional arrests in the treatment group that would not have occurred without DNA processing and that the cost of these additional arrests was just over US$ 14,000.

Especially in the current financial climate, where labour accounts for such a large proportion of restricted police budgets, if fewer investigative resources are used on unsolvable investigations, 'it seems logical that detectives would have a better chance of clearing the smaller number of remaining solvable cases' (Williams and Sumrall 1982, p. 112). Solvability analysis also allows for the crime-screening process to be streamlined and for predictions to be made in relation to whether cases are solvable. This would, in turn, allow policing agencies to allocate resources differently.

The first option for policing agencies would be to use the same quantity of resources on a smaller number of crimes, thus allowing for more depth of investigation and greater potential for solving more crimes. Alternatively, the reduction in allocated cases could be used to free up resources, which could then be reallocated to gathering other types of evidence in the initial investigation, such as DNA in the work conducted by Roman et al. (2009). The resources so made available for reallocation could also be used to investigate—or proactively target—higher-harm crimes such as child sexual exploitation, allowing policing agencies to redesign the capabilities of their resources whilst retaining existing levels of crime-solving.

Predicting the Outcome of the Case

Knowing the factors that are more prevalent in solved cases has therefore been shown to benefit policing in numerous ways. In order to solve more crimes, many police forces conduct crime screening, and where it does not occur formally, officers will frequently screen cases to concentrate on those seen as most promising (Waegel 1982; Brandl and Frank 1994; Coupe and Griffiths 1996). However, even formal mechanisms are predominantly based on officer-derived experiential judgements and public interest assessments (Gill et al. 1996; Robinson and Tilley 2009), which differ between forces and provide for vast inconsistencies (Coupe and Griffiths 1996).

Despite such a wide body of evidence indicating that crime solvability can be predicted and the fact that private businesses are using predictive algorithms to solve various business problems (Ayres 2007), Sherman (2013) states that, as of 2012, it was still difficult to find a police agency that used a statistical model of solvability to allocate investigative resources.

The argument in relation to whether clinicians make better predictions than algorithms has been ongoing for many decades. Meehl (1954) disputed Sarbin's (1944) wholesale dismissal of the importance of the clinician in prediction, but both concluded that statistical predictions are generally more accurate.

In relation to algorithmic prediction, Meehl (1986, p. 373) stated:

> there is no controversy in social science that shows such a large body of qualitatively diverse studies coming out so uniformly in the same direction as this one. When you are pushing 90 investigations, predicting everything from the outcome of football games to the diagnosis of liver disease and when you can hardly come up with a half dozen studies showing even a weak tendency in favour of the clinician, it is time to draw a practical conclusion, whatever theoretical differences may still be disputed. Why, then, is such a strongly and clearly supported empirical generalization not applied in practice, particularly because there are no plausible theoretical reasons to have expected otherwise in the first place?

In 1996, Grove and Meehl examined 136 studies covering a wide range of topics and demonstrated that the mechanical or statistical method is almost invariably equal or superior to the clinical or practitioner method. They concluded (Grove and Meehl 1996, p. 320) that 'to use the less efficient of two prediction procedures in dealing with such matters is not only unscientific and irrational, but it is also unethical. To say that the clinical–statistical issue is of little importance is preposterous'.

Later chapters in this book present research relating to violent crimes (Chapter "Targeting Factors that Predict Clearance of Non-domestic Assaults") and pickpocketing on the UK railway network (Chapter "Pickpocketing on Railways"), both of which have demonstrated—through split sample testing with the use of large data sets—not only that it is possible to predict whether crimes will be solved or not but also that allocation of cases is more accurate when performed by an algorithmic model than by experienced practitioners. Therefore, even if police officers could previously argue that they were an exception to the above statements about clinicians, this volume provides evidence that this does, in fact, also apply to policing. There is therefore much to be gained from identifying solvability factors and building predictive models that can be compared to existing practice in order to improve the ways in which crime is investigated. This volume draws together a variety of empirical studies of property, violent and sexual crimes that demonstrate how police agencies can make gains in investigative effectiveness and efficiency by harnessing predictive models based on the statistical analysis of solvability factors.

References

Addington, L. A. (2006). Using national incident-based reporting system murder data to evaluate clearance predictors: A research note. *Homicide Studies, 10*(2), 140–152.

Ahlberg, J., & Knutsson, J. (1990). The risk of detection. *Journal of Quantitative Criminology, 6*(1), 117–130.

Alderden, M. A., & Lavery, T. A. (2007). Predicting homicide clearances in Chicago: Investigating disparities in predictors across different types of homicide. *Homicide Studies, 11*(2), 115–132.

Antrobus, E., & Pilotto, A. (2016). Improving forensic responses to residential burglaries: Results of a randomized controlled field trial. *Journal of Experimental Criminology, 12*(3), 319–345.

Association of Chief Police Officers. (1996). *Using forensic science effectively*. London: ACPO.

Audit Commission. (1993). *Helping with enquiries: Tackling crime effectively*. London: HMSO.

Ayres, I. (2007). *Supercrunchers: How anything can be predicted*. London: Murray.

Balemba, S., Beauregard, E., & Martineau, M. (2014). Getting away with murder: A thematic approach to solved and unsolved sexual homicides using crime scene factors. *Police Practice and Research, 15*(3), 221–233.

Baskin, D., & Sommers, I. (2010). The influence of forensic evidence on the case outcomes of homicide incidents. *Journal of Criminal Justice, 38*(6), 1141–1149.

Baskin, D., & Sommers, I. (2012). The influence of forensic evidence on the case outcomes of assault and robbery incidents. *Criminal Justice Policy Review, 23*(2), 186–210.

Beauregard, E., & Martineau, M. (2014). No body, no crime? The role of forensic awareness in avoiding police detection in cases of sexual homicide. *Journal of Criminal Justice, 42*(2), 213–220.

Bieck, W., & Kessler, D. A. (1977). *Response time analysis*. Kansas City: Missouri Board of Police Commissioners.

Blake, L., & Coupe, R. T. (2001). The impact of single and two-officer patrols on catching burglars in the act. *The British Journal of Criminology, 41*(2), 381–396.

Bloch, P. B., & Bell, J. (1976). *Managing investigations: The Rochester system*. Washington, DC: The Police Foundation.

Bond, J. (2007). Value of DNA evidence in detecting crime. *Journal of Forensic Sciences, 52*(1), 128–136.

Bradbury, S., & Feist, A. (2005). *The use of forensic science in volume crime investigations: A review of the research literature* (Home Office Online Report 43/05). London: Home Office.

Brandl, S. G., & Frank, J. (1994). The relationship between evidence, detective effort, and the disposition of burglary and robbery investigations. *American Journal of Police, 13*(3), 149–168.

Briody, M. (2004). The effects of DNA evidence on homicide cases in court. *Australian & New Zealand Journal of Criminology, 37*(2), 231–252.

Brown, J. M., Hamilton, C., & O'Neill, D. (2007). Characteristics associated with rape attrition and the role played by scepticism or legal rationality by investigators and prosecutors. *Psychology, Crime & Law, 13*(4), 355–370.

Brown, K. M., & Keppel, R. D. (2012). Child abduction murder: The impact of forensic evidence on solvability. *Journal of Forensic Sciences, 57*(2), 353–363.

Burrows, J., Tilley, N. (2005). *An overview of attrition patterns*. Online Report 45/05. London: Home Office.

Burrows, J., Hopkins, M., Hubbard, R., Robinson, A., Speed, M., & Tilley, N. (2005). *Understanding the attrition process in volume crime investigations* (Home Office Research Study 295). London: Home Office.

Burrows, J., & Tarling, R. (1982). *Clearing up crime*. London: HMSO.

Cardarelli, A. P., & Cavanagh, D. (1992). *Uncleared homicides in the United States: An exploratory study of trends and patterns*. Paper presented at the annual meeting of the American Society of Criminology, New Orleans.

Chaiken, J. M. (1975). *The criminal investigation process: Volume II: Survey of municipal and county police departments*. Santa Monica, CA: The RAND Corporation.

Chaiken, J. M., Greenwood, P. W., & Petersilia, J. (1976). *The criminal investigation process: A summary report*. Santa Monica, CA: The RAND Corporation.

Clawson, C., & Chang, S. K. (1977). Relationship of response delays and arrest rates. *Journal of Police Science and Administration, 5*(1), 53–68.

Cordner, G. W. (1989). Police agency size and investigative effectiveness. *Journal of Criminal Justice, 17*(3), 145–155.

Corwin, M. (1997). *The killing season: A summer inside an LAPD homicide division*. New York: Simon and Schuster.

Coupe, R. T. (2014). *An evaluation of the effects of police resources and incident solvability on crime detection* (Legal Studies Research Paper Series, Paper 46). Cambridge: University of Cambridge, Faculty of Law.

Coupe, R. T. (2016). Evaluating the effects of resources and solvability on burglary detection. *Policing & Society: An International Journal of Research and Policy, 26*(5), 563–587.

Coupe, R. T., & Blake, L. (2005). The effects of patrol workloads and response strength on burglary emergencies. *Journal of Criminal Justice, 33*(3), 239–255.

Coupe, R. T., & Blake, L. (2006). Daylight and darkness strategies and the risks of offenders being seen at residential burglaries. *Criminology, 44*(2), 431–463.

Coupe, R. T., & Girling, A. J. (2001). Modelling police success in catching burglars in the act. *Omega, 29*(1), 19–27.

Coupe, T., & Griffiths, M. (1996). *Solving residential burglary* (Police Research Group Crime Detection and Prevention Services Paper 77). London: Home Office.

Coupe, T., & Griffiths, M. (2000). Catching offenders in the act: An empirical study of police effectiveness in handling 'immediate response' residential burglary. *International Journal of the Sociology of Law, 28*(2), 163–176.

Coupe, R. T., & Kaur, S. (2005). The role of alarms and CCTV in detecting non-residential burglary. *Security Journal, 18*(2), 53–72.

D'Alessio, S. J., & Stolzenberg, I. (2003). Race and the probability of arrest. *Social Forces, 81*(4), 1381–1397.

Davis, R. C., Jensen, C. J., Burgette, L., & Burnett, K. (2014). Working smarter on cold cases: Identifying factors associated with successful cold case investigations. *Journal of Forensic Sciences, 59*(2), 375–382.

Donnellan, P. G. (2011). *To what extent is burglary detection a consequence of effective investigation?* (Unpublished MSt thesis). University of Cambridge.

Eck, J. E. (1979). *Managing case assignments: The burglary investigation decision model replication*. Washington, DC: Police Executive Research Forum.

Eck, J. E. (1983). *Solving crimes: The investigation of burglary and robbery*. Washington, DC: Police Executive Research Forum.

Eitle, D., Stolzenberg, I., & D'Alessio, S. J. (2005). Police organizational factors, the racial composition of the police, and the probability of arrest. *Justice Quarterly, 22*(1), 30–57.

Fallik, S., & Wells, W. (2015). Testing previously unsubmitted sexual assault kits: What are the investigative results? *Criminal Justice Policy Review, 26*(6), 598–619.

Fitzgerald, J. (2006). *The attrition of sexual offences from the New South Wales criminal justice system*. Sydney: New South Wales Bureau of Crime Statistics and Research.

Folk, J. F. (1971). *Municipal detective systems—A quantitative approach* (Technical Report Number 55). Boston: Operations Research Center, Massachusetts Institute of Technology.

Geberth, V. J. (1996). *Practical homicide investigation: Tactics, procedures and forensic techniques*. Boca Raton, FL: CRC Press.

Gill, M., Hart, J., Livingstone, K., & Stevens, J. (1996). *The crime allocation system: Police investigations into burglary and auto crime* (Police Research Series Paper 16). London: Home Office.

Gottfredson, M. R., & Hindelang, M. J. (1979). A study of the behavior of law. *American Sociological Review, 44*(1), 3–18.

Greenberg, B., Elliot, C. V., Kraft, L. P., & Procter, S. H. (1977). *Felony investigation decision model—An analysis of investigation elements of information*. Washington, DC: US Government Printing Office.

Greenwood, P. W. (1970). *An analysis of the apprehension activities of the New York City Police Department*. Santa Monica, CA: The RAND Corporation.

Greenwood, P. W., Chaiken, J. M., Petersilia, J., & Prusoff, L. (1975). *The criminal investigation process: Volume III: Observations and analysis*. Santa Monica, CA: The RAND Corporation.

Greenwood, P. W., & Petersilia, J. (1975). *The criminal investigation process: Volume I: Summary and policy implications*. Santa Monica, CA: The RAND Corporation.

Grove, W. M., & Meehl, P. E. (1996). Comparative efficiency of informal (subjective, impressionistic) and formal (mechanical, algorithmic) prediction procedures: The clinical–statistical controversy. *Psychology, Public Policy, and Law, 2*(2), 293–323.

Hester, M. (2006). Making it through the criminal justice system: Attrition and domestic violence. *Social Policy and Society, 5*(1), 79–90.

Hohl, K., & Stanko, E. A. (2015). Complaints of rape and the criminal justice system: Fresh evidence on the attrition problem in England and Wales. *European Journal of Criminology, 12*(3), 324–341.

Home Office. (2011). *User guide to Home Office crime statistics*. London: Home Office.

Hopkins, M. (2009). Why are arson detection rates so low? A study of the factors that promote and inhibit the detection of arson. *Policing: A Journal of Policy and Practice, 3*(1), 78–88.

Ingemann-Hansen, O., Brink, O., Sabroe, S., Sørensen, V., & Charles, A. V. (2008). Legal aspects of sexual violence—Does forensic evidence make a difference? *Forensic Science International, 180*(2–3), 98–104.

Innes, M. (2002). The 'process structures' of police homicide investigations. *The British Journal of Criminology, 42*(4), 669–688.

Isaacs, H. (1967). *A study of communications, crimes and arrests in a metropolitan police department. Task force report: Science and technology*. Washington, DC: UN Government Printing Office.

Jiao, A. Y. (2007). Explaining homicide clearance: An analysis of Chicago homicide data 1965–1995. *Criminal Justice Studies, 20*(1), 3–14.

Keel, T. G., Jarvis, J. P., & Muirhead, Y. E. (2009). An exploratory analysis of factors affecting homicide investigations: Examining the dynamics of murder clearance rates. *Homicide Studies, 13*(1), 50–68.

Killmier, B. (2014). *Offenders and their offences: Convicted burglars in Adelaide* (MSt thesis). University of Cambridge.

Klinger, D. A. (1997). Negotiating order in patrol work: An ecological theory of police response to deviance. *Criminology, 35*(2), 277–306.

Lamme, M., & Bernasco, W. (2013). Are mobile offenders less likely to be caught? The influence of the geographical dispersion of serial offenders' crime locations on their probability of arrest. *European Journal of Criminology, 10*(2), 168–186.

Langworthy, R. H., & Hindelang, M. J. (1979). Effects of police agency size on the use of police employees: A re-examination of Ostrom, Parks and Whitaker. *Police Studies: The International Review of Police Development, 2*(1), 11–19.

Lee, C. (2005). The value of life in death: Multiple regression and event history analyses of homicide clearance in Los Angeles County. *Journal of Criminal Justice, 33*(6), 527–534.

Litwin, K. J. (2004). A multilevel multivariate analysis of factors affecting homicide clearances. *Journal of Research in Crime and Delinquency, 41*(4), 327–351.

Litwin, K. J., & Xu, Y. (2007). The dynamic nature of homicide clearances: A multilevel model comparison of three time periods. *Homicide Studies, 11*(2), 94–114.

Lockwood, B. (2014). What clears burglary offenses? Estimating the influences of multiple perspectives of burglary clearance. *Policing: An International Journal of Police Strategies and Management, 37*(4), 746–761.

Marché, G. E. (1994). The production of homicide solutions: An empirical analysis. *American Journal of Economics and Sociology, 53*(4), 385–401.

Meehl, P. E. (1954). *Clinical vs. statistical prediction: A theoretical analysis and a review of the evidence*. Minneapolis: University of Minnesota Press.

Meehl, P. E. (1986). Causes and effects of my disturbing little book. *Journal of Personality Assessment, 50*(3), 370–375.

Menaker, T. A., Campbell, B. A., & Wells, W. (2016). The use of forensic evidence in sexual assault investigations: Perceptions of sex crimes investigators. *Violence Against Women, 23*(4), 399–425.

Mouzos, J., & Muller, D. (2001). Solvability factors of homicide in Australia: An exploratory analysis. In *Trends and issues in crime and criminal justice*. Canberra: Australian Institute of Criminology.

Newburn, T. (2007). Understanding investigation. In T. Newburn, T. Williamson, & A. Wright (Eds.), *Handbook of criminal investigation*. Cullompton: Willan Publishing.

Newiss, G. (2002). *Responding to and investigating street robbery* (unpublished). In K. Jansson (Ed.), *Volume crime investigations—A review of the research literature* (Home Office Online Report OLR 44/05). London: Home Office.

Olphin, T. W. L. (2015). *Solving violent crime: Targeting factors that predict clearance of non-domestic violent offences* (Unpublished MSt thesis). University of Cambridge.

Ostrom, E., Parks, R., & Whitaker, G. (1978). Police agency size: Some evidence on its effects. *Police Studies, 1*(1), 34–46.

Ousey, G. C., & Lee, M. R. (2010). To know the unknown: The decline in homicide clearance rates, 1980–2000. *Criminal Justice Review, 35*(2), 141–158.

Paine, C. (2012). *Solvability factors in dwelling burglaries in Thames Valley* (unpublished MSt thesis). University of Cambridge.

Paine, C., & Ariel, B. (2013). *Solvability analysis: Increasing the likelihood of detection in completed, attempted and in-progress burglaries*. Paper presented at the 6th International Evidence-Based Policing Conference, Cambridge, 8–10 July 2013.

Paré, P., Felson, R. B., & Ouimet, M. (2007). Community variation in crime detection: A multilevel analysis with comments on assessing police performance. *Journal of Quantitative Criminology, 23*(3), 243–258.

Parkinson, P. N., Shrimpton, S., Swanston, H. Y., O'Toole, B. I., & Oates, R. K. (2002). The process of attrition in child sexual assault cases: A case flow analysis of criminal investigations and prosecutions. *The Australian & New Zealand Journal of Criminology, 35*(3), 347–362.

Pelfrey, W. V., Jr., & Hanna, C. A. (2011). The role of suspect and victim information in investigation outcomes: Revisiting Eck's triage theory. *Law Enforcement Executive Forum, 11,* 91–100.

Peterson, J. L., Hickman, M. J., Strom, K. J., & Johnson, D. J. (2013). Effect of forensic evidence on criminal justice case processing. *Journal of Forensic Sciences, 58*(S1), S78–S90.

Peterson, J., Sommers, I., Baskin, D., & Johnson, D. (2010). *The role and impact of forensic evidence in the criminal justice process*. Washington, DC: National Institute of Justice.

Ponce, C., Salfati, C. G., Barton, S. M., & Shon, P. C. (2007). Homicide solvability factors in El Salvador: An initial exploration. *Law Enforcement Executive Forum, 7*(1), 151–172.

Puckett, J. L., & Lundman, R. J. (2003). Factors affecting homicide clearances: Multivariate analysis of a more complete conceptual framework. *Journal of Research in Crime and Delinquency, 40*(2), 171–193.

Randol, B. M., & Sanders, C. M. (2015). Examining the barriers to sexual assault evidence processing in Washington State: What's the hold up? *Criminology, Criminal Justice, Law and Society, 16*(2), 1–13.

Regoeczi, W. C., Jarvis, J., & Riedel, M. (2008). Clearing murders: Is it about time? *Journal of Research in Crime and Delinquency, 45*(2), 142–162.

Regoeczi, W. C., Kennedy, L. W., & Silverman, R. A. (2000). Uncleared homicides: A Canada/United States comparison. *Homicide Studies, 4*(2), 135–161.

Riedel, M., & Rinehart, T. A. (1996). Murder clearances and missing data. *Journal of Crime and Justice, 19*(2), 83–102.

Robb, P., Coupe, R. T., & Ariel, B. (2015). 'Solvability' and detection of metal theft on railway property. *European Journal on Criminal Policy and Research, 21*(4), 463–484.

Roberts, A. (2007). Predictors of homicide clearance by arrest: An event history analysis of NIBRS incidents. *Homicide Studies, 11*(2), 82–93.

Roberts, A. (2008). The influences of incident and contextual characteristics on crime clearance of nonlethal violence: A multilevel event history analysis. *Journal of Criminal Justice, 36*(1), 61–71.

Roberts, A. (2014). Adjusting rates of homicide clearance by arrest for investigation difficulty: Modelling incident- and jurisdiction-level obstacles. *Homicide Studies, 19*(3), 273–300.

Robinson, A., & Tilley, N. (2009). Factors influencing police performance in the investigation of volume crimes in England and Wales. *Police Practice and Research: An International Journal, 10*(3), 209–223.

Roman, J. K., Reid, S. E., Chalfin, A. J., & Knight, C. R. (2009). The DNA field experiment: A randomized trial of the cost-effectiveness of using DNA to solve property crimes. *Journal of Experimental Criminology, 5*, 345–369.

Rydberg, J., & Pizarro, J. M. (2014). Victim lifestyle as a correlate of homicide clearance. *Homicide Studies, 18*(4), 342–362.

Sarbin, T. R. (1944). The logic of prediction in psychology. *Psychological Review, 51*(4), 210–228.

Sherman, L. W. (2013). The rise of evidence-based policing: Targeting, testing, and tracking. *Crime and Justice, 42*(1), 377–451.

Skogan, W. G., & Antunes, G. E. (1979). Information, apprehension and deterrence: Exploring the limits of police productivity. *Journal of Criminal Justice, 7*(3), 217–241.

Snyder, H. N. (1999). The overrepresentation of juvenile crime proportions in robbery clearance statistics. *Journal of Quantitative Criminology, 15*(2), 151–161.

Spelman, W., & Brown, D. K. (1981). *Calling the police: Citizen reporting of serious crime*. Washington, DC: Police Research Executive Forum.

Stevens, J. M., & Stipak, B. (1982). Factors associated with police apprehension productivity. *Police Science and Administration, 10*(1), 52–57.

Telep, C. W., & Weisburd, D. (2011). *What is known about the effectiveness of police practices*? John Jay College of Criminal Justice. http://www.jjay.cuny.edu/Telep_Weisburd.pdf. Accessed May 24, 2014.

Tilley, N., & Burrows, J. (2005). *An overview of attrition patterns* (Home Office Online Report 45/05). London: Home Office.

Tilley, N., & Ford, A. (1996). *Forensic science and crime investigation* (Crime Prevention and Detection Series, Paper 73). London: Home Office.

Tilley, N., Robinson, A., & Burrows, J. (2007). The investigation of high volume crime. In T. Newburn, T. Williamson, & A. Wright (Eds.), *Handbook of criminal investigation* (pp. 226–254). London: Willan Publishing.

Tillyer, M. S., & Tillyer, R. (2015). Maybe I should do this alone: A comparison of solo and co-offending robbery outcomes. *Justice Quarterly, 32*(6), 1064–1088.

Tillyer, M. S., Tillyer, R., & Kelsay, J. (2015). The nature and influence of the victim–offender relationship in kidnapping incidents. *Journal of Criminal Justice, 43*(5), 377–385.

Waegel, W. B. (1982). Patterns of police investigation of urban crimes. *Journal of Police Science and Administration, 10*(4), 452–465.

Webbink, D., van Erp, J., & van Gastel, F. (2017). The effect of media exposure of suspects on solving crime. *The Economic Journal, 127*(600), 547–570.

Weisburd, D., & Eck, J. E. (2004). What can the police do to reduce crime, disorder and fear? *The Annals of the American Academy of Political and Social Science, 593*(1), 42–65.

Wellford, C., & Cronin, J. (1999). *An analysis of variables affecting the detection of homicides: A multivariate study*. Washington, DC: Justice Research Statistics Association.

Williams, V. L., & Sumrall, R. O. (1982). Productivity measures in the criminal investigation function. *Journal of Criminal Justice, 10*(2), 111–122.

Wolfgang, M. E. (1958). *Patterns in criminal homicide*. Philadelphia: University of Pennsylvania.

Assessing Solvability Factors in Greater Manchester, England: The Case of Residential Burglaries

Patrick Gerard Donnellan and Barak Ariel

Residential burglary is always a national concern. It is a volume contributor to overall crime statistics. The perpetrators attack the personal space and belongings of their victims, some of which are the most vulnerable members of society. They can occur at any time of day or night, which adds to the damage they cause not just to physical property and sense of security, but to our general perceptions of fear of crime more broadly.

Clearance rates are often very low in burglary crime, with often not more than a fifth of incidents cleared by the police (Braga et al. 2011). However, as Chapter "Existing Research on Solvability" suggested, both Greenberg et al. (1977) and Eck (1979) have offered a promising investigation decision model that can point the police in the direction of 'solvable cases'. Replication of these earlier works did not take place in Europe. Here, we present what we believe is the first of such explorations.

The original solvability factors model incorporated six variables in the model that carry strong predictive validity—'Witness Present', 'Discovered by the Police', 'Usable Fingerprints', 'Suspect Developed', 'Vehicle Involved', and 'Response Time'. Yet since the 1970s, prominent developments were made in forensic sciences and technology, with CCTV and DNA testing to name a few. New methods of investigations emerged, such as social network analysis, electronic tagging and mobile tracking technologies. Therefore, additional variables investigated are required to be instigated as well.

This chapter aims to replicate the original solvability factors models (Greenberg et al. 1977; Eck 1979), and to enhance it with additional variables. We used a total of 400 burglary crimes from the period 1 April 2008 to the 31 March 2009, 200

P. G. Donnellan (✉)
Greater Manchester Police, Manchester, UK
e-mail: GerryP.Donnellan@gmp.police.uk

B. Ariel
Institute of Criminology, University of Cambridge, Cambridge, UK

Institute of Criminology, Faculty of Law, The Hebrew University, Mount Scopus, Jerusalem, Israel

R. T. Coupe et al. (eds.), *Crime Solvability Factors*,
https://doi.org/10.1007/978-3-030-17160-5_3

detected crimes and 200 non-detected crimes, which were randomly selected from a pool of nearly 35,000 break-ins in the Greater Manchester Police area. Our study seems to be the first major replication of solvability factors decision-making model in Europe.

Seventy seven offences of burglary where violence has been used against the occupiers were also selected for the purpose of the analysis. The 77 crimes were all the burglary crimes involving violence or threats of violence during the same period, but were classified originally as violent crimes—an important lesson for future studies on solvability factors (i.e., that the classification of crimes can often be erroneous or misleading). We then compared the prevalence of each of these factors in the solved versus the unsolved crime, in order to estimate the potential contribution of each of these variables in residential burglary solvability.

Research Settings—Greater Manchester Police

The Greater Manchester Police Force area is divided into 12 geographical policing areas known as divisions. Each division has its own unique features ranging from a busy and vibrant city centre to areas of severe deprivation and diverse communities. Recorded crime data for Greater Manchester Police shows that between 2003 and 2007 recorded levels of residential burglary had fallen. In 2008/09, the recorded number of burglaries however increased compared to the previous year by 9.9% to 23,770. The detection rate of these burglaries remained constant over the years, around 12%; however, the rates for the 12 divisions in 2008/09 ranged broadly, from 7.7 to 17.6%.

Early Solvability Decision-Making Models for Burglary Offences

As Chapter "Existing Research on Solvability" has shown, there are key studies in the area of initial crime screening models. The earliest work was developed by Greenberg et al. (1977) in 'Felony Investigation Decision Model—An Analysis of Investigative Elements of Information'. Greenberg's et al. (1977) model identified 25 factors, but linked six elements directly to the arrest of an offender (listed below). When tested the model on 500 burglary crimes in four police departments in the USA, Greenberg discovered that it predicted the arrest in between 67 and 92% of cases. Heterogeneity was explained based on 'inconsistent policies governing the criteria by which a burglary case was cleared' (Greenberg et al. 1977, p. xxvii).

Greenberg's et al. (1977) model included factors that virtually any crime recording system contains. The preliminary initial investigation by the first officer attending the crime can highlight if any of the six variables were present. This feature is critically important for replication and generalisability; if a set of factors is unique to a particular department that is, for example, rich in resources, then the model would not be transferrable to other jurisdictions. Instead, Greenberg included key features that, when present, are linked to higher clearance rates.

A few years later, Eck (1979) replicated Greenberg's work (1977), but incorporated a weighting system for the six solvability factors, depending on their contribution to an arrest. The 'known suspect' factor received the greatest weighting (9), with usable fingerprints and witnesses' reports weighted as '7', and time range weighted as '5' in the model. According to the model, cases receiving a score greater than 10 should be allocated for further investigation, and those with a score of 10 or less should be filed as 'closed investigations'. Eck (1979) applied the variables to over 12,000 burglary cases and was able to predict solvability with an accuracy of 85%—that is, the model's predictive accuracy of an arrest was 85% of recorded offences of burglary, plainly based on the preliminary investigation of the first officer attending. This gave the burglary investigation decision model both reliability and validity. Operationally, it could allow significant caseloads to be screened out and resources to be redeployed to cases that would become solvable with more police investigative attention. This has significant connotations in the current economic climate.

The Original Six Solvability Factors

1. **On-view report of offence (i.e. if a police officer was first to observe the offence)**. Being caught 'in the act' or burglars being sighted nearby is dependent on the ability of police resources to respond extremely quickly, or to be lucky enough to be in the area, while the burglary was in progress. Coupe and Blake (2005) confirm this recognising that quick response is important, but the number of patrols that respond also determines if arrests are to be made. They found that 'the police were almost twice as successful when they reached the scene within 4 min of the alert being sounded than they were when they arrived after 6 min' (2005, p. 244). This is supported by Burrows et al. (2005) who made similar findings and Greenwood and Petersilia (1975) who asserted that most crimes are detected as a consequence of arrests made at the scene of the burglary and information from witnesses.
2. **Suspect information developed, including his or her description or name**. Previously, Eck (1983) has concluded that without a suspect name or identity being given to the police, there is little likelihood of detecting that crime. However, in the original model, Eck (1979:20) defined the 'suspect developed' variable as situations when 'the police obtained the suspect's name or nickname, or a portion of a name, and/or a description of the suspect. This description could involve physical characteristics, words spoken, mannerisms, or an address'. This is wide ranging. Aspects of the definition will be more productive, for example, the suspect's name compared to a vague description. Still, suspect element was clearly seen by Eck (1979) as key to detecting the crime. If a name had been

obtained for the person responsible, this will very likely be a significant predictor of solvability. Eck however included here a description of the offender. This may or may not be helpful in detecting crimes as the description can vary ranging from something vague to one containing detail. It was identified by Burrows et al. (2005, p. 57) that not all burglaries are 'stranger crimes' as 19.3% of detected crimes were committed by offenders who knew the victim.

3. **Witness's report of offence**. Recognising that witnesses are important in detecting burglaries, Coupe and Blake (2006) examined if the degree of importance was influenced by when the burglary was committed, that is, daytime or during the night. Burglars would have 'the cover of darkness' during the night, but it would increase the risk of arrest if selecting occupied dwellings. 'Daytime burglars' would conversely increase the risk of arrest and identification by witnesses unless they selected the dwellings with increased cover. They concluded that there were 'greater chances of being seen and ultimately caught in daylight' (2006, p. 443).
4. **Estimated range of time of occurrence (the time delay between the burglary being reported and the arrival of the police)**. The factors influencing crimes of burglary being detected have also been studied by Coupe and Griffiths (1996) and Coupe and Blake (2006). In these studies, the offender was caught at or near the scene in 43% of cases, from witness accounts in 34% of cases and forensic evidence produced detections in only 6% of cases examined. A quick response by patrols also enables an early scene assessment to be made and the forensic investigation to be commenced. This is essential for external scenes during adverse weather. This increases the opportunities to identify a named suspect. A quick response was also evident when Greenwood et al. (1976) found that nearly 30% of detections for burglary were as a result of officers responding to the scene. This is supported by Coupe and Blake (2005) who ascertained that the more patrols that attended the scene, the more burglars were arrested.
5. **Usable fingerprints (fingerprints which are believed to belong to the offender)**. Greenwood and Petersilia (1975) claimed at up to 1.5% of all burglary detections are as a result of fingerprints recovered from the crime scene. Coupe and Griffiths (1996) put the figure for fingerprints used in detected offences of burglary at 17%. The significance of forensic evidence should not be underestimated as Bradbury and Feist assert that 'forensic evidence greatly increases the odds of detecting an offence especially when other forms of evidence are absent' (2005, p. 12). The Association of Chief Police Officers (1996) identified that forensic evidence can assist in identifying an unknown offender and can corroborate existing evidence. In 1972, Parker and Peterson found that physical evidence existed at 92% of burglary scenes, but it seems from the facts above that this was not, at this time, transferred into evidence to the limited techniques that existed at this time. Greenwood and Petersilia (1975) asserted that if an offender was not identified at the time the burglary was reported, it was unlikely that the offender would ever be identified. They concluded that if investigators conducted thorough primary investigations and uncover fingerprints, for example, they would detect the majority of crimes. The value of fingerprint evidence was

found by Eck (1979) to be relevant in 9% of burglaries. The value of forensic evidence is appreciated and supported by Coupe and Griffiths (1996) and Bradbury and Feist (2005) but not by Jansson (2005) who concludes that forensic evidence is central only in a minority of criminal investigations.
6. **Vehicle description**. This factor refers to information about a car or any other transportation that enabled the offender to reach the crime scene or away from it. This includes, among other details, a licence plate, car make and model, or any other feature that can identify the perpetrator following some investigation about the vehicle.

Additional Solvability Factors

The six information elements are still valid and relevant but need to be updated and to take into account advancements in forensic capabilities. We list these variables below, but two areas are of particular interest. First, the six elements identified by Eck and Greenberg do not take into account the value of property stolen or if it is traceable or indeed if the victim sustained an injury during the course of the crime. These factors can also influence not just solvability but also the public interest factor in investigating the crime. This point is argued by O'Reilly (1992) who has added them to the six elements. Interestingly, he also includes in his solvability checklist a question asking if the victim has been informed of the status of the investigation. This approach attempts to incorporate a victim-focussed approach.

Second, forensic evidence and advancements in forensic sciences are not part of the model, as they were not part of the modern crime scene investigation apparatus. DNA testing was not included in the model, as well as other types of forensic tests, like footwear impressions, or E-fits of suspects. As rightly claimed by Tilley and Ford (1996: 46), 'the forensic problem in volume crime appears to be generally less well thought through'. Improvements in forensic capability should provide greater opportunities to identify suspects. Furthermore, since the 1970s, there has been a proliferation of CCTV especially in cities like London or New York City, where a network of cameras is recording constantly the movement of people as well as vehicles.

Data and Procedures

The first contact made by a victim or witness to the police, in the majority of occasions, does not result in the creation of a crime report. At least in England and Wales, the contact is usually by telephone and results in the creation of a force wide incident number (FWIN), which is a computer log of the circumstances. This FWIN is then the catalyst to despatch officers to the scene. The FWIN is created by the call operator asking the victim or witness a series of questions that will elicit the urgency that needs to be given to allocating resources to the report of crime. This is effectively a triage of all calls by the call takers against a police service standard consistent with the National Call Handling Standards. This graded response policy dictates that attendance will be: (a) within 15 min for emergency calls; this includes cases where an offender is actually committing a crime, been detained and they pose a risk, has just been disturbed and made off; (b) within 1 h for priority calls; this includes cases where the offender has made off, been detained and they do not pose a risk or if burglary has been deemed a priority crime for that area; (c) within 4 h for routine calls.

The quantitative data owned by Greater Manchester Police routinely captures the times between which the crime occurred, circumstances of the crime, police reports, forensic results, offender information, stolen property and vehicle details if applicable. For each burglary recorded the FWIN, there are about fifty variables collected by the police and recorded in the crime reports. Such a data-rich document makes it an ideal source to use, but its attractiveness is also because the data are not available from anywhere else. The crime report also includes other data such as the modus operandi of the crime. The information is captured by the officer who attends the crime and undertakes the primary investigation. This officer then causes the information to be inputted onto the electronic crime report allowing the data to be analysed and mapped. The quality of the data is dependent upon the attention to detail and professionalism of the officer conducting the primary investigation.

There are five Home Office burglary dwelling codes, which included attempted burglary. These crime categories formed the prominent crime codes for our study. However, if during the course of a burglary a witness/victim was assaulted, then the incident would be recorded as an assault (e.g. personal injury), according to the National Crime Recording Standards, hence taking precedence over the property aspect of a crime. Therefore, the most accurate methodology to conduct this work was to create a search of all recorded crimes for the research period which had been generated from a FWIN (computer log) opened as a burglary.

There were 34,924 burglary crimes recorded during the twelve months of the study, period 1 April 2008 to 31 March 2009, but we required cases that were finalised (i.e. deemed closed). For the study period, there were 23,770 closed burglary investigations. Of this total closed crimes, 2947 (12.4%) had been cleared and 20,823 (87.6%) had not.

Nevertheless, as the system did not populate the data in analysable format in order to extract the presence of solvability factors in each case, a manual read of each investigation case was required for the purpose of the analysis. Given time constraints, we randomly selected a sample of detected crimes and a sample of undetected crimes. Random selection was performed using the pseudo-random number formula available within Microsoft Excel which was applied to each crime number. This process was applied to both cleared and non-cleared burglary dwelling crimes. Power calculations identified that a total sample size of 400 crimes—200 cleared and 200 not cleared—satisfies the power requirements of detecting small to medium effects with a $p < .05$ and power of 80%. This sample represented 1.7% of all the closed burglary crimes.

To these burglary crimes, we added all 77 burglaries that occurred during the time of the study where violence was included in the incident, so the overall classification was 'violence', even though the modus operandi was clearly a break-in with an intent to steal property. These included 20 detected violent burglary crimes and 57 undetected violent burglary crimes. Thus, in total, our sample included 477 cases of burglary.

Solvability Factors Crime Variables

The following variables were examined for all our 477 detected versus undetected burglary crimes. There may be several crime scenes, so each one of these variables can appear multiple times, as well as for multiple offenders.

1. Offence reporting party
2. Method of reporting
3. Disposal code (arrest, cautions, no further action, etc.)
4. Day of week
5. Time of day
6. Attempted burglary or not
7. Suspect named
8. Suspect described
9. Documentation provided or not
10. Documentation type
11. Footprints at primary scene
12. Fingerprints at primary scene
13. DNA at primary scene
14. Other forensic evidence at primary scene
15. CCTV
16. Value of property stolen.
17. Vehicle information

Statistical Procedure

The analysis examined the differences between; (a) Detected and Undetected burglaries and (b) Detected and Undetected Violent Burglaries. Chi-square tests and t-tests were performed to test for statistically significant differences between detection status and Eck's (1979) variables and the additional factors listed above. The overall analysis focuses primarily at establishing that the significant correlations between the solvability factors and solvability reported in the US are replicable in a UK context. For this focus, our test statistics are sufficient (for granular analysis of effect sizes, see Chapter "Population-Level Analysis of Residential Burglaries").

Table 1 Original six solvability factors: prevalence in solved and unsolved cases in Greater Manchester Police (1 April 2008–31 March 2009)—burglaries

Variable	Factor present/not present	Detected burglary ($n = 200$)	Undetected burglary ($n = 200$)	χ^2/t-test
Witness present	Present	87 (43.5%)	32 (16.0%)	36.19**
	Not present	113 (56.5%)	168 (84.0%)	
Discovered by the police	Present	5 (2.5%)	0 (0%)	5.06*
	Not present	195 (97.5%)	200 (100%)	
Usable fingerprints	Present	90 (45.0%)	42 (21.0%)	26.05**
	Not present	110 (55.0%)	158 (79.0%)	
Suspect developed	Present	89 (44.5%)	38 (19.0%)	30.00**
	Not present	111 (55.5%)	162 (81.0%)	
Vehicle involved	Present	5 (2.5%)	30 (15.0%)	−19.57**
	Not present	195 (97.5%)	170 (85.0%)	
Police response time		1′30″ (SD = 3′15″)	2′23″ (SD = 4′04″)	−2.35*

*$p < .05$; **$p < .01$; ***$p < .001$

Findings

Detected Versus Undetected Burglary

Our analyses suggest that in six out of six factors, statistically significant differences emerged between solved and unsolved cases, in terms of the presence of solvability factors. With the exception of the vehicle information, prevalence of solvability factors increases the likelihood of the case being solved. For example, a witness was present in 44% of detected burglaries in comparison with only 16% in undetected cases. This was expected as a witness can provided valuable information to identify the offender. Likewise, information in possession of the police during the primary investigation regarding the suspect ('suspect developed'), significantly differed for detected and undetected burglaries (45% vs. 19%, respectively). These and other findings are reported in Table 1.

While it was anticipated that there would be *more* detections that result in details of a vehicle, only 2.5% of detected cases had a vehicle information, whereas 15% of the undetected cases have had information on a vehicle. It is possible that the vehicle information was simply wrong (e.g. the wrong licence plate number reported by a member of the public).

We note that only five burglaries were discovered by police (but all were detected) but none of the undetected burglaries were discovered by the police. This has major implications in terms of our expectation from the police to tackle burglars in progress through police-initiated activities.

The new variables that are presently in existence in police records are listed in Table 2—again, with the breakdown in terms of solved and unsolved cases and the prevalence of each variable in the two categories. As shown, no differences emerged between the two groups based on the entity reporting or method of reporting the crime to the police, or in terms of the temporal characteristics of the crime; in both groups the highest frequency of detected (33.7%) and undetected burglaries (32.0%) occurred in the morning period, when the residents are often not home. Furthermore, if the burglary was unsuccessful or 'just' attempted without any goods stolen from the property, significant differences emerged in terms of detection, with 8% of detected burglaries were an attempt, compared to 16% of undetected cases. In terms of stolen goods, it appears that value of property stolen was available for 134 detected burglaries and 163 undetected burglaries, but no significant differences were found.

Statistically significant differences were detected in terms of the prevalence of named suspects in solved (15%) versus unsolved investigations (3%). However, when witnesses provided only a description of the suspect (e.g., height, skin colour, clothes), they did not enhance clearance rates ($t = 1.82$; $p > .05$).

The forensic variables examined—footprints, fingerprints, DNA and other forensic evidence—suggest that their presence in the scene is linked to case clearances, except footprint evidence (33.2% vs. 24.00% for fingerprints; 22.4% vs. 10.00% for DNA). CCTV was also a predictor of solvability ($\chi^2 = 11.10, p < .01$), with 9.2% of detected burglaries had CCTV present (compared to 1.5% of undetected cases; but cf. Welsh and Farrington 2009).

Detected Versus Undetected Violent Offences

As noted, 77 burglaries involved a degree of violence exhibited towards the victim or witness (20 solved). However, these are nevertheless 'break-ins' that can potentially be utilised via a screening model. Each variable was examined in isolation, producing the findings (Table 3). Witness—other than the victim—present at the scene was a significant contributor for solvability; notice that in none of the unsolved cases a witness was present at the scene. Similarly, notice that in all solved burglaries with violence a suspect's description was developed. It may have to do something with the discovery by the police through other investigations (30% vs. 2%). As with the non-violent burglaries, vehicle description was a negative contributor to solvability, potentially because of false information. Finally, we found statistically significant differences in terms of clearance rates the faster the police reach the scene. In fact, the data suggests time of arrival was 2.5 longer on unsolved cases compared to solved cases (9 min vs. 23 min, respectively). It is important, however, to point out that the model does not allude to causality, and this correlation may reflect a deeper relationship between time of arrival and solvability, which we discuss below.

Next (Table 4), we observe the differences between the solved and unsolved violent burglaries with the new variables not included in the original decision-making

Table 2 Additional solvability factors: prevalence in solved and unsolved cases in Greater Manchester Police (1 April 2008–31 March 2009)—burglaries

Variable	Factor present/not present	Detected burglary ($n = 200$)	Undetected burglary ($n = 200$)	χ^2/t-test
Offence reported by	3rd Party	33 (16.80%)	45 (22.80%)	2.35
	Police	5 (2.50%)	4 (2.00%)	
	Victim	159 (80.70%)	148 (75.10%)	
Method of reporting	999	106 (53.00%)	102 (51.05%)	4.51
	In-person	6 (3.00%)	2 (1.00%)	
	Found by police	7 (3.50%)	3 (1.50%)	
	Phone	81 (40.50%)	93 (46.50%)	
Day of week	Mon	36 (18.00%)	28 (14.00%)	6.57
	Tue	23 (11.50%)	29 (14.50%)	
	Wed	22 (11.00%)	24 (12.00%)	
	Thu	23 (11.50%)	37 (18.50%)	
	Fri	36 (18.00%)	33 (16.50%)	
	Sat	30 (15.00%)	27 (13.50%)	
	Sun	30 (15.0%)	22 (11.00%)	
Time of offence	Morning 06:00–11:59	65 (33.70%)	63 (32.00%)	4.49
	Afternoon 12:00–17:59	50 (25.90%)	60 (30.50%)	
	Evening 18:00–23:59	40 (20.70%)	49 (24.90%)	
	Night 00:00–05:59	38 (19.70%)	25 (12.70%)	
Attempted burglary	Present	16 (8.00%)	31 (15.50%)	5.43*
	Not present	184 (92.00%)	169 (84.50%)	
Suspect named	Present	29 (14.50%)	6 (3.00%)	16.56**
	Not present	171 (85.50%)	194 (97.00%)	
Suspect described	Present	38 (19.00%)	28 (14.00%)	1.82
	Not Present	162 (81.00%)	172 (86.00%)	
Documentation provided	Present	185 (98.40%)	195 (98.00%)	.093
	Not Present	3 (1.50%)	4 (2.00%)	
Documentation type	Report	7 (3.70%)	5 (2.50%)	14.04**
	Statement	177 (94.10%)	176 (88.40%)	
	FWIN only	0 (0%)	14 (7.00%)	
	Not provided	4 (2.10%)	4 (2.00%)	
Footprints at primary scene	Present	37 (18.60%)	34 (17.20%)	.137
	Not present	162 (81.40%)	164 (82.80%)	

(continued)

Table 2 (continued)

Variable	Factor present/not present	Detected burglary ($n = 200$)	Undetected burglary ($n = 200$)	χ^2/t-test
Fingerprints at primary scene	Present	66 (33.20%)	48 (24.00%)	4.11*
	Not present	133 (66.80%)	152 (76.00%)	
DNA at primary scene	Present	41 (22.40%)	19 (9.50%)	11.9**
	Not present	142 (77.60%)	180 (90.50%)	
Other forensic evidence at primary scene	Present	29 (14.60%)	23 (11.60%)	.762
	Not present	170 (85.40%)	175 (88.40%)	
CCTV	Present	14 (9.20%)	3 (1.50%)	11.1**
	Not present	138 (90.80%)	196 (98.50%)	
Value of stolen property		£1711.92 (SD = £5707.87)	£1233.78 (SD = £3,007.80)	.925

*$p < .05$; **$p < .01$; ***$p < .001$

Table 3 Original six solvability factors: prevalence in solved and unsolved cases in Greater Manchester Police (1 April 2008–31 March 2009)—burglaries with violence

Variable	Factor present/not present	Detected violent burglary ($n = 20$)	Undetected violent burglary ($n = 57$)	χ^2/t-test
Witness present	Present	15 (75.0%)	57 (100%)	15.24**
	Not present	5 (25.0%)	0 (0%)	
Discovered by the police	Present	6 (30%)	1 (1.8%)	14.29*
	Not present	14 (70%)	56 (98.2%)	
Usable fingerprints	Present	3 (15.0%)	19 (33.3%)	2.44
	Not present	17 (85.0%)	38 (66.7%)	
Suspect developed	Present	20 (100%)	52 (91.2%)	1.88
	Not present	0 (0%)	5 (8.8%)	
Vehicle involved	Present	0 (0%)	13 (22.8%)	−5.49*
	Not present	20 (100%)	44 (77.2%)	
Response time		9′00″ (SD = 0′10″)	23′01″ (SD = 0′43″)	2.365*

*$p < .05$; **$p < .01$; ***$p < .001$

model. We are cognizant that the number of cases is limited (although we have used the entire cohort of cases with no exclusion), and therefore, the statistical analyses should be taken with some caution. We emphasise the results that 'stick out' most profoundly.

It appears that once a violent burglary is reported by a third party, the likelihood of detection is diminished (none of the solved violent burglaries were reported by a third party, and 80% were reported to the police by the victim). We have also found a significant difference existed in terms of having a described suspect, however as a backfiring contributor: the suspect was described in 35.1% (20) of undetected cases but in none of the detected cases. Similarly, it seems that technology (CCTV) and forensic evidence (DNA, fingerprints and footprints) are not associated with solvability of violent burglaries.

Discussion

The aim of this study was to evaluate the reliability of the case screening model in respect of burglary cases in England, with more recent data end points. We complicated the original Eck's (1979) model, by incorporating 16 additional variables beyond the six solvability factors that are collated and stored in contemporary investigations of burglary cases. We further expanded the study, by looking at burglaries that were categorised as 'robbery' or 'assault' crimes (following the Home Office rules), because while they started as a break-in, the aggression and violence that characterise these incidents have led to classifying them as a crime category other than burglary (against person crime classification). We would argue that future studies in solvability factors analysis should pay close attention to the 'closing code' of each case and include the entire population of relevant cases when considering the distribution of solvabiilty factors.

To facilitate this study, we collected data on a random sample of 400 burglary cases from across the Greater Manchester Police, with an even split between solved and unsolved cases. All violent burglaries that took place during the study period were also analysed ($n = 77$). The first major finding is that the original decision-making model is still relevant more than thirty years later. Virtually all factors are significantly more prevalent in detected burglaries—witness present, discovered by the police, the presence of usable fingerprints, suspect developed and response time. Similar trends emerged in terms of detected violent burglaries, however not necessarily significant at the .05 level, given the small samples we used. 'Vehicle involved', i.e. details provided on potential methods of travel linked to the offence, was found to be a negative contributor. This suggests that information held on this modus operand is not necessarily linked to successful investigations. More research is needed in this area, but it is possible that it has to do with the ability of witnesses to recall details in an accurate way—which has already been shown to suffer from issues and biases.

One area where we see great strides since the 1970s is forensic evidence. Nearly half of the solved cases included usable fingerprints—as opposed to less than 10%

Table 4 Additional solvability factors: prevalence in solved and unsolved cases in Greater Manchester Police (1 April 2008 to 31 March 2009)—violent burglaries

Variable	Factor present/not present	Detected burglary (n = 200)	Undetected burglary (n = 200)	χ^2/t-test
Offence reported by	3rd Party	0 (0%)	8 (14.00%)	214.27***
	Police	4 (20.00%)	0 (0%)	
	Victim	16 (80.00%)	49 (86.00%)	
Method of reporting	999	17 (85.00%)	49 (86.00%)	3.27
	In-person	0 (0%)	1 (1.80%)	
	Found by police	1 (5.00%)	0 (0%)	
	Phone	2 (10.00%)	7 (12.30%)	
Day of week	Mon	5 (25.00%)	11 (19.30%)	5.11
	Tue	4 (20.00%)	7 (12.30%)	
	Wed	0 (0%)	8 (14.00%)	
	Thu	2 (10.00%)	9 (15.80%)	
	Fri	3 (15.00%)	10 (17.50%)	
	Sat	3 (15.00%)	8 (14.00%)	
	Sun	3 (15.00%)	4 (7.00%)	
Time of offence	Morning 06:00–11:59	1 (5.00%)	5 (8.80%)	8.83*
	Afternoon 12:00–17:59	6 (30.00%)	3 (5.30%)	
	Evening 18:00–23:59	7 (35.00%)	26 (45.60%)	
	Night 00:00–05:59	6 (30.00%)	23 (40.40%)	
Attempted burglary	Present	1 (5.00%)	6 (10.50%)	.547
	Not present	19 (95.00%)	51 (89.50%)	
Suspect named	Present	2 (10.00%)	0 (0%)	5.85*
	Not present	18 (90.00%)	57 (100%)	
Suspect described	Present	0 (0%)	20 (35.10%)	−6.39*
	Not present	13 (100%)	37 (64.90%)	
Documentation type	Report	5 (25.00%)	13 (22.80%)	.04
	Statement	15 (75.00%)	44 (77.20%)	
Footprints at primary scene	Present	5 (25.00%)	25 (43.90%)	2.21
	Not present	15 (75.00%)	32 (56.10%)	
Fingerprints at primary scene	Present	3 (15.00%)	16 (28.10%)	1.36
	Not present	17 (85.00%)	41 (71.90%)	
DNA at primary scene	Present	2 (10%)	16 (28.10%)	2.70
	Not present	18 (90%)	41 (71.90%)	

(continued)

Table 4 (continued)

Variable	Factor present/not present	Detected burglary ($n = 200$)	Undetected burglary ($n = 200$)	χ^2/t-test
Other forensic evidence at primary scene	Present	0 (0%)	6 (10.50%)	2.28
	Not present	20 (100%)	51 (89.50%)	
CCTV	Present	0 (0%)	8 (14.00%)	3.13^
	Not present	20 (100%)	49 (86.00%)	

$^*p < .05$; $^{**}p < .01$; $^{***}p < .001$; $^\wedge p = .070$

of solved cases in the 1970s. We suspect that police officers are trained more these days to secure the scene, to collect evidence in a professional way and to look for clues where they can be found. The proliferation of fingerprint collection kits—as well as DNA and other types of evidence—clearly helped make such a transition.

Furthermore, when we compare the original solvability factors model and the findings from this study, we can see improvements made in the primary investigation by the officers initially despatched to the cases. The importance of the primary investigation cannot be underestimated, as the first few steps in the investigation will identify witnesses and suspect information.

One final note about the original screening model is the inability of the police to 'be at the right place in the right time' and to discover a burglary in progress or immediately thereafter; in only five out of 200 burglary cases, the police solved a case which it detected first-hand. It raises the question of the value in proactive initiatives to combat burglary, if the outcome of interest is making a 'positive arrest'. On the other hand, nearly a third of detected violent crimes were discovered by the police officers. It might be that the police are better at solving violent crimes that they are in solving property crimes. It is also equally probable that this correlation is coincidental, given the small samples and the largely nonsignificant differences between the solved and unsolved cases. More research is needed, with larger samples—an avenue which is offered in Chapter "Population-Level Analysis of Residential Burglaries".

Our findings emphasise the importance of forensic sciences in detecting burglaries and are supported by Coupe and Griffiths (1996) and Bradbury and Feist (2005, p. V) who assert that 'the presence of forensic material greatly increases the odds of detection where other types of evidence are not available. Overall, therefore, forensic material makes the greatest contribution to detecting harder to solve crimes'. Moreover, in 2/3 of crimes no usable fingerprints were found in the scene either. One reason commonly cited by burglary investigators is the number of unusable fingerprints which are classified as legitimate access. This of course is an issue when the offender is known to the victim and therefore, when no break-ins are part of the crime and therefore ruling out suspects becomes more difficult. Skilled interviewers are needed who can tactfully disclose evidence in a structured and considered manner. This will increase the yield from forensic identifications of fingerprints. This is where substantial gains can be made, and it is worthy of further research. For example, an experiment on the value of DNA and fingerprint evidence has shown how innovative evidence collection tools can enhance clearance rates (Antrobus and Pilotto 2016). The randomized controlled trial illustrated that when using these technological innovations unavailable to police departments two decades ago, scenes attended by experimental officers were significantly more likely to be solved (27% of scenes) than scenes attended by control officers (20% scenes). Although admittedly the overall clearance rate is low, a 26% change attributable to the implementation of technology in crime scene investigations illustrates the potential for improvement using forensic sciences.

A perhaps obvious challenge was DNA. This was present in 22.4% of detected cases and 10% of detected cases involving violence. Both fingerprints and DNA provided important evidence, allowing the investigator to approach the interview with the suspect on the front foot. In some cases, this will be sufficient in itself to yield a detection, but in others, it may require a skilful interview to secure the detection. This aspect was not part of this research although our study found that the suspects admitted the offence in 33.8% of the detected cases and 22.7% of cases involving violence.

Our evidence does not support the utility of footprint evidence. This is important, as it has implications for future investments in this tool. If our results are credible, the findings are indicative of a forensic platform that does not justify its utility. Similar contentions were made by Coupe in Chapter Resources, Solvability and Detection: A Theoretical Model. However, we stress that our study is not causal and is based on a limited number of burglary cases. More research is needed, and in other research cites as well, before firm conclusions are made in this regard.

Finally, in recent years there has been a proliferation of CCTV, which was present in 9.2% of detected cases, but was absent in most cases involving violence. What is not clear from the evidence is how well the CCTV is utilised in conjunction with other variables.

This Study's Limitations

The sample size of 400 crimes, 200 detected and 200 undetected crimes, although meeting statistical requirements for reliability and representativeness, did not allow to measure interaction effects. While independently some factors were found to be weak predictors of solvability, they may work differently when interacting with other variables. For example, footprints might predict solvability when interrelating with CCTV or other forensic evidence. Likewise, the effect of vehicle details may flip and become a positive predictor when working in conjunction with CCTV evidence. However, our study was limited in size and large-scale studies, like those discussed in Chapter "Pickpocketing on Railways", can provide a more reliable estimate for each factor and for a combination of factors.

While being one of the earliest studies we know outside the USA on solvability, there is a great need for more replications. It is not enough to rely on one study, nor to rely on replications of particular decision-making models that are more than thirty years old and, by definition, do not account for the tremendous leaps made in both investigation theory and forensic capabilities. Certainly officers today are more attuned to securing a scene of a crime and are more informed about the types of evidence that can lead to case clearance. At any rate, we introduce other studies that have looked at the solvability factors model with more recent data, with a larger data set and in different research settings. We discuss the generalisability of these findings, in the context of our study, in Chapter "Conclusions" below.

Whether a solvability factors decision-making model will lead to more productive outcomes is presently speculative. A significant drawback is that the model is correlational at best, where different variables are modelled to predict certain outcomes. Therefore, we cannot conclude from these findings that by focusing on the factors that were found to be associated with higher clearance rates in the *statistical model*, the police will *actually* increase the clearance rates. For example, there may be additional variables that have a stronger effect on clearance rates, but for which we did have data. There may also be interaction effects, which we did not compute either, given our limited sample sizes. Therefore, more research and with other populations is required—certainly randomised experiments, in which the predictive validity of the solvability factors model will be tested.

References

Antrobus, E., & Pilotto, A. (2016). Improving forensic responses to residential burglaries: results of a randomized controlled field trial. *Journal of Experimental Criminology, 12*(3), 319–345.

Association of Chief Police Officers/Forensic Science Service. (1996). *Using forensic science effectively.* London: ACPO:FSS.

Bradbury, S. A., & Feist, A. (2005). *The use of forensic science in volume crime investigations: A review of the research literature*. Paper 43, London: Home Office.

Burrows, J., Hopkins, M., Hubbard, R., Robinson, A., Speed, M., & Tilley, N. (2005). *Understanding the attrition process in volume crime investigations* (No. 295). Home Office research study no. 295. London: Home Office Research, Development and Statistics Directorate.

Coupe, T., & Blake, L. (2005). The effects of patrol workloads and response strength on arrests at burglary emergencies. *Journal of Criminal Justice, 33,* 239–255.

Coupe, T., & Blake, L. (2006). Daylight and darkness targeting strategies and the risk of being seen at residential burglaries. *Criminology, 44*(2), 431–464.

Coupe, T., & Griffiths, M. (1996). *Solving residential burglary*. Police Research Group Crime Detection and Prevention Services, Paper 77, London: Home Office.

Eck, J. E. (1979). *Managing case assignments: The burglary investigation decision model replication*. Police Executive Research Forum, Washington, DC: Library of Congress.

Eck, J. E. (1983). *Solving crimes: The investigation of burglary and robbery*. Police Executive Research Forum, Washington, DC: Library of Congress.

Greenberg, B., Elliot, C. V., Kraft, L. P., & Procter, S. H. (1977). *Felony investigation decision model—An analysis of investigation elements of information*. Washington, DC: U.S. Government Printing Office.

Greenwood, P. W., & Petersilia, J. (1975). *The criminal investigation process: Volume I: Summary and policy implications*. Washington, DC: U.S. Government Printing Office, National Institute of Law Enforcement and Criminal Justice.

Greenwood, P. W., Chaiken, J. M., & Petersilia, J. (1976). *The criminal investigation process: A summary report*. Lexington: DC Heath.

Jansson, K. (2005). *Volume crime investigations—A review of the research literature*. Online report OLR 44/05. London: Home Office.

Sherman, L. W. (2013). The rise of evidence-based policing: Targeting, testing, and tracking. *Crime and justice, 42*(1), 377–451.

Tilley, N., & Ford, A. (1996). *Forensic science and crime investigation*. Police Research Group Paper 73, London: Home Office.

Welsh, B. C., & Farrington, D. P. (2009). Public area CCTV and crime prevention: an updated systematic review and meta-analysis. *Justice Quarterly, 26*(4), 716–745.

Population-Level Analysis of Residential Burglaries

Colin Paine and Barak Ariel

Introduction

In Chapter "Assessing Solvability Factors in Greater Manchester, England: The Case of Residential Burglaries", we illustrated the value of replicating the original decision-making model (Greenberg et al. 1977; Eck 1979) in the UK context. Analysis of a random sample of 400 residential burglaries in the Greater Manchester area, with the addition of 77 burglaries that included violence as well, illustrated the value not only of the solvability factors model outside the USA and over time, but also of forensic sciences.

However, as we point out in Chapter "Assessing Solvability Factors in Greater Manchester, England: The Case of Residential Burglaries", the major shortcoming of the Manchester study was its size. Patrick Donnellan, who was writing his master's dissertation at the time, was unable to read more than 35,000 criminal investigation logs and synthesize the data within the constrained time. At the time, the computerized Manchester data sets were not as sophisticated as they are today, so a stratified sampling technique was required.

Another drawback of the original solvability screening models, as well as the study in Chapter "Assessing Solvability Factors in Greater Manchester, England: The Case of Residential Burglaries", is their rather crude statistical approaches. Chi-square tests are generally involved with basic statistics, and they can give us only limited information about the relevant contribution of each solvability factor. More broadly speaking, statistical tests that provide an 'either/or' test of significance

C. Paine (✉)
Thames Valley Police, London, UK
e-mail: Colin.Paine@thamesvalley.pnn.police.uk

B. Ariel
Institute of Criminology, University of Cambridge, Cambridge, UK

Institute of Criminology, Faculty of Law, The Hebrew University, Mount Scopus, Jerusalem, Israel

R. T. Coupe et al. (eds.), *Crime Solvability Factors*,
https://doi.org/10.1007/978-3-030-17160-5_4

are limited in their capacity to teach us lessons. Instead of—or at the very least in conjunction with—the classic tests of significance, we need to measure magnitudes. Effect size analyses of each of the associated variables, as well as overall summary effect sizes, will be used in this chapter to measure the magnitude of the differences between solved and unsolved cases in terms of the prevalence of these factors.

Given the shortcomings of the earlier work (Greenberg et al. 1973; Eck 1979), which we discussed more extensively in Chapter "Existing Research on Solvability", we sought to advance our understanding of solvability factors in several ways. First, we sought to identify, using population-level data, the factors that make the largest contribution to residential burglary solvability. Using descriptive analysis of the prevalence of solvability factors in solved and unsolved burglary cases, the aim was to identify the variables most strongly associated with solved cases.

Second, the literature thus far has placed limited emphasis on modern forensic scientific advancements. The use of DNA, footprints, and similar residue from the offender that can now be used to identify an offender more reliably and (arguably) more easily than ever before has not been introduced in any of the published work about solvability factor analysis. Finally, this study uses an unusually large cohort of cases, which enables a more sensitive analysis of the solvability factors. The analysis utilizes the entire data set of burglaries from a major police force in England and Wales, which provides a rich source of information, particularly for some variables that may have only a small—yet not insignificant—effect on case clearance.

Methods

Data Sources

We were fortunate to collaborate with the Thames Valley Police on this project. The Thames Valley is a geographically large, diverse area covering three counties with a population of 2.3 million people. It covers 5700 km and includes large urban towns and cities such as Slough, Reading, Oxford, Wycombe and Milton Keynes, together with large rural areas such as Aylesbury Vale, South Oxfordshire and West Oxfordshire.

The area has just below the average number of domestic burglary offences by force per 1000 of population. As such, it is likely that the results of the analysis can be generalized to the population of all UK burglaries. The sample included all residential burglaries recorded in the Thames Valley Police area from 1 March 2010 to 31 October 2011 ($N = 14{,}306$). These burglaries represented 14,306 of the 289,764 crimes recorded in Thames Valley during the time period. Thus, residential burglaries accounted for 4.93% of the total recorded crime. This breaks down further into 2537 (17.73%) attempted burglaries and 11,769 (82.26%) successful, or completed, burglaries. Using these data sources we have focused on the 11,769 successful burglaries, of which 1257 were solved and 10,512 were unsolved. An additional breakdown of the data shows that, of the detected offences, 1257 were full residential burglaries with a detection rate of 10.68%. As the number of attempted burglaries was limited in scope, we excluded these from the current analysis.

The sample excluded non-residential burglaries ($n = 18{,}029$), attempted distraction burglaries ($n = 83$), full distraction burglaries ($n = 279$), attempted aggravated burglaries ($n = 1$) and full aggravated burglaries ($n = 60$). The sample also excluded 'no crimes', that is, suspected offences that after investigation were proven not to have occurred ($n = 329$).

The majority of burglary offences in the sample occurred during the daytime, with a dip in the early evening between 20:00 and 22:00. The numbers fall off considerably after 01:00 until 07:00.

The data were drawn from the Thames Valley Police crime recording system (CEDAR), the investigation management application (IMM), the incident resourcing system (Command and Control) and the forensic recording system (Socrates). The police service is a data-rich environment, and automating the extraction of data makes it possible to have a substantial data set that covers the entire population of reported residential burglaries within the Thames Valley.

Statistical Analysis

Unlike the analysis In Chapter "Assessing Solvability Factors in Greater Manchester, England: The Case of Residential Burglaries", that implemented inferential statistics, our analysis will focus on magnitude. We used a meta-analytic approach to evaluate between-group differences—that is, solved versus unsolved cases. We observed the prevalence of each factor for each solved and unsolved case and computed the standardized mean differences. These data were presented in terms of Cohen's *d* (Cohen 1988). We used the Comprehensive Meta-Analysis V.2 software (CMA) to then synthesize the results from each factor and present the overall results (Lipsey and Wilson 2001). The data inputted into CMA consisted of (a) the number of solved and unsolved factors and (b) the number of times each factor appeared in each of the two groups' incidents. Thus, the study will identify which variables can most effectively predict the case outcome by reference to their effect size.

Attention should be drawn to the forest plots in the figures presented in this chapter (right-hand side). Each point estimate represents the magnitude of the difference between the groups. Anything to the right of the null line (0.00) implies that the difference 'favours' the solved cases, and anything to the left of the line indicates that the factor was more prevalent in the unsolved investigations. The further away the point estimate is from the null line, the larger the magnitude of the difference. The horizontal lines crossing the point estimates represent the confidence intervals, and when they cross through the vertical null line, it indicates that the effect is not statistically significant. The diamond represents the average treatment effect. This approach is increasingly utilized in criminal justice research (see: Ariel 2012; Ariel et al. 2016a, b, 2017; Robb et al. 2015).

Findings

Solvability Variables

Table 1 illustrates the relative presence of each variable in solved and unsolved cases. As can be seen, the frequency with which the key variables occur varies considerably.

A Closer Look at the Critical Variables

Suspect Named

During the analysis, it became clear that this variable is unusable as it is always added once a case is detected. As such, it was present in each of the 1257 detected cases, making any analysis in terms of the victim or another person naming the suspect impossible.

Footprint Marks Recovered

This variable relates to whether or not a footprint mark was recovered at or near the scene. Out of a total of 1257 detected cases, a footprint mark was recovered in 62 cases (4.93%). In contrast, footprint marks were recovered in only 29 (0.27%) of the 10,512 undetected cases. The very large effect size is also statistically significant ($d = 1.616, p < .001$).

DNA Recovered

This variable relates to whether an article has been recovered at or near the scene that potentially holds the perpetrator's DNA. DNA was recovered in 167 (13.29%) of the 1257 detected burglaries. In comparison, DNA was recovered in only 95 (0.9%) of the 10,512 undetected cases. A chi-square test was conducted in order to determine whether or not the difference is statistically significant ($\chi^2 = 790.805, p < .001$). The effect size is large, and the finding is statistically significant ($d = 1.556, p < .001$).

Fingerprints Recovered

This variable relates to the recovery of one or more fingerprints from inside or outside the scene that had not yet been compared to eliminate the aggrieved party. In 267 (21.24%) of the 1257 detected burglaries, a fingerprint was recovered, compared to only 388 (3.61%) of the 10,512 undetected cases. A chi-square test was conducted

Table 1 Burglary dwelling solvability factors—prevalence in solved and unsolved cases—investigative, forensic and offender's Modus Operandi (MO) variables

		Solved cases (N = 1257)		Unsolved cases (N = 10,512)		χ^2
		n	%	n	%	
Investigative	Witness report of offence	279	22.2	963	9.2	202.087***
	Suspect description recorded	20	1.6	87	0.8	7.264**
	Offender disturbed	227	18.1	1045	9.9	112.522***
	Offender seen	277	22.0	904	8.6	270.795***
	Offender's vehicle sighted	51	4.1	206	2.0	48.995***
	Description of offender's vehicle recorded	11	0.9	69	0.7	.795
	CCTV preserved	412	32.8	3476	33.1	.043
	Media appeal completed	71	5.6	404	3.8	9.446**
	Reported as burglary in progress	106	8.4	406	3.9	224.522***
	Any stolen property recovered	248	19.7	1145	10.9	13.728**
Forensic	Fingerprints recovered	267	21.2	388	3.7	657.967***
	DNA recovered	167	13.3	95	0.9	790.805***
	Footprint marks recovered	62	4.9	29	0.3	317.300***
Offender MO	Vehicle stolen in the crime	100	8.0	502	4.8	29.403***
	Property stolen	956	76.1	7894	75.1	13.728**
	Anything left at scene by the offender	165	13.1	811	7.7	79.103***
	Premises was subject to a previous burglary	173	13.8	1550	14.7	36.574***
	Offender MO: tidy search	569	45.3	4821	45.9	4.281*
	Offender MO: untidy search	305	24.3	3274	31.1	13.204***
	Offender MO: thorough search	80	6.4	702	6.7	.058

(continued)

Table 1 (continued)

	Solved cases (N = 1257)		Unsolved cases (N = 10,512)		χ^2
	n	%	n	%	
Offender MO: search whole house	357	28.4	3649	34.7	8.506**
Antiques stolen	2	0.2	45	0.4	1.731
Camcorder/camera stolen	81	6.4	757	7.2	.112
Cash stolen	40	3.2	291	2.8	1.676
Cheque book/credit cards stolen	70	5.6	569	5.4	.711
Clothing stolen	18	1.4	114	1.1	1.979
Computer stolen	298	23.7	2530	24.1	1.418
Household electrical stolen	39	3.1	341	3.2	.032
Jewellery stolen	155	12.3	1866	17.8	18.695***
Power tools stolen	11	0.9	118	1.1	.313
Committed during darkness	454	36.1	3447	32.8	7.874*
Committed during daylight	384	30.5	3151	30.0	3.498
Premises were occupied	474	37.7	3178	30.2	32.958***
Premises were unoccupied	592	47.1	6163	58.6	53.253***

*$p < .05$; **$p < .01$; ***$p < .001$

in order to test whether the difference is statistically significant ($\chi^2 = 657.967$***, $p < .001$). The effect size was calculated as very large, and is statistically significant ($d = 1.076$, $p < .001$).

Offender Seen

An offender is recorded as being seen if any person involved believes themselves to have seen the suspect either during the commission of the crime or shortly thereafter. Out of 1257 detected burglaries, an offender was seen in 277 cases (22.03%). In contrast, the offender was seen in only 904 (8.59%) of the 10,512 undetected burglaries. A chi-square test was conducted in order to ascertain the statistical significance of this difference ($\chi^2 = 270.795$, $p < .001$). The effect size was calculated as medium ($d = 0.606$, $p < .001$).

Witness Recorded

Whether an offence is recorded as having been witnessed is much broader than Greenberg's original definition of 'anyone who sees or hears a suspicious circumstance at or near the time of the occurrence and in close proximity of the crime scene' (Greenberg et al. 1973, p. A-6). A witness is recorded against a burglary if anyone other than the victim has observed the offence or if they have any evidential role in relation to the offence. Thus, this is a much broader variable than 'offender seen'. One or more witnesses were recorded in 279 (22.19%) of the 1257 detected cases, compared to 963 (9.16%) of the 10,512 undetected cases. A chi-square test was conducted in order to test the statistical significance of the finding ($\chi^2 = 202.087$, $p < .001$). The effect size was calculated as medium ($d = 0.573, p < .001$).

Reported as a Burglary in Progress

This variable relates to whether the crime initially came to police attention as a result of a report stating that the event was a crime in progress. One hundred and six (8.43%) of the 1257 detected cases were reported as burglaries in progress, compared to 406 (3.86%) of the 10,512 undetected burglaries. A chi-square test was completed in order to test whether the difference is statistically significant ($\chi^2 = 224.552$, $p < .001$). The effect size was calculated as medium ($d = 0.457, p < .001$).

The number of reported burglaries in progress varies significantly by the hour of the day. The highest number of occurrences is reported between 03:00 and 04:00, and the lowest incidence is between 07.00 and 08.00. Similarly, the number of burglaries in progress that are subsequently detected also varies significantly by the hour of the day, with most detected burglaries in progress occurring between 14:00 and 15:00.

Offender's Vehicle Sighted

A record is made of the offender's vehicle being sighted if any person identifies a vehicle that they believe to belong to the offender. In 51 (4.06%) of the 1257 detected cases, the offender's vehicle was seen. In comparison, 206 undetected cases (1.96%) featured offender vehicle sightings, out of a total of 10,512 undetected cases. A chi-square test was completed in order to determine the statistical significance of the difference ($\chi^2 = 48.995, p < .001$). The effect size was calculated as medium ($d = 0.457, p < .001$).

Table 2 Burglary dwelling solvability factors—temporal variations in solved and unsolved cases

Variable name	Solved cases			Unsolved cases			t
	Mean	SD	n	Mean	SD	n	
Time to attend (minutes)	132.26	532.75	1051	171.26	492.97	9826	−2.418*
Offence duration (minutes)	13.14	60.93	1106	20.08	104.42	9174	−2.164*

Stolen Property Recovered

This variable relates to whether any of the property stolen in the burglary was subsequently recovered, either before or after the arrest of any suspect. In 248 (19.72%) of the 1257 detected cases, some property was recovered. In contrast, property was recovered in 1145 (10.89%) of the 10,512 undetected cases. A chi-square test was completed in order to determine whether the difference is statistically significant ($\chi^2 = 13.728$, $p = .001$). The effect size was calculated as small to medium ($d = 0.385$, $p < .001$).

Offence Duration

Table 2 sets out the temporal variations in terms of offence duration and the time to attendance of the first officer on scene between solved and unsolved cases. The offence duration is calculated as the difference between the time at which the premises were last left secure and the time at which the burglary was discovered. For detected burglaries, the mean offence duration was 23.12 h (SD = 175.57), as compared to a mean offence duration of 15.48 h (SD = 68.99) for undetected burglaries. An independent samples t test was conducted in order to measure the difference between the mean offence durations for detected and undetected burglaries ($t = -2.164$, $p = .030$). The effect size was calculated as very small ($d = -0.069$, $p = .030$).

Time to Attendance of First Officer

The time to the attendance of the first officer was calculated in minutes as the difference between the time at which the offence was reported to the police and the time at which the first member of police personnel arrived on the scene. The mean time to attendance was 134.35 min (SD = 456.41) for detected burglaries and 184.08 min (SD = 502.29) for undetected ones. An independent samples t test was conducted in order to measure the difference between the mean offence durations for detected and undetected burglaries ($t = -2.418$, $p = .016$). The effect size was calculated as very small ($d = -0.078$, $p = .016$).

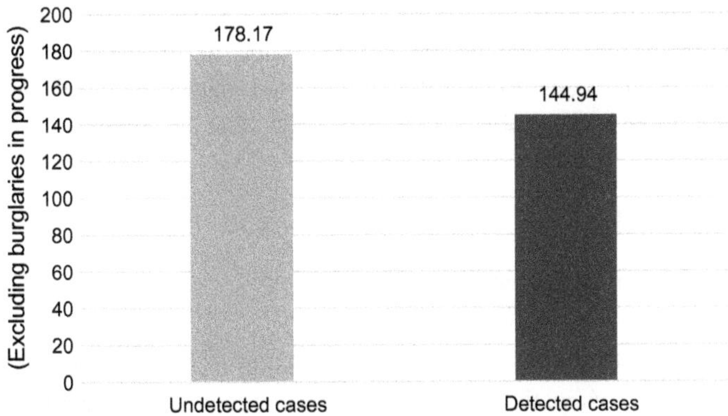

Fig. 1 Average (mean) time to attendance of first officer (minutes, excluding burglaries in progress)

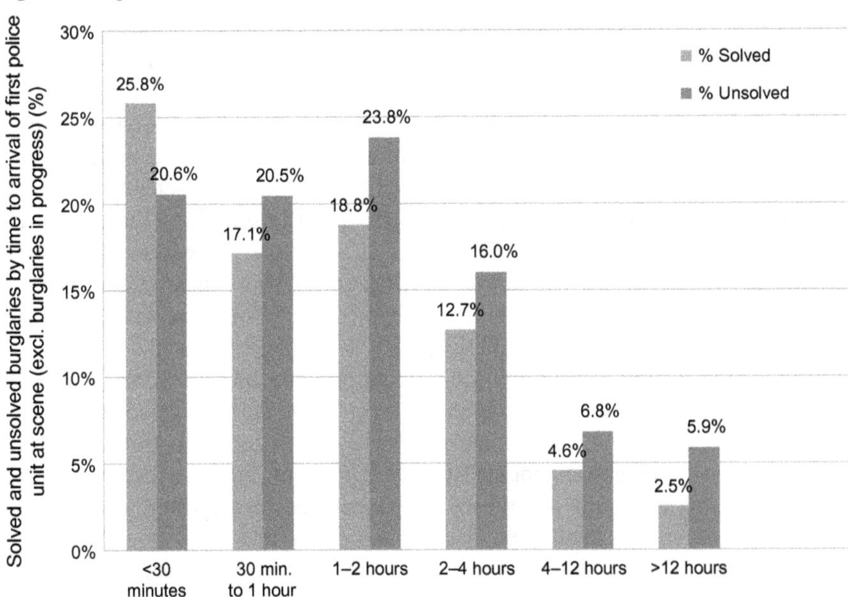

Fig. 2 Percentage of solved and unsolved burglaries by time to arrival of first police unit at scene (01 March 2010–31 October 2011, excluding burglaries in progress)

For the sample of detected burglaries, excluding burglaries in progress, the mean time to attendance was 144.94 min (SD = 559.817). For undetected burglaries, excluding burglaries in progress, the mean time to attendance was 178.17 min (SD = 502.184) (Fig. 1. An independent samples t test was conducted in order to measure the difference between the mean time to attendance for both detected and undetected cases ($t = -1.918$, $p = .030$). The effect size was calculated as very small, but statistically significant ($d = -0.0655, p = .030$).

For detected attempted burglaries, excluding burglaries in progress, the mean time to attendance was 86.95 min (SD = 189.47), compared to 260.51 (SD

= 555.259) for the undetected cases of attempted burglary (Fig. 2). An independent samples t test was conducted in order to measure the difference between the mean times to attend for detected and undetected cases (t = −2.258, p = .003). The effect size was calculated as small (d = −0.264, p = .003).

Predictive Power of Solvability Factors

To determine the effectiveness of these solvability factors in predicting the outcomes of burglary investigations, each solvability factor was tested against the sample of 11,769 burglaries (Fig. 3a–d; Table 3).

The top 14 factors were identified as solvability factors by reference to their effect size. All factors with a more than trivial effect size were included, including 'footprint marks recovered', 'DNA recovered', 'fingerprints recovered', 'offender seen', 'witness report of offence', 'burglary in progress', 'offender's vehicle sighted', 'stolen property recovered', 'offender disturbed', 'offender description recorded', 'anything left at scene', 'vehicle stolen in crime', 'media appeal completed' and 'premises were occupied'. An analysis of these 14 factors was conducted to determine the total predictive accuracy of each solvability factor in isolation (Table 4). Each factor had surprisingly high predictive power, with all but one of the factors predicting the final case outcome with an accuracy in excess of 80%. Only 'premises were occupied' fell short, accurately predicting just 61% of final case outcomes, and was therefore eliminated as a solvability factor. 'Media appeal completed' was also eliminated as a solvability factor, since it could produce 100% case assignment if officers were able to conduct a media appeal on *any* case they wished to investigate. The description of the offender's vehicle and whether clothing was stolen were not included, as the findings were not statistically significant. Whether the offence was committed during the hours of darkness and the offence duration were excluded, as the effect sizes were too small to be reasonably meaningful.

Table 5 sets out the results of the analysis of the frequency with which these solvability factors occur within the cohort of burglaries. The most powerful solvability factor, the recovery of forensic material, occurs infrequently.

The 12 remaining solvability factors were then tested against the full sample of 11,769 burglaries to determine the accuracy of any one or more of these factors in predicting case outcomes. As the number of solvability factors per case increases, the numbers of cases that are predicted to be solved and that are in fact solved fall, as does the number of wasted investigations. However, as the number of solvability factors rises, the numbers of cases predicted *not* to be solved and that are in fact are not solved increase, as does the number of lost detections (Fig. 4). The total number of cases assigned for investigation falls until it reaches the point of solvability factors at which it becomes a no-assignment model.

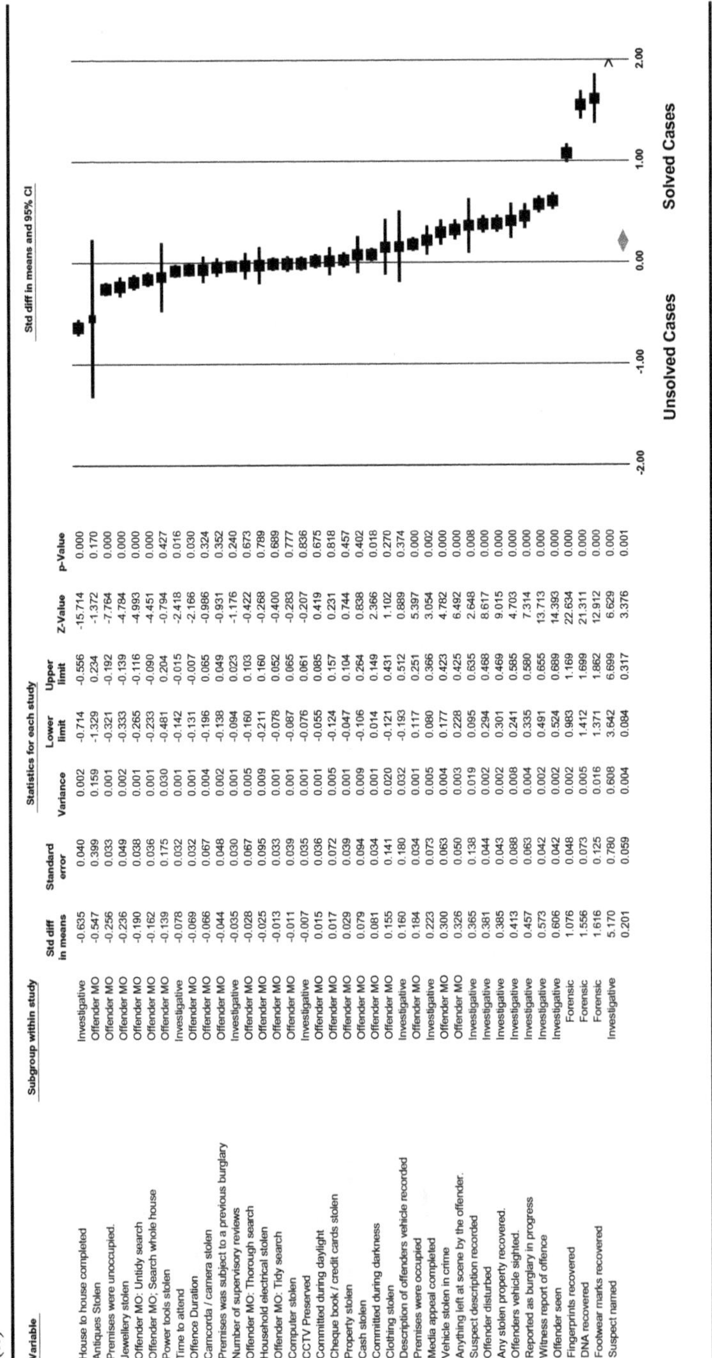

Variable	Subgroup within study	Statistics for each study						
		Std diff in means	Standard error	Variance	Lower limit	Upper limit	Z-Value	p-Value
House to house completed	Investigative	-0.635	0.040	0.002	-0.714	-0.556	-15.714	0.000
Antiques Stolen	Offender MO	-0.547	0.399	0.159	-1.329	0.234	-1.372	0.170
Premises were unoccupied.	Offender MO	-0.256	0.033	0.001	-0.321	-0.192	-7.764	0.000
Jewellery stolen	Offender MO	-0.236	0.049	0.002	-0.333	-0.139	-4.784	0.000
Offender MO: Untidy search	Offender MO	-0.190	0.038	0.001	-0.265	-0.116	-4.993	0.000
Offender MO; Search whole house	Offender MO	-0.162	0.036	0.001	-0.233	-0.090	-4.451	0.000
Power tools stolen	Offender MO	-0.139	0.175	0.030	-0.481	0.204	-0.794	0.427
Time to attend	Investigative	-0.078	0.032	0.001	-0.142	-0.015	-2.418	0.016
Offence Duration	Offender MO	-0.069	0.032	0.001	-0.131	-0.007	-2.166	0.030
Camcorda / camera stolen	Offender MO	-0.066	0.067	0.004	-0.196	0.065	-0.986	0.324
Premises was subject to a previous burglary	Offender MO	-0.044	0.048	0.002	-0.138	0.049	-0.931	0.352
Number of supervisory reviews	Investigative	-0.035	0.030	0.001	-0.094	0.023	-1.176	0.240
Offender MO: Thorough search	Offender MO	-0.028	0.067	0.005	-0.160	0.103	-0.422	0.673
Household electrical stolen	Offender MO	-0.025	0.095	0.009	-0.211	0.160	-0.268	0.789
Offender MO: Tidy search	Offender MO	-0.013	0.033	0.001	-0.078	0.052	-0.400	0.689
Computer stolen	Offender MO	-0.011	0.039	0.001	-0.087	0.065	-0.283	0.777
CCTV Preserved	Investigative	-0.007	0.035	0.001	-0.076	0.061	-0.207	0.836
Committed during daylight	Offender MO	0.015	0.036	0.001	-0.055	0.085	0.419	0.675
Cheque book / credit cards stolen	Offender MO	0.017	0.072	0.005	-0.124	0.157	0.231	0.818
Property stolen	Offender MO	0.029	0.039	0.001	-0.047	0.104	0.744	0.457
Cash stolen	Offender MO	0.079	0.094	0.009	-0.106	0.264	0.838	0.402
Committed during darkness	Offender MO	0.081	0.034	0.001	0.014	0.149	2.366	0.018
Clothing stolen	Offender MO	0.155	0.141	0.020	-0.121	0.431	1.102	0.270
Description of offenders vehicle recorded	Investigative	0.160	0.180	0.032	-0.193	0.512	0.889	0.374
Premises were occupied	Offender MO	0.184	0.034	0.001	0.117	0.251	5.397	0.000
Media appeal completed	Investigative	0.223	0.073	0.005	0.080	0.366	3.054	0.002
Vehicle stolen in crime	Offender MO	0.300	0.063	0.004	0.177	0.423	4.782	0.000
Anything left at scene by the offender.	Offender MO	0.326	0.050	0.003	0.228	0.425	6.492	0.000
Suspect description recorded	Investigative	0.365	0.138	0.019	0.095	0.635	2.648	0.008
Offender disturbed	Investigative	0.381	0.044	0.002	0.294	0.468	8.617	0.000
Any stolen property recovered.	Investigative	0.385	0.043	0.002	0.301	0.469	9.015	0.000
Offenders vehicle sighted.	Investigative	0.413	0.088	0.008	0.241	0.585	4.703	0.000
Reported as burglary in progress	Investigative	0.457	0.063	0.004	0.335	0.580	7.314	0.000
Witness report of offence	Investigative	0.573	0.042	0.002	0.491	0.655	13.713	0.000
Offender seen	Investigative	0.606	0.042	0.002	0.524	0.689	14.393	0.000
Fingerprints recovered	Forensic	1.076	0.048	0.002	0.983	1.169	22.634	0.000
DNA recovered	Forensic	1.556	0.073	0.005	1.412	1.699	21.311	0.000
Footwear marks recovered	Forensic	1.616	0.125	0.016	1.371	1.862	12.912	0.000
Suspect named	Investigative	5.170	0.780	0.608	3.642	6.699	6.629	0.000
		0.201	0.059	0.004	0.084	0.317	3.376	0.001

Fig. 3 Burglary effect size analysis: **a** all variables, residential burglaries, **b** forensic subgroup, **c** investigative subgroup, **d** offender modus operandi subgroup

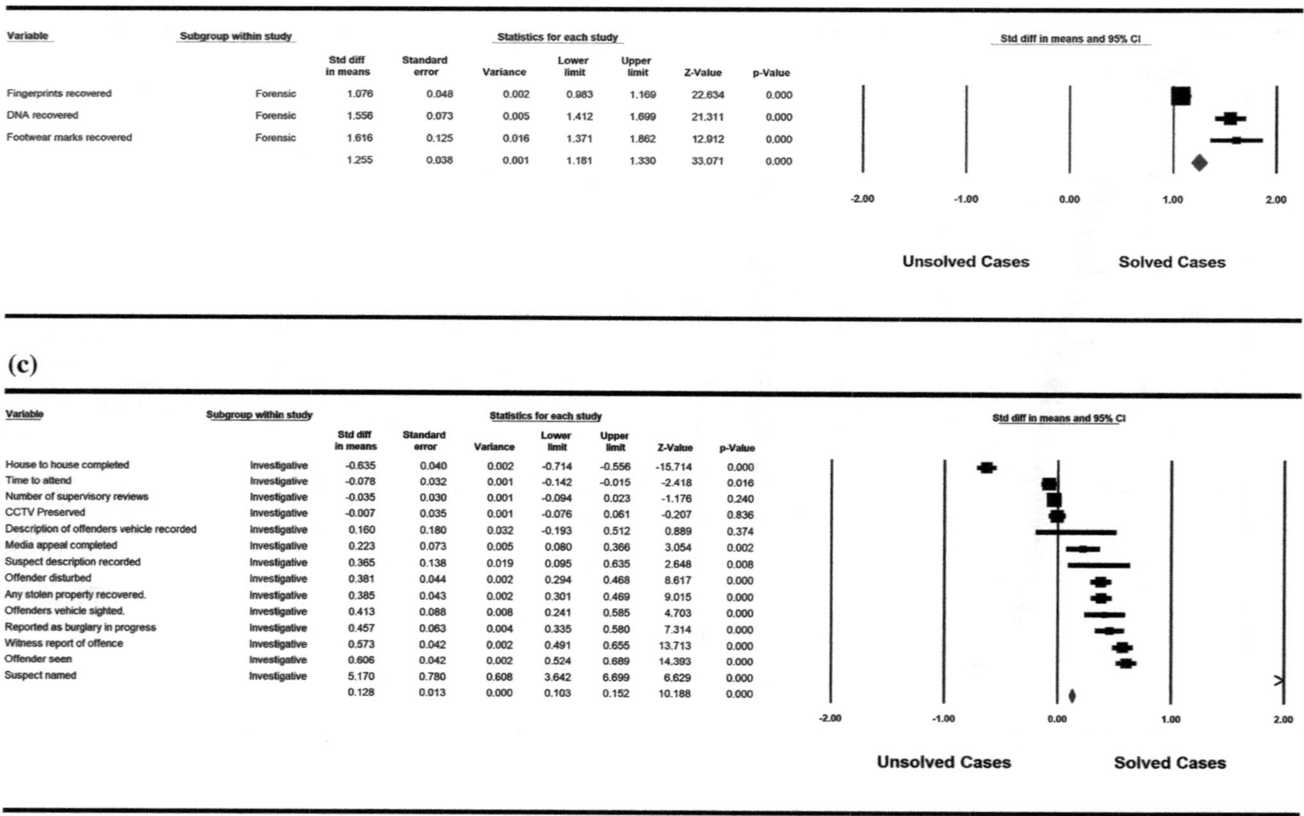

(b)

Variable	Subgroup within study	Std diff in means	Standard error	Variance	Lower limit	Upper limit	Z-Value	p-Value
Fingerprints recovered	Forensic	1.076	0.048	0.002	0.983	1.169	22.634	0.000
DNA recovered	Forensic	1.556	0.073	0.005	1.412	1.699	21.311	0.000
Footwear marks recovered	Forensic	1.616	0.125	0.016	1.371	1.862	12.912	0.000
		1.255	0.038	0.001	1.181	1.330	33.071	0.000

(c)

Variable	Subgroup within study	Std diff in means	Standard error	Variance	Lower limit	Upper limit	Z-Value	p-Value
House to house completed	Investigative	-0.635	0.040	0.002	-0.714	-0.556	-15.714	0.000
Time to attend	Investigative	-0.078	0.032	0.001	-0.142	-0.015	-2.418	0.016
Number of supervisory reviews	Investigative	-0.035	0.030	0.001	-0.094	0.023	-1.176	0.240
CCTV Preserved	Investigative	-0.007	0.035	0.001	-0.076	0.061	-0.207	0.836
Description of offenders vehicle recorded	Investigative	0.160	0.180	0.032	-0.193	0.512	0.889	0.374
Media appeal completed	Investigative	0.223	0.073	0.005	0.080	0.366	3.054	0.002
Suspect description recorded	Investigative	0.365	0.138	0.019	0.095	0.635	2.648	0.008
Offender disturbed	Investigative	0.381	0.044	0.002	0.294	0.468	8.617	0.000
Any stolen property recovered.	Investigative	0.385	0.043	0.002	0.301	0.469	9.015	0.000
Offenders vehicle sighted.	Investigative	0.413	0.088	0.008	0.241	0.585	4.703	0.000
Reported as burglary in progress	Investigative	0.457	0.063	0.004	0.335	0.580	7.314	0.000
Witness report of offence	Investigative	0.573	0.042	0.002	0.491	0.655	13.713	0.000
Offender seen	Investigative	0.606	0.042	0.002	0.524	0.689	14.393	0.000
Suspect named	Investigative	5.170	0.780	0.608	3.642	6.699	6.629	0.000
		0.128	0.013	0.000	0.103	0.152	10.188	0.000

Fig. 3 (continued)

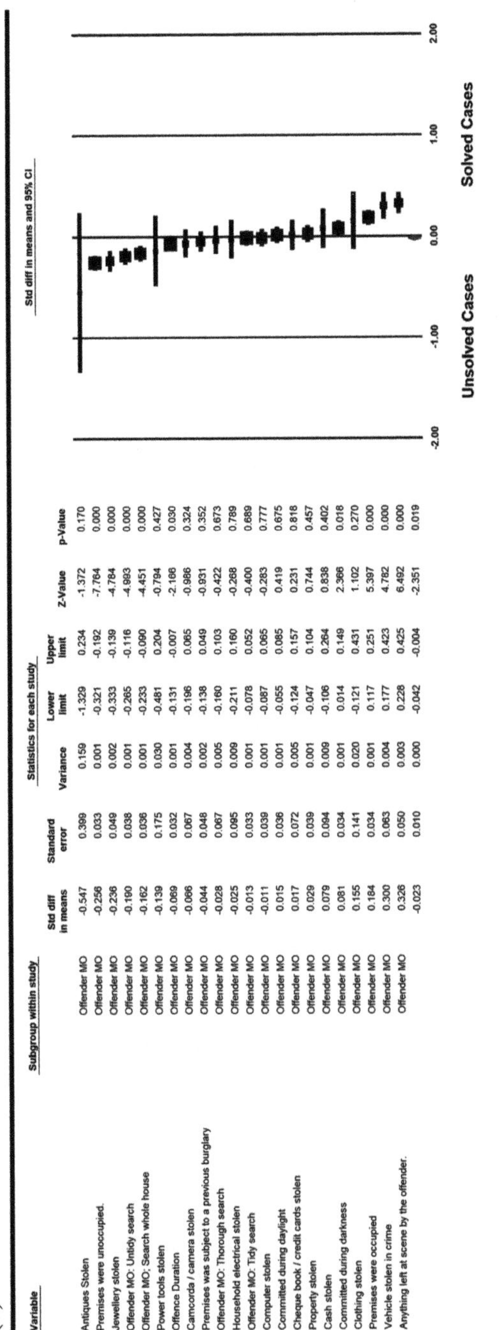

(d)

Variable	Subgroup within study	Statistics for each study						
		Std diff in means	Standard error	Variance	Lower limit	Upper limit	Z-Value	p-Value
Antiques Stolen	Offender MO	-0.547	0.399	0.159	-1.329	0.234	-1.372	0.170
Premises were unoccupied.	Offender MO	-0.256	0.033	0.001	-0.321	-0.192	-7.764	0.000
Jewellery stolen	Offender MO	-0.236	0.049	0.002	-0.333	-0.139	-4.784	0.000
Offender MO: Untidy search	Offender MO	-0.190	0.038	0.001	-0.265	-0.116	-4.993	0.000
Offender MO; Search whole house	Offender MO	-0.162	0.036	0.001	-0.233	-0.090	-4.451	0.000
Power tools stolen	Offender MO	-0.139	0.175	0.030	-0.481	0.204	-0.794	0.427
Offence Duration	Offender MO	-0.069	0.032	0.001	-0.131	-0.007	-2.166	0.030
Camcorda / camera stolen	Offender MO	-0.066	0.067	0.004	-0.196	0.065	-0.986	0.324
Premises was subject to a previous burglary	Offender MO	-0.044	0.048	0.002	-0.138	0.049	-0.931	0.352
Offender MO: Thorough search	Offender MO	-0.028	0.067	0.005	-0.160	0.103	-0.422	0.673
Household electrical stolen	Offender MO	-0.025	0.095	0.009	-0.211	0.160	-0.268	0.789
Offender MO: Tidy search	Offender MO	-0.013	0.033	0.001	-0.078	0.052	-0.400	0.689
Computer stolen	Offender MO	-0.011	0.039	0.001	-0.087	0.065	-0.283	0.777
Committed during daylight	Offender MO	0.015	0.036	0.001	-0.055	0.085	0.419	0.675
Cheque book / credit cards stolen	Offender MO	0.017	0.072	0.005	-0.124	0.157	0.231	0.818
Property stolen	Offender MO	0.029	0.039	0.001	-0.047	0.104	0.744	0.457
Cash stolen	Offender MO	0.079	0.094	0.009	-0.106	0.264	0.838	0.402
Committed during darkness	Offender MO	0.081	0.034	0.001	0.014	0.149	2.366	0.018
Clothing stolen	Offender MO	0.155	0.141	0.020	-0.121	0.431	1.102	0.270
Premises were occupied	Offender MO	0.184	0.034	0.001	0.117	0.251	5.397	0.000
Vehicle stolen in crime	Offender MO	0.300	0.063	0.004	0.177	0.423	4.782	0.000
Anything left at scene by the offender.	Offender MO	0.326	0.050	0.003	0.228	0.425	6.492	0.000
		-0.023	0.010	0.000	-0.042	-0.004	-2.351	0.019

Fig. 3 (continued)

Table 3 Effectiveness of solvability factors in predicting case outcomes for dwelling burglary

	Correctly predicted to be solved	% correctly predicted to be solved	Correctly predicted not to be solved	% correctly predicted not to be solved	Total predictive accuracy	% total predictive accuracy	Predicted to be solved but was not solved; wasted investigations	% wasted investigations	Predicted not to be solved but was solved lost detections	% lost detections	Total cases assigned for investigation
All cases	**1257**	**100**	**10,512**	**100**			**10,512**	**100**	**0**	**0**	**11,769**
Footprint impression recovered	64	5.09	10,483	99.7	10,547	89.6	29	0.2	1195	95.0	91
DNA recovered	167	13.2	10,417	99.0	10,584	89.9	95	0.9	1090	86.7	262
Fingerprint	267	21.2	10,124	96.3	10,391	88.2	388	3.6	990	78.7	655
Offender seen	277	22.0	9608	91.4	9885	83.9	904	8.5	980	77.9	1181
Witness	279	22.1	9549	90.8	9828	83.5	963	9.1	978	77.8	1242
Burglary in progress	106	8.4	10,106	96.1	10,212	86.7	406	3.8	1151	91.5	512
Offender's vehicle sighted	51	4.0	10,306	98.0	10,357	88.0	206	1.9	1206	95.9	257
Stolen property recovered	248	19.7	9367	89.1	9615	81.6	1145	10.8	1009	80.2	1393
Offender disturbed	227	18.0	9467	90.0	9694	82.3	1045	9.9	1030	81.9	1272

(continued)

Table 3 (continued)

	Correctly predicted to be solved	% correctly predicted to be solved	Correctly predicted not to be solved	% correctly predicted not to be solved	Total predictive accuracy	% total predictive accuracy	Predicted to be solved but was not solved; wasted investigations	% wasted investiga- tions	Predicted not to be solved but was solved lost detections	% lost detections	Total cases assigned for investi- gation
Suspect description recorded	20	1.5	10,425	99.1	10,445	88.7	87	0.8	1237	98.4	107
Offender left evidence at scene	165	13.1	9701	92.2	9866	83.8	811	7.7	1092	86.8	976
Media appeal completed	71	5.6	10,108	96.1	10,179	86.4	1186	11.2	404	32.1	475
Vehicle stolen in the crime	100	7.9	10,010	95.2	10,110	85.9	502	4.7	1157	92.0	602
Premises were occupied	474	37.7	7234	68.8	7708	65.4	100	0.9	770	61.2	3652

Table 4 Effectiveness of solvability factors in predicting case outcomes

Number of solvability factors presented in the case	Number of cases assigned for investigation	Correctly predicted to be solved (true positive)	Correctly predicted not to be solved (true negative)	Total predictive accuracy	Predicted to be solved, but was not solved (false positive)	Predicted not to be solved, but was solved (false negatives)
1	4979 (42.31%)	922 (73.35%)	6455 (61.41%)	7377 (62.68%)	4057 (38.59%)	335 (26.65%)
2	2051 (17.43%)	519 (41.29%)	8980 (85.43%)	9499 (80.71%)	1532 (14.57%)	738 (58.71%)
3	943 (8.01%)	286 (22.75%)	9855 (93.75%)	10,141 (86.17%)	657 (6.25%)	971 (77.25%)
4	410 (3.48%)	154 (12.25%)	10,256 (97.56%)	10,410 (88.45%)	256 (2.44%)	1103 (87.75%)
5	133 (1.13%)	65 (5.17%)	10,444 (99.35%)	10,509 (89.29%)	68 (0.65%)	1192 (94.83%)
6	29 (0.25%)	19 (1.51%)	10,502 (99.90%)	10,521 (89.40%)	10 (0.00%)	1238 (98.50%)
7	5 (0.00%)	4 (0.32%)	10,511 (99.99%)	10,515 (89.34%)	1 (0.00%)	1253 (99.68%)
Total cases	11,769 (100%)	1257 (10.68%)	10,512 (89.32%)	11,769 (100%)	10,512 (89.32%)	1257 (10.68%)

Table 5 Frequency of solvability factors for residential burglaries ($N =$ 12,269)

Solvability factor	Frequency (%)	n
Footprint identified	0.77	91
DNA identified	2.23	262
Fingerprint identified	5.57	655
Offender seen	10.03	1181
Witness	10.55	1242
Burglary in progress	4.35	512
Offender's vehicle sighted	2.18	324
Any stolen property	11.84	1393
Offender disturbed in progress	10.81	1272
Suspect's description recorded	0.91	107
Anything left at the scene by offender	8.29	976
Vehicle stolen in the crime	5.12	602
Premises were occupied	31.03	3652

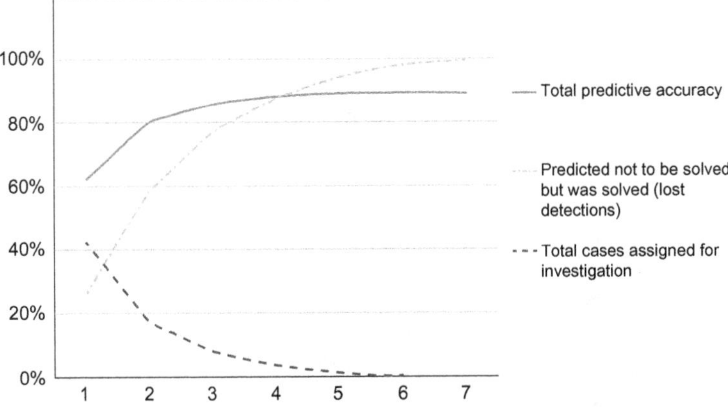

Fig. 4 Relationship between predictive accuracy, lost detections and case assignment

Discussion

Many of the results from this study were expected, and in line with existing research. However, other results were surprising and have far-reaching implications.

The study design was unable to test whether the presence of a particular variable provided the first link between the crime and the suspect or whether it was definitive in securing the evidence required to make an arrest, in contrast to previous studies (Burrows et al. 2005). This study was also unable to demonstrate any causative link between solvability factors and case outcomes. However, it has been able to demonstrate that a number of factors are strongly correlated with case outcomes. The factors present some notable similarities to and differences from Greenberg et al.'s (1973) original work.

Greenberg et al. identified the recovery of usable fingerprints as a solvability factor. Others have identified the recovery of DNA as an equally powerful solvability factor (Burrows et al. 2005; Robinson and Tilley 2009; Chapter "Assessing Solvability Factors in Greater Manchester, England: The Case of Residential Burglaries"). Indeed, there has been a substantial investment in improving the capability of forensic investigation in the UK through the development of the National Automated Fingerprint Identification system (NAFIS) and the National DNA Database (NDNAD). The substantial effect size for these elements therefore comes as no surprise. What is unexpected, however, is the new finding that the recovery of footprint marks has such a sizeable and statistically significant effect. It is peculiar that a footprint mark, which does not definitively link a suspect to a scene, should have such a correlation. This is in contrast to Greenberg et al. who found that, 'of the three major categories of physical evidence that generally would be collected at the crime scene of burglaries—fingerprints, tool marks and footprints—only fingerprints appeared to have been useful' (1973, p. 25). The increasing importance of footprint marks could perhaps be explained by the presence of a dedicated footprint unit within the Thames

Valley Police that processes and matches footprint marks at crime scenes and the footprints of burglars at the point of arrest. It would seem that Sherlock Holmes rightly noted that 'there is no branch of detective science which is so important and so much neglected as the art of tracing footsteps' (Doyle 1887, p. 57).

The role of witnesses in solving burglaries is unsurprisingly of critical importance. Greenberg et al. assigned the same weight to the presence of a witness as to the recovery of usable fingerprints. Whilst this research confirms the importance of witnesses to the solving of burglary cases, the effect size is substantially smaller than that of recovered fingerprints. This finding may reflect the problematic role of witnesses in investigation.

Hogan-Howe (2012) identified three ways of solving crime: catching the offender in the act, forensics and identification by a third party. Indeed, Coupe and Blake (2005) revealed that arresting offenders at or near the crime scene makes a remarkably large contribution to overall burglary detection rates. Robinson and Tilley (2009) confirmed that catching offenders at or near the scene is the single factor most likely to have the greatest impact on subsequent case detection. The relative importance of burglaries being reported whilst in progress has again been confirmed by this study for both successful and attempted burglaries, although—in contrast to Robinson and Tilley's (2009) findings—it is not the most important factor in solving a case. This is perhaps due to the relative priority that Thames Valley Police has assigned to these emergencies in terms of the importance of forensic recovery after the event. It is most interesting to note that the effect size for burglaries in progress is much greater for attempted offences than completed offences. This could perhaps be explained by the increased rate at which these offences, by their very nature, are witnessed and disturbed.

Greenberg et al. (1973) identified offence duration as of particular importance, assigning a substantial weighting to offences of less than an hour in duration. This research has confirmed the correlation between shorter offence durations and positive case outcomes; however, the effect size is substantially smaller than expected for both attempted and successful burglaries, leading to its rejection as a solvability factor.

The time to attendance of the first officer was not identified as a solvability factor by Greenberg et al. (1973), but was identified as such by Eck (1979). The correlation between time to attendance and case solution is not unexpected. What is unexpected, however, is that, even when burglaries in progress are removed from the data, there remains a statistically significant correlation between time to attendance and solved cases, although the effect size is small. Further research could identify whether this correlation relies on an increase in the likelihood of other more fundamental solvability factors, such as identifying witnesses before they leave the scene or obtaining forensic evidence before it is destroyed by the elements or other people. However, the overall effect size of the correlation between time to attendance and case outcome was not sufficiently large to warrant its selection as a solvability factor.

Furthermore, whether the offender left anything, such as a tool or gloves, at the scene is a newly discovered solvability factor with a moderate effect size. This study has been unable to analyse whether the nature of the item left behind itself influences the effect size. Further research may also be able to analyse whether or not the correlation to solved cases derives from the nature of the object itself, such as a dropped driving licence, or from a more fundamental solvability factor, such as a fingerprint recovered from the item.

The recovery of stolen property is also a newly discovered solvability factor. Unfortunately, the way in which these data were stored prevented any analysis to determine whether or not the property was discovered before or after the identification of the suspect. Nevertheless, it is interesting to note that the effect size for this solvability factor is much greater for completed residential burglaries than attempted ones.

The discovery that house-to-house enquiries are correlated with unsolved cases is an unexpected finding requiring explanation. The purpose of house-to-house enquiries is to identify witnesses to the offence or to other suspicious activity that may be associated with the burglary. It would be expected that house-to-house enquiries would be completed for all burglaries—and indeed, an 88% frequency of completion suggests a high degree of compliance. However, it is surprising to find that there are in fact fewer recorded witnesses in cases where house-to-house enquiries are completed than in cases where such enquiries are not conducted. It is conceivable that, in cases that are quickly solved, investigators may feel under a reduced obligation to record these enquiries than would be the case in unsolved investigations.

The recent proliferation of CCTV, not only in town centres but also in residential settings, has resulted in much more criminal activity being caught on camera. It was therefore expected that preserving CCTV would be strongly correlated with solved burglaries, but this is not the case. However, it is perhaps less surprising when it is considered that this study obtained data only on whether CCTV was *preserved*, not on whether it was viewed or formed an active part of an investigation. It is not unreasonable to suppose that CCTV is frequently preserved 'just in case' it may be of investigative value. Unfortunately, it was not possible to extract any other variables in relation to CCTV, such as whether it was viewed or whether an image of a suspicious person was captured. It is reasonable to suppose that such variables *would* be more strongly correlated with solved cases.

It is unfortunate that this research has been unable to study the effect of the suspect-named variable introduced in Greenberg et al.'s (1973) research, rendering a full replication of his weighted model impossible. However, the study of cases solved in the *absence* of any solvability factors revealed that victims name suspects with some frequency. It would not be unreasonable to suppose that, if the data were available in a format accessible to this study, that 'suspect named' would also have been identified as a solvability factor.

Predictive Accuracy

This study has demonstrated that it is possible to predict, using the 12 identified solvability factors, case outcomes with a high degree of accuracy. The total predictive accuracy of 62.68% when one factor is present and 80.71% when two factors are present compares very favourably to Greenberg et al.'s (1973) model, which was able to predict case outcomes with an accuracy of 67–92%, depending on the police department. This research is also comparable to Eck's (1979) replication, which achieved predictive accuracy of 85%. These studies assigned differing weights to each of their six identified variables. It might be that, with further statistical work, weights could be assigned to each of the solvability factors identified by the present study that could perhaps further increase the predictive accuracy of the model.

The predictive accuracy of this model is as good as that of Greenberg et al. or Eck in view of the fact that it adopts a much higher standard for a case solution. The decision to use sanction detections rather than case clearances or arrests will have adversely affected the predictive accuracy. However, once the 'suspect-named' variable is added and further statistical work is done to weight the 12 variables, it is likely that this model will show further increases in predictive accuracy.

As the model stands, it provides the information required by police leaders to make judgements as to whether to set a cut-point and save resources. The model identified could be further developed to attach cash savings to each cut-point based on the fact that each burglary investigation takes, on average, 3.7 h (Mawby 2001), at the cost per officer hour. Whilst the popular press might urge that it is never acceptable to screen out efforts to solve a burglary case, such arguments might be tempered by a demonstration of the cash benefits to taxpayers of doing so. The resource savings effected by adopting a cut-point are very substantial indeed, given that this model would screen out at least 67.69% of cases. In comparison, Greenberg et al.'s (1973) model screened out a massive 86.7% of investigations, whilst the Rochester model screened out a mere 32% (Bloch and Bell 1976).

The concerns of the media may be alleviated if the level of lost detections never rises as high as the model predicts. There is some reason for supposing this may be the case, as greater investigative effort can be spent on the remaining investigations. The Rochester system found that 'because the team closed their cases early they were able to concentrate on those that remained open' (Bloch and Bell 1976, p. 45). Indeed, 'officer workload is a much more important factor than mere police presence in determining the clear up rate' (Burrows and Tarling 1982, p. 9). This research has identified that very substantial numbers of cases have solvability factors present, yet do not result in detection. It could be that, if more investigator time was available for these cases, the level of lost detections would be much lower—perhaps non-existent. Perhaps, therefore, the argument about case screening could be reframed in terms of allowing investigators the time to focus on the most promising cases rather than chasing those that offer no solid chance of identifying the perpetrator.

Conclusions

The detection of crime, and in particular the detection of burglary, is central to the policing mission. Stubbornly low national detection rates and an era of austerity must focus activity on what can be done to bring more offenders to justice whilst conserving valuable resources.

The effect size analysis of the variables led to the identification of 12 solvability factors that are able to predict case outcomes with a high degree of accuracy. In a replication of previous research, this study produced a screening model that would enable police leaders to set a solvability threshold to determine a desired balance between allocated cases and lost detections. The resource savings made possible by this model may prove attractive in the current financial climate. Given that 38.59% of burglaries with solvability factors present are not solved, it may follow that more cases could be solved if investigators were able to devote more time to them. The next steps would be to conduct an experiment to determine the extent to which the adoption of this model would produce lost detections whilst saving investigative resources.

References

Ariel, B. (2012). Deterrence and moral persuasion effects on corporate tax compliance: findings from a randomized controlled trial. *Criminology, 50*(1), 27–69.

Ariel, B., Sutherland, A., Henstock, D., Young, J., Drover, P., Sykes, J., ... & Henderson, R. (2016a). Report: Increases in police use of force in the presence of body-worn cameras are driven by officer discretion: A protocol-based subgroup analysis of ten randomized experiments. *Journal of Experimental Criminology, 12*(3), 453–463.

Ariel, B., Sutherland, A., Henstock, D., Young, J., Drover, P., Sykes, J., ... & Henderson, R. (2016b). Wearing body cameras increases assaults against officers and does not reduce police use of force: Results from a global multi-site experiment. *European Journal of Criminology, 13*(6), 744–755.

Ariel, B., Sutherland, A., Henstock, D., Young, J., Drover, P., Sykes, J., ... & Henderson, R. (2017). "Contagious accountability" a global multisite randomized controlled trial on the effect of police body-worn cameras on citizens' complaints against the police. *Criminal Justice and Behavior, 44*(2), 293–316.

Bloch, P. B., & Bell, J. (1976). *Managing investigations: The Rochester system*. Washington DC: The Police Foundation.

Burrows, J. (1986). *Burglary: Police actions and victims' views* (Home Office Research and Planning Unit Paper 37). London: Home Office.

Burrows, J., Hopkins, M., Hubbard, R., Robinson, A., Speed, M., & Tilley, N. (2005). *Understanding the attrition process in volume crime investigations* (Home Office Research Study 295). London: Home Office.

Burrows, J., & Tarling, R. (1982). *Clearing up crime*. London: HMSO.

Cohen, J. (1988). *Statistical power analysis for the behavioral sciences* (2nd ed.). Hillsdale, NJ: Lawrence Erlbaum.

Coupe, R. T., & Blake, L. (2005). The effects of patrol workloads and response strength on burglary emergencies. *Journal of Criminal Justice, 33*(3), 239–255.

Coupe, T., & Griffiths, M. (1996). *Solving residential burglary* (Police Research Group Crime Detection and Prevention Services, Paper 77). London: Home Office.

Donnellan, P. G. (2011). *To what extent is burglary detection a consequence of effective investigation?* (unpublished M.Sc. thesis). University of Cambridge.

Doyle, A. C. (1887). *A study in scarlet*. London: Ward, Lock and Co.

Eck, J. E. (1979). *Managing case assignments: The burglary investigation decision model replication*. Washington, DC: Police Executive Research Forum.

Eck, J. E. (1983). *Solving crimes: The investigation of burglary and robbery*. Washington DC: Police Executive Research Forum.

Eck, J. E., & Spelman, W. (1987). Who ya gonna call? The police as problem busters. *Crime & Delinquency, 33*(1), 31–52.

Greenberg, B., Elliot, C. V., Kraft, L. P., & Procter, S. H. (1977). *Felony investigation decision model—An analysis of investigation elements of information*. Washington, DC: US Government Printing Office.

Greenberg, B., Yu, O., & Lang, K. (1973). *Enhancement of the investigative function* (Vol. I). Menlo Park, CA: Stanford Research Institute.

Hogan-Howe, B. (2012, July 9). *Total policing*. Unpublished Lecture, Criminology Faculty, Cambridge University.

Lipsey, M. W., & Wilson, D. B. (2001). *Practical meta-analysis*. Thousand Oaks, CA: SAGE Publications.

Robb, P., Coupe, T., & Ariel, B. (2015). 'Solvability' and detection of metal theft on railway property. *European Journal on Criminal Policy and Research, 21*(4), 463–484.

Robinson, A., & Tilley, N. (2009). Factors influencing police performance in the investigation of volume crimes in England and Wales. *Police Practice and Research: An International Journal, 10*(3), 209–223.

Solvability Indicators for 'First Officers': Targeting Eyewitness Questioning at Non-residential Burglaries

Richard Timothy Coupe

Introduction

Most burglaries are solved as a result of suspects being seen by witnesses, who are most commonly either the victims or their neighbours. Four-tenths of residential and non-residential detected cases result from burglaries being witnessed while 'in progress' and patrol officers arresting offenders at or near the scene (Paine and Ariel 2013; Coupe and Griffiths 1996; Robinson and Tilley 2009). In addition, as many detected cases are attributable to suspect descriptions collected by patrol officers subsequently questioning neighbours or burglary victims. Only a small proportion of the 15% of burglaries reported while in progress, however, is solved. At the unsolved 'in-progress' incidents and the 85% of burglaries where patrols made a routine response, patrol officers could question neighbours, some of whom actually see offenders and call in alerts. Others, however, may see a burglar but not realize at the time that an offence had been or was about to be committed. Unfortunately, there is only a small subset of burglary incidents where neighbours are likely to be able to provide first officers with suspect descriptions good enough to identify a culprit. To save resources, therefore, it is desirable to narrow down the numbers of incidents where neighbours are questioned by focusing on those with a high probability of providing the evidence that results in arrest. If this can be achieved, resources currently wasted on many cases that are very unlikely to be solved can be allocated to more solvable cases, some of which might involve neighbours able to provide valuable eyewitness evidence that might otherwise missed by first officers.

The purpose of this chapter is to examine ways of identifying those burglary incidents where neighbours are most likely to have seen an offender and provide definite suspect information that leads to arrest. Its focus is, therefore, on the solvability indicators that point to the incidents most likely to possess the key solvability factors

R. T. Coupe (✉)
Institute of Criminology, University of Cambridge, Cambridge, UK
e-mail: rtc23@cam.ac.uk

R. T. Coupe et al. (eds.), *Crime Solvability Factors*,
https://doi.org/10.1007/978-3-030-17160-5_5

that result in detection, so that the efforts of first officers at the scene may be more cost-effectively targeted. To determine which scenes should be visited to question witnesses, the objective is to identify indicators for screening in incidents where neighbours are most likely to be able to provide a definite suspect identification. For burglaries reported while in progress by neighbours, those who saw rather than heard the burglar are likely to be more promising. For the bulk of incidents reported some time after the event, often when employees or owners arrive at premises in the mornings or when householders return home, neighbours who have a line of sight to target scenes—particularly access and exit points—are most likely to be able to provide suspect information. For the latter, identifying those neighbours of burglary victims most likely to have seen offenders and be able to provide a suspect description, however, will enable officer resources to be used sparingly at only those incidents with a high probability of detection.

Witness Evidence at Burglary Scenes

Existing research highlights the importance of focusing police attention on witness evidence. Most burglaries are solved as a result of rapid patrol response and capture or, subsequently, due to suspect information obtained from witnesses (Burrows et al. 2005; Coupe and Griffiths 1996; Robinson and Tilley 2009). Over 40% of residential and rather fewer non-residential burglaries are solved as a result of 'in-progress' alerts that lead to offenders being caught in the act (Coupe and Griffiths 1996; Coupe et al. 2002). A further 34% of residential and 44% of non-residential arrests are due to the identification of suspects using witness evidence (Coupe and Griffiths 1996; Coupe et al. 2002). The importance of these characteristics as solvability factors is confirmed by other studies (e.g. Burrows et al. 2005; Donnellan 2012; Paine and Ariel 2013; Coupe 2016).

Even though in-progress burglaries and those with witness evidence are the most solvable, relatively few of even these sorts of cases are actually solved. As many as 15% of burglaries are reported while 'in progress', and there is witness evidence at over 70% (Coupe and Fox 2015), but responses to less than a fifth of 'in-progress' alerts and fewer than 1 in 17 cases with witness evidence result in the culprit's arrest (Coupe and Fox 2015). Thus, despite offering very good prospects for detection, only small proportions of these cases are actually detected. This indicates that many, in practice, may not be so easily solved, but it is also possible that officers fail to question witnesses at every solvable incident and, conversely, waste resources questioning witnesses who are unlikely to provide useful evidence. Selectivity, therefore, must be exercised in questioning eyewitnesses in order to, as far as is possible, allocate officer resources only to those who will produce evidence likely to result in arrest. At many burglaries not reported while in progress, many neighbours realize only when questioned that they had, in fact, seen somebody who was likely to have been an offender but had not regarded the perpetrator's behaviour as suspicious at the time. An ability to pick out the burglaries at which neighbour witnesses will be able to provide suspect evidence that will result in arrests would mean that far less first-officer time would be spent on fruitless questioning. Visiting neighbours can be particularly time-consuming if they are no longer at the premises or at home and special return visits by police officers are necessary.

The objective in this chapter is therefore to identify the characteristics of burglary events and features of burglary scenes that are the best indicators of those incidents witnessed by neighbours and most likely provide definite suspect evidence of a quality that enables arrest and case clearance. Data on these more detailed characteristics of non-residential burglary incidents are drawn from surveys of victims, first officers and sites, supplemented by incident logs, which illustrate how incidents may be identified at which neighbours are most likely to have seen offenders and provide eyewitness evidence that leads to arrest. The chapter is concerned with identifying those cases that are solvable in terms of providing suspect information that results in arrest.

Methodology

Research Design and Instruments

The evidence presented in this chapter is based on research into non-residential burglaries committed in 2000. The use of historic data is justified by their unique type and quality. The research instruments included surveys of officers, incident logs, victim interviews and site surveys. All data were linked to individual burglary incidents, permitting arrests and case detections to be linked to police actions, resources, victim and burglary characteristics and evidence collected at each stage of investigations. Significantly for this chapter, it was possible to relate the environmental features of burglary sites to whether or not neighbours provided definite suspect evidence and whether this resulted in arrest. It is the incident characteristics collected in victim interviews and site surveys that enable the identification of more solvable cases where arrests are made more likely either by rapid response alerts by neighbours or by questioning neighbours.

The non-residential burglary sample comprises 1008 incidents—308 detected and 700 non-detected—drawn from a population of 6329 non-residential burglaries. The officer surveys had a 90% response rate. A sample of 299 cases was randomly selected for victim interviews and site surveys, stratified with half detected and half undetected. These surveys provide the environmental data that enables us to identify and predict the characteristics of incidents where neighbours can provide valuable eyewitness evidence.

Sampling Frame

This non-residential burglary study was undertaken in nine of the operational command units of a large UK conurbation force serving a population of three million people and policed by 3000 officers. The sampling frame incorporates a major city of three quarters of a million people and three important industrial towns, with a variety of burglary targets. These range from city centre shops and offices to factories and warehouses on industrial estates, science parks, restaurants, hotels, public houses, religious and leisure facilities, and public service facilities, such as schools, colleges, health centres, hospitals and government offices. This suggests that findings should be generalizable to burglaries in other large urban areas, if not, in certain respects, to rural areas.

The study's findings have a contemporary value owing to the relatively few changes in the investigation and detection of burglaries during the last 20 years and the not-dissimilar pressures being placed on staffing resources. Cases are still screened using procedures not grounded in statistical measurement (Robinson and Tilley 2009), and the principal ways of solving them have altered little, with catching burglars red-handed or on the basis of eyewitness evidence about suspects still dominant (Tilley et al. 2007; Robinson and Tilley 2009, cf. Coupe and Griffiths 1996). Few are solved now, as previously, by tracing stolen property or vehicle registrations, or by using informants. A growing—but still relatively small—number of burglary detections, however, do now result from forensic evidence collected from crime scenes, often footprints, fingerprints and DNA samples (Donnellan 2012; Paine and Ariel 2013), whereas few did so two decades ago. There has been an increase in 'car-key' burglary (Carden 2012), in which offenders break into properties for car keys in order to steal cars, but remote hacking of the electronic key fobs common on expensive modern cars is making such burglary redundant.

Furthermore, despite the increased use of proactive policing approaches (Newburn 2007), these appear to be more effective at preventing crime (Tilley et al. 2007), playing little role in the investigation of burglary and other high-volume crime, most of which is still dealt with reactively (Jansson 2005; Tilley et al. 2007; Robinson and Tilley 2009; Donnellan 2012; Paine and Ariel 2013). Examples of proactive policing of burglary include using informants for crimes to be subsequently committed, using undercover officers to open a false stolen property 'fence' to intercept offenders, or installing silent and delayed audible alarms (e.g. Chenery et al. 1997) at premises in order to catch repeat offenders. Now, as in 1994, these appear to be of little importance in solving burglary (Coupe and Kaur 2005). Only the increased use of forensic samples to detect burglary cases is notable (Paine and Ariel, Chapter "Population-Level Analysis of Residential Burglaries"; Antrobus and Pilotto 2016).

Improving Cost-Effective Evidence Collection: Questioning Neighbours at Non-residential Burglaries

Importance of Sighting Burglars

A burglar being seen is one of the strongest solvability factors. This is not only because there is potential to catch offenders in the act, as many subsequent arrests are attributable to eyewitness evidence, and most of these are incidents at which neighbours see offenders. Burglars were seen at almost a third of non-residential incidents. These incidents were over seven times as likely to result in arrest as burglaries where no offender was seen: 42% arrested compared with only 5.4%, respectively, (χ^2(2, 1008) = 371.64, $p < .001$, $V = .61$). This resulted in nine times as many detections: 36% compared with 5.4% (χ^2(2, 1006) = 364.69, $p < .001$, $V = .60$). If the offender is not caught red-handed at or near the scene, then good quality suspect information, preferably a definite suspect identification, will often help clear the case.

Incident Characteristics at Incidents Where Neighbours See Burglars

The characteristics that predict the incidents at which neighbours see burglars and whether or not they have valuable suspect evidence depend on intervisibility between the target and neighbouring properties. The key factors are, first, the numbers of neighbouring properties with a line of sight to burglars' entry and exit points and, second, the distances between targets and neighbouring properties. During darkness, target visibility is lower; thus, more neighbours are needed to spot burglars at night, and audibility can be as important as vision in alerting onlookers. Poorer night-time visibility may be mitigated by better street lighting.

Suspects were seen at non-residential burglaries when burgled and neighbouring properties were in closer proximity to one another ($F = 7.92$, $p < .01$), an average of 39 yards compared with 65 yards when offenders were not seen in daylight, dropping to 29 yards compared with 68 yards at night ($F = 12.98$, $p < .001$). At incidents where offenders were seen, there were also more neighbouring properties with either an upstairs ($F = 17.30$, $p = .001$) or downstairs view of targets ($F = 9.98$, $p < .01$); more neighbours are needed to spot offenders from upstairs than downstairs. The deterioration in visibility during darkness is reflected in the larger number of neighbours needed for burglar sighting at night (Table 1).

Table 1 Non-residential burglar sightings: mean neighbour numbers for whether or not burglars seen by daylight/darkness and number of upstairs and downstairs neighbours with line of sight to targets (Coupe and Kaur 2005)

		Upstairs	Downstairs
Daylight	Seen	4.8	3.4
	Not seen	2.3	1.1
Darkness	Seen	7.5	6.9
	Not seen	4.9	4.9

Definite Suspect Identification Evidence

Solvability indicators for the burglaries where questioning neighbours more frequently provides definite suspect identification will help determine how useful such visits are likely to be. It would enable the screening out of the majority of incidents that would involve special or separate visits to talk to victims' neighbours. Such indicators can improve the cost-effective collection of eyewitness evidence.

Most definite suspect ID evidence is collected from neighbours rather than victims or passers-by. Sometimes, the suspect's name or a description that identifies a suspect will be provided by neighbours when an alert is called in, and this can help catch the offender close to the burglary scene—or at it, if it is extensive, such as a factory, or is partly open to the public, such as a college, medical centre or group of shops and offices. Patrol officers often question neighbours when they respond but may need to return, especially if the response has been 'routine' and neighbours are not at home or in nearby premises. Equally, not every incident called in by victims receives a patrol response.

A journey to question neighbours therefore frequently involves additional effort, particularly if multiple trips are needed to make contact, but only in a small minority of cases is a definite suspect ID obtained. Officers questioned neighbours at 21% of non-domestic burglaries and obtained definite suspect information at only 3.4%. Questioning of neighbours by first officers at 'in-progress' incidents provided about 40% of the definite suspect IDs collected from neighbours; subsequent questioning of neighbours at incidents that received routine patrol responses provided the other 60%. Many definite suspect IDs were collected at 'in-progress' incidents at which offenders were not caught at or near the scene and facilitated subsequent arrest. All neighbours who call in alerts while the burglary is in progress should clearly be questioned by officers if the offender is not arrested at that time.

Definite suspect ID evidence almost doubled the probability of an arrest from 11% to 20% ($\chi^2 = 44.24, p < .001$) compared with poorer quality suspect evidence. It was associated with high secondary detection (when a suspect admits the burglary offence while being questioned about a different offence) rates of 10%, compared with 1.6% for cases without such evidence.

Table 2 Binary logistic regression, with whether or not a definite suspect ID was obtained as the dependent variable

Variable	*B*	SE	Wald	*p*	Exp(*B*)
Whether or not in-progress burglary	2.025	.692	8.571	.003	7.578
Number of neighbours questioned	−.810	.221	13.476	.000	.445
Number of neighbours with target view from downstairs	−.1.14	.34	11.03	.001	.32
Constant	.828	.925	.800	.370	2.288

Definite Suspect ID Evidence at 'In-Progress' and 'Routine' Incidents

Since patrol officers at in-progress burglaries can usually question neighbours who called in alerts when they first respond, few resources are wasted at these incidents, the more so because a neighbour calling in an alert has often seen the offender. Only infrequently must patrols disengage to respond to another emergency. However, at the other 86% of incidents to which a 'routine' response is made, resources can be wasted questioning neighbours who are unlikely to have seen the burglar. Equally, evidence can be missed if not every neighbour who might have seen the offender is questioned. At incidents graded as 'routine', police responses take longer and neighbours who have seen burglars may no longer be at their premises. A response may not normally be made to every non-residential incident so that definite suspect ID evidence may be missed if screening-out decisions take no account of the solvability indicators discussed here.

Indicators of Definite Suspect Identification Evidence

The three best predictors of the incidents where definite suspect IDs could be obtained from neighbours were as follows: whether or not the incident was an 'in progress' burglary; more neighbours were questioned; and there were more neighbouring properties with a line of sight to the target from downstairs (Table 2). The odds of obtaining a suspect ID were more than seven times higher at in-progress burglaries and were three times higher for every additional neighbour with a downstairs view of the target so that they were 18 times higher at incidents with six or more neighbours than a single neighbour.

Table 3 Indicators of non-residential burglaries where neighbours provided a definite suspect identification

Indicator variable	Suspect ID		Statistical
	No	Yes	Significance
Mean number of residential properties with rear view of target	2.5	6.6	$F = 5.8, p = .019$
Mean number of non-residential premises with view of target from upstairs	2.9	7.6	$F = 7.3, p = .009$
Mean number of non-residential premises with view of target from downstairs	1.3	6.7	$F = 13.5, p = .000$

Incidents Where Neighbours Were Questioned

For the 17% of sample incidents at which neighbours were questioned, the solvability indicators for neighbours providing definite suspect IDs relate to the numbers of residential or non-residential properties with a line of sight to the burgled premises from different positions (Table 3). As offenders break into premises or burglary sites, they are liable to be seen clearly from residential property situated to the rear of the target and if there are larger numbers of neighbouring non-residential properties with a view of the target from either upstairs or downstairs. The number of neighbours with a view of the target from downstairs is the strongest predictor of neighbours providing a definite suspect description.

Having six or more neighbouring properties with a line of sight to the target from downstairs is the level at which the likelihood of a neighbour providing a definite suspect description becomes strikingly higher. Where neighbours were questioned, victims with six or more neighbours were 16 times more likely to have neighbours who were able to provide a definite ID: IDs were provided by neighbours at only 1% of premises with fewer than six neighbours, but at 16% of those with six or more neighbours ($\chi^2 = 52.26, p < .001, df = 1$). This may reflect other characteristics of premises and streets with more neighbours, notably being better lit after dark and during twilight, since the number of neighbours with a target view from downstairs was positively correlated with distance from the nearest street light ($r_s = -213, p <$ $.001$) and distance between street lights ($r_s = -.277, p < .001$). Larger numbers of neighbouring premises intervisible with targets also reflect higher-density land use and the proximity of larger numbers of neighbours to targets.

The numbers of residential properties with a view of the rear of premises and numbers of properties with a view from upstairs were highly correlated with those with a downstairs view ($r = .80, p < .001$; $r = .84, p < .001$, respectively). Binary logistic regression analysis applied to the full sample shows that they add next to nothing to the level of explanation of definite suspect ID outcomes, raising Nagelkerke's R^2 value from .242 to .243.

Binary logistic regression applied only to those incidents where neighbours were questioned, with whether or not there was a definite suspect ID as the dependent variable, indicates that, at burglaries with six or more neighbours with a downstairs target view, the odds of obtaining an ID are improved by 8.1:1 compared with five or fewer neighbours ($p = .003$, Nagelkerke's $R^2 = .20$). At routine incidents, only where neighbours were questioned, these odds were improved by 10.25:1 ($p = .016$; Nagelkerke's $R^2 = .18$). Only questioning neighbours at routine incidents if there are six or more with a downstairs view of the target will be cost-effective. Questioning neighbours who call in alerts at in-progress burglaries also effectively contribute to clearing up more offences.

Missed Opportunities and Wasted Visits

In practice, a great deal of effort was expended to secure only a handful of definite IDs: patrol officers questioned neighbours at 17% of all burglaries, but definite suspect ID evidence was obtained at only 2%. Current practice is undiscriminating and results in missed opportunities and wasted visits. Many neighbours are questioned at premises whose occupants are very unlikely to have seen anything. This waste is far greater if officers are unable to visit neighbours when they initially respond to incidents and must return later. Officers questioned neighbours at targets with fewer than six neighbouring premises at 16% of all burglaries, of which only 1% provided definite suspect IDs—equivalent to .17% of all burglaries.

An average of 1.7 neighbours were visited at the 17% of targets where neighbours were questioned. The distribution of neighbour numbers visited is shown in Fig. 1. Where there was definite suspect ID information, an average of 46 min was spent on questioning, while interviews took only 10 min on average when there was no information. Where there was useful information, an average of 28 min was spent talking with neighbours. Although little questioning time is wasted at incidents where no information was obtained, making special trips to visit neighbours takes up patrol officers' travel time and requires time to establish contact with neighbours before officers are able to question them.

There were almost certainly missed opportunities at 4.7% of all burglaries which had six or more neighbouring premises and were not 'in-progress' alerts. Since neighbours provided suspect IDs at 16% of incidents where there were six or more neighbours, every 1 in 6.25 of these might have been expected to yield definite suspect IDs, potentially boosting overall arrests by .8%, from 11.9 to 12.7%.

The potential to cost-effectively use line of sight by neighbours as a solvability indicator of definite suspect ID evidence is limited by the proportion of incidents with six or more neighbours. At non-residential burglaries, only 7% of incidents have six or more neighbours with a downstairs target view. It is predictably higher for 'in-progress' incidents—at 9%. The potential is, therefore, not likely to involve more than 1% of detections at non-domestic burglaries. Nevertheless, directing effort at only the 7% of incidents likely to provide evidence makes a contribution, which, if replicated in other investigative areas, could in combination notably improve burglary detections. Electronic cadastral plans enable the identification of those targets with six neighbouring premises likely to have a downstairs target view. Allowing for estimating these so as to not miss any opportunities might result in neighbours being questioned at perhaps a tenth rather than just 7% of promising incidents.

Checking Missed Potential: Comparing Incidents with More Than Five Neighbours Where Neighbours Were and Were not Questioned

This potential depends on the comparison of routine incidents with six or more neighbouring premises where neighbours were and were not questioned, specifically as to whether these two groups are similar with regard to the characteristics that affect sighting. The security, premises function, employee numbers and site characteristics—including cover, access, surrounding land use, street lighting, distance and numbers of neighbouring premises—of the incidents in these two groups did not differ. From a raft of 54 measures, there were differences only in open ground at the backs of premises [more with open ground at incidents where neighbours were not

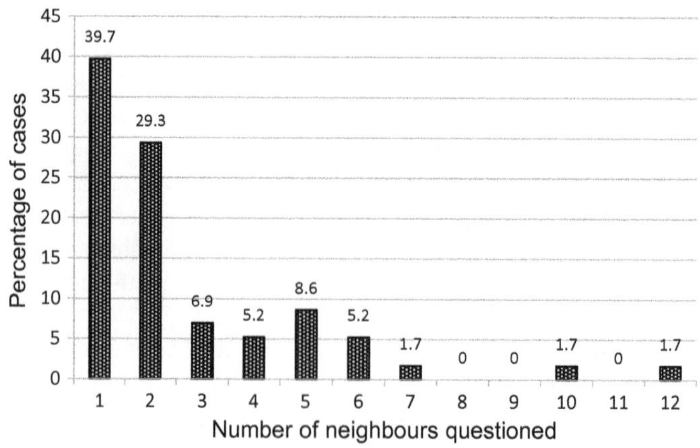

Fig. 1 Numbers of neighbours questioned at incidents where police visited neighbours

questioned ($\chi^2 = 3.70$, $p = .054$, $df = 1$)] and in repeat burglaries. Open ground, when controlling for all other factors, makes it more likely that burglars were seen ($p = .008$, BLR odds ratio = 2.51), so that the potential is, if anything, better where neighbours were not visited. Burglaries where officers did not question neighbours also had fewer—only a quarter as many: 13% versus 57%—multiple repeat incidents during the six months prior to the incidents in this study ($\chi^2 = 6.42, p = .04, df = 2$). More repeat burglaries indicate that guardianship was poorer at incidents where neighbours were questioned (Coupe and Mueller-Johnson, Chapter "Improving Offence Solvability and Detection Rates at Non-residential Burglary: Predicting Single and Multiple Repeat Incidence"), since multiple repeat burglaries occur particularly at premises with poor guardianship, indicating that the potential for definite suspect IDs may be even higher at the premises that patrol officers did not visit.

Discussion and Conclusion

Solvability indicators of the burglaries at which questioning neighbours will provide definite suspect identification help improve the use of 'first-officer' resources and increase case detections. By prioritising incidents where there are far higher odds of obtaining definite suspect ID evidence from neighbours, a statistical basis for incident prioritization and case screening can inform patrol officer deployment. Such indicators can help pinpoint efforts to collect eyewitness evidence.

Findings indicate that neighbour questioning at non-residential burglaries can be better targeted by using solvability indicators. The promising subgroups for collecting definite suspect IDs are 'in-progress' incidents where no offenders were caught red-handed (c. 6% of the sample), and premises with six or more neighbours with a line of sight to the target promises. These could provide almost two-thirds of the sample's definite suspect IDs possessed by neighbours, while visiting only 13% of incidents. Visits to only 7% of routine incidents promise to provide a third of the sample's definite suspect ID evidence. Clearly, IDs could sometimes be collected by telephone from neighbours who call in an alert, and this information is often better obtained when the alert call is made since it can help rapid response patrols catch offenders, as well help with detecting cases where offenders, who commonly discard stolen property, are caught near the scene and in nearby streets. Further investigative activities and additional evidence are needed for four-fifths of those burglars caught at or near scenes by rapid response patrols (Coupe, Chapter "Investigative Activities, Resources and Burglary Detection").

Daylight in-progress burglaries are self-evidently a promising source of suspect evidence, particularly from neighbouring properties, but also from the victims themselves. This has been illustrated in this chapter with a study of non-residential burglary. Eyewitness evidence is also superior in daylight at non-residential burglaries, though more occur outside the working day and at weekends, when neighbouring properties are often unoccupied, unless burgled premises are situated—as many are—in residential areas or burglaries take place in the private parts of buildings that otherwise stay open to the public at these times, such as restaurants, bars, railway stations or hospitals.

This chapter illustrates the benefits of examining solvability indicators that enable resources to be targeted at the most promising subsets of incidents where suspects have been seen and where definite suspect IDs may be obtained. Solvability factors tell us that cases where a suspect has been seen ought to be investigated since this factor has a very strong positive correlation with detection and is the most prevalent of all burglary solvability factors. A minority of these incidents, nevertheless, is detected. Solvability indicators consider how resources ought to be selectively and cost-effectively targeted at specific subsets of cases where offenders have been seen and where neighbours are most likely to possess ID evidence. Rather than investigating all cases where suspects have been seen with similar effort, effort should be tailored so that the most solvable subset of cases is prioritised. Using incident and site characteristics as indicators enables the more solvable incidents to be identified and the less solvable ones to be screened out. Targeting resources at the most solvable minority of burglaries enables cost-effective case clearance with few solvable incidents neglected and detections maximized.

References

Antrobus, E., & Pilotto, A. (2016). Improving forensic responses to residential burglaries: Results of a randomized controlled field trial. *Journal of Experimental Criminology, 12*(3), 319–345.

Burrows, J., Hopkins, M., Hubbard, R., Robinson, A., Speed, M., & Tilley, N. (2005). *Understanding the attrition process in volume crime investigations* (Home Office Research Study 295). London: Home Office.

Carden, R. (2012). *Car key burglaries: An exploratory analysis*. Paper presented at the 5th International Evidence-Based Policing Conference, Cambridge, July 9–11, 2012.

Chenery, S., Holt, J., & Pease, K. (1997). *Biting back II: Reducing repeat victimisation in Huddersfield* (Crime Detection and Prevention Series, Paper 82). London: Home Office.

Coupe, R. T. (2016). Evaluating the effects of resources and solvability on burglary detection. *Policing & Society: An International Journal of Research and Policy, 26*(5), 563–587.

Coupe, R. T., Erwood, N., & Kaur, S. (2002). *Solving non-residential burglary* (unpublished Home Office report). London: Home Office.

Coupe, R. T., & Kaur, S. (2005). The role of alarms and CCTV in detecting non-residential burglary. *Security Journal, 18*(2), 53–72.

Coupe, T., & Fox, B. H. (2015). A risky business: How do access, exposure and guardians affect the chances of non-residential burglars being seen? *Security Journal, 28*(1), 71–92.

Coupe, T., & Griffiths, M. (1996). *Solving residential burglary* (Police Research Group Crime Detection and Prevention Services, Paper 77). London: Home Office.

Donnellan, G. (2012). *Burglary solvability factors*. Paper presented at 4th International Evidence-Based Policing Conference, Cambridge, July 4–6, 2011.

Jansson, K. (2005). *Volume crime investigations—A review of the research literature* (Home Office Online Report OLR 44/05). London: Home Office.

Newburn, T. (2007). Understanding investigation. In T. Newburn, T. Williamson, & A. Wright (Eds.), *Handbook of criminal investigation*. Cullompton: Willan Publishing.

Paine, C., & Ariel, B. (2013). *Solvability analysis: Increasing the likelihood of detection in completed, attempted and in-progress burglaries*. Paper presented at the 6th International Evidence-Based Policing Conference, Cambridge, July 8–10, 2013.

Robinson, A., & Tilley, N. (2009). Factors influencing police performance in the investigation of volume crimes in England and Wales. *Police Practice and Research: An International Journal, 10*(3), 209–223.

Tilley, N., Robinson, A., & Burrows, J. (2007). The investigation of high volume crime. In T. Newburn, T. Williamson, & A. Wright (Eds.), *Handbook of criminal investigation* (pp. 226–254). London: Willan Publishing.

Pickpocketing on Railways

Stephanie Sharp and Richard Timothy Coupe

Introduction

The objectives of this chapter are to examine the solvability of pickpocketing offences on railway property policed by the British Transport Police (BTP), with a view to improving detection rates and securing resource efficiencies. Specifically, this study will identify the key solvability factors and develop a screening model for filtering out promising cases for further cost-effective investigation. It will also outline a randomized controlled trial that will provide evidence of the effects on clearance and generate further data about the tactics employed during secondary investigations.

Pickpocketing involves the theft of items from the victim and is perpetrated by individuals or by coordinated groups of offenders. It is one of the most prevalent offences on the UK rail network, where passengers standing or sitting close together on crowded trains, platforms and concourses often present attractive targets for thieves. BTP deals with over 7,000 pickpocketing offences a year. Though only 5% of these are detected, 90% are screened in for further investigation, indicating that there is considerable potential for saving resources by only investigating cases with reasonable prospects of being solved. Accurately identifying solvable cases is likely to not only save resources currently wasted on fruitless investigations, but also increase the number of cases that are detected.

Case-screening decisions about pickpocketing cases are currently made on a formal basis using the experience and subjective judgements of operatives in approximately 25 BTP Case Management Units. Practice varies geographically, with some local areas enforcing mandatory secondary investigations for pickpocketing. Approaches that allow for discretion to be exercised, however, tend to result in

S. Sharp (✉)
British Transport Police, London, UK
e-mail: Stephanie.Sharp@btp.pnn.police.uk

R. T. Coupe
Institute of Criminology, University of Cambridge, Cambridge, UK

R. T. Coupe et al. (eds.), *Crime Solvability Factors*,
https://doi.org/10.1007/978-3-030-17160-5_6

inconsistent screening decisions, with greater effort expended on non-routine cases (Waegel 1982) and the value of circumstantial factors for solving cases being undervalued (Gill et al. 1996; Jansson 2005), particularly, if investigating officers have heavy workloads (Waegel 1982). The use of statistical modelling to predict solvability and inform case screening decisions promises a more consistent and accurate allocation of investigative resources only to those cases that it is possible to detect.

In the absence of any earlier published studies of pickpocketing solvability and detection, this study aims to complement existing work on the solvability of burglary (e.g. Eck 1983) and robbery (Brandl and Frank 1994) and studies that seek to explain why pickpocketing occurs (Andersson 2014; Newton et al. 2014). While key solvability factors for burglary and robbery point to the importance of in-progress witnessing of the offence, other eyewitness evidence and selected forensic evidence (e.g. Brandl and Frank 1994; Eck 1983; Paine 2012), other studies, such as those of metal theft solvability on railway property (Robb et al., Chapter "Metal Theft Solvability and Detection") or assault (Olphin 2015), indicate a broader range of factors that also include the region in which offences occur and other situational factors, as well as factors specific to the crime, such as what is stolen and the type of place where the theft or assault occurred. It is likely that comparable circumstantial and situational factors, such as visibility, lighting and the presence of CCTV or fewer tourists and resources, including higher staffing levels, will have a bearing on solving incidents of pickpocketing on the railways.

Pickpocketing on the Railway

Railways present circumstances that are ideal for pickpocketing, since concentrated congestion and high passenger densities offer greater anonymity to thieves and lower the likelihood of their apprehension (Newton et al. 2014). Pickpocketing is particularly rife during the morning and late afternoon peak travel times (Newton et al. 2014), when congestion in places such as lifts and carriages inhibits eyewitness and meaningful CCTV evidence. Pickpocketing is a 'stealth' crime (Smith 2008) in which the skilled perpetrator deploys distractions to ensure the offence goes unnoticed (Pickpocketing 1995). These include spilling a drink or bumping into the victim to disguise a theft and make contact appear accidental (Andersson 2014). Other tactics of pickpockets on railways include a single 'dip' into a bag or pocket, slashing open a bag and a group surrounding or jostling a target. Victims often notice that belongings are missing only a considerable time after the theft has occurred and are frequently unable to pinpoint the time or even the train or station where the crime took place. The circumstantial context under which pickpocketing occurs on the railways, therefore, has an important bearing on the factors likely to help detection, such as CCTV recordings or eyewitness accounts from victims, witnesses or the police. If crowds lower solvability, there may be higher proportions of solvable cases on less congested trains, platforms, lifts and escalators and at times of day when there are fewer passengers.

Methodology

Setting and Data

The study uses data from BTP crime records on 36,260 pickpocketing offences that occurred between September 2010 and August 2015 on the London Underground system and in the six 'over-ground' railway subdivisions policed by the BTP in England, Wales and Scotland. There is an assumed delay of up to 310 days in dealing with cases, so that investigations will have been completed for at least 95.3% of the population, for which disposition as solved or unsolved will be known. The identification of the culprit, who is charged, summonsed, cautioned or dealt with by other means, including a penalty notice for disorder, community resolution or a youth restorative disposal, defines a solved or detected case in England and Wales. Some cases, in which the offender had died or where the Crown Prosecution Service decided that prosecuting the offender would not be in the public interest, were also classified as detected (Table 1). In Scotland, the definition of a detected case also involves identification of the culprit, including the accused being charged, being notified of intended prosecution or a fixed penalty, or being the subject of a juvenile judicial procedure (Table 1). The application of these definitions leads to their classification as a 'positive outcome' by the BTP. Data included 34,460 undetected cases and 1,800 detected cases.

Solvability Factors

Twenty-two factors related to the solvability of pickpocketing offences were identified by reviewing existing screening procedures based on operational experience and with reference to existing solvability studies (e.g. Eck 1979; Paine 2012; Olphin 2015). These relate to the geographical and temporal characteristics of cases, victim details, stolen property, reporting delays, suspect information and whether the offence was witnessed or whether CCTV footage is available (Table 2).

Analysis Plan

The first part of the analysis considers which solvability factors are important for solving pickpocketing incidents. Standardised differences of means were used to measure the relative magnitude of the effect of each factor (Cohen 1988), that is, when present, how often each individual factor is related to cases being solved. A forest plot is used to present these results. Next, the relative importance of different factors in solving cases is considered, using a multivariate approach with binary logistic regression.

Table 1 Criteria for counting a case as detected in England and Wales and Scotland

England and Wales		Scotland	
C01	(a) Charged	Det1	Accused charged and report sent to Procurator Fiscal
	(b) Summonsed/postal requisitioned		
C02	(a) Caution—youth	Det2	Accused charged and released on a written undertaking to appear at court
	(b) Caution—youth conditional		
C03	(a) Caution—adult	Det3	Offender detected by means of notice of intended prosecution
	(b) Caution—adult conditional		
C04	Taken into consideration	Det4	Accused not charged—evidence available and warrant craved report submitted
C05	The offender has died (all offences)	Det5	Accused charged and detained in custody for court
C06	Penalty notice for disorder	Det6	Accused dealt with by means of a fixed penalty notice number
C07	Cannabis warning	Det7	Offender detected but not being reported
C08	(a) Community resolution	Det8	Accused identified—Police Direct Measure applied (>18 years)
	(b) Youth restorative disposal		
C09	Not in the public interest (CPS decision—all offences)	Det9	Early and effective intervention juvenile judicial procedure (<18 years)

Table 2 Solvability factors for analysis

Subdivision	Victim age	Suspect age	Stolen property value	Offence witnessed
Location type: train, platform, concourse, inner station, shops	Victim gender	Suspect gender	Stolen property >£500	CCTV available
Journey type: static or moving	Victim ethnicity	Number of suspects	Phone or electronic device stolen	Alcohol or drugs involved
Season	Victim vulnerable	Suspect description		Victim intimidated
Time of offence				
Time delay: commission-report				
Victim's perceived range of offence time				

The second part of the analysis entails developing a model that predicts whether or not cases are solved. The regression results are used to specify the values of each of the solvability factors in the predictive model according to their effect sizes, which, combined, explain whether or not an offence is solved.

The predictive model is then used to inform a pickpocketing screening decision tool. By scoring and summing the values of each of the solvability factors, an overall solvability score for each offence will be determined. If this exceeds the threshold value below which offences are unlikely to be solved and at which there is a high likelihood resources will be wasted, then the offence will be screened in for further investigation; if, however, the overall score falls below this critical threshold, the offence will be filed as undetected.

Findings

Individual Solvability Factors

The significance of individual factors was measured using the appropriate bivariate statistical test and the standard difference in means used to determine effect size. Additional two-category variables were created from existing factors. The time the offence was committed, for example, had four categories—morning, afternoon, evening and night; new variables that compared morning with the other three time periods, afternoon with the other three periods, and so forth, were tested against whether or not cases were solved. Pickpocketing is one of the least-solved offences, with only 5.1% of sample cases being detected.

29 of the 63 independent variables were significantly related to whether or not incidents were solved. More cases were detected when there was more precise knowledge of when the incident occurred, shorter delays between crime commission and report, when incidents did not take place on moving trains, when there was a suspect description, the offence was witnessed, CCTV was available, and there were additional suspects. In addition, at solved incidents, victims were older and more victims were female. Incidents involving Chinese victims were more likely, and those involving black victims less likely, to be detected. In contrast, suspect ethnicity, whether or not drugs or alcohol were involved, the value of the stolen property and whether a phone or electronic device was stolen were not significantly related to detection.

Effect size analysis improves our understanding of the comparative importance of factors in boosting detection probabilities. Table 3 provides a perspective by comparing the odd ratios and the standard difference in means between the detected and undetected cases for each of the solvability factors. Suspect descriptions and additional suspects are very strong predictors, making detection, respectively, 150 and 93 times more likely. If the offence is witnessed, this improves the likelihood of detection sixfold. Cases are over 20 times more likely to be solved when CCTV records are available, and incidents with younger suspects—aged under 30 years—are twice as likely to be solved. Though less than a seventh of cases involve female suspects, these have triple the likelihood of detection. Shorter delays in reporting offences and better pinpointing of when the crime occurred are confirmed as factors with large effect sizes. Incidents with black suspects have 60% lower odds of being detected.

Multivariate Analysis and Predictive Modelling

Analysis based on individual variables takes no account of the interaction effects of other independent variables or the ways in which factors combine to co-occur in the same subsets of incidents. Binary logistic regression analysis was applied to isolate the independent statistical effects of each factor and to identify a 'best-fit' predictive model that would provide the basis for a 'tool' for screening in solvable cases. The aim was to describe a model that contained significant independent factors with large effect sizes that, in combination, would explain the highest degree of variation in detection outcomes.

Factors with high multicollinearity (a VIF > 10) were removed to identify those with a more stable coefficient and lower variance to be entered into the regression equation. Factors available for larger numbers of incidents that would preserve the power of the predictive model were given priority: for instance, the suspect description was retained at the expense of the intercorrelated alternatives, suspect gender, ethnicity and age, since this renders the model more powerful without sacrificing size effects.

Variable combinations were tested iteratively to produce a best-fit, operationally viable model that balances high explanatory power in relation to outcome variance against individual factor significance, full model significance and the percentage of correct classifications in solved and unsolved groups. The final model, which explains a high level of variance and identifies the variables to be used for practical screening purposes, is shown in Table 4. The predictive model is significant ($\chi^2 = 2{,}722.6$, $p < 0.000$ and $n = 17{,}773$) and accounts for 43.5% of the variance between solved and unsolved cases (Nagelkerke's $R^2 = 0.435$).

Factors with the largest effect sizes were 'suspect description', which improved the odds of detection 55 times, and CCTV availability, which boosted them nearly eightfold (Table 4). Victim intimidation and shorter offence durations of less than 15 min also notably raised detection odds. Offences occurring on static trains, on platforms or within the confines of a station, in the morning or on the London underground system also had better odds of being solved. Male suspects and the theft of a phone or other electronic device lowered the odds of a successful detection (Table 4).

Table 3 Bivariate analysis: detected/not detected by each solvability factor

	Odds ratio	Lower limit	Upper limit	Std. diff in means	Standard error
Suspect Gender: Male	0.366	−1.133	0.025	−0.554	0.296
Suspect Ethnicity: Mixed	0.397	−1.000	−0.018	−0.509	0.251
Victim Ethnicity: Black	0.544	−0.523	−0.149	−0.336	0.095
Victim Gender: Male	0.619	−0.343	−0.186	−0.264	0.040
Sub Division: Wales	0.631	−0.889	0.382	−0.254	0.324
Sub Division: East	0.705	−0.313	−0.072	−0.192	0.062
Suspect Ethnicity: Black	0.709	−0.483	0.105	−0.189	0.150
Victim Ethnicity: Mixed	0.836	−0.356	0.157	−0.099	0.131
Suspect Ethnicity: Asian	0.872	−0.554	0.403	−0.075	0.244
Sub Division: Western	0.875	−0.425	0.278	−0.074	0.179
Time Committed: Evening	0.901	−0.144	0.029	−0.058	0.044
Season: Spring	0.910	−0.139	0.035	−0.052	0.044
Phone or Electronic Device	0.926	−0.116	0.032	−0.042	0.038
Location Type: On Train	0.941	−0.112	0.044	−0.034	0.040
Victim Ethnicity: Asian	0.944	−0.152	0.089	−0.032	0.061

(continued)

Table 3 (continued)

	Odds ratio	Lower limit	Upper limit	Std. diff in means	Standard error
Time Committed: Afternoon	0.961	−0.098	0.054	−0.022	0.039
Season: Autumn	0.970	−0.101	0.067	−0.017	0.043
Season: Summer	0.985	−0.096	0.079	−0.008	0.045
Victim Ethnicity: White	1.012	−0.081	0.094	0.007	0.045
Sub Division: Transport for London	1.045	−0.051	0.100	0.024	0.039
Property Value Over £500	1.046	−0.065	0.114	0.025	0.046
Location Type: Inner Station	1.066	−0.091	0.161	0.035	0.065
Location Type: Concourse/Outside Station	1.067	−0.120	0.191	0.036	0.080
Time Committed: Morning	1.070	−0.048	0.123	0.037	0.043
Location Type: Commercial Property	1.095	−0.163	0.263	0.050	0.109
Sub Division: South	1.096	−0.051	0.152	0.050	0.052
Season: Winter	1.140	−0.010	0.154	0.072	0.042
Sub Division: Scotland	1.143	−0.349	0.496	0.074	0.215
Time Committed: Night	1.143	−0.029	0.177	0.074	0.053
Sub Division: Pennine	1.154	−0.067	0.225	0.079	0.075
Location Type: Platforms	1.189	−0.043	0.234	0.095	0.071

(continued)

Table 3 (continued)

	Odds ratio	Lower limit	Upper limit	Std. diff in means	Standard error
Sub Division: Midland	1.358	−0.039	0.376	0.169	0.106
Vulnerable Victim	1.364	0.002	0.340	0.171	0.086
Alcohol or Drugs Involved	1.564	−0.549	1.043	0.247	0.406
Delay from Commit to Report: 1 h	1.672	0.184	0.383	0.283	0.051
Suspect Ethnicity: White	1.704	0.007	0.580	0.294	0.146
Victim Ethnicity: Chinese	1.921	0.212	0.508	0.360	0.076
Delay from Commit to Report: 1 Week	1.993	0.226	0.534	0.380	0.079
Committed Range < 120 Mins	2.044	0.140	0.648	0.394	0.130
Suspect Age: Under 30	2.218	0.083	0.795	0.439	0.182
Delay from Commit to Report: 24 h	2.322	0.380	0.549	0.464	0.043
Committed Range < 60 Mins	2.485	0.357	0.647	0.502	0.074
Suspect Gender: Female	2.732	−0.025	1.133	0.554	0.296
Committed Range < 45 Mins	2.880	0.450	0.717	0.583	0.068
Delay from Commit to Report: 30 Mins	2.955	0.439	0.756	0.597	0.081

(continued)

Table 3 (continued)

	Odds ratio	Lower limit	Upper limit	Std. diff in means	Standard error
Suspect Ethnicity: Other	3.285	−0.929	2.240	0.656	0.808
Committed Range < 30 Mins	3.432	0.571	0.788	0.680	0.055
Committed Range < 25 Mins	4.114	0.679	0.880	0.780	0.051
Journey Type: Static	4.475	0.749	0.904	0.826	0.040
Committed Range < 20 Mins	4.574	0.747	0.930	0.838	0.047
Committed Range < 15 Mins	5.071	0.808	0.982	0.895	0.044
Committed Range < 10 Mins	5.523	0.861	1.024	0.942	0.042
Committed Range < 5 Mins	5.741	0.886	1.041	0.963	0.039
Intimidated Victim	5.812	0.532	1.409	0.970	0.224
Committed Range: Exact Time Known	5.886	0.902	1.053	0.977	0.038
Offence Witnessed	6.040	0.799	1.184	0.992	0.098
CCTV Available	20.718	1.591	1.751	1.671	0.041
Additional Suspects	92.893	2.120	2.877	2.498	0.193
Suspect Description	149.73	2.620	2.903	2.762	0.072
Fixed	N/A	0.338	0.368	0.353	0.008

Table 4 Binary logistic regression with detected/undetected outcome as dependent variable

Detected versus non-detected						95% CI for EXP (B)	
Variable	B	*SE*	Wald	*p*	Exp (B)	Lower	Upper
CCTV available	2.058	0.097	449.776	0.000	7.827	6.471	9.466
Phone or electronic device stolen	−0.278	0.090	9.483	0.002	0.758	0.635	0.904
Journey type: static	0.381	0.102	14.107	0.000	1.464	1.200	1.786
Committed time range: within 15 mins	0.736	0.103	50.826	0.000	2.089	1.706	2.557
Victim gender: male	−0.355	0.092	14.816	0.000	0.701	0.585	0.840
Location type: platforms	0.310	0.161	3.701	0.054	1.363	0.994	1.869
Victim intimidated	1.255	0.587	4.567	0.033	3.509	1.110	11.094
Transport for London subdivision	0.126	0.091	1.918	0.166	1.134	0.949	1.356
Time: morning	0.193	0.100	3.706	0.054	1.213	0.996	1.477
Suspect description	4.010	0.147	742.743	0.000	55.140	41.326	73.571
Constant	−12.502	1.301	92.290	0.000	0.000		

*$n = 17{,}773$ (98.5% of a possible 18,039 cases)

The Predictive Model

The logit formula (Eq. 1), derived from the binary logistic regression analysis, provides a single solvability score for each pickpocketing case on a linear scale. This is the basis for an evidence-based decision tool to help determine which solvable cases should be screened in for further investigation.

$$\begin{aligned}\text{logit(p)} = {} & 12.502 + (\text{CCTV available} \times 2.058)\\ & + (\text{phone or electronic device stolen} \times -0.278)\\ & + (\text{journey type:static} \times 0.381)\\ & + (\text{committed time range within 15 min.} \times 0.736)\\ & + (\text{victim gender:male} \times -0.355)\\ & + (\text{location type:platforms} \times 0.310) + (\text{victim intimidated} \times 1.255)\\ & + (\text{suspect description} \times 4.010) + (\text{subdivision:TfL} \times 0.126)\\ & + (\text{time:morning} \times 0.193) \qquad (1)\end{aligned}$$

A solvability score above −11.7 virtually guarantees that a case will be detected, whereas failure to detect a case is more or less assured if the case has a solvability score lower than −4.5. The appropriate solvability score above which cases would

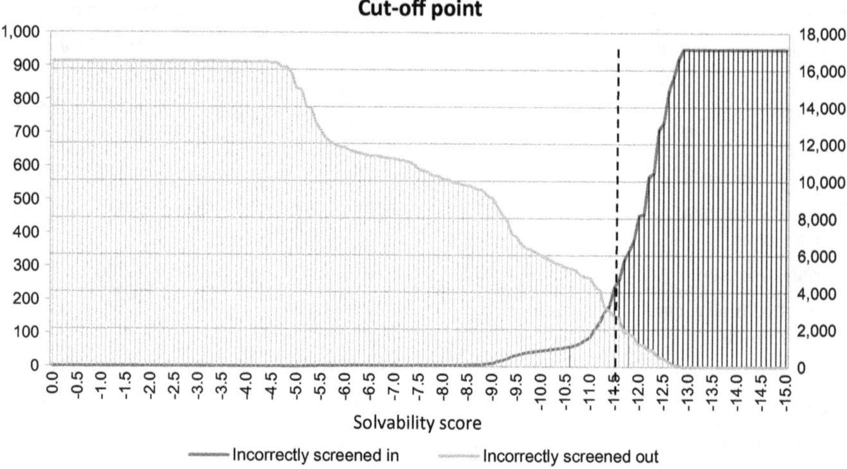

Fig. 1 Identification of the screening model's cut-off value

be screened in and below which they would be screened out was selected as −11.7. This cut-off point balances the numbers of cases correctly screened in and out against those incorrectly screened in and out (Fig. 1). It also balances the minimisation of false positive (unsolvable cases incorrectly screened in, resulting in wasted effort) and false negative rates (solvable cases screened out, resulting in a missed opportunity to detect), while prioritising low missed opportunities over a little more wasted effort, a strategy that meets BTP preferences. Even so, the −11.7 cut-off point precedes a marked increase in the anticipated wasted effort while containing missed opportunities at an estimated 40 cases per year.

Screening decisions also took account of three characteristics not considered in the solvability analysis. If an offence involved stolen property valued at over £5,000 or if there was a named suspect or a reputational risk associated with not investigating, it was screened in, even if its solvability score was below the −11.7 solvability cut-off value. Owing to the absence of reliable data for named suspects and reputational risk, these factors are excluded from the following test of the screening model's predictive accuracy.

The Screening Model's Accuracy

Existing practice for pickpocketing offences occurring in BTP's jurisdiction has been to screen in over 90% of cases. This is likely to result in high numbers of false positives, with considerable effort wasted in investigating undetected cases, though minimising false negatives, with few solvable cases left undetected. The current

Table 5 Accuracy of existing screening practice

		Real case outcome	
		Case cleared	Case not cleared
Model-predicted case outcome	Case cleared	100% (908)	90.1% (15,596)
	Case not cleared	0% (0)	9.9% (1,717)
Total accuracy = 908 + 1,717 ÷ 18,221 × 100 = 14.4%			

Table 6 Accuracy of predicted screening model

		Real case outcome	
		Case cleared	Case not cleared
Model-predicted case outcome	Case cleared	87.1% (791)	26.0% (4,496)
	Case not cleared	12.9% (117)	74.0% (12,817)
Total accuracy = 791 + 12,817 ÷ 18,221 × 100 = 74.7%			

screening practice is 14.4% accurate, with 90% of all unsolved cases incorrectly screened in for investigation (Table 5).

In contrast, the accuracy of the predictive screening model that also takes account of cases in which property valued at over £5,000 was stolen is 74.7% (Table 6). Thirteen per cent of offences that were, in practice, solved, would be incorrectly screened out, while 87% would be correctly screened in. These detected cases that would be missed are balanced by a considerable saving of effort since only 30% of unsolved cases would be investigated. Internal BTP data indicate that pickpocketing investigations average 4.5 h, so that over 104, 590 h were wasted on fruitless secondary investigation of pickpocketing offences during the five-year sample period.

Secondary Investigation of Pickpocketing Offences

The total number of secondary investigative actions (i.e. those subsequently carried out by detectives) for each case were available for the full sample of 36,242 cases, though data on the types of actions and any additional evidence collected were not. There were no differences between the solved cases, which were all screened in, and the unsolved cases screened in for further investigation in terms of the numbers of case actions (MW, $p = 0.512$), investigative actions (MW, $p = 0.766$), supervisory actions ($p = 0.924$), victim actions (MW, $p = 0.146$) or total actions (MW, $p = 0.304$). This suggests that as much effort was expended on further investigation of unsolved as solved cases, confirming the waste of resources due to non-statistical case-screening practices. Hierarchical regression analysis (Table 7) confirms that the addition of investigative actions does not improve the statistical explanation of the clearance of pickpocketing offences and offers no solvability advantage over the statistically significant predictive model.

Developing a Screening Tool

A screening tool was built in Excel to support statistically based case-screening decisions. This is based on the ten solvability factors and effect sizes from the predictive logit formula (Eq. 1) plus the three additional screen-in factors. The operator indicates which factors are present in a case and the effect sizes for the factors that are present are summed. If these exceed −11.7 or some other defined solvability score, the case is screened in. Even if the score is below −11.7, the presence of an additional factor would also result in the case being screened in.

Discussion

This study has identified a variety of pickpocketing solvability factors. Cases with suspect descriptions were 55 times likelier to be solved, confirming the findings of other research into a range of crimes (Isaacs 1967; Reiss and Bordua 1967; Greenwood 1970; Greenwood et al. 1975; Chaiken et al. 1976; Eck 1979; Brandl and Frank 1994; Coupe and Kaur 2005; Burrows et al. 2005; Eitle et al. 2005; Peterson et al. 2010; Olphin 2015). Eighty-three per cent of cases with suspect information in the initial report were solved. CCTV recordings markedly boosted detection odds, indicating that it may be worthwhile examining the locations of the CCTV cameras that produce the most valuable evidence, with a view to installing more cameras in comparable parts of the transport system not currently covered. Other factors boosting the odds of a detection are female suspects, incidents with more precisely known occurrence times, thefts not involving electronic devices, and incidents occurring in the morning, on the London underground system, and somewhere other than on a moving train.

Pickpocketing is a low-solvability crime: only 5% of offences are solved, even though 90% are screened in for further investigation. Consequently, a great deal of investigative effort is wasted on offences that are never detected. If the statistical model had been used for case-screening decisions with a solvability cut-off score of −11.7 over the five-year sample period, there would have been 23,242 fewer wasted secondary investigations. At an average time investment of 4.5 h per investigation, this would have saved 104,589 h of detectives' time over five years. This is the equivalent of 12 detectives working throughout the year (220 eight-hour days), or saving of over £600,000 per annum, excluding overhead spending.

Table 7 Hierarchical regression summary

Model	Change statistics								
	R	*R* square	Adjusted *R* square	Std. error of the estimate	*R* square change	*F* change	*df*1	*df*2	Sig, *F* change
Circumstance-based (step 1)	0.620	0.384	0.384	0.171	0.384	1,966.784	10	31,518	0.000
Circumstance and effort-based (step 2)	0.620	0.384	0.384	0.171	0.000	1,965	4	31,514	0.097

The predictive model will likely make investigation more cost-effective, markedly reducing wasted effort. At the solvability threshold selected to screen cases in or out, decision-making would be more than five times more accurate than current practice, with only 30% of cases being screened in for further investigation, compared to 90% under the existing screening system. Rather fewer cases would be solved; however, 87% of existing detections would be cleared.

The solvability score used as the threshold for screening cases in or out can be varied according to BTP's preferences regarding the balance between wasted effort and missed detections. To ensure that 95% of existing detected cases were still solved, for instance, would require a lower solvability threshold score entailing the investigation of more cases, with the drawback that rather more resources would be wasted on unsolved cases incorrectly—though necessarily—screened in for investigation. On the other hand, if fewer cases were to be screened in for further investigation, fewer resources would be wasted, but at the cost of lowering the number of detected cases.

The volume of investigative actions was not related to case solvability, so that additional detectives may not boost the number of detected cases. Further research into the types of actions taken in secondary investigations of particular cases is needed to assess whether the ways in which such cases are investigated can be cost-effectively improved. Analysis of the types of investigative activities, resource inputs and evidence outputs for residential burglary confirms that further investigations have weaker effects on detection rates than information and evidence collected by first officers (Coupe, Chapter "Investigative Activities, Resources and Burglary Detection"). Despite this, overall, police officer time resource input per incident has a strong effect on detections, and resources, together with case solvability, determine whether incidents are solved (Coupe, Chapter "Investigative Activities, Resources and Burglary Detection").

Solvability depends partly on where offences take place on the railway network, with the prospects for detection being far higher in the south-east subdivision, and particularly on London's underground railway system. This confirms other railway crime solvability (Robb et al., Chapter "Metal Theft Solvability and Detection") and burglary solvability (Paine and Ariel, Chapter "Population-Level Analysis of Residential Burglaries") studies, which show that the environment affects crime solvability factors and, hence, the proportion of crimes solved.

Conclusions

This study extends knowledge of crime solvability to pickpocketing and promises to markedly improve the efficiency and cost-effectiveness of the way in which pickpocketing offences are investigated. It identifies solvability factors that enable prediction of 44% of case outcomes, providing bases for a predictive model and a practical case-screening decision tool. The statistical model is five times as accurate as existing screening practices, and the improvements in accuracy are particularly due to reductions in the fruitless investigation of low-solvability offences that are incorrectly screened in for investigation. Since such a high proportion of cases currently investigated, it is hardly surprising that there is also a slight fall in detected cases. There is currently immense strain on investigative resources due to over-investigation of cases that it is either impossible or exceptionally difficult to detect. These findings indicate how this may be relieved by targeting the solvable cases.

Some predictors of more solvable pickpocketing cases appear similar to those in other offences. These are suspect descriptions, witness statements, prompt crime reporting, the ability to pinpoint the timing of offences to within 15 min and the availability of CCTV. Other factors, such as suspect age, the involvement of Chinese or female victims and whether a phone or electronic device was stolen are possibly limited to pickpocketing. Those more specific to transit crime include whether the offence took place on a moving train or a station platform, the time of day and the part of the railway system in which the offence occurred. These are in line with factors affecting the detection of sexual offences on railway property (Jones et al., Chapter "Reporting, Detection and Solvability of Sex Offences on Railways"). The addition of other factors may improve the predictive model; boosting the prediction of detection outcomes to 60% would enable even more accurate case screening. Reporting factors, for instance, have an important bearing on whether sexual offences on BTP property are solved, with reports made directly to BTP police or railway personnel resulting in higher detection rates than those reported to Home Office police (Jones et al., Chapter "Reporting, Detection and Solvability of Sex Offences on Railways"). This may also affect the solvability of pickpocketing offences.

High-volume crime on railways is not limited to pickpocketing. There are also large numbers of cycle thefts, low-level violence and antisocial behaviour offences, while the effects of other crimes (Robb et al., Chapter "Metal Theft Solvability and Detection") can be to either disrupt railway services, as is the case with metal theft, or result in serious harm and concerns about using rail services, as happens with certain sexual offences. The application of the principles identified in this solvability study to assessing solvability and carrying out more accurate screening of other crime types would enable a more comprehensive evidence-based solution to crime detection on railway property.

Among this study's strengths are its evaluation of a large number of factors as potential solvability predictors and the large population of pickpocketing offences that raises statistical power and permits a split-sample test of the predictive solvability model. There are no published random controlled experiments of solvability factors that have confirmed the predicted benefits of the resources saved by using statistical case screening without significant loss of detected cases. The predictive solvability factors identified in this study are currently being considered for implementation by the BTP. The effectiveness of statistical screening of pickpocketing offences is planned to be assessed, which will extend to evaluating the effectiveness of further investigations. This will provide much needed insights into the reliability of predictive models derived using non-experimental methods, thereby filling an important theoretical gap in our knowledge of crime solvability.

References

Andersson, P. K. (2014). 'Bustling, crowding, and pushing': Pickpockets and the nineteenth-century street crowd. *Urban History, 41*(2), 291–310.

Brandl, S. G., & Frank, J. (1994). The relationship between evidence, detective effort, and the disposition of burglary and robbery investigations. *American Journal of Police, 13*(3), 149–168.

Burrows, J., Hopkins, M., Hubbard, R., Robinson, A., Speed, M., & Tilley, N. (2005). Understanding the attrition process in volume crime investigations (Home Office Research Study 295). London: Home Office.

Chaiken, J. M., Greenwood, P. W., & Petersilia, J. (1976). *The criminal investigation process: A summary report*. Santa Monica, CA: The RAND Corporation.

Cohen, J. (1988). *Statistical power analysis for the behavioral sciences* (2nd ed.). Hillsdale, N.J.: Lawrence Erlbaum.

Coupe, R. T., & Kaur, S. (2005). The role of alarms and CCTV in detecting non-residential burglary. *Security Journal, 18*(2), 53–72.

Eck, J. E. (1979). *Managing case assignments: The burglary investigation decision model replication*. Washington, DC: Police Executive Research Forum.

Eck, J. E. (1983). *Solving crimes: The investigation of burglary and robbery*. Washington DC: Police Executive Research Forum.

Eitle, D., Stolzenberg, I., & D'Alessio, S. J. (2005). Police organizational factors, the racial composition of the police, and the probability of arrest. *Justice Quarterly, 22*(1), 30–57.

Gill, M., Hart, J., Livingstone, K., & Stevens, J. (1996). *The crime allocation system: Police investigations into burglary and auto crime (Police Research Series, Paper 16)*. London: Home Office.

Greenwood, P. W. (1970). *An analysis of the apprehension activities of the New York City Police Department*. Santa Monica, CA: The RAND Corporation.

Greenwood, P. W., Chaiken, J. M., Petersilia, J., & Prusoff, L. (1975). *The criminal investigation process: Volume III: Observations and analysis*. Santa Monica, CA: The RAND Corporation.

Isaacs, H. (1967). *A study of communications, crimes and arrests in a metropolitan police department*. Task force report: Science and technology. Washington, DC: UN Government Printing Office.

Jansson, K. (2005). *Volume crime investigations—A review of the research literature (Home Office Online Report OLR 44/05)*. London: Home Office.

Newton, A., Partridge, H., & Gill, A. (2014). Above and below: Measuring crime risk in and around underground mass transit systems. *Crime Science, 3*(1), 1–14.

Olphin, T. W. L. (2015). *Solving violent crime: Targeting factors that predict clearance of non-domestic violent offences* (unpublished MSt thesis). University of Cambridge.

Paine, C. (2012). *Solvability factors in dwelling burglaries in Thames Valley* (Unpublished MSt thesis). University of Cambridge.

Peterson, J., Sommers, I., Baskin, D., & Johnson, D. (2010). *The role and impact of forensic evidence in the criminal justice process*. Washington, D.C.: National Institute of Justice.

Pickpocketing: A survey of the crime and its control (1995). *University of Pennsylvania Law Review, 104*(3), 408–420.

Reiss, A., & Bordua, D. J. (1967). Environment and organisation: A perspective on the police. In D. J. Bordua (Ed.), *The police: Six sociological essays*. New York: Wiley.

Smith, M. J. (2008). Addressing the security needs of women passengers on public transport. *Security Journal, 21*(1–2), 117–133.

Waegel, W. B. (1982). Patterns of police investigation of urban crimes. *Journal of Police Science and Administration, 10*(4), 452–465.

Metal Theft Solvability and Detection

Paul Robb, Richard Timothy Coupe and Barak Ariel

Introduction

Few metal theft offences on railway property are detected, and police services need to identify those cases and investigative activities likely to lead to arrest. Rail metal thefts have increased in recent years in response to escalating global scrap metal prices (Sidebottom et al. 2011), which the new manufacture of metals like copper cannot alone satisfy. Railways have large amounts of various types of metal, much of which is in the track network, and therefore diffuse and vulnerable, particularly in remote places with poor guardianship. A statistical basis for 'triaging' decisions is likely to be helpful in identifying solvable cases. The objectives of this chapter are to describe the different sorts of metal goods stolen from railways in England and Wales, examine geographical differences in solvability and detection, and compare detected and undetected incidents in order to identify those offences to which investigative resources should be allocated. By these means, the solvability factors for 'triaging' metal theft incidents can be established.

Potential Solvability Factors for Metal Theft on Railways

The circumstances of the offence—whether it is seen while in progress or the presence of eyewitnesses who can provide good suspect descriptions—often have an important bearing on its solvability (Burrows et al. 2005). Most evidence that aids detection is collected at crimes scenes (e.g. Jansson 2005), and this includes forensic evidence. The quality of the latter for metal theft will depend on the type of metal stolen and whether it was located indoors or outdoors. While tracing stolen property tends to be

P. Robb · R. T. Coupe (✉) · B. Ariel
Institute of Criminology, University of Cambridge, Cambridge, UK
e-mail: rtc23@cam.ac.uk

R. T. Coupe et al. (eds.), *Crime Solvability Factors*,
https://doi.org/10.1007/978-3-030-17160-5_7

far less important for solving offences (e.g. Coupe and Griffiths 1996; Tilley et al. 2007), this is often because most property is not easily identifiable. Similarly, much of the metal taken from railway property can be difficult to trace and identify once it has been removed, even though its eventual destination, principally China (Kooi 2010), may be known.

One aim of this study is to establish which sources of evidence and investigative approaches are important in detecting metal theft and appreciate the bases on which incidents need to be screened in for investigation. A timely response may be important for metal theft offences witnessed and reported by passersby or residents, especially if they occur outdoors, where forensic clues do not survive long in the damp UK climate. If there is a signalling failure due to the cutting of rail-side cabling and if railway engineers' arrival on scene precedes that of the police, this may lead to a loss of evidence. A timely patrol response may, therefore, be an important predictor, not only of capture, but also of arrest due to further investigation.

Further investigation often depends on information from witnesses, and this is contingent on their cooperation with the police. Cooperation, in turn, is affected by witnesses' views about the fairness of police procedures and police effectiveness (Skogan 2006; Bradford 2012; Kochel et al. 2013; Dirikx and van den Bulck 2014). Railway employees often witness in-progress thefts, but their views about their employers as well as the police may affect cooperativeness. Even if unwitting receivers of stolen metal, scrap dealers may not always be helpful with police enquiries. Nevertheless, tracing stolen property may be more effective for metal theft than other offences, such as burglary, given its bulk and because it is easier to identify scrap metal dealers, the main purchasers of stolen metal.

Objectives

The aims of this chapter are to classify the different sorts of metal theft offences committed on railway property and identify their solvability characteristics. By modelling offence characteristics and detections for initial responses and subsequent investigations, case-screening procedures can be defined so that future metal theft offences can be cost-effectively investigated and detections maximized. The chapter also examines regional differences in railway metal theft and solvability and its implications for screening and resource targeting.

Metal theft pushes up the costs of rail services due to the need to replace stolen property and the demands it places on policing resources. Some thieves cut power or signalling cables critical to the safe provision of train services. These result in extra costs owing to travel delays, which lower service quality and inconvenience passengers, who may require compensation. Tampering with live cables can, occasionally, result in the serious injury or death of offenders, often a costly matter. Better targeting of resources may improve safety and reduce injuries as well as cost-effectively increase detection rates.

Methodology

Sampling Frame and Data

The analysis is based on data from British Transport Police crime reports and incident logs on 4001 thefts of metal that occurred between January 2009 and December 2010 in the five 'over-ground' railway basic command units (BCUs) in England and Wales. Of this sample, 510 cases were detected and 3491 undetected. Only incidents where metal was likely to have been stolen for its scrap value were included. Data on investigations and the ways in which offences were detected were added. The definition of a solved or detected offence was an offender being arrested and charged.

Formal crime-screening procedures based on officer experience were in use in 2009 in BCUs with large numbers of metal thefts, and in all BCUs in 2010 following a substantial rise in the number of offences due to a surge in global scrap metal demand (Sidebottom et al. 2011).

Solvability Factors

Twelve factors related to the solving of cases were identified through an examination of solved cases and with reference to existing solvability studies (e.g. Greenberg et al. 1977; Eck 1979). These factors consisted of alerts made by eyewitnesses, sometimes having disturbed offenders while the offence was in progress or having recorded vehicle registrations. This, together with the activation of alarms at the sides of tracks, sometimes led to patrols intercepting metal thieves at or near the crime scene. Other sources of evidence that helped detect offences were covert automatic number plate recognition (ANPR) matches, intelligence or surveillance, and stolen goods awaiting collection which were hidden near crime scenes. Further investigative activities involved scrap dealer checks, CCTV footage and the matching of suspect and vehicle descriptions and forensic samples from the scene against known-offender records. There were also data on the types of metal stolen, and when and where the thefts took place.

Railway employees were largely responsible for disturbing offenders committing offences, but sometimes security guards or members of the public working close to railway property who alerted the police were involved. Although witnessing incidents may improve detections, disturbing offenders is liable to reduce them, since offenders often realize they have been seen and quickly leave crime scenes. Witnessed alerts where offenders were disturbed are therefore distinguished as a separate solvability factor.

Analysis Structure

First, descriptive statistics are used to profile the importance of the principal types of railway metal theft and the differences in their detection rates. The effects of the key solvability factors on solving incidents will then be examined. These are used to measure the comparative effect of each factor individually (Cohen 1988), and a forest plot is used to portray them. Factors are considered in terms of their individual 'strength' in solving cases based on standardised differences of means using forest plots, incidence levels in detected and undetected cases and with respect to the correlation between solvability factors. Next, a multivariate approach with binary logistic regression was used to isolate each factor and assess the comparative effects of factors in solving cases. Hierarchical classification software was used to describe how combinations of solvability factors of different strengths result in different detection rates.

Geographical differences in solvability and detections between the five railway basic command units were then considered. Finally, analyses of cut signal cable offences and copper cable thefts are used to examine how variations in investigative practice appear to affect the geographical variation in solvability factors and detection rates and to examine missed detections and the potential to improve detections.

Findings

Types of Metal Theft

There are seven types of metal theft on railways:

1. cut cable, generally from or near the trackside, is often hidden nearby and removed by thieves later;
2. cable theft, generally cut from the trackside;
3. thefts from railway compounds or depots, including fenced-off areas where work is being carried out on tracks and areas close to warehouses, engine sheds and other buildings;
4. burglary of railway buildings and thefts of building parts, such as lead roofing, gutters and copper heating pipes;
5. theft of individual metal objects, such as signs, gates, fencing and scrap metal;
6. lengths of rail and associated equipment, including clips, plates and sleepers, often at tracksides; and
7. theft from electric substations servicing electric trains, despite these buildings often being protected with secure fencing and high-quality alarm systems.

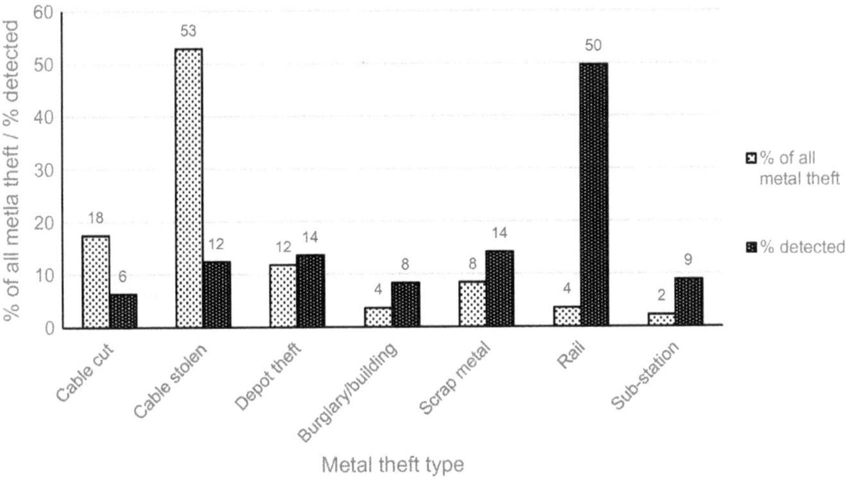

Fig. 1 Metal theft types: importance and detection rates (from Robb et al. 2015)

Importance of Different Types of Theft and Detections

Cable cuts and theft represented 70% of all metal thefts, with scrap metal theft, theft from depots and thefts of scrap responsible for the bulk of the remainder (Fig. 1). Of the entire sample of crimes, 12.7% were detected, but this varied from 49% for the theft of steel rail to only 6% for cut copper cable. Stealing lengths of rail requires vehicles with heavy lifting gear and is visually conspicuous. Detection rates for theft from depots and of cable and scrap were close to the average (Fig. 1).

The Importance of Different Solvability Factors

The importance of solvability factors involves their strength as predictors of detections and their prevalence or the proportions of sample cases in which they are present. Strength may be assessed by effect size; if a factor is present in a high proportion of detected cases compared with undetected cases, it is likely to be more effective in contributing evidence to case solution. Forest plots (Fig. 2) show the importance of individual factors in terms of the strength of their relationship with detected compared to undetected cases. The highest, positive standard differences in means were where a check was carried out on scrap metal dealers, covert activities were used, or an arrest took place. Other factors with high odds of detection were discovery by patrols, the identification of suspect offenders using forensic samples, vehicle registration checks and incidents at which there were eyewitnesses (Fig. 2). Disturbing suspects, CCTV and alarmed alerts were weaker factors and few detections resulted from offenders returning to crime scenes to retrieve hidden metal. Detection

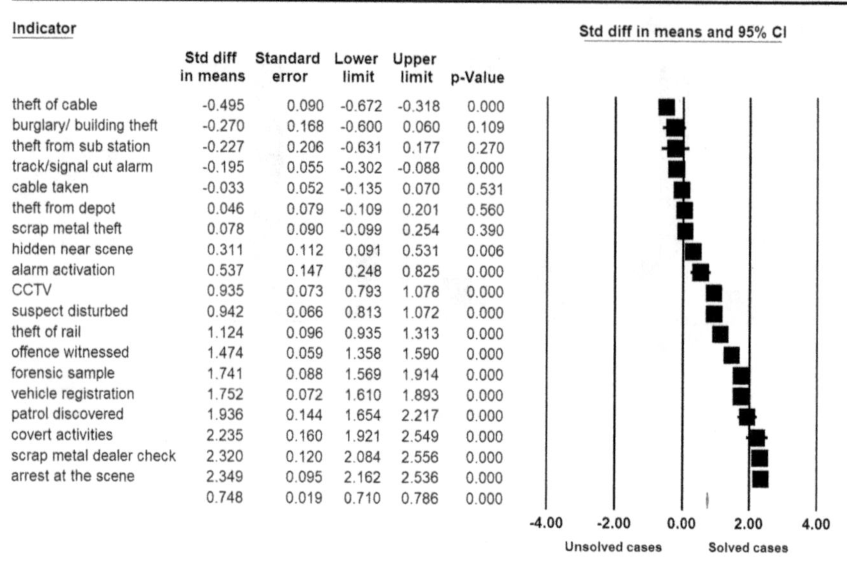

Indicator	Std diff in means	Standard error	Lower limit	Upper limit	p-Value
theft of cable	-0.495	0.090	-0.672	-0.318	0.000
burglary/ building theft	-0.270	0.168	-0.600	0.060	0.109
theft from sub station	-0.227	0.206	-0.631	0.177	0.270
track/signal cut alarm	-0.195	0.055	-0.302	-0.088	0.000
cable taken	-0.033	0.052	-0.135	0.070	0.531
theft from depot	0.046	0.079	-0.109	0.201	0.560
scrap metal theft	0.078	0.090	-0.099	0.254	0.390
hidden near scene	0.311	0.112	0.091	0.531	0.006
alarm activation	0.537	0.147	0.248	0.825	0.000
CCTV	0.935	0.073	0.793	1.078	0.000
suspect disturbed	0.942	0.066	0.813	1.072	0.000
theft of rail	1.124	0.096	0.935	1.313	0.000
offence witnessed	1.474	0.059	1.358	1.590	0.000
forensic sample	1.741	0.088	1.569	1.914	0.000
vehicle registration	1.752	0.072	1.610	1.893	0.000
patrol discovered	1.936	0.144	1.654	2.217	0.000
covert activities	2.235	0.160	1.921	2.549	0.000
scrap metal dealer check	2.320	0.120	2.084	2.556	0.000
arrest at the scene	2.349	0.095	2.162	2.536	0.000
	0.748	0.019	0.710	0.786	0.000

Fig. 2 Importance of individual metal theft factors (from Robb et al. 2015)

frequency was highest for scrap metal theft and lowest for cut cable left at the crime scene, which is indicative of attempted theft.

Incidence of Solvability Factors

Cases with solvability factors that occur in a high proportion of solved cases and a low proportion of unsolved cases, such as scrap metal dealer checks, covert police activities, vehicle registration details and useful forensic samples, are more cost-effective to investigate than those that occur in higher proportions in unsolved incidents compared with solved incidents, such as offences witnessed, alarm activation or where stolen goods are hidden near the scene.

The frequency with which factors are present in metal theft cases also affects their importance. If a stronger factor—such as scrap dealer checks, with high odds of being detected—crops up in fewer cases, then it can be more cost-effectively investigated and detected, but may result in fewer detected cases than a weaker factor that has a higher incidence, such as a witnessed offence. The volume of incidents in which a solvability factor is present affects its importance to investigating officers. The prevalence of solvability factors is not related to effect size (Fig. 3; $r = -0.38$, $p = 0.28$), and both measures must be considered when screening in cases for investigation.

Incidents with 'stronger' factors, such as discovery by a patrol, covert police activities, scrap metal dealer checks, details of vehicle registrations or usable forensic

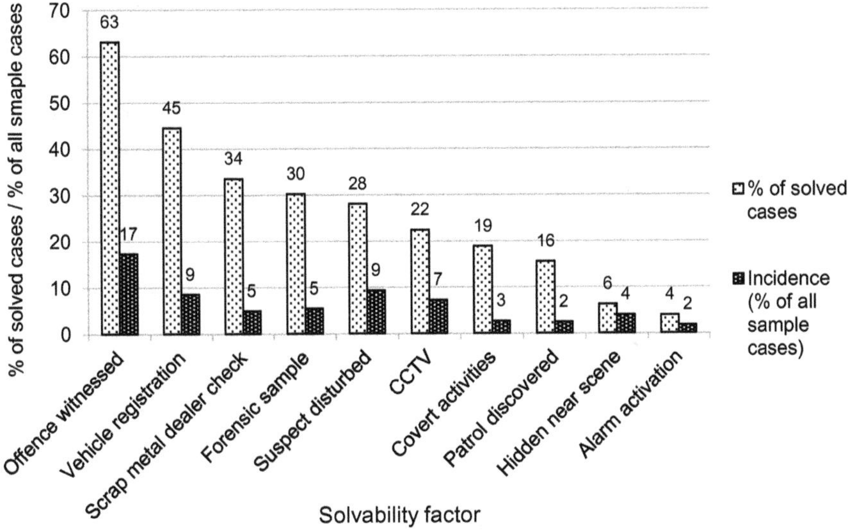

Fig. 3 Percentage of cases with different solvability factors that were detected and the percentage of population cases with each factor present (from Robb et al. 2015)

samples, are more cost-effective to investigate. In contrast, weaker factors, such as 'witnessed offences', that occur in larger volumes of cases are also important since they present the potential to detect more cases. Since the 'offence witnessed' factor has the highest prevalence in the sample cases, it holds significant potential for detection, but more cases that will not be solved must be investigated less cost-effectively. Factors with low effect sizes, such as goods 'hidden near the scene', or those occurring in a large proportion of sample cases, need more effort per detected case.

Solvability factors are more favourable for detecting offences if they have a higher incidence in the sample and a 'stronger' effect size.

Multivariate Analysis of Solvability Factors

Most solvability factors occur alongside other factors, especially in detected cases, so that the odds of detection will differ in a multivariate analysis that measures the effect size for each solvability factor while considering the statistical effects of all other factors. Solvability factors often occur in combination at the outset of cases, but others are added as officers follow the initial evidence and focus their efforts on cases featuring stronger factors with larger effect sizes. The most highly correlated factors form two main clusters (Fig. 4). One of these concerns checks on scrap metal dealers, covert police activities and vehicle registration information, while the other

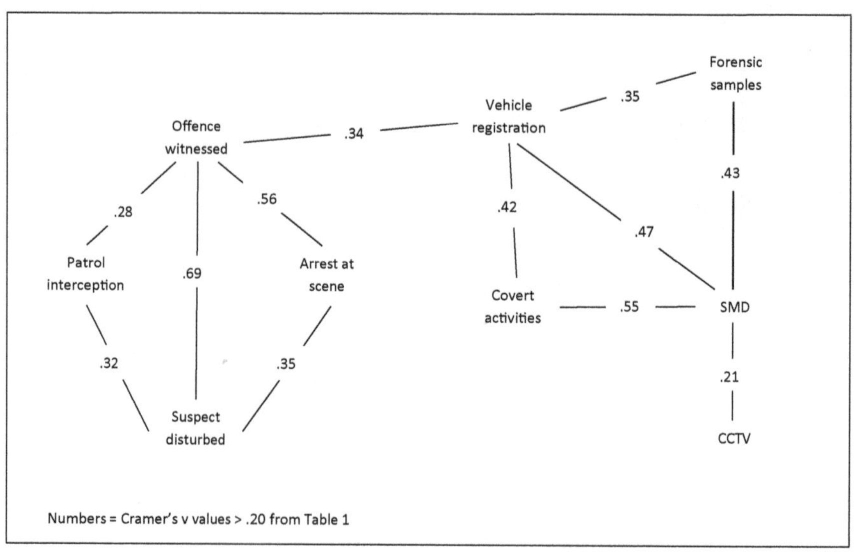

Fig. 4 Strongly correlated solvability factors (from Robb et al. 2015)

includes offences being witnessed and suspects being disturbed or arrested at or near crime scenes.

The aim is, separately for arrests at or near the crime scene and for all detections, to understand the independent effects ofeach solvability factor on detection outcomes.

Arrest at or Near the Crime Scene

Offenders were arrested at or near the crime scene at 58% of detected incidents. In 53% of these, no other factors contributed to the detection of the case. Therefore, an interception at the crime scene by patrols was solely responsible for 31% of detected cases. Suspect evidence from eyewitnesses or forensic evidence contributed to solving other incidents where there had been arrests.

'Alerts raised by witnesses' had a very large effect size, and 55% of the variation in on-scene arrest (Nagelkerke's $R^2 = 0.552$) was due to this factor and the sounding of alarms, which together led to successful patrol responses (Table 1). The odds of arrest were particularly high when the crime was witnessed and high when there was a patrol interception. Capture odds are halved for cases where offenders are disturbed at the scene since they are frequently aware of having been compromised and quickly take flight. Cutting signal cable had no effect on the capture of offenders at or near the scene, probably because they were initially thought to be system faults rather than offences.

Table 1 Binary logistic regression with whether or not there was an on- or near-scene arrest the dependent variable (from Robb et al. 2015)

Solvability factors	B	*SE*	Wald	*p*	Exp(B)
Metal theft witnessed	4.650	0.245	359.41	0.000	104.56
Suspect disturbed	−0.730	0.175	17.36	0.000	0.482
Patrol interception	0.2.921	0.323	81.52	0.000	18.55
Alert due to alarm sounding	1.007	0.481	4.382	0.036	2.74
Alert due to signalling cable cuts	−0.032	0.188	0.029	0.865	0.969
Constant	−5.050	0.228	489.660	0.000	0.006

[a]$N = 4001$

Table 2 Binary logistic regression with detected/not detected the dependent variable (from Robb et al. 2015)

Solvability factors	B	*SE*	Wald	*p*	Exp(B)
Scrap metal dealer visit	3.476	0.294	140.215	0.000	32.344
Witnessed	3.331	0.189	310.657	0.000	27.979
Patrol discovery	3.279	0.319	105.466	0.000	26.547
Forensic evidence	2.385	0.242	97.437	0.000	10.862
Covert activities	2.148	0.467	21.152	0.000	8.564
Alarm sounded	1.382	0.382	13.117	0.000	3.985
CCTV	1.190	0.205	33.691	0.000	3.289
Vehicle registration	0.957	0.192	24.866	0.000	2.603
Track or signal cut alarm	0.370	0.165	5.001	0.025	1.447
Property hidden at the scene	0.350	0.313	1.247	0.264	1.419
Suspect disturbed	−1.082	0.202	28.754	0.000	0.339
Constant	−4.292	0.158	735.603	0.000	0.014

[a]$N = 4001$

All Detection Outcomes

Together, solvability factors explained 64% of the variation in detection outcomes (Nagelkerke's $R^2 = 0.638$). The factors with the largest detection odds were scrap metal dealer checks, the availability of eyewitness accounts and interception of offenders by patrols (Table 2; Fig. 5). Usable forensic samples and covert policing activities had medium detection odds, while the presence of vehicle registration information, CCTV, triggered alarms and property hidden at the crime scene increased detection odds to a smaller extent (Table 2). Disturbing criminals at the scene depressed detection odds (Table 2; Fig. 5), indicating that thefts reported where this happens ought to be accorded lower priority than other thefts witnessed while in progress, given the poorer prospects for a positive outcome.

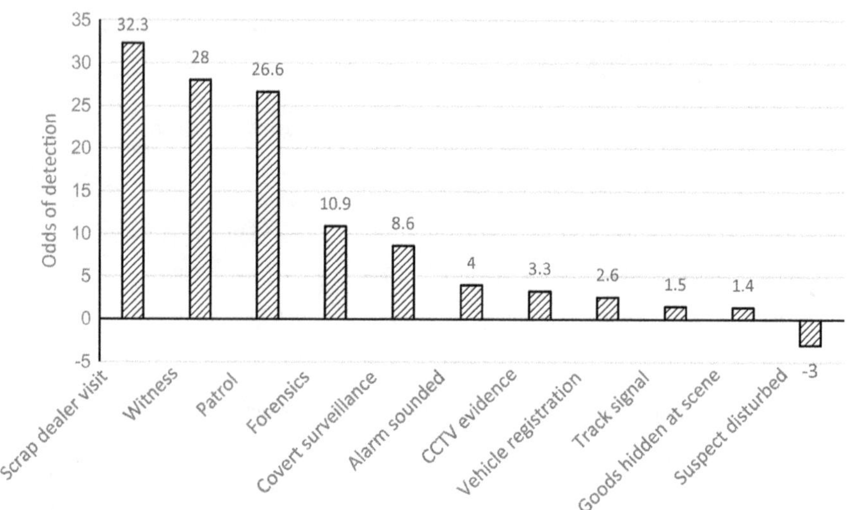

Fig. 5 Detection odds for metal theft solvability factors based on binary logistic regression (from Robb et al. 2015)

Number of Solvability Factors Per Offence and Offence Solvability

Case detection strongly reflects the number of solvability factors present in each incident. The solvability factor numbers in cases explain 61% of detection outcomes (Nagelkerke's $R^2 = 0.61$), with each additional factor increasing detection odds more than fivefold (Exp(B) = 5.123). In addition, the number of solvability factors is a perfect measure of overall metal theft solvability (Nagelkerke's $R^2 = 0.998$, solvability factor numbers regressed on the 12 principal solvability factors). It is evident that almost none of those cases with either no or only a single solvability factor present can be detected, while, with each additional factor, the probability of detection progressively improves, so that five factors make it a virtual certainty and six or more factors guarantee it (Fig. 6). Detected incidents have a median of three factors compared with one factor for undetected cases (U, $p < 0.001$).

Combinations of Factors of Different Solvability

For metal theft, a larger number of factors are associated with stronger factors with larger effect sizes, and it is the combination of factors of varying strength in different cases that determines case outcomes. Solvability factors may be classified into four groups according to their independent strength, based on logistic regression odds ratios (Table 3), and combinations of these factors have varying detection probabili-

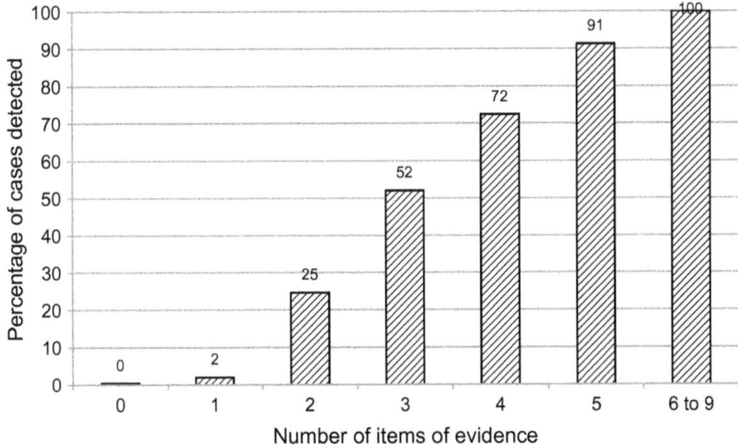

Fig. 6 Percentage of cases with different numbers of solvability factors (items of evidence) that were solved (from Robb et al. 2015)

Table 3 Solvability factor strength

Solvability factor strength	Solvability factor
Strong (*odds ratio*: *26–32:1*)	Scrap metal dealer visits
	Event witnessed
	Patrol discovery
Medium strength (*odds ratio*: *8.5–11:1*)	Forensic evidence
	Covert activities
Low strength (*odds ratio*: < *4:1*)	Alarm sounded
	CCTV
	Vehicle registration
	Track or signal cut alarm
	Property hidden at the scene
Low strength negative (*odds ratio: 3:1*)	Suspect disturbed

ties (Table 4). Subsets of cases within these combined factors have between four and five to—albeit very infrequently—six solvability factors, and the larger the numbers of additional factors, the fewer the incidents that possess them.

There are two principal clusters of solvability factors: those associated with scrap metal dealer visits and those where offences were witnessed (Table 4). Certain factors also occur in the same cases, such as scrap metal dealer visits with vehicle registration evidence. Where larger numbers of strong solvability factors were present together in a case, the highest detection rates resulted. Scrap metal dealer checks were effective singly, but far more so when combined with vehicle registration evidence and covert activity (Table 4). Covert activities, whenever present, confer very high solvability.

Table 4 Effectiveness of factors in detecting cases (from Robb et al. 2015)

Solvability factors	Detected		Undetected		Total
	n	%	*n*	%	
Scrap dealer visit	45	68	21	32	66
Scrap dealer visit + vehicle registration	47	90	5	10	52
Scrap dealer visit + vehicle registration + covert activities	79	100	0	0	79
Offence witnessed	116	46	137	54	253
Offence witnessed + discovered by patrol	69	86	11	14	80
Offence witnessed + covert activities	7	100	0	0	7
Offence witnessed + suspect disturbed	54	22	193	78	247
Offence witnessed + suspect disturbed + CCTV	13	36	23	64	36
Forensic sample	33	49	35	51	68
Discovered by patrol	6	46	7	54	13
Vehicle registration	9	22	32	78	41
Solved via other factor combinations/no factors	32	1.5	3027	98.5	3059
Totals	510	12.7	3491	87.3	4001

[a]Figures based on SPSS hierarchical classification software

'Offence witnessed', singly, is associated with 46% of cases solved (Table 4); if 'discovered by patrol' is combined therewith, detections are elevated to 86% while, if 'covert activities' evidence is also added, 100% are detected. However, the combination of 'suspects disturbed', a negative solvability factor, with 'offence witnessed' halves the percentage detected from 46 to 22%; even the addition of 'CCTV' evidence, a weak solvability factor, is sufficient to offset this by increasing the percentage detected to 36 from 22% (Table 4). Therefore, detecting cases rests on the numbers of solvability factors of differing strength, whose combined effect is to increase and decrease proportions of detected incidents (Table 5). These factors are indicative of the presence of items of evidence of varying strength that influence whether cases are solved.

However, almost 47% of incidents with the various combinations of solvability factors identified as enabling detection remained unsolved. These amounted to 11.5% of unsolved cases. It is possible that, among these cases with solvability factors present, as well as perhaps others, there is potential for detection that was not realized due to insufficient police resources being available or resources not being applied to the right activities in a timely way. Without fuller information about what investigative activities were undertaken and the effort expended, it is difficult to estimate this missed potential. Sometimes, there may be no unrealized potential, with cases remaining unsolved even though every investigative avenue has been followed up. For instance, there may be no further investigative options available if, in the

Table 5 Metal theft solvability factor combinations and percentages solved

Solvability factor number + strength	Solved as % of cases with factor combination	% of all solved cases
1 very strong + 1 medium (+1 weak)	100	17
1 very strong + 1 weak	90	9
2 strong	86	14
1 strong	50	33
1 medium	49	7
1 strong + 1 weak + 1 negative	36	3
1 strong + 1 negative	22	11
1 weak	22	2
Other	2	6

absence of other evidence, neither checking a registration number nor visiting the closest three scrap metal dealerships do not produce evidence that results in case detection.

Geographical Variation in Metal Theft Solvability and Detections

Metal theft solvability, solvability factors and detection levels vary between the five different regional police areas or basic command units (BCUs). The detection levels in the worst-performing BCU (London South) (9.2%) were only half those in the best performing BCU (North West) (19.2%). This is mirrored by differences in the mean numbers of solvability factors per case, which were lowest in the London South Area (0.78) and highest in the North West Area ($M = 1.37$). Detection rates were higher in areas with higher proportions of incidents with two or more solvability factors (Fig. 7). The London South Area's lowest detection rates relate to only 18% of offences with two or more solvability factors, whereas the North West Area's highest detection rate is associated with 32.7%.

Geographical variation in the detection rates partly reflect the incidence of different types of metal theft offences between the areas (cut cable: $\chi^2(N = 4) = 57.9$, $p < 0.000$, $V = 0.12$, $p < 0.000$; cable theft: $\chi^2(N = 4) = 75.2$, $p < 0.000$, $V = 0.14$, $p < 0.000$; depot: $\chi^2(N = 4) = 59.9$, $p < 0.000$, $V = 0.12$, $p < 0.000$; burglary: $\chi^2(N = 4) = 81.6$, $p < 0.000$, $V = 0.14$, $p < 0.000$; scrap: $\chi^2(N = 4) = 16.5$, $p = 0.002$, $V = 0.06$, $p = 0.002$; rail: $\chi^2(N = 4) = 51.2$, $p < 0.000$, $V = 0.11$, $p < 0.000$; substation: $\chi^2(N = 4) = 437.3$, $p < 0.000$, $V = 0.33$, $p < 0.000$). Detected rail theft offences have, on average, almost four solvability factors and have the highest detection rates at 49%. They represent 9.3% of the North West Area's metal theft, contributing to high

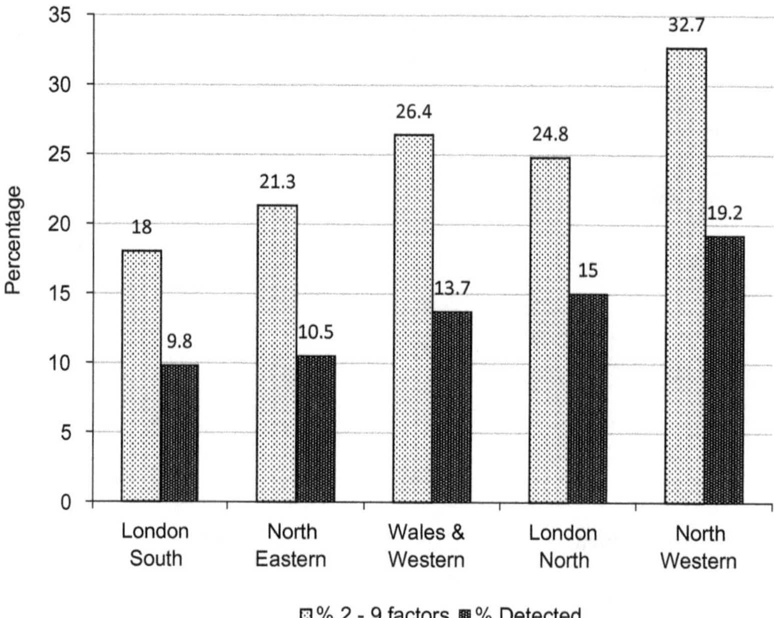

Fig. 7 Percentage of cases detected and with two to nine solvability factors by railway area (from Robb et al. 2015)

detection rates there, but only 2.8% of metal theft in the other areas. In contrast, substation and burglary thefts make up 16.2 and 11%, respectively, of London South Area metal thefts, but only 0.5 and 2.7% of theft in the other areas. Only 8.6% of burglary and substation thefts were detected, and there were only 0.6 solvability factors per case, contributing to London South Area having the lowest detection rates. The type of metal theft varied geographically, and its contribution to regional differences in detection rates is confirmed by the ordinal regression of area detection levels (Table 6).

Geographical differences in solvability factors, however, are not only a reflection of differences in metal theft types. The mean numbers of solvability factors differ regionally even within different offence types. The level of these differences is revealed by comparing the regions with the highest and lowest mean numbers of solvability factors for each offence type (Fig. 8). The largest solvability contrasts concerned substation theft, which was prevalent only in the London South Area (where there were 17 times as many solvability factors as in other areas), burglary (with 5.9 times as many solvability factors in South London as the North East), and scrap metal theft (with 2.4 times more solvability factors in the North East as in the South London Area). Notably, cable theft solvability was 90% higher in the North West (a mean of 1.56 solvability factors per case) than the London South Area (a mean of 0.82 solvability factors per case) (Fig. 8).

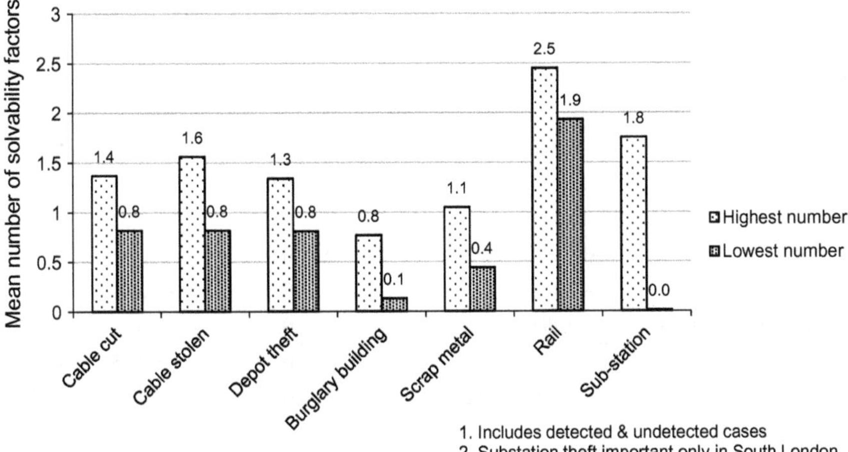

Fig. 8 For each metal theft offence type, mean number of solvability factors for the areas with highest and lowest means of solvability factors per offence (from Robb et al. 2015)

It is evident that offence solvability varies geographically, which may reflect differences in the environments in which metal theft occurs. In sparsely populated areas, there may be fewer eyewitnesses, and patrols may have to travel farther to reach crime scenes. In the North West Area, for instance, it rains more heavily and frequently, so that less forensic evidence may be collected. The amounts of metal stolen can also affect solvability. Some offences, such as rail theft, the incidence of which varies regionally, involve co-offenders using goods vehicles and sometimes lifting gear; there can also be small-scale thefts by single offenders using wheelbarrows or wheeled dustbins. Geographical variations in solvability may also be attributable to differences in crime-screening procedures, and greater resources per offence are likely to result in more thorough investigations in some regions.

Multivariate Analysis of BTP Area Variation

An ordinal measure of area detection rate variation was defined, based on the five BTP areas' ranked average detection rates, with the area with the lowest average rate scored as 1 and the highest as 5. This was regressed on solvability factors and metal offence types (Table 6).

Differences in regional detection outcomes reflected geographical variation in every offence type (Table 6). Differences in solvability factors also helped explain detection outcomes, notably scrap metal dealer visits, CCTV evidence, alerts due to track or signal cable being cut, metal hidden at the crime scene and forensic

Table 6 Ordinal regression of ranked area detection level on solvability factors and metal offence types (from Robb et al. 2015)

Variable	Estimate	*SE*	Wald	*p*	95% CI	
					Lower	Upper
Area detection level 1	−20.496	1.342	233.285	0.000	−23.126	−17.866
Area detection level 2	−18.153	1.332	185.611	0.000	−20.765	−15.542
Area detection level 3	−17.111	1.332	165.149	0.000	−19.721	−14.502
Area detection level 4	−16.171	1.331	147.540	0.000	−18.781	−13.562
Scrap metal dealer visit	−0.464	0.174	7.125	0.008	−0.804	−0.123
Track or signal cut alarm	0.291	0.069	17.957	0.000	0.156	0.425
Forensic sample	−0.338	0.147	5.306	0.021	−0.625	−0.050
CCTV	0.256	0.119	4.600	0.032	0.022	0.489
Goods hidden at scene	−0.309	0.148	4.335	0.037	−0.599	−0.018
Alarm sounded	−0.400	0.219	3.340	0.068	−0.829	0.029
Offence witnessed	0.045	0.113	0.161	0.688	−0.176	0.267
Suspect disturbed	−0.052	0.141	0.134	0.714	−0.328	0.225
Patrol discovery	−0.319	0.198	2.605	0.107	−0.707	0.068
Vehicle registration	−0.066	0.131	0.256	0.613	−0.324	0.191
Covert activities	−0.204	0.219	0.871	0.351	−0.633	0.225
Cable cut	−3.375	0.258	171.221	0.000	−3.881	−2.870
Cable stolen	−3.389	0.252	181.099	0.000	−3.882	−2.895
Scrap metal theft	−3.154	0.268	138.101	0.000	−3.680	−2.628
Rail theft	−3.680	0.297	153.358	0.000	−4.262	−3.097
Depot theft	−3.724	0.264	198.235	0.000	−4.242	−3.205
Burglary/building	−2.667	0.294	82.445	0.000	−3.242	−2.091

evidence. Therefore, incident solvability varies geographically, independently of spatial variation in the types of metal offence committed.

Assessment of Missed Detection Potential

Cases with fewer solvability factors were detected: almost three quarters of cases with four solvability factors were solved, compared to half of those with three factors and only a quarter of those with two factors. However, many incidents were not detected, even though they had between two and four solvability factors. Cuts to signalling cable and cable thefts are considered below in terms of missed detection potential.

Cable Thefts

Over half of metal thefts concerned the theft of cable, but 43% of incidents with two to four solvability factors were detected (two factors: 28% detected; three factors: 50% detected; four factors: 74% detected). A full 26% of cases with four solvability factors were not solved. The most prominent factor with the strongest effect was police visits to scrap metal dealers to find stolen metal and gain intelligence by checking transaction records and questioning dealers and employees. The majority (79%) of cable theft cases were solved when dealer visits were made, but only 36% of such cases were detected when no dealer visit occurred ($\chi^2 = 44.22$, $p < 0.000$, 1 *df*). However, such visits were made in less than a fifth of cases, and no visit was made for 93% of the *unsolved* cable theft cases with between two and four solvability factors. If visits had been made in all of these cases and, as a result, half of them had gained an additional solvability factor, the additional cases with two, three and four solvability factors might have elevated cable theft detection rates by 3% and all metal theft detections by 1.6%.

The results of regional contrasts in scrap metal dealer checks were striking. Visits occurred in eight times as many incidents in the North West Area as the London South Area. Visits relating to 32% of cable theft offences resulted in 50% of such offences being detected in the North West, whereas visits were made to only 4% of incidents in the London South Area, contributing to a low detection rate of 25% in this area. It appears that investigative practices and resource allocation may also be responsible for detection differences, which is suggestive of missed detection potential.

Signal Cable Cut Offences

The poorest cable cut detection rates were in the North East Area, where officers detected only 6.2% of such offences—a mere third of the highest detection rate, 20.1%, in the North West Area. This reflects large differences in the mean number of solvability factors per case ($F = 3.89$; $p < 0.004$; North East = 0.82 factors; North West = 1.37 factors) and the fact that the North East Area had only half as many signal cut cases with two or more solvability factors (Fig. 9). This may be the result of area differences in whether these offences are treated as technical signalling faults until repair units arrive at the scene.

Therefore, incident solvability and detection rates display spatial variation, which can be substantial. This may reflect environmental differences in offence types or their solvability, but may also be due to resource allocation differences, which may sometimes be a response to demand differences and differing priorities.

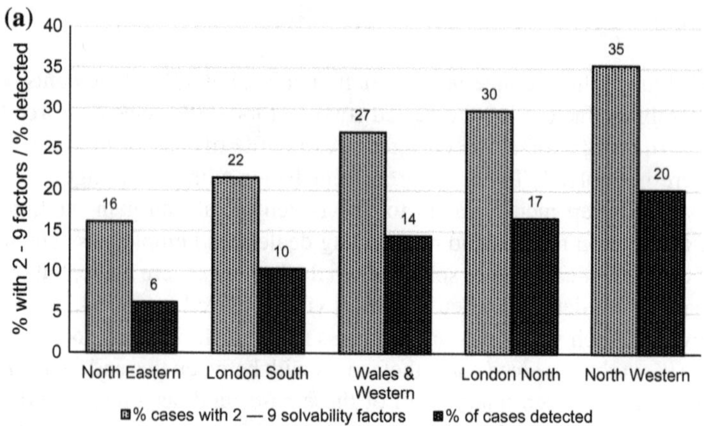

Fig. 9 Signal cut offences detected and with more than two solvability factors by Area (from Robb et al. 2015)

Discussion and Conclusions

Nine solvability factors enable the detection of railway metal theft: arrest at the scene, scrap metal dealer visits, offences being witnessed, covert activities, patrol interception, suspects being disturbed, vehicle registration details and the presence of CCTV footage and forensic evidence. Both solvability and the odds of detection are improved when there are more factors per case and their combined strength is greater. The model explains almost two-thirds of the variation in the cases that are either solved or not solved. There are two notable clusters of solvability factors. One centres on scrap metal dealer visits which have the highest detection outcomes. These are further improved in cases where police covert activities were undertaken and vehicle registration details were available. The other is 'witnessed incidents', also a predictor of high detection rates, particularly when combined with a rapid patrol response or covert police activities. However, when combined with 'disturbed offender', which is a negative solvability factor, detection odds are strikingly lowered. Usable forensic samples in isolation offer good prospects for solving cases.

While the absence of solvability factors is the reason that most unsolved cases are not detected, almost half of cases with between two and six solvability factors present also remain unsolved. These tend to be cases with fewer or weaker factors, but this failure to detect appears to also reflect investigative decisions, some of which may be due to insufficient resources to meet demand. It is likely that there is missed potential to solve cases such as cable cuts because of this. A third of variation in detections is, moreover, not explained by the solvability model, and the inclusion of resource inputs in the model would be likely to boost explanation. Opportunities to investigate solvable offences may have been neglected while investigative resources may have been spent—without benefit—on cases with poor prospects of being cleared. It is unlikely that scrap metal dealer checks were carried out at every solvable case that might have benefited from this activity.

There were marked geographical variations in incident solvability and detection rates. Detection rates in the North West Area were double those in the London South Area; significant differences exist in the incidence of different types of metal theft offences and these, with variations in offence solvability, affect detection rates. Spatial differences in the types of metal theft partly account for this, but solvability and detections varied between regions even for the same offence type. Given the marked differences in scrap metal dealer checks and detected signal cable cut cases, it is evident that different investigative responses affected outcomes. Far fewer dealer checks were made in the London South Area, where more resources were spent on personal theft from passengers on trains and at stations.

These findings can inform the policing and investigation of railway metal theft. Investigations can be built around cases with stronger and more numerous solvability factors. Cases with a number of factors of a combined strength predicted by the model in this chapter to be highly likely to be solved ought to be a particular focus: for all but the smallest quantities of metal theft, visiting the closest three scrap metal dealers with prior convictions would appear appropriate. Detection targets should differ between regions according to solvability potential, which this chapter's findings indicate reflect the incidence of different types of metal theft as well as environmental differences, such as weather that affects usable forensic evidence. Similarly, investigative resources should be tailored to regional solvability and detection potential, so that police capacity—in terms of the available resources per solvable case—is comparable.

The findings indicate that metal theft incidents could be solved more cost-effectively if investigative effort were tailored to the combinations of solvability factors identified in this chapter as being the best predictors of detections. The identification of strong solvability factors indicates that 'triaging' of cases using statistical screening would be likely to improve detections cost-effectively. This is an issue that may be better resolved with a randomized controlled test of metal theft offences that compares the outcomes of statistical and non-statistical screening and investigative practice.

References

Bradford, B. (2012). Policing and social identity: Procedural justice, inclusion and cooperation between police and public. *Policing and Society: An International Journal of Research and Policy, 24*(1), 22–43.

Burrows, J., Hopkins, M., Hubbard, R., Robinson, A., Speed, M., & Tilley, N. (2005). Understanding the attrition process in volume crime investigations (Home Office Research Study 295). London: Home Office.

Cohen, J. (1988). *Statistical power analysis for the behavioral sciences* (2nd ed.). Hillsdale, N.J.: Lawrence Erlbaum.

Coupe, T., & Griffiths, M. (1996). *Solving residential burglary (Police Research Group Crime Detection and Prevention Services, Paper 77)*. London: Home Office.

Dirikx, A., & van den Bulck, J. (2014). Media use and the process-based model for police cooperation. *The British Journal of Criminology, 54*(2), 344–365.

Eck, J. E. (1979). *Managing case assignments: The burglary investigation decision model replication*. Washington, DC: Police Executive Research Forum.

Greenberg, B., Elliot, C. V., Kraft, L. P., & Procter, S. H. (1977). *Felony investigation decision model—An analysis of investigation elements of information*. Washington, DC: US Government Printing Office.

Jansson, K. (2005). *Volume crime investigations—A review of the research literature (Home Office Online Report OLR 44/05)*. London: Home Office.

Kochel, T. R., Parks, R., & Mastrofski, S. D. (2013). Examining police effectiveness as a precursor to legitimacy and cooperation with police. *Justice Quarterly, 30*(5), 895–925.

Kooi, B. R. (2010). *Theft of scrap metal*. Problem-Specific Guides Series, No. 58. US Department of Justice, Office of Community-Oriented Policing Services.

Robb, P., Coupe, T., & Ariel, B. (2015). 'Solvability' and detection of metal theft on railway property. *European journal on criminal policy and research, 21*(4), 463–484.

Sidebottom, A., Jyoti, B., Bowers, K., Thompson, L., & Johnson, S. (2011). Theft in price-volatile markets: On the relationship between copper price and copper theft. *Journal of Research in Crime and Delinquency, 48*(3), 396–418.

Skogan, W. (2006). Asymmetry in the impact of encounters with the police. *Policing and Society: An International Journal of Research and Policy, 16*(2), 99–126.

Tilley, N., Robinson, A., & Burrows, J. (2007). The investigation of high volume crime. In T. Newburn, T. Williamson, & A. Wright (Eds.), *Handbook of criminal investigation* (pp. 226–254). London: Willan Publishing.

Detecting and Combating Internet Telephony Fraud

Colin Duffy and Richard Timothy Coupe

Introduction

The rapid growth in cybercrime is difficult to combat. One reason for this is that offenders often live in a different country from their victims. This poses problems for national police services, which can investigate crime and carry out arrests only in their own jurisdictions and must seek the assistance of foreign police agencies to locate and detain offenders living abroad. Internet telephone fraud is illustrative of the increasing amount of electronic crime, particularly financial fraud, that now takes place internationally. Two of its principal forms are the remote hacking of business telephone systems and the use of stolen credit and debit cards to steal telephone calls. The objectives of this chapter are to understand the characteristics of these offences and how they can be prevented. The challenges involved in identifying and arresting the perpetrators are considered.

Fraud due to remote hacking often involves setting up overseas premium rate telephone numbers, then hacking into business telephone systems connected to the internet and calling those numbers. The criminal either owns the premium telephone number or is in partnership with the number owner. By international agreement, payments for call charges incurred must be honoured. Even though the calls have been stolen, therefore, the owners of the distant premium numbers receive payment from the originating telephone networks for connecting them in their countries. As well as the charges due to the premium rate number itself, each routing stage between the hacked phone system and the premium rate number receives its due portion of the call charges.

Card fraud, in contrast, involves a criminal registering as a customer with an internet telephone service provider using a stolen credit or debit card and accumulating substantial call charges before the company discovers the customer to be a fraudu-

C. Duffy (✉)
iNet Telecom Ltd. (Voipfone), London, UK
e-mail: colin@voipfone.co.uk

R. T. Coupe
University of Cambridge, Cambridge, UK

R. T. Coupe et al. (eds.), *Crime Solvability Factors*,
https://doi.org/10.1007/978-3-030-17160-5_8

lent user. As with telephone hacking, criminals call premium line numbers created specifically to enable the fraud. Unlike hacking, which leaves the business customer footing the bill, card fraud leaves the telephone service provider with unpaid charges.

The purpose of this study is to examine how criminals use the internet telephone network to commit these frauds and to recommend pragmatic and cost-effective methods of fraud detection and interdiction. It uses original call data from an internet telephone service provider and telephone industry call fraud data to identify the principal attack methods and the characteristics of stolen telephone calls, including their destinations, and provides insights into how these crimes may be best identified and prevented.

Existing Research and Internet Telephone Systems Crime

Internet telephony fraud is entirely unexplored in criminology literature. There is, however, evidence sourced from the telecommunications industry that provides insights into the scale, modi operandi and characteristics of these crimes.

Two-fifths of the world's population—including a fifth of people in poorer countries—are now able to access the internet (Internet World Statistics 2004). The internet is ubiquitous, with communications technology embedded in a large variety of fixed and mobile devices, many vulnerable to being remotely scanned and controlled by criminals. An internet technology called Voice over Internet Protocol (VoIP) allows telephone calls to be made over the internet so that telephones are prime targets for cybercriminals.

Telephony fraud is estimated to cost $46 billion globally and £953 million in the UK every year and is growing rapidly (Communications Fraud Control Association [CFCA] 2013; National Fraud Authority [NFA] 2013). VoIP hacking fraud is its fastest-growing form and is estimated to cost $3.6 billion a year (CFCA 2013). The annual costs of PBX hacking, premium services and international revenue sharing are, respectively, $4.4, $4.7 and $1.8 billion (CFCA 2013). Prepaid subscription/plastic telephone call fraud is an unknown percentage of $5.2 billion (CFCA 2013). Even with double counting due to confusion regarding the attack methods (e.g. PBX hacking) and monetising mechanisms (e.g. premium rate sharing fraud) utilised, the criminal costs of VoIP fraud are understated. Both the criminal gains and the harm it causes victims can be significant.

Internet Telephone Systems and Fraud

VoIP is replacing time-division multiplexing (TDM) as the global standard for transmitting telephone calls. Most countries use it—some, such as Austria, exclusively (Wood 2014)—and all BT's customers will be served by VoIP networks by 2025 (CommsBusiness 2015).

VoIP technology means that the telephone system is no longer a separate network using its own specialised signalling, and, as computers are attached to the internet, VoIP telephones can be attacked from the internet by remote scanning and control.

The abuse of revenue-sharing agreements, such as premium rate and international share, has been a problem for previous technologies, such as mobile telephony. As a consequence, corporations that own communications networks have developed fraud detection systems based on sophisticated neural network and pattern recognition software and a secure international data exchange system, the Near Real-Time Roaming Data Exchange, to combat attacks (GSM Association [GSMA] 2007). However, the small VoIP companies providing internet telephone services, of which there are 120 in the UK, do not have these expensive protection systems and are vulnerable to remote hacking. Moreover, the characteristics of this new form of fraud render non-real-time systems ineffective, no matter how sophisticated they may be in detecting fraud after the act.

The internet telephone service providers provide VoIP Private Branch eXchange (PBX) services to connect customers' telephones to the Public Switched Telephone Network (PSTN). These sophisticated telephone exchanges are located at telephone companies' premises and can remotely monitor and maintain customers' telephones. Customers do not need them on site, although some customers prefer to own and install PBX equipment on their premises, carrying out their own switchboard functions. The connection between a VoIP telephone and the telephone company's network is by means of a session initiation protocol (SIP), which allows multiple simultaneous telephone calls to be made. This 'SIP trunk' enables large savings, but, unfortunately, also allows hackers to remotely create multiple calls from a single device such as a telephone or PBX and run up large bills very quickly.

The Crimes

Internet telephone fraud occurs when criminals gain control of the telephone company customer's telephones or use stolen credit or debit cards to register as customers and call expensive numbers, usually in distant countries.

The fraudulent use of credit and debit cards to steal telephone calls from telephone companies is an offence under s. 125 of the Communications Act 2003 and the Fraud Act 2006. Once the fraudulent customer is registered with a telephone company, VoIP telephones are used to make calls to high-value numbers.

Remote hacking of telephones in order to steal calls is an offence under the Computer Misuse Act 1990 and s. 125 of the Communications Act 2003. The criminal breaches the security of the telephone equipment, normally the PBX, and makes calls to high-value numbers, generating profits as for plastic card fraud. Whereas plastic card theft defrauds telephone companies, hacking most often defrauds individual business customers. While plastic card fraud may be viewed as a 'traditional crime using computers' (Wall 2003), internet telephone hacking can be classified as a 'hybrid cybercrime' (Wall 2003) that exploits the fresh opportunities provided by VoIP technology.

Offenders either own the service on which the numbers terminate or are in partnership with owners and take a share of the fraud revenue or the premium rate number revenue. International premium rate numbers are readily available for purchase on the internet, frequently offering services like astrology, psychic readings, sex chat lines or TV voting.

Internet Telephone Call Charging System

The price of a telephone company charges for a call to another country consists of its own operating costs and profits, plus the 'termination charge': the amount charged by the telecommunications company in the destination country to deliver the call there. This is paid according to what is known as the inter-carrier call accounting financial settlement process. There are often many stages in a chain of global communications that form a complex web of international accounting and contractual arrangements. Stages are owned by different operators, most or all of which may be acting legally. They are obliged to pass along payments for the up-chain termination of telephone calls. Termination charges are not simply a function of distance, but are set by each country and can be extremely expensive. The telephone company in this study charges 1.8 ppm (pence per minute) to send a call to France, the USA and Australia and 2 ppm for calls to China. Calls to Burma, however, cost 39 ppm, while Diego Garcia calls cost 294 ppm and those to the Maldives 240 ppm.

Target Selection

Telephone hackers search for targets while hidden behind a succession of proxy networks, using free software tools such as Shodan, which is able to automatically and systematically locate vulnerable equipment anywhere in the world. A Shodan scan for network telephones (SIP devices) with vulnerable-to-access ports was carried out by the first author on 14 May 2015, uncovering 2,783 open devices, of which a quarter was in the USA, a tenth each in the UK and Mexico and another tenth in Brazil and Turkey.

Having located vulnerable devices, hackers can use free tools, such as the SIPVicious 'Friendly Scanner' (SIPVicious 2012), to gain access to telephones on PBXs using a brute-force password cracker. Then, hackers can start 'Making Direct Phone Calls and Causing Havoc' (Gauci 2008, p. 22).

Attacking internet telephone companies by plastic card fraud requires stolen credit and debit card details, which are traded in closed user forums (Holt and Lampke 2010). Symantec's 'underground economy list' ranks and prices illicit products, including credit cards (Table 1).

Table 1 Symantec's underground economy list (Fossi et al. 2008)

Rank for sale	Rank requested	Goods and services	Percentage for sale (%)	Percentage requested (%)	Range of prices
1	1	Bank account credentials	18	14	\$10–\$1000
2	2	Credit cards with CVV2 numbers	16	13	\$0.50–\$12
3	5	Credit cards	13	8	\$0.10–\$25
4	6	Email addresses	6	7	\$0.30/MB–\$40/MB
5	14	Email passwords	6	2	\$4–\$30
6	3	Full identities	5	9	\$0.90–\$25
7	4	Cash-out services	5	8	8–50% of total value
8	12	Proxies	4	3	\$0.30–\$20
9	8	Scams	3	6	\$2.50–\$100/week for hosting; \$5–\$20 for design

Hackers select an internet telephony company that allows credit card payments, register for service using stolen card details and make calls using their own telephone equipment. They commonly use 'privacy' networks such as HideMyArse to conceal their online identities and anonymising software such as Tor (the onion router), a network of virtual tunnels that enables people to meet, communicate and offend with impunity.

Inter-carrier Payment Policy

As the incumbent telecommunications company in the UK, BT handles interconnected traffic from most UK telecommunications providers, passing traffic through its international gateways to partners in the terminating countries. It lawfully receives payment for interconnected traffic, fraudulent or otherwise. In the UK, BT operates a scheme intended to limit the practice of 'traffic pumping' or, to use its official label, the artificial inflation of traffic (AIT) by withholding payments for calls that have been generated in bad faith. However, this applies only to domestic traffic. For international payments, the AIT Group concluded:

> it was simply not practicable to extend the domestic AIT scheme for the Standard Interconnect Agreement to take in outgoing IDD [International calls]. [...] There is not, and it seems unlikely that there ever will be a facility to withhold international payments. (BT 2015)

The European Union's Universal Service Directive allows member states to withhold payment for fraudulent calls (Body of European Regulators for Electronic Communications [BEREC] 2013). However, this is operable only inside the EU, has not yet been implemented and is fraught with inter-operator contractual difficulties.

Globally, the Resolution 61 proposal, which aims to regulate 'number misuse', has been put to the United Nations Telecommunications Union regulations committee but has not yet been adopted (International Telecommunication Union, Telecommunication Standardization Sector [ITU] 2012).

Methodology

Research Design

This chapter is based on four sets of secondary telephone call data. Three of these consist of call data drawn from the records of one of the 120 UK telephone companies providing VoIP telephone services. They enable comparison of the times, duration, destination telephone numbers and costs of fraudulent and non-fraudulent calls. Call data records are computer generated for billing purposes, are regulated under the Communications Act 2003 and are complete, accurate and auditable. The first data set contains the key characteristics of 7666 *fraudulent* telephone calls made between August 2011 and August 2014. The second consists of the records of 1,750,548 *non-fraudulent* calls made in June 2014. Given the size of the data set, this is likely to be representative of the 'normal' telephone call characteristics of business customers. At almost 2 million calls a month, three matching years of data would not only be unmanageable analytically but are also unavailable.

A third file provided by the telephone company has call data on 215 hacking alerts (or potential 'attacks') sampled systematically by selecting every second case from a population of 439 potential attacks that occurred between July 2014 and July 2015. The telephone company introduced an anti-fraud system in July 2014, and its effectiveness can be assessed by comparing these data, which post-date the introduction of the anti-fraud system, with the 7666 fraudulent calls made during the three years prior to its introduction.

The fourth data set enables examination of the destinations and prices of fraudulent calls from an industry-wide perspective. It contains a list of 15,461 fraudulently used telephone numbers (known as 'hot numbers') reported to the Telecommunications UK Fraud Forum ([TUFF] 2015) by UK telecommunications companies. The call numbers are shared between the companies to block further use.

Data and Analysis Plan

The telephone company's three files contain data on telephone call duration, price, time and date, total attack cost and destination numbers. For fraudulent calls, there are data on the type of 'attack'—hacking or plastic card—and, for card fraud only, the time and date of registration with the company. A corruption index value for the country of each destination telephone number has been added. Transparency International's 2013 corruption perception index (CPI) (Transparency International [TI] 2014) for world nations has been used. This enables assessment of the degree to which fraudulent and non-fraudulent call destinations are located in countries with high corruption rates.

The analysis and description of findings compare the ways in which the characteristics of fraudulent and non-fraudulent telephone calls differ. We also examine how fraudulent calls may be blocked to minimise theft by drawing on selected distinctive features of fraudulent calls. The analysis supports the paper's objectives of understanding how fraudulent calls may be identified and prevented, while they are being committed, so as to minimise loss. Through its analysis of the locations of destination call numbers, it also provides insights into the solvability of stolen telephone call crime, while an examination of monetising mechanisms offers insight into the difficulties of identifying and arresting offenders, as well as the potential for preventing the crime.

The collection, ordering, cleaning and analysis of data were challenging and exceptionally time-consuming and were carried out by the first author. In view of 'workspace' difficulties encountered with the use of SPSS on large call data files, Stata was also used for data analysis.

Findings

Fraudulent and non-fraudulent or 'normal' calls are compared in terms of their incidence across the day and the week, duration, price and destination numbers. The call destination countries in which bogus premium numbers are to be found are also considered, and the destination countries of fraudulent and normal calls are examined with respect to corruption levels. Aspects of this information can be used to help prevent telephone call theft.

Incidence of Fraudulent Calls

Fraudulent telephone calls due to remote hacking occur at distinctively different times of day and days of the week from non-fraudulent or 'normal' calls. Non-fraudulent call frequency is high on weekdays when business customers use telephones, between

8.30 and 17.30, albeit with slight dips for midday lunch periods, and low at other times (Fig. 1).

Remotely hacked calls, in contrast, commonly occur outside business hours when offices are empty and the telephone company's customers are not themselves using telephones. Hacking attacks stand out as striking 'spikes' of exceptionally high call frequency. One such attack on a business customer is shown in Fig. 1 at approximately 02.00. It is generating call revenues at twice the rate of 30,000 normal telephones at their peak call volume, using multiple auto-dialling of a telephone system at a speed impossible for humans to achieve. Such attacks test a range of fraudulent numbers, with 'hot numbers' (i.e. known fraudulent telephone numbers) being blocked by telephone company software until the hacking software finds numbers that have not yet been flagged as fraudulent.

Three years of fraudulent calling data confirm the heaviest incidence of fraudulent calls in the small hours (Fig. 2), with a smaller period of activity during the late afternoon and early evening that reflects weekend hacking attacks. Very few normal calls occur out of business hours, between 20.00 and 08.00 the next day, compared with fraudulent calls: only 4% of non-fraudulent calls occur during these hours on weekdays, compared with 60% of fraudulent calls ($\chi^2(1, N = 1{,}728{,}731) = 52{,}167.5$, $p < .001$, $V = .174$), while only 8% of normal, compared with 67% of fraudulent, calls are made during this window over the whole seven-day week ($\chi^2(1, N = 1{,}804{,}726) = 36{,}199$, $p < .001$, $V = .142$).

Similarly, more fraudulent calls due to hacking occur at weekends, with 18% of fraudulent calls, but only 4% of normal calls, occurring on Saturdays and Sundays ($\chi^2(1, N = 1{,}813{,}510) = 39{,}150$, $p < .001$, $V = .147$, $n = 181{,}351$). Few businesses operate after 17.00 on Saturdays and 16.00 on Sundays, and weekend fraud traffic is concentrated during the early evening.

It is clear that hackers seek to exploit the times that business premises are least likely to be occupied by employees using telephones, who might otherwise disrupt

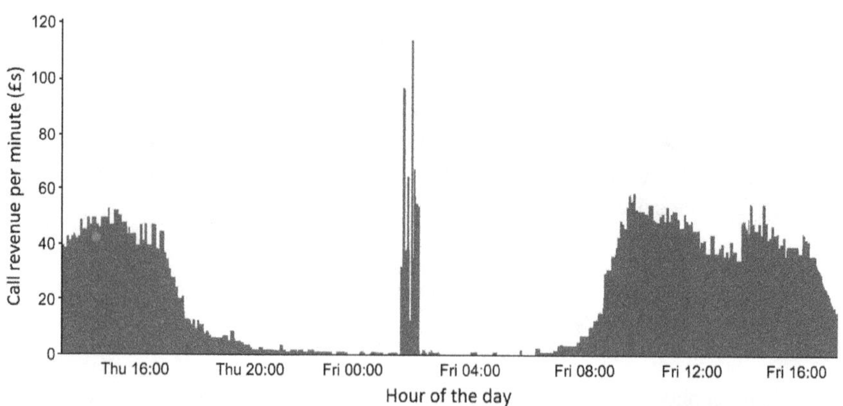

Fig. 1 Single fraudulent hacking attack showing as an out-of-hours 'spike' of calls between two working days of 'normal' calls

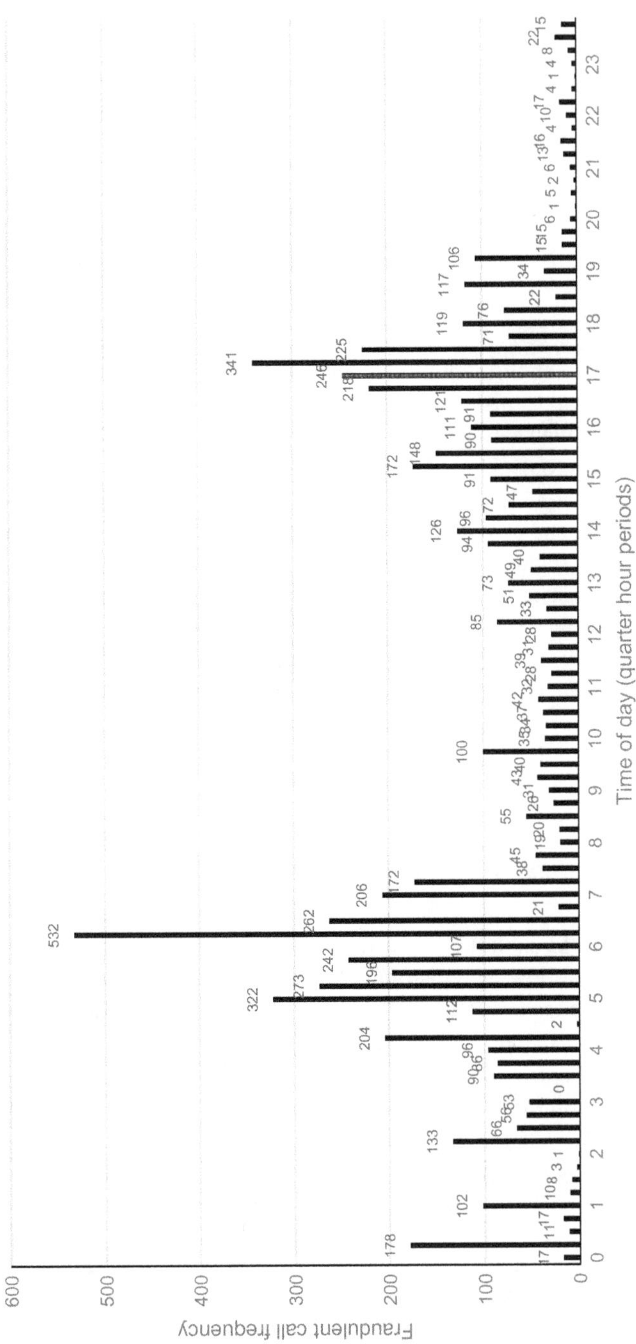

Fig. 2 Fraudulent calls by time of day based on three years of telephone company data

remote call hacking. The differences between the working day and the evening and night-time hours and between weekdays (Fig. 3a) and weekends (Fig. 3b) appear, therefore, to reflect offender awareness of the routine activities of victims, with offence timing coinciding with periods when weak guardianship is most likely (Cohen and Felson 1979).This is also a characteristic of telephone call theft that can potentially be used in its prevention.

Incidence of Remote Hacking Compared with Plastic Card Fraud

The timing of calls stolen through remote hacking differs from that of those due to card fraud. Though both forms of fraud predominantly occur outside business hours, more remote hacking than card fraud occurs between 20.00 and 08.00 on weekdays, with 74% compared to only 56% of card fraud occurring outside business hours on weekdays ($\chi^2(1, N = 1{,}813{,}541) = 39{,}145.0$, $p < .001$, $V = .15$). At weekends, the incidences of hacking and card fraud do not differ by time of day, although far more hack attacks than card fraud take place over the weekends: 44% of hack attacks occur on Saturdays and Sundays, compared with only 8% of card frauds ($\chi^2(1, N = 9031) = 871.6$, $p < .001$, $V = .31$). More card fraud occurs on weekdays and even during business hours because fraudulent card use more often mirrors normal telephone use since such fraudsters are posing as ordinary telephone customers. Hackers attack and render telephone systems unusable by the victims, while credit card fraudsters use their own equipment to make calls that can be detected only by service providers.

Other Characteristics of Credit Card Fraud

Credit card fraud attacks exhibit other distinctive characteristics. One is a distinctive decay rate for attacks following registration for service with the telephone company. Seventy per cent of attacks occur on the day on which the fraudster registers as a customer. By the next day, 84% of attacks by accounts that would eventually be identified as fraudulent had already taken place. A full 98% of attacks by such accounts occurred within the first 30 days (Fig. 4). It is clear that most card fraud is perpetrated as quickly as possible before the telephone company becomes aware that the card being used is stolen.

The other notable feature of card fraud is that international customers are 9.4 times more likely to attempt fraud than domestic, UK customers ($\chi^2(1, N = 215) = 38.9$, $p < .001$, $V = .43$). Though many appear to be UK customers, fraudsters often disguise their location so that the international fraud rate is likely to be understated.

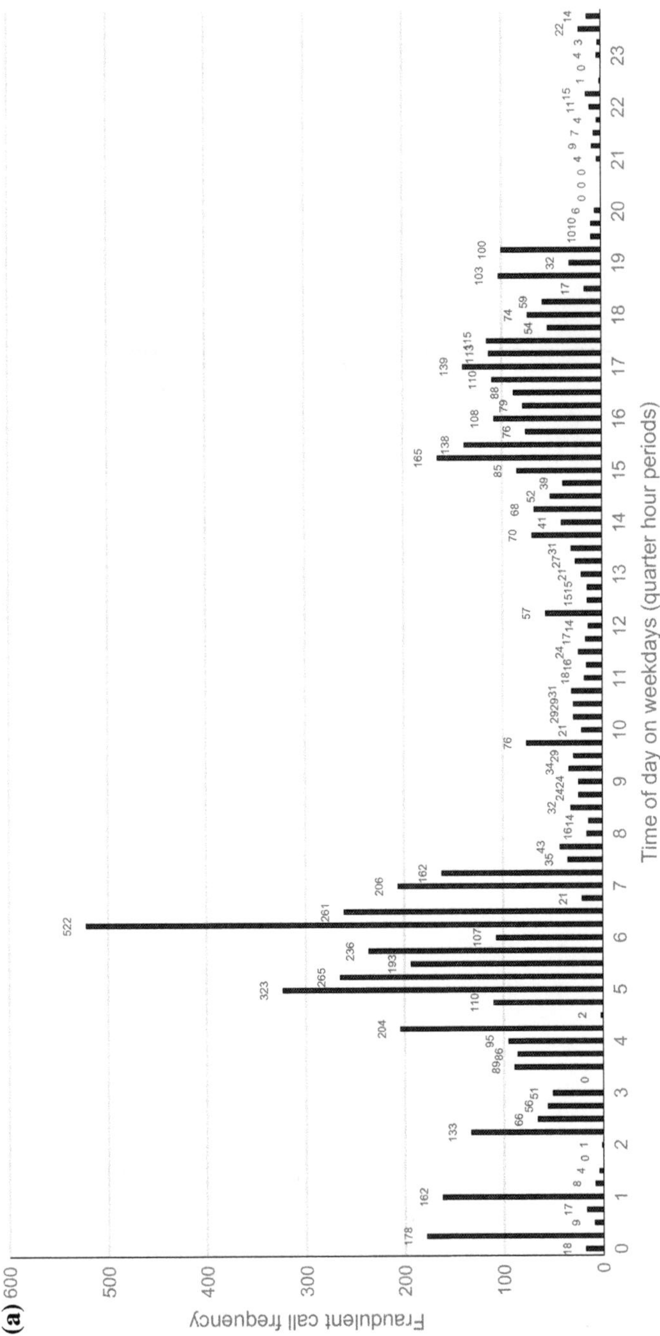

Fig. 3 Fraudulent calls by time of day for **a** weekdays, **b** weekends (telephone company data)

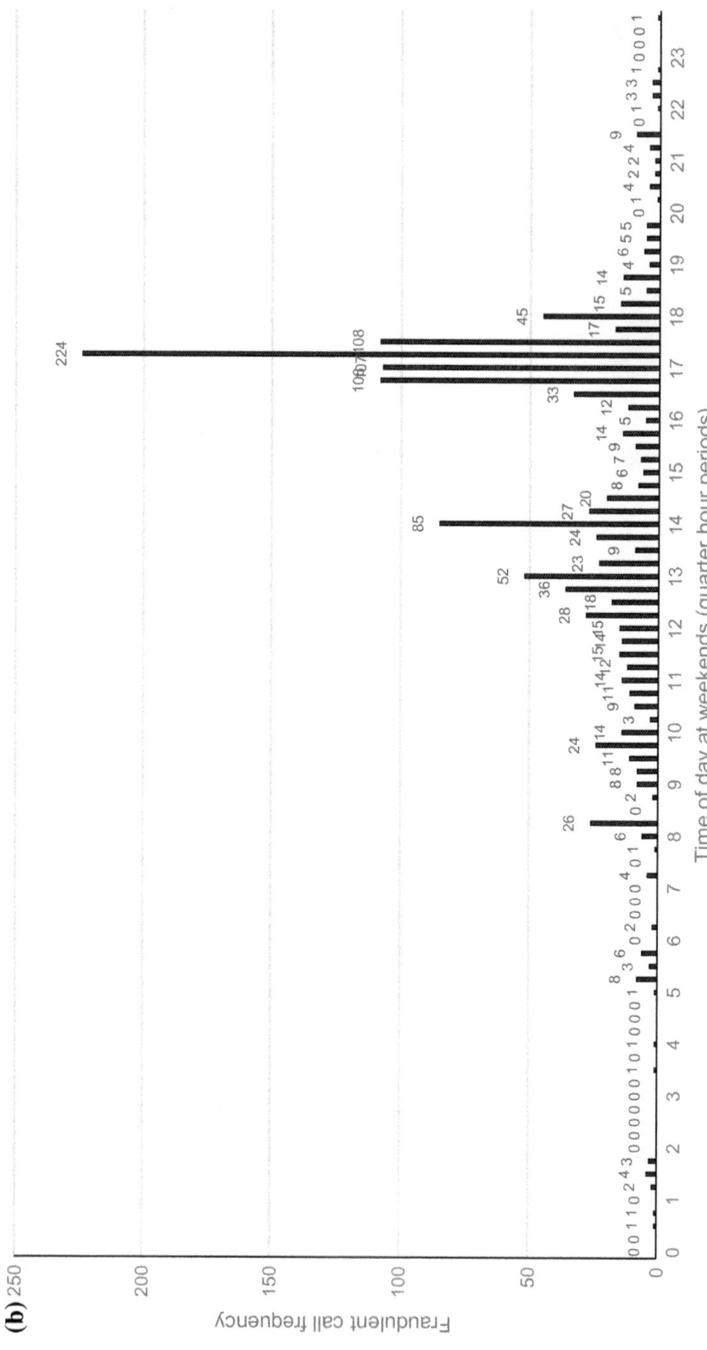

Fig. 3 (continued)

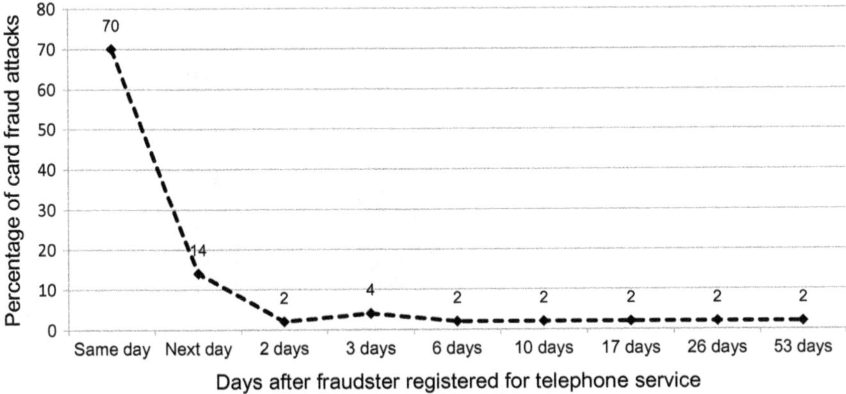

Fig. 4 Incidence of plastic card fraud attacks by time from customer registration

Duration of Fraudulent and Non-fraudulent Calls

Comparison of the telephone company's data shows that fraudulent calls are 2.4 times longer than normal calls (t-test, $p < .001$, $d = 1.34$, $n = 7666$, 1,750,542), averaging 336 s (SD = 412 s) compared to only 137 s (SD = 318 s) for non-fraudulent calls. Despite this, 99.9% of both fraudulent and non-fraudulent calls have durations of under an hour, and 95% of both sorts of call are surprisingly similar, averaging just over 18 min. These similarities make duration data an unreliable indicator of telephone theft and less helpful than expected for developing security software.

Frequency of Calling

Fraudulent attacks involve high-frequency calling, averaging a call every 43 s (SD = 34.8, maximum = 118, minimum = 0.4 s). Extremely high frequencies of a call every 0.4 s can be achieved only with automatic dialling equipment.

Price Analysis of Fraudulent and Non-fraudulent Calls

Fraudulent calls are far more expensive than normal calls (U, $z = -973.3$, $p < .001$, $n = 1{,}811{,}738$), with fraudulent calls 16.3 times as expensive than normal calls according to the TUFF data and 5.8 times as expensive as normal calls according to the internet telephone company data (Fig. 5). As with call duration, call prices are not normally distributed (skewness = 136; kurtosis = 62,600; Q–Q plot confirmed).

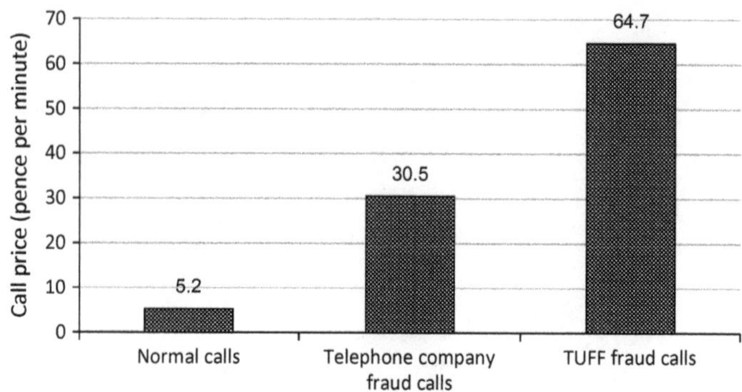

Fig. 5 Prices of fraudulent and non-fraudulent (normal) calls

This reflects the preponderance of low-cost non-fraudulent calls, of which 53% are to standard UK landline numbers at 1.2 ppm, 29% to UK mobiles at 12 ppm and 8% to European or other Western destination landlines (1.8 ppm) or mobiles (12 ppm). Over 82% of fraudulent calls are to 'rest-of-world' destinations, which have 483 individual and often more expensive prices, compared with only 4% of non-fraudulent calls (Fig. 6).

Moreover, fraudulent calls to rest-of-world destinations are far more expensive than non-fraudulent ones—approximately three to six times as costly—since criminals select the most expensive destinations in which to locate premium numbers (Fig. 7).

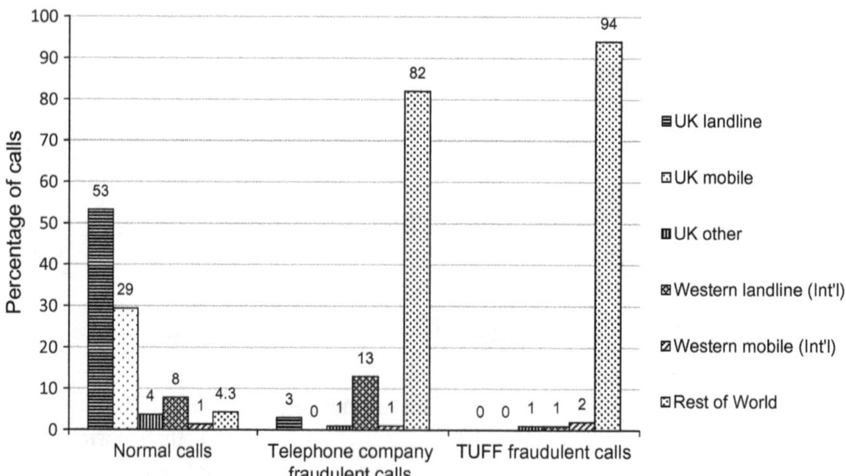

Fig. 6 Importance of destinations of fraudulent and non-fraudulent (normal) calls

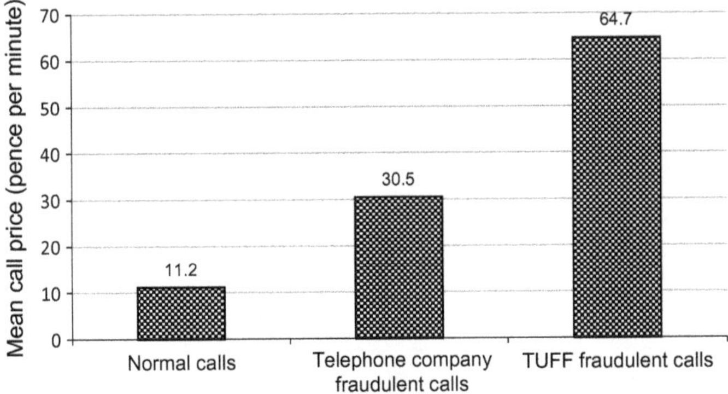

Fig. 7 Mean prices of fraudulent and non-fraudulent calls to 'rest-of-world' destinations

Even within the UK, TUFF data show that, the higher the charge for calling the destination number, the more often it is used for fraudulent calls ($r = .61, p < .01$). With progressively more expensive telephone numbers, the proportion of fraud rises, from 1% of 01 and 02 numbers to 22% of 08 numbers, 37% of 070 numbers and 40% of 09 numbers. Despite this, there is no significant correlation between call price and fraud count for either the TUFF or telephone company data set, indicating that, while this is a necessary condition for fraud, many expensive calls are made legitimately.

Therefore, theft of telephone calls is profitable to criminals because of the substantial call costs that can be accumulated over short periods. As well as lasting longer and being made, automatically, with a greater frequency per unit time, fraudulent calls are made to expensive numbers in the most costly destinations.

Destinations of Fraudulent and Non-fraudulent Telephone Calls

Even within the rest-of-world destinations, many fraudulent numbers are located in certain types of country (Fig. 8). The TUFF data show that most destination countries for telephone call fraud are located primarily in North-West and North-East Africa, Eastern Europe, the Caribbean and parts of Asia, the Middle East and South-East Asia. Fewer fraudulent calls are made to numbers in the Western developed world, with the exception of the UK, the USA and Spain. Few are also made to Latin America, except for Chile and Bolivia, while China and India, despite their size, receive almost no fraudulent calls.

Table 2 shows the top 50 fraud destinations for the TUFF, telephone company and CFCA data sets. Despite certain destination countries featuring on all three lists, and 19 out of 50 being common to TUFF and the study's telephone company data, there are other countries that are fraudulent call destinations for TUFF companies

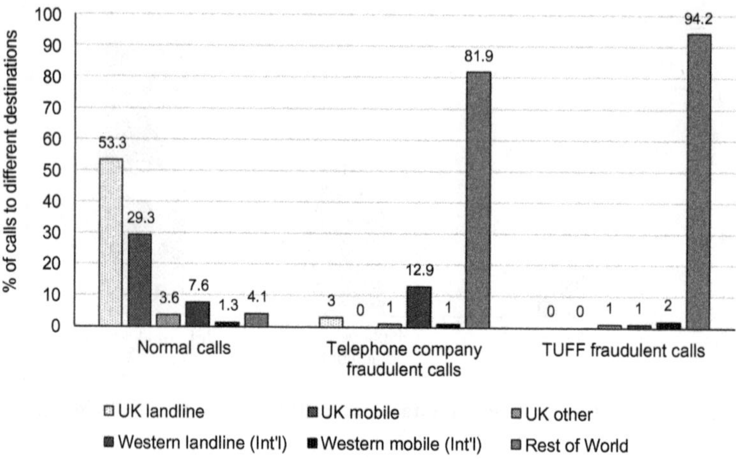

Fig. 8 Comparison of normal and fraudulent call destinations

but not for the telephone company's customers and vice versa. This points to criminals, possibly different criminals, using numbers in different countries and targeting different sorts of UK business customers.

It is, however, notable that small islands feature particularly prominently as fraudulent call destinations in the study's telephone company data. No non-fraudulent calls were made to two-thirds of these 24 countries, and few to the other third, though the fraudulent call traffic is relatively high (Table 3). The average cost of calling these islands is also high, at 72 ppm (SD = 102 ppm), and it is likely that this helps account for their use by criminals.

Differences in the destination countries between the TUFF, telephone company and CFCA data may reflect the targeting of different sorts of business organisations by fraudsters in different countries, and there may be differences between the types of business customer attracted by the 120 internet telephone companies. The telephone company used for this study may have a bias towards certain sorts of business customer who are more frequently targeted by criminals with premium numbers in certain countries. The existence of differences suggests that businesses are selectively targeted by criminals, presumably on the basis of the perceived size of their telephone systems, the absence of guardianship at premises and their vulnerability in terms of their inability to prevent fraudulent calls through early detection of attacks or speedy identification of stolen card use.

Destination Countries and Corruption Perception Index

Transparency International's corruption perception index (CPI) measures countries' corruption on 100-point scale, on which a low value indicates a high level of cor-

Table 2 Most frequent target destinations of fraudulent calls

Fraudulent call destination by rank	Voipfone	TUFF	CFCA[a]
1	Croatia[b]	Gambia[d]	Latvia[d]
2	Bosnia Herzegovina[b]	Cuba[c]	Gambia[d]
3	France (special)	Guinea	Somalia[d]
4	Tanzania	Morocco[b]	Sierra Leone[d]
5	Sri Lanka	Haiti	Guinea
6	Liberia	UK[e]	Cuba[c]
7	Macedonia[b]	Latvia[d]	East Timor
8	UK[e]	Bhutan	Lithuania[d]
9	Azerbaijan[b]	Romania	Taiwan[c]
10	Burkina Faso	Thailand	UK[e]
11	Sudan	Turkey[b]	
12	Australia	Algeria	
13	Serbia[b]	Ethiopia[b]	
14	Afghanistan[b]	Laos	
15	Morocco[b]	Croatia[b]	
16	Poland[b]	Lithuania[d]	
17	Mali[b]	Somalia[d]	
18	Malaysia	Bosnia[b]	
19	Bulgaria[b]	Kenya	
20	Ethiopia[b]	Taiwan[c]	
21	Chad	Chile[b]	
22	Cuba[c]	Bolivia	
23	Turkey[b]	Estonia	
24	Palestine	Russia[b]	
25	Syria	Spain	
26	USA[b]	Bulgaria[b]	
27	El Salvador	Mali[b]	
28	Qatar	East Timor	
29	Pakistan[b]	Sierra Leone[d]	
30	South Africa	Serbia[b]	
31	Philippines	Afghanistan[b]	
32	Taiwan[c]	North Korea	
33	Canada	Sao Tome	
34	United Arab Emirates	USA[b]	
35	Germany	Azerbaijan[b]	

(continued)

Table 2 (continued)

Fraudulent call destination by rank			
	Voipfone	TUFF	CFCA[a]
36	Bangladesh	Belarus	
37	Egypt	Zimbabwe	
38	Madagascar	Honduras	
39	Saudi Arabia	Pakistan[b]	
40	Lebanon	Eritrea[b]	
41	Dominica	Moldova	

[a]Communications Fraud Control Association
[b]Country present in both study's telephone company data and TUFF data
[c]Country present in data of study's telephone company, TUFF and the CFCA top 10
[d]Country present in data of TUFF and CFCA top 10
[e]Country present in data of study's telephone company and CFCA top 10

ruption. Since the UK telephone company data used for this study is dominated by UK traffic, its mean of 75 (SD = 5.3) is, as expected, almost identical to the UK's CPI score of 76. However, the average CPI score for the destination countries of the telephone company's fraudulent traffic is significantly lower, at 45 (SD = 16.2; t-test, $p < .001$), with a very large effect size ($d = 5.54$), confirming the appeal of corrupt countries for internet telephone crime. TUFF's fraudulent calls were made to even more corrupt countries, with a mean CPI score of 36 (SD = 14.2; t-test, $p < .001$, $d = 7.1$).

Combating Fraud with Security Software

Following a sustained attack in 2014, the telephone company that provided data for this study developed an anti-fraud software tool. This identifies and disables accounts subject to plastic fraud and hacking attacks using an algorithm that takes account of calling rates per minute and high-risk destinations. As indicated in the findings, these are two of the hallmarks of hacking frauds. The algorithm uses high call frequency to trigger an alert and automatically disables an account when calls to high-risk destinations exceed a set level.

The anti-fraud tool's effects were immediate, reducing fraud losses from an average of £200 to £0.33 per event. It traps 100% of all frauds, but these represent only 30% of the accounts it disables. It also, therefore, disables accounts from which legitimate calls to overseas destinations are being made. Since these occur at a rate of less than one false positive account per day, this requires few resources from the company's customer support services. Such accounts can be enabled following com-

Table 3 Fraudulent and non-fraudulent calls, call prices and populations of small island countries

Country	Price (ppm)	Population	Fraud count	Normal calls
Easter Island	132.00	5761	114	0
San Marino	5.28	31,448	30	8
Cook Islands	144.00	19,569	20	1
Ascension	240.00	880	16	4
Niue	120.00	1611	15	0
Norfolk Island	156.00	2302	9	0
Diego Garcia	264.00	4239	9	0
Vanuatu	86.40	252,763	8	1
New Caledonia	31.20	262,000	8	3
Nauru	144.00	9378	7	0
Wallis and Futuna Islands	78.24	15,500	7	0
Kiribati	86.88	102,351	6	0
Solomon Islands	157.68	561,231	6	0
British Virgin Islands	20.00	27,800	5	0
Falkland Islands	126.24	2932	5	3
St Helena	238.56	4255	5	0
Aruba Mobile	30.72	102,911	5	1
St Pierre and Miquelon	55.20	6080	3	0
Palau	81.60	20,918	3	0
Tonga	67.20	105,323	3	0
French Polynesia	45.84	276,831	3	4
Netherlands Antilles	18.00	304,759	3	0
Micronesia	30.72	103,549	2	0
Tuvalu	73.68	9876	1	0
Marshall Islands	42.00	52,634	1	0

munications with the customers involved and can be 'white-listed' to prevent further false positives. Between June 2014 and June 2015, the anti-fraud tool prevented an estimated 2500 fraudulent calls.

Given the association identified between credit card fraud and overseas customers and the high incidence of card fraud within the first few days of registration as a customer, short-term credit control practices would be effective in countering such fraud, especially if applied to overseas customers.

Discussion

The analysis of internet telephone fraud data indicates that there are a number of potential approaches to combating the theft of telephone calls using remote hacking and stolen plastic cards. One, which has been described above, involves anti-fraud software to detect and disable accounts that are under attack from hacking fraudsters. This is very effective.

The method is also effective in stopping credit card fraud, as both forms of fraud ultimately result in high-frequency calls to expensive destinations. However, additional measures could be available for card fraud. The enabling of new accounts could be delayed, especially for higher-risk overseas customers, for the length of time usually required for the telephone company to become aware of accounts involving a stolen card. International customers could be required to make their first payment by bank transfer, thereby guaranteeing payment to the service provider. This would remove the likelihood of future attack and ensure that far fewer fraudulent calls would be made.

None of these preventive measures, however, would result in the arrest of the criminals responsible. Such offenders will almost certainly continue to commit telephone fraud, as well as being very likely to commit other forms of cybercrime against citizens of the UK and other countries. Disabling the international telephone payment system so that payments cease to be made in cases where fraud is known to have occurred would, if agreement could be reached, effectively put an end to the majority of internet telephone fraud. While this might face opposition from corrupt countries and transit operators who may benefit financially from this global fraud, the ethical arguments for maintaining payments that are knowingly obtained though fraud are weak if indeed they exist at all. Banning premium price numbers within the UK alone would, in itself, markedly reduce local fraud, but would interfere with the many legitimate uses for these numbers. Some providers block calls to such numbers, only opening them to vetted customers on demand.

However, these offences are solvable in terms of the potential to arrest the criminals responsible. Since the charges paid to the owners of premium numbers that have been used in connection with remote hacking or plastic card fraud must leave an audit trail, stopping such payments at this stage would also be feasible, given compliance from the jurisdictions involved. Equally, it appears feasible to link criminals with the accounts into which stolen telephone call charges from premium numbers are paid. The technical solvability of these offences is, therefore, linked with forensic accounting. However, like much cybercrime, given the international nature of these offences, their solvability also hinges on international politics and the exertion of power to gain compliance. The USA's 'outreach' policies are an example of how such criminals living in overseas jurisdictions may be arrested and extradited for crimes committed in US territory and against US citizens. The explosion in internet crimes perpetrated in many countries from many others highlights the potential benefits of international collaboration between police agencies in combating international crimes. Internet telephone theft is an international crime and demands an international solution if its solvability is to be exploited and culprits arrested.

Conclusions

Telephony theft is a costly crime for businesses, amounting to almost £1 billion pounds a year in the UK alone. Fortunately, fraudulent calls possess highly distinctive characteristics. Theft of calls using remote hacking, the dominant mode of offending for internet telephony, occurs outside business hours and is marked by high call frequency, often to premium numbers in overseas countries. Known 'hot' fraudulent numbers can be pre-blocked, while accounts being used to make excessive numbers of calls to 'rogue' countries known to be popular destinations for fraudulent calls can be disabled in real time. Card fraud has distinctive 'time-decay' characteristics so that, with real-time technologies, delays in enabling the accounts of new customers, particularly those from overseas countries with a disproportionately higher incidence of stolen plastic cards, could prevent calls from being stolen.

As well as exploitation of the distinctive features of network telephone theft to develop software or procedures for preventing it, the monetisation mechanisms for international payment also offer potential for a more certain way of deterring criminals. If payments were not to be made for local charges connected to numbers used in telephone fraud, there would be no gains for offenders, and internet telephone fraud—in the principal forms in which it currently occurs—would cease.

However, these offences are potentially solvable with respect to clearing them with the arrest of the criminals involved. Even if prevented from committing telephone fraud, it appears very likely that criminals will switch to other forms of internet crime so that their arrest will help stop this and deter others. Doing so is technically challenging, and there are also often insuperable legal barriers to face. Forensic auditing is needed to identify the criminal owners of premium numbers used in frauds. International policing cooperation is also a precondition for collecting this type of investigative evidence and using it to enable arrest.

Internet telephone fraud is, like most cybercrimes, international, and it is clear from the rapid escalation in cybercrime that preventive approaches are failing to keep it in check. It seems likely that exploiting the solvability of cybercrimes such as internet telephone fraud to arrest the criminals responsible would help deter such crimes, while a lack of deterrence will certainly encourage it. Combating international crime effectively will involve investigating and arresting its perpetrators. Unless police agencies in less corrupt countries, whose citizens are often the victims of international cybercrime, secure the cooperation of police in countries where such crimes are enabled, it will continue to be difficult to arrest any criminals and deter others who, not unjustifiably, view cybercrime as a safe and profitable means of offending.

References

Body of European Regulators for Electronic Communications. (2013). Article 28(2) USD Universal Service Directive: A harmonised BEREC cooperation process—BEREC Guidance Paper. *BoR, 13,* 37.

BT Group. (2015). International tariff guide for residential customers. http://www.bt.com/static/wa/account/pricechanges/International_Tariff_Guide.pdf?s_cid=con_FURL_internationalpricing. Accessed February 2, 2015.

Cohen, L. E., & Felson, M. (1979). Social change and crime rate trends: A routine activity approach. *American Sociological Review, 44*(4), 588–608.

CommsBusiness. (2015). BT set firm date to switch off ISDN network! http://commsbusiness.co.uk/news/bt-set-firm-date-to-switch-off-isdn-network/. Accessed August 24, 2015.

Communications Fraud Control Association. (2013). 2013 global fraud loss survey. http://www.cfca.org. Accessed June 10, 2014.

Fossi, M., Johnson, E., Turner, D., Mack, T., Blackbird, J., McKinney, D., et al. (2008). Symantec report on the underground economy July 07–June 08. http://eval.symantec.com/mktginfo/enterprise/white_papers/b-whitepaper_underground_economy_report_11-2008-14525717.en-us.pdf. Accessed February 4, 2018.

Gauci, S. (2008). Storming SIP security. https://resources.enablesecurity.com/resources/22_29_storming_sip.pdf. Accessed November 9, 2014.

GSM Association. (2007). GSMA speeds up the transfer of roaming call records. Press release. http://www.gsma.com/newsroom/press-release/gsma-speeds-up-the-transfer-of-roaming-call-records/. Accessed October 7, 2015.

Holt, T., & Lampke, J. (2010). Exploring stolen data markets online: Products and market forces. *Criminal Justice Studies: A Critical Journal of Crime, Law and Society, 23*(1), 33–50.

International Telecommunication Union, Telecommunication Standardization Sector. (2012). *Resolution 61—Countering and combating misappropriation and misuse of international telecommunication numbering resources*. Resolution approved at World Telecommunication Standardization Assembly, November 20–29, 2012, Dubai.

Internet World Statistics. (2004, Q4). World internet usage and population statistics. http://www.internetworldstats.com/stats.htm. Accessed August 23, 2014.

National Fraud Authority. (2013). Annual fraud indicator. https://www.gov.uk/government/uploads/system/uploads/attachment_data/file/206552/nfa-annual-fraud-indicator-2013.pdf. Accessed March 30, 2015.

SIPVicious. (2012). Blog. http://blog.sipvicious.org. Accessed January 29, 2015.

Telecommunications UK Fraud Forum. (2015). www.tuff.co.uk. About Us. Accessed April 10, 2015.

Transparency International. (2014). Corruption Perceptions Index 2013. https://www.transparency.org/cpi2013/results. Accessed June 22, 2014.

Wall, D. S. (2003). Mapping out cybercrimes in a cyberspatial surveillant assemblage. In F. Webster & K. Ball (Eds.), *The intensification of surveillance: Crime, terrorism, and warfare in the information age* (pp. 112–136). London: Pluto.

Wood, N. (2014). Telekom Austria migrates to VoIP. http://www.totaltele.com/view.aspx?ID=485461. Accessed June 6, 2014.

Targeting Factors that Predict Clearance of Non-domestic Assaults

Tom Olphin and Katrin Mueller-Johnson

Introduction

Whether it is due to the direct injury that is caused, the financial cost to society of the treatment of injuries and repair of damaged property, or the psychological impact of the incident, violent crime causes a dramatic amount of harm. In the UK, violent crime accounts for an estimated quarter of offences in volume and 58% of the total tangible costs of crime (Brand and Price 2000). Despite the suggestion that violent offenders are more likely to be described or identified, something that prior solvability research has shown to improve solvability, not all violent crimes are solved, with detection rates in the UK remaining at around 40% between 2008 and 2013 (Smith et al. 2013). Greenberg et al. (1977) found it difficult to identify solvability factors for violent offences, and there have been a few other solvability studies of non-fatal violent crimes. Although studies of many types of high-volume crime have been prevalent, few of these have examined large-enough samples to identify factors with low prevalence.

Targeting allows prioritisation of scarce resources, so it is important to consider whether investigative resources can be allocated through prediction of the outcome following the initial investigation into a violent crime. At the time of this research, West Midlands Police (WMP) screened crimes based on initial investigative evidence in relation to offender identity, forensic opportunities, CCTV, vehicle details, the availability of witnesses and other factors. WMP gathers a wealth of data in relation to solvability factors due to this screening, making it ideal for conducting research of this sort. Whilst these data are collected, and whilst screening crimes is likely to result in a more rational and systematic allocation of investigative resources, the WMP screening tool was based upon officer experience and intuition rather than analysis of solvability factors. This poses a risk that cases are incorrectly allocated

T. Olphin (✉) · K. Mueller-Johnson
Institute of Criminology, University of Cambridge, Cambridge, UK
e-mail: to288@cam.ac.uk

R. T. Coupe et al. (eds.), *Crime Solvability Factors*,
https://doi.org/10.1007/978-3-030-17160-5_9

or filed, which may waste resources or cause victims to be let down, whilst offenders escape justice.

Despite Meehl (1954) identifying that predictive formulae are frequently superior and seldom, if ever, inferior to human decision-makers, Sherman (2013) noted that, as of 2012, it was still difficult to find a police agency that used a statistical model of solvability to allocate investigative resources. We were also unable to find a direct comparison between a predictive allocation model and an experiential crime screening model such as those used by most policing agencies. Therefore, there is much to be gained from identifying solvability factors and building an algorithmic predictive model which can be compared to a real-world experiential model using a large data set. These authors therefore set about addressing this gap by identifying a police force with a well-documented experiential allocation tool from which a large sample of high-quality crime data could be recovered and analysed to determine solvability factors for non-domestic violent offences, which could then be used to build an algorithmic model to predict whether crimes would be solvable or not based upon the evidence gleaned during the initial investigation.

Previous Research into the Solvability of Violent Offences

Since Greenberg et al. (1977) found it difficult to identify solvability factors for violent offences, few studies have examined the solvability of non-lethal violent crime. However, Roberts (2008) used logistic regression to examine the effect of the incident and contextual characteristics on arrest rates for non-lethal violence and found that, for robbery and aggravated assault, incidents with multiple victims or with concomitant offences were more likely to be cleared. Consistent with other research, victim injury (D'Alessio and Stolzenberg 2003) and the offender being known (Eitle et al. 2005; Peterson et al. 2010) were also found to be associated with a higher likelihood of clearance. Eyewitness reports and victim or witness testimony also appear relevant to solvability (Baskin and Sommers 2012; Tilley et al. 2007). Offences that occurred in dwellings were found by Eitle et al. (2005) to be more likely to be solved, though this could be due to the higher likelihood of the offender(s) being known to the victim. There is some conflict over the benefit of forensic evidence in relation to the clearance of violent offences. Peterson et al. (2010, 2013) demonstrated clear links between the collection and analysis of physical evidence and arrest of suspects, whilst Baskin and Sommers (2012) found no such link.

Some factors have also previously been found to be more prevalent in unsolved cases of violent crime; use of a firearm in commission of the offence and time elapsed since the offences were factors found by Roberts (2008) to be contraindicative of solvability, whilst D'Alessio and Stolzenberg (2003) found that robbery and assault incidents were less likely to be solved when involving violence between strangers.

This research therefore sets out to expand our knowledge of solvability factors in relation to non-domestic violent crime through the use of a large data set taken from an agency whose crime data have been assessed as being of high quality, with crime classifications recorded correctly (Her Majesty's Inspectorate of Constabulary and Fire & Rescue Services [HMIC] 2012).

Methodology

Defining Clearance

As of April 2014, solved offences are now recorded by the Home Office as offences having definite positive outcomes; this includes all outcomes, both sanction and non-sanction, where the evidential standard required to charge an offender has been met, and is the current mechanism for recording crime clearance in the UK. The research described in this chapter uses positive crime outcome as the method for measuring clearance, as this provides the most accurate and complete outcome measure available.

Data Selection

Implementation of the Crime Service Team (CST) improved the quantity, quality and homogeneity of solvability data recorded by WMP. The CST was implemented throughout WMP by 27 February 2012; thus, 1 March 2012 was selected as the start point for data collection. A preliminary analysis of offences between January 2010 and May 2014 demonstrated that 99% of the violent offence investigations conducted during that period were finalised, by recording a closing categorisation, within 221 days. The outcome data were downloaded in September 2014, so data were downloaded for offences reported between 1 March 2012 and 31 December 2013 in order to allow for 221 days to have passed for all crimes in the data set.

All crimes with special interest markers for child abuse, vulnerable adult and domestic violence were removed due to their intra-familial nature, as it was felt that these crimes may differ inherently in terms of solvability. In addition, certain other offences were removed. Murder and manslaughter were removed because they differ from other violent crimes by having no living victim available, and they generally receive much greater investigative resourcing. Attempted murder of a victim under one-year-old was removed, as children are nearly always killed by someone known to them (Regoeczi et al. 2008). Driving-related violent offences and public order offences were removed to minimise offence heterogeneity, and conspiracy offences were removed as they may involve suspects who were not part of the original incident. Finally, all offences relating to arrest (such as the use of violence to escape arrest) and offences against public officials (such as assaults on police or prison officers) were removed, as these generally have much higher detection rates (Jansson 2005; Smith et al. 2013). Use of these dates and inclusion rules provided 29,105 cases for analysis.

Data Sources and Variables Identified

Data were retrieved from numerous electronic systems to provide information relating to the offence and report method, location and temporal data, details in relation to weapon use, modus operandi, outcome, forensic attendance and evidence recovery and details of all documents scanned during the investigation. Some of the data, such as location type, included vast lists of different responses, so dummy variables were created which were consistent with those used by other researchers (Litwin 2004; Puckett and Lundman 2003), such as whether the offence occurred in a private indoor location (Riedel and Boulahanis 2007).

In addition, WMP currently base case allocation on 14 factors identified through officer experience and intuition. Data for these 14 factors are recorded by CST staff by asking several questions of the initial attending officer. Suspect information is present if the officer is aware of any information relating to the identity of the offender. 'Witness outstanding' identifies cases where witnesses are known about who have not yet provided their evidence. Some crimes are recorded as mandatory for investigation (including, but not limited to, most serious violence and hate crimes). Where an offence relates to a critical incident, receives significant media attention or relates to community tension issues, this is recorded, along with incidents in which significant financial losses have been incurred or where the offence is high profile. Forensic evidence is identified in this measure by the presence of any evidence that the officer believes may be worthy of forensic recovery. The officer then records whether the offence is part of a series, whether the identifiable or flagged property has been taken, whether they are aware of any vehicle information and whether CCTV footage may be available (although not whether it has been viewed and shows the offence). If the case is already resolved, this is also recorded. However, the field for recording whether a crime was solved initially is overwritten whenever the crime is cleared and so cannot be used in this analysis. These CST questions make up the experiential model currently used by WMP to determine whether crimes should be allocated for investigation, and so were also included in the analysis.

Analytical Procedures

Cases were given unique reference numbers and were randomly split into two groups using a random sequence generator (random.org n.d.) in order to prevent overfitting of data once the predictive algorithm was built. One half ($n = 14{,}553$) was used to build the model, and the other half ($n = 14{,}552$) was used to test the accuracy of the model.

Potential factors were examined individually to begin with using independent samples t-tests or chi-square tests, as appropriate, to assess whether there was a difference in the prevalence of each factor between solved and unsolved cases. The effect size was assessed for each of the factors identified using the Campbell Collaboration effect size calculator, based on work by Lipsey and Wilson (2001), to assess each variable's individual impact on whether a case is solved.

To assess the degree to which case solvability can be predicted, all factors that were significant at the $p < 0.05$ level in the earlier bivariate tests, and any that were believed to be of tactical value, containing information not covered by other factors, were then examined for inter-variable correlation. For variable combinations with Pearson's r value exceeding 0.9, one of the variables was removed to avoid multicollinearity errors before the remaining variables were included in logistic regression, using whether the case was cleared or not as the dichotomous dependent variable. The output of the logistic regression was then used to design a statistically weighted predictive model, which was applied to the second half of the data to establish its predictive accuracy, and this was then compared to the accuracy of the experiential solvability model in use by WMP at the time.

Findings

Factors Included in the WMP Experiential Model

The 14 factors composing the experiential model used by WMP to predict solvability were examined in bivariate analyses, the results of which are shown in Fig. 1. Despite the mean number of WMP model variables present being significantly higher in cleared cases ($t[13{,}721.782] = 16.746, p < 0.001$), only suspect information, officer-identified forensic opportunities and the offence being part of a series were significant positive predictors of solvability when examined in bivariate analyses.

Cases with outstanding witnesses (witnesses that have been identified but not yet interviewed) or additional officer-defined factors (evidence that is not included in other parts of the experiential model, but that the officer feels makes the case solvable) did not differ significantly in prevalence between cleared and uncleared cases. This is surprising, as they would appear on the surface to offer additional evidence. However, it is possible that many of these witnesses or pieces of additional evidence do not actually aid investigations and therefore could be misleading. The classification of the incident as mandatory to investigate, critical, of media interest or high profile, or its association with community tension or high financial impact, has no relation with solvability. However, these variables will be included in multivariate models as they reduce reputational risk and limit the potential damage to public confidence that could arise from crimes with these characteristics not being investigated.

Three factors were more prevalent in uncleared cases than cleared ones: the potential for CCTV footage, property taken in the offence being flagged or marked in some way and recorded vehicle registration mark (VRM) details being available. The mechanisms by which these are associated more with uncleared cases than cleared ones are not entirely understood. However, the negative impact of the flagged or marked property being taken in the offence could reflect an effect of concomitant theft-related

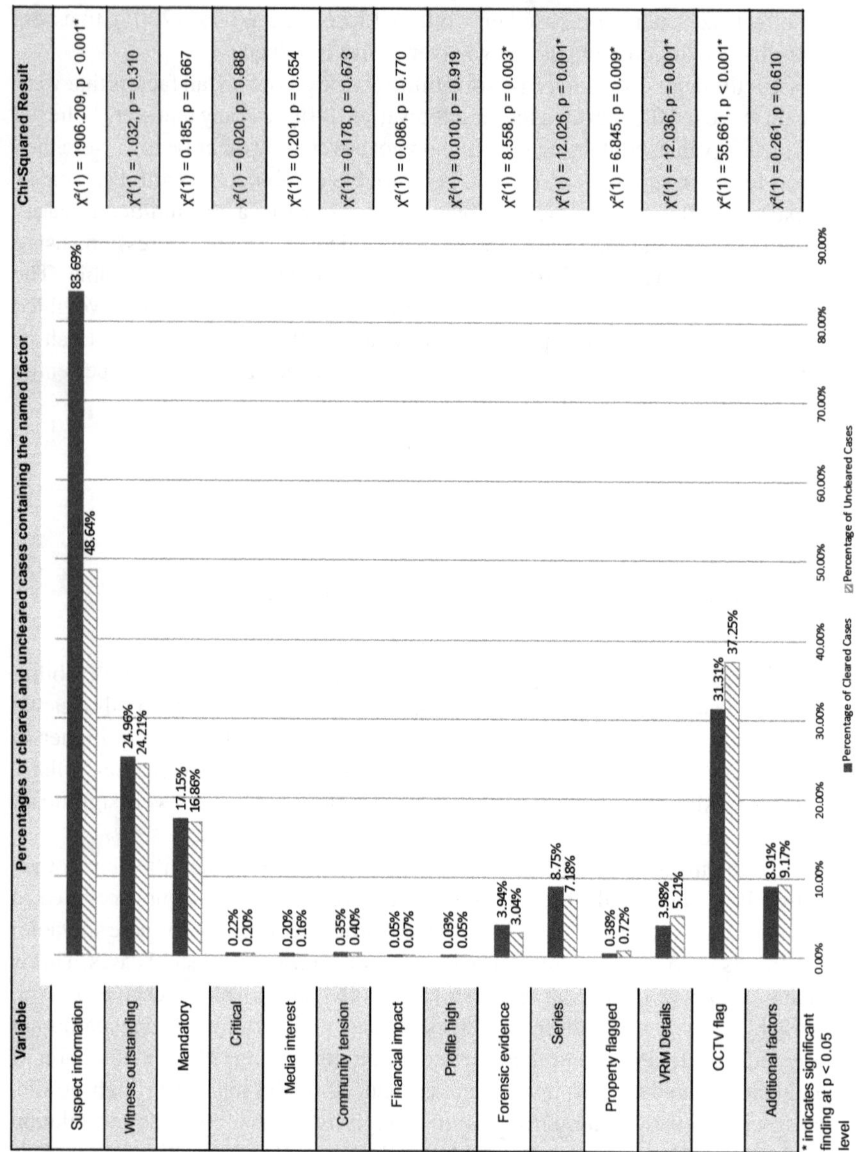

Fig. 1 Results of chi-square tests for prevalence of WMP-identified variables for cleared and uncleared cases

offences, and the negative finding in relation to the presence of VRM information could indicate that, when this information is collected, it is not accurate enough to increase the odds of solving a crime. The presence of CCTV is understandably suggested as a solvability factor by WMP and has been demonstrated to be so by other researchers (Robb et al. 2015). However, in this research, it shows a greater prevalence in uncleared cases.

As it was improbable that adding CCTV evidence to an investigation would reduce the likelihood of solving the crime, this variable was examined more closely. Inspection revealed that the variable was actually measuring whether the officer thinks there might be CCTV. This would therefore include many different outcomes, ranging from CCTV that the officer has seen and that clearly shows the offender committing the crime, to no CCTV being present despite the officer having thought there might be. Therefore, it is recommended that more accurate measures of the presence of CCTV are created to facilitate its use in the prediction of solvability. The mean of total WMP-model solvability variables present was significantly higher for cleared than for uncleared cases ($t[13{,}721.782] = 16.746, p < 0.001$): *n* compared with only n for uncleared cases.

Identification of Other Solvability Factors

Forty-four other factors were examined by means of chi-square tests to determine their prevalence in cleared and uncleared cases. These are presented in Figs. 2 and 3. Figure 2 includes the offence code (common assault, assault occasioning actual bodily harm, wounding, assault occasioning grievous bodily harm (GBH) without intent, assault occasioning grievous bodily harm with intent and attempted murder), whether there is a relationship or link between the victim and the offender, whether injuries are visible, a hate crime marker, whether a weapon was used (knife, lethal firearm, opportunistic weapons such as a rock, non-lethal or imitation firearm, blunt instrument, vehicle or other) and what the weapon was used for (injury or damage, threat, carried but not used or use not recorded).

Figure 3 includes the type of location in which the offence occurred (private indoor, private outdoor, public indoor or public outdoor), whether the offence occurred on licensed premises or in a dwelling, the method of reporting (police station front office, contact centre or patrol), whether the time between the conclusion of the offence and the crime being reported was less than 5 min and whether the duration of the offence was under 15 min.

Offences that occurred in daylight were identified by working out the sunrise and sunset times for every offence date using the US Naval Observatory ([USNO] 2014) Sun or Moon Rise/Set Table with the coordinates 52° 29′N, 1° 54′W. The days between the first and last offence committed were calculated, and cases where this exceeded one were counted as not definitely daylight as offence time is unknown. The remainder were compared to the USNO (2014) table using the offence start time as the comparison.

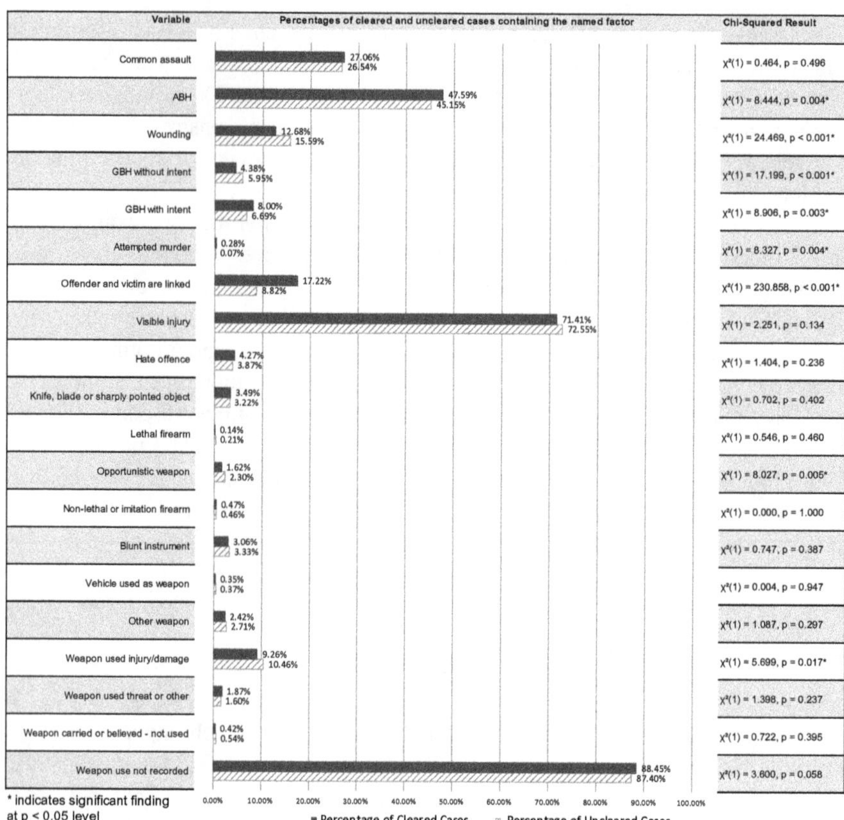

Fig. 2 Results of chi-square tests for prevalence of variables relating to offence type, victim–offender link, injury, weapon type and weapon usage in cleared and uncleared cases

Different markers are present on WMP systems, so the next two items examined were the presence of the 'alcohol involved' and 'drugs involved' markers. These are added to the crime report if the officer believes that the commission of the crime involved alcohol or drugs, either as a result of an inebriated person being involved in the offence, or due to the suspicion that a theft was motivated by the desire to purchase drugs, or that an assault relates to the enforcement of a drugs debt. Whether a forensic scene investigator (FSI) attended or retrieved something evidential are the next variables, shown in Fig. 3. Finally, the system that stores paper copies of evidence completed and scanned in by officers was examined: MG11 s are witness statements, so it was examined whether there were zero, just one or more than one scanned onto the system; PROP describes forms produced by the property system whenever items have been seized and booked into evidence; SOCO is used if officers scan in reports produced by forensic officers; DRAW denotes photographs and drawings scanned onto the system; MISC denotes miscellaneous papers, and SUSP denotes forms on

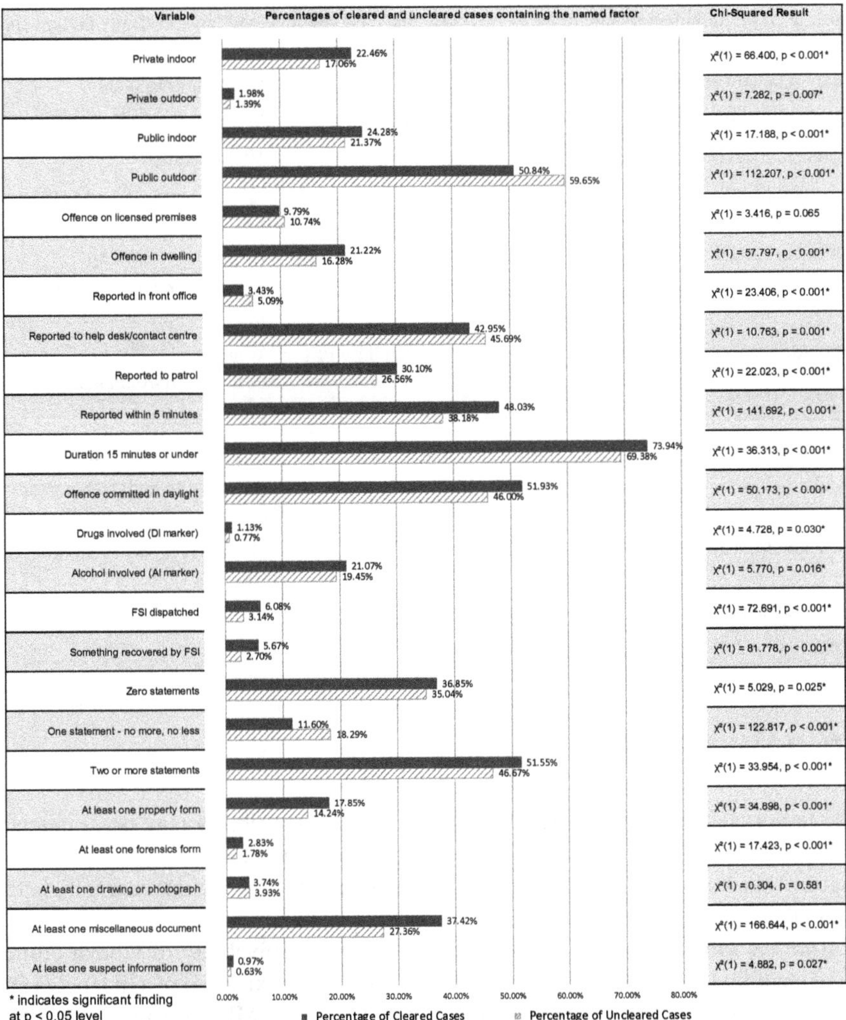

Fig. 3 Results of chi-square tests for prevalence of variables relating to offence location, reporting of offences, offence timings, special interest markers, forensic evidence and paperwork items in cleared and uncleared cases

which the description of an unknown suspect is noted down. Table 1 breaks all of the factors included in Figs. 1, 2 and 3 into solvability factors (factors more prevalent in cleared cases) and case-limiting factors (those more prevalent in uncleared cases).

Table 1 Individual factors identified by bivariate analysis broken down into solvability factors and case-limiting factors

Individual solvability factors		Case-limiting factors
Suspect information	Duration ≤15 min	Property flagged
Forensic evidence	Offence committed in daylight	VRM details
Series	Drugs involved marker	CCTV flag
Offence—ABH	Alcohol involved marker	Offence—wounding
Offence—GBH with intent	FSI dispatched	Offence—GBH without intent
Offender and victim are linked	Something recovered by FSI	Weapon used—injury/damage
Private indoor	Zero MG11s	Public outdoor
Private outdoor	Two or more MG11s	Reported in front office
Public indoor	At least one PROP	Reported to helpdesk/contact centre
Offence in dwelling	At least one SOCO	One MG11—no more, no less
Reported to patrol	At least one MISC	
Reported within 5 min	At least one SUSP	

Effect Size Analysis

The importance of different variables in determining solvability may be examined by the statistical strength of their relationship with cleared and uncleared offences. Figure 4 shows the statistical effect size of variables examined in this research, both in tabular format and as a forest plot.

The five most important factors in determining the solvability of violent crime were identified as: possession of suspect information, the existence of a link between suspect and victim, the presence of at least one item in the MISC documents folder, the offence having been reported within 5 min of its occurrence and the retrieval of forensic evidence. Many other factors play a smaller, yet not insignificant, part in determining whether violent crimes are cleared.

Cases Without Suspect Information

Previous research has shown suspect information to be the strongest indicator of solvability by far. There is a risk, though, that the effects of weaker factors are not seen when suspect information is present. Therefore, the above analysis was repeated, but only for cases where no suspect information was available. When these cases

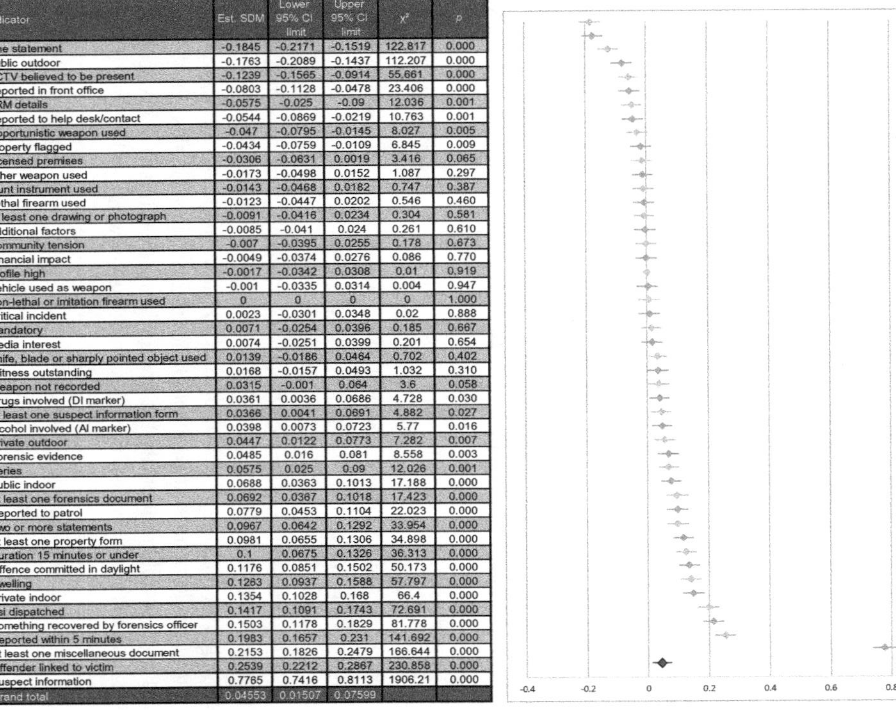

Indicator	Est. SDM	Lower 95% CI limit	Upper 95% CI limit	X^2	p
One statement	-0.1845	-0.2171	-0.1519	122.817	0.000
Public outdoor	-0.1763	-0.2089	-0.1437	112.207	0.000
CCTV believed to be present	-0.1239	-0.1565	-0.0914	55.661	0.000
Reported in front office	-0.0803	-0.1128	-0.0478	23.406	0.000
VRM details	-0.0575	-0.025	-0.09	12.036	0.001
Reported to help desk/contact	-0.0544	-0.0869	-0.0219	10.763	0.001
Opportunistic weapon used	-0.047	-0.0795	-0.0145	8.027	0.005
Property flagged	-0.0434	-0.0759	-0.0109	6.845	0.009
Licensed premises	-0.0306	-0.0631	0.0019	3.416	0.065
Other weapon used	-0.0173	-0.0498	0.0152	1.087	0.297
Blunt instrument used	-0.0143	-0.0468	0.0182	0.747	0.387
Lethal firearm used	-0.0123	-0.0447	0.0202	0.546	0.460
At least one drawing or photograph	-0.0091	-0.0416	0.0234	0.304	0.581
Additional factors	-0.0085	-0.041	0.024	0.261	0.610
Community tension	-0.007	-0.0395	0.0255	0.178	0.673
Financial impact	-0.0049	-0.0374	0.0276	0.086	0.770
Profile high	-0.0017	-0.0342	0.0308	0.01	0.919
Vehicle used as weapon	-0.001	-0.0335	0.0314	0.004	0.947
Non-lethal or imitation firearm used	0	0	0	0	1.000
Critical incident	0.0023	-0.0301	0.0348	0.02	0.888
Mandatory	0.0071	-0.0254	0.0396	0.185	0.667
Media interest	0.0074	-0.0251	0.0399	0.201	0.654
Knife, blade or sharply pointed object used	0.0139	-0.0186	0.0464	0.702	0.402
Witness outstanding	0.0168	-0.0157	0.0493	1.032	0.310
Weapon not recorded	0.0315	-0.001	0.064	3.6	0.058
Drugs involved (DI marker)	0.0361	0.0036	0.0686	4.728	0.030
At least one suspect information form	0.0366	0.0041	0.0691	4.882	0.027
Alcohol involved (AI marker)	0.0398	0.0073	0.0723	5.77	0.016
Private outdoor	0.0447	0.0122	0.0773	7.282	0.007
Forensic evidence	0.0485	0.016	0.081	8.558	0.003
Series	0.0575	0.025	0.09	12.026	0.001
Public indoor	0.0688	0.0363	0.1013	17.188	0.000
At least one forensics document	0.0692	0.0367	0.1018	17.423	0.000
Reported to patrol	0.0779	0.0453	0.1104	22.023	0.000
Two or more statements	0.0967	0.0642	0.1292	33.954	0.000
At least one property form	0.0981	0.0655	0.1306	34.898	0.000
Duration 15 minutes or under	0.1	0.0675	0.1326	36.313	0.000
Offence committed in daylight	0.1176	0.0851	0.1502	50.173	0.000
Dwelling	0.1263	0.0937	0.1588	57.797	0.000
Private indoor	0.1354	0.1028	0.168	66.4	0.000
Fsi dispatched	0.1417	0.1091	0.1743	72.691	0.000
Something recovered by forensics officer	0.1503	0.1178	0.1829	81.778	0.000
Reported within 5 minutes	0.1983	0.1657	0.231	141.692	0.000
At least one miscellaneous document	0.2153	0.1826	0.2479	166.644	0.000
Offender linked to victim	0.2539	0.2212	0.2867	230.858	0.000
Suspect information	0.7765	0.7416	0.8113	1906.21	0.000
Grand total	0.04553	0.01507	0.07599		

Fig. 4 Effect size of individual solvability factors

were examined, two factors emerged that appeared to affect clearance rates. Once cases with suspect information were removed from the sample, the presence of VRM information was more prevalent in cleared cases than uncleared ones ($\chi^2(1) = 13.989$, $p < 0.001$), a finding that contradicts the results for all cases (as shown in Fig. 1, the previous finding was that VRM information was more prevalent in uncleared cases than in cleared ones: $\chi^2(1) = 12.036$, $p < 0.05$). In the same way, the availability of other information, as identified by officers, also becomes more prevalent in cleared cases than uncleared ones. Whilst this finding is not significant ($\chi^2(1) = 2.462$, $p < 0.117$), the change of direction appears worthy of acknowledgement. The change in prevalence of these two variables does indicate that there may be other variables which, despite being relevant, were not available to this research and would not be found without an in-depth review of all information contained in free-text or paper records.

Multivariate Analysis and Predictive Modelling

As indicated above, it is crucial to take account of the interactions between variables when examining solvability. Because some factors may alter in importance based on the presence of other factors, a logistic regression analysis was conducted to identify the statistical impact of each factor, and to design a predictive algorithm which could be used as a tool to predict solvability in future cases. To control for multicollinearity, all variables were compared to all other variables using the Pearson correlation tests. 'Private indoor location' and 'offence occurring in a dwelling' were strongly positively correlated ($r(14{,}553) = 0.968$, $p < 0.001$), and 'FSI dispatched' and 'something recovered by FSI' were also strongly positively correlated ($r(14{,}553) = 0.949$, $p < 0.001$). As 'private indoor location' encompasses more than 'dwelling' does, and 'FSI dispatched' can be manually altered by policy or situational decisions, the variables for 'offence occurring in a dwelling' and 'FSI dispatched' were not included in the logistic regression. The presence of SOCO paperwork was also removed as such information should be identified through other forensic variables. Furthermore, because it was not possible to identify the precise nature of those papers scanned as miscellaneous, and as future process changes could unknowingly alter this, affecting the model, the presence of miscellaneous papers was removed to avoid the potential for it to become misleading once a model is built and implemented. A decision was made to include three factors that were not significant in the individual analyses: 'offence occurring in licensed premises', due to it nearing significance; 'availability of additional factors', as it showed an interesting relationship with suspect information; and a measure of outstanding witnesses, as this is otherwise unavailable to the model. The variables included in the model are shown in Table 2.

The logistic regression model was statistically significant ($\chi^2(26) = 2539.100$, $p < 0.001$). The model explained 21.5% (Nagelkerke's R^2) of the variance in clearance and correctly classified 66.9% of cases. Sensitivity (true positives) was 69.0%, specificity (true negatives) was 65.3%, positive predictive value was 60.7% and negative

Table 2 Variables included in the logistic regression analysis

Variable	Description
PrivateIn	Offence location private indoor
PrivateOut	Offence location private outdoor
PublicIn	Offence location public indoor
RepPatrol	Offence reported to patrol
ForensicsRec	Forensic items recovered
WMPSusInfo	WMP suspect information
WMPWitOut	WMP witness outstanding
WMPForensic	WMP forensic
WMPSeries	WMP series
WMPVRM	WMP VRM information
WMPCCTV	WMP CCTV flag
WMPAddFact	WMP additional factors
TwoMG11	Two or more statements
OnePROP	One or more property forms
OffLink	Offender linked to victim
Dur15Min	Duration under 15 min
DIMarker	Drugs involved marker
AIMarker	Alcohol involved marker
Rep0to5 m	Reported in under 5 min
Daylight	Offence occurred in daylight
PublicOut	Offence location public outdoor
Licensed	Offence on licensed premises
RepFO	Reported in front office
RepHDCC	Reported to help desk/contact centre
OppWeap	Opportunistic weapon used
JustOneMG11	Just one statement

predictive value was 73.1%. Of the 26 predictor variables, 17 emerged as statistically significant. All factors are detailed in Table 3.

Cases with suspect information were more than five times likelier to be solved than cases without, and the likelihood of solving cases with forensic evidence was 2.52 times higher than for those without. Offences that occurred in public indoor locations, were reported to patrol, were part of a series, had additional factors available, had at least one property sheet scanned, where the victim was linked to the offender, lasted less than 15 min, had an alcohol involved marker, were reported within 5 min of the end of the offence or occurred in daylight were significantly more likely to be cleared than those without. Cases where officers believed there might be CCTV, where statements were scanned onto CrimeScan, that occurred on licensed premises,

Table 3 Results of the logistic regression analysis

Variable	B	S.E.	Wald	*df*	*p*	Odds ratio	95% C.I. for EXP(B)	
							Lower	Upper
Offence location private indoor	0.219	0.264	0.689	1	0.406	1.245	0.742	2.087
Offence location private outdoor	0.482	0.296	2.651	1	0.103	1.620	0.906	2.894
Offence location public indoor	0.614	0.266	5.347	1	0.021	1.848	1.098	3.110
Offence reported to patrol	0.136	0.051	6.983	1	0.008	1.145	1.036	1.266
Forensic items recovered	0.923	0.101	83.512	1	0.000	2.516	2.064	3.067
WMP suspect information	1.655	0.043	1471.640	1	0.000	5.231	4.807	5.692
WMP witness outstanding	−0.005	0.044	0.013	1	0.908	0.995	0.913	1.084
WMP forensic	−0.124	0.105	1.398	1	0.237	0.883	0.719	1.085
WMP series	0.179	0.068	7.036	1	0.008	1.196	1.048	1.366
WMP VRM information	0.055	0.091	0.365	1	0.546	1.057	0.883	1.264
WMP CCTV flag	−0.118	0.044	7.276	1	0.007	0.889	0.815	0.968
WMP additional factors	0.139	0.065	4.631	1	0.031	1.149	1.012	1.304
Two or more statements	−0.141	0.044	10.376	1	0.001	0.869	0.797	0.946
One or more property forms	0.255	0.054	21.997	1	0.000	1.290	1.160	1.435
Offender linked to victim	0.338	0.056	36.368	1	0.000	1.403	1.257	1.566

(continued)

Table 3 (continued)

Variable	B	S.E.	Wald	*df*	*p*	Odds ratio	95% C.I. for EXP(B)	
							Lower	Upper
Duration under 15 min	0.225	0.041	30.018	1	0.000	1.253	1.156	1.358
Drugs involved marker	0.232	0.191	1.471	1	0.225	1.261	0.867	1.833
Alcohol involved marker	0.140	0.050	7.679	1	0.006	1.150	1.042	1.270
Reported in under 5 min	0.325	0.038	73.868	1	0.000	1.384	1.285	1.490
Offence occurred in daylight	0.196	0.039	24.864	1	0.000	1.217	1.127	1.315
Offence location public outdoor	0.261	0.262	0.996	1	0.318	1.298	0.777	2.169
Offence on licensed premises	−0.235	0.082	8.285	1	0.004	0.791	0.674	0.928
Reported in front office	−0.164	0.099	2.739	1	0.098	0.848	0.698	1.031
Reported to help desk/contact centre	−0.073	0.047	2.445	1	0.118	0.929	0.847	1.019
Opportunistic weapon used	−0.409	0.139	8.707	1	0.003	0.664	0.506	0.872
Just one statement	−0.562	0.058	93.104	1	0.000	0.570	0.509	0.639
Constant	−2.060	0.269	58.603	1	0.000	0.127		

involved an opportunistic weapon, or had only one statement scanned were associated with lower odds of being solved.

The predictive formula was created using the base of $\text{logit}(p) = b0 + b1X1 + b2X2 + b3X3 + bkXk$ (Medcalc Software 2014a), and the resultant formula can be seen in Eq. 1 below. Where any of the variables are present in the data set, they are coded as one and, where not present, as zero.

Predictive Formula

$$
\begin{aligned}
\text{Predictive Model Logit}(p) &= -2.06012231166749 \\
&+ (\text{Private Indoor} \times 0.21896234166784) \\
&+ (\text{Private Outdoor} \times 0.482221853049798) \\
&+ (\text{Public Indoor} \times 0.614168153975186) \\
&+ (\text{Reported to Patrol} \times 0.135507823875585) \\
&+ (\text{Something Recovered by FSI} \times 0.922678539797806) \\
&+ (\text{Suspect Information} \times 1.65451761371856) \\
&- (\text{Witness Outstanding} \times 0.00509247368812278) \\
&- (\text{Forensic Evidence} \times 0.124114369542983) \\
&+ (\text{Series} \times 0.179382232899131) \\
&+ (\text{VRM Details} \times 0.0552156712817925) \\
&- (C\text{CTV Flag} \times 0.118196466193996) \\
&+ (\text{Additional Factors} \times 0.13909164461101) \\
&- (\text{Two or More Statements} \times 0.140966342491925) \\
&+ (\text{At least one Property Form} \times 0.254753361095196) \\
&+ (\text{Duration 15 minutes or under} \times 0.225334514108994) \\
&+ (\text{Drugs Involved Marker} \times 0.23158147033591) \\
&+ (\text{Alcohol Involved Marker} \times 0.139861549604373) \\
&+ (\text{Reported within 5 minutes} \times 0.324619578460559) \\
&+ (\text{Offender Link to Victim} \times 0.338284590056064) \\
&+ (\text{Daylight Offence} \times 0.196372030404582) \\
&+ (\text{Public Outdoor} \times 0.261198299233381) \\
&- (\text{Licensed Premises} \times 0.234972861437699) \\
&- (\text{Reported in Front Office} \times 0.164408083792076) \\
&- (\text{Reported to Help Desk or Contact Centre} \times 0.0734407903273885) \\
&- (\text{Opportunistic Weapon Used in Offence} \times 0.409479586358932) \\
&- (\text{One Statement Exactly} \times 0.561505039063743) \qquad (1)
\end{aligned}
$$

The basic result from the logistic regression uses a cut-off point of 0.5 for determining accuracy. However, this balances the errors equally between incorrect allocation and incorrect filing, which may lead to victims of solvable crimes being let down. Eck (1979) noted that the balance between resource usage and detection levels can be altered by moving the cut-point in a weighted model. To give political weight to any model, the number of solvable crimes that are filed must be minimised, whilst balancing these against the number of incorrectly allocated crimes, as including fewer of these may mean that more crimes can be solved overall. To select an appropriate cut-off point, error rates were calculated for a range of cut-off scores; these are displayed in Table 4.

$P = 0.39$ was determined as being the most appropriate significance level to minimise the number of incorrectly filed reports (victims who are let down) whilst still reducing resource wastage through incorrect allocation.

The model outlined in Eq. 1 was compared to the logit(p) value for $p = 0.39$ using a logit transformation table (Medcalc Software 2014b). Logit(p) for $p = 0.39$ is -0.4473. Therefore, all cases with a logit(p) value exceeding -0.4473 are screened in. This calculation makes up the main part of the model. In addition to the calculation, a number of additional screen-in factors were incorporated in order to take into account of both the seriousness of the offence and the type of offence to avoid causing serious damage to force reputation or public confidence by failing to investigate certain crimes. These factors are set out in Table 5, and all assessments of model accuracy include all offences that are screened in, regardless of whether they were included by the model or as a result of the automatic screen-in criteria.

Accuracy of Screening Models

Using a graphical representation adapted from Eck (1979) (Fig. 5), the predictive accuracy of the current WMP allocation model (Fig. 6) and of the new statistical model produced through this research (Fig. 7) is presented below.

The overall accuracy of the model is then calculated using the following formula:

$$\text{Accuracy}(\%) = (\text{Correct Prediction} + \text{Correct Prediction})/\text{Total Cases} \times 100$$

Figure 6 shows the percentages (and numbers) of cases that are correctly and incorrectly predicted by the current WMP model. Due to the existence of 1296

Fig. 5 Model accuracy. Adapted from Eck (1979)

		Real case outcome	
		Case cleared	Case not cleared
Model-predicted case outcome	Case cleared	Correct Prediction	Wasted Investigation
	Case not cleared	Lost Clearance	Correct Prediction

Table 4 Comparison of screen-out values for logistic regression

Screen-out criteria—logistic regression *p*-value	Correctly allocated	Incorrectly allocated	Incorrectly filed	Correctly filed	% Correctly allocated	% Correctly filed	% Overall correct
Lower than 0.10	6345	8006	18	184	99.72	2.25	44.86
Lower than 0.20	5958	5590	405	2600	93.64	31.75	58.81
Lower than 0.30	5488	4170	875	4020	86.25	49.08	65.33
Lower than 0.31	5466	4136	897	4054	85.90	49.50	65.42
Lower than 0.32	5428	4097	935	4093	85.31	49.98	65.42
Lower than 0.33	5419	4072	944	4118	85.16	50.28	65.53
Lower than 0.34	5398	4030	965	4160	84.83	50.79	65.68
Lower than 0.35	5374	4004	989	4186	84.46	51.11	65.69
Lower than 0.36	5351	3961	1012	4229	84.10	51.64	65.83
Lower than 0.37	5318	3911	1045	4279	83.58	52.25	65.95
Lower than 0.38	5294	3874	1069	4316	83.20	52.70	66.03
Lower than 0.39	5250	3823	1113	4367	82.51	53.32	66.08
Lower than 0.40	5210	3779	1153	4411	81.88	53.86	66.11
Lower than 0.41	5185	3729	1178	4461	81.49	54.47	66.28
Lower than 0.42	5109	3644	1254	4546	80.29	55.51	66.34
Lower than 0.43	5060	3591	1303	4599	79.52	56.15	66.37

(continued)

Table 4 (continued)

Screen-out criteria—logistic regression p-value	Correctly allocated	Incorrectly allocated	Incorrectly filed	Correctly filed	% Correctly allocated	% Correctly filed	% Overall correct
Lower than 0.44	5009	3522	1354	4668	78.72	57.00	66.49
Lower than 0.45	4926	3436	1437	4754	77.42	58.05	66.52
Lower than 0.46	4841	3356	1522	4834	76.08	59.02	66.48
Lower than 0.47	4738	3213	1625	4977	74.46	60.77	66.76
Lower than 0.48	4698	3149	1665	5041	73.83	61.55	66.92
Lower than 0.49	4552	2989	1811	5201	71.54	63.50	67.02
Lower than 0.50	4392	2841	1971	5349	69.02	65.31	66.93
Lower than 0.60	2381	1282	3982	6908	37.42	84.35	63.83
Lower than 0.70	586	258	5777	7932	9.21	96.85	58.53
Lower than 0.80	101	25	6262	8165	1.59	99.69	56.80
Lower than 0.90	3	0	6360	8190	0.05	100.00	56.30

Table 5 Automatic screen-in criteria

Screen-in category	Description of specific screen-in factor	Rationale
Incident type	Hate crime	These are offence types that may cause severe reputational damage if investigation does not occur
	Media interest	
	Community tension	
	Critical incident	
	High-profile offence	
Case is resolved	Case is already resolved and has been cleared	Case is already solved
Allocated by logit model	Case is allocated based on its score on the solvability equation	Case is deemed by the equation to be solvable
Offence severity	GBH without intent (or attempt)	These are offences where serious injury has been caused or intended
	GBH with intent (or attempt)	
	Attempt murder	
Overwhelming evidence	It has not been possible to create these yet but examples would be; CCTV which is clear shows the offender and the offence taking place or offence witnessed by a police officer	These are pieces of evidence where officers can identify that there is sufficient evidence, even if in evidential areas that the model would usually determine to be weak, to permit a prosecution

Fig. 6 Model accuracy of WMP current experiential model

		Real case outcome	
		Case cleared	Case not cleared
Model-predicted case outcome	Case cleared	100% (6,334)	84% (6,922)
	Case not cleared	0% (0)	16% (1,296)
Total accuracy = 6,334 + 1,296 ÷ 14,552 × 100 = 52.4%			

Fig. 7 Model accuracy of new statistical model

		Real case outcome	
		Case cleared	Case not cleared
Model-predicted case outcome	Case cleared	93% (5,864)	58% (4,761)
	Case not cleared	7% (470)	42% (3,457)
Total accuracy = 5,864 + 3,457 ÷ 14,552 × 100 = 64.1%			

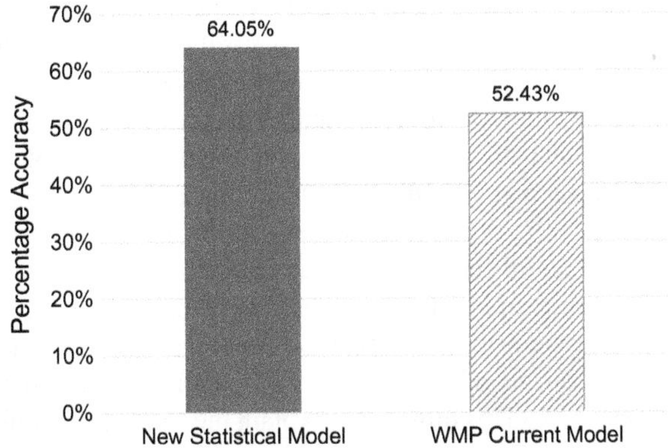

Fig. 8 Difference in model accuracy

unallocated cases, the actual error rate for cases incorrectly filed may not be zero, as some of these cases may in fact be solvable. The current WMP model correctly predicted 7630 out of 14,552 cases, giving the model an overall accuracy of 52.43%.

Figure 7 shows the percentages (and numbers) of cases correctly and incorrectly predicted by the statistical model designed through this research. The weighted statistical model correctly predicted 9321 out of 14,552 cases, giving the model an overall accuracy of 64.05%. As it was impossible to identify cases solved during the initial investigation, it is possible that, upon implementation, this accuracy would improve, since some incorrectly filed cases may be allocated by virtue of them having already been solved.

Predictive accuracy is increased by 22.16% through the use of the statistical model produced by this research. This is shown graphically in Fig. 8 and equates to an additional 1691 crimes being accurately predicted. This increase in accuracy would see WMP saving valuable resources by identifying thousands of unsolvable crimes per year without expending resources only to find that they were not solvable. This would facilitate either an increase in service level for crimes that are allocated, which may improve overall clearance rates or financial savings due to requiring fewer investigators to maintain current levels of service. These authors would hope that resource levels would be retained at current levels, resulting in a better level of service for victims of violent crime across the West Midlands.

Discussion

Despite previous researchers (Greenwood et al. 1975) having struggled to identify solvability factors for violent crime, this study identified 38 factors associated with the clearance of violent crimes, whether as positive (solvability) factors or as negative (case-limiting) factors. This study has also developed previous research by using both bivariate analyses of individual factors and logistic regression to identify factors using a large randomized sample of 14,553 cases and has advanced solvability research by building a predictive model which was then tested against current screening protocols on the other half ($n = 14{,}552$) of the data set.

Twenty-five positive solvability factors were identified using bivariate analyses. As in much previous research on a wide variety of crime types (Burrows et al. 2005; Coupe and Griffiths 1996; Coupe and Kaur 2005; Eck 1979; Eitle et al. 2005; Newiss 2002; Stevens and Stipak 1982), suspect information emerges as by far the most powerful individual predictor of solvability. Given the importance of suspect information and earlier findings that witness evidence is key (Baskin and Sommers 2012), it is unsurprising that the presence of two or more statements scanned onto CrimeScan and of a known link between the victim and offender were both indicative of clearance. This might also explain the finding that offences committed in daylight were more likely to be cleared, consistent with the findings of Coupe and Blake (2006). As with other research (Bond 2007, 2009; Coupe and Griffiths 1996; Paine 2012), measures of forensic evidence—forensic investigator dispatched, forensic evidence recovered, officer-identified forensic opportunities and at least one forensic form scanned—were more prevalent in solved cases. The fact that forensic evidence is not a particularly prevalent factor, yet is a strong predictor of solvability, suggests that other studies that have disputed the value of forensic evidence (Burrows et al. 2005) may have suffered from low statistical power. Many of the solvability factors relate to offence timing, with short offence durations (under 15 min), short delays before reporting (less than 5 min) and rapid reporting methods (to patrol) being consistent with other findings (Bieck and Kessler 1977; Spelman and Brown 1981). Lower aoristic risk may act as a possible proxy for faster response times due to lower demand (Blake and Coupe 2001; Clawson and Chang 1977).

Other factors identified as indicative of solvability included information about the location (private indoor location, dwelling, public indoor location or private outdoor location); whether the offence was part of a series; whether alcohol or drugs were involved; crimes that were more serious (GBH with intent, attempted murder); property, suspect or miscellaneous forms scanned onto police systems; and controlling for other factors, the presence of additional officer-identified factors.

Thirteen case-limiting factors were also identified by means of bivariate analyses: only one statement, public outdoor offence location, officer-identified potential for CCTV, reported in front office, reported to help desk or control centre, opportunistic weapon used, ABH, minor wounding, GBH without intent, flagged property, offence on licensed premises, weapon used to cause injury and officer-identified VRM information—though the last item changes to a positive factor if suspect information is controlled for. This study therefore demonstrates that there are differences between solvability factors with and without suspect information. A change of direction for some variables once suspect information is removed indicates that it is possible for weaker variables to be overshadowed; therefore, previous researchers may have missed variables that would otherwise have been found to be relevant. In addition, previous research that has stopped after the stage of identifying factors through bivariate analysis may have provided an incomplete picture when attempting to create tools that policing agencies could use for crime-screening purposes. That more serious assaults enhance, and less serious ones depress, detections may reflect the greater investigative effort applied to the former.

At the time of this research, WMP allocated crime for secondary investigation mandatorily if the offence related to a critical incident, had received significant media attention, involved community tension issues, was a high-profile offence or involved significant financial impact. Notably, none of these factors differs in prevalence between solved and unsolved cases. It is therefore worth considering whether it would be a better use of resources to investigate cases based on algorithmic assessment of their solvability, whilst safeguarding victims in cases involving vulnerability, as this may have a greater impact on the continued safety of those victims.

Most of the factors identified through bivariate analyses were examined further using logistic regression analysis, which was then reverse-engineered to create a predictive algorithm. Various cut-off points above which cases are screened in for investigation were assessed to ensure that the model screened in as many solved cases as possible, as the political ramifications of the public feeling that police will not investigate reported crime could be severe (Gill et al. 1996). The model therefore incorporated a selection of automatic inclusion criteria, and—despite these criteria making the model less accurate in terms of prediction—when tested on the second randomly selected 14,552 cases, it correctly predicted the outcome in 64.05% of cases. This was then directly compared to the accuracy of the current screening method, which is based upon an assessment of the important criteria by experts and correctly predicts the outcome in only 52.43% of cases.

The data used in this research provided for an extremely large-scale, powerful analysis, which facilitated the discovery of factors that are less prevalent and may not have shown up in previous research. However, it does not allow for the identification of non-electronically recorded variables. It was therefore not possible to break down certain variables, such as suspect information, to examine whether different levels of description would provide differential links to clearance. This, along with a lack of accessible electronically recorded data in some areas, also resulted in some variables—such as whether there were concomitant offences, which has been demonstrated to be relevant in other research (Roberts 2008)—not being usable for this research.

It may be possible to identify other factors that could improve the model's accuracy if a mechanism for coding free-text and paper-based records can be established. This might also improve our understanding of the mechanisms by which factors link to solvability and may allow a glimpse into areas such as intelligence reports and the importance of proactive tactics, so is an area for development in future work.

Whilst limited by the factors detailed above, this research conducted the largest-scale examination of solvability factors to date. The use of a massive data set has enabled many disparate solvability factors and case-limiting factors to be identified as relevant to the non-domestic violent crime, an area in which others have struggled to identify solvability factors. Using these factors, this research has combined traditional techniques with novel examinations of information to produce a predictive model that has been demonstrated to be capable of increasing the accuracy of allocation for WMP by just over 22%.

Conclusions

This research demonstrates that Meehl's (1954) assertion that algorithmic models often outstrip, and seldom if ever underperform when compared to, expert judgement or experiential models also applies to policing and the prediction of whether crimes can be solved. This research designed an algorithmic alternative to an experiential case-screening model in current use and tested it directly against the existing experiential model on a novel data set. The algorithmic model improved the accuracy of prediction by over 22% over the baseline provided by the experiential model.

Various implications arise from this research. Firstly, researchers in the field of solvability must recognise the impact that solvability factors, especially the presence of suspect information, have on one another. Failure to address inter-variable effects may reduce the external validity of any such study. Researchers must also ensure that their data sets are of a sufficient size to allow for the identification of factors with low prevalence, though it would also be of benefit to conduct in-depth analysis of smaller samples to assess the impact of currently unidentified additional factors, such as covert and proactive tactics, and parts of the secondary investigation that may identify actions, such as identification of linked investigation through modus operandi comparison, that might be more effective if performed in the primary investigation but are currently associated with secondary investigations. In addition, it would be beneficial for police forces to record data in a manner that facilitates research. Improvements in the accuracy of electronic recording and the auditability of data changes would improve the potential for future research.

The next step would be to assess the impact of implementing a model such as this on clearance rates, legitimacy, victim satisfaction and cost. This model is best implemented using a randomized controlled trial (Lösel 2007), which would allow for the measurement and assessment of its impact and for the completion of a cost-benefit analysis (Dhiri and Brand 1999). Overall, this research has demonstrated that, at a time when policing resources are scarce, failure to use algorithmic models to allocate those resources may well be causing police forces to neglect other areas of business that they could free up resources to work on. With algorithmic prediction being used in so many other aspects of our lives (Ayres 2007), it now appears fair to ask why police forces have not caught up with the rest of the modern world.

References

Ayres, I. (2007). *Supercrunchers: How anything can be predicted*. London: Murray.

Baskin, D., & Sommers, I. (2012). The influence of forensic evidence on the case outcomes of assault and robbery incidents. *Criminal Justice Policy Review, 23*(2), 186–210.

Bieck, W., & Kessler, D. A. (1977). *Response time analysis*. Kansas City: Missouri Board of Police Commissioners.

Blake, L., & Coupe, R. T. (2001). The impact of single and two-officer patrols on catching burglars in the act. *The British Journal of Criminology, 41*(2), 381–396.

Bond, J. (2007). Value of DNA evidence in detecting crime. *Journal of Forensic Sciences, 52*(1), 128–136.
Bond, J. (2009). The value of fingerprint evidence in detecting crime. *International Journal of Police Science & Management, 11*(1), 77–84.
Brand, S., & Price, R. (2000). *The economic and social costs of crime* (Home Office Research Study 217). London: Home Office.
Burrows, J., Hopkins, M., Hubbard, R., Robinson, A., Speed, M., & Tilley, N. (2005). *Understanding the attrition process in volume crime investigations* (Home Office Research Study 295). London: Home Office.
Clawson, C., & Chang, S. K. (1977). Relationship of response delays and arrest rates. *Journal of Police Science and Administration, 5*(1), 53–68.
Coupe, R. T., & Blake, L. (2006). Daylight and darkness strategies and the risks of offenders being seen at residential burglaries. *Criminology, 44*(2), 431–463.
Coupe, R. T., & Kaur, S. (2005). The role of alarms and CCTV in detecting non-residential burglary. *Security Journal, 18*(2), 53–72.
Coupe, T., & Griffiths, M. (1996). *Solving residential burglary* (Police Research Group Crime Detection and Prevention Services, Paper 77). London: Home Office.
D'Alessio, S. J., & Stolzenberg, I. (2003). Race and the probability of arrest. *Social Forces, 81*(4), 1381–1397.
Dhiri, S., & Brand, S. (1999). *Analysis of costs and benefits: guidance for evaluators*. London: Home Office.
Eck, J. E. (1979). *Managing case assignments: The burglary investigation decision model replication*. Washington, DC: Police Executive Research Forum.
Eitle, D., Stolzenberg, I., & D'Alessio, S. J. (2005). Police organizational factors, the racial composition of the police, and the probability of arrest. *Justice Quarterly, 22*(1), 30–57.
Gill, M., Hart, J., Livingstone, K., & Stevens, J. (1996). *The crime allocation system: Police investigations into burglary and auto crime* (Police Research Series, Paper 16). London: Home Office.
Greenberg, B., Elliot, C. V., Kraft, L. P., & Procter, S. H. (1977). *Felony investigation decision model—An analysis of investigation elements of information*. Washington, DC: US Government Printing Office.
Greenwood, P. W., Chaiken, J. M., Petersilia, J., & Prusoff, L. (1975). *The criminal investigation process: Volume III: Observations and analysis*. Santa Monica, CA: The RAND Corporation.
Her Majesty's Inspectorate of Constabulary and Fire & Rescue Services. (2012). *Review of police crime and incident reports: West Midlands Police*. London: HMIC.
Jansson, K. (2005). *Volume crime investigations—A review of the research literature* (Home Office Online Report OLR 44/05). London: Home Office.
Lipsey, M. W., & Wilson, D. B. (2001). *Practical meta-analysis*. Thousand Oaks, CA: SAGE Publications.
Litwin, K. J. (2004). A multilevel multivariate analysis of factors affecting homicide clearances. *Journal of Research in Crime and Delinquency, 41*(4), 327–351.
Lösel, F. (2007). Doing evaluation research in criminology: Balancing scientific and practical demands. In R. D. King & E. Wincup (Eds.), *Doing research on crime and justice* (pp. 141–170). Oxford: Oxford University Press.
MedCalc Software. (2014a). MedCalc manual: Logistic regression, version 14.12.0—last modified December 3, 2014. http://www.medcalc.org/manual/logistic_regression.php. Accessed December 31, 2014.
MedCalc Software. (2014b). MedCalc manual: Logit transformation, version 14.12.0—last modified December 3, 2014. http://www.medcalc.org/manual/logit_transformation_table.php. Accessed December 31, 2014.
Meehl, P. (1954). *Clinical vs. statistical prediction: A theoretical analysis and a review of the evidence*. Minneapolis: University of Minnesota Press.

Newiss, G. (2002). Responding to and investigating street robbery. In K. Jansson (Ed.), *Volume crime investigations—A review of the research literature* (Home Office Online Report OLR 44/05). London: Home Office.

Paine, C. (2012). *Solvability factors in dwelling burglaries in Thames Valley* (unpublished MSt thesis). University of Cambridge.

Peterson, J., Sommers, I., Baskin, D., & Johnson, D. (2010). *The role and impact of forensic evidence in the criminal justice process*. Washington, D.C.: National Institute of Justice.

Peterson, J. L., Hickman, M. J., Strom, K. J., & Johnson, D. J. (2013). Effect of forensic evidence on criminal justice case processing. *Journal of Forensic Sciences, 58*(S1), S78–S90.

Puckett, J. L., & Lundman, R. J. (2003). Factors affecting homicide clearances: Multivariate analysis of a more complete conceptual framework. *Journal of Research in Crime and Delinquency, 40*(2), 171–193.

Random.org. (n.d.). Random sequence generator. https://www.random.org/sequences/. Accessed September 12, 2014.

Regoeczi, W. C., Jarvis, J., & Riedel, M. (2008). Clearing murders: Is it about time? *Journal of Research in Crime and Delinquency, 45*(2), 142–162.

Riedel, M., & Boulahanis, J. G. (2007). Homicides exceptionally cleared and cleared by arrest: An exploratory study of police/prosecutor outcomes. *Homicide Studies, 11*(2), 151–164.

Robb, P., Coupe, R. T., & Ariel, B. (2015). 'Solvability' and detection of metal theft on railway property. *European Journal on Criminal Policy and Research, 21*(4), 463–484.

Roberts, A. (2008). The influences of incident and contextual characteristics on crime clearance of nonlethal violence: A multilevel event history analysis. *Journal of Criminal Justice, 36*(1), 61–71.

Sherman, L. W. (2013). The rise of evidence-based policing: Targeting, testing, and tracking. *Crime and Justice, 42*(1), 377–451.

Smith, K., Taylor, P., & Elkin, M. (2013). *Crimes detected in England and Wales 2012/13*. London: Home Office.

Spelman, W., & Brown, D. K. (1981). *Calling the police: Citizen reporting of serious crime*. Washington, DC: Police Research Executive Forum.

Stevens, J. M., & Stipak, B. (1982). Factors associated with police apprehension productivity. *Police Science and Administration, 10*(1), 52–57.

Tilley, N., Robinson, A., & Burrows, J. (2007). The investigation of high volume crime. In T. Newburn, T. Williamson, & A. Wright (Eds.), *Handbook of criminal investigation* (pp. 226–254). London: Willan Publishing.

United States Naval Observatory. (2014). Sun or moon rise/set table for one year. http://aa.usno.navy.mil/data/docs/RS_OneYear.php. Accessed December 13, 2014.

Solvability Factors and Investigative Strategy for Faith Hate Crime: Anti-Semitic and Islamophobic Assault, Criminal Damage and Public Order Offences in London

Simon Rose, Richard Timothy Coupe and Barak Ariel

Introduction

There is a very long history of hate and conflict connected with religious differences. This has involved alienation between different Christian denominations, particularly after the development of Protestantism in Northern Europe and England, which resulted in wars and migrations in Europe, within the British Isles and to the Americas. Antagonism between Christianity and Islam has been evident in medieval fighting over the Holy Land and subsequent movement of people of Muslim faith into Spain and briefly France, while the fall of Constantinople also brought the geographical border between predominantly Islamic and Christian territories, closer to Europe. This has been paralleled on the Asian subcontinent by antagonism between Muslims, Hindus and Sikhs and, following the deconstruction of the USSR in the late 1980s, between Orthodox Christian Russia and the Muslim-dominated former republics to the South. In recent decades, migration has brought substantial populations of people of Muslim and other faiths into Europe, Russia and North America so that the 'religious interface' is now within European and Russian cities. What was once an issue that affected areas, such as the Balkans, the Middle East or Egypt, where the worlds of different religions met geographically, has become a matter of daily interaction on the streets, at work and in residential neighbourhoods in Western countries and Russia.

The situation of minority Muslim populations in most Western and Southern European countries, therefore, now mirrors that of Jewish people, who have been present in Europe for many centuries. 'Muslim-on-Jewish' antagonism increasingly complements the 'Christian-on-Jewish' antagonism (Boyes 2017) that has been evi-

S. Rose (✉)
Metropolitan Police Service, London, UK
e-mail: simon.rose@met.police.uk

S. Rose · R. T. Coupe · B. Ariel
University of Cambridge, Cambridge, UK

R. T. Coupe et al. (eds.), *Crime Solvability Factors*,
https://doi.org/10.1007/978-3-030-17160-5_10

dent in many European countries and Russia over the centuries (e.g., Dubnow 1918). By comparison, conflicts between Sikhs and Hindus and between these groups and Muslims, and between Muslims of different denominations, which threaten peace in the Middle East and on the Asian subcontinent, appear to be of far less importance in terms of hate crime in England and Wales, although Catholic–Protestant discord still pervades Northern Ireland and Belgium. Equally, hate offences against white Caucasians by minorities in the UK are more likely to find expression as racial crimes and to be infrequently reported. Certain types of terrorism offences are an exception but, due to their special characteristics and separate classification, these will not be considered in this chapter, despite the presence in many of these criminal acts of an element of implied underlying faith hate, such as those committed by 'hate preachers'. Their effects on the incidence of the faith hate crimes examined in this chapter, however, will be highlighted.

This chapter is focused on the most numerous of reported faith hate crimes in England and Wales: anti-Semitic and Islamophobic crimes. They can be related to many types of crime, ranging from verbal offences, damage to property and assaults with physical injury to, rarely, homicide. In this chapter, these offences will be classified in terms of three crime types, which include virtually every faith hate crime, namely assaults, criminal damage and public order offences. The aim is to identify and assess those solvability factors that enable their successful investigation and detection and determine the scope for improving cost-effective faith hate crime investigation and elevating detection rates.

Existing Work

Anti-Semitic data has been available in the UK only since the establishment of the Community Security Trust, a Jewish charity for promoting the safety and security of Jewish communities, in 1994. The Metropolitan Police Force, whose Greater London jurisdiction is the origin of the data used in this chapter, has formally recorded faith hate and anti-Semitic crime only since the MacPherson Report (Macpherson 1999) on the racist murder of Stephen Lawrence, and 'flags' to enable the tracking of Islamophobic crimes were introduced in 2006. In the UK, the victim's perception of an incident determines the classification of an offence as racist or involving faith hate, whereas classification as a 'bias' crime in the USA depends on the investigating officer, which predisposes to under-recording there (Jenness and Grattet 2001).

As a result, there are striking differences in recorded faith hate crime rates, with such offences occurring 88 times more frequently in London (2.3 per 1000 population) than in the USA (0.03 per 1000 population) (Kielinger and Paterson 2007). This means it can be difficult to compile a sample of US crimes involving faith hate of sufficient size for solvability factor analysis. It is hardly surprising, therefore, that Messner et al. (2004) identified only 43 out of 438,191 US assaults, and Phillips (2009) identified only 15 out of 643 bias crimes, as faith hate offences. Despite the larger volumes of UK offences, even faith hate studies there have relied on small samples (Iganski 2007). Kielinger and Paterson (2007) sampled only 156 offences from a four-year data set of 1296 cases, while the subset of faith hate crime incidents in the Leicester Hate Crime Project (Leicester Centre for Hate Studies 2014) consisted of 215 victims, of which 136 were Islamophobic and seven anti-Semitic.

Existing studies have focused more on the characteristics of faith hate crime and explanations for changes in its incidence than on solvability factors and detection outcomes. Almost a third involved aggravating factors to an existing altercation or opportunistic rather than premeditated hate acts, and few reflected extremism or organised offending (Kielinger and Paterson 2007). There appear to be few equivalents of the organised anti-Semitic attacks by British fascists on Jewish buildings in the 1930s (Rubin 2010). Whereas Kielinger and Paterson (2007) found anti-Semitic crime to be directed at individuals rather than property, the converse has been concluded in the USA (Cheng et al. 2013). Victim gender and age affect the probabilities of faith hate crime being reported (Harlow 2005), and victims have low confidence in and satisfaction with the police (Leicester Centre for Hate Studies 2014).

In both the USA and UK, faith hate crimes reported to the police have been rising during the past decade. In the USA, it accounted for only a tenth of US bias crime in 2003–2006 (Sandholtz et al. 2013) compared to 28% in 2014 (Wilson 2014). In London, there has also been a progressively upward trend in recorded offences since 2010 (Metropolitan Police Service [MPS] 2017; Fig. 1). Recorded figures do not match victim survey evidence, which indicates stable or even declining faith hate offending (Goodhart 2017), suggesting that increases in recorded offending reflect higher reporting rates.

Faith hate offending in both the USA and UK has matched international events. There have been surges in anti-Semitic offences in the USA (Deloughery et al. 2012) and in Islamophobic crime in London, which has matched media reports of Islamic

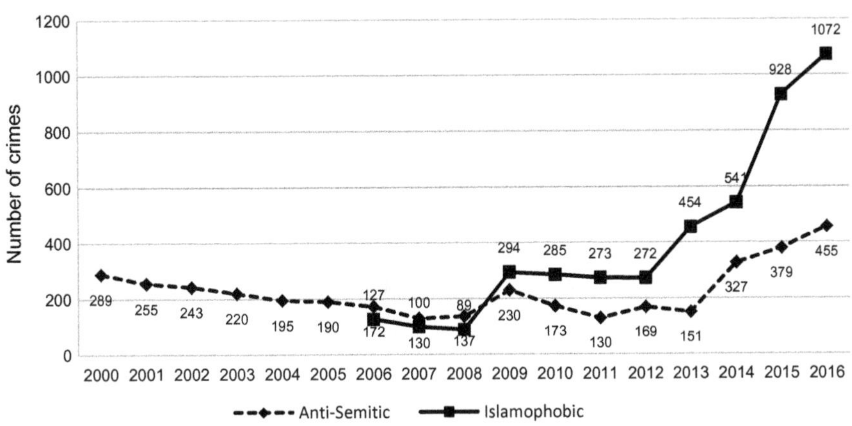

Fig. 1 Anti-Semitic and Islamophobic crimes in London by year of incidence

terrorism offences, notably the murder of drummer Lee Rigby, the attacks on Paris's Bataclan Theatre and the Berlin lorry attack (Fig. 1; MPS 2017). These terrorist offences may be viewed as the most serious faith hate crimes, which have effects on multiple reciprocal faith-hate offences of assault, criminal damage and public order.

There is only a small amount of published research into faith hate crime solvability and detection. The clearance of US bias offences depends on available evidence but also reflects police discretion (Lyons and Roberts 2014). This discretion is influenced by victim and offender characteristics, including gender, age, race, ethnicity and social standing (Lyons and Roberts 2014), with the application of the law, as Black (1976) suggests, reflecting the relative status of the parties involved.

Based on 418 anti-Semitic and 297 Islamophobic US bias crimes, Walfield et al. (2017) carried out the only study of faith hate crime solvability factors. They identified seven factors, with arrests more likely if the offence was anti-Christian rather than anti-Semitic (+45%), involved multiple victims (+69%), was committed at a religious institutional venue (+73%), if other crimes were simultaneously committed (+75%), if it was a Western rather than a Southern jurisdiction (+99%), if there was a major victim injury (+138%), and if there was a minor victim injury (+263%). Walfield et al.'s (2017) NIBRS data relate to 557 police agencies covering only a third of the US population, particularly smaller US police forces in the American South and Midwest. Owing to this and to systematic errors due to the classification of some offences as anti-Arab, the conclusions for large city forces in the USA may differ.

Although London has few reported anti-Christian offences, and the US regional differences do not apply to England and London, the importance of victims who have suffered injury, concomitant offences and particular venues are, as in large US cities, likely to be important solvability factors. As well as investigating the overall solvability factors for faith hate crime in London, this chapter examines the factors for anti-Semitic and Islamophobic crimes separately. Its large samples also facilitate analysis of faith hate offences that involve verbal comments, personal assaults and property offences separately in order to derive factors to support screening decisions that may be applied to the specific types of faith hate incidents. This, it is anticipated, will help to clarify the points at which the investigation of different types of crime might be discontinued, enabling maximisation of cost-effectiveness and the tailoring of investigations to crime harm.

This chapter presents a review of the recent changes in reported faith hate crime in London and its incidence across the 32 London boroughs; an analysis of the solvability factors; the measurement of incident solvability and detection odds; and an examination of the geographical distribution of the differences in solvability and its relationship with detections across the boroughs.

Methodology

The study uses data from Metropolitan Police records for a population of 4723 Islamophobic and 3967 anti-Semitic hate offences committed in London between January 2000 and April 2017.

Whether or not a crime was detected is defined in terms of a 'sanction detection' rather than the alternatives of 'clearance' or 'detection'. A sanction detection means that either a suspect has been charged, or reported for summons, or cautioned, or been issued with a penalty notice for disorder or the offence has been taken into consideration when an offender is sentenced.

Analysis Structure

The findings initially consider changes in levels of faith hate crime in London, the crimes to which faith hate is linked and how Islamophobic and anti-Semitic faith hate offences are distributed across the London police jurisdictions, which are coterminous with its 32 boroughs. The variation in detection rates across jurisdictions is also examined.

Bivariate relationships between solvability factors and sanction detection outcomes were investigated for the whole sample and separately for each of Islamophobic and anti-Semitic crimes. Binary logistic regression analysis was used to identify the significant solvability factors of varying effect sizes for all faith hate crimes, and separately for Islamophobic and anti-Semitic offences. Separate binary logistic regression tests were carried out for assaults and criminal damage and public order offences, and then for these offence types within the Islamophobic and anti-Semitic incident groups, in order to determine whether solvability factors differed markedly between them. The presence of distinctive solvability factors for the six different combinations of faith hate and crime type would enable more accurate identification of cases of varying solvability and, therefore, of which cases offer the best potential for investigation leading to an arrest.

Summary solvability scores were calculated for faith hate crimes as a whole, for Islamophobic and anti-Semitic crimes, and for the three different crime types by summing the product of each significant solvability factor's odds ratio for each data case. The distribution in solvability scores may be used to identify cases with different probabilities of being detected and provide insights about the cost-effectiveness of investigating crimes with different characteristics and evidence. The solvability analyses can also help specify the cut-off points for ceasing investigation, so that potential savings from hitherto fruitless investigative effort can be calculated and the characteristics of offences which justify further investigation established. Crime type was also an input for specifying the cut-off points, with more serious, harmful offences accorded a more conservative point at which to cease investigation. Knowing the characteristics of crimes very unlikely to be solved enables agencies to make an informed choice about whether to screen out subsets of cases highly unlikely to be detected or to accept the resource implications of exhaustively investigating every crime—most of which will not, in the event, be detected—should this be the preferred agency approach.

Finally, the spatial distribution of solvability scores across the 32 London boroughs was examined and related to the borough distribution of detection rates for the different faith hate groups and the three crime-type groups: assaults and criminal damage and public order offences.

Findings

Characteristics of Faith Hate Offences

Faith hate crime incidents reported to the police have increased for both Jewish and Muslim victims during the last decade (Fig. 1). The rate of increase has been higher for Islamophobic offences, and this may, in part, reflect the growing numbers of people of Muslim faith living in London. The anti-Semitic crime rate in London (1:1313 population) is approximately 2.8 times that of the Islamophobic crime rate (1:3710 population), since there are far fewer Jewish than Muslim residents in London (172,000 compared with 1,012,800) (Office for National Statistics 2012).

The spatial distribution of faith hate crimes reflects the large numbers and wider geographical spread of Muslim households compared with households who are visibly Jewish (Figs. 2 and 3). More than half (59%) of anti-Semitic crimes were committed in just four of London's 32 boroughs and 77% in eight boroughs. Barnet and Hackney, where two large orthodox Jewish communities are situated, saw 44% of such crime. Half the other boroughs accounted for less than 1% of anti-Semitic crime. In contrast, Islamophobic crimes occurred in almost every borough, with only one borough accounting for less than 1% of offences and only two boroughs—Tower Hamlets and Westminster—seeing more than 6% of them. Muslims are evidently identifiable throughout London.

Types of Faith Hate Crime and Detection Rates

The overall detection rate for faith hate crime in London is 19%, but at 22%, the detection rate for Islamophobic crime is higher than that for anti-Semitic crime, which stands at 15%. Faith hate crime may be categorised into 18 principal types, for which the incidence (Fig. 4) and detection rates (Fig. 5) vary markedly. Public order or harassment offences constitute 59% of faith hate crimes and criminal damage, assault and malicious communication account for most of the rest (Fig. 4). As expected, public order offences have a detection rate close to the average for these offences:

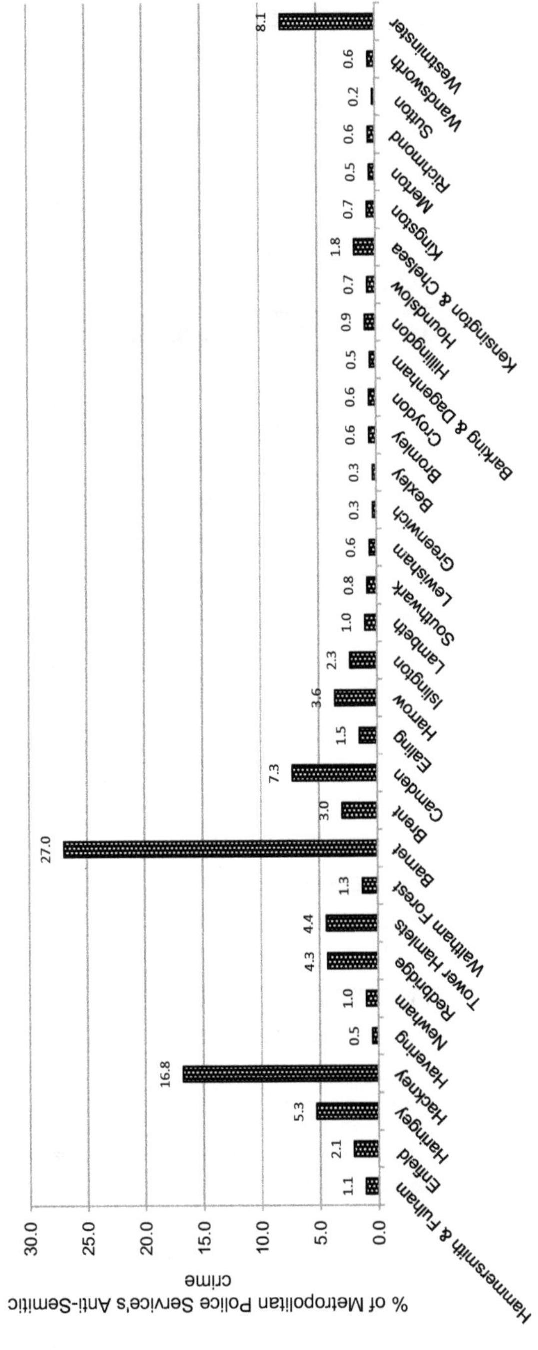

Fig. 2 Geographical distribution of anti-Semitic crime in London–percentage of the MPS' total anti-Semitic crime per London borough

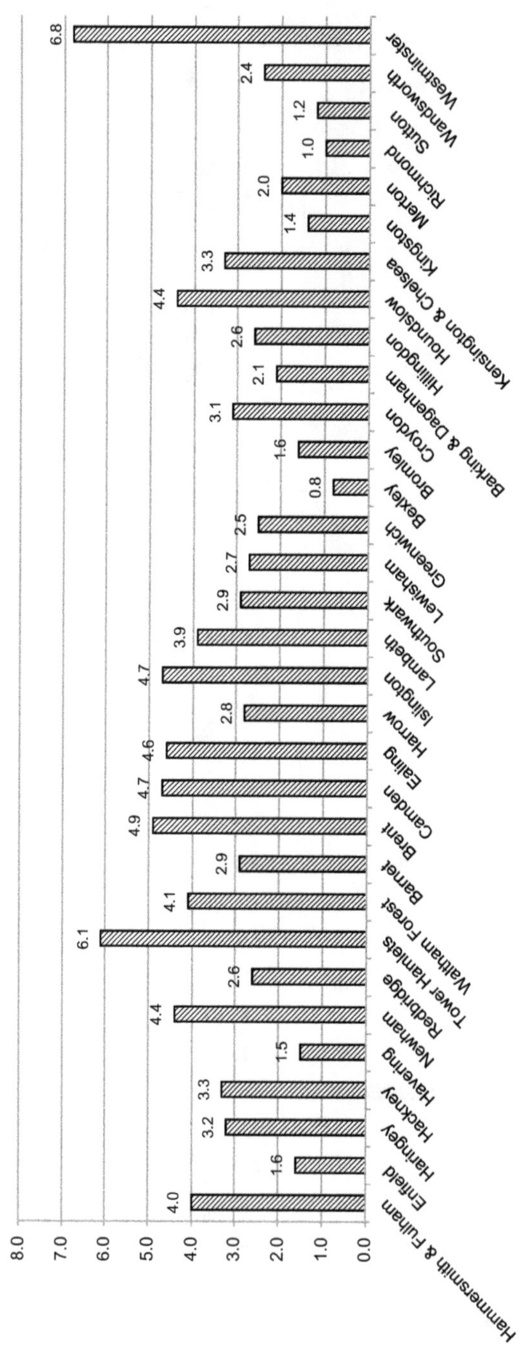

Fig. 3 Geographical distribution of Islamophobic crime in London–percentage of the MPS' total Islamophobic crime per London borough

20%. Other crimes with which faith hate crime is linked also have detection rates similar to comparable non-faith hate offences, with sexual assault at 33% and burglary at 14% (Fig. 5). Detection rates for assault are higher for more serious assaults, with grievous bodily harm (GBH) at 39% and actual bodily harm (ABH) at 34%, compared with only 17% for common assault, suggesting that more serious cases receive more resources and have better odds of being solved.

For the purposes of this chapter's analysis, the 18 offence types are classified into three groups: assaults, and criminal damage and public order offences (Fig. 6). The higher detection rates for Islamophobic compared with anti-Semitic crimes persist for every crime type (Fig. 7).

Detection rates vary between boroughs; four have rates of 26% or higher, while seven have rates ranging from 11 to 17% (Fig. 8). It is likely that variation in detection rates will reflect not only differences in the incidence of Islamophobic and anti-Semitic crimes and the types of offences committed, but also other factors, including the resources allocated to faith hate crime investigation in different jurisdictions. The relationships between jurisdictional detection rates and solvability will be explored in the final part of the chapter.

Solvability of Faith Hate Crimes

Solvability factors were initially identified on the basis of prior solvability studies and from a qualitative examination of a sample of 50 detected anti-Semitic and Islamophobic crimes. These factors were: investigating borough, specialist or borough investigators, day committed, time committed, delay in reporting, type of crime, investigating officer rank, how police were notified, venue type, the existence of CCTV, victim age, victim gender, severity of victim injury, repeat victim status, victim occupation, forensic tasking, how the suspect was identified, and Islamophobic or anti-Semitic crime.

These were re-specified, if necessary, as binary variables and their relationship with whether or not crimes were detected was tested for all faith hate offences together, and for anti-Semitic and Islamophobic crimes separately.

Seventeen significant factors were identified for all faith hate crimes (Table 1). These include victim characteristics, such as gender, ethnicity, and whether the victim is of working age or a repeat victim; event characteristics, such as crime type, whether the victim was injured, the venue, any delay in reporting and the reporting method; and investigative characteristics, including the deployment of forensic investigators, availability of CCTV records and the rank of the police investigator. It is notable that the involvement of uniformed police constables enhanced detections compared with the use of detective constables or sergeants. Whether investigations were carried out by specialist or local borough police teams had no bearing on detection outcomes.

Almost every one of these factors persisted as one of the 16 significant solvability factors predicting whether Islamophobic crimes were detected (Table 1), though whether or not the crime was a public order offence was no longer significant, nor,

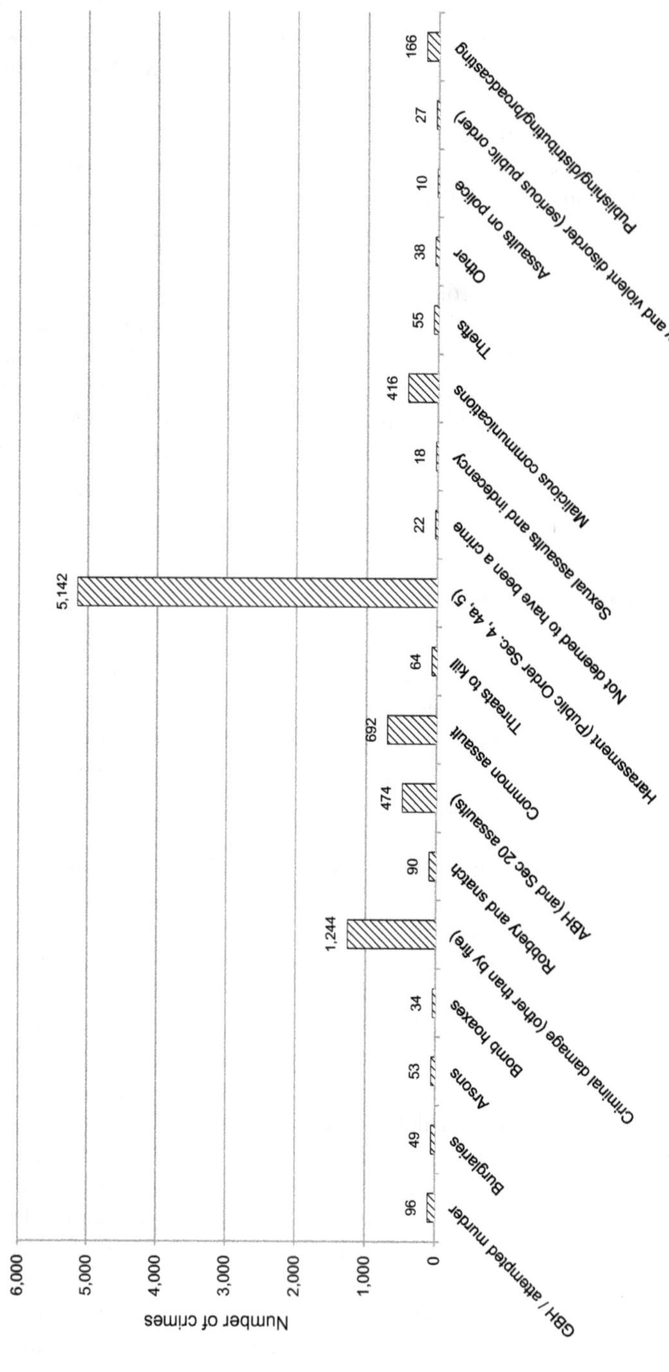

Fig. 4 Incidence of different types of faith hate crime

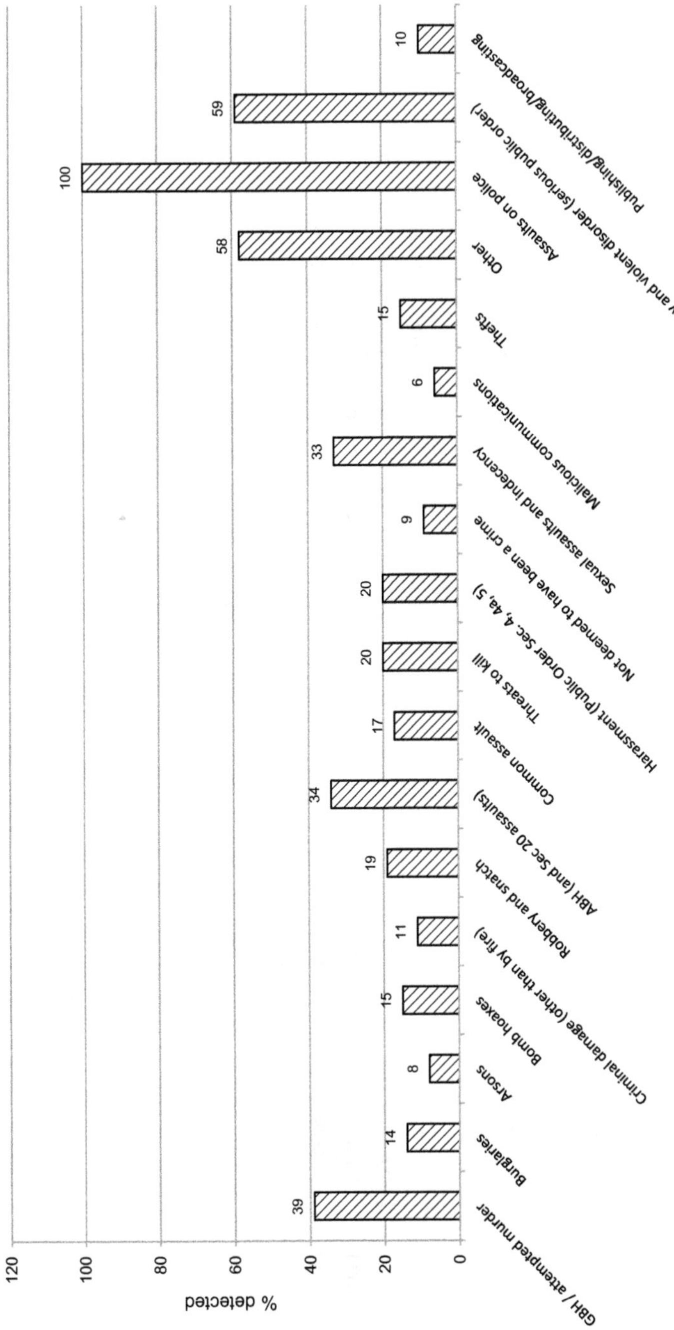

Fig. 5 Faith hate crime type by detection rate

Table 1 Bivariate associations between detection of faith hate crimes and solvability factors

		All faith hate crimes				Anti-Semitic				Islamophobic			
Solvability factor	Criteria	Detect rate %	χ^2	p	d	Detect rate %	χ^2	p	d	Detect rate %	χ^2	p	d
Gender	Male/female	21/16	37.2	<0.001	0.13	15/14	1.4	0.239	0.04	28/17	71.6	<0.001	0.26
Corporate/personal victim	Individual/company	19/18	0.6	0.444	0.02	15/15	0.0	0.946	<0.01	22/22	0.1	0.719	0.01
Forensic deployment	Yes/no	15/19	7.1	0.008	0.06	12/15	2.1	0.144	0.05	18/23	4.0	0.046	0.06
Type of faith hate	Anti-Semitic/Islamophobic	15/22	73.5	<0.001	0.18	15/22	73.5	<0.001	0.18	15/22	74.0	<0.001	0.18
Existence of CCTV	Yes/no	29/19	68.1	<0.001	0.23	24/18	9.8	0.002	0.15	31/20	54.8	<0.001	0.25
Team dealing	On borough/specialist	19/17	0.2	0.666	0.01	15/25	1.9	0.169	0.04	22/14	2.4	0.120	0.05
Repeat victim	Yes/no	17/20	4.0	0.05	0.05	14/15	0.4	0.548	0.02	19/23	4.5	0.033	0.06
Ethnicity	White/not white	17/22	37.2	<0.001	0.14	15/15	0.0	0.954	<0.01	23/23	0.2	0.699	0.01
Person injured	Injured/not injured	28/18	46.7	<0.001	0.16	22/14	15.0	<0.001	0.03	34/21	35.4	<0.001	0.18
When reported	Weekday/weekend	18/22	13.3	<0.001	0.08	15/16	2.2	0.141	0.05	21/26	12.1	0.001	0.10
Delay in reporting	None (<15 min)/>15 min	28/11	432.2	<0.001	0.46	13/10	124.7	<0.001	0.36	33/12	278.3	<0.001	0.50
Method of reporting	Direct/indirect	22/9	151.5	<0.001	0.27	18/8	56.0	<0.001	0.24	25/10	75.8	<0.001	0.26

(continued)

Table 1 (continued)

		All faith hate crimes				Anti-Semitic				Islamophobic			
Solvability factor	Criteria	Detect rate %	χ^2	p	d	Detect rate %	χ^2	p	d	Detect rate %	χ^2	p	d
Victim of working age	18–65/1–17, 66+	20/13	28.2	<0.001	0.12	16/10	12.2	<0.001	0.12	23/17	7.0	0.008	0.08
Rank of investigator	PC/DC, supervisor	23/15	79.0	<0.001	0.19	18/13	19.4	<0.001	0.14	26/7	151.2	<0.001	0.36
Crime type	Assault/not assault	25/18	42.9	<0.001	0.13	19/14	10.7	0.001	0.10	31/21	38.2	<0.001	0.18
Crime type	Criminal damage/any other	11/20	69.9	<0.001	0.18	8/17	42.0	<0.001	0.21	15/23	15.1	<0.001	0.11
Crime type	Public order/any other	20/17	13.3	<0.001	0.08	17/13	11.1	0.001	0.10	23/22	0.6	0.437	0.02
Venue	Public open space/any other	20/20	1.0	0.328	0.02	16/16	0.4	0.546	0.02	25/21	6.2	0.013	0.07
Venue	In/on transport	23/20	2.8	0.95	0.04	16/16	0.0	0.869	<0.01	25/22	1.6	0.201	0.04
Venue	In residential address/any other	15/22	42.1	<0.001	0.15	14/17	23.0	0.085	0.06	15/	45.9	<0.001	0.20
										25			
										26			
Venue	In public venue/any other	24/19	21.6	<0.001	0.11	19/15	5.1	0.024	0.08	22/22	11.1	0.001	0.10
Venue	In private venue/any other	20/20	0.0	0.959	0.01	18/16	0.8	0.371	0.03	23	0.1	0.710	0.01
Police witnessed offence	Yes/no	91/15	1763.1	<0.001	1.01	89/11	872.6	<0.001	1.07	92/18	903.3	<0.001	0.97

(continued)

Table 1 (continued)

		All faith hate crimes				Anti-Semitic				Islamophobic			
Solvability factor	Criteria	Detect rate %	χ^2	p	d	Detect rate %	χ^2	p	d	Detect rate %	χ^2	p	d
Reported on/off peak (09.00–21.00)	Peak/off peak	17/26	77.3	<0.001	0.19	14/19	13.9	<0.001	0.12	20/31	69.2	<0.001	0.24
Victim occupation	Police, driver, security/other	42/17	205.2	<0.001	0.31	31/14	31.4	0.001	0.18	47/20	147.9	<0.001	0.36
Investigating borough	4 boroughs[a]/others	28/18	38.1	<0.001	0.18	24/15	9.94	0.002	0.10	30/21	18.3	<0.001	0.07
Number of witnesses	3 or fewer/4 or more	15/33	319.7	<0.001	0.35	12/30	31.4	0.001	0.18	18/35	157.1	<0.001	0.37

[a]Islington, Bromley, Kensington and Chelsea, Richmond

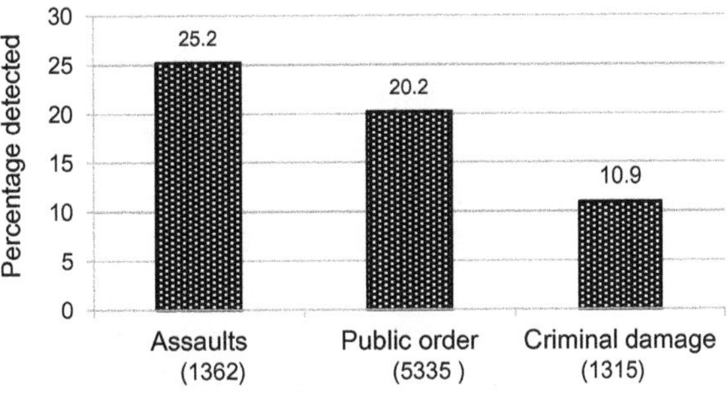

Fig. 6 Detection by principal crime types (numbers of cases in parentheses)

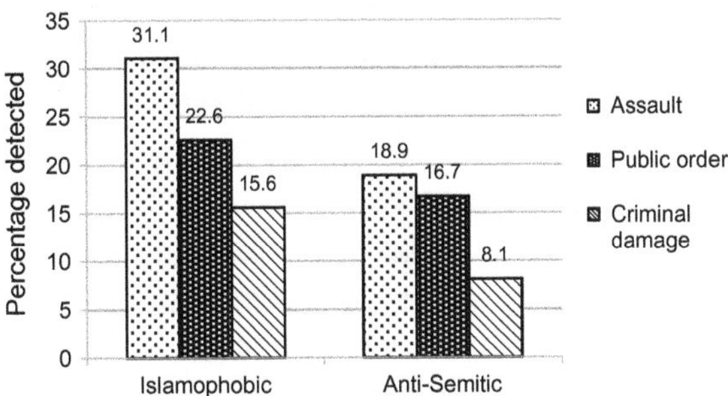

Fig. 7 Percentage of crimes detected by crime type and faith hate type

predictably, was ethnicity, while whether the offence occurred on public open space became significant. In contrast, there were only 11 significant solvability factors for anti-Semitic crimes (Table 1). Neither ethnicity, repeat victimisation, whether an offence was reported at the weekend or on a weekday, nor the deployment of forensic officers had any bearing on detection (Table 1). Reporting methods and delays, however, affected detection, as did the availability of CCTV evidence, whether the victim was injured, and the nature of the crime committed.

Crimes witnessed by police officers predictably had far higher detection rates; 4.3% of all faith hate crimes were witnessed by police officers, but this percentage was higher for assaults (6.3%) and lower for criminal damage offences (2.6%). Examining solvability factors with these cases excluded, however, resulted in only small changes to the significant detection predictors for Muslims, and none for Jewish victims. For crimes against Jewish people, the same 11 solvability factors persisted. For Muslim victims, there were 15 significant factors rather than 16, with 13 of these remaining unchanged. Being of working age and forensic deployment no longer, respectively, elevated and depressed detections, while a team from the local borough, rather than a specialist team, investigating an offence boosted detections. The better performance of uniformed constables and local teams may partly reflect the allocation of more challenging cases to more senior and specialist officers.

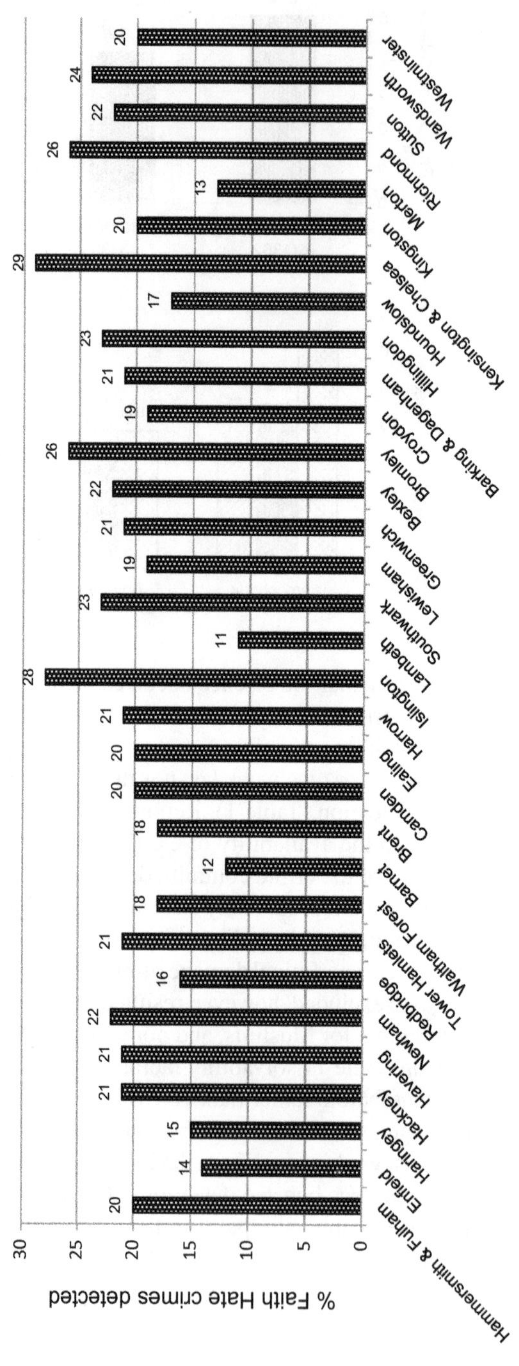

Fig. 8 Faith hate crime detection rates by London borough, 2000–2017

Multivariate Analysis of Solvability Factors

Solvability Factors for Anti-Semitic and Islamophobic Offences

Binary logistic regression analyses were used to identify the solvability factors for each of the anti-Semitic and Islamophobic sets of crimes (Table 2).

Five significant factors explain 31% of anti-Semitic crime detections and nine factors 34% of Islamophobic detection outcomes (Table 2). Offences witnessed by the police largely involved hate offences committed against the police and, predictably, had very high odds of detection (55:1 and 200:1 for anti-Semitic and Islamophobic crimes, respectively). As for many other offences examined in this volume (e.g., burglary in Chapters. "Assessing Solvability Factors in Greater Manchester, England: The Case of Residential Burglaries", "Population-Level Analysis of Residential Burglaries" and "Solvability Indicators for 'First Officers': Targeting Eyewitness Questioning at Non-residential Burglaries"; pickpocketing in Chapter "Pickpocketing on Railways"; non-domestic assaults in Chapter "Targeting Factors that Predict Clearance of Non-domestic Assaults"; and sex offences on railways in Chapter "Reporting, Detection and Solvability of Sex Offences on Railways"), eyewitnesses evidence and speedy reporting helped solve offences. The presence of four or more witnesses and the absence of delay in reporting captured these effects, with each factor approximately doubling the odds of solving cases, with stronger effects for Islamophobic offences (Table 2). Faith hate assaults had higher odds of being solved than public order or criminal damage offences, rather more so for victims of anti-Semitism (Table 2). Being injured as a result of an anti-Semitic crime boosted detection odds, but injury had no bearing on the clearance of Islamophobic cases. Four other factors boosted the odds of detecting Islamophobic incidents, but not anti-Semitic ones: investigation by a police constable (rather than a more senior officer), an offence being reported during off-peak hours, a victim working as a driver, in the security industry or as a police officer and an offence occurring in one of the four boroughs of Bromley, Islington, Kensington and Chelsea, or Richmond.

Solvability Factors for Different Crimes: Assault, Criminal Damage, Public Order

Faith hate offences involve different types of crime. There have been few, if any, studies of either public order offence or criminal damage solvability, and studies of non-domestic assault solvability, such as the one reported in this volume (Olphin and Mueller-Johnson, Chapter "Targeting Factors that Predict Clearance of Non-domestic Assaults"), are rare. This chapter provides insights into these offences as well as providing solvability factors for different sorts of faith hate offending.

The different best-fit binary logistic regressions for assault, criminal damage and public order faith hate offences (Tables 3(i), 4(i) and 5(i)) share five solvability factors: victim occupation (police, driver or security), witnessed by the police, four or more witnesses, a delay in reporting, and whether the offence occurred in one of four London boroughs (Kensington and Chelsea, Richmond, Bromley or Islington).

Table 2 Binary logistic regressions with best-fit solutions: solvability factors for anti-Semitic crimes and Islamophobic crimes

	Anti-Semitic						Islamophobic					
Solvability factor	*B*	*SE*	Wald	*df*	*p*	Exp(*B*)	*B*	*SE*	Wald	*df*	*p*	Exp(*B*)
Victim male or female	−0.09	0.18	0.24	1	0.622	0.92	−0.40	0.11	12.9	1	0.000	0.67
Repeat victim (Y/N)	0.38	0.21	3.17	1	0.075	1.46	−0.11	0.14	0.55	1	0.458	0.90
Vitim ethnicity white (Y/N)	−0.21	0.48	0.37	1	0.543	0.81	−0.26	0.14	3.44	1	0.064	0.77
Victim Injured (Y/N)	0.64	0.32	4.11	1	0.043	1.90	0.26	0.20	1.73	1	0.188	1.30
Victim working age (Y/N)	0.46	0.25	3.47	1	0.062	1.58	0.05	0.19	0.080	1	0.777	1.06
Victim was police, driver or security industry	−0.57	0.30	3.60	1	0.058	0.56	−0.93	0.16	35.1	1	0.000	0.39
Venue public open space (Y/N)	0.33	0.28	1.32	1	0.250	1.38	0.07	0.17	0.14	1	0.707	1.07
Venue residential (Y/N)	0.06	0.31	0.04	1	0.844	1.06	0.32	0.20	2.67	1	0.102	1.38
Venue public (Y/N)	−0.04	0.31	0.02	1	0.902	0.96	0.07	0.18	0.14	1	0.707	1.07
Venue covered by CCTV	−0.15	0.18	0.69	1	0.405	0.86	0.13	0.12	1.26	1	0.262	1.14
Witnessed by police (Y/N)	−5.0	0.73	47.7	1	0.000	0.01	−4.0	0.36	126.0	1	0.000	0.02
Rank of investigating officer PC (Y/N)	−0.23	0.16	2.06	1	0.151	0.80	−0.21	0.10	4.22	1	0.040	0.81

(continued)

Table 2 (continued)

	Anti-Semitic						Islamophobic					
Solvability factor	*B*	*SE*	Wald	*df*	*p*	Exp(*B*)	*B*	*SE*	Wald	*df*	*p*	Exp(*B*)
Forensic tasks undertaken	0.03	0.34	0.01	1	0.936	1.03	−0.13	0.23	0.33	1	0.568	0.88
Kensington and Chelsea, Richmond, Bromley or Islington	−0.31	0.31	1.00	1	0.318	0.73	−0.40	0.15	6.95	1	0.008	0.67
Four or more witnesses	0.72	0.17	18.00	1	0.000	2.05	0.79	0.11	55.98	1	0.000	2.20
Assault (Y/N)	−0.98	0.43	5.08	1	0.024	0.38	−0.65	0.31	4.42	1	0.036	0.52
Criminal damage (Y/N)	0.06	0.45	0.02	1	0.895	1.06	−0.39	0.33	1.35	1	0.245	0.68
Public order (Y/N)	−0.68	0.38	3.24	1	0.072	0.51	−0.39	0.27	2.01	1	0.156	0.68
Reported at weekend (Y/N)	−0.28	0.18	2.23	1	0.136	0.76	0.12	0.11	1.14	1	0.286	1.12
Time reported on/off peak	−0.26	0.18	2.02	1	0.155	0.77	−0.29	0.11	6.45	1	0.011	0.75
Direct or indirect reporting	−0.49	0.29	2.80	1	0.094	0.61	−0.31	0.20	2.34	1	0.127	0.76
Delay in reporting (Y/N)	−0.61	0.17	13.3	1	0.000	0.54	−0.94	0.12	61.30	1	0.000	0.39
Constant	5.2	1.3	16.0	1	0.000	173.8	5.19	0.83	38.8	1	0.000	179.4
	$\chi^2 = 307.438, p < 0.001, df = 22, N = 1374$ Nagelkerke's $R^2 = 0.31$						$\chi^2 = 737.626, p < 0.001, df = 22, N = 2857$ Nagelkerke's $R^2 = 0.34$					

To these were added other solvability factors, some common to criminal damage and public order offences (victim's faith and reported at peak times of day), and others unique to particular offences. Factors that help explain detection outcomes only for particular offences are (for public order incidents only) victim gender, whether the victim is of working age, whether reporting is direct or indirect, and whether the offence was investigated by police attached to the borough, and (for assaults only) whether forensic tasks were undertaken and whether the crime venue was public.

There are eight, seven and twelve significant solvability factors, respectively, for assaults, criminal damage and public order offences (Tables 3(i), 4(i) and 5(i)). Seven of these (namely whether the victim was a police officer, driver or security worker, whether the offence was witnessed by the police, whether the investigating officer was a police constable, whether the offence occurred in the boroughs of Kensington and Chelsea, Richmond, Bromley or Islington, whether there were four or more witnesses and whether there was a reporting delay) helped explain every offence type, so that, respectively, one, two and five additional solvability factors were distinctive in explaining individual offence types, particularly public order offences. It therefore makes sense to apply solvability factor analysis to each individual type of faith hate offence.

A police witness stood out as the strongest factor for every type of offence. Most other factors had quite low odds of improving detection outcomes, typically c. 2:1. A few solvability factors had better odds, notably whether public order offences were investigated by the local police (in the same borough), and, for criminal damage offences, occurrence in one of the four boroughs (Kensington and Chelsea, Richmond, Bromley, Islington) and whether the victim was in a particular occupation (a police officer, driver, or in the security industry). These factors had odds of between 4:1 and 6:1. Significant solvability factors explain a rather higher proportion of detection outcomes for assaults (36%) and criminal damage (37%) offences than public order crimes (30%) (Tables 3(i), 4(i) and 5(i)).

Solvability Factors for Islamophobic and Anti-Semitic Assaults and Criminal Damage and Public Order Offences

Six separate binary logistic regression analyses were carried out for each of the three crime types for the two faith hate victim groups to assess whether this would improve the proportion of detection outcomes explained by solvability factors. Narrowing down analyses to specific faith-crime-type subgroups should enable solvability factors and investigative decisions to be more closely tailored to specific sorts of crime. Binary logistic regression results for the six faith-crime-type subgroups are shown in Tables 3(ii) and (iii), 4(ii) and (iii), and 5(ii) and (iii). There was overlap between the six faith-type–crime-type groups in terms of the significant solvability factors, though only two factors were common to every faith–crime-type subgroup: whether or not the victim was a police officer, driver or security employee and whether or not the police witnessed the offence.

Investigating faith hate crimes in terms of faith hate crime-type subgroups—rather than just faith-type or offence-type groups—improves accuracy a little. Different

Table 3 Binary logistic regressions with best-fit solutions: solvability factors for assaults

	(i) All assaults						(ii) Islamophobic assaults						(iii) Anti-Semitic assaults					
Solvability factor	*B*	*SE*	Wald	*df*	*p*	Exp(*B*)	*B*	*SE*	Wald	*df*	*p*	Exp(*B*)	*B*	*SE*	Wald	*df*	*p*	Exp(B)
Male/female victim													0.55	0.28	3.78	1	0.052	1.73
Victim was police, driver or security industry	1.1	0.27	15.1	1	0.000	0.56	1.1	0.31	12.1	1	0.001	2.88	1.3	0.48	7.65	1	0.006	3.78
Venue residential or not	−0.74	0.22	11.5	1	0.001	0.48	−0.52	0.25	4.2	1	0.041	0.60						
Venue public venue or not	−0.43	0.20	4.8	1	0.029	0.65												
Witnessed by police or not	5.0	0.73	46.7	1	0.000	143.8	5.1	1.0	24.7	1	0.000	164.7	5.53	1.0	28.3	1	0.000	250.8
Rank of investigating officer PC or not																		
Forensic tasks undertaken	0.60	0.29	4.3	1	0.039	1.81							1.7	0.47	13.3	1	0.000	5.45
Kensington and Chelsea, Richmond, Bromley or Islington	0.60	0.28	4.7	1	0.031	1.82	0.73	0.31	5.5	1	0.019	2.08						

(continued)

Table 3 (continued)

	(i) All assaults						(ii) Islamophobic assaults						(iii) Anti-Semitic assaults					
Solvability factor	*B*	*SE*	Wald	*df*	*p*	Exp(*B*)	*B*	*SE*	Wald	*df*	*p*	Exp(*B*)	*B*	*SE*	Wald	*df*	*p*	Exp(B)
Four or more witnesses	0.86	0.16	29.4	1	0.000	2.35	0.82	0.19	18.6	1	0.000	2.27	1.34	0.25	28.4	1	0.000	3.81
Direct or indirect reporting							1.5	0.34	18.7	1	0.000	4.37	1.12	0.34	10.7	1	0.001	3.05
Time reported on/off peak																		
Delay in reporting (Y/N)	1.0	0.16	30.8	1	0.000	2.78												
Constant	−3.0	0.49	37.3	1	0.000	0.049	−3.1	0.54	34.4	1	0.000	0.043	−3.35	0.35	94.0	1	0.000	0.04
	$\chi^2 = 344.7, p < 0.001, df = 8, N = 1217$						$\chi^2 = 179.6, p < 0.001, df = 6, N = 688$						$\chi^2 = 187.2, p < 0.001, df = 6, N = 663$					
	Nagelkerke's $R^2 = 0.36$						Nagelkerke's $R^2 = 0.32$						Nagelkerke's $R^2 = 0.40$					
	80.4% of cases correctly predicted						75.6% of cases correctly predicted						87.3% of cases correctly predicted					

Table 4 Binary logistic regressions with best-fit solutions: solvability factors for criminal damage

	(i) All criminal damage offences						(ii) Islamophobic criminal damage						(iii) Anti-Semitic criminal damage					
Solvability factor	*B*	*SE*	Wald	*df*	*p*	Exp(*B*)	*B*	*SE*	Wald	*df*	*p*	Exp(*B*)	*B*	*SE*	Wald	*df*	*p*	Exp(*B*)
Victim was police, driver or security industry	1.8	0.58	9.67	1	0.002	6.02	1.8	0.80	5.1	1	0.024	6.03	2.02	0.88	5.21	1	0.022	7.52
Venue residential or not	0.76	0.26	8.6	1	0.003	2.15	1.1	0.36	9.14	1	0.003	3.00						
Venue public venue or not													−0.9	0.42	4.65	1	0.031	0.41
Witnessed by police or not	6.1	1.1	33.0	1	0.000	448.1	4.8	2167	0.00	1	0.000	117.1	5.66	1.1	25.9	1	0.000	287.4
Rank of investigating officer PC or not	0.95	0.24	16.2	1	0.000	2.59	1.1	0.31	11.4	1	0.001	2.89	0.72	0.37	3.85	1	0.050	2.05
Kensington and Chelsea, Richmond, Bromley or Islington	1.4	0.34	17.3	1	0.000	4.01	1.5	0.43	11.3	1	0.001	4.30	1.57	0.54	8.43	1	0.004	4.83
Four or more witnesses	1.2	0.29	16.2	1	0.000	3.23	1.4	0.35	15.4	1	0.000	3.95						
Time reported on/off peak	0.63	0.25	6.21	1	0.013	1.87							1.14	0.37	9.45	1	0.002	3.11

(continued)

Table 4 (continued)

	(i) All criminal damage offences						(ii) Islamophobic criminal damage						(iii) Anti-Semitic criminal damage					
Solvability factor	*B*	*SE*	Wald	*df*	*p*	Exp(*B*)	*B*	*SE*	Wald	*df*	*p*	Exp(*B*)	*B*	*SE*	Wald	*df*	*p*	Exp(*B*)
Delay in reporting (Y/N)	0.83	0.24	12.4	1	0.000	2.29	0.68	0.30	5.0	1	0.026	1.96	1.23	0.37	10.9	1	0.001	3.42
Anti-Semitic or Islamophobic victim	−0.71	0.24	9.04	1	0.003	0.49	–	–	–	–	–	–	–	–	–	–	–	–
Constant	−6.3	0.99	40.6	1	0.000	0.002	−3.1	0.54	34.4	1	0.000	0.043	−8.2	1.2	47.2	1	0.000	0.00
	$\chi^2 = 228.8, p < 0.001, df = 9, N = 1083$						$\chi^2 = 103.3, p < 0.001, df = 7, N = 465$						$\chi^2 = 119.0, p < 0.000, df = 7, N = 618$					
	Nagelkerke's $R^2 = 0.37$						Nagelkerke's $R^2 = 0.34$						Nagelkerke's $R^2 = 0.40$					
	91.2% of cases correctly predicted						88.0% of cases correctly predicted						94.3% of cases correctly predicted					

Table 5 Binary logistic regressions with best-fit solutions: solvability factors for public order offences

	(i) All public order offences						(ii) Islamophobic public order offences						(iii) Anti-Semitic public order offences					
Solvability factor	*B*	*SE*	Wald	*df*	*p*	Exp(*B*)	*B*	*SE*	Wald	*df*	*p*	Exp(*B*)	*B*	*SE*	Wald	*df*	*p*	Exp(*B*)
Male/female victim	−0.4	0.09	22.0	1	0.000	0.65	−0.6	0.11	24.2	1	0.000	0.58						
Victim was police, driver or security industry	0.89	0.13	45.3	1	0.000	2.42	0.93	0.15	36.8	1	0.000	2.53	0.73	0.26	7.78	1	0.005	2.07
Venue residential or not	0.76	0.26	8.6	1	0.003	2.15	0.37	0.14	6.62	1	0.010	1.45						
Witnessed by police/not	4.6	0.34	185.8	1	0.000	96.32	4.1	0.38	114.1	1	0.000	60.14	4.9	0.52	88.5	1	0.000	132.9
Rank of investigating officer PC or not	0.32	0.09	13.8	1	0.000	1.37	0.36	0.11	11.0	1	0.001	1.43	0.38	0.13	8.20	1	0.004	1.46
Kensington and Chelsea, Richmond, Bromley or Islington	0.35	0.14	6.55	1	0.010	1.42	0.35	0.16	5.1	1	0.025	1.42						
Borough/other police investigation	−1.5	0.65	5.12	1	0.024	0.23	−1.5	0.63	5.5	1	0.019	0.23						

(continued)

Table 5 (continued)

	(i) All public order offences						(ii) Islamophobic public order offences						(iii) Anti-Semitic public order offences					
Solvability factor	*B*	*SE*	Wald	*df*	*p*	Exp(*B*)	*B*	*SE*	Wald	*df*	*p*	Exp(*B*)	*B*	*SE*	Wald	*df*	*p*	Exp(*B*)
Four or more witnesses	0.85	0.09	90.1	1	0.000	2.33	0.82	0.11	56.2	1	0.000	2.25	0.93	0.15	40.7	1	0.000	2.54
Time reported on/off peak	0.22	0.10	5.27	1	0.022	1.25	0.35	0.12	8.6	1	0.003	1.42						
Direct or indirect reporting	0.28	0.14	4.36	1	0.037	1.32												
Delay in reporting (Y/N)	0.82	0.09	77.1	1	0.000	2.27	0.98	0.11	74.4	1	0.000	2.67	0.79	0.13	36.0	1	0.000	2.21
Anti-Semitic or Islamophobic victim	−0.2	0.09	4.91	1	0.027	0.82	–	–	–	–	–	–	–	–	–	–	–	–
Constant	−2.8	0.77	13.5	1	0.000	0.059	−3.4	0.72	22.0	1	0.000	0.034	−3.87	0.29	175.4	1	0.000	0.02
	$\chi^2 = 1009.5, p < 0.001, df = 12, N = 4799$						$\chi^2 = 639.4, p < 0.001, df = 10, N = 2784$						$\chi^2 = 397.8, p < 0.000, df = 5, N = 2174$					
	Nagelkerke's $R^2 = 0.30$						Nagelkerke's $R^2 = 0.31$						Nagelkerke's $R^2 = 0.28$					
	84.4% of cases correctly predicted						82.0% of cases correctly predicted						87.1% of cases correctly predicted					

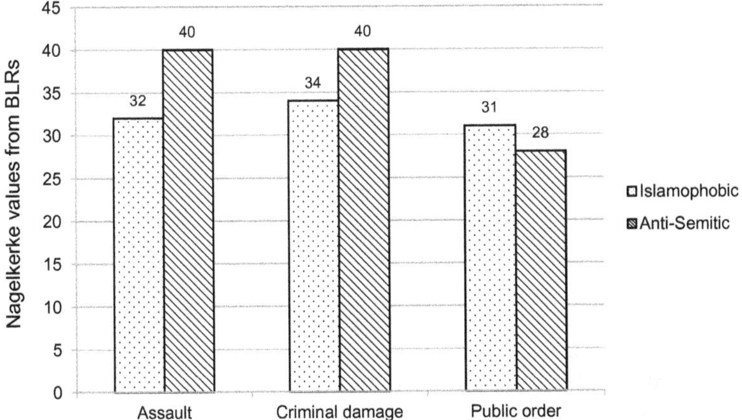

Fig. 9 Nagelkerke's R^2 values for faith hate crime-type binary logistic regressions (i.e., percentage of detected/undetected outcomes explained by significant solvability factors)

solvability factors more precisely explain detection outcomes between Islamophobic and anti-Semitic criminal damage offences, with five out of seven factors common to both faiths (Table 4(ii) and (iii)), between Islamophobic and anti-Semitic public order offences (where the Islamophobic regression has twice the number of significant solvability factors, ten vs. five, (Table 5(ii) and (iii)), and between Islamophobic and anti-Semitic assaults, which share four out of six solvability factors (Table 3(ii) and (iii)). Some significant factors are present in most faith-crime-type models, such as 'four or more witnesses', which affects detection outcomes for every faith-crime-type subgroup bar anti-Semitic criminal damage offences. Other factors are prevalent for some offence types but not others, such as reporting delay, which is a significant factor for public order and criminal damage offences but not for assaults, where a quicker patrol response may be the norm. Other factors affect certain faiths. Whether the offence, for example, occurred in one of the four boroughs (Kensington and Chelsea, Richmond, Bromley, Islington) helped account for the detection outcomes of only Islamophobic offences; there are very few Jewish victims in Richmond and Bromley and only small numbers in Islington and Kensington and Chelsea.

Investigating offences in terms of both faith hate type and crime type together also provides a more accurate insight into the proportion of detections explained by solvability factors.

Summary Nagelkerke values of $R^2 = 0.31$ for all Islamophobic offences taken together and 0.34 for all anti-Semitic offences, and values of $R^2 = 0.36$ for all assaults, 0.37 for all criminal damage offences and 0.30 for all public order offences, irrespective of faith type, become more precise when regression analysis is applied to the six faith–hate–crime-type subgroups (Fig. 9). The level of statistical explanation is, in fact, higher for Jewish than Muslim victims of assault and criminal damage (respectively, Nagelkerke's $R^2 = 0.40$, 0.40 for anti-Semitic vs. 0.32, 0.34 for Islamophobic offences). This is reversed for public order offences, for which explanation levels are lower (Fig. 9).

Summary Solvability Measures, Detections and Targeting Investigative Effort

Single summary solvability measures for individual incidents were calculated by multiplying the odds ratios of significant solvability factors by each case's binary value and summing these to create a single solvability score for each data case. Different solvability scores were calculated for the same cases when analysed in terms of different subgroups. An anti-Semitic assault case might, for instance, have an anti-Semitic solvability score based on the solvability factors and odds ratios from the binary logistic regression including only anti-Semitic incidents. The same case would have a slightly different score when based on the solvability factor odds ratios from the binary logistic regression including only assault cases, and yet another for a regression that included only anti-Semitic assault cases.

By comparing the distribution of solvability scores with detections for any defined population subgroup, it is possible to assess how well solvability scores predict detection outcomes, identify subsets of cases with varying probabilities of being solved and, therefore, to determine the types of cases for which investigative effort may be more and less cost-effectively used.

Summary Solvability Measures for Anti-Semitic and Islamophobic Crimes

Detected anti-Semitic incidents had far higher anti-Semitic solvability scores: an average of 41.7 compared with only 9.4 for undetected cases ($F = 1113.5, p < 0.000$, $n = 1, 3850$). The higher the solvability score, the more cases were detected (Fig. 10). The most solvable 4% of anti-Semitic incidents (scores >25.0) had a 94% chance of being detected, since almost all involved a police officer witness. The next most solvable 11% (scores 12.1–25.0) and 10% (scores of 11.1–12.0) had, respectively, a 30% and 19% chance of being detected (Fig. 10). Hence, the most solvable 25% of cases—which constituted 61% of all detections—had good 36% odds (2.8:1) of being detected. Less solvable cases, with scores between 9 and 11, constituted 27% of anti-Semitic cases and had odds of only 10% of being solved, so that considerable investigative effort was required to secure these detections. The least solvable cases constituted over a quarter of the anti-Semitic offences and, with only 5% detection odds, were the most cost-ineffective cases in terms of investigative resources. It would be worthwhile monitoring incidents with scores indicating good prospects for detection in order to help ensure that the 65% of them that are not detected have received a thorough investigation.

Detected Islamophobia incidents also had far higher Islamophobia solvability scores—an average of 48.0 compared with only 6.6 for undetected cases ($F = 902.7$, $p < 0.000$, n = 1, 4594). The most solvable 4.5% of Islamophobia incidents (scores >25.0) had a 95% chance of being detected, since almost all involved a police offi-

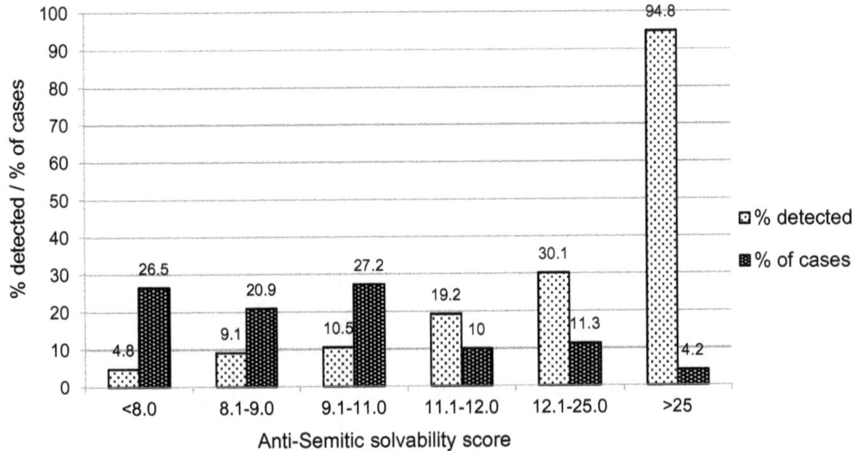

Fig. 10 Percentage of anti-Semitism incidents detected and percentage of cases by anti-Semitic solvability scores

cer witness. The next most solvable 11% (scores of 17.2–25.0) and 9% (scores of 15.8–17.2) had, respectively, a 50 and 32% chance of being detected (Fig. 11). Hence, the most solvable 25% of cases, which constituted 59% of all detections, had good 52% odds (1.9:1) of being detected. Therefore, it is more cost-effective to secure detected outcomes from the most solvable 60% of Islamophobia incidents than from the equivalent anti-Semitic incidents, which have only 36% odds of detection. The next most solvable cases, constituting 26% of Islamophobia cases, had 20% odds of being detected—double that of the equivalent anti-Semitic group. The least solvable cases have comparable detection rates to anti-Semitic incidents: 17% of Islamophobia detections (and 19% of anti-Semitic ones) were, therefore, cost-ineffective to investigate and solve.

Overall, the solvability scores of the two faith hate crimes are not dissimilar. Islamophobic incidents, however, can be solved rather more cost-effectively in terms of the percentage of cases that needs to be investigated to produce a given detection outcome (Fig. 12). It may be that the better detection rates of Islamophobia crimes reflect greater resources as well as inherent incident characteristics, of which one is the type of crime.

Summary Solvability Measures for Assaults and Criminal Damage and Public Order Offences

For all types of offence, detected cases had far higher solvability scores than undetected ones (assaults: mean scores of 40.1 vs. 3.9; $F(1, 1215) = 299.3$, $p < 0.001$; criminal damage: mean scores of 21.5 vs. 15.5; $F(1, 1081) = 267.4$, $p < 0.001$;

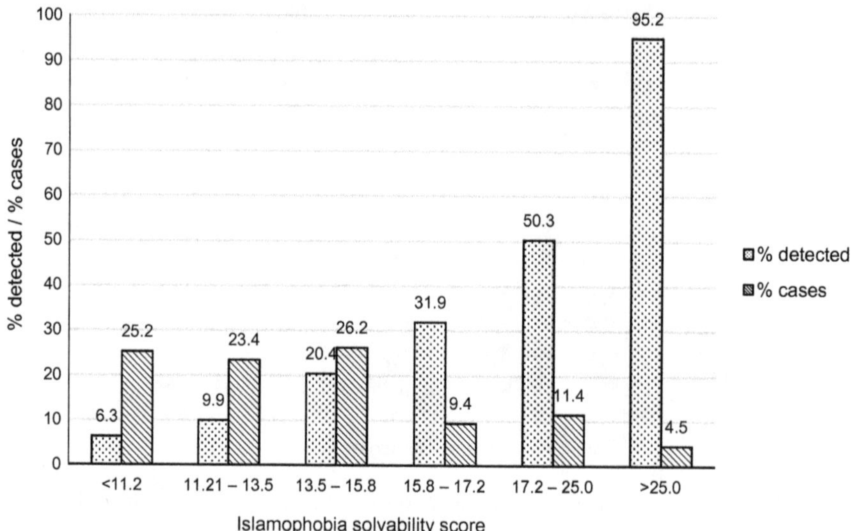

Fig. 11 Percentage of Islamophobia incidents detected and percentage of cases by Islamophobia solvability scores

public order: mean scores of 25 vs. 3.9; $F(1, 4797) = 1098$, $p < 0.001$). The very high detection rates for the highest solvability score group for every crime type are attributable to police witnessing offences (Figs. 13, 14 and 15). Even excluding cases

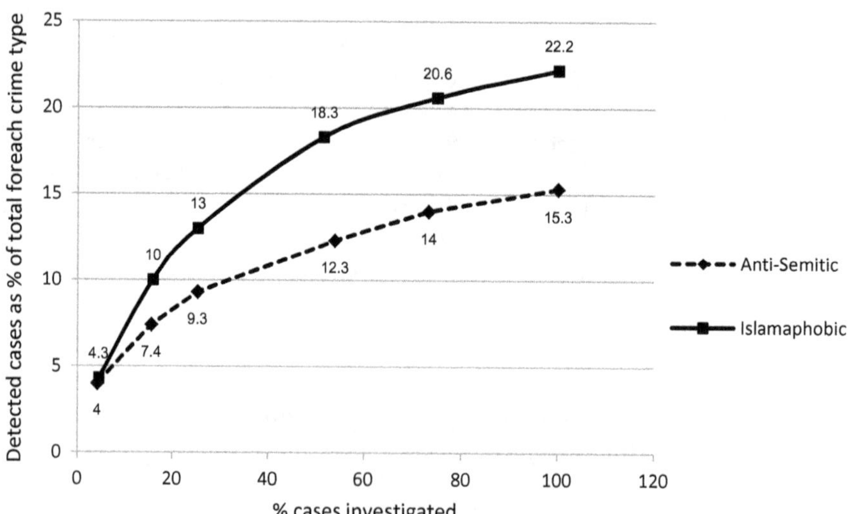

Fig. 12 For each hate faith offence, cumulative percentage of cases investigated by cumulative percentage of cases detected, from low (values 0) to high case solvability scores

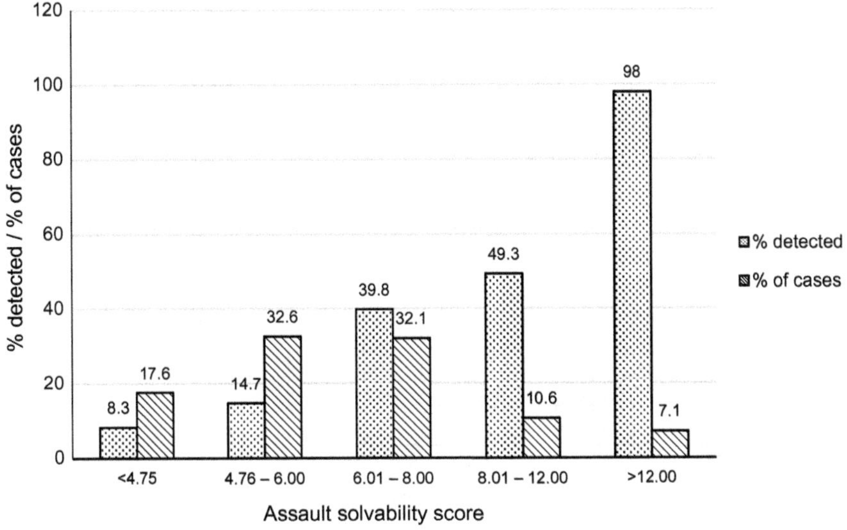

Fig. 13 Percentage of assaults detected and percentage of cases by assault solvability scores

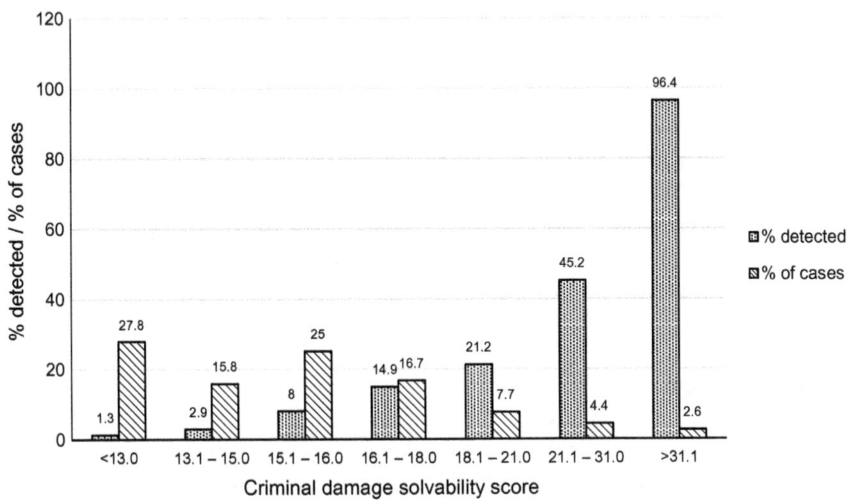

Fig. 14 Percentage of criminal damage offences detected and percentage of cases by criminal damage solvability scores

where police witnessed offences, the higher criminal damage solvability scores of detected cases persisted, with, for instance, criminal damage offences averaging 19.0 for detected cases compared with 15.4 for undetected cases ($F(1, 1053) = 135.7$, $p < 0.001$).

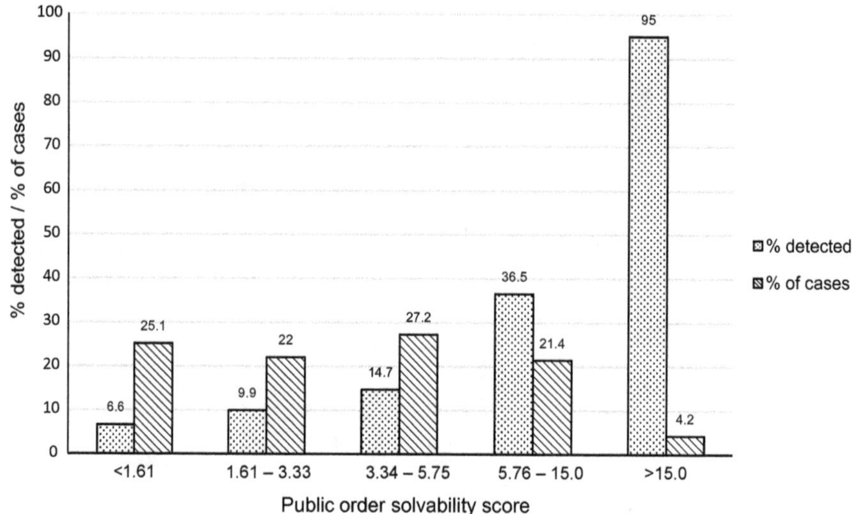

Fig. 15 Percentage of public order offences detected and percentage of cases by public order solvability scores

Assaults

For assaults, the most solvable 7% of faith hate assault incidents (scores >13.0) had a 97% chance of detection, while the next most solvable 12% (scores of 7.51–13.0) and 11% (scores of 6.01–7.5) had, respectively, a 55% and 38% chance of being detected (Fig. 13). Cases with lower solvability scores can only be solved less cost-effectively. Nearly a third (30%) of assault incidents are characterised by high solvability scores and might be prioritised for investigation.

Criminal Damage

Excluding the 2.6% of criminal damage incidents witnessed by police officers, which often involve an on-the-spot arrest, a further 29% of cases, identifiable using a scoring system based on the solvability factors identified by this study, offer good prospects—overall, a 21% likelihood—of being solved. For lower solvability cases, which make up over two-thirds of all criminal damage offences, the prospects for detection drop markedly (Fig. 14).

Public Order Incidents

Ninety-five per cent of public order incidents with scores exceeding 15 (reflecting cases where the police witnessed the offence) and 37% of those with scores between

5.76 and 15 were solved (Fig. 15). These represent a quarter of all public order cases. Other, less solvable, public order incidents offer deteriorating prospects of detected outcomes: only 15% of cases in the next most solvable group (scores of 3.34–5.75) were detected, representing 27% of incidents. The prospects of detected cases drop further for the remaining cases, making up almost half of all public order offences (Fig. 15).

Comparative cost-effectiveness of different crime-type investigations

Figure 16 illustrates the potential differences in the cost-effectiveness of investigations for the various crime-type subsets of cases. The graph portrays the detected cases that result from investigating offences of varying solvability as currently defined on the basis of the analysis. The investigation of the most solvable offences results in the highest detection outcomes (bottom left-hand corner), after which the number of detected cases resulting from investigations progressively falls as fewer detected cases result from the investigation of progressively less solvable offences (towards top right-hand corner). The differences in the investigative input versus the detected case output reflect differences in the overall detection rates, with assaults more cost-effectively solved than public order offences, and these, in turn, more cost-effectively solved than criminal damage offences. Hence, more criminal damage cases than public order offences must be investigated to produce a given number of detected cases,

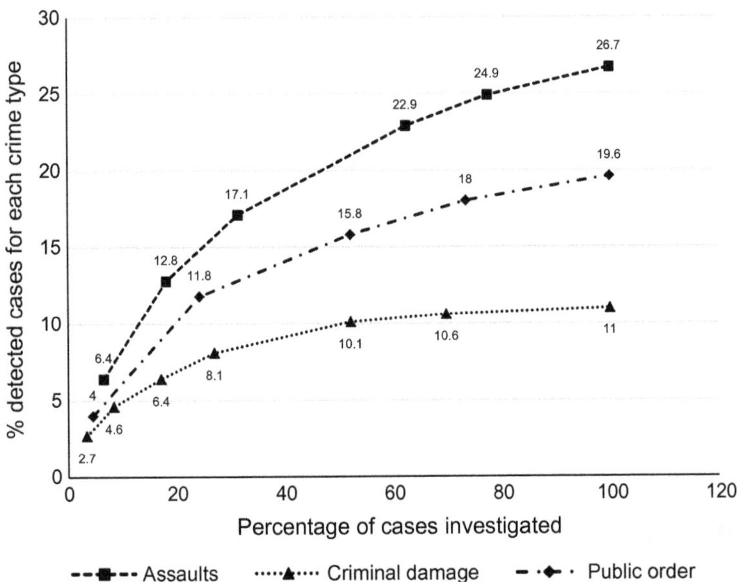

Fig. 16 For each crime type, detected cases as percentage of all cases by percentage of cases investigated

and more of the latter must in turn be investigated than assault cases. It is possible that the costs of investigating the different types of crime may differ, so that the ratio between cases investigated and detected on its own may be made more accurate given an understanding of investigative costs. These can present significant additional costs if further investigations that do not merely follow up on evidence collected by first officers are undertaken but also involve significant additional investigative effort, only part of which may, in practice, be fruitful (see Coupe Chapter "Investigative Activities, Resources and Burglary Detection"). The higher detection rates for assaults may be due partly to more further investigations being carried out by detectives than for criminal damage and public order offences.

Solvability of Assault, Criminal Damage and Public Order Offences with Muslim and Jewish Victims

Summary solvability scores were calculated separately for each of the six faith hate-type–offence-type subgroups. Each solvability score was based on the significant solvability factors from each of the six binary logistic regressions, with detection outcome as the dependent variable (Tables 4(ii) and (iii), 5(ii) and (iii), and 6(ii) and (iii)). As above, solvability scores were calculated by multiplying each case's binary value by the odds ratios for every significant solvability factor and summing the products, so that a case in which every solvability factor was present would take the highest score and one where no solvability factor was present would be allocated the lowest. Solvability scores summarise the combined odds of a case being detected.

As expected, mean solvability scores were far higher for detected cases for all of the six different faith-type–crime-type subgroups (Table 6(A)). The differences persisted when incidents witnessed by the police were excluded (Table 6(B)).

Figures 17, 18, 19, 20, 21 and 22 show the percentage of cases detected compared with the percentage of cases investigated for the six faith-type–crime-type subgroups. Each bar chart indicates the investigative effort that must be potentially expended to achieve the detection outcomes if the solvability factors identified in the chapter were to be used to guide investigative decisions. For every faith-type–crime-type subgroup, high-solvability cases have higher detection rates and present scope for more cost-effective detection. With declining case solvability, the proportions of detected cases fall until, for the least solvable cases, far more cases must be investigated to produce fewer detections (Figs. 17, 18, 19, 20, 21 and 22). There are differences between the faith-type–crime-type subgroups in the proportions of cases that must be investigated in order to solve cases cost-effectively, and these are now outlined.

Assaults

Half of Islamophobic assault cases have at least 40% odds of being detected, and these can be identified using solvability factors (Fig. 17). Therefore, there are good prospects for cost-effectively solving 25% of the 31% of cases currently detected

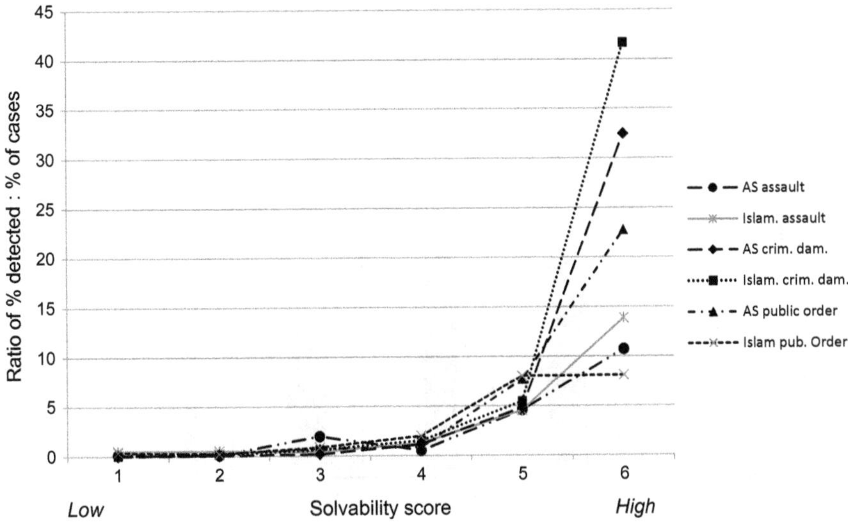

Fig. 17 Islamophobic assault solvability score by percentage detected and percentage of sample cases

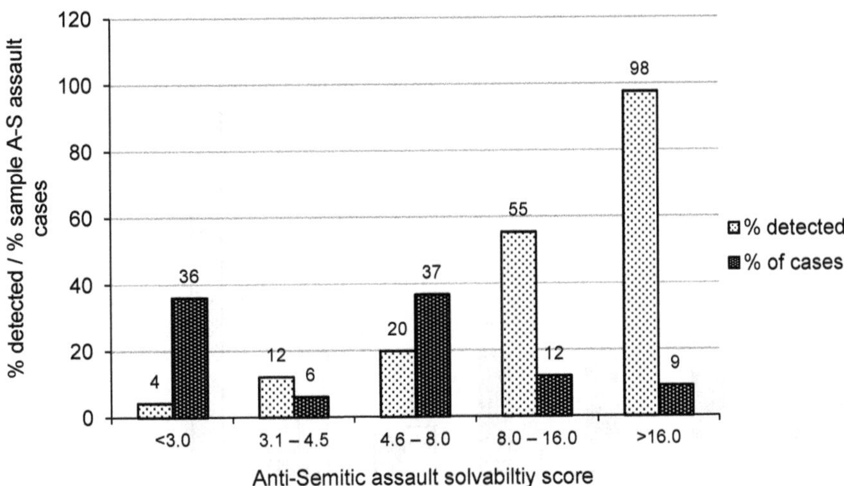

Fig. 18 Anti-Semitic assault solvability score by percentage detected and percentage of sample cases

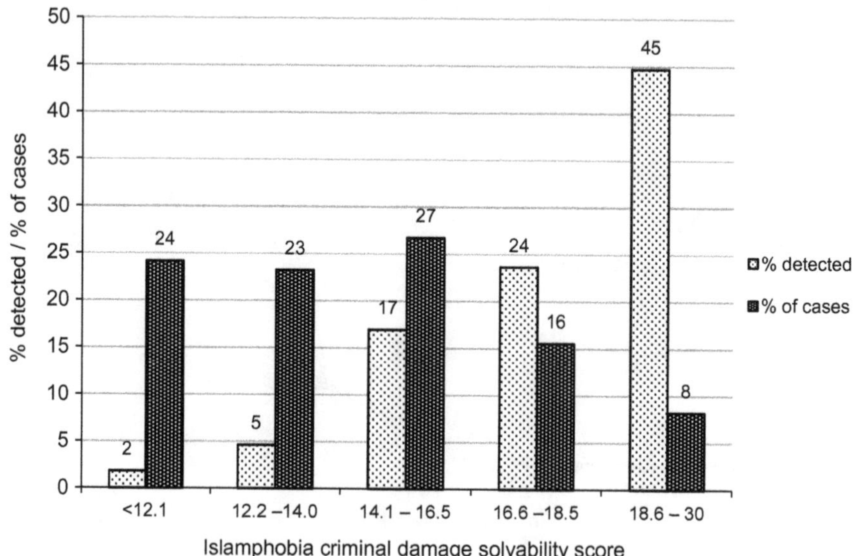

Fig. 19 Islamophobic criminal damage solvability score by percentage detected and percentage of sample cases

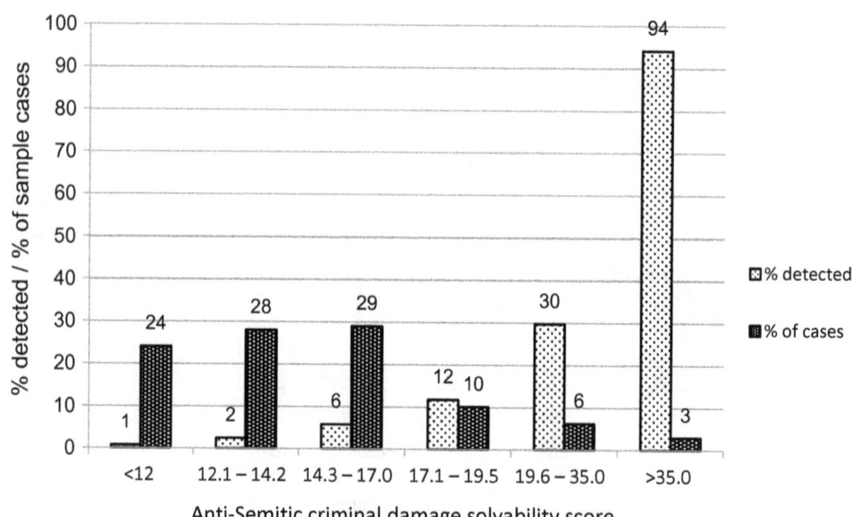

Fig. 20 Anti-Semitic criminal damage solvability score by percentage detected and percentage of sample cases

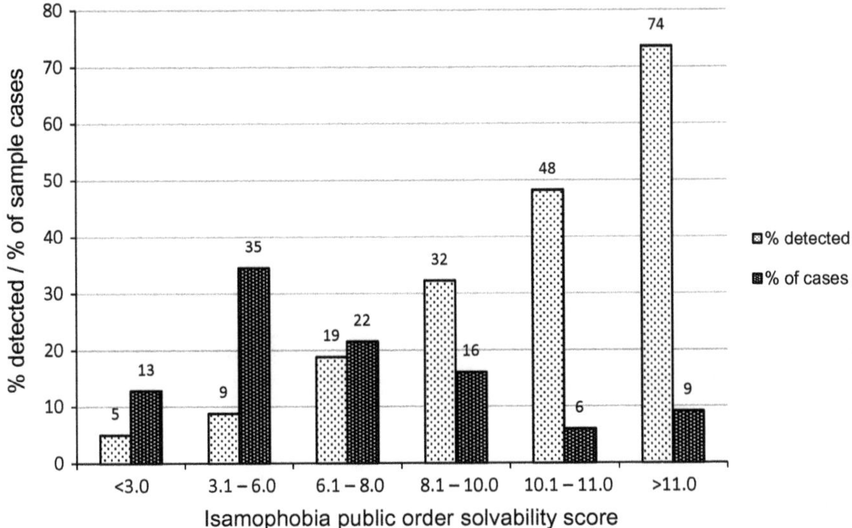

Fig. 21 Islamophobic public order offence solvability score by percentage detected and percentage of sample cases

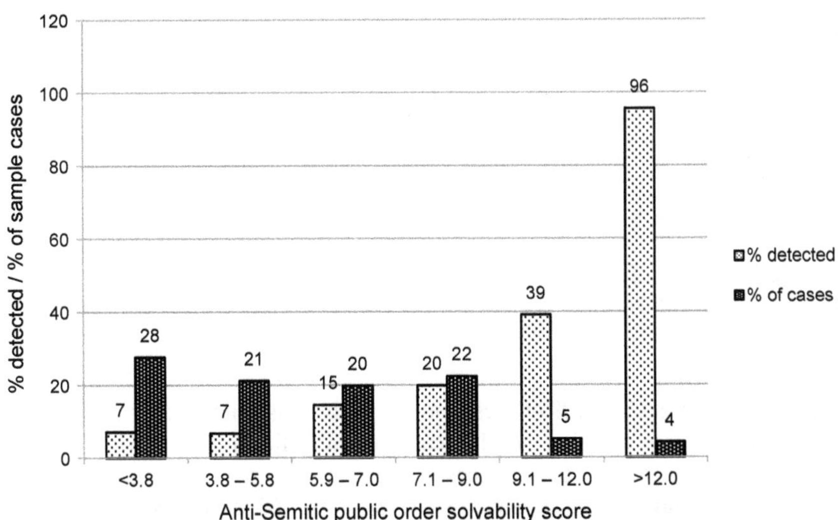

Fig. 22 Anti-Semitic public order offence solvability score by percentage detected and percentage of sample cases

Table 6 Differences in mean solvability score between undetected and detected cases for the six faith-type–crime-type subgroups for (A) all sub-group cases (B) sub-group cases excluding those where police witnessed offences

(A)	Undetected mean solvability score	Detected mean solvability score	*F* test (*df*)	*p*
Islamophobic assaults	5.3	43.2	(1686) = 140.9	0.000
Anti-Semitic assaults	3.8	76.7	(1661) = 215.1	0.000
Islamophobic criminal damage	13.7	34.5	(1463) = 90.2	0.000
Anti-Semitic criminal damage	15.0	106.7	(1616) = 246.9	0.000
Islamophobic public order	6.0	19.2	(12,782) = 618.4	0.000
Anti-Semitic public order	5.9	38.7	(12,172) = 566.5	0.000
(B)	Undetected mean solvability score	Detected mean solvability score	*F* test (*df*)	*p*
Islamophobic assaults	5.0	6.6	(1636) = 66.4	0.000
Anti-Semitic assaults	3.3	5.9	(1624) = 85.3	0.000
Islamophobic criminal damage	3.3	17.1	(1452) = 73.4	0.000
Anti-Semitic criminal damage	14.4	18.5	(1599) = 61.4	0.000
Islamophobic public order	5.8	8.3	(12,660) = 387.2	0.000
Anti-Semitic public order	5.6	6.7	(12,088) = 105.8	0.000

(i.e., 80% of them). Only 7% of these more solvable cases involve a police officer witness, so a large proportion of other cases where officers neither witnessed nor were themselves victims of the offences may be solved.

A fifth of the anti-Semitic assault cases have at least 55% odds, and a further 37% have 20% odds of being detected. These, too, can be identified using solvability factors (Fig. 18). Therefore, there are good prospects for identifying and cost-effectively solving 22.5% of the 25% of cases currently being detected. Nine per cent of the more solvable cases involve a police officer witness, so a good proportion of other cases where officers neither witnessed nor themselves fell victim to assault may be solved.

Criminal Damage

Apart from the 2.4% of Islamophobic criminal damage incidents certain to be detected when the police witnessed the incident, a further 8 and 16% of incidents have, respectively, 45 and 24% chances of being detected (Fig. 19). These account for 10% of the 16% of cases currently detected. To improve this to 14%, it would be necessary to investigate a further 27% of cases with 17% odds of detection.

Overall detection rates for anti-Semitic criminal damage incidents are low, at 8.2%. Apart from the 3% of incidents virtually certain to be detected when the police witness the incident (Fig. 20), a further 6 and 10% of incidents have, respectively, 30 and 12% chances of being detected (Fig. 20). Together, these account for 70% of the cases currently detected, and 19% of cases would have to be investigated to make these arrests. To elevate the proportion to 90% of the cases currently being solved, a further 29% of cases with only a 6% chance of detection would need to be investigated. This is a considerable amount of additional work, even though only half of incidents need to be investigated to achieve this outcome.

Public Order Offences

The 22% detection rate for Islamophobic public order cases is double that for criminal damage. The third of incidents with solvability scores in excess of 8 have very good prospects for detection and account for two-thirds of all detections (Fig. 21). The next 17% most solvable cases (scores of 6–8) have 19% odds of being detected and can be solved reasonably cost-effectively (Fig. 21).

The overall detection rate for anti-Semitic public order offences was 16.7%, lower than Islamophobic public order offences, and only half the rate of criminal damage cases. Apart from the highly solvable 4% of cases witnessed by the police, which have 96% detection rates, the next most solvable 5, 22 and 20% of cases, had, respectively, 39, 20 and 15% detection rates (Fig. 22). Half of those cases identified as being the most solvable would need to be investigated in order to detect 80% of the cases currently being detected.

Summary

This review of incident solvability indicates that the summary solvability scores derived from significant binary logistic regression variables are good predictors of the odds of detecting different subsets of faith hate crime-type incidents. For each subset of cases based on either crime type or a combination of faith hate type and crime type, there is a distinctive 'curve' of incident solvability. Using these summary solvability measures, it is possible to scale cases from the least to the most solvable, providing scope to prioritise the investigation of cases that show the greatest promise for detection. Knowing the odds of cases being solved also points to the subsets of incidents that, on the basis of their solvability scores, might have been expected to be detected but which, in practice, remained undetected. Verifying that relevant investigative activities have been carried out for potentially solvable cases is another useful application of solvability analysis.

Figure 23 illustrates the potential differences in the cost-effectiveness of investigations for the various crime-type–faith-type subsets of cases. The graph portrays the detected cases that result from investigating offences of varying solvability. The investigation of the most solvable offences results in the highest detection outcomes (bottom left-hand corner) and then the number of detected cases resulting from investigations progressively falls as few detected cases result from the investigation of progressively less solvable offences (towards top right-hand corner). The differences in investigation input-detected case output reflect differences in overall detection rates, with Islamophobic offences more cost-effectively solved for every crime type than anti-Semitic offences, assaults more cost-effectively solved than public order offences, and these more so than criminal damage offences. Hence, more criminal damage cases must be investigated to produce a given number of detected cases than public order offences, and more of the latter must be investigated than assault cases. It is possible that the costs of investigating the different types of crime may differ, so

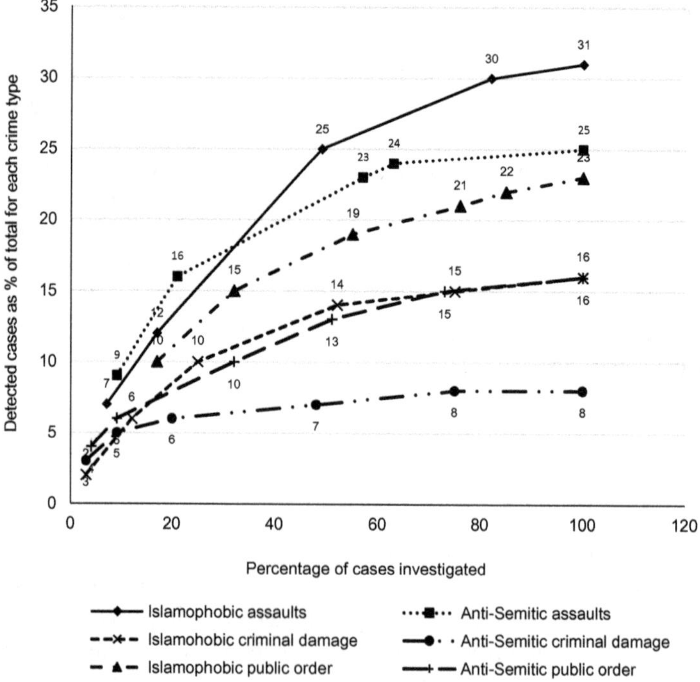

Fig. 23 For each faith hate offence-type group, cumulative percentage of cases investigated by cumulative percentage of cases detected (grouped in order from low (values 0) to high case solvability scores)

that the ratio between cases investigated and detected on its own may be made more accurate from an understanding of investigative costs. These can present significant additional costs if further investigations that do not merely follow up on evidence collected by first officers are undertaken (see Coupe Chapter "Investigative Activities, Resources and Burglary Detection"). The higher detection rates for assaults may be due partly to more further investigations being carried out by detectives than for criminal damage and public order offences.

Geographical Variation in Detections and Solvability

Spatial Variation in Faith Hate Detections and Solvability

Incident solvability shows considerable geographical variation (Fig. 24), with mean solvability scores ranging from 42 to 8 for Islamophobic incidents and 26–14 for anti-Semitic incidents. Mean borough Islamophobic and anti-Semitic solvability scores are not significantly related ($r = -0.019$, $p = 0.92$, $n = 32$). This may reflect, in part, the differences in the spatial distribution of different types of faith hate crimes experienced by Jewish and Muslim victims, which vary in terms of solvability.

Spatial variation in detection rates for Islamophobic crimes reflects solvability differences across the boroughs ($r = 0.52$, $p = 0.002$, $n = 32$), indicating that 27% ($R^2 = 0.27$) of spatial variation in detection rates is attributable to differences in case solvability. Anti-Semitic borough detection rates, in contrast, were not significantly linked to the spatial distribution of solvable cases ($r = 0.19$, $p = 0.30$, $n = 32$).

Therefore, boroughs that detected more Islamophobic crimes did not detect more anti-Semitic crimes (Fig. 25, $r = 0.11$, $p = 0.56$, $n = 32$; $r_s = 0.10$, $p = 0.59$, $n = 32$), indicating either that investigative performance for the two faith hate offences was at odds or that case solvability varied for the two types of faith hate crimes. This partly reflects the fact that fewer Jewish people were the victims of public order offences, which have higher detection rates, and more experienced criminal damage to property, which had lower detection rates (Fig. 26; χ^2 (2, 8012) = 206.4, $p < 0.001$), though the effect size is low ($V = 0.16$, $p < 0.001$), indicating other influences, such as variation in incident solvability and investigative resources.

There are few significant relationships between solvability scores and detection rates between assaults and criminal damage and public order offences, or between these different offences when examined for either Islamophobia or anti-Semitism victims separately.

Detection rates across the 32 boroughs for the three main offence types—assault, criminal damage and public order offences—were unrelated (assaults vs. criminal damage: $r = 0.05$, $p = 0.78$; assaults vs. public order: $r = -0.31$, $p = 0.09$, $p = 0.61$; criminal damage vs. public order: $r = 0.09$, $p = 0.61$), so that boroughs with higher detection rates for one sort of offence did not necessarily have high rates for the others.

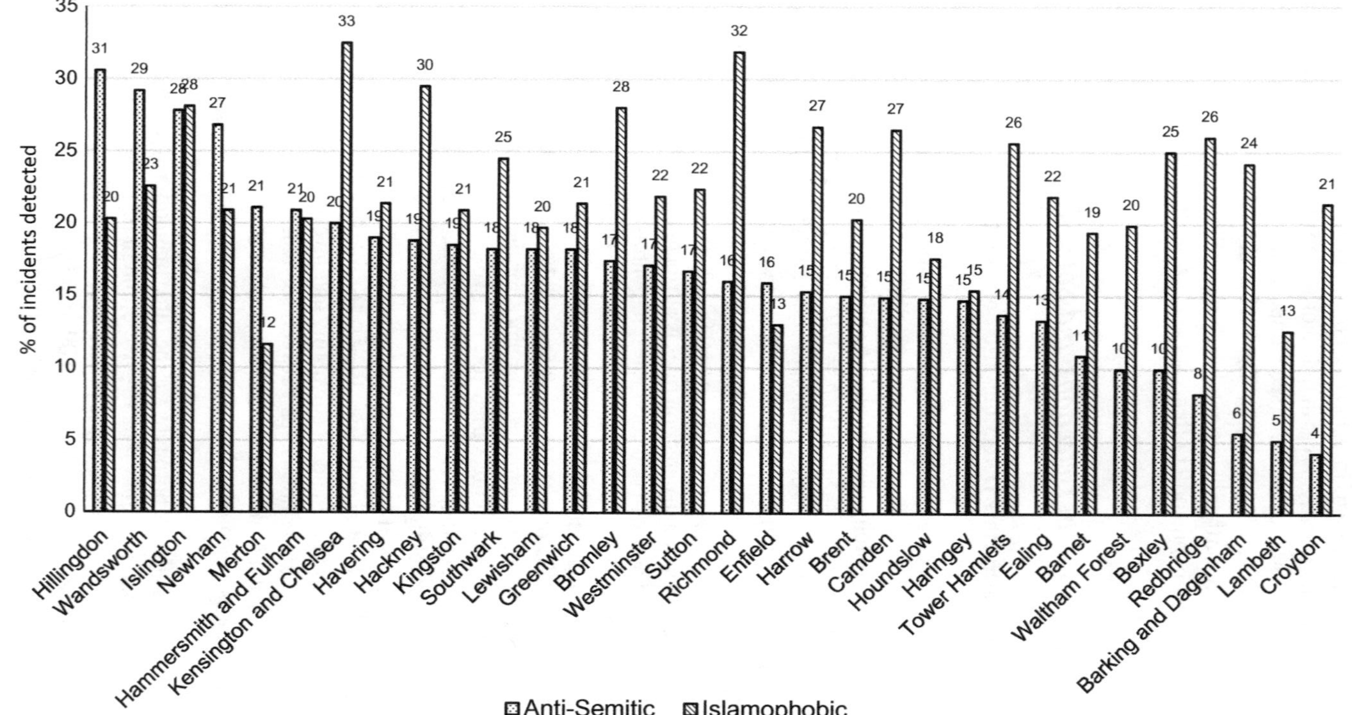

Fig. 24 Anti-Semitic and Islamophobic solvability scores for 32 London boroughs

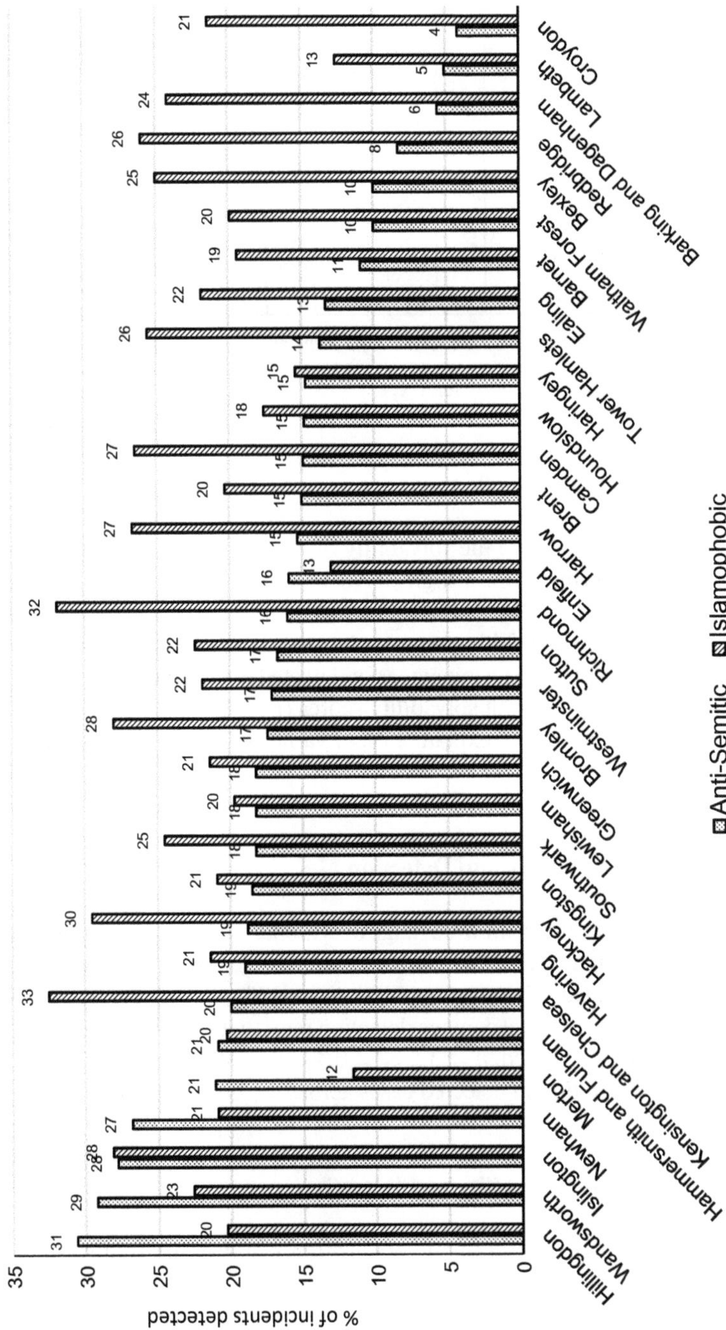

Fig. 25 Percentages of Islamophobic and anti-Semitic incidents detected by borough

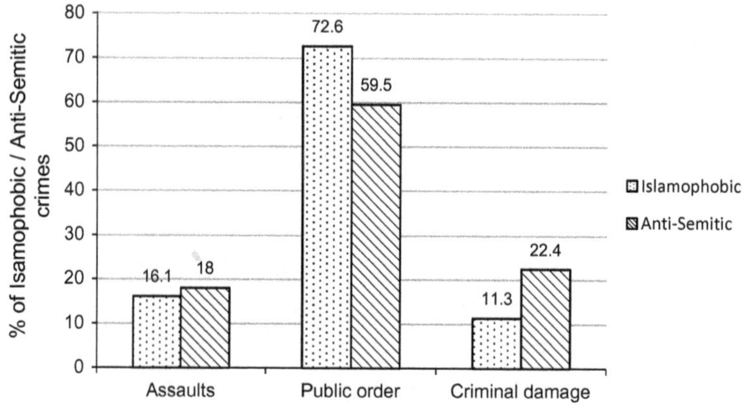

Fig. 26 Percentages of different crimes by faith type

Assaults—Solvability and Detection

There is considerable variation in the solvability of faith hate assault crimes across London's boroughs, varying from a high of 70 in Richmond to a low of 0.6 in Bromley.

Borough detection rates for faith hate assaults are not always closely related to solvability (Fig. 27), although the percentages of detected assault cases for boroughs are correlated with borough assault solvability scores ($r = 0.50, p = 0.004, n = 32$; $r_s = 0.49, p = 0.005, n = 32$) and explain 23% of variation in detected cases across the boroughs ($R^2 = 0.226$).

Criminal Damage—Solvability and Detection

As with faith hate assaults, there is a wide range of criminal damage solvability scores across the London boroughs (Fig. 28), from a high of 97 in Hammersmith and Fulham to a low of 14 in Westminster. Using borough means, the criminal damage solvability score is weakly related to criminal damage detection rates, with a low–medium effect size ($r = 0.34, p = 0.03$, 1–tailed, $n = 32$; $r_s = 0.49, p = 0.002$, 1–tailed, $n = 32$), and explains 11% of variation in detected cases across the boroughs ($R^2 = 0.116$).

Public Order Offences—Solvability and Detection

There is, similarly a wide range of public order offence solvability scores for both faiths across the London boroughs (Fig. 29), from a high of 97 in Hammersmith and Fulham to a low of 14 in Westminster. Using borough means, the criminal damage solvability score is weakly related to criminal damage detection rates, with

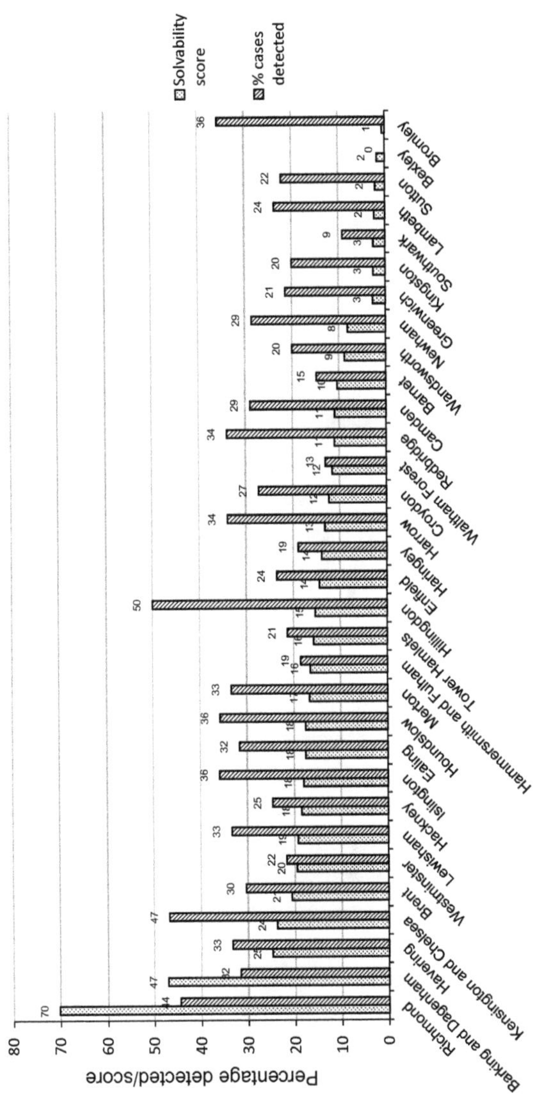

Fig. 27 Percentage of assault cases detected and assault solvability score by borough for both faiths

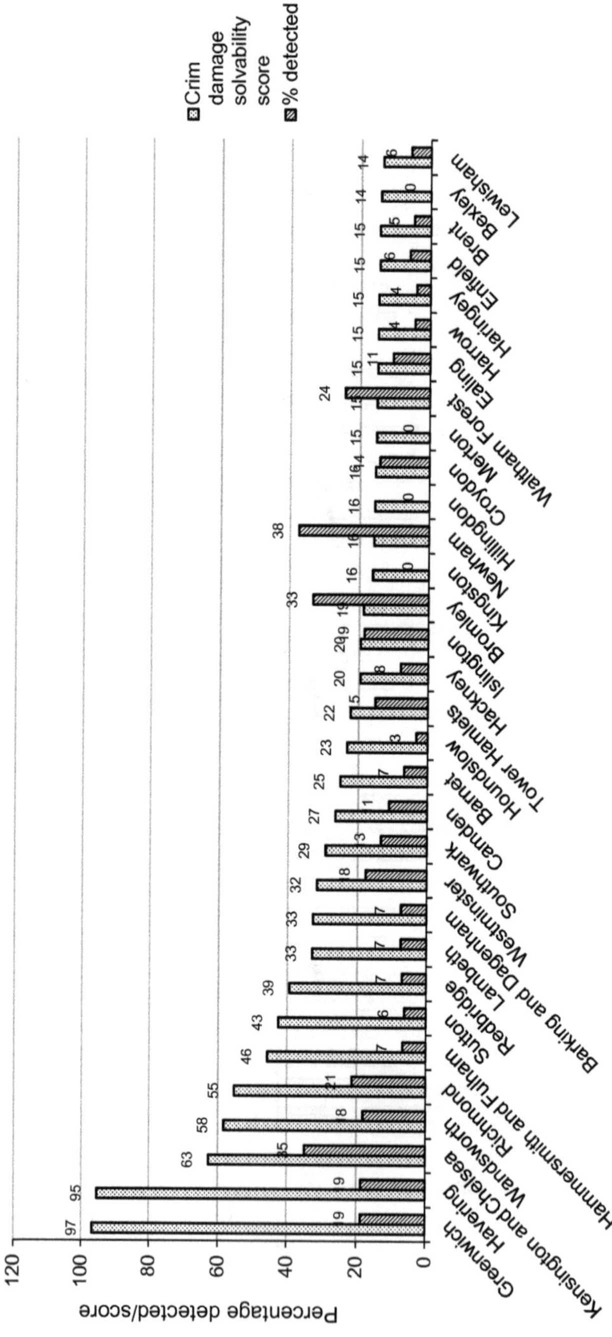

Fig. 28 Percentage of criminal damage cases detected and assault solvability score by borough for both faiths

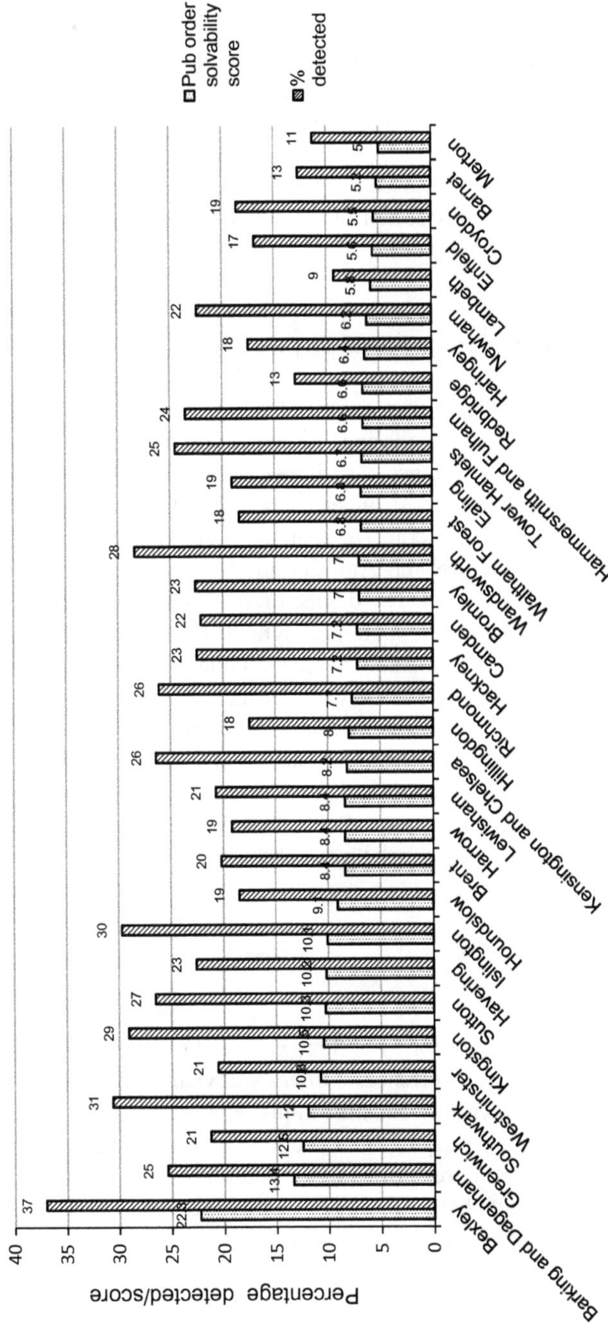

Fig. 29 Percentage of public order offences detected and public order solvability score by borough for both faiths

a low–medium effect size ($r = 0.34$, $p = 0.03$, 1–tailed, $n = 32$; $r_s = 0.49$, $p = 0.002$, 1–tailed, $n = 32$), and explains 11% of the variation in detection rates across the boroughs ($R^2 = 0.116$).

The range of faith hate public order solvability scores across the London boroughs was narrower than for faith hate assaults or faith hate criminal damage offences. The highest value was 32 in Bexley and the lowest 5 in Merton (Fig. 23). Using borough means, the public order offence solvability score is shown to be strongly related to public order detection rates ($r = 0.693$, $p < 0.001$, $n = 32$; $r_s = 0.633$, $p < 0.001$, 1–tailed, $n = 32$), explaining almost half of the variation in the number of detected cases across the boroughs ($R^2 = 0.48$).

Summary of Spatial Variations in Solvability and Detection

There were marked geographical variations in solvability scores for all types of faith hate crime, and particularly for assaults and criminal damage offences. The solvability scores for all faith hate crime types were imperfectly related to detections at the borough scale, though this link was stronger for public order offences and assaults and for Islamophobic crimes in general. The spatial association between public order solvability and detection was weaker. Anti-Semitic borough detection rates were unrelated to solvability differences. The degree of spatial mismatch between solvability and detections indicates that some boroughs detect more or fewer offences than can be expected from these solvability scores. Other solvability factors which this study has not uncovered may affect detections and influence differences in borough detection rates. There is also the likelihood that the proportions of solvable cases that are investigated may vary from borough to borough, partly because there are borough differences in allocated investigative resources, and that this may have varied for the three different crime groups. Some detection may also reflect randomly occurring factors and circumstances relating to specific offences.

Conclusions

Faith hate offences are particular forms of three principal types of crime—assaults, criminal damage and public order offences—directed at victims identified as belonging to, in this study, the Jewish or Muslim faiths. Hate crimes are expressed by assaulting minority victims, damaging their property and directing verbal abuse at them. They can also involve more serious terrorist offences, not considered in this chapter. Almost a fifth of faith hate offences in London examined in this study were detected. As for the equivalent non-faith–hate offences, more assaults than public order and more public order than criminal damage cases were solved. More faith hate offences with Muslim victims than Jewish victims were detected; this persisted for assaults and public order offences, but not for criminal damage offences.

About 4% of detected cases involved police witnessing incidents on arrival at the scene and, sometimes, officers were victims themselves. Crimes witnessed by officers were virtually certain to be solved. The other solvability factors had smaller effects on detection outcomes. Notable factors included having a victim who was a police officer, driver or security worker, a reporting delay, larger numbers of eye-witnesses and a residential venue. Some solvability factors were related to policing provision, and some could be manipulated to improve outcomes. These included the rank of investigating officer, with police constables proving more successful in detecting cases, whether local borough officers or a specialist MET team conducted the investigation, and whether the offence occurred in one of the high-performing boroughs in terms of detecting hate crimes. More detailed analysis of faith (Jewish or Muslim victims)-type and crime-type subgroups resulted in rather more precise identification of 'tailored' solvability factors and specified more accurately the levels of statistical explanation of detection outcomes.

The officers who dealt with cases also affected detection outcomes. That constables rather than sergeants or inspectors boosted detections may reflect the allocation of more challenging cases to the latter, as well as police constables more often being the personnel who deal with such incidents and more frequently themselves being the victims of faith hate offences. Equally, it is likely that off-borough specialist teams were allocated more difficult cases to solve, including some that initially looked promising but were, in practice, otherwise.

Assuming that all cases required similar investigative resources, the potential for solving cases using the solvability factors identified in this chapter can be assessed. Assaults have the potential to be solved more cost-effectively, and public order offences notably less so, while criminal damage presents the poorest prospects for cost-effective detection. This is in line with, and partly reflects, the differences in detection rates for the different crimes.

There were marked differences in faith hate crime detection rates between the 32 London boroughs. These partly reflect differences in the solvability of offences, which reflected variations in the characteristics of cases and the policing of faith hate crimes, particularly the sorts of police officer and investigative resources directed at incidents which could help 'unlock' solvability. In addition to the resources available to deal with faith hate crime, borough police services are likely to vary in terms of the successful investigative targeting of the more solvable cases so that there will be a varying potential to detect cases that is not being realised. Many apparently highly solvable offences were not detected. A systematic approach to identifying the more solvable offences on the basis outlined in this chapter would help ensure that the full potential of faith hate crime solvability is being exploited.

The study shows that it is possible to identify more and less easily detected faith hate offences of different types by carrying out solvability factor analyses. Solvability scores based on the effect sizes of important factors from regression analyses can predict detection odds and help guide the prioritisation of cases for investigation so that investigative resources may be better targeted.

References

Black, D. (1976). *The behavior of law*. New York: Academic Press.

Boyes, R. (2017, December 17). Muslim migrants behind rise in anti-Semitism. *The Times*.

Cheng, W., Ickes, W., & Kenworthy, J. B. (2013). The phenomenon of hate crimes in the United States. *Journal of Applied Social Psychology, 43*(4), 761–794.

Deloughery, K., King, R., & Asal, V. (2012). Close cousins or distant relatives? The relationship between terrorism and hate crime. *Crime & Delinquency, 58*(5), 663–668.

Dubnow, S. M. (1918). *History of the Jews in Russia and Poland, from the earliest times until the present day*. Bergenfield, New Jersey: Avotaynu.

Goodhart, D. (2017, December 10). No, there isn't a surge in hate crime. It's confusion that's running riot. *The Sunday Times*, p. 28.

Harlow, C. W. (2005). Hate crime reported by victims and police. Bureau of Justice Statistics Special Report NCJ 209911. Washington, DC: US Department of Justice.

Iganski, P. (2007). Too few Jews to count? Police monitoring of hate crime against Jews in the United Kingdom. *American Behavioral Scientist, 51*(2), 232–245.

Jenness, V., & Grattet, R. (2001). *Making hate a crime: From social movement to law enforcement*. New York, NY: Russell Sage Foundation.

Kielinger, V., & Paterson, S. (2007). Policing hate crime in London. *American Behavioral Scientist, 51*(2), 196–204.

Leicester Centre for Hate Studies. (2014). *The Leicester Hate Crime Project*. Leicester, UK: University of Leicester.

Lyons, C. J., & Roberts, A. (2014). The difference 'hate' makes in clearing crime: An event history analysis of incident factors. *Journal of Contemporary Criminal Justice, 30*(3), 268–289.

Macpherson, W. (1999). *The Stephen Lawrence Inquiry: Report of an inquiry by Sir William Macpherson of Cluny*. London: Home Office.

Messner, S. F., McHugh, S., & Felson, R. B. (2004). Distinctive characteristics of assaults motivated by bias. *Criminology, 42*(3), 585–618.

Metropolitan Police Service. (2017).

Office for National Statistics. (2012).

Phillips, N. D. (2009). The prosecution of hate crimes: The limitations of the hate crime typology. *Journal of Interpersonal Violence, 24*(5), 883–905.

Rubin, B. (2010). The rise and fall of British fascism: Sir Oswald Mosley and the British Union of Fascists. *Intersections, 11*(2), 323–380.

Sandholtz, N., Langton, L., & Planty, M. (2013). *Hate crime victimization, 2003–2011* (US Department of Justice Special report NCJ 241291). Washington, DC: Bureau of Justice Statistics.

Walfield, S. M., Socia, K. M., & Powers, R. A. (2017). Religious motivated hate crimes: Reporting of law enforcement and case outcomes. *American Journal of Criminal Justice, 42*(1), 148–169.

Wilson, M. (2014). *Hate crime victimization, 2004–2012—Statistical tables* (US Department of Justice Special Report NCJ 244409). Washington, DC: Bureau of Justice Statistics.

Reporting, Detection and Solvability of Sex Offences on Railways

Anthony Jones, Richard Timothy Coupe and Katrin Mueller-Johnson

Introduction

Trains and railway property are attractive environments for certain types of offending, since there are large numbers of potential victims and places where offences can be committed, many of which can be difficult to police. Railway systems are especially prone to pickpocketing (Sharp and Coupe Chapter "Pickpocketing on Railways") and metal theft (Robb et al. Chapter "Metal Theft Solvability and Detection"). Passengers, particularly female travellers, also constitute attractive targets for sex offenders. Trains, platforms, passageways, station concourses, stairs and escalators, waiting rooms, buffet and retail facilities present opportunities for different sorts of sexual offences at both busy and quiet times of the day. The reporting of sex offences, however, may be impeded by the inherent nature of the crime, which can be the source of shame or embarrassment for some victims. Even after reporting the offence, some victims fail to make or maintain direct contact with investigating officers, hampering detection. For minor sexual offences, such as indecent exposure, reporting rates can be further depressed by the effort required to make contact and register an offence, something that may deter travellers pressed for time. Almost three quarters of railway sexual offences occur in and around London, the busiest part of the railway network, where commuters and tourists—many foreign—predominate, the former often in a rush to reach work or home, the latter less informed about how to report offences, sometimes unable to speak English and unlikely to be available beyond their planned visit to respond to police requests to help identify suspects.

The objective of this study is to examine how the ways in which sexual offences are reported affect detection outcomes. It uses six years of British Transport Police

A. Jones (✉)
Metropolitan Police, Westminster, UK
e-mail: acjones25@googlemail.com

R. T. Coupe · K. Mueller-Johnson
University of Cambridge, Cambridge, UK

R. T. Coupe et al. (eds.), *Crime Solvability Factors*,
https://doi.org/10.1007/978-3-030-17160-5_11

(BTP) data that cover the 5842 sex offence cases for which reporting medium and source are available. The focus is on the incident reporting medium and source, that is, how it was reported and by whom, and the subsequent cooperation of victims with investigating officers, in order to assess how these factors affect sex crime solvability and detection. Eyewitness evidence, including that from victims, plays a key role in solving violent contact (e.g. Olphin and Mueller-Johnson, Chapter "Targeting Factors that Predict Clearance of Non-domestic Assaults") and sex crimes, by either enabling on-scene capture or subsequent arrest resulting from suspect identification evidence. Victims' willingness to pursue an offence may depend on a number of factors, including its seriousness, the identity of the victim and whether he or she is easily able to access and maintain contact with the police, where and when the offence took place, and the investigative efforts made by officers. Findings from this chapter promise to help enhance detection rates by informing the BTP about those methods of reporting sex offences that may help officers investigating crimes to establish and maintain contact with victims and other witnesses, and by improving our understanding of the factors affecting the clearance of sexual offences. This can inform policy and provide advice to the travelling public who either witnesses to or the victims of sex offences.

Existing Studies of Sex Crime Reporting and Detection

Sexual offending and harassment are prevalent on transport networks, not only in London (SPA Future Thinking 2013), but in many other cities, including Paris (Winter 2014), New York (Stringer 2007), Mexico City (Dunckel-Graglia 2013) and Baku (Jafarova et al. 2014). As many as 90% of survey respondents in Mexico City and Baku reported having experienced sexual harassment or assault, while 94% of female respondents in Paris had received unwanted sexual attention, which three quarters had sought to combat when on the Metro by adapting their clothing (Winter 2014). Nine per cent of travellers in London reported being sexually assaulted, over a third of which were less serious, consisting of groping, rubbing or touching victims (TfL 2013).

Sexual offences are most prevalent when public transport is crowded (Stringer 2007; Lambillion 2012), when unwanted sexual behaviour can go unnoticed (Stringer 2007), and bystander intervention is depressed due to uncertainty about whether actions were deliberate or accidental and a reduction in individual responsibility (Nickerson et al. 2014). Given these impediments (Latané and Darley 1970), it is perhaps unsurprising that few bystanders report sexual offences on transport systems (Stringer 2007).

Sexual offences are often heavily underreported, despite increases in the reporting of violent offences between 1994 and 2008 in England and Wales (Tarling and Morris 2010). Underreporting particularly characterises less serious sexual offences, which victims can regard as too trivial or inappropriate to report to the police; they may feel that it is not a 'real crime', may be uncertain that harm was intended or may have dealt with it themselves (Lievore 2003). Only 4% of the tenth of New York subway travellers subjected to sexual assault reported it to the police (Stringer 2007), while only a tenth of females subjected to sexual harassment or assaults on public transport in London reported these offences (Future Thinking 2015). Despite reporting rates being higher for more serious offences (Bennett and Wiegand 1994), including sexual offences (Fitzgerald et al. 1988; Brooks and Perot 1991), even the most serious sexual offences such as rape can have low reporting levels, for instance among students, who may not view themselves as victims (Koss 1985). While reporting rates were higher with stranger perpetrators, even for this group, reporting rates fell if victims thought they had too little information to enable the identification of assailants (Williams 1984; Skogan 1994). Barriers to reporting all but the more serious sexual assaults include age, gender, sexual orientation, crime context and feelings of shame, guilt, self-blame and embarrassment (Taylor and Gassner 2010). The normalisation of sexual harassment may also affect habituation to unwanted sexual behaviour and depress reporting levels of less serious offences (Stringer 2007).

There are few, if any, studies of the importance of different media for reporting various crimes and how these affect the service provided, police investigations and detections. Existing research provides insights into how initial questioning by call handlers can alter information quality and distort witnesses' memories (Ambler and Milne 2006; Leeney and Mueller-Johnson 2011), but there is relatively little evidence on how technical innovations such as mobile telephones and iPhones affect reporting capability and behaviour. It appears likely that, since reliance on landlines limits the timing and levels of reporting (Spelman and Brown 1981), the removal of this restriction will enable victims and those who witness crimes to contact police authorities more freely. It is to be expected that more crimes will be reported and that there will have been disproportionate increases in very speedy and possibly 'real-time' communication.

In order to overcome possible reporting barriers, in 2013, BTP and TfL launched public advertisement campaigns, 'Project Guardian' and 'Report it to Stop it', to raise awareness of sexual assaults on London's buses, trams, trains and railway property. It appears that these led to marked increases of over 30% in sexual offence reporting (TfL 2016). However, reporting increases during 2015 were associated with a fall in detection outcomes, which is thought to be attributable to changes in reporting mediums involving the use of telephone texts with victims or witnesses, who then cooperated less with police officers.

The objective in this study is to explore the media and sources of reporting in order to assess their links with successful sexual offence investigation and detection. Media coverage of historic sex abuse of children and child sexual exploitation, as in Rotherham (Travis 2015) in the UK, may have improved the willingness to report sexual offences, but transient minor offending on public transport, even if reported, may not be actively pursued by victims due to reporting barriers linked to victim circumstances and offence characteristics as well as perceived difficulties in identifying offenders once they have left the scene of the offence. By examining the reporting media for different types of sexual offences committed against victims in different places at different times on railway property, this chapter aims to identify the effectiveness of reporting media and sources in terms of detection outcomes and, hence, to inform reporting policy and outline a strategy to enable and encourage victims to report offences using the most effective media and sources.

Methodology

Research Design

The study is based on a population of 5842 sexual offences committed on UK railway property between April 2010 and March 2016. Data on reporting media and sources were added, as were data on the type of offence, when and where it occurred in terms of BTP jurisdiction, and whether on a train, platform, or elsewhere on railway property.

A sample of 361 cases was randomly drawn from this population in order to examine victim contact with BTP investigators. This sample size complied with 'sample size determination test' calculations (Lachin 1981) to be certain of sufficient statistical power to meet testing needs. Data on attempted and successful victim contacts were compiled by the first author from descriptive data in the 'crime action' fields, case by case, for the various sexual offences.

Measurement of Key Variables

The variable 'reporting source' identifies who made the report to the BTP force control room, and seven distinct categories were identified relating to police, public and railway staff. Police officers can be either from the BTP or other forces, while public reports can be from witnesses, victims or their family members. Rail staff can be on trains or stations or in control rooms. The variable 'reporting medium' measured how the report was made, for instance, by radio (e.g. BTP officer), landline telephone, email, text or social media.

Both reporting source and medium depend on the circumstances at the time of the offence and the victim, who chooses how to report it and to whom. If a victim immediately contacts a BTP officer on the station concourse who reports the offence to the BTP control room by radio, the police officer would be the reporting source and 'radio' the medium. If, however, a victim reports an offence to the control room using a telephone text message, the reporting source would be the victim, and the medium, 'text'. If a victim delayed reporting an offence until reaching home and used a non-emergency telephone line to inform the control room, the source would be the victim, and the medium, 'public non-emergency'.

A detected case involves either an offender being charged, summonsed, or cautioned. It can also include circumstances where an offence is taken into account when the offender is charged with another offence, a community resolution, and when an offender responsible for an offence has died.

Structure of the Analysis

The analysis is organised to meet the chapter's main aims. These are to understand the characteristics of sex offending on railway property, including the importance of different types of offence, where and when they occur and any jurisdictional variation, and to examine the possible effects of these offence characteristics on detection outcomes. The other key aim is to examine the ways in which offences are reported to the police and the effect this has on detections. Reporting characteristics can affect victim–investigator contact; this, in turn, is likely to affect detection outcomes and will also be considered. Identifying the role that offence and reporting characteristics play in framing detections will help inform BTP on how to best facilitate and encourage reporting procedures.

Findings

Detection Rates, Offence Types and Locations

There are six main types of sexual offence, which differ in terms of incidence and seriousness. As can be seen from Fig. 1, the most common was sexual assault, almost all of which were non-penetrative, while public indecency and exposure made up most of the rest. Together, these offences accounted for 96% of all sexual offences. Rape and penetrative sexual assault were far less common, constituting, respectively, 1 and 0.6% of sexual offences. There were also few voyeurism offences.

Offence Type and Location

Almost 70% of offences occurred on trains or trams, a fifth in station buildings and a tenth on railway platforms. The types of sexual offences vary in terms of where they take place on railway property ($\chi^2(12, N = 5842) = 333.71, p < 0.000, V = 0.17$). More of the high-volume offences of low and medium seriousness occur on trains or trams, while the most serious offence of rape and the less common offence of voyeurism more often take place in station buildings (Fig. 2). Far fewer rapes than other sexual offences took place on trains, trams and railway platforms, where there is presumably less seclusion or privacy to commit these acts ($\chi^2(1, N = 5842) = 353.30, p < 0.000$). Two-thirds of rapes, but only a fifth of other sexual offences, occurred in station buildings, toilets and other parts of stations, and other places on railway property, including restaurants and bars.

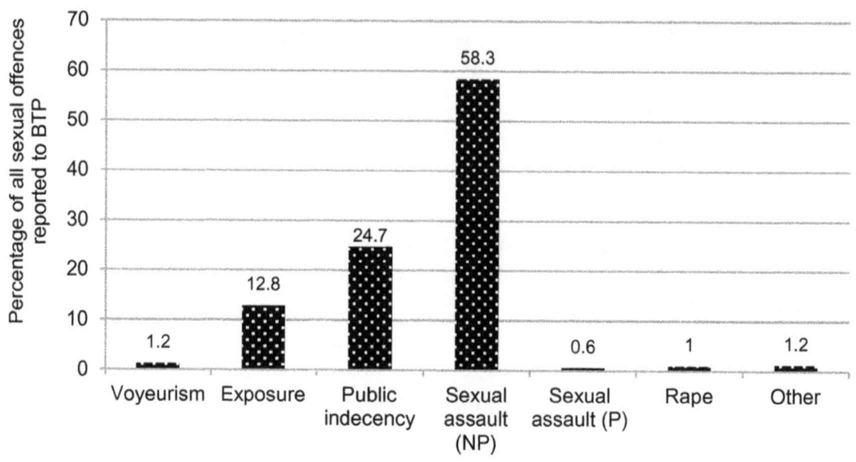

Fig. 1 Importance of different sexual offences

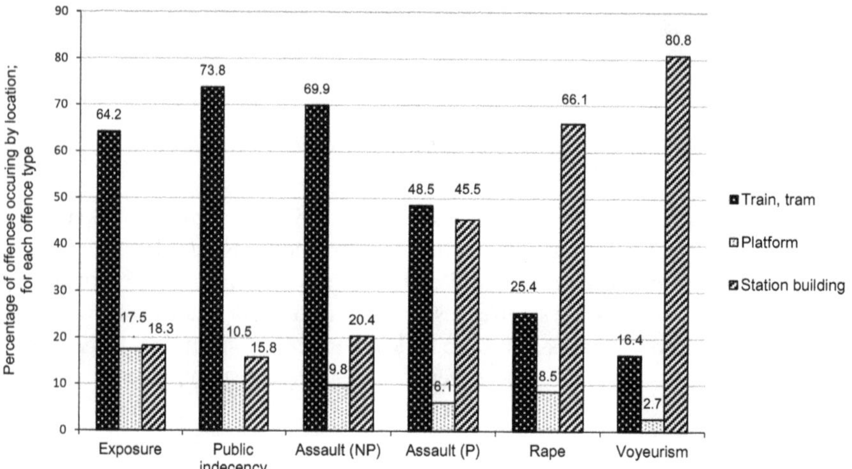

Fig. 2 Offence type by location

Penetrative assault also occurred less frequently on platforms ($\chi^2(1, N = 5842) = 11.03, p < 0.001$) but was equally common on trains and in station buildings (Fig. 2). Victims were particularly susceptible to penetrative assaults on stairs and escalators and in retail, food and other locations within station buildings, excluding toilets. Such assaults on escalators may be facilitated by victim immobility and height differences with victims on higher escalator stair treads and offenders lower down.

There is less variation in the proportion of offences occurring on platforms, though voyeurism—most common in male toilets, where 70% of such offences took place—occurs least frequently on platforms as well as on trains.

The vast majority (81%) of high-volume, low- and medium-severity sexual offences—non-penetrative assault, public indecency and exposure, which account for 96% of all sexual offences—take place on trains, trams or station platforms. Just over a third (35%) of all sexual offences are committed on the London Underground system, mainly on trains, and are mostly lower severity, non-penetration offences involving sexual touching over clothing.

Offence Type and Reporting

The most severe sexual offences were mostly reported by victims to either BTP staff or the police. However, a small number of victims used text to make reports. For non-penetrative assaults, public indecency and exposure, the most common way to report was using the public non-emergency phone number. For voyeurism, reporting directly to BTP staff was the most common method of notifying authorities (Fig. 3).

Reporting source also varied by offence type. As expected, police were more frequently the reporting source for more serious offences, including rape and penetrative assault, compared with less serious ones (Fig. 4). This number was particularly low for voyeurism, which, like rape and penetrative assault, is a low-volume sexual offence. For the higher-volume sexual offences, the sources differed less, though

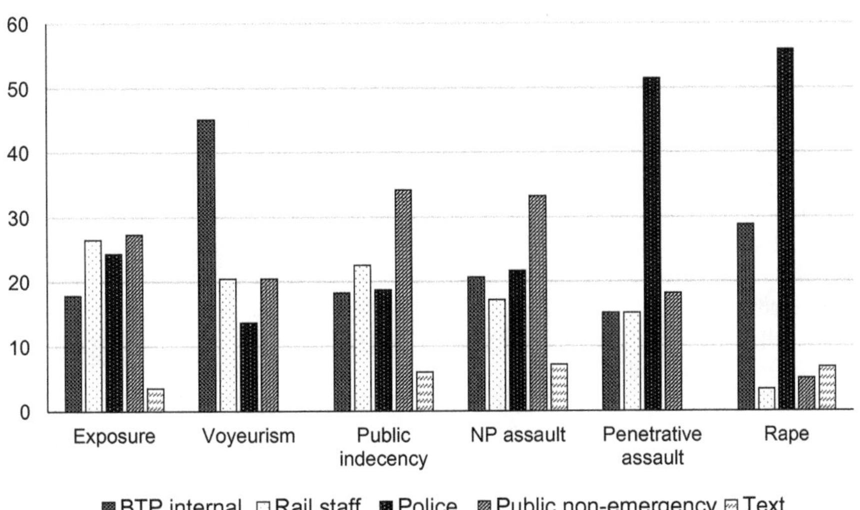

Fig. 3 Reporting medium by offence type

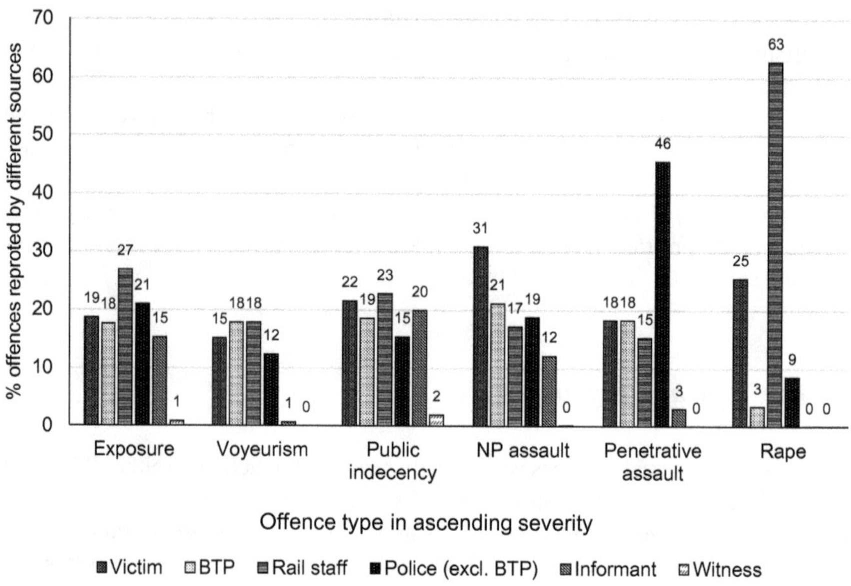

Fig. 4 Reporting source by offence type

reports sourced from victims were higher for non-penetrative assaults than for public indecency, and, in turn, higher for these than for indecent exposure incidents (Fig. 4).

Reporting Characteristics by Offence Location

Reporting characteristics varied considerably by location (Fig. 5) and by BTP jurisdiction (Fig. 6). Offences with reporting origins involving text, email and social media tend to derive from victims, witnesses and informant sources and particularly concern offences committed on trains, where contact with Rail staff or BTP officers is more difficult (Fig. 5). This is likely to result in lower detection rates for offences from this source using these media. The tendency for low detection rates is likely to be compounded by victims of offences committed on trains being too busy or unavailable to follow up complaints with further police assistance, given the numbers taking place in the London subdivision and especially on Underground trains.

Reporting media (origins) differed markedly between BTP divisions and subdivisions ($\chi^2(8, N = 5827) = 288.51, p < 0.000, V = 0.16$). Far higher proportions of reports (43%) were made by telephone, email, text or social media in the London, South and East divisions than in the other BTP areas, particularly Scotland (13%) (Fig. 6). The converse was the case for reports made by BTP officers and Rail staff, which accounted for 74% of offences in Scotland but only 35% of those in the London, South and East divisions (Fig. 6).

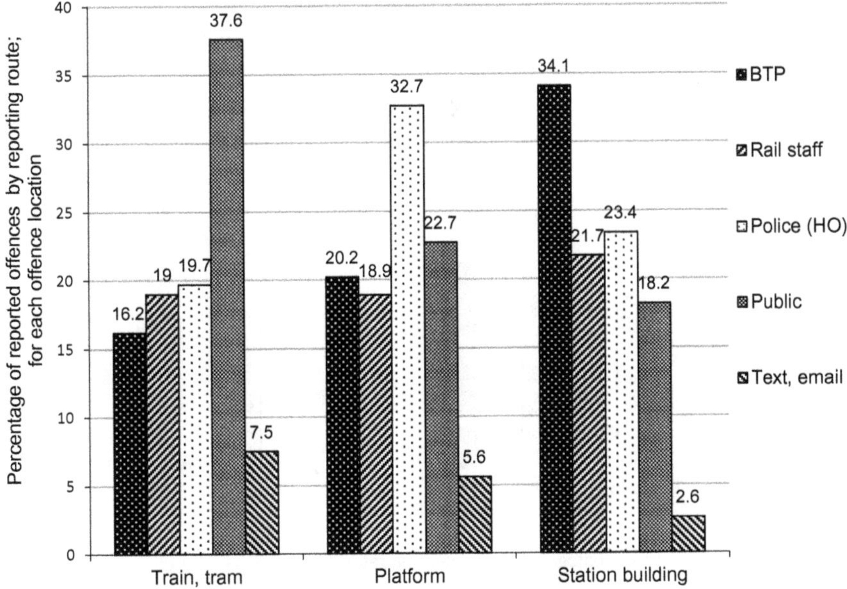

Fig. 5 Reporting medium (origin) by offence location

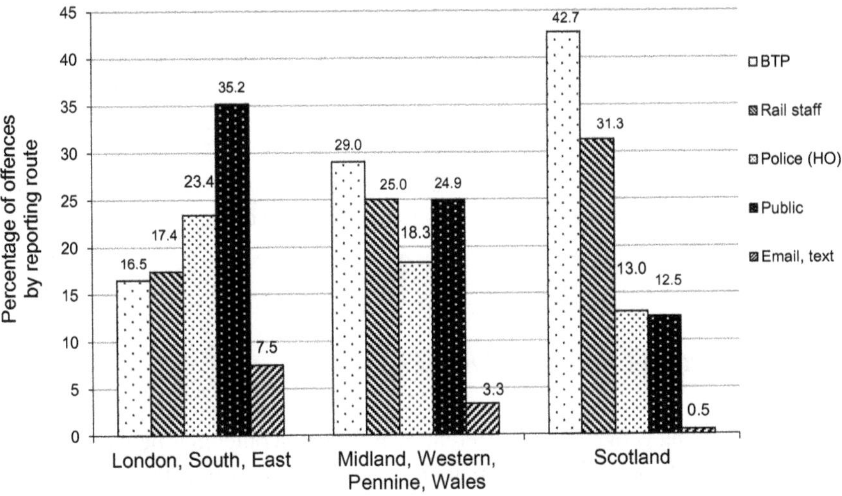

Fig. 6 Reporting medium (origin) by BTP division

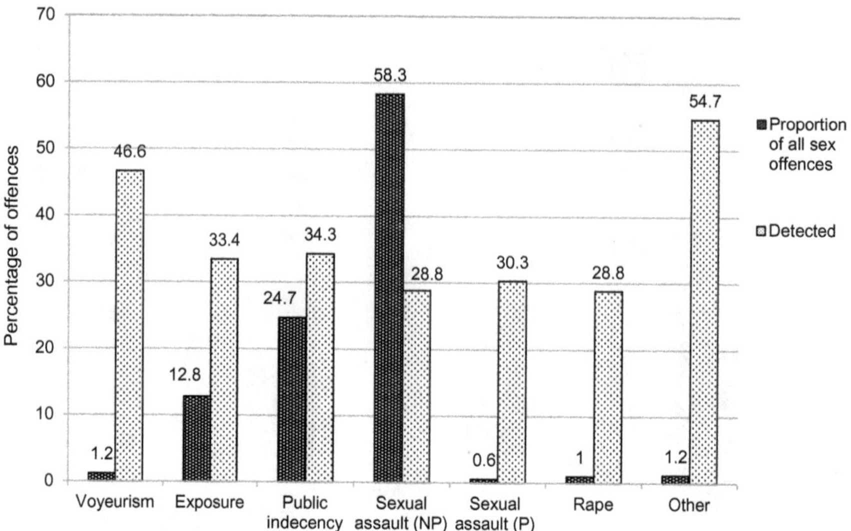

Fig. 7 Sexual offence types: categories and detection rates

Detection Rates

Overall, 32% of sexual offences were detected over the six-year period. Detection rates varied according to the type of sexual offence (Fig. 7), being rather lower for rape and non-penetrative assault (29%) and higher for voyeurism (47%). Detection rates were lower for offences committed on trains, trams or platforms than elsewhere at railway stations ($\chi^2(1, N = 5842) = 42.52, p < 0.001, V = 0.09$)—29% compared with 39% elsewhere—though, even at stations, this varied according to particular locations (Fig. 8).

BTP Jurisdiction and Detections

There were striking geographical differences in detection outcomes between the different BTP subdivisions (Fig. 9). Scotland's detection rate was more than twice that of London, at 58% compared with 25%. Detection rates were lower in subdivisions with a higher incidence of sexual offences ($r = -0.75, p = 0.03$), indicating that larger investigative demand may depress successful outcomes. The London and South subdivisions had by far the most sexual offences, together accounting for 58% of the UK's sexual offending on railways and the lowest detection rates (25 and 27%). Twenty-seven per cent of sex offences occurred in five other subdivisions—Midlands, Wales, Pennine, Western and Scotland combined—with an average detection rate of 45%.

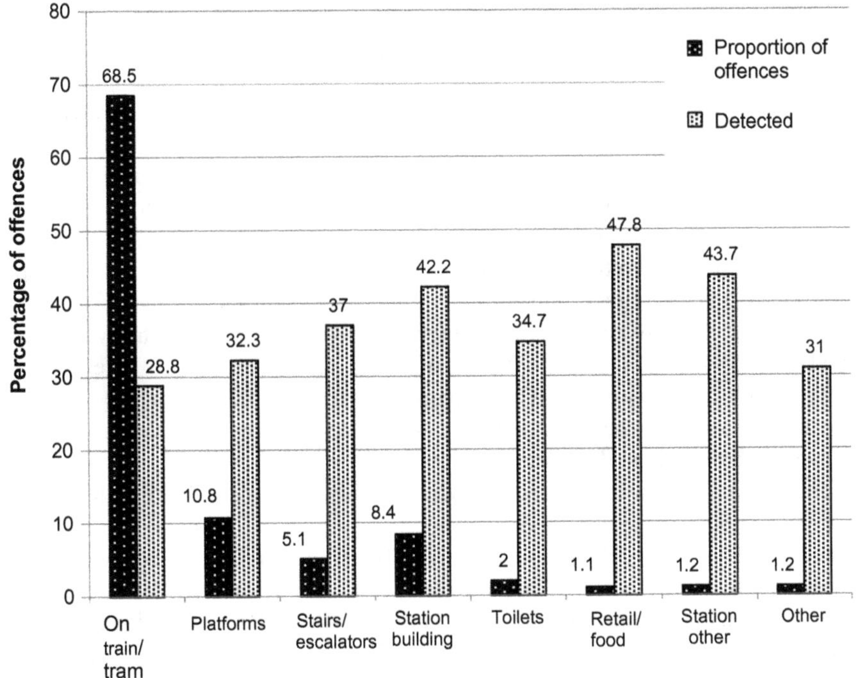

Fig. 8 Crime location and detection rates

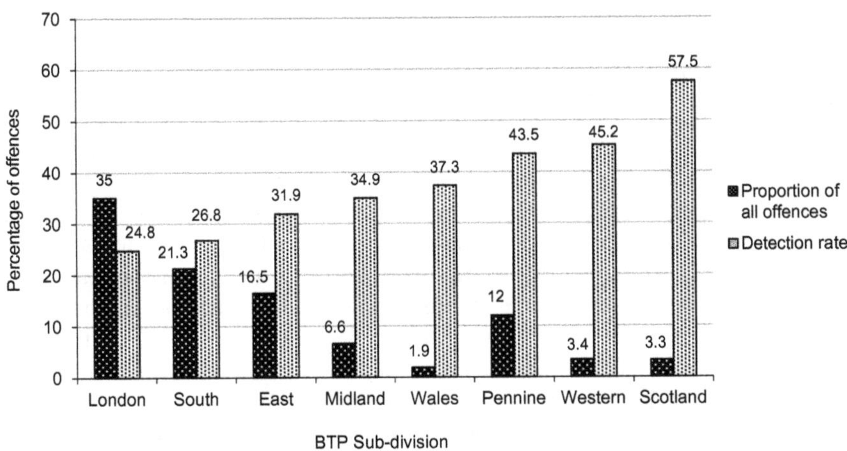

Fig. 9 Proportion of all sexual offences and detection rates by BTP subdivision

Differences in detection rates also reflected significant variations in the incidence of different types of sexual offence between regions ($\chi^2(42, N = 5841) = 464.59$, $p < 0.000$, $V = 0.12$). Scotland's very high detection rate of 57.5% is partly attributable to its markedly high incidence of voyeurism and 'other' sexual offences, which have the highest detection rates ($\chi^2(1, N = 5841) = 66.2$, $p < 0.000$). These constitute 17% of the Scottish region's offences but only 8.5% of all the other regions combined. The Pennine, Western and Wales regions had double the incidence of the most serious sexual offences—rape and penetrative assault ($\chi^2(1, N = 5841) = 17.94$, $p < 0.000$)—compared with the other regions: 4.2% compared with only 1.9%, perhaps a reflection of fewer high-volume, less serious sexual offences.

The London subdivision had a far higher incidence of non-penetrative assault ($\chi^2(1, N = 5841) = 135.97$, $p < 0.000$), with this high-volume sexual offence constituting 69% of sexual offences here compared with only 53% elsewhere. The low detection rates for non-penetrative assault contributed to London's rating as the subdivision with the lowest detection rates.

The striking contrasts in detection rates between London, which has the lowest at 25%, and Scotland, with the highest at 58%, may, in part, reflect differences in offences (χ^2 $(12, N = 5842) = 23.8$, $p < 0.000$, $V = 0.16$), for instance, with more non-penetrative assaults and public indecency in London, South and East compared with Scotland: 86% compared with 66% of offences. Better Scots detection outcomes also reflected a tendency ($\chi^2(4, N = 5842) = 50.11$, $p < 0.000$, $V = 0.07$) for more offences there to take place in station buildings (29 vs. 20%) and fewer on trains (62 vs. 71%) compared with the London, South and East BTP subdivisions.

Offence Timing and Detections

A fifth fewer offences, 26% compared with 33%, occurring at three particular periods of the day were solved ($\chi^2 = 23.8$, $p < 0.000$, 1 df, $V = 0.064$, $N = 5842$), namely the morning rush hour (07.00–09.00), late morning (11.00–12.00), and very late at night (00.00–02.00). Although more offences occur when transport is most crowded (Stringer 2007; Lambillion 2012), there is less success in solving offences not only during crowded periods but also during quieter periods like late mornings and even quiet times like late night–early morning. This reflects the sorts of offences that take place at these times and their location on railway property. In contrast, there was no marked drop in the detection of offences committed during the evening 'rush-hour' period, possibly in part because the journey home after work is spread over a longer time span.

Taken together, these three periods of the day when detection rates were low were associated particularly with offences committed on trains, trams, escalators and stairs ($\chi^2(7, N = 5872) = 62.64$, $p < 0.000$, $V = 0.104$): 27% of these took place during these five hours, compared with only 17.7% of those in other locations, such as on platforms and in station buildings. Both penetrative and non-penetrative assaults were rather more likely to occur at these times—28% of them compared with 21%

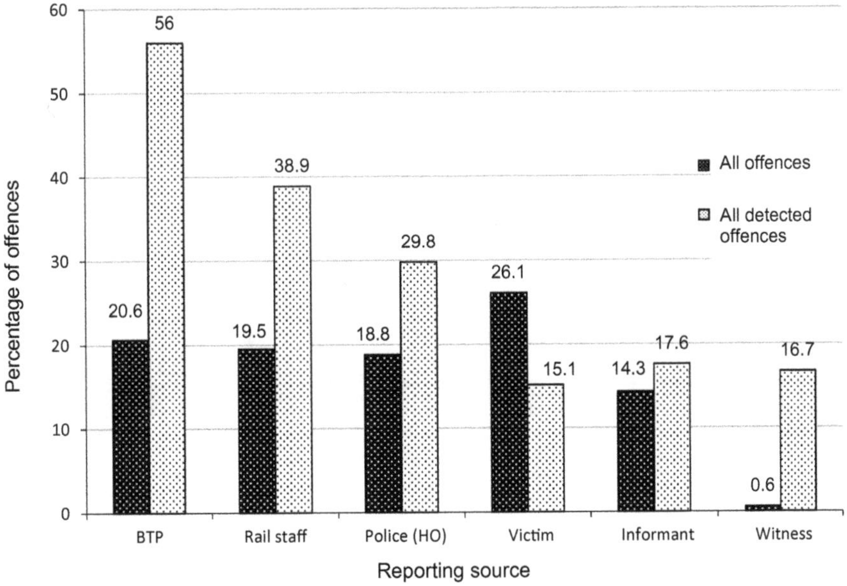

Fig. 10 Detection rates and importance of the different reporting sources

of other offences ($\chi^2(1, N = 5842) = 38.29, p < 0.000, V = 0.081$)—and the fact fewer offences were solved at these periods partly reflects the low clearance rates for these particular offences.

Reporting Medium and Source

Reporting sources and media/origin are shown in Figs. 10 and 11. Reporting sources are linked to multiple media or origins; for example, reports made to BTP officers may be called in by internal telephone or radio, while police services other than the BTP fall into three categories: Home Office (HO) police, the Metropolitan Police Service, covering London, and other services. About twice as many incidents were reported via police as Rail staff, and together they accounted for 59% of reporting sources (Fig. 10). Most of the rest were reported by victims and informants directly to the BTP control room. Given the close relationship between reporting source and medium, police and Rail staff were the origin of 62% of incident reports to the BTP control room, of which 20% were Rail staff; police officers from forces other than the BTP were almost as important as BTP officers themselves (Fig. 10). The remaining 38% of reports originated directly from the public by telephone, with a notable minority using text, email and social media (Fig. 11).

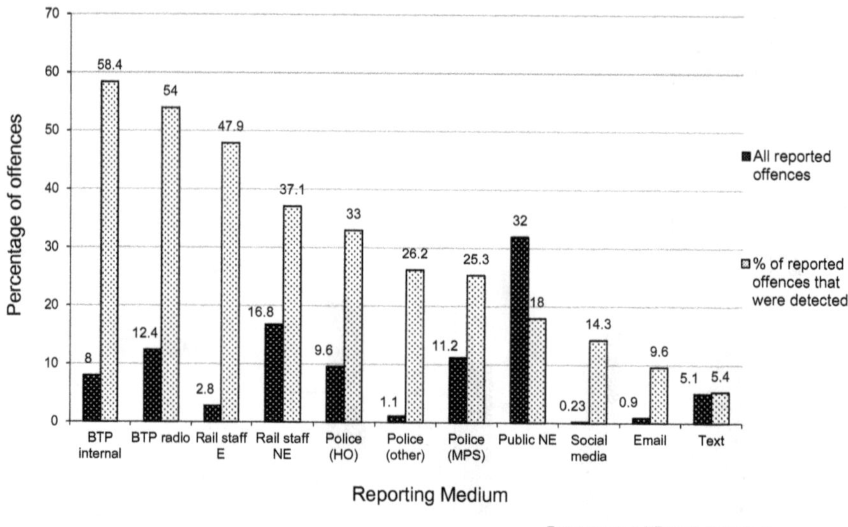

Fig. 11 Detection rates and importance of the different reporting media/origins

Reporting Characteristics and Detections

Reporting source and media both had strong relationships with whether or not cases were detected. About twice as many incidents were reported via police than via Rail staff, and together they accounted for 59% of reporting sources (Fig. 10). Most of the rest were reported by victims and informants directly to the BTP control room. Detection rates varied strikingly by reporting source ($\chi^2(6, N = 5842) = 634.09$, $p < 0.000$, $V = 0.33$). Those reported or observed by BTP officers had particularly high detection rates (56%), while those reported by Rail staff also had detection rates above the average of 31% (Fig. 10). Incidents sourced from Home Office territorial police officers had a detection rate of 16%, close to the mean and almost double that of incidents reported by witnesses, informants or victims themselves. Reporting incidents via police officers or Rail staff was therefore more effective than victims, witnesses or informants contacting the BTP control room directly. However, this partly reflects the association of reporting source with reporting medium and offence characteristics, including the location, timing and seriousness of different offences.

Reporting medium or origin was also related to detection outcomes ($\chi^2(10, N = 5842) = 640.80, p < 0.000$), with which it had a high effect size ($V = 0.33$), similar to that of reporting source, with which it is highly correlated ($\chi^2(30, N = 5842) = 14{,}239.0, p < 0.000, V = 0.70$), particularly when the principal source and medium scale items are amalgamated ($\chi^2(15, N = 5842) = 13{,}858.50, p < 0.000, V = 0.89$).

Like reporting source, offences reported via radio or internal telephone to the BTP control room that originated from BTP officers resulted in more detections than those from Rail staff, which, in turn, were superior to those where victims, informants or witnesses contacted the control room (Fig. 11). Telephoning the control room (public non-emergencies) was more successful than using email, text and social media reporting (Fig. 11). The differences partly reflect the links between reporting medium and offence location ($\chi^2(8, N = 5842) = 355.31, p < 0.000, V = 0.18$), and reporting medium and offence type ($\chi^2(8, N = 5842) = 355.31, p < 0.000, V = 0.18$).

The Relative Importance of Offence Characteristics and Reporting Characteristics in Explaining Detections

In order to statistically isolate the effects of reporting on detections, three sets of analyses involving multivariate tests were needed (Fig. 12). Offence characteristics could affect detections either directly or via reporting characteristics and victim–investigator contact. Similarly, reporting characteristics, partly shaped by offence characteristics, could affect detections either directly or via victim–investigator contact. The first analysis measures the influence of offence characteristics on reporting (Fig. 12, number 1), and the second considers the relationship between reporting on the one hand and offences and victim contact on the other, and between contact and detections (Fig. 12, number 2). The third examines the effects of reporting on detections while taking account of offence characteristics and any other relevant factors, such as victim contact (Fig. 12, number 3).

The Effects of Offence Characteristics on Reporting (Fig. 12, Number 1)

Binary logistic regression analyses with reporting source as the outcome variable indicate that offence type, location and timing have an important bearing on reporting origins, even when controlling for BTP jurisdiction (Table 1). BTP officers, Rail staff and other police officers, compared with the public using telephones, texts and emails, were far more likely to report offences that occurred on platforms and particularly in station buildings rather than on trains. The odds of offences being reported by police and Rail staff were similarly a fifth higher at quieter periods when there were fewer sexual offences reported overall. The odds of reports originating with BTP officers and Rail staff were elevated for more serious offences (Table 1(A)). This tendency all but disappeared for reports from BTP officers alone (Table 1(C)) and for reports made by texting and emailing (Table 1(D)), for which the only significant relationship was for exposure, which had 3.1 times lower odds of being reported by these media. Public indecency and non-penetrative assault cases had, respectively, 2.9 and 3 times the odds of not being reported to Rail staff and all types of police officers (Table 1(B)).

Table 1 Binary logistic regressions: reporting origins as dependent variable with four different categorisations

Variable	(A) Dependent variable: BTP and Rail staff/other report origins						(B) Dependent variable: Police officers and Rail staff/public origins: telephone, email, text, social media					
	B	SE	Wald	df	p	Exp (B)	B	SE	Wald	df	p	Exp (B)
Location: station, platform, train			136.7	2	0.000				198.1	2	0.000	
Location: station versus train	0.83	0.07	134.4	1	0.000	2.28	1.07	0.08	173.9	1	0.000	2.80
Location: platform versus train	0.06	0.09	0.4	1	0.537	1.06	0.64	0.10	44.8	1	0.000	1.90
Division: Scotland (D); Western–Wales–Pennine–Midlands (C); London SE (B)			198.9	2	0.000				90.1	2	0.000	
D versus B division	1.5	0.18	73.6	1	0.000	2.20	1.32	0.22	36.3	1	0.000	3.74
C versus B division	0.8	0.07	145.0	1	0.000	1.23	0.54	0.07	60.3	1	0.000	1.72
Time of day: busy versus quiet	0.20	0.07	9.1	1	0.003	1.23	0.20	0.07	9.3	1	0.002	1.22
Offence type			27.3	5	0.000				22.0	5	0.001	
Exposure versus rape	1.1	0.30	13.1	1	0.000	3.00	−0.78	0.42	3.4	1	0.065	0.459
Voyeurism versus rape	1.4	0.39	13.5	1	0.000	4.14	−0.89	0.51	3.1	1	0.080	0.410
Public indecency versus rape	1.1	0.30	13.0	1	0.000	2.94	−1.06	0.42	6.4	1	0.011	0.348
Non-penetrative assault versus rape	0.9	0.30	9.6	1	0.002	2.50	−1.10	0.42	7.0	1	0.008	0.334
Penetrative assault versus rape	0.1	0.49	0.1	1	0.817	1.12	−0.26	0.62	0.2	1	0.675	0.770
Constant	−2.2	.32	46.8	1	0.000	0.11	0.74	0.43	3.0	1	0.084	2.10
BLR model summary	Nagelkerke's $R^2 = 0.096$; Model: $\chi^2 = 424.6, p < 0.000$, 10 df; 65% of cases correctly predicted						Nagelkerke's $R^2 = 0.096$; Model: $\chi^2 = 424.7, p < 0.000$, 10 df; 63% of cases correctly predicted					

(continued)

Table 1 (continued)

Variable	(C) Dependent variable: BTP/other report origins						(D) Dependent variable: Police officers and Rail staff and victims by telephone, email, text, social media					
	B	SE	Wald	df	p	Exp (B)	B	SE	Wald	df	p	Exp (B)
Location: station, platform, train			136.4	2	0.000				26.0	2	0.000	
Location: station versus train	0.92	0.08	136.0	1	0.000	2.51	−0.99	0.20	25.9	1	0.000	0.37
Location: platform versus train	0.22	0.11	4.1	1	0.043	1.25	−0.18	0.19	0.9	1	0.341	0.84
Division: Scotland (D); Western–Wales–Pennine–Midlands (C); London SE (B)			114.9	2	0.000				25.2	2	0.000	
D versus B division	1.1	0.17	42.6	1	0.000	2.99	−2.39	1.01	5.6	1	0.018	0.09
C versus B division	0.7	0.08	88.7	1	0.000	2.04	−0.73	0.16	20.0	1	0.000	0.48
Time of day: busy versus quiet	0.14	0.08	2.7	1	0.100	1.15	−0.29	0.12	6.0	1	0.015	0.75
Offence type			17.0	5	0.004				10.8	5	0.057	
Exposure versus rape	−0.09	0.32	0.1	1	0.775	0.91	−1.14	0.57	4.0	1	0.044	0.32
Voyeurism versus rape	0.73	0.39	3.6	1	0.059	2.07	−18.28	4587.2	0.0	1	0.997	0.00
Public indecency versus rape	0.08	0.31	0.07	1	0.793	1.09	−0.71	0.54	1.7	1	0.193	0.49
Non-penetrative assault versus rape	0.21	0.30	0.48	1	0.490	1.23	−0.53	0.54	1.0	1	0.324	0.59
Penetrative assault versus rape	−64	0.58	1.23	1	0.268	0.53	−18.8	6794.3	0.0	1	0.998	0.00
Constant	−2.3	0.34	44.8	1	0.000	0.11	−1.25	0.57	4.8	1	0.028	0.29
BLR model summary	Nagelkerke's $R^2 = 0.080$; Model: $\chi^2 = 298.4, p < 0.000$, 10 df; 80% of cases correctly predicted						Nagelkerke's $R^2 = 0.052$; Model: $\chi^2 = 114.0, p < 0.000$, 10 df; 94% of cases correctly predicted					

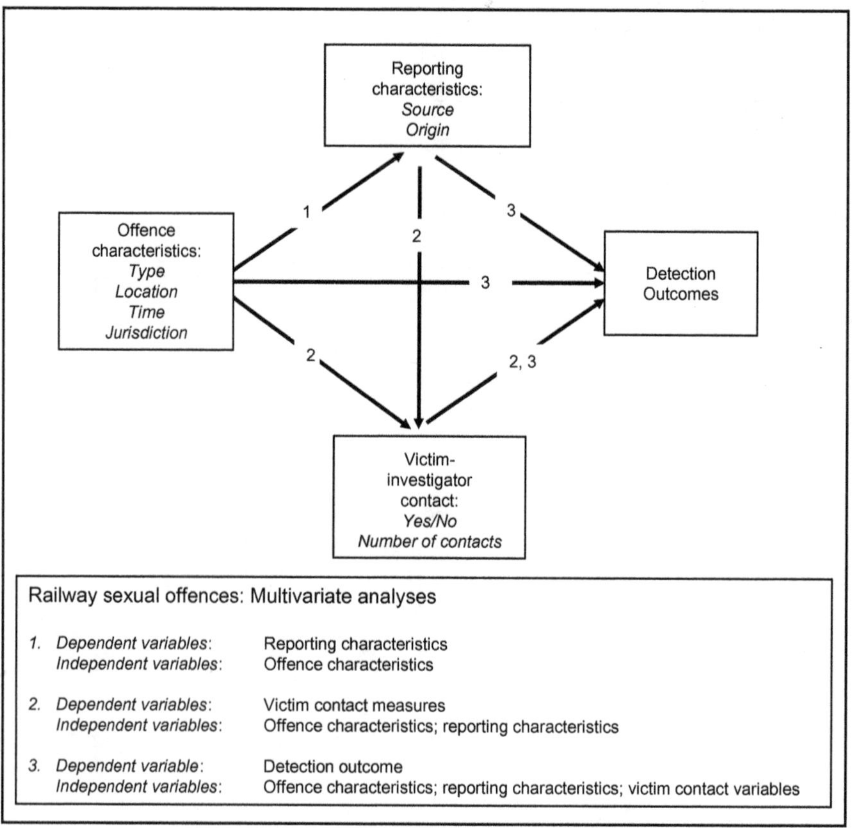

Fig. 12 Railway sexual offences: multivariate analyses

Reporting characteristics, therefore, were notably dependent on offence characteristics, even when controlling for BTP jurisdiction. Offence characteristics, including jurisdictional effects, accounted for a little under a tenth of variation in reporting origins.

With regard to variation in reporting not accounted for by these factors, it is likely that much reporting of sexual offences of low and medium seriousness (i.e. neither assaults nor rape) depends on the preference of the victim, witness or informant, who may often not wish to be inconvenienced by or have the time to spend, seeking out a police officer or Rail staff member. Still others may decide it is not worthwhile reporting an offence by telephone or text or may not have a BTP telephone number to hand. Such effects may be random. Higher reporting to BTP officers and Rail staff in places like Scotland, even when controlling for other offence characteristics, may partly reflect better their availability and accessibility, levels of officer workload demand, or fewer tourists.

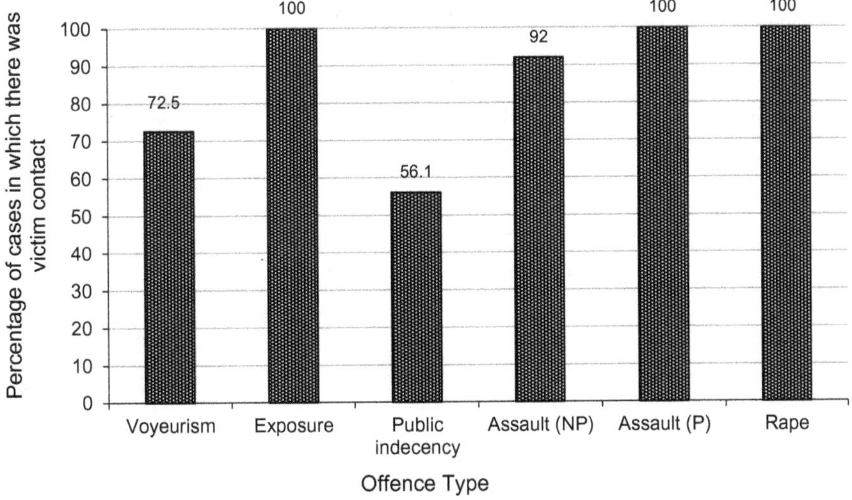

Fig. 13 Victim contact with BTP investigators by offence type

Reporting Characteristics and Victim–Investigator Contact (Fig. 12, Number 2)

Reporting is likely to influence victim–investigator contact, which, in turn, may affect investigations, making solving offences more or less difficult and consequently either facilitating or hampering detections. Many busy commuters and foreign tourists in London as well as other UK-resident victims who report less serious sexual offences, however, may not regard it as worthwhile, given the time involved and probable journey delays (London Assembly Police and Crime Committee 2016), or be available to respond positively to subsequent police requests to assist, for instance, by providing suspect descriptions or identifying suspects. Some reports may be made to police officers and Rail staff specifically because victims want the offence to be investigated, but reporting medium and source also reflect whether or not offences take place on trains, where it is more difficult to contact officers or Rail staff and where more of the less serious offences that dominate sex offending on railways take place. The question is whether, even despite these factors, differences in reporting characteristics still affect victim contact.

Based on the random sample of 361 cases drawn from the population for which contact and attempted contact data were collected, it is evident that there was contact between police and victims in a very high proportion (81%) of cases. For these cases, there was a mean of 3.4 contacts (SD = 2.2). The larger the number of attempts, the higher the numbers of contacts ($r_s = 0.21$, $p < 0.001$, $n = 361$), and fewer attempts to contact victims by BTP police were made in cases where there was no contact ($F = 8.35$, $p = 0.004$, df = 1, 359), an average of only 0.75 (SD = 1.41) attempts compared with 1.44 (SD = 1.85) where victim contact occurred (Fig. 13).

Whether or not BTP investigators managed to contact victims varied by offence type ($\chi^2 = 55.70$, $p < 0.000$, 5 df, $V = 0.39$, $n = 361$), but not by offence location, time, BTP division or subdivision or report origin. While contacts were made with fewer victims of exposure and public indecency, contact levels were, as expected, far higher for reports of assault (both penetrative and non-penetrative), rape and voyeurism (Fig. 13). Contact was also related to report source, albeit weakly (χ^2(3, $n = 361$) $= 9.42$, $p < 0.000$, $V = 0.16$), being lower for Rail staff (73%) and BTP (76%) than for reports made to the BTP control room by victims, witnesses or informants (87%) or to other police officers (86%).

These effects were confirmed in a binary logistic regression with whether or not contact was made as the dependent variable (Table 2). Each change to a more serious offence (from exposure to voyeurism, to public indecency, to non-penetrative assault, to penetrative assault, to rape) raised contact odds by 64% (Exp(B) = 1.64:1). The odds of contact were 2.5 times higher in the Midlands, Western, Wales and Pennine subdivisions than in London–South-East (Table 2). Reporting characteristics—source or origin—had no bearing on victim contact, nor did offence location and timing. Eleven per cent of variation in whether or not contact was made was explained by these variables (Nagelkerke's $R^2 = 0.107$, $n = 357$), with 81% of outcomes correctly predicted. A PLUM ordinal regression showed that no variables were significantly related to the number of successful contacts.

However, whether investigators managed to contact victims was not significantly related to whether or not cases were detected ($\chi^2(12, N = 361) = 16.23, p = 0.181$, $V = 0.21$). This reflects, in part, cases with zero contacts but positive outcomes, representing 41% of solved cases involving those offences, namely public indecency and exposure, where a victim is not required in law or those where the Crown Prosecution Service (CPS) charged an offender without a victim contact or statement. When public indecency and exposure offences were excluded, there was a marginally significant relationship between victim contact and detection ($\chi^2(1, N = 225) = 3.85$, $p = 0.050$, $V = 0.13$). Here, cases with victim contact had a 35% detection rate compared with only 12% without contact.

Detection and Reporting and Offence Characteristics (Diagram 1, Number 3)

Reporting characteristics have been shown to have stronger, and offence characteristics rather less strong, bivariate relationships with case detection. The relationship between reporting source and detections persisted strongly when controlling for offence type (Table 2, χ^2 *controlling for offence type* $= 682.0$, $p < 0.000$, 62 df) and offence location (Table 2, χ^2 *controlling for offence location* $= 672.0$, $p < 0.000$, 72 df). When controlling for reporting source, in contrast, significant relationships between offence type and detection outcomes disappear, while those between location and detection outcomes are weakly significant in a few categories, confirming

Table 2 Binary logistic regression: dependent variable: contact (no/yes)

Offence type (exposure, voyeurism, public indecency, NP assault, P assault, rape)	0.50	0.12	16.0	1	0.000	1.64
Location: station, platform, train			1.7	2	0.426	
Location: station versus train	−0.38	0.35	1.2	1	0.281	0.69
Location: platform versus train	−0.46	0.49	1.0	1	0.341	0.63
Time of day: busy versus quiet	−0.29	0.37	0.6	1	0.432	0.75
Reporting origin			4.8	4	0.314	
BTP versus text, email, social media (TES)	−0.05	0.67	0.0	1	0.943	0.95
Rail staff versus TES	−0.06	0.67	0.0	1	0.930	0.94
Police (other) versus TES	0.80	0.68	1.4	1	0.238	2.23
Public (telephone) versus TES	0.18	0.65	0.1	1	0.778	1.20
Division: Scotland (D); Western–Wales–Pennine–Midlands (C); London SE (B)			7.2	2	0.027	
D versus B division	1.62	1.09	2.2	1	0.136	5.08
C versus B division	0.90	0.39	5.5	1	0.019	2.46
Constant	0.12	0.98	0.014	1	0.905	1.12
BLR model summary	Nagelkerke's $R^2 = 0.107$; Model: $\chi^2 = 24.3, p < 0.001$, 7 df; 81% of cases correctly predicted $N = 357$					

the far greater strength of the link between reporting and detections. Offence type, location and timing, however, also differ by BTP jurisdiction, which also affects detection.

However, as indicated above, neither victim contact nor number of contacts were related to whether cases were detected, except for voyeurism, assault and rape cases. A binary logistic regression with detection outcome as the dependent variable (Table 3) confirms that victim contact has no significant effect on detection, particularly when taking into account other independent factors. Since victim contact measures have little or no bearing, statistically speaking, on detections, they were excluded from the multivariate tests used to examine the effects of reporting characteristics on solving sexual offences.

Binary logistic regressions that exclude measures of victim–BTP investigator contact and consequently include the full population of 5842 cases indicate that reporting source and origin had very strong effects on detection outcomes when controlling for other factors. The odds of detection were markedly higher for incident reports originating with BTP officers, Rail staff, and other police officers compared with those communicated by text, email and social media (Table 3(A)). Specifically, reports made to BTP officers had 17.6 times the odds of being detected as reports made by text, email and social media, with those to Rail staff having 8.7 times the odds and those to other police officers 1.5 times (Table 3(A)). Even those cases where

Table 3 Binary logistic regressions: dependent variable: not detected/detected

Variable	(A) Dependent variable: Not detected/detected						(B) Dependent variable: Not detected/detected					
	B	SE	Wald	df	*p*	Exp(B)	B	SE	Wald	df	*p*	Exp(B)
Offence type			18.5	5	0.000				19.1	5	0.002	
Exposure versus rape	0.40	0.32	1.6	1	0.207	1.49	0.46	0.32	2.1	1	0.148	1.58
Voyeurism versus rape	0.55	0.39	2.0	1	0.158	1.74	0.58	0.39	2.2	1	0.138	1.79
Public indecency versus rape	0.53	0.31	2.9	1	0.086	1.70	0.65	0.31	4.3	1	0.038	1.91
Non-penetrative assault versus rape	0.25	0.31	0.6	1	0.423	1.28	0.36	0.31	1.4	1	0.248	1.43
Penetrative assault versus rape	0.25	0.49	0.3	1	0.614	1.28	−0.24	0.50	0.2	1	0.635	1.26
Location: station, platform, train			1.3	2	0.515				1.7	2	0.439	
Location: station versus train	0.09	0.08	1.29	1	0.257	1.09	0.09	0.08	1.3	1	0.248	1.09
Location: platform versus train	0.0	0.10	0.00	1	0.978	1.03	−0.03	0.10	0.1	1	0.75	0.97
Time of day: busy versus quiet	0.18	0.07	5.7	1	0.017	1.19	0.1	0.07	1.9	1	0.163	1.11
Reporting origin			499.1	4	0.000				441.5	4	0.000	
BTP versus text, email, social media (TES)	2.9	0.23	92.1	1	0.000	17.61	2.8	0.23	150.6	1	0.000	15.87
Rail staff versus TES	2.2	0.23	84.1	1	0.000	8.65	2.1	0.23	84.1	1	0.000	7.90
Police (other) versus TES	1.8	0.23	60.2	1	0.000	5.74	1.7	0.23	58.5	1	0.000	5.61
Public (telephone) versus TES	1.1	0.22	25.9	1	0.000	3.13	1.1	0.22	24.6	1	0.000	3.05
Division: Scotland (D); Western–Wales–Pennine–Midlands (C); London SE (B)									51.7	2	0.000	

(continued)

Table 3 (continued)

Variable	(A) Dependent variable: Not detected/detected						(B) Dependent variable: Not detected/detected					
	B	SE	Wald	df	p	Exp(B)	B	SE	Wald	df	p	Exp(B)
D versus B division							0.88	0.17	27.8	1	0.000	2.42
C versus B division							0.39	0.07	31.1	1	0.000	1.48
Constant	−3.3	0.39	71.8	1	0.000	0.04	−3.37	0.39	73.3	1	0.084	0.03
BLR model summary	Nagelkerke's $R^2 = 0.151$; Model: $\chi^2 = 654.8, p < 0.000$, 12 df; 71% of cases correctly predicted						Nagelkerke's $R^2 = 0.163$; Model: $\chi^2 = 706.4, p < 0.000$, 14 df; 71% of cases correctly predicted					
Variable	(C) Dependent variable: Not detected/detected						(D) Dependent variable: Not detected/detected					
	B	SE	Wald	df	p	Exp (B)	B	SE	Wald	df	p	Exp (B)
Offence type			19.4	5	0.002				19.8	5	0.002	
Exposure versus rape	0.40	0.32	1.59	1	0.208	1.49	0.45	0.32	2.0	1	0.158	1.56
Voyeurism versus rape	0.56	0.39	2.1	1	0.152	1.75	0.58	0.40	2.2	1	0.139	1.79
Public indecency versus rape	0.53	0.31	3.0	1	0.086	1.70	0.64	0.31	4.1	1	0.042	1.89
Non-penetrative assault versus rape	0.24	0.31	0.6	1	0.437	1.27	0.34	0.31	1.2	1	0.276	1.40
Penetrative assault versus rape	0.19	0.49	0.2	1	0.698	1.21	0.18	0.50	0.1	1	0.723	1.19
Location: station, platform, train			0.8	2	0.656				1.2	2	0.540	
Location: station versus train	0.07	0.08	0.7	1	0.402	1.07	0.07	0.08	0.8	1	0.381	1.07
Location: platform versus train	−0.2	1.0	0.0	1	0.842	0.98	−0.05	0.10	0.2	1	0.622	0.95
Time of day: busy versus quiet	0.17	0.07	5.3	1	0.022	1.18	0.1	0.07	1.9	1	0.169	1.11
Reporting origin			41.2	4	0.000				41.4	4	0.000	

(continued)

Table 3 (continued)

Variable	(C) Dependent variable: Not detected/detected						(D) Dependent variable: Not detected/detected					
	B	SE	Wald	df	*p*	Exp (B)	B	SE	Wald	df	*p*	Exp (B)
BTP versus text, email, social media (TES)	1.6	0.32	25.8	1	0.000	5.01	1.6	0.32	24.3	1	0.000	4.81
Rail staff versus TES	1.6	0.28	31.9	1	0.000	4.93	1.6	0.28	30.6	1	0.000	4.78
Police (other) versus TES	1.4	0.25	32.5	1	0.000	4.18	1.5	0.25	34.3	1	0.000	4.33
Public (telephone) versus TES	1.1	0.23	25.5	1	0.000	3.11	1.1	0.23	24.3	1	0.000	3.04
Reporting source			43.1	3	0.000				36.941.4	3	0.000	
BTP versus public (victim, witness, etc.)	1.4	0.24	32.9	1	0.000	3.90	1.3	0.24	29.4	1	0.000	3.66
Rail staff versus public	0.67	0.19	12.7	1	0.000	1.95	0.60	0.19	10.3	1	0.001	1.83
Police (other) versus public	0.46	0.15	9.0	1	0.003	1.58	0.38	0.15	6.2	1	0.013	1.46
Division: Scotland (D); Western–Wales–Pennine–Midlands (C); London SE (B)									51.7	2	0.000	
D versus B division							0.84	0.17	25.2	1	0.000	2.32
C versus B division							0.37	0.07	26.3	1	0.000	1.44
Constant	−3.4	0.39	73.8	1	0.000	0.03	−3.4	0.39	74.5	1	0.000	0.03
BLR model summary	Nagelkerke's $R^2 = 0.162$; Model: $\chi^2 = 700.2, p < 0.000$, 15 df; 71% of cases correctly predicted						Nagelkerke's $R^2 = 0.171$; Model: $\chi^2 = 745.3, p < 0.000$, 17 df; 71% of cases correctly predicted					

Independent variables: offence type, location, time, reporting origin (A), with BTP jurisdiction added (B), reporting source added (C), and BTP jurisdiction and reporting source added (D) victims telephoned incident details to the control room had three times the odds of being solved. Communicating offence reports to the BTP control room by text, email or social media was strikingly less likely to result in detected cases.

Reporting medium may, however, be a marker for solvability rather than influencing it. The victim's perception of the likelihood of detection may affect their chosen reporting method: if the offender has not left or is thought to be still close to the crime scene, victims may regard it as worthwhile to find a BTP officer, whereas, if they think that finding offenders will be difficult, they may not take the time to report the offence in person, preferring text.

When reporting source is added to the model (Table 3(C)), the absolute importance of reporting origin is lowered, given the high intercorrelation between origin and source. The improved odds of detection due to BTP officers calling incidents into the control room become similar to those of Rail staff at 5:1, though the odds of calling in incident details by telephone remain similar at 3:1. The odds associated with report origin are therefore 'captured' partly by reporting source.

Although offence type is significantly related to detection outcomes, and there is an 8% drop in the odds of a case being solved with each increase in crime type seriousness, no individual offence type is significant (Table 3(A)). Neither offence location nor time helps to explain whether or not cases are detected, though these factors help explain reporting characteristics (Table 3) and, in this way, have indirect effects on detection outcomes.

BTP jurisdiction has significant effects on detection, even when controlling for reporting characteristics and offence characteristics (Tables 3(B) and (D)). Sexual offences in Scotland have 2.4 times, and those in Western, Pennine, Wales and Midlands subdivisions 1.5 times, the odds of being detected than those in the London, South and South-East jurisdictions.

Differences in reporting characteristics between divisions and in offence type explain 17% (Nagelkerke's $R^2 = 0.17$) of the variation in whether or not cases were detected, and reporting characteristics make the main contribution to this statistical outcome: the addition of the jurisdiction variable adds 1% to the explanation.

Hence, the ways in which sexual offences are reported are strongly related to whether cases are solved and may be regarded as notable solvability factors. Reporting method may, however, partly reflect other factors related to case solvability, including whether the offender remains at or near the scene and whether the victim is able to describe the offender in a way that would enable his eventual arrest. Even taking account of reporting differences, offence location and type, Scottish and other BTP jurisdictions outside the London, South and East divisions solved more offences—a likely reflection of demand relative to officer supply, given the high levels of sex offending on railways in the London–South-East Division, particularly London. In London, detection rates are also likely to be depressed by the higher number of tourists and other non-English-speakers, while Transport for London has recently encouraged reporting of sex offences by victims, witnesses and informants using telephones, text, emails and social media. While this has successfully enhanced reporting, these are the least promising media for detecting offences with the least subsequent cooperation with investigating officers. It is also possible that BTP officers in Scotland and parts of the Western–Pennine–Midlands–Wales division may be deployed in different ways, with a larger proportion patrolling railway property, especially station buildings, making them more accessible to victims.

There may be other explanations for the scale of sex offending in the London–South-East division. These may include the fact that the level of passenger numbers at busy periods in other jurisdictions may not match those in London, and especially on the London Underground, which may make assaults when passengers are standing at close quarters easier to perpetrate. The particular characteristics of the London Underground, such as the need to use escalators and staircases where offences can be committed when victims are positioned on higher steps than perpetrators, and underground pedestrian pathways, which can be empty at quiet times, may make victims more vulnerable, while more frequent train stops are likely to allow offenders to more quickly flee crime scenes. Equally, there may be more sexual offenders in London, and this study did not include data on offender characteristics. On the other hand, there may also be more trains operating during the early morning and after midnight in London, when low passenger numbers may also facilitate assault as well as exposure and public indecency offences.

Predicting Detections

Summary Solvability Scores

Summary solvability scores were derived by converting all the significant variables in Table 3(A) into individual binary variables, multiplying the odds ratios from a binary regression equation by whether or not the factor was present (0, 1) and summing them to produce a score for each case. A solvability score was calculated for reporting characteristics and all of the significant offence characteristics, and another was calculated on the basis of reporting characteristics alone. The solvability score makes it possible to assess the extent to which detection outcomes may be accurately predicted from, for the first score, all the significant offence and reporting variables (Fig. 14), and, for the second score, from the reporting characteristics alone (Fig. 15).

The relationship between the reporting solvability score and detections demonstrates that reporting incidents via more effective origins or sources proved to be highly beneficial for solving sexual offences. These scores reflect a hierarchy of reporting sources and origins in terms of outcomes. Higher reporting solvability scores are attributable to incidents reported particularly to BTP officers and Rail staff. Reporting offences by telephone and particularly by text, email and social media appears to be far less beneficial in terms of detections, even when taking into account the effects of different offence types, locations, timing and jurisdiction.

The highest reporting solvability scores, achieved by a little over a fifth of the population, give cases a 57% likelihood of being solved when controlling for offence type, location, timing and BTP jurisdiction (Fig. 15). It appears that, through more cases being reported via the best performing—in terms of detection outcomes—

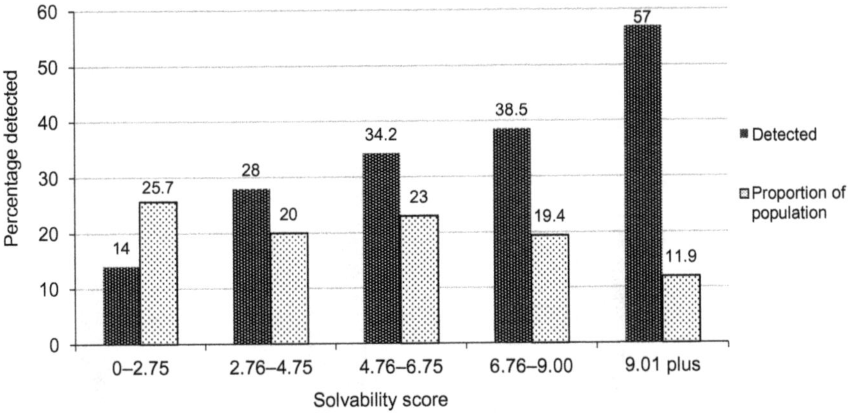

Fig. 14 Solvability score by percentage detected and as a proportion of the population of incidents

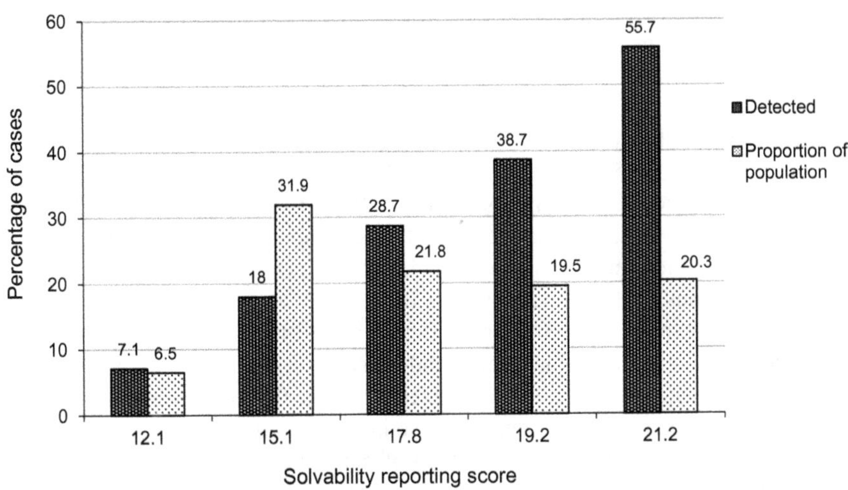

Fig. 15 Reporting solvability score by percentage detected and as a proportion of the population of incidents

origins, there is potential to boost the detection rate for sexual offences on railways. The ways in which offences are reported are a solvability factor that, if used to inform officer deployment and accessibility and to inform potential victims, might hold potential to elevate detection rates without significant additional resources. Reporting offences using texts may reflect difficulties in locating BT police officers at stations at particular times, so that improved reporting might be achieved by staffing particular places to meet demand at particular times. Equally, investigating time–space demand for reporting may require additional officer resources or officers who can respond quickly to reports communicated by victims on trains by intercepting offenders as trains stop and they attempt to leave the crime scene.

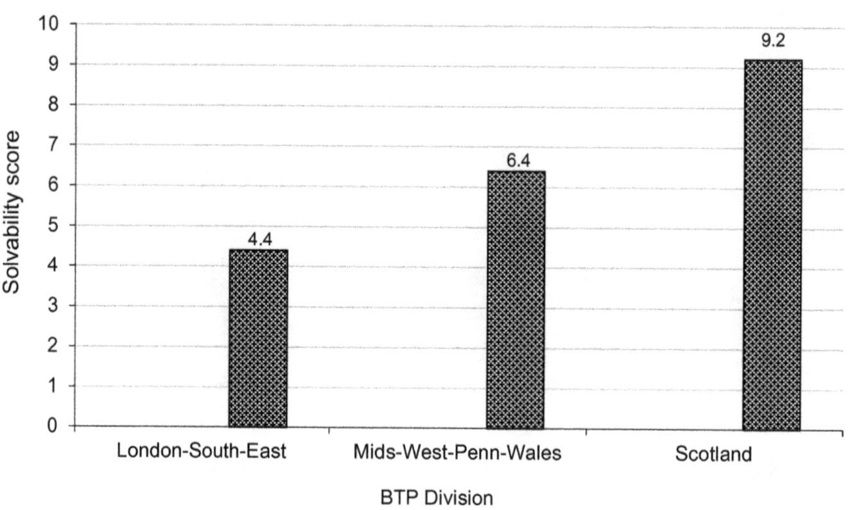

Fig. 16 Mean solvability score for offences in the BTP jurisdictions

While the solvability score is far higher for solved than unsolved cases ($F = 554.1$, $p < 0.001$, $n = 15{,}840$; *M*s: 4.3, 6.6; SDs = 3.5, 3.2), it appears that the score based on reporting origin odds ratios alone (the 'reporting solvability' score), when controlling for offence characteristics and other significant factors, is a rather better predictor of detection outcomes ($F = 658.4$, $p < 0.001$, $n = 15{,}840$), given smaller standard deviations relative to value ranges (SDs = 2.3 vs. 2.6 for solvability score). Reporting score explains 14.6% (Nagelkerke's $R^2 = 0.146$) of the variation in detection outcomes, and adding in the offence and jurisdiction characteristics elevates this by only a small amount to 16.4% (Nagelkerke's $R^2 = 0.164$). The reporting solvability score may be regarded as superior also in that the highest predicted detection group contains almost twice the proportion of population cases—a fifth compared with a tenth—for the solvability score's highest detection group (Fig. 15, cf. Fig. 14).

Jurisdictional Differences in Solvability

As a result of differences in offence type, location, timing and volume between the BTP jurisdictions, there are striking variations in offence solvability, which results in the marked differences in detection outcomes highlighted above, with Scotland's detections (58%) more than twice those of London–South-East (25%), and with Midlands–Pennine–Western–Wales intermediate to these at 40% (Fig. 16).

There were significant differences in both solvability score ($F(25{,}839) = 344.6$, $p < 0.001$; Fig. 16) and reporting solvability score ($F(25{,}839) = 130.7$, $p < 0.001$) between BTP divisions. A PLUM ordinal logistic regression, with BTP division ranked in terms of detection rate the dependent variable, indicates that the differences in detection outcomes reflect geographical differences in reporting characteristics and offence seriousness, location and timing. In contrast with London–South-East, Scotland has more serious offences, fewer offences committed at busy times on trains, and more offences committed at stations where reporting to BTP and Rail staff is higher, partly as a result of better accessibility relative to where offences take place.

Discussion and Conclusion

Reporting characteristics evidently had an important bearing on whether or not sexual offences were solved, irrespective of the type or seriousness of the sexual offence, where on railway property it occurred or when, or BTP jurisdiction; reporting differences accounted for 17% of detection outcomes. There was a reporting hierarchy in terms of detection prospects, with reports to BTP officers the most likely to result in detected cases, followed by Rail staff members, police officers from the territorial police services, telephoned reports from victims, witnesses or informants, and finally, email, texts or social media reporting. The findings indicate that it would be possible to achieve far higher detection rates if victims, witnesses and other informants would report cases to or via BTP officers or Rail staff members, whatever the circumstances of the offence.

Achieving this will be more difficult for offences committed on trains, since more trains are now being crewed by only drivers as, on many services, guards are being dispensed with to save on Rail staffing costs. Unfortunately, a majority of offences take place on trains. A means of contacting and reporting offences that occur on train journeys immediately on the victims' arrivals at their destinations or while in transit would help enhance detections and deter offenders. On longer-distance trains, a means of easily reporting the coach number and train while in transit, so that offenders might be intercepted at the next station, would improve the odds of intercepting offenders. For offences on the London Underground, even with active BTP teams at the busiest sex offending periods, even immediate real-time reporting while in transit would present a challenge to BTP officers, given the short distances and travel times between stations in central London, where many offences take place. Offences that take place on Underground trains in London's suburbs, where the travel times between stations are longer, may provide more scope for timely interception. Such operations might be undertaken randomly as well as at specific times, informed by periods of high incidence of sexual offending on particular railway lines and parts of the Underground system. Enhancing BTP officer availability at stations, particularly during the peak hours of sexual offence incidence—and especially if these coincide with pickpocketing, robbery and other offences—would be likely, therefore, to assist in boosting detections.

It appears that modern electronic communications do not lend themselves to improved detections. Direct contact with the officers employed to police the railways and, secondarily, Rail staff, rather than contact with local police services or offence reporting by telephone or electronic messaging, are superior means for reporting sexual offences. However, telecommunications may be harnessed to good effect if offences are called in as 'on-train emergencies', given that offenders will find it difficult to flee any train until it arrives at a station. Onboard CCTV, both visible (to deter) and covert (to identify offenders), on the train routes where passengers are most vulnerable would support detections.

Offence characteristics, including offence type and location, and the BTP jurisdiction in which they occur, affect detections indirectly through their effects on reporting characteristics. Offence jurisdiction and offence type also have small independent and direct effects on detections, elevating explained variation a little. Victim–investigator contact, though affected by reporting and other offence characteristics, could not be shown to have any effect on detection outcomes when all offences were considered together. Only once those offences where victim cooperation was not needed were excluded and only cases where victim contact played a role were considered was there a significant link between investigator contact and detections.

Future research on sexual offence solvability on railways would benefit from a fuller set of solvability factors, but most especially from information on victim cooperation and the quality of evidence they provide. As it is, a fuller understanding of the mechanism whereby reporting via BTP officers and staff, rather than by police officers from other forces, and by these officers rather than by victims themselves, results in far better prospects for detections requires measures of the quality of victim and other members of the public's assistance with police investigations. Reporting medium was linked to offence severity, with more serious offences being reported to territorial police officers, as opposed to British Transport police officers. It also depended on where offences take place: more offences occurring in station buildings were reported to BTP officers, BTP staff and territorial police officers where they were accessible to victims. Far more of the offences on trains, which constitute the majority of sexual offences, were reported by telephone—almost certainly a reflection of the difficulties inherent in contacting officers and staff, of whom there are far fewer on moving trains. Reporting medium also varied by BTP subdivision, with far more offences reported by telephone in London and the South-East, and the fewest in Scotland. This reflected in part the greater severity of offences and higher proportion of offences committed at stations in Scotland where, as a result, more police and staff were accessible to victims. In contrast, in London and the South-East, higher proportions of offences were less serious offences occurring on trains, where the absence of police and staff resulted in far more telephone reporting. Findings indicate, however, that jurisdiction, offence severity and location help explain detection outcomes independently of their effects on reporting medium.

Offence location, severity and jurisdiction, however, barely explain a tenth of the differences in reporting medium. Even for offences committed at stations, victims' choice of medium may depend on other factors, such as whether the perpetrator is still on station premises and victims' perceptions of the likelihood of offenders being arrested. It would be important to ascertain why victims choose a particular reporting medium. It may be that, in some circumstances, when the perpetrator is still in the station and a BTP officer, police officer or member of Rail staff can be found, this is the most promising way to report the offence. When no officer can easily be found, the victim may have to report the crime by phone. In a situation where the offender has left the station and the victim may believe themselves to be unable to describe the offender in a unique way, he/she may believe that there is too little to go on to apprehend the offender. As a consequence, the victim may decide not to invest the time to report the offence in person or on the phone, instead resorting to text or social media. All this is, at this point, conjecture. A study of victim decision-making could shed light on this issue. This would then provide guidance on whether reporting medium is indeed a solvability factor in itself, or just a marker of different underlying offence or victim characteristics.

This study indicates, nevertheless, that channelling sexual offence reports via BTP officers and Rail staff—that is, encouraging 'in-house' reporting—will be beneficial, especially for the high-volume, low-to-medium-seriousness offences that account for all but 4% of all sexual offences. This may be a reflection of better BTP resources for investigating such offences, which accords them a higher priority, a timeliness in dealing with them, as well as information on known offenders who have previously used the railways as their preferred sexual offending venue. Studies of the reporting and contact process for other offences, in both the BTP and other police forces, of the effects of reporting procedures on detections and of the impact of victim contact on evidence of varying quality are likely to yield findings that also have implications for successful detection outcomes, promising to minimise potentially solvable cases that remain undetected.

References

Ambler, C., & Milne, R. (2006). *Call handling centres—An evidential opportunity or a threat?* Paper Presented at the Second International Investigative Interviewing Group Annual Conference, Portsmouth, UK.

Baxter (2008).

Bennett, R. R., & Wiegand, R. B. (1994). Observations on crime reporting in a developing nation. *Criminology, 32*(1), 135–148.

Brooks, L., & Perot, A. R. (1991). Reporting sexual harassment: Exploring a predictive model. *Psychology of Women Quarterly, 15*(1), 31–47.

Dunckel-Graglia, A. (2013). 'Pink transportation' in Mexico City: Reclaiming urban space through collective action against gender-based violence. *Gender and Development, 21*(2), 265–276.

Fitzgerald, L. F., Shullman, S. L., Bailey, N., Richards, M., Swecker, J., Gold, Y., et al. (1988). The incidence and dimensions of sexual harassment in academia and the workplace. *Journal of Vocational Behavior, 32*(2), 152–175.

Future Thinking. (2015). Safety and security annual report 2014. http://content.tfl.gov.uk/safety-and-security-annual-report-2014-15.pdf. Accessed [date].

'Half of French women' alter clothes to avoid harassment. (2016, June 15). *The local*. http://www.thelocal.fr/20160615/half-of-french-woman-alter-clothes-to-avoid-harassment. Accessed [date].

Jafarova, T., Campbell, S., & Rojas, W. S. (2014). *AZE: Rapid assessment on sexual harassment in the Baku metro rail—Final report*. Philippines: Asian Development Bank.

Koss, M. P. (1985). The hidden rape victim: Personality, attitudinal, and situational characteristics. *Psychology of Women Quarterly, 9*(2), 193–212.

Lachin, J. M. (1981). Introduction to sample size determination and power analysis for clinical trials. *Controlled Clinical Trials, 2*(2), 93–113.

Lambillion, A. (2012). *Serious sexual offences problem profile*. London: British Transport Police.

Latané, B., & Darley, J. M. (1970). *The unresponsive bystander: Why doesn't he help?*. Engelwood Cliffs, NJ: Prentice Hall.

Leeney, D. G., & Mueller-Johnson, K. (2011). Examining the forensic quality of police call-centre interviews. *Psychology, Crime & Law, 18*(7), 669–688.

Lievore, D. (2003). *Non-reporting and hidden reporting of sexual assault: An international literature review*. Archive. Canberra: Australian Institute of Criminology.

London Assembly Police and Crime Committee. (2016). *Crime on public transport*. London: Greater London Authority.

Nickerson, A. B., Aloe, A. M., Livingston, J. A., & Feeley, T. H. (2014). Measurement of the bystander intervention model for bullying and sexual harassment. *Journal of Adolescence, 37*(4), 391–400.

Skogan, W. G. (1994). *Contacts between police and public: Findings from the 1992 British Crime Survey (Home Office Research Study 134)*. London: HMSO.

SPA Future Thinking. (2013). *Safety and security annual report 2013/14*. London: Transport for London. http://content.tfl.gov.uk/safety-and-security-annual-report-2013-14.pdf. Accessed [date].

Spelman, W., & Brown, D. K. (1981). *Calling the police: Citizen reporting of serious crime*. Washington, DC: Police Research Executive Forum.

Stringer, S. M. (2007). *Hidden in plain sight: Sexual harassment and assault in the New York City subway system*. NY: Office of the Manhattan Borough President.

Tarling, R., & Morris, K. (2010). Reporting crime to the police. *The British Journal of Criminology, 50*(3), 474–490.

Taylor, S. C., & Gassner, L. (2010). Stemming the flow: Challenges for policing adult sexual assault with regard to attrition rates and under-reporting of sexual offences. *Police Practice and Research: An International Journal, 11*(3), 240–255.

Transport for London. (2013). *Safety and security annual report*. London: Transport for London. http://content.tfl.gov.uk/safety-and-security-annual-report-2013-14.pdf.

Transport for London. (2016). *Report it to stop it (campaign)*. London: Transport for London.

Travis, A. (2015, April 09). Reported child sexual abuse has risen 60% in last four years. *The Guardian*. https://www.theguardian.com/society/2015/apr/09/reported-child-sexual-abuse-has-risen-60-in-last-four-years-figures-show. Accessed [date].

Williams, L. S. (1984). The classic rape: When do victims report? *Social Problems, 31*(4), 459–467.

Winter, J. (2014). *French feminist group storms Paris underground with anti-harassment posters in 'Take Back the Metro' campaign to end subway intimidation of women*. [Online]. http://www.dailymail.co.uk/femail/article–2831482/French-feminist-group-storms-Paris-underground-anti-harrassment-posters-Metro-campaign.html, http://www.thelocal.fr/20160615/half-of-french-woman-alter-clothes-to-avoid-harassment.

Offender–Offence Profiling: Improving Burglary Solvability and Detection

Bronwyn Killmier, Katrin Mueller-Johnson and Richard Timothy Coupe

Introduction

Burglary is one of the most common crimes, yet frequently remains unsolved. Little more than 13% of incidents are solved in the UK (Taylor and Bond 2012) and Australia (Killmier 2013). Around four-fifths of solved incidents rely mainly on eyewitness evidence that facilitates capture at or near the burglary scene or subsequent arrest due to suspect descriptions (Coupe and Griffiths 1996; Burrows et al. 2005; Paine and Ariel 2013). Although there is evidence that more thorough forensic work at burglary scenes, particularly on fingerprints, and better-performing forensic investigators can markedly boost detections (Antrobus and Pilotto 2016), improved forensic procedures have not, in general, increased detection rates as much as anticipated, even for those cases involving DNA samples (Roman et al. 2009). In the bulk of cases, however, there is not even eyewitness or forensic evidence or probable suspect information available to guide police to the arrest of burglars (Coupe and Blake 2006). As a result, cases are left unsolved, victims suffer and perpetrators are free to burgle again.

Research consistently indicates that different types of burglars commit different types of burglaries (Farrington and Lambert 2006; Miethe et al. 2006; Coupe and Blake 2006; Fox and Farrington 2012), and the objective of this study is to explore the links between offender and burglary target characteristics in order to create specific typologies of burglary offenders and offences for use in future police investigations. Using latent class analysis, subtypes of burglar traits and criminal histories will

B. Killmier
Formerly of South Australia Police, Adelaide, SA, Australia

K. Mueller-Johnson (✉) · R. T. Coupe
Institute of Criminology, University of Cambridge, Cambridge, UK
e-mail: kum20@cam.ac.uk

R. T. Coupe
e-mail: rtc23@cam.ac.uk

R. T. Coupe et al. (eds.), *Crime Solvability Factors*,
https://doi.org/10.1007/978-3-030-17160-5_12

be derived and related to offence styles and burglary characteristics, so that subsets of offenders with distinctive combinations of characteristics may be predicted from known offence characteristics at unsolved burglaries. In this way, this chapter promises to provide a means of helping to identify not just the types of offenders but, by matching offences with lists of known local offenders, the likely culprits for some of the majority of incidents at which there is little or no evidence and which, consequently, remain unsolved (Coupe and Griffiths 1996).

As well as improving 'known offender targeting' by detectives, it is likely that the application of typology information will assist in directing patrol effort at burglars who may still be in possession of stolen property following burglary incidents. Linking certain types of burglars to distinctive types of targets can also inform intensive forensic investigation on burglaries of certain sorts of homes, identified by spatio-temporal and demographic characteristics, with a view to putting evidence in place that may, in the future, help identify offenders who are rarely caught. If burglary target types can be matched to specific subsets of offender types, these would enable the formalisation and systematisation of police 'known offender targeting', which could, as a result, be carried out more comprehensively and cost-effectively. The technique promises to help combat changes in police expertise and offender behaviour. Fewer officers are now local to the areas they police, and there is higher officer turnover, so that offenders may be less well known to officers. Equally, some burglars are more mobile, because fewer now make burglary journeys on foot, while others target more distant areas where they formerly lived to carry out burglaries either alone or alongside former friends (Bernasco 2010). Target characteristics are likely to vary by time of day (Tompson and Coupe 2017), the presence of daylight or darkness (Coupe and Blake 2006), co-offending, the age of the offender and the distance travelled, and other relationships between burglary offence characteristics and offender traits are likely to exist.

This study aims to classify burglars and burglaries in Adelaide, South Australia, and considers the extent to which it is possible to identify distinctive associations between offence types and offender types with a view to predicting the offenders most likely to be responsible for unsolved offences. By these means, it promises to help boost the numbers of solvable burglary cases.

Existing Research on Offender–Offence Profiling

Most offender profiling studies have been carried out on serious offences, such as homicide and rape. Few have considered high-volume property crimes, such as burglary and theft of and from vehicles, which have far lower detection rates (e.g., Taylor and Bond 2012). Despite claims for the success of offender profiling, existing typologies are not statistically grounded in empirical data, making their validity and reliability questionable (Kocsis and Cooksey 2002). The few exceptions to this include serial murder, rape and arson (Kocsis et al. 2002; Kocsis and Cooksey 2002; Promish and Lester 1999), which have detection rates of 50–79% in the USA, compared with only 14% for burglary (Taylor and Chaplin 2011). This is not dissimilar to the UK burglary clear-up rates, which, despite the increased use of forensic investigation (Donnellan 2012; Paine and Ariel 2013), repeat and near-repeat burglary investigation and prolific burglar targeting, also remain very low (Tilley et al. 2007).

Whereas, much existing offender profiling considers repeat or serial offenders to help identify specific 'psychological signatures' for individual offenders (Farrington and Lambert 2006), burglary's high prolificacy is likely to counter the identification of specific psychological signatures for each unsolved incident where the offender is unknown. Rather, the identification of the types of burglars associated with different types of burglaries—identified by when and where they occur—and the victim, property and incident characteristics—such as whether the crime scene is organised or disorganised, the means and place of entry, inter-visibility with neighbouring premises, house type and age, victim age and family type—are as likely to help predict the different types of burglars responsible.

Fox and Farrington (2012) applied such an approach to burglary data from the state of Florida, deriving distinctive offence and offender typologies by using latent class analysis to classify a sample of 405 cases. They identified four offence styles, four offender types and four offending history groups. The offence styles were termed 'opportunistic', 'organised', 'disorganised' and 'interpersonal'. The *opportunistic* type was described by the absence of forced entry, no use of tools, a tidy search and, despite interruption in most cases, a lower likelihood of leaving evidence. The *organised* type was characterised by planning: tools were brought to the scene, the search was tidy, and high-value items were stolen. The *disorganised* type, on the other hand, showed a lack of preparation or control, with untidy searches, tools or evidence left behind, and often nothing actually stolen. The final type, the *interpersonal,* occurred mainly at occupied premises during night-time, where the victim confronted the burglar, who used no tools and left a tidy scene. According to Fox and Farrington (2012), such offences were motivated by anger or interpersonal disputes. Four types of offenders were identified: 'older white males', 'younger whites', 'older black males' and 'younger minorities'. The paper also attempts to describe the appearance of these offenders, using eye and hair colour, as well as height and weight. The offending history classification consisted of 'starters', 'low rates', 'high rates' and 'chronics'.

Using these identified classes, Fox and Farrington (2012) attempted to link offences and offenders, offenders and offending history, as well as offences and offending history. Offender type and offence type were indeed related. Older white males, for instance, were particularly likely to commit 'opportunistic' and 'organised' offences. 'Disorganised' offences were more often committed by 'younger white' offenders, while the 'older black' group was particularly represented in the interpersonal offence type. It was also possible to link offender type and offending history. Younger and older offenders, as well as younger minority offenders, were in the 'starter' group, 'low-rate' offenders were likely to be either younger or older whites, and 'chronic' offenders were most likely to be older white or black offenders. The final link, however—that between offence and offending history—could not be identified in their data. This is a critical link, since types of offenders could be identified from existing records using measures of offender age, prior offences, versatility and prolificacy if only it were possible to predict these from the observable offence types. The fact that this link was not significant presents questions about how feasible it will be to use offender–offence links to solve more burglaries.

It is an empirical question as to whether the offence and offender clusters found by Fox and Farrington (2012) generalise to other data or locations. Compared with European countries or Australia, Florida has distinctive offenders, dwelling environments, climatic conditions and legal frameworks. Florida's housing environments are often of low density and without streetlights, and Florida's latitude limits seasonal changes in weather and in the balance of daylight–darkness, so that some of the temporal and seasonal swings that commonly affect the incidence of different types of burglary (Tompson and Coupe 2017) are likely to be absent. The US definition of burglary includes burglary vagrancy, murder, rape and murder, as well as burglary theft, so that US offender typologies demarcate distinctions between these groups, which would be classified as different offences in Australia, as much as between types of burglaries involving only theft, which is the focus of the current study.

Furthermore, there are offender differences and notable differences in offender behaviour and burglary characteristics between Daytona, Florida, and Australia. One is that prior offences may be taken into account in Australia, while, in Florida, information on prior offences results in lengthier sentences, so that fewer offenders admit to them. Consequently, prolificacy in Florida is counted in a handful of cases, whereas in Australia, prolific burglars commonly have committed hundreds of offences. Whether US prior offence numbers accurately differentiate between high and low prolificacy is questionable. While female burglars are rare in Florida and, as in the UK, often co-offend with males, in Adelaide, lone adult female burglars are more common.

This chapter will investigate whether the links between offence and offender types are sufficiently strong in a different environment, an Australian setting, to help improve detection rates. It aims to help remedy the limited burglary research into offender–offence typologies for high-volume crime by improving our understanding of the key characteristics of burglars and burglaries in metropolitan Adelaide and by developing offender, offence and offender–offence typologies using latent class analysis. In doing so, its findings aim to both extend academic knowledge and provide insights into an approach to profiling burglaries that promises to eventually help police investigations and detection rates through improved solvability.

Methodology

Research Design and Data

The research is based on data on offender and offence characteristics taken from police records. A sample was compiled of the 265 unique offenders convicted for committing 349 domestic burglaries in the metropolitan jurisdiction of Adelaide in 2010. Serious criminal trespass (residence), the equivalent in South Australia of burglary, is committed if a person enters a dwelling in order to harm its occupants or to steal or damage property. In 2010, there were 8518 serious criminal trespass offences with a 9% 'arrested and charged' rate and a conviction rate of 4%. This study is based on the 349 cases where arrestees were prosecuted and convicted. The substantial attrition between arrest and conviction is a matter of concern for the police who undertake prosecutions in South Australia.

Two-thirds of South Australia's population, or 1.2 million people, live in Adelaide (Australian Bureau of Statistics 2011), which covers an area of 1820 km^2. Residential densities are low at 660 persons per km^2, and housing stock is dominated by low-rise, single-family dwellings and few apartments.

Data Sources and Characteristics

The study relies on secondary data on incident characteristics, offender behaviour at the scene and offender traits and histories taken mainly from South Australia Police databases. Demographic and housing socioeconomic ratings were taken from the Australian Bureau of Statistics (2013). It was assumed that offenders started burglary journeys from their homes. The distances of journeys to the crime scene were calculated using the 'where-is.com' software (2013), which assumes use of the road network.

Police data were collected from reports compiled by arresting officers for intelligence and prosecution purposes. These include the offender's demographic details, criminal history, modus operandi, motive and entry method, forensic evidence, whether or not the offender was disturbed and by whom, the use of tools, and the value of stolen property. The first author collected data on crime and conviction histories by individually accessing each offender's records from a number of police systems.

In summary, there is a full range of data on the time and date of offence, time and method of discovery, means and location of entry, dwelling type and occupancy, types of items stolen, amount of victims' losses, demographic characteristics of victims, whether or not the offence was a repeat burglary, whether the offender was sighted, and the date on which the offence was cleared. There are also details about dwelling security. Offender data include age, ethnicity, gender, age of crime onset, distance travelled to burglary, presence and number of co-offenders, motive for the burglary, and whether the offence involved violence or was drug-related. There were also data on offending and sentencing histories, including convictions, that enable the determination of prolificacy, specialisation and versatility, and a measure of expertise in terms of the numbers of arrests compared with levels of offending.

Method of Analysis

Analysis of these data was conducted in three principal stages. Firstly, a descriptive analysis of the characteristics of offenders and offences was undertaken to gain a better understanding of the sample and the most prevalent characteristics of offenders and offences.

Secondly, latent class analyses, which prior research had suggested would highlight discrete groupings of offender variables (Vaughn et al. 2008), was used to identify (a) an empirical classification of burglary offenders, with each offender assigned to a group that his or her individual characteristics most accurately fit, (b) an empirical classification of offending histories, and (c) an empirical classification of burglary offences, based on crime scene information.

Finally, we assessed the extent to which it was possible to link offence groups and offender groups, offender groups and offending history types, and offence group and offending history types.

Findings

Adelaide's Burglar and Burglary Characteristics

The variables used to measure criminal histories, offender characteristics and offence characteristics are shown in Table 1(A–C). They constitute the inputs to classifications using latent class analysis. They also highlight the principal ways in which burglars and burglaries in South Australia differ from those in Europe and the USA, though these figures refer to only the subset of solved cases. These are unlikely to reflect the bulk of unsolved cases, which involve more older offenders who travel greater distances to commit burglary (Lammers 2014).

In some respects, the sample has similarities with northern hemisphere burglary. Co-offending is more common among younger offenders (τ_b ($N = 349$) $= -0.482, p < 0.001$), who tend to target homes in daylight and on weekdays, and visit more rooms (τ_b ($N = 349$) $= 0.101, p = 0.043$). As elsewhere (van Koppen and Jansen 1998 in the Netherlands; Snook 2004 in Canada; Wright 2013 in England), older offenders also tend to travel farther ($r = 0.268, p < 0.01, n = 349$). They also target higher-valued homes in South Australia ($r_s = 0.285, p < 0.001, n = 349$), though the evidence for this elsewhere varies. In England, for instance, it depends on whether burglars are on foot or use a vehicle (Coupe and Blake 2006) and may apply better to rural than urban areas (Wright 2013). Younger offenders tended more often to leave burglary scenes untidy ($F(1, 348) = 8.21, p = 0.004$). The tendency of offenders targeting houses in areas of higher socioeconomic status to themselves live in upmarket areas ($\chi^2(4, N = 349) = 75.6, p < 0.001$) and leave more DNA than fingerprint samples at the scene ($F(1, 348) = 7.13, p = 0.008$) may apply only to South Australia. Equally, they may well be replicable in European or US burglary samples, though few, if any,

Table 1 Descriptive statistics for all offender and offence characteristics ($N = 349$)[a]

Sample %		Sample %	
(A) *Criminal history*			
Criminal record	93.4	Medium prior SCT offences (26–50)	6.3
No record	6.6	High prior SCT offences (>50)	6.3
Child start (1–10 years)	6.0	No prior drug/alcohol offences	47.0
Adolescent start (11–18 years)	73.1	Low prior drug/alcohol offences (1–25)	52.7
Young adult start (19–25 years)	11.2	Medium prior drug/alcohol offences (26–50)	.3
Adult onset (>26 years)	9.5	High prior drug/alcohol offences (>50)	0
No prior offences	6.6	No prior dishonesty offences	11.7
Low prior offences (1–25)	27.2	Low prior dishonesty offences (1–25)	59.6
Medium prior offences (26–50)	19.5	Medium prior dishonesty offences (26–50)	18.9
High prior offences (>50)	46.7	High prior dishonesty offences (>50)	9.7
0 years offending	6.0	No prior traffic offences	22.1
1–10 years offending	48.4	Low prior traffic offences (1–25)	71.3
11–20 years offending	32.1	Medium prior traffic offences (26–50)	6.0
>21 years offending	13.5	High prior traffic offences (>50)	.6
No prior violent offences	25.5	Offended alone	61.4
Low prior violent offences (1–25)	71.1	Offended in company	38.6
Medium prior violent offences (26–50)	1.7	Knew victim	25.5
High prior violent offences (>50)	1.7	Did not know victim	74.5
No prior SCT offences	14.3		
Low prior SCT offences (1–25)	73.1		
(B) *Offender traits* ($N = 349$)			
Male	84.8	Brown eyes	45.6
Female	15.2	Other eye colour	15.5
Child (<18 years)	37.9	Blue eyes	33.2
Adolescent (18.1–26.9)	17.0	Green eyes	5.7
Younger adult (27–35)	25.0	Brown hair	60.5
Male	84.8	Brown eyes	45.6
Female	15.2	Other eye colour	15.5
Child (<18 years)	37.9	Blue eyes	33.2
Adolescent (18.1–26.9)	17.0	Green eyes	5.7

(continued)

Table 1 (continued)

Sample %		Sample %	
Younger adult (27–35)	25.0	Brown hair	60.5
Adult (>35.1)	20.1	Black hair	22.1
Caucasian	70.8	Blond hair	14.3
Aboriginal/Torres Strait Islander	21.5	Other colour hair	3.2
Other	7.7	Thin	34.4
Short	15.8	Average weight	52.7
Average height	81.7	Large	12.9
Tall	2.6	Offender employed	14.3
Low-value offender residence	67.9	Offender student	30.7
Average-value offender residence	14.3	Offender unemployed	55.0
High-value offender residence	17.8	Alcohol/drug affected at time of offence	12.9
		Not alcohol/drug affected at time of offence	87.1
(C) *Offence characteristics*			
Forced entry	55.6	House alarmed	2.9
No forced entry	44.4	House not alarmed	97.1
Tools used	31.8	Utilitarian motive	74.5
No tools used	68.2	Excitement motive	7.2
Evidence left at scene	73.1	Anger/dispute/revenge motive	14.0
No evidence left at scene	26.9	Other motive	4.3
DNA left at scene	18.6	Daytime	71.9
Fingerprints left at scene	27.2	Darkness	28.1
Other forensic evidence left at scene	55.0	Weekday	75.1
Untidy scene	25.5	Weekend	24.9
Tidy scene	74.5	Offender disturbed	56.7
Crime successful	88.0	Offender not disturbed	43.3
Attempt only	12.0	Alarm disturbed	1.4
Low distance travelled (<2 km)	32.0	Resident disturbed	38.7
Medium distance travelled (2.1–6 km)	21.9	Guardian disturbed	49.9
High distance travelled (>6 km)	46.1	No property stolen	22.9
Victim age child (<18)	2.9	Low-value property stolen ($1–$500)	25.2
Victim age adolescent (18.1–26.9)	12.0	Medium-value property stolen ($501–$3000)	29.5
Victim age younger adult (27–35)	16.6	High-value property stolen (>$3001)	22.3
Victim age adult (>35)	64.8	Low-value victim residence	44.7

(continued)

Table 1 (continued)

Sample %		Sample %	
Front door entry	22.63	Average-value victim residence	19.5
Front window entry	10.31	High-value victim residence	35.8
Side window entry	10.60	No rooms visited (0)	6.6
Side door entry	4.5	Some rooms visited (1–3)	48.4
Back door entry	30.37	All rooms visited (4–5)	45.0
Back window entry	20.63	Victim employed	60.2
Roof entry	0.85	Victim not employed	29.8
		Victim retired	10.0

[a]Percentages calculated excluding missing values

other studies have yet reported these facts—possibly, in part, because few studies have related offenders to offences and environmental characteristics.

Other characteristics, however, differ markedly from those of burglars and burglaries in other jurisdictions. Journeys to crime are far longer in Adelaide, with most offenders travelling over 6 km ($M = 9.7$ km; Mdn = 5.2 km; SD = 11.7), and the numbers of prior offences are far higher—with half the sample having committed over 50 prior dishonesty offences—than in the USA, where a prolific offender is defined as having committed only a handful of prior offences (e.g., Fox and Farrington 2012). A utilitarian motive is also more predominant in Adelaide than in Daytona, Florida, where excitement and thrills motivate a quarter of all solved residential burglaries - more than three times as many as in Adelaide. Unlike Adelaide, the large numbers of holiday homes in Daytona may prove attractive to these burglars. Adelaide, in common with rural South Australia, has a distinctive ethnic minority group, the Aboriginal/Torres Strait Islanders, and a disproportionate number of mature women with lengthy criminal careers from this group are actively involved in domestic burglary. This differs from the ethnic minority characteristics of burglars in Europe and the USA, who, in contrast, tend to be younger, male and either African American in the USA or West Indian in the UK.

There are notable differences, as well as some similarities, in terms of burglary and burglar characteristics between this study and existing studies. Adelaide typologies are unlikely to match those in the USA or research on typologies yet to be carried out there or elsewhere, including Europe. This suggests that typologies that help identify the kinds of offenders likely to be responsible for unsolved burglaries will need to be tailored to distinctive 'local' burglar–burglary characteristics and that there are unlikely to be universal typologies that apply to every jurisdiction, particularly those in other countries.

Latent Class Analysis

Latent class analysis is a statistical technique that groups persons in a data set based on their characteristics. Those similar in terms of the chosen characteristics are grouped together, while those who are dissimilar from each other are grouped into different clusters (Muthen and Muthen 2000). Unlike more traditional statistical tests, like *t*-tests, there is no single significance test which tells the user if a model is significant. Instead, a number of goodness-of-fit indices are reported for a number of models with a different number of class solutions, such as the Akaike Information Criterion (AIC), the Bayesian Information Criterion (BICO), and the Consistent Akaike Information Criterion (CAIC). The solution with the lowest values on these indices is chosen, as lower values indicate a better fit than higher values. It is common that one solution will not have the lowest value on all fit indices at the same time. In this situation, the model with highest number of lowest measures is typically selected.

Three different sets of latent class analyses were conducted: first, on offence characteristics; second, on offender information, and finally on offender history characteristics. Table 2 represents the fit indices for all potential class solutions for these three sets of analyses.

Classifying Offences

The key inductively derived variables that enabled differentiation in the latent class analysis were whether the burglary was committed in daylight or darkness, whether entry happened via a door or window, whether entry was forced or unforced, whether the search of the property was tidy or untidy, whether the offender was disturbed, whether evidence was left at the scene, and how much was stolen.

A five-cluster solution provided the best fit (Table 2). The modal values for these clusters are presented in Table 3, and the cluster profiles are depicted in Fig. 1a–e.

The largest cluster—the 'disorganised, disturbed' offence group—included a third of all offences (33.6%), and involved forced entry through the door, was equally likely to occur during daytime or night-time, and was mostly committed without tools. The search was tidy, and the offender was disturbed and left evidence at the scene. Nothing or only low-value items (<$500) were stolen.

The second-largest group—the 'organised window entry' type—included 30.9% of offences and involved entry entered during the daytime through a window, the use of force and tools, a tidy search, and the theft of high-value items (worth > $500). The offender was not disturbed but left evidence at the scene.

The third group—the 'opportunistic door entry' type—comprised a fifth of the sample (19.7%) and was characterised by unforced entry through the door during the day, without the use of tools. The offender searched in a tidy manner, stole high-value items and was disturbed, but left no evidence at the scene.

The fourth cluster (10.1% of offences)—the 'opportunistic window entry' type—involved unforced daytime entry through a window, no tool use, and typically a tidy

Table 2 Fit indices for all potential class solutions using latent class analysis

	LL	BIC(LL)	AIC(LL)	CAIC(LL)	Npar	*df*	*p*	Class.Err.
Offenders								
1-Cluster	−1837.30	3744.87	3698.61	3756.87	12.00	337	0.000	0.00
2-Cluster	−1749.15	3621.26	3540.31	3642.26	21.00	328	0.002	0.06
3-Cluster	−1722.51	**3620.67**	**3505.02**	**3650.67**	30.00	319	0.090	0.10
4-Cluster	−1709.09	3646.52	3496.17	3685.52	39.00	310	0.250	0.18
5-Cluster	−1699.86	3680.77	3495.73	3728.77	48.00	301	0.380	0.23
6-Cluster	−1689.90	3713.55	3493.81	3770.55	57.00	292	0.550	0.21
Offender history								
1-Cluster	−1757.36	3614.26	3548.73	3631.26	17.00	332	0.000	0.00
2-Cluster	−1630.44	3401.40	3308.88	3425.40	24.00	325	0.000	0.03
3-Cluster	−1545.08	3271.66	3152.15	3302.66	31.00	318	0.000	0.05
4-Cluster	−1501.75	3225.99	3079.50	3263.99	38.00	311	0.003	0.03
5-Cluster	−1485.07	3233.62	3060.14	3278.62	45.00	304	0.032	0.15
6-Cluster	−1467.62	**3239.71**	**3039.25**	**3291.71**	52.00	297	0.210	0.12
7-Cluster	−1455.60	3256.64	3029.20	3315.64	59.00	290	0.450	0.15
Offences								
1-Cluster	−1915.87	3890.28	3851.73	3900.28	10.00	339	0.000	0.00
2-Cluster	−1857.37	3831.84	3754.73	3851.84	20.00	329	0.000	0.13
3-Cluster	−1828.29	3832.23	3716.58	3862.23	30.00	319	0.007	0.15
4-Cluster	−1813.78	3861.77	3707.56	3901.77	40.00	309	0.033	0.16
5-Cluster	−1801.00	**3894.76**	**3702.00**	**3944.76**	50.00	299	**0.100**	0.16
6-Cluster	−1794.78	3940.86	3709.56	4000.86	60.00	289	0.110	0.20
7-Cluster	−1787.85	3985.56	3715.70	4055.56	70.00	279	0.140	0.22

Note LL = log likelihood; BIC = Bayesian Information Criterion; AIC = Akaike Information Criterion; CAIC = Consistent Akaike information Criterion; npar = number of parameters; *df* = degrees of freedom. The values in bold correspond to the best class solution for the data

search. The offender was not disturbed, high-value items were stolen, and evidence was left at the scene.

The final cluster—the 'organised door entry' type—representing only 5% of the sample, consisted of unforced daytime entries through the door, tool use, and either a tidy or untidy search. Here, the offender was not disturbed, left no evidence at the scene, and stole high-value items.

Classifying Offender Traits

The application of latent class analysis to offender data resulted in the identification of three offender groups. The modal values for each group are described in Table 4, and

Table 3 Summary of characteristics of five groups of offence characteristics

LCA cluster	% of sample	Daylight/darkness	Entry	Tool use	Search	Disturbed	Stolen property value	Evidence left at scene
1	33.6	Day/night	Forced (door)	No	Tidy	Yes	Nothing stolen/low value	Yes
2	30.9	Day	Forced (window)	Yes	Tidy	No	High-value	Yes
3	19.7	Day/night	Unforced (door)	No	Tidy	Yes	Low/high-value	No
4	10.1	Day/night	Unforced (door/window)	No	Tidy	No	High value	Yes
5	05.6	Day	Unforced (door)	Yes	Tidy/untidy	No	High value	No

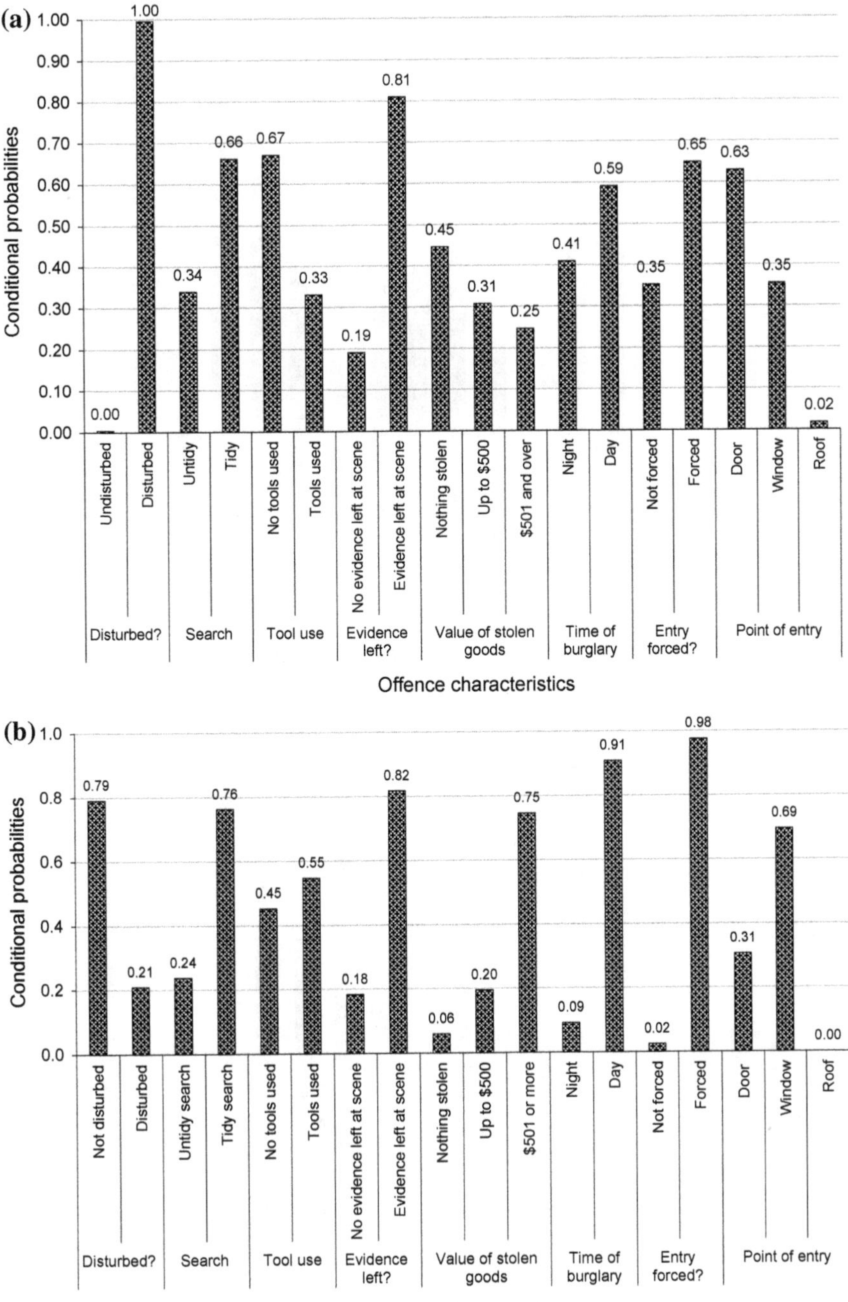

Fig. 1 Conditional probabilities for offence characteristics by offence cluster—**a** Cluster 1 'disorganised, disturbed' (33.6%). **b** Cluster 2 'organised, entry through window' (30.9%). **c** Cluster 3 'opportunistic, entry through door' (19.7%). **d** Cluster 4 'opportunistic, entry through window' (10.1%), **e** Cluster 5 'organised, entry through door' (5.6%)

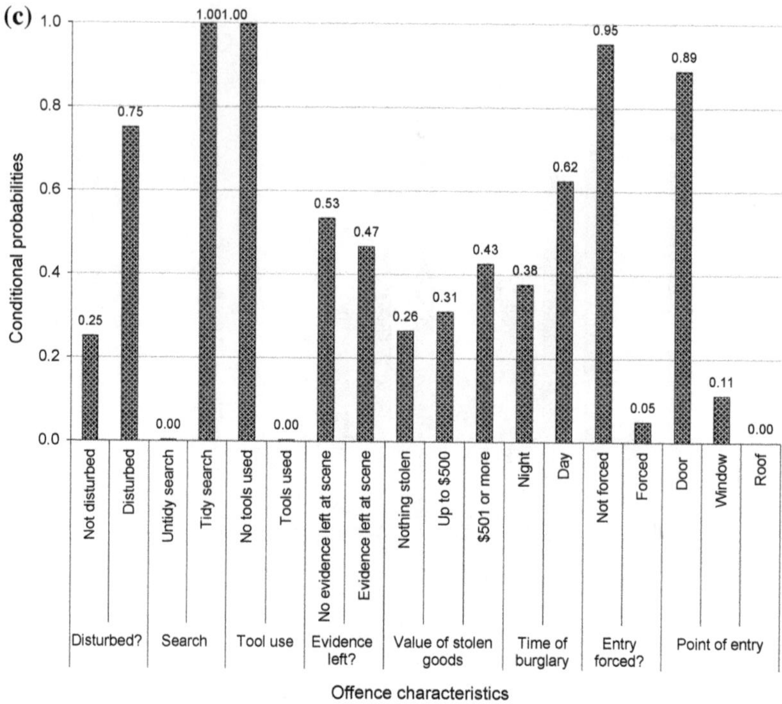

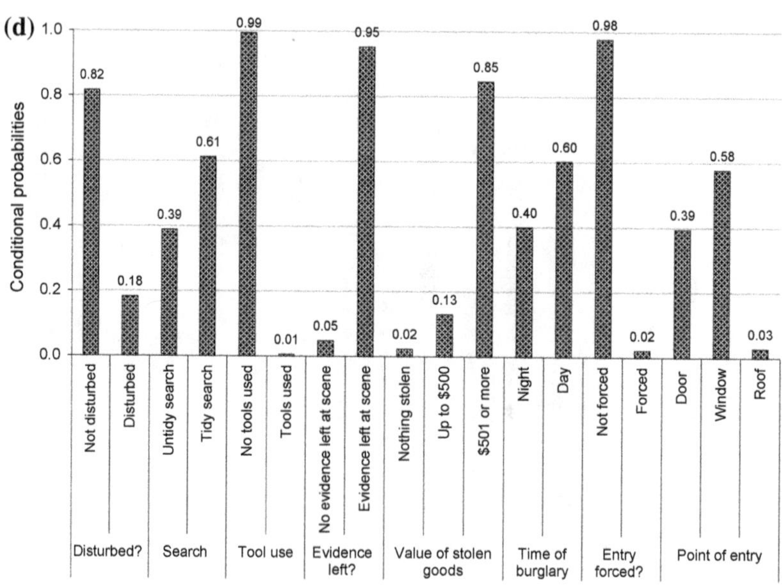

Fig. 1 (continued)

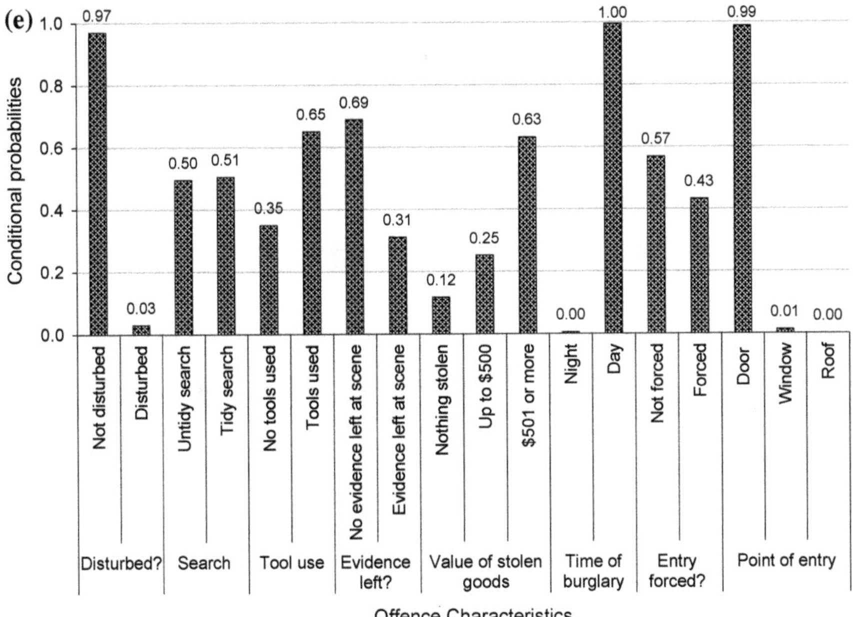

Fig. 1 (continued)

more detailed profiles for clusters are shown in Fig. 2. The key inductively derived variables that enable differentiation between offender types are offender age, gender and ethnicity, whether co-offending or alone, crime journey distance, and whether victims are family, acquaintances or strangers.

Cluster 1, comprising about half the sample (52.3%), was characterised by male, predominately—but not exclusively—Caucasian offenders, working alone, who burgled strangers mostly more than 6 km away from where they lived.

Cluster 2 (35.7% of the sample) typically consisted of young Caucasian males under the age of 18 who committed the offence together with two or more co-offenders, mostly only a short distance (less than 2 km away) from where they lived, and who predominantly burgled strangers.

Cluster 3 (12.0% of the sample) comprised Caucasian males in their late 20s or older, who committed the offence alone and typically against an acquaintance, mainly close to where they lived.

Classifying Offender Histories

A six-cluster solution emerged as the best fit for classifying offender histories (Fig. 3a–f). The variables used were age at first offence and number of traffic, theft, burglary, and violent offences.

Table 4 Summary characteristics of three groups of offender traits

LCA cluster	Percentage of sample (%)	Age	Offender number	Gender	Journey to crime	Victims	Ethnicity
1	52.3	Adults (>18 years)	1	Male	Long distances (>6 km)	Strangers	Caucasian/aboriginal
2	35.7	Youths (<18 years)	3+	Male	Short distance (<2 km)	Strangers	Caucasian
3	12.0	Adults in late 20s or older	1	Male	Short distance (<2 km)	Acquaintances	Caucasian

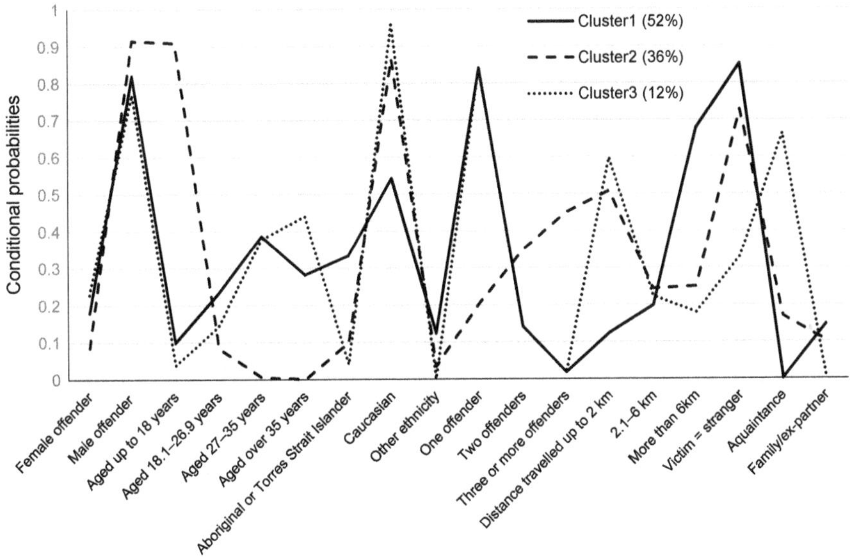

Fig. 2 Three cluster profiles—offender traits

Thirty per cent of the sample was in cluster 1 (30.2%). This group was most likely to have the earliest onset of delinquency, with 12% having offended by the age of 12 and 83% by the age of 18. They had prolific and varied criminal careers, with up to 25 previous offences in each of the measured offence types: traffic, theft, previous burglaries, violent and drug offences.

In cluster two (27.6% of the sample), most offenders had a teenage onset and previous records for, predominantly, theft and burglary offences (up to 25 offences in each of these); the majority had also committed prior violent or traffic offences, but had no drug involvement.

Offenders in cluster three (18.0% of the sample) also had a teenage onset and were very prolific, with up to and in excess of 51 previous theft and burglary offences, respectively. They also had up to 25 previous traffic, violent or drug offences.

Cluster four (9% of the sample) had an unspecific onset, with fewer than half of offenders with onset before 18, a quarter by the age of 25 and another quarter by 26 years of age or older. Most of this group had up to 25 previous violent or drug offences. About half had up to 25 previous burglary offences, slightly more than had none, and a quarter had no previous record for theft offences.

Cluster five (8.5% of the sample) comprised teenage onset, first-time offenders, with no previous offences in any of the five offence types.

Cluster six (6.6% of the sample) involved offenders with late onset, mainly after the age of 26. They had no prior violent offences, and two-thirds of these also had no drug offences. The majority had some traffic and burglary offences (up to 25 each) and were prolific in theft offences (up to 50).

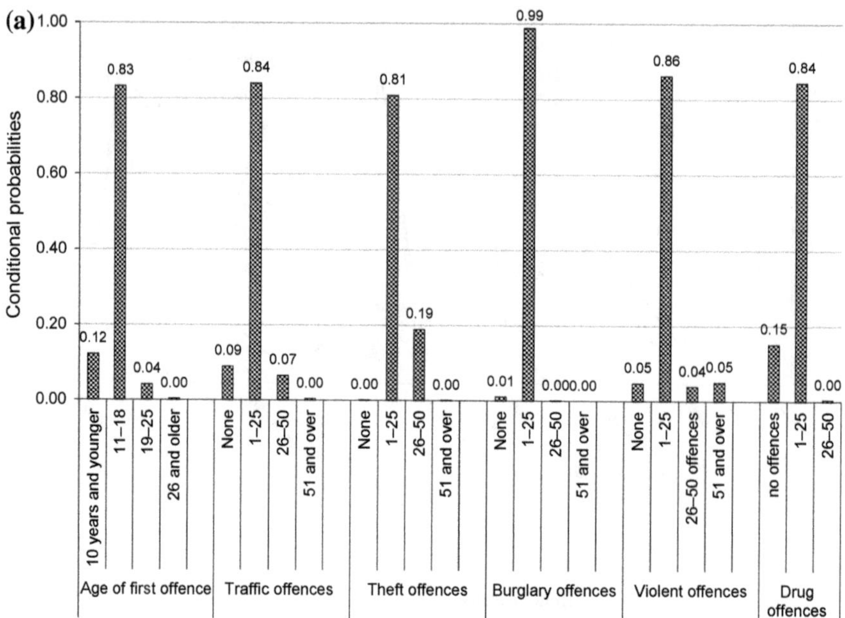

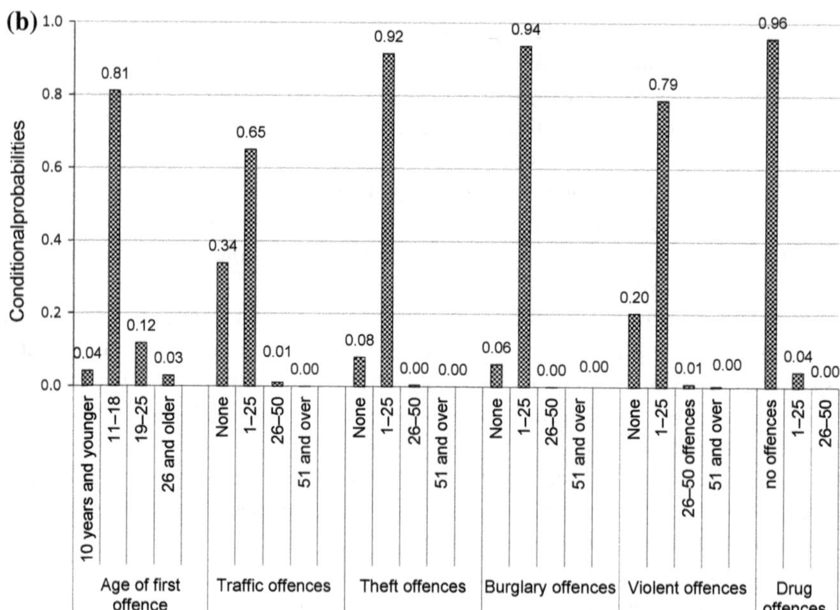

Fig. 3 **a** Cluster 1 'teenage onset, low intensity, great diversity, including drugs' (30.2%). **b** Cluster 2 'teenage onset, low intensity, specialised property and violent offences, no drugs' (27.6%). **c** Cluster 3 'teenage onset, high-intensity property offending, but also lower intensity other crimes types' (18.1%). **d** Cluster 4 'unspecific onset, low intensity, varied crime types' (9.03%). **e** Cluster 5 'starters' (8.5%). **f** Cluster 6 'late-onset property offenders' (6.6%)

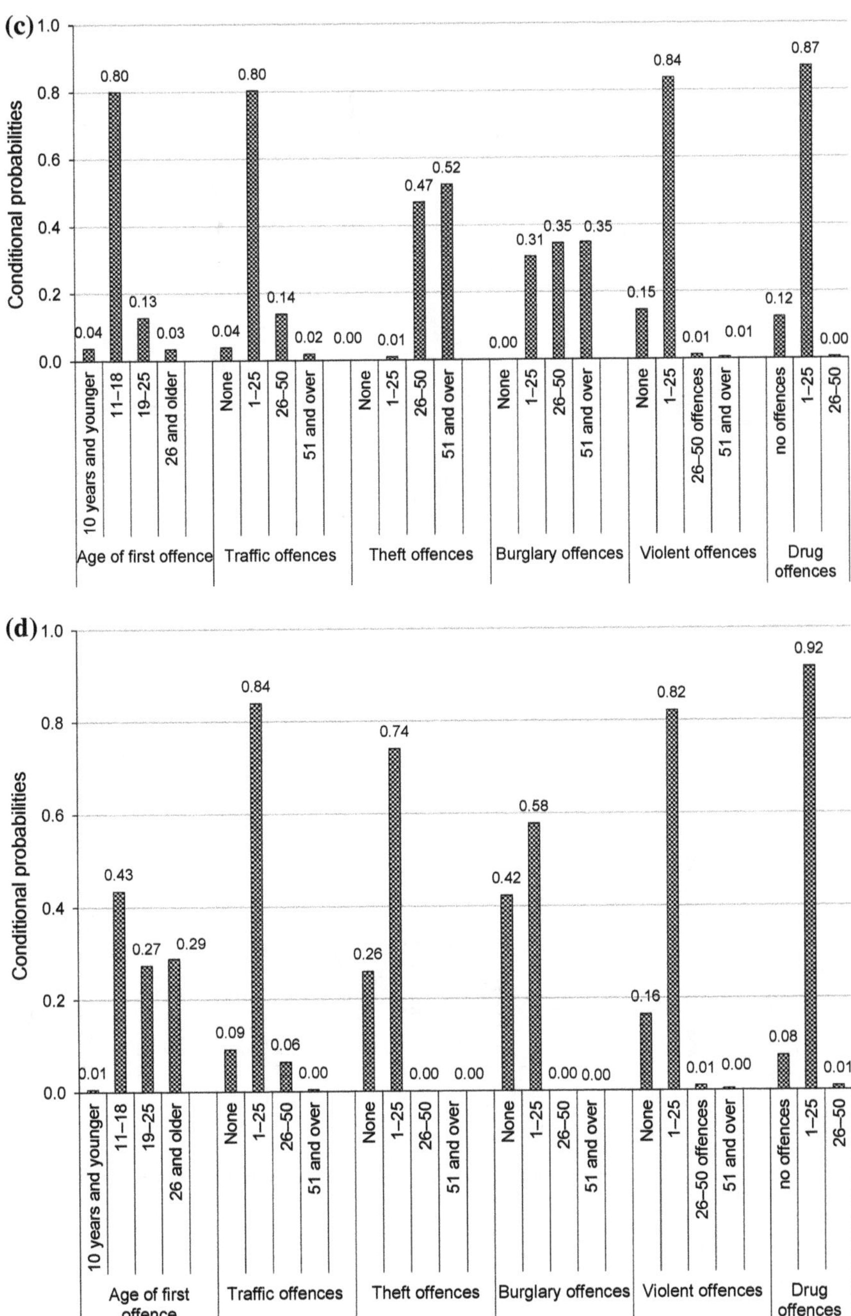

Fig. 3 (continued)

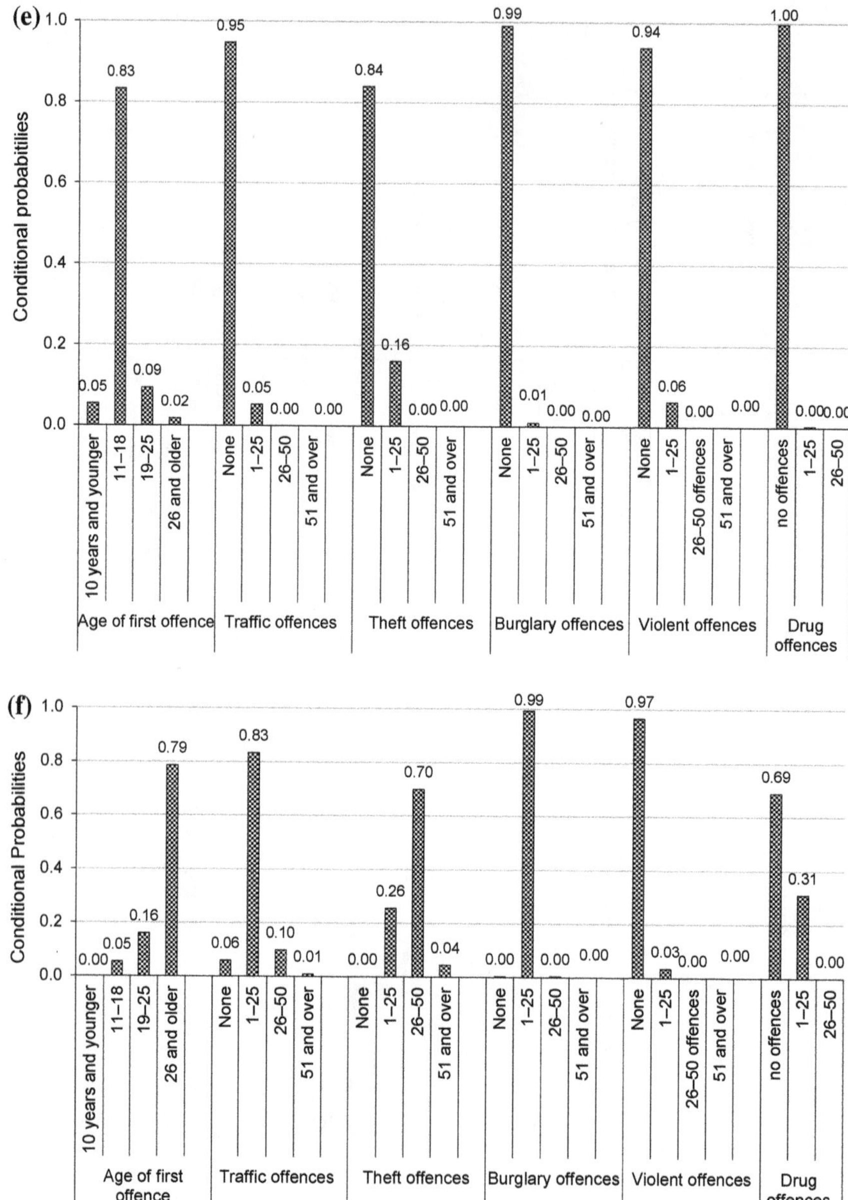

Fig. 3 (continued)

Matching Offender and Offence Typologies

Matching Offenders and Offences

In a further step, we attempted to determine whether it was possible to match offender clusters with offence clusters. There was indeed a significant relationship between offender clusters and offence clusters ($\chi^2(8, N = 349) = 21.38$, $p = 0.008$; $\phi = 0.25$, $p = 0.006$). Table 5 reports the chi-square test results and the adjusted standard residuals for each offender–offence combination. Adjusted standardised residuals (ASR) over +2 and lower than −2 denote that a particular variable combination occurs more often (in the case of an ASR > 2) or less often (in the case of an ASR < –2) than would be expected if there was no relationship between the two variables.

Offenders of the first cluster, that is, adult offenders who travelled longer distances to burgle strangers, were particularly likely to show a cluster 2 modus operandi (MO)—'organised window entry' (as evidenced by the ASR = 2.6)—and were particularly unlikely to be associated with the offence characteristics seen in offence clusters 4 ('opportunistic window entry') (ASR = –2.1) and 5 ('organised door entry') (ASR = = –2.3).

Offenders in cluster 2, that is, teenage offenders who committed their burglaries together with at least one other person, were overrepresented in offence clusters 4 (the 'opportunistic window entry' class (ASR = 2.4)) and cluster 5 (the 'organised door entry' group (ASR = 2.6)). As such, their offences involved predominantly unforced entry and the taking of high-value items without being disturbed.

Offenders in cluster 3, that is, older burglars who committed offences against acquaintances, were particularly likely to commit offences with the characteristics from offence cluster 1 [the 'disorganised, disturbed' class (ASR = 2.1)] and were unlikely to show offence characteristics from offence cluster 2 (the 'organised window entry' group (ASR = –2.1)). Thus, these offenders were associated with forced entry through doors, with a tidy search, being disturbed, where evidence was left and where nothing or only items of low value were taken.

Linking Offenders and Offence History

Next, we linked offender clusters and offence histories (Table 6). The relationship was statistically significant (χ^2 (8, $N = 349$) = 149.30, $p < 0.001$; $\Phi = 0.65$, $p < 0.001$). Cluster 1 offenders—adult burglars who travelled longer distances—were particularly likely to have the most prolific burglary and theft records (offence history cluster 2) and were also likely to have committed some violent and drug offences. They were underrepresented in the second offending history cluster, being restricted mainly to property offences, but had committed fewer of these than those offenders in offending history cluster 1. Cluster 1 offenders were also underrepresented in the young first offenders criminal history type (offending history cluster 5). Offenders in cluster 2—the young co-offending group—were likely to have a teenage onset

Table 5 Offender types by offence type

Offender groups	Offence types					
	Cluster 1 'disorganised, disturbed'	Cluster 2 'Organised window entry'	Cluster 3 'Opportunistic door entry, disturbed'	Cluster 4 'Opportunistic window entry'	Cluster 5 'Organised door entry'	Total
Cluster 1 Lone burglars who travel longer distances	55	71	45	14	3	188
	(29.30)	(37.80)	(23.90)	(7.40)	(1.60)	(100.00)
	(50.00)	(64.00)	(57.70)	(37.80)	(23.10)	(53.90)
Adjusted standardised residual	−1	2.6	0.8	−2.1	−2.3	
Cluster 2 Teenage co-offenders who target closer strangers	38	34	24	20	9	125
	(30.40)	(27.20)	(19.20)	(16.00)	(7.20)	(100.00)
	(34.50)	(30.60)	(30.80)	(54.10)	(69.20)	(35.80)
Adjusted standardised residual	−0.3	−1.4	−1.1	2.4	2.6	
Cluster 3 Older lone acquaintance burglars	17	6	9	3	1	36
	(47.20)	(16.70)	(25.00)	(8.30)	(2.80)	(100.00)
	(15.50)	(5.40)	(11.50)	(8.10)	(7.70)	(10.30)
Adjusted standardised residual	2.1	−2.1	0.4	−0.5	−0.3	
Total	110	111	78	37	13	349
	(31.50)	(31.80)	(22.30)	(10.60)	(3.70)	(100.00)
	(100.00)	(100.00)	(100.00)	(100.00)	(100.00)	(100.00)

Note X^2 $(8, N = 349) = 21.38, p = 0.008$; $\Phi = 0.25, p = 0.006$; frequencies, column and row percentages as well as adjusted standardised residuals are shown. Column and row percentages are shown in brackets and be mainly restricted to property offences, although at a lower level of intensity than offenders in cluster 1. Cluster 3 offenders—older burglars committing offences against acquaintances—were overrepresented in offending history cluster 4, having an unspecific onset with low intensity offending but committing crimes of various types, and they were underrepresented in offending history cluster 2, the teenage onset, low intensity but specialised group.

Linking Offences and Offending History

There was no significant association between offence characteristics and offending history[1] (Table 7). Thus, while it was possible to statistically link offence characteristics and offender types, and offender types with offender histories, it was not possible to connect offence characteristics directly with offending history. This is the vital link to be established in order to predict the characteristics of offenders responsible for different types of unsolved burglary incidents.

Discussion

This study set out to investigate the possibility of identifying distinctive types of residential burglary offences and offenders and connecting them with each other. Such an approach would, if successful, have the potential to assist case 'triage' and suspect prioritization by identifying burglars likely to have been responsible for specific sorts of burglaries. Given the different setting of this study—Australia as opposed to the USA—and the corresponding differences in crime definitions, criminal justice systems, population composition and the physical and built environments, it is unsurprising that findings differ in some ways from earlier work.

As with the US study by Fox and Farrington (2012), it was possible to create cluster analysis solutions for offences, offenders and offending history. It was similarly possible to connect offences with offending types, and offending types with offending histories. As with the Florida results, it was not possible to significantly link offences with offending histories, a finding that means the technique is unlikely to be of much help in policing burglaries. It makes it less likely that this approach can, in practice, help identify probable culprits from lists of known offenders using predicted offending history variables. However, this chapter shows that the specific variables used to identify groups, and the characteristics of the resulting groups, depend on

[1]A chi-square test was also conducted to see whether it was possible to link offence characteristics with burglars' offending histories. This is a critical linkage for predicting the offender characteristics held in police records from offence characteristics. As both sets of clusters involved cluster groups containing only 5% of the sample, there was a violation of the assumptions of the chi-square test with regard to the requirement that not more than 20% of the cells should have an expected count of less than 5. For this reason, the chi-square test was run only with the four largest offence clusters and the four largest offending history clusters.

Table 6 Offender types by offending history type

Offender types	Offending history types						
	Cluster 1 Teenage onset, low intensity, diverse	Cluster 2 Teenage onset, low intensity, specialised	Cluster 3 Teenage onset, high-intensity property; lower intensity other	Cluster 4 Unspecific onset, low intensity, varied crime types	Cluster 5 Starters	Cluster 6 Late onset, property-specific	Total
Cluster 1 Burglars who travel longer distances	60	35	53	19	1	20	188
	(31.9)	(18.6)	(28.2)	(10.1)	(0.5)	(10.6)	(100.0)
	(57.1)	(33.3)	(91.4)	(67.9)	(3.4)	(83.3)	(53.9)
Adjusted standardised residual	0.8	−5	6.3	1.5	−5.7	3	
Cluster 2 Teenage burglars who offend in groups	29	67	1	1	27	0	125
	(23.2)	(53.6)	(0.8)	(0.8)	(21.6)	(0.0)	(100.0)
	(27.6)	(63.8)	(1.7)	(3.6)	(93.1)	(0.0)	(35.8)
Adjusted standardised residual	−2.1	7.2	−5.9	−3.7	6.7	−3.8	
Cluster 3 Older acquaintance burglars	16	3	4	8	1	4	36
	(44.4)	(8.3)	(11.1)	(22.2)	(2.8)	(11.1)	(100.0)
	(15.2)	(2.9)	(6.9)	(28.6)	(3.4)	(16.7)	(10.3)
Adjusted standardised residual	2	−3	−0.9	3.3	−1.3	1.1	
Total	105	105	58	28	29	24	349
	(30.1)	(30.1)	(16.6)	(8.0)	(8.3)	(6.9)	(100.0)
	(100.0)	(100.0)	(100.0)	(100.0)	(100.0)	(100.0)	(100.0)

Note X^2 $(8, N = 349) = 149.30, p < 0.001$; $\Phi = 0.65, p < 0.001$; frequencies, column and row percentages as well as adjusted standardised residuals are shown. Column and row percentages are shown in brackets

Table 7 Offence characteristics clusters by offending history clusters

Offence cluster	Offending history cluster				
	Cluster 1 Teenage onset; low intensity; diverse	Cluster 2 Teenage onset; low intensity; specialised	Cluster 3 Teenage onset; high-intensity property; lower intensity other	Cluster 4 Unspecific onset; low intensity; diverse	Total
Cluster 1 'Disorganised disturbed'	37	32	18	13	100
	(37.0)	(32.0)	(18.0)	(13.0)	(100.0)
	(37.0)	(32.0)	(31.0)	(46.4)	(35.0)
Adjusted standardised residual	0.5	−0.8	−0.7	1.3	
Cluster 2 'Organised window entry'	31	29	20	5	85
	(36.5)	(34.1)	(23.5)	(5.9)	(100.0)
	(31.0)	(29.0)	(34.5)	(17.9)	(29.7)
Adjusted standardised residual	0.3	−0.2	0.9	−1.4	
Cluster 3 'Opportunistic door entry'	20	25	14	10	69
	(29.0)	(36.2)	(20.3)	(14.5)	(100.0)
	(20.0)	(25.0)	(24.1)	(35.7)	(24.1)
Adjusted standardised residual	−1.2	0.3	0	1.5	
Cluster 4 'Opportunistic window entry'	12	14	6	0	32
	(37.5)	(43.8)	(18.8)	(0.0)	(100.0)
	(12.0)	(14.0)	(10.3)	(0.0)	(11.2)
Adjusted standardised residual	0.3	1.1	−0.2	−2	
Total	100	100	58	28	286
	(35.0)	(35.0)	(20.3)	(9.8)	(100.0)
	(100.0)	(100.0)	(100.0)	(100.0)	(100.0)

Note $X^2(9, N = 286) = 9.75, p = 0.371; \Phi = 0.19, p = 0.371$; frequencies, column and row percentages as well as adjusted standardised residuals are shown. Column and row percentages are shown in brackets local data: offence, offending and offender history groups vary geographically for the same crime. This is an important finding. It indicates that the profiling of high-volume crimes will need tailoring to jurisdictional circumstances. Like crime-type profiles and solvability factors, the characteristics of specific types of crime differ in response to population and environmental circumstances, so that it may be difficult to apply a model developed in one place to other places.

Adelaide residential burglaries could be grouped into four different classes, differentiated by the levels of organisation and opportunism involved, as well as the point of entry to the target property. The largest group, comprising a third of the sample, were the disorganised, disturbed burglaries, which were likely to use force but unlikely to use prepared tools, where items of varying value were stolen, and evidence was very likely to be left at the scene. The second-largest class were organised burglaries using mostly the window as the point of entry (30%), followed by two opportunistic groups (together comprising 29% of the sample), and a smaller organised group that used a door as the entry point. This model is slightly more fine-grained than that of Fox and Farrington (2012), whose groups differed only by level of organisation and opportunism. Differences between the two studies also occur because some of the variables included in the model differ. The Florida model, for instance, included offender motivation as attributed by the investigating officer as part of the crime scene information. We thought this too subjective and therefore excluded it from our model.

In the offender type analysis, we observed three groups: two adult groups that differed from each other in the nature of the offender's relationship to the victim (with one group targeting strangers and the other predominantly burgling acquaintances) and in the distance travelled to the burglary location. Acquaintance burglars travelled shorter distances, a likely reflection of the fact that most people tend to have acquaintances close to home. There was also a teenage group that tended to commit their offences in the presence of at least one co-offender. Our classification system differed from that of the Florida study in that their data yielded four groups differentiated by ethnicity and age. All the Adelaide groups were most likely to be Caucasian, although, in the first cluster of older offenders who travelled longer distances, there was a 30% probability of the offender being Aboriginal, many of whom were Torres Strait Island women. In contrast, the probability of this was less than 10% in the other two offender types.

With regard to offending history, the Adelaide model had a beginner group and a lower-rate group—similar to Florida—but it also had a late-onset group, a group with a property-specific criminal record, as well as offenders with a criminal history across all measured crime types.

These differences between the models have implications for the transfer and applicability of the Fox and Farrington findings to countries other than the USA, or even to other US states, given the differences in the definitions of burglary and in police and court procedures. For instance, in Florida, it is unlikely that offenders will admit to previous offences to allow these to be taken into consideration, while in South Australia this is a common practice. This resulted in Fox and Farrington's (2012) data not being characterised by lengthy prior offending histories, while in our data a lengthy prior offending history was the norm rather than the exception. In addition, the physical, social and built environments may differ greatly between locations and characteristics. This includes the density of population and of houses, house types, vegetative or other visual cover around houses, social control via the presence of neighbours during the daytime, and the level of physical or technological target hardening, which may affect the ease, and therefore the risk, of burglary in different locations. This, then, as Fox and Farrington (2012) rightly suggest, might affect the prevalence of the different types of burglaries, or, as we have also found, might result in different offence or offender types. In Florida, for instance, most burglars (47.5% of the total) were opportunistic, while in our group both opportunistic groups together made up only 29%. It is possible that a setting with many holiday homes, some for rent, and often left empty, may encourage opportunistic burglaries motivated by thrill, excitement or occupation by vagrants, whereas these opportunities are more limited in Adelaide with its permanent households.

Conclusion

There are more studies of burglaries than of burglars, few burglary studies have information on both offenders and offences, and far more is known about urban than rural burglary (Marshall and Johnson 2005). This chapter not only develops the first empirically-based burglary offender–offence profiles for Australia but also improves knowledge of offender profiling and assesses the scope for its application to the high-volume and highly undetected crime of burglary.

Given the absence of the most potent forms of evidence, such as forensic evidence, eyewitness evidence or confessions, for the majority of burglaries (Bennell and Canter 2002), being able to infer a group of likely suspects from crime site characteristics would be very helpful. This study provides some empirical support for the possibility of such an approach, though no significant connection was found between offences and offender histories. Our data showed that, for Adelaide, if a crime scene involved the characteristics of the organised window entry type, the most likely suspects may come from the group of older offenders who travel longer distances. Where the crime scene suggests a disorganised, disturbed burglary, the burglar could belong to any of the offender groups, but is more likely to be an older acquaintance. As these offenders do not travel as far for their burglaries, the burglar could be searched for closer to the burgled property. This indicates the potential to use geographical profiling to identify likely perpetrators. Finally, opportunistic window entry burglaries, as well as those featuring organised door entry, were particular likely to be committed by teenage offenders, who rarely act alone, so the investigation could be widened to look for more than one suspect or known co-offenders.

If stronger links could be found between offences and offender histories for high-volume offences, a randomized controlled trial could be implemented to determine any effects on detection outcomes. Such a trial would require allocation of the same police officer resources per burglary to test and control samples for the specific investigative activities for which offender–offence profiling would be beneficial and comparison of the detection outcomes of each sort of investigative activity.

However, as the next step, the relationships between offences, offenders and offending history that we were able to establish here need to be tested with new data in order to establish accuracy rates for the predictions and to see whether the information derived from the model is specific enough to be of any practical use. The offender groups identified in this chapter are quite broad. It is possible that future studies with larger samples and, more importantly, more specific offender information might derive more nuanced groups. In another step, it is also important to study the temporal stability of burglars' modi operandi, since a profiling system such as the one presented here only makes sense if there is sufficient stability across offences.

Finally, the differences between the results from Florida and from Adelaide are an important reminder that, for burglaries, geographical context does matter and that police forces interested in applying such a tool—even if rudimentary—for suspect prioritization should, as a first step, seek to develop their own model using their own force data.

References

Antrobus, E., & Pilotto, A. (2016). Improving forensic responses to residential burglaries: Results of a randomized controlled field trial. *Journal of Experimental Criminology, 12*(3), 319–345.

Australian Bureau of Statistics. (2011). Census quick stats, all people—Usual residents, greater capital city statistical areas, Greater Adelaide, Code 4GADE (GCCSA). http://www.censusdata.abs.gov.au/census_services/getproduct/census/2011/quickstat/4GADE?opendocument&navpos=220.

Australian Bureau of Statistics. (2013). Socio-Economic indexes for areas (SEIFA) using 2011 census data for greater capital city statistical areas, Greater Adelaide, Code 4GADE (GCCSA). http://www.abs.gov.au/ausstats/abs@.nsf/mf/2033.0.55.001.

Bennell, C., & Canter, D. V. (2002). Linking commercial burglaries by modus operandi: tests using regression and ROC analysis. *Science & Justice, 42*(3), 153–164.

Bernasco, W. (2010). A sentimental journey to crime: Effects of residential history on crime location choice. *Criminology, 48*(2), 389–416.

Burrows, J., Hopkins, M., Hubbard, R., Robinson, A., Speed, M., & Tilley, N. (2005). Understanding the attrition process in volume crime investigations (Home Office Research Study 295). London: Home Office.

Coupe, R. T., & Blake, L. (2006). Daylight and darkness strategies and the risks of offenders being seen at residential burglaries. *Criminology, 44*(2), 431–463.

Coupe, T., & Griffiths, M. (1996). *Solving residential burglary (Police Research Group crime detection and prevention services, Paper 77)*. London: Home Office.

Donnellan, G. (2012). *Burglary solvability factors*. Paper Presented at 4th International Evidence-Based Policing Conference, Cambridge, 4–6 July 2011.

Farrington, D., & Lambert, S. (2006). Predicting offender profiles from offence and victim characteristics. In R. N. Kocsis (Ed.), *Criminal profiling: International perspectives in theory practice and research*. Totowa, NJ: Humana Press.

Fox, B., & Farrington, D. (2012). Creating burglary profiles using latent class analysis: A new approach to offender profiling. *Criminal Justice and Behavior, 39*(12), 1582–1611.

Killmier, B. (2013). *Offenders and their offences: Convicted burglars in Adelaide.* (Unpublished MSt thesis). University of Cambridge.

Kocsis, R. N., & Cooksey, R. (2002). Criminal psychological profiling of serial arson crimes. *International Journal of Offender Therapy and Comparative Criminology, 46*(6), 631–656.

Kocsis, R. N., Cooksey, R., & Irwin, H. (2002). Psychological profiling of offender characteristics from crime behaviours in serial rape offences. *International Journal of Offender Therapy and Comparative Criminology, 46*(6), 144–169.

Lammers, M. (2014). Are arrested and non-arrested serial offenders different? A test of spatial offending patterns using DNA found at crime scenes. *Journal of Research in Crime and Delinquency, 51*(2), 143–167.

Marshall, B., & Johnson, S. D. (2005). *Crime in rural areas: A review of the literature for the rural evidence research centre*. Jill Dando Institute of Crime Science: University College London.

Miethe, T., McCorkle, R., & Listwan, S. (2006). *Crime profiles: The anatomy of dangerous persons, places, and situations* (3rd ed.). Los Angeles, CA: Roxbury.

Muthen, B., & Muthen, L. (2000). *Mplus user's guide*. Los Angeles: Muthen and Muthen.

Paine, C., & Ariel, B. (2013). *Solvability analysis: Increasing the likelihood of detection in completed, attempted and in-progress burglaries*. Paper Presented at the 6th International Evidence-Based Policing Conference, Cambridge, 8–10 July 2013.

Promish, D., & Lester, D. (1999). Classifying serial killers. *Forensic Science International, 105*(3), 155–159.

Roman, J. K., Reid, S. E., Chalfin, A. J., & Knight, C. R. (2009). The DNA field experiment: A randomized trial of the cost-effectiveness of using DNA to solve property crimes. *Journal of Experimental Criminology, 5,* 345–369.

Snook, B. (2004). Individual differences in distance travelled by serial burglars. *Journal of Investigative Psychology and Offender Profiling, 1*(1), 53–66.

Taylor, P., & Bond, S. (2012). *Crimes detected in England and Wales 2011/12 (Statistical Bulletin 08/12)*. London: Home Office.

Taylor, P., & Chaplin, R. (2011). *Crimes detected in England and Wales 2010/11 (Statistical Bulletin 10/11)*. London: Home Office.

Tilley, N., Robinson, A., & Burrows, J. (2007). The investigation of high volume crime. In T. Newburn, T. Williamson, & A. Wright (Eds.), *Handbook of criminal investigation* (pp. 226–254). London: Willan Publishing.

Tompson, L., & Coupe, R. T. (2017). Time and criminal opportunity. In G. J. N. Bruinsma & S. D. Johnson (Eds.), *The Oxford handbook of environmental criminology*. Oxford: Oxford University Press.

van Koppen, P. J., & Jansen, R. W. J. (1998). The road to the robbery: Travel patterns in commercial robberies. *The British Journal of Criminology, 38*(2), 230–246.

Vaughn, M. G., DeLisi, M., Beaver, K., & Howard, M. (2008). Toward a quantitative typology of burglars: A latent profile analysis of career offenders. *Journal of Forensic Science, 53*(6), 1387–1392.

where-is.com software (2013). Accessible at http://www.whereis.com/.

Wright, O. (2013). *Urban to rural: An exploratory analysis of burglary and vehicle crime with a rural context* (unpublished MSt thesis). University of Cambridge.

Boosting Offence Solvability and Detections: Solving Residential Burglaries by Predicting Single and Multiple Repeats

Richard Timothy Coupe and Katrin Mueller-Johnson

Introduction

Burglary is one of the most common but least frequently solved crimes. Many burglaries occur when premises are unoccupied and are discovered only when householders return home. There is often little or no evidence to point to the identity of the culprits. The prediction of repeat burglary incidence by profiling the distinctive characteristics of these offences, however, would provide means to help tackle some of the 87% of UK burglary cases that would otherwise go unsolved (FBI 2008; Taylor and Bond 2012). Burglary constitutes 26% of all property crime in the USA, and 88% of cases remain unsolved, so that there is even greater potential there from forecasting repeat incidence. Low clear-up rates mean that many burglars are able to commit at least 50 burglaries or more prior to being caught, while a tenth or more of burglars may never be apprehended (Ahlberg and Knutsson 1990). However, little is currently known about the features that distinguish repeat residential burglary targets from properties that are burgled only once. This is perhaps surprising given its practical potential for solving burglaries that would otherwise remain unsolved.

Such increased detections might be achieved through deploying silent and delayed audible alarms and covert CCTV cameras at predicted repeats, as well as installing tracking devices on or inside the sorts of goods previously stolen, and, therefore, most likely to be stolen again (Chenery et al. 1997), perhaps even planting goods known from prior burglaries to be attractive. Over-victimisation at repeat targets could become a potent vehicle for catching the culprits, so that 'repeat burglars' become the agents of their own downfall. In this way, what might appear to be wise and rational targeting may turn out to be the very converse, with the most safe targets becoming the least so.

R. T. Coupe (✉) · K. Mueller-Johnson
Institute of Criminology, University of Cambridge, Cambridge, UK
e-mail: rtc23@cam.ac.uk

R. T. Coupe et al. (eds.), *Crime Solvability Factors*,
https://doi.org/10.1007/978-3-030-17160-5_13

In this study, residential single and multiple repeat burglaries and non-repeat incidents are compared with regard to the characteristics of victims, site visibility and exposure, access, security characteristics, and stolen goods. In this way, indicator variables are identified that provide the basis for predicting repeat burglary. This will enable the forecasting of small subsets of premises facing high risks of re-victimisation. These premises then could be targeted with interventions to entrap offenders, thus having the potential to boost burglary solvability and to arrest more burglars, including those who are not known to the police, earlier in their criminal careers, which in turn, will help prevent further burglaries and other offences.

Existing 'Repeat Burglary' Research

Repeat burglary has principally considered its incidence and concentration (e.g., Tseloni and Pease 2003; Johnson et al. 1997) or the prediction of 'near repeats' using spatial analytic techniques (Townsley et al. 2003; Johnson and Bowers 2004; Bowers and Johnson 2005). Offenders commit repeat burglary soon after the initial incident (Bowers et al. 1998; Farrell and Pease 1993; Farrell 1995; Pease 1998; Robinson 1998; Spelman 1995), and a third of residential repeats take place in the month following the first burglary (Johnson et al. 1997). Nine-tenths of the residential repeats within the following three months involve the same offenders returning (Bernasco 2008; Johnson 2008). The timing of subsequent burglaries in itself (Polvi et al. 1991; Ericsson 1995; Ashton et al. 1998; Palmer et al. 2002) indicates that it is likely to be the same offenders returning to familiar premises to steal goods not taken earlier or replacement goods. Familiarity with premises and goods enable quicker search and escape (Ericsson 1995), occasionally facilitated by key theft (Budd 1999). If this is the case, repeat burglary will reflect 'event dependency' (Tseloni and Pease 2004; Johnson et al. 2009), where prior knowledge boosts repeat burglary odds. This need not rule out the effects of 'heterogeneous risk', since low risk for offenders can also help 'flag' (Tseloni and Pease 2003) initial and repeat selection. It is possible that some repeat offences do not occur due to an unfavourable risk evaluation of premises on arrival at the scene. Some may be displaced to 'near-repeat' burglaries (Coupe 2017b).

The scale of repeat victimisation provides considerable potential for entrapment, particularly if the likely repeat targets may be narrowed down by prediction. In England and Wales, annual domestic burglary repeat rates have varied between 15 and 17–22% per annum during the last two decades (Ministry of Justice [MOJ] 2010), and 32% of incidents with entry (Budd 1999) are repeats.

Despite the profiling of burglary incident characteristics using both aggregated (e.g., Sampson and Wooldredge 1987; Tseloni and Pease 2003) and individual data (e.g., Hough 1987; Coupe and Blake 2006, 2010; Coupe and Fox 2015), there has been little, if any investigation of the distinctive target characteristics of repeat incidents. Moreover, little, if anything is known about the distinctive features—if there are any—of multiple repeat targets when compared with single repeat incidents.

This research profiles the target characteristics of residential repeat burglaries, comparing non-repeat incidents, single repeats, and multiple repeats to determine whether they exhibit distinctive characteristics. By comparing 'one-off' or non-repeat incidents with single repeats, and single repeats with multiple repeats, their distinctive characteristics can be identified and a basis for predicting their occurrence formed. It also promises to enable the arrest of burglars, who tend to be versatile (Shover 1991), sooner, thereby preventing not just burglaries but also other crimes. In this way, the paper provides an approach to predicting and entrapping burglars that promises to prevent other crimes, especially property offences that are far more difficult to solve (Thanassoulis 1995; Smit et al. 2004). Improvements in solving burglary cases, therefore, are likely also to benefit the victims of other crimes.

The objective of this study is primarily to seek out the combination of variables that best predicts the incidence of single and multiple repeat residential burglaries. It is hypothesised that premises which are repeatedly burgled will have readily saleable goods to steal and offer safer, lower-risk targets to offenders than other burglary premises, so that they will be characterised by weaker guardianship and lower exposure. Multiple repeats, it is predicted, will be even safer for offenders than single repeat targets. Since arrest at burglaries relates strongly to burglars being seen (Eck 1979; Coupe and Griffiths 1996), it is likely that measures of exposure and neighbour guardianship will be good predictors for repeats, since poor guardianship and low exposure will favour burglars at repeat targets.

Methodology

Research Design and Research Instruments

Data were collected from police incident logs, burglary site surveys, and questionnaires completed by police officers and victims for a sample of residential burglaries committed in 1994. The burglaries took place between April and September in two operational command units of a police force incorporating most of a major UK city, with a population of over 1.75 million people and a wide variety of burglary targets. Specifically, domestic dwellings varied from apartments to terraced, semi-detached and detached dwellings, and included privately rented, state-funded and owner-occupied housing.

Questionnaires detailing the initial police response and case outcomes were completed by 563 of the 704 sampled officers, a response rate of 80%. The sample consists of 354 undetected and 209 detected incidents. From this principal sample, a subsample was randomly compiled in order to conduct additional victim interviews and burglary site surveys. These surveys provided victim interviews and site survey data for 200 burglary incidents. The randomization of both the selection of the principal sample and the compilation of the second-stage sample helps to methodologically assure the generalisability of the findings to comparable UK environments. The characteristics of burglaries and dwellings within the completed victim and site survey responses did not significantly differ from those of the principal sample, indicating random non-response. The predictive analyses in this chapter are based on the subsample of incidents.

Incorporating data on offence characteristics from a variety of sources means that few key target features have been omitted from the study and enables links to be drawn between target characteristics and whether premises had suffered single or multiple repeat burglaries in order to identify the subset of variables that best explains repeat incidence with a view to developing prediction measures.

Data

Burglary characteristics were collected for the full sample with a self-completed questionnaire survey of patrol officers attending the incidents and incident logs. The characteristics were chosen so that they could be easily scored by officers responding to incidents. The police logs provided data on when the burglaries were reported and whether an offender had been spotted at or near the scene. The questionnaires included details about occupancy at the time of the offence and where the offender entered and exited the premises, as well as confirming the incident log data.

The burglary site survey dealt with the situation of burgled dwellings with respect to neighbouring houses, whether or not there was rear access, and distances from other properties and the road. Surveillability or visibility of the target from neighbours was measured using the number of properties and the estimated distances from properties intervisible with the target premises, whether it was light or dark at the time of the burglary, and the cover surrounding the dwelling. The height and density of hedges, shrubs and trees, and the height and disposition of fences and walls, were used as the basis for estimating the amounts of front and rear cover. Four surveyors implemented the site surveys and victim questionnaires for the residential surveys. Accuracy in grading vegetation cover and assessing distances was improved by undertaking practice estimates between different points until they coincided with measured distances.

The victim questionnaire survey provided data on victims' occupancy of the premises and whether there had been other burglaries during the prior six and twelve months, so that the sampled incident could be identified as a non-repeat, the first (or a single) repeat or the second or subsequent burglary in a series of multiple repeats. Victims were also asked whether security had been upgraded following earlier burglaries.

These multifaceted dwelling burglary data sets, each drawn from four sources, enable the linking of repeat burglary incidence with target and victim characteristics. They afford the information needed to identify the distinctive features of non-repeat, single repeat, and multiple repeat residential burglaries, so that their incidence may be forecasted. These predictor variables are likely to be of value for repeat burglary prediction in similar residential environments. The findings also provide an analytic and procedural template for sifting out variables that are accurate predictors of repeat burglary incidence in environments outside the UK.

A Retrospective Rather Than a Prospective Approach

Victims were questioned about prior burglaries in order to establish whether the sample burglary was the first, second, third, or nth burglary to take place during the last six months. Burglaries at dwellings occupied by households for less than six months were excluded from the sample. Knowledge of the numbers of burglaries that have occurred is based on retrospective questioning of victims, and the characteristics of premises at the time of surveying victims and sites are used to differentiate between premises with just a one-off burglary, a single repeat and multiple repeats, even though certain features of dwellings may have varied over the six-month sample period in the case of multiple burglaries.

The method used in this chapter is, therefore, based on the assumption that the target characteristics at the time of the site and victim surveys had changed insufficiently to prevent them being used to compare single and multiple burglaries that occurred at different times over the prior six-month period.

Many of the predictive variables used in this study are static. These include the presence of a road at the side or rear of the premises, the distances to neighbouring premises or streetlights, the numbers of neighbouring premises with a view of the entrance or approaches to the target, and the type and age of the dwelling. Others are dynamic variables. Those relevant to the regression equations used for predicting repeat burglary incidence include the number of rooms visited by offenders, vegetative cover, daylight and darkness conditions, and security changes to the premises. Details about prior security measures were collected, and a measure of security lights prior to the burglary is used in comparing non-repeats and repeats. Vegetative cover changes may have modified risks at the premises due to seasonal changes in deciduous leaf cover. However, key elements of the 'cover' variable involve evergreen vegetation and the disposition of buildings, walls, and fences—aspects of the environment that do not change.

Since over nine-tenths of repeat residential burglaries are committed by the same offenders (Bernasco 2008; Johnson 2008) at the same times and days of the week (Bowers and Johnson 2005) as initial incidents, burglars appear to be exploiting victims' routine activities in a consistent way. It seems reasonable to assume that repeat targeting decisions will exhibit consistency in other respects, such as the number of rooms visited and whether the burglary occurs in daylight or darkness—variables used in the analysis in this chapter. If a burglar has previously targeted a premises when a single-adult occupant is absent during darkness in the evening, it is likely the offender will repeat this pattern of victimisation. It would be odd if a subsequent attempt to burgle occurred during daylight hours, when the dwelling was occupied. Many repeat burglaries affect single-adult households (Table 1) with predictable windows of absence that permit a burglar monitoring the occupant's absence to undertake lengthier searches including all rooms. It is assumed that repeat burglars' decisions will continue to take advantage of weak occupant guardianship.

The methodological approach is therefore, strictly speaking, to determine whether retrospective measures of premises characteristics can be used to successfully explain

Table 1 Residential burglary: comparing characteristics of repeats and non-repeats

Routine activity concept	Variable	Repeats: mean or %	Non-repeats: mean or %	*t*	*p*	Effect size (*d*)
Guardianship	Occupancy by victim	14%	35%	$\chi^2 = 5.92$	0.015	OR = 0.30, 95% CI [0.15; 0.60]
	Single-adult households	34%	19%	$\chi^2 = 3.66$	0.056	OR = 2.20, 95% CI [1.15; 4.20]
Access	*No significant variables*					
Exposure	Cover index	11.3	8.52	$F= 7.38$	0.007	$d = 0.57$; 95% CI [0.15; 1.00]
	Rear cover index	7.32	5.85	$F= 6.68$	0.011	$d = 0.54$; 95% CI [0.12; 0.97]
	Height of front cover (in *m*)	1.12	0.71	$F= 2.71$	0.101	$d = 0.32$; 95% CI [−0.05; 0.70]
Guardianship	Front door deadlocks	35%	16%	$\chi^2 = 5.58$	0.034	OR = 2.89, 95% CI [1.47; 5.67]
Objects	Security lighting					
	Burglar alarms					
Attractiveness	*No significant variables*					
Dwelling type	Dwelling terraced	53%	19%	$\chi^2 = 14.2$	0.007	OR = 4.80, 95% CI [2.55; 9.08]
	Dwelling age (years)	63.5	50.2	$F= 4.26$	0.041	$d = -0.48$; 95% CI [−0.93; −0.02]
	Dwelling tenure: rented	63%	46%	$\chi^2 = 3.78$	0.052	OR = 1.99, 95% CI [1.14; 3.52]
Area character	Number of rooms burglar/s visited	4	3.19	$F= 5.83$	0.017	$d = -0.47$; 95% CI [−0.86; −0.08]
	Burglary occurred during evening	46%	28%	$\chi^2 = 5.21$	0.073	OR = 2.19, 95% CI [1.22; 3.94]
	Area with high male unemployment	34%	16%	$F= 6.48$	0.012	$d = -0.46$; 95% CI [−0.83; −0.09]

differences between non-repeats and repeat incidents, and between single and multiple repeat burglaries. On this basis, the chapter aims to assess whether it would be feasible to predict which types of dwelling are most at risk of repeat burglary and which, compared with single repeat incidents, face different degrees of risk of multiple repeat burglary.

Analytical Procedure

In order to identify predictors for repeat and multiple repeat burglaries, two sets of analyses were conducted. Firstly, the data were used to compare premises that were only burgled once with those that had at least one repeat. In the second set of analyses, premises that had only one repeat burglary were compared with those that had more than one repeat.

To do so, initial bivariate analyses were conducted. A variety of burglary characteristics were drawn from the site surveys, victim interviews, officer questionnaires, and police logs. These cover the target environment, the occupants, the dwelling, its security, accessibility, entry and exit points, and surrounding land uses.

Significant variables with larger size effects were then used to identify the best combination of predictors of single repeat and multiple repeat burglary.

A comparison of premises burgled only once with those burgled at least twice was achieved using a logistic regression analysis to determine the best combination of variables for predicting repeat incidence with the greatest confidence. As the aim is a 'best-fit' equation, testing was iterative, and those variables with lower significance and smaller effect sizes were removed in order to find the variable combination that maximises statistical explanation. Then, a single summary prediction score was created by summing the products of each case's binary value and the regression odds ratios for the significant variables. This provides a prediction score weighted according to the effect sizes of every significant variable, with a value for every sample data case. The summary prediction score for each case was then compared for cases involving single burglaries and those involving at least one repeat in order to identify the cut-off points where the predictive summary score forecasts repeat burglary incidence with a high probability.

As multiple repeat residential burglaries are quite rare, there is a relatively small subset of cases, so that it was not possible to use the same approach to compare single and multiple repeats. Instead of the logistic regression approach, a single summary score was derived by combining the Cramer's V scores for each significant variable, while controlling for the other significant variables. Cramer's V scores provide a measure of the strength of bivariate relationships and, combined, they indicate the cumulative effect size of the input variables. This predictive score was then compared with the likelihood of single versus multiple repeats in order to identify a cut-off point at which a score value indicates a high probability of multiple repeat burglary incidence.

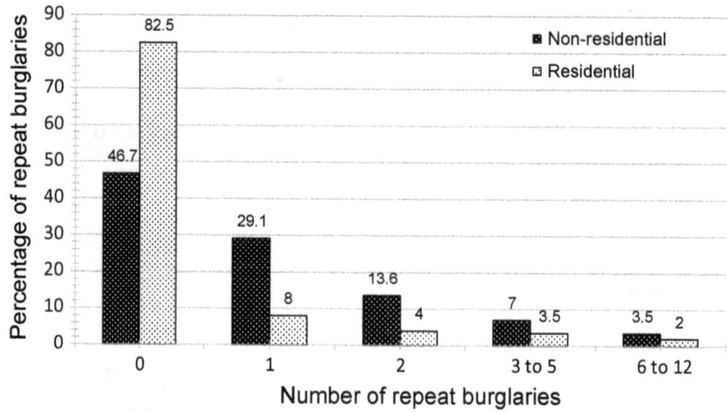

Fig. 1 Incidence of repeat residential burglary

Findings

Levels of Repeat Burglary

Seventeen per cent of dwellings were repeat burgled during the six months prior to the sample incident, a figure in line with annual repeat residential burglary rates of 15–22% during the last two decades for England and Wales (MoJ 2010). The level of non-residential burglary repeats is far higher—54%—and similar to that in Mirrlees-Black and Ross' national survey (1996) (Fig. 1).

Once a repeat burglary had occurred, 54% of these dwellings were the target of one or more additional repeats within six months (or multiple repeats), a level not dissimilar to the 48% of non-residential premises burgled multiple times. Ten per cent of dwellings and a quarter of non-residential premises were therefore affected by multiple repeat burglary (i.e., burgled more than twice).

The potential to save costs on entrapment equipment at dwellings is greater since these may be avoided at over 83% of incidents, given repeat rates of 17%. The potential savings at both dwellings and non-dwellings are comparable once a single repeat burglary has taken place, since there is an approximate 50% probability of a further repeat at all sorts of burglaries.

Predicting Non-repeat and First-Time Repeat Burglaries

In order to predict which burgled dwellings were more or less likely to be repeat burgled, bivariate analyses were conducted. Repeat incidents affected dwellings that tended to be older, rented, and situated in areas with high male unemployment (Table 1). Repeat targets were especially terraced houses (53% vs. 19%), with

Table 2 Residential burglary: binary logistic regression results predicting repeat burglary versus single burglary

	B	*SE*	Wald	*df*	*p*	Exp(*B*)
Terraced versus other dwelling type	−1.510	0.507	8.880	1	0.003	0.221
Apartment versus other dwelling type	−1.755	0.724	5.886	1	0.015	0.173
Security lights prior to first burglary	1.370	0.480	8.160	1	0.004	3.937
Burglar visited fewer versus all rooms	0.953	0.429	4.929	1	0.026	2.593
Level of cover at rear of dwelling (low/high)	−0.169	0.061	7.654	1	0.006	0.845
Property age: built before/after 1945	0.905	0.471	3.685	1	0.055	2.471
Constant	0.183	1.773	0.011	1	0.918	1.201

Note −2LL 152.08, $X^2 = 33.41$, $df = 6$, $p < .001$; Cox and Snell $R^2 = 0.154$, Nagelkerke's $R^2 = 0.254$

fewer detached (3% vs. 15%), and semi-detached properties (15.6% vs. 37.7%). Even though repeat burglaries occurred particularly during the evenings (Table 1), there were less than half as many victims at home at the time of the burglary, making it safer for burglars. This probably reflects the fact that twice as many dwellings repeatedly burgled were home to single adults (Table 1), normally unoccupied for longer periods of time. This makes it easier for burglars, who often wait for the sole occupant to leave, to be certain that the home is empty, unlike dwellings with larger families, where it is more difficult to keep track of where every person is and not be caught out by an occupant's unexpected return home.

In terms of exposure (Table 1), the cover around repeat targets was superior to that surrounding non-repeat dwellings, in particular rear cover. Burglars visited more rooms at repeat targets, possibly because they realised they had more time to do it, or perhaps because there were more often co-offenders involved. Repeats were also characterised by better security, probably a response to a history of repeat burglary, with superior front door deadlocks, security lighting, and burglar alarms fitted.

There were no differences between repeats and non-repeats in terms of neighbour guardianship measures, stolen property value or goods, means of access and exit from targets, visibility of targets to neighbours, whether burglars were spotted or arrested or a large number of small census data measures and socio-demographic measures of victims.

Variables that significantly differed between non-repeat and repeat incidents (Table 1) were iteratively tested using binary logistic regression analysis to produce a best-fit model (Table 2) that incorporated measures that could be used by police officers, either through direct observation or from information provided by victims. This model explained a quarter of the variation in whether or not a premises would be burgled again (Nagelkerke's $R^2 = 0.254$).

A summary score for predicting repeat burglary was derived by multiplying the values (0 or 1, according to whether the characteristic is present or absent) of each of the six variables by the associated odds ratio for each burglary case. This score

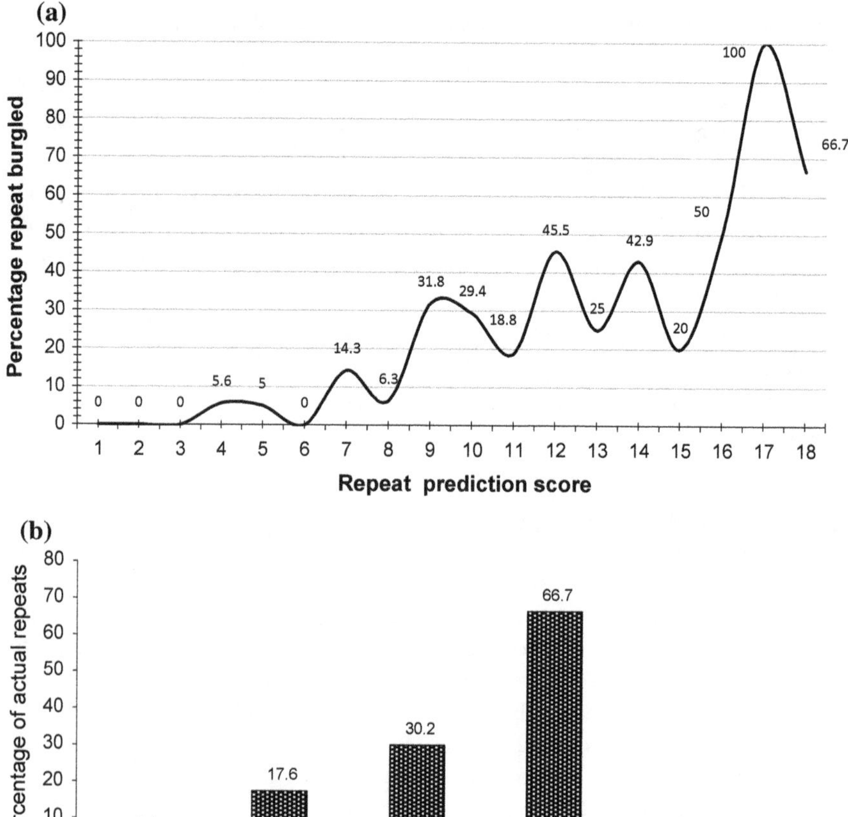

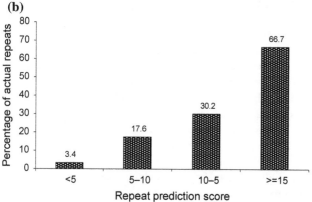

Fig. 2 Percentage of repeat residential burglaries for cases with different prediction scores: **a** Individual scores, **b** Grouped scores

produces a weighted sum of the six input variables according to effect sizes based on odds ratios for each case. A score of 1 equates to a very low risk of a repeat burglary, whereas a high score (>15), indicates an exceptionally high risk. The repeat prediction score was strongly positively correlated with and explains almost three-quarters of the variation in, repeat burglary incidence ($r = 0.84$, $p < 0.001$, $R^2 = 0.71$). As such, it provides a basis for forecasting repeat incidence that can inform operational practice.

Figures 2a, b and 3 indicate the potential to identify subgroups that might be cost-effectively targeted for intervention. Burgled properties with prediction scores under 5 have a low (3.4%) risk of being repeat burgled (Fig. 3); these constitute 29% of all sample burglaries. Being the least prone to repeat burglary, these would be least

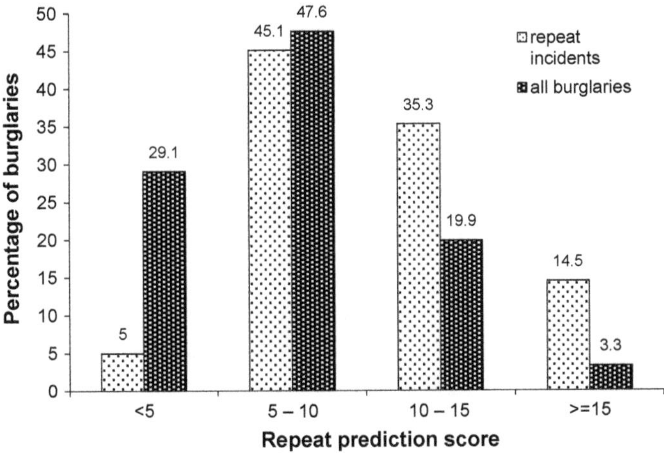

Fig. 3 Repeat prediction score by percentage of repeat residential burglaries and all residential burglaries

cost-effective if targeted for entrapment intervention. Those with scores between 5 and 10 constitute 48% of the population of burglaries, and these have a risk in line with the average repeat burglary rate for sample dwellings of 17%—rather more promising for intervention, but nevertheless costly.

Cases with prediction scores in excess of 15 have a 66.7% chance of suffering a repeat burglary (Fig. 2a, b) and constitute 14.5% of all repeat burglaries but only 3.3% of all sample burglaries (Fig. 3). For this subset of properties, it would be highly cost-effective to either entrap burglars or strengthen security markedly (Fig. 2a, b).

Even burgled dwellings in the next most promising group, with scores of 10–15, constitute only a fifth of all burgled properties and have a 30% chance of being repeat burgled. Though rather less cost-effective to equip with entrapment devices or to prioritise for rapid patrol response to the triggering of covert alarms, they account for 35% of all repeat burglaries (Fig. 3). By focusing on the 23% of burglaries with repeat prediction scores of 10 and over, there is potential to target half of all repeat burglaries, since these cases contain 35.3 and 14.5%, respectively, of all repeat incidents (Figs. 2a, b and 3).

A calculator into which a police officer, informed after responding or by telephone or email, is able to input Yes/No responses to the six indicator variables and which produces a predictive score determining the probability of a repeat burglary occurring could inform police patrols and dwelling occupants. This advice could support the installation of devices designed to entrap and provide an early alert for police patrols, who would be aware that such an alert is highly likely to be a genuine burglary in progress. The installation of delayed audible and silent alarms sited deeper inside premises should enable such incidents to be distinguished from other alarmed alerts (Coupe and Kaur 2005), many of which turn out to be false alarms (Cahalane 2001) or offenders testing premises to see whether triggering an alarm elicits a patrol response (Coupe 2017a, b).

Predicting Multiple Repeat Burglaries from a Sample of Single (First-Time) Repeat Incidents

If a repeat burglary has already occurred, the probability of further repeat incidences may be forecasted. The aim of this section is to identify the characteristics that discriminate between single repeats and multiple repeats of between 2 and 12 incidents with a view to predicting from the single repeats those most at risk of further repeat burglaries.

Few variables were significantly associated with single or multiple repeat incidence due to the small sample of repeat burglaries (Table 3).

Three key variables predict which premises where a single repeat has occurred will be re-victimised a third time or more. The inputs are number of rooms visited, number of other properties with a view of the entry or break-in point, and whether the target is an apartment.

As there were too few multiple repeat burglaries to allow running a logistic regression, a multiple burglary prediction score was derived by multiplying each of these three significant variables by their Cramer's *V* values from their individual associations with single or multiple repeats, while controlling for the other two variables, and then summing these to produce an overall prediction score for each data case.

Multiple repeat burglary incidents have far higher repeat prediction scores ($F = 19.72, p < 0.001, M_{\text{singles}} = 27; M_{\text{multiples}} = 66$). A score of 50, intermediate to these means, demarcates high and low scores: 90% of multiple repeats had high scores, compared with only 31% of single repeats ($\chi^2 = 12.61, p < 0.001, V = 0.60$).

Overall, single repeats have a 54% risk of re-victimisation, but cases with high prediction scores have a 77% risk, compared with only 15% for those with low scores (Fig. 4). The prediction score based on Cramer's *V* values, therefore, helps pick out the single repeats most at risk of being re-victimised. Eleven per cent of sample cases are single repeats with high prediction scores. Since 77% of those with high scores are likely to be re-burgled, the prospects are good for cost-effective interventions that enable arrest and case detection. These include rapid patrol responses in response to silent or delayed audible alarms, the use of high-quality covert CCTV to help identify suspects and bugging goods likely to be stolen with a view to tracking burglars who would otherwise evade arrest. Only 15% of single repeats with low prediction scores (equivalent to 1.3% of sample burglaries) experience multiple repeat burglary (Fig. 4), so that it appears few opportunities will be missed. Equally, only 23% of single repeats with high scores are not re-victimised (Fig. 4), so little effort is likely to be wasted, and successful arrests at high-score single repeats are far likelier than unsuccessful ones.

Table 3 Residential burglary: comparing characteristics of single repeats and multiple repeats

Routine activity concept	Variable	Single repeats: av. or %	Multiple repeats: av. or %	*t*	*p*	Effect size (*d*)
Guardianship	No. of neighbours with view of target entry point	1.56	1.32	$t = 1.5$	0.150	$d = .51$ [−0.16; 1.18]
	Mean distance of houses with view of approaches to target	1.69	1.26	$t = 2.7$	0.011	$d = 0.92$ [0.22; 1.61]
	20 or more dwellings with view of approaches to target	69	26	$\chi^2 = 6.30$	0.012	
	Single-adult household	31	37	$\chi^2 = 0.12$	0.728	OR = 0.77 [0.42; 1.38]
	Victim at home during burglary	19	16	$\chi^2 = 2.95$	0.086	OR = 1.23 [0.59; 2.56]
Access	House situated in middle of street versus at corner or next to alley	58	38	$\chi^2 = 1.5$	0.229	
Exposure	Height of rear cover (vegetation, walls, fencing)	4.4	4.3	$t = 0.09$	0.909	$d = 0.03$ [−0.63;.69]
	Burglaries committed in darkness	42%	44%	Fisher's =0.61	0.992	
Guardianship objects	Burglar alarm fitted prior to burglary	19%	16%	$\chi^2 = .05$	0.817	OR = 1.23 [0.59; 2.56]
	Security lights fitted prior to burglary	50%	32%	$\chi^2 = 1.23$	0.268	
Attractiveness	Targets where electrical goods, cash, jewellery stolen	50	58%	$\chi^2 = 0.22$	0.640	OR = 0.72 [0.41; 1.26]
	More than one room in target visited	81%	100%	$\chi^2 = 3.89$	0.048	
Dwelling type	Whether an apartment	0%	32%	$\chi^2 = 6.09$	*0.014*	OR = 0.56 [0.26; 1.19]
	Whether a terraced dwelling	63%	53%	$\chi^2 = 0.35$	0.557	OR = 1.51 [0.86; 2.66]
	Dwelling age: whether built prior to 1945	69%	79%	$\chi^2 = 0.47$	0.492	
	Dwelling is an apartment	0.0%	31.6%	$\chi^2 = 6.09$	0.014	

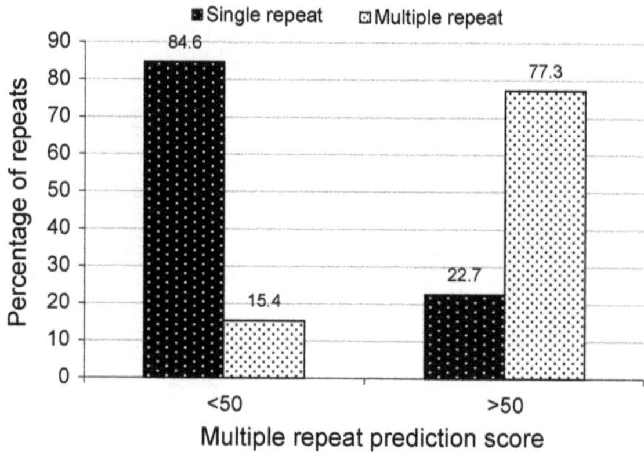

Fig. 4 Percentage of single and multiple repeat residential burglaries by high and low prediction scores

As with the prediction of single repeat incidents, the multiple repeat prediction score helps pick out the single repeats most at risk of being re-victimised.

Prediction Scores, Solvability, and Detections

Neither prediction score was related to whether or not cases were detected (non-repeat/single repeat: $F(1, 196) = 0.22$, $p = 0.64$,); single/multiple repeat: $F(1, 35) = 1.76$, $p = 0.19$), nor were there any differences in detection rates between non-repeats, single repeats and multiple repeats ($\chi^2 = 0.27$, $p = 0.87$, $n = 198$). The sample detection rate was 6.3%.

Potential to Improve Solvability and Detections

By targeting the 23% of all burglaries with higher repeat prediction scores, there is potential to detect half of single repeat burglaries, constituting 8% of sample burglaries, so that up to an additional 8% of cases might be detected—7.5% when taking account of cases detected otherwise. There is, equally, opportunity to elevate sample detection rates by up to 5.4% (taking account of those solved by other means) by targeting the 63% of repeats with high prediction scores that account for 77% of multiple repeats. Since 23% of the sample burglaries must be targeted to achieve the potential detections (7.5%) based on repeat burglary predictions, but only 11% to achieve those based on multiple repeat predictions (i.e., 5.4%), the latter will be more effective. Earlier arrest at single repeat incidents would, however, prevent multiple repeats, 90% of which are the work of the same offenders (Bernasco 2008; Johnson

2008). However, with only 7.7% of single repeats and 5.3% of multiple repeats in this sample detected, there is considerable scope for improvement in arrests. Earlier success would confer advantages in terms of burglary reduction only if arrestees were incapacitated via imprisonment or tracked electronic tagging, although such offenders might not be expected to re-victimise a prior target that led to their arrest.

A likely operational scenario for using these predictions would be to focus on the subset of burglaries at high risk of being re-victimised as first-time repeats, plus those with a high risk of being further re-victimised as multiple repeats. A small proportion of first incidents will be detected using customary investigative approaches, and some of the first-time repeats are likely to be successfully detected using the entrapment interventions suggested in this chapter. For those burglaries that remain unsolved, the remaining dwellings can be addressed on the basis of the forecasts from the multiple repeat prediction scores.

In practice, it may prove difficult to realise the full potential for additional arrest and detections outlined above. Not every suspect is known to the police so that it may not be possible to identify every offender from CCTV recordings, some of which may, in any case, fail if offenders cover their faces. Entrapment attempts connected to the first repeat, such as a 'near miss' by a patrol responding to a silent alarm alert, might frighten offenders and deter further victimisation. The approach, therefore, promises to elevate solvability, but its true potential for improving detections will need to be tested through practical implementation.

Discussion and Conclusions

These findings indicate that repeat burglaries may be predicted using their distinctive characteristics with a degree of confidence sufficient to isolate relatively small sample subsets at a far higher risk of further victimisation. By these means, for instance, the 3% of sample burglaries with a 67% risk that suffers 15% of all repeat victimisation can be identified. Similarly, it is possible to pick out the 63% of single repeats that have a 77% risk of being re-victimised.

The ability to predict the incidents most likely to suffer further victimisation at these two stages in the repeat burglary chain presents potential for targeting by police agencies. This could be done using entrapment devices that either covertly photograph the offender or trigger a covert alarm connected either to an alarm company or directly to police services. These techniques offer the potential to boost solvability and detect more burglary cases. Rapid responses to incidents where a covert alarm has been triggered and where the offender spends longer at the scene searching every room because he does not expect the householder to return home offer improved scope for on-scene arrest. Previous work on entrapment devices has demonstrated that installing temporary alarms in burgled properties in Huddersfield improved arrests (Chenery et al. 1997). Levels of domestic burglary and repeat burglary also were markedly reduced without evidence of burglary displacement to police divisions bordering the Huddersfield jurisdiction (Chenery et al. 1997). Tracking devices installed inside goods that match those previously stolen will allow for known offenders to be pinpointed more easily following the incident and may even indicate where goods are being 'fenced', depending on tracking range.

It seems that these techniques offer the potential to enhance arrests on, at least, a non-continuous basis, since offenders may realise that these interventions are being employed and take evasive action, such as covering faces to avoid recognition on CCTV recordings or staying on premises for shorter periods than it takes for a police patrol to respond. It might be expected that some will cease to re-burgle dwellings if they realise that what they had viewed as a safe target has become very unsafe. The random use of the approach in different parts of large police jurisdictions in order to catch unsuspecting burglars would appear appropriate. The approach may be expected to be of particular value in rural areas where burglary detection rates are far lower partly as a result of weaker patrol cover and the greater involvement of older offenders (Wright 2013), fewer of whom are arrested (Lamme and Bernasco 2013).

This study extends existing analyses of repeat and near-repeat burglary incidence based on only spatio-temporal measures to environmental and burglary site variables, including those measuring neighbour intervisibility. It has involved the use of 'static' variables, complemented by others involving retrospective questioning of burglary victims, to establish prior burglary circumstances, such as those relating to security improvements. The actual potential for improving solvability using an 'entrapment and arrest' approach can be better assessed either with 'static' variables alone or with data collected prospectively. The predictive outputs, furthermore, must ideally be experimentally tested to determine the probable benefits of an entrapment approach for solvability and detection. A prospective 'starting' sample of the order of perhaps 4,000 burglaries, or 14 times the size of the sample used in this study, eventually involving over 5,000 victim interviews and site surveys, would be needed to enable the comparison of 'single' and 'multiple' repeats and to facilitate 'split-sample' testing of predictive variables. Even so, this study presents evidence indicating that, even with non-prospective survey data, it is feasible to identify the distinctive characteristics of 'single' and 'multiple' repeat burglaries with sufficient accuracy to enable their prediction.

As for all research, it appears likely that external validity of the findings will be limited to housing environments comparable to those in this study, that is, urban housing environments in the UK and certain large towns in Ireland. Equivalent studies, such as that by Killmier et al. (Chapter "Offender–Offence Profiling: Improving Burglary Solvability and Detection"), which uses a burglary sample from Adelaide, indicate that different housing environments may present differences in access, occupancy guardianship and the visibility of targets from neighbouring premises. This is likely to affect re-victimisation. In Perth, Western Australia, for instance, only 6% of burglaries are near-repeats (Zanetti 2015) compared with over half of the burglaries in Merseyside, UK (Bowers et al. 2005). Spatio-temporal variations in solvability and in detections due to environmental and housing differences are likely to affect the use of this approach and compound other differences attributable to variation in investigative techniques and resourcing. For the UK, however, the variables identified would be a promising basis for identifying those properties most at risk of being repeat burgled and could be of value for policing practice.

References

Ahlberg, J., & Knutsson, J. (1990). The risk of detection. *Journal of Quantitative Criminology, 6*(1), 117–130.

Ashton, J., Brown, I., Senior, B., & Pease, K. (1998). Repeat victimisation: Offender accounts. *International Journal of Risk, Security and Crime Prevention, 3*(4), 269–279.

Bernasco, W. (2008). Them again? Same-offender involvement in repeat and near repeat burglaries. *European Journal of Criminology, 5*(4), 411–431.

Bowers, K., Hirschfield, A., & Johnson, S. (1998). Victimisation revisited: A case study of non-residential repeat burglary on Merseyside. *The British Journal of Criminology, 38*(3), 429–452.

Bowers, K., & Johnson, S. (2005). Domestic burglary repeats and space–time clusters: The dimensions of risk. *European Journal of Criminology, 2*(1), 67–92.

Bowers, K. J., Johnson, S. D., & Pease, K. (2005). Victimisation and re-victimisation risk, housing type and area: A study of interactions. *Crime Prevention and Community Safety: An International Journal, 7*(1), 7–17.

Budd, T. (1999). *Burglary of domestic dwellings: Findings from the British Crime Survey (Home Office Statistical Bulletin 4/99)*. London: Home Office.

Cahalane, M. (2001). Reducing false alarms has a price—so does response: Is the real price worth paying? *Security Journal, 14*(1), 31–53.

Chenery, S., Holt, J., & Pease, K. (1997). *Biting back II: Reducing repeat victimisation in Huddersfield (Crime Detection and Prevention Series, Paper 82)*. London: Home Office.

Coupe, R. T. (2017a). Resources, solvability and detection. In R. T. Coupe & B. Ariel (Eds.), *Crime solvability, police resources and crime detection*. Springer.

Coupe, T. (2017b). Burglary decisions. In W. Bernasco, H. Elffers, & J.-L. van Gelder (Eds.), *The Oxford handbook on offender decision making*. Oxford: Oxford University Press.

Coupe, R. T., & Blake, L. (2006). Daylight and darkness strategies and the risks of offenders being seen at residential burglaries. *Criminology, 44*(2), 431–463.

Coupe, R. T., & Blake, L. (2010). The effects of target characteristics on the sighting and arrest of offenders at burglary emergencies. *Security Journal, 24*(2), 157–178.

Coupe, R. T., & Kaur, S. (2005). The role of alarms and CCTV in detecting non-residential burglary. *Security Journal, 18*(2), 53–72.

Coupe, T., & Fox, B. H. (2015). A risky business: How do access, exposure and guardians affect the chances of non-residential burglars being seen? *Security Journal, 28*(1), 71–92.

Coupe, T., & Griffiths, M. (1996). *Solving residential burglary (Police Research Group Crime Detection and Prevention Services, Paper 77)*. London: Home Office.

Eck, J. E. (1979). *Managing case assignments: The burglary investigation decision model replication*. Washington, DC: Police Executive Research Forum.

Ericsson, U. (1995). Straight from the horse's mouth. *Forensic Update, 43*, 23–25.

Farrell, G. (1995). Preventing repeat victimisation. In M. Tonry, & D. P. Farrington (Eds.), *Building a safer society. Crime and Justice, Vol. 19: Strategic approaches to crime prevention*. Chicago: University of Chicago Press.

Farrell, G., & Pease, K. (1993). *Once bitten, twice bitten: Repeat victimisation and its implications for crime prevention (Crime Prevention Unit Series, Paper 46)*. London: Home Office Police Department.

Federal Bureau of Investigation. (2008). *Crime in the United States*. Washington, DC: Uniform Crime Reporting Program.

Hough, M. (1987). Offenders' choice of target: Findings from victim surveys. *Journal of Quantitative Criminology, 3*(4), 355–369.

Johnson, D. (2008). The near-repeat burglary phenomenon. In S. Chainey & J. Ratcliffe (Eds.), *Crime mapping case studies: Practice and research*. Chichester: Wiley.

Johnson, S. D., Bowers, K. J., & Hirschfield, A. (1997). New insights into the spatial and temporal distribution of repeat victimisation. *The British Journal of Criminology, 37*(2), 224–241.

Johnson, S. D., & Bowers, K. J. (2004). The burglary as clue to the future: The beginnings of prospective hot-spotting. *European Journal of Criminology, 1*(2), 237–255.

Johnson, S. D., Summers, L., & Pease, K. (2009). Offender as forager? A direct test of the boost account of victimisation. *Journal of Quantitative Criminology, 25*(2), 181–200.

Lamme, M., & Bernasco, W. (2013). Are mobile offenders less likely to be caught? The influence of the geographical dispersion of serial offenders' crime locations on their probability of arrest. *European Journal of Criminology, 10*(2), 168–186.

Ministry of Justice. (2010). *Burglary statistics*. London: MoJ.

Mirrlees-Black, C., & Ross, A. (1996). *Crime against retail and manufacturing premises: Findings from the 1994 Commercial Victimisation Survey (Home Office Online Report 37/05)*. London: Home Office.

Palmer, E. J., Holmes, A., & Hollin, C. R. (2002). Investigating burglars' decisions: Factors influencing target choice, method of entry, reasons for offending, repeat victimisation of a property and victim awareness. *Security Journal, 15*(1), 7–18.

Pease, K. (1998). *Repeat victimisation: Taking stock (Crime Detection and Prevention Series, Paper 90)*. London: Home Office.

Polvi, N., Looman, T., Humphries, C., & Pease, K. (1991). The time course of repeat burglary victimisation. *The British Journal of Criminology, 31*(4), 411–414.

Robinson, M. B. (1998). Burglary revictimisation: The time period of heightened risk. *The British Journal of Criminology, 38*(1), 78–87.

Sampson, R. J., & Wooldredge, J. D. (1987). Linking the micro- and macro-level dimensions of lifestyle—Routine activity and opportunity models of predatory victimisation. *Journal of Quantitative Criminology, 3*(4), 371–393.

Shover, N. (1991). Burglary. In M. Tonry & N. Morris (Eds.), *Crime and justice: An annual review of research* (pp. 73–113). Chicago: University of Chicago Press.

Smit, P., Meijer, R. F., & Groen, P.-P. J. (2004). Detection rates, an international comparison. *European Journal on Criminal Policy and Research, 10*(2–3), 225–253.

Spelman, W. (1995). Once bitten, then what? Cross-sectional and time-course explanations of repeat victimisation. *The British Journal of Criminology, 35*(3), 366–383.

Taylor, P., & Bond, S. (2012). *Crimes Detected in England and Wales 2011/12 (Home Office Statistical Bulletin 08/12)*. London: Home Office.

Thanassoulis, E. (1995). Assessing police forces in England and Wales using data envelopment analysis. *European Journal of Operational Research, 87*(3), 641–657.

Townsley, M., Homel, R., & Chaseling, J. (2003). Infectious burglaries: A test of the near repeat hypothesis. *The British Journal of Criminology, 43*(3), 615–633.

Tseloni, A., & Pease, K. (2003). Repeat personal victimisation. 'Boosts' or 'flags'? *The British Journal of Criminology, 43*(1), 196–212.

Tseloni, A., & Pease, K. (2004). Repeat personal victimisation: Random effects, event dependence and unexplained heterogeneity. *The British Journal of Criminology, 44*(6), 931–945.

Wright, O. (2013). *Urban to rural: An exploratory analysis of burglary and vehicle crime with a rural context (unpublished MSt thesis)*. University of Cambridge.

Zanetti, P. (2015). Personal communication with the author.

Improving Offence Solvability and Detection Rates at Non-residential Burglary: Predicting Single and Multiple Repeat Incidence

Richard Timothy Coupe and Katrin Mueller-Johnson

Introduction

Non-residential burglary is a common offence, but has a low detection rate of 13% (Taylor and Bond 2012). Many non-residential burglaries occur when premises are unoccupied and are discovered only when workers arrive at premises at the start of the working day. Burglaries committed during weekends are frequently discovered and reported early on Monday mornings. There can often be little or no evidence to point to the identity of the culprits. The prediction of repeat burglary incidence by profiling the distinctive characteristics of these offences, however, would provide means to help tackle some of the 87% of UK burglaries that would otherwise remain unsolved (Taylor and Bond 2012). Low clear-up rates reflect the large numbers of burglaries offenders are able to commit before being caught (Ahlberg and Knutsson 1990); some may never be apprehended. The findings from this study promise to enhance burglary solvability and enable the arrest of more burglars earlier in their criminal careers, thus helping prevent further offending. Using repeat burglary predictions to enhance arrests involves the entrapment of offenders at the crime scene. In this study, non-residential single and multiple repeat burglaries are compared with non-repeat incidents with regard to the characteristics of victims, site visibility and exposure, access, security characteristics, stolen goods, and whether cases were solved. In this way, indicator variables are identified for predicting repeat burglary.

Little is currently known about the features of repeat burglary targets, other than that they tend to be non-residential rather than domestic premises (Mirrlees-Black and Ross 1996). This chapter aims to address the significant gaps in our knowledge in order to discover reliable predictor variables. It is likely that repeatedly burgled premises will involve lower risks for offenders and have readily saleable goods to steal, so that they will be characterised by weaker guardianship, better access, lower

R. T. Coupe (✉) · K. Mueller-Johnson
University of Cambridge, Institute of Criminology, Cambridge, UK
e-mail: rtc23@cam.ac.uk

R. T. Coupe et al. (eds.), *Crime Solvability Factors*,
https://doi.org/10.1007/978-3-030-17160-5_14

exposure, and the theft of distinctive types of property. Multiple repeat targets, it is hypothesised, will be even safer for offenders than single repeat targets, so that an ability to identify those premises that will most frequently be victimised will help solve cases that may be among the least easily solved. If premises at high risk of repeat burglary can be identified, offenders may be caught by deploying silent and delayed audible alarms and covert CCTV cameras and by installing tracking devices on or inside the sorts of goods previously stolen and, therefore, most likely to be stolen again (Chenery et al. 1997). By these means, what burglars perceive as safer targets may become far more risky, and repeat victimisation a powerful means of catching the culprits. In this way, what might appear to be wise and rational targeting may turn out to be the very converse, with the safest targets becoming the least so. The findings promise to provide a means of solving not only burglaries but also other offences subsequently committed by burglars, many of whom are versatile offenders (Blumstein et al. 1988; Shover 1991).

The objectives in this chapter are to identify variables that help explain variation in the incidence of single and multiple repeat burglaries. On this basis, predictive indicators of single and multiple repeat non-domestic burglary incidents will be derived to enable the identification of subsets of premises at high risk of being re-burgled.

Existing Repeat Non-residential Burglary Research

Existing research has principally considered repeat burglary incidence and concentration (e.g., Tseloni and Pease 2003; Johnson et al. 1997) and the prediction of 'near-repeats' patterns (Townsley et al. 2003; Johnson and Bowers 2004; Bowers and Johnson 2005). Most repeat burglary occurs soon after the initial incident (Bowers et al. 1998; Farrell and Pease 1993; Farrell et al. 1995; Pease 1998; Spelman 1995): over 40% of non-residential repeats (Bowers et al. 1998) take place in the month following the first burglary (Johnson et al. 1997). Since nine-tenths of residential repeats within the following three months involve the return of the same offenders (Bernasco 2008; Johnson 2008), it appears likely that many non-residential repeats will similarly be due to the return of the same culprits. Given the higher rate of non-residential than residential burglary repeats (Mirrlees-Black and Ross 1996; cf. Budd 1999) combined with the smaller number of promising non-residential than residential burglary targets, it may be that fewer of these repeats are committed by the same offender. Nevertheless, the timing of subsequent non-residential burglaries indicates that, as for residential repeats (Polvi et al. 1991; Ericsson 1995; Ashton et al. 1998; Palmer et al. 2002), the same offenders will often be returning to familiar premises to steal goods not taken earlier or replacement goods and that 'event dependency' (Tseloni and Pease 2004; Johnson et al. 2009) as well as 'heterogeneous risk' (Tseloni and Pease 2003) influences repeat victimisation.

The scale of repeat victimisation at non-residential burglaries creates potential opportunities for apprehending returning burglars. By identifying those properties most at risk, entrapment could be carried out cost-effectively. As many as half of non-dwelling burglaries are repeats occurring within six months of the initial burglary (Mirrlees-Black and Ross 1996), and there is a notably high incidence of multiple repeat burglary (burgled on more than two occasions) at commercial premises. Two-thirds of shop burglaries and three-quarters of factory burglaries are repeats, and these types of premises also suffer greatly from multiple repeat burglary: over 40% experienced two or three burglaries, and a quarter of all types of commercial targets were burgled on four or more occasions (Mirrlees-Black and Ross 1996). A remarkable number of non-residential premises are burgled three times or more. Factories, warehouses and shops therefore present potential for cost-effective entrapment at subsequent burglaries, even without the use of prediction to narrow down the target list to those most at risk.

Despite being subjected to far higher levels of repeat targeting (Mirrlees-Black and Ross 1996), far fewer studies have attempted to profile non-residential burglary characteristics. Exceptions include research by Coupe and Fox (2015) and Hakim and Shachmurove (1996). Little, if anything, is known about the distinctive features, if indeed any exist, of multiple repeat non-residential targets when compared with single repeat incidents.

This research profiles the target characteristics of non-residential burglaries, comparing non-repeat incidents with single repeats and multiple repeats to determine whether they exhibit distinctive characteristics. By comparing 'one-off' or non-repeat incidents with both single and multiple repeats, their distinctive characteristics can be identified and a solid basis for predicting their incidence established. It is, perhaps, surprising that there has been so little research in this area, given its practical potential for solving burglaries that would otherwise remain unsolved. It also promises to speed the arrest of burglars, who tend to be versatile (Shover 1991), thereby preventing not just further burglaries—almost a fifth of which are aggravated by violence (Mirrlees-Black and Ross 1996)—but also other crimes. In this way, the chapter provides an approach to predicting and entrapping burglars that promise to prevent other crimes, especially other property offences that are more difficult to solve (Thanassoulis 1995; Smit et al. 2004). Improvements in solving burglary cases, therefore, are likely also to benefit the victims of other crimes.

The objective of the study is primarily to seek out the combination of variables that best predicts the incidence of single and multiple repeat burglaries at non-residential premises. To be of practical value, subsets of indicators that may be easily observed and scored by police officers must be selected, and means of implementing entrapment schemes and devices outlined. Such an approach can be used for longer and make a larger contribution to detections if offenders remain ignorant about how they have been caught. Indicator variables for single and multiple repeat incidents will be identified and input to best-fit binary logistic regressions, from which summary prediction scores will be derived. These scores can then be compared with the actual incidence of single compared with non-repeats and with the incidence of multiple compared with single repeats.

Methodology

Research Design and Research Instruments

Data were collected from police incident logs, burglary site surveys, and questionnaires of police officers and victims for a sample of non-residential burglaries committed in 2000. Burglaries took place between April and September in 12 operational command units of a UK conurbation police force, covering over 250 square miles. This incorporates most of a major city and a number of important industrial towns, with a population of over 1.75 million people and a wide variety of burglary targets. Specifically, non-residential premises range from locally owned shops and offices to factories and warehouses on industrial estates and science parks. These constituted two-thirds of non-residential targets. Other premises include hotels, public houses and restaurants, schools and colleges, gas stations, religious and leisure facilities, health centres, and other public service facilities.

Questionnaires detailing the initial police response and case outcomes were completed by 1,008 of the 1,117 sampled first officers at the scene and officers investigating non-residential burglary cases, a response rate of 90%. As at February 2001, 308 incidents were recorded as detected, while a further 700 incidents—most of which had been filed undetected—were yet to be solved.

From this principal sample, a subsample was randomly compiled in order to conduct additional interviews with victims and burglary site surveys. These surveys provided 299 non-residential burglary cases with successful victim interviews and site survey data. The randomization of both the selection of the principal sample and the compilation of the second-stage sample helps to methodologically ensure the generalisability of the findings. The characteristics of the burglary, security, and premises types within the completed victim and site survey responses did not significantly differ from those of the principal sample, indicating random non-response. The findings discussed in this chapter are based on the subsample of 299 incidents.

Incorporating data on offence characteristics from a variety of sources means that few key target features have been omitted from the study and enables links to be drawn between target characteristics and whether premises had been 'repeat' burglarised in order to identify the subset of variables that best predicts repeat incidence.

Data

The burglary site survey dealt with the situation of burgled premises with respect to neighbouring properties, whether or not there was rear access, and the distances from premises to other properties and the road. Surveillability or visibility of the target from neighbouring premises was measured using the number of properties and the estimated distances from properties intervisible with the target premises, whether it was light or dark at the time of the burglary, and the cover surrounding the dwelling.

The height and density of hedges, shrubs and trees, and the height and disposition of fences and walls, were used as the basis for estimating amounts of front and rear cover. Distances between targets and street lights, and distances between streetlights, were used as indicators of street lighting provision. Three surveyors implemented the site surveys and victim survey questionnaires. Accuracy in grading vegetation cover and assessing distances was improved by undertaking practice estimates between different points until they coincided with measured distances. Features affecting the vulnerability of premises were also recorded. These included the presence of side or rear alleys and open ground, the types of properties contiguous with targets, and security details.

The victim questionnaire survey provided data on victims' occupancy of the premises, the nature of the business carried out, the type and value of goods stolen, access to the site and the premises, and security measures, including details of CCTV, alarms, and security patrols. Victims were also questioned about whether there had been other burglaries during the prior six and twelve months, so that the sampled incident was either a non-repeat, the first or single repeat, or the last of a series of multiple repeats. Victims were also asked whether security had been upgraded since the earlier burglaries occurred.

This multifaceted data set, drawn from four sources, enables the linking of repeat burglary incidence with target and victim characteristics. This enables the distinctive features of non-repeat, single repeat and multiple repeat burglaries to be identified, so that their incidence may be forecasted. These predictor variables are likely to be of value for repeat burglary prediction in similar UK environments and other countries with similar industrial, warehousing, office, educational, religious, recreational and retailing environments. The findings also provide an empirical and procedural template for sifting out variables that are accurate predictors of repeat burglary incidence.

Reliance on a Retrospective Rather Than a Prospective Approach

Information about the outcome variable (single burglary, repeat burglary, multiple repeat burglaries) was elicited by questioning victims about the number of burglaries they had experienced during the six months prior to the sample burglary. The data collection method is, therefore, retrospective. For this reason, the method used in this chapter is based on the assumption that the target characteristics at the time of the site and victim surveys had changed insufficiently to invalidate their use for comparing single and multiple burglaries that occurred at different times over the six-month period.

Many of the predictive variables used in this study are static. These include the presence of a road at the side or rear of the premises, distances to neighbouring premises or streetlights, the type of organisation and the goods made, stored or sold.

Others are dynamic, including the presence of daylight or darkness, the security features of premises, such as locks, CCTV and alarm numbers, and the type of vegetative cover, changes in which can have implications for the accuracy of a retrospective method. Respondents were questioned about changes to security features. Sixteen per cent of premises owners had made changes to security during the prior six months, but this did not differ between non-repeat, first repeat and multiple repeat premises ($\chi^2(4, N = 299) = 2.75, p = 0.253$). While deciduous vegetative cover may be subject to seasonal change, key elements of the 'cover' variable involve the disposition of buildings, walls, and fences—aspects of the environment that do not change. The principal 'dynamic' variables used in the predictive models in this chapter were measures of security objects, and changes to these during the during the 6 months prior to this sample being collected are known from victim interviews.

The methodological approach, strictly speaking, is to determine whether premises characteristics—given they are assumed either to be static or, if dynamic, their status at the time of incidents is known—can be used to successfully explain differences between non-repeats and repeat incidents and between single and multiple repeat burglaries. On this basis, the chapter aims to assess whether it would be feasible to predict which types of premises are most at risk of repeat burglary and which, compared with single repeat incidents, face different degrees of risk of multiple repeat burglary.

A prospective survey approach that starts with a set of first-time incidents at premises and measures the target conditions using a series of surveys repeated as and when repeat burglaries occurred would be preferable, so that circumstances prevailing at the time of the offence could be known with certainty. However, even implementing prospective surveys at premises can involve delays of two to three weeks from burglary incidence, so that victim questioning is often retrospective in any event. This can result in confusion about the precise burglary event that is the subject of the questionnaire, especially at large premises with a number of security personnel that may have been victimised up to twelve times over a short period. There are circumstances, particularly if attitude measurement is involved, where prospective approaches with cross-sectional surveys may be misleading compared with retrospective methodologies (Coupe and Onodu 1997). It is possible for longitudinal, cross-sectional survey responses to show changes through time, but for these to be at odds with retrospective questioning, to which the same respondents indicate that there have been no changes—an inconsistency that reflects the subjectivity of assessments conducted at specific points in time without reference to prior circumstances (Coupe and Onodu 1997).

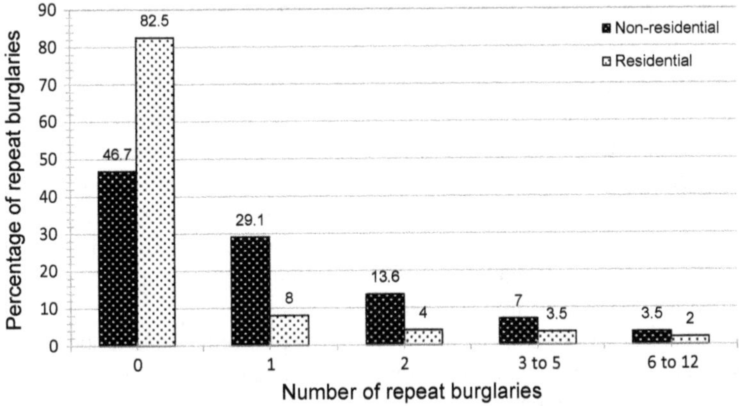

Fig. 1 Incidence of repeat non-residential burglary during prior six months

Findings

Levels of Repeat Burglary

A very high proportion—54%—of non-residential premises had been burgled during the six months prior to the sample incident. This re-victimisation rate is far higher than for residential burglary (Fig. 1). The rate mirrors that in Mirrlees-Black and Ross' (1999) national survey and is comparable in that there were very high concentrations of repeat burglary at certain retail and manufacturing premises, which feature prominently in this sample.

Once a repeat burglary had occurred, 48% of non-residential premises experienced one or more additional repeats within six months (Fig. 1). A quarter of non-residential premises and 10% of dwellings, therefore, were burgled more than twice.

It is clear that a very high proportion of burgled non-residential premises are the subject of continuing burglar interest. This suggests that it is likely to be cost-effective to employ entrapment approaches even without narrowing down repeat targets using predictive techniques. Even so, there is considerable scope to save on costs with accurate prediction. There are also potential savings once a single repeat burglary has taken place. The greater the number of burglaries that occurred at a non-residential target, the sooner the first repeat occurred ($\tau_b = -0.54$, $p < 0.001$), so that the timing of the first repeat is one of the indicators of multiple repeats and highlights the targets where more putative repeats may be prevented by entrapment operations.

Repeat Burglary Measures and Structure of the Analysis

The principal objective is to identify those target features that are associated with single and multiple repeat burglaries, so that the risk of incidence can be estimated with some confidence. With this information, interventions can be made to arrest more burglars, thereby combating the most intensive burglary victimisation. Since arrest at burglaries relates strongly to burglars being seen (Eck 1979; Coupe and Griffiths 1996), it is likely that measures of exposure and neighbour guardianship will be good predictors, since poor guardianship and low exposure will favour burglars at repeat targets, and particularly at 'multiple repeat' targets.

This chapter therefore aims to sift out the strong correlates and associations with larger size effects so that the best combination of predictors of single and multiple repeat burglary may be identified.

Depending on the point in a repeat burglary 'chain' that intervention is to take place, two approaches are used to determine the best predictors of repeat burglary incidence. These are to compare:

1 the characteristics of 'one-off' burglaries with those of repeat targets; and
2 the characteristics of single repeats with those of multiple repeats.

The approach is to initially identify the bivariate relationships with large effect sizes between repeats and non-repeats and between single and multiple repeats. From these, variables that can be easily scored by police officers responding to incidents or speaking by telephone with premises occupants will be entered into logistic regressions to determine the best combination of variables for predicting repeat incidence with the greatest confidence. As the aim is a 'best-fit' equation, testing will be iterative and variables with lower significance will be removed in order to find the optimal variable combination that maximizes statistical explanation. For each of the two logistic regressions, a single predictive variable will be derived by taking a weighted average of the regression odds ratios. Case values for each predictive variable will be compared with whether or not a repeat or multiple repeat burglary occurred in order to identify the cut-off points where the predictive variable forecasts repeat burglary incidence with a high probability.

Characteristics of Repeat Burglaries Compared with 'One-Off' Incidents

The key risk for burglars is being seen while committing burglary, and this is lower where burglary premises and sites have weaker guardianship and lower exposure (Coupe and Fox 2015). Targets at which offenders were seen had been subjected to over a third fewer repeat burglaries ($F = 5.32, p < 0.02$) during the six months prior to the sample incident. This indicates that repeat burglary occurs at safer, lower-risk targets with poorer guardianship and lower exposure, and that multiple repeat incidents will show this to an even greater degree.

Repeat targets were distinctive in terms of variables describing guardianship, guardianship objects, exposure and access and with regard to the type of organisation and goods stolen (Table 1).

Guardianship from neighbours and passersby was notably weaker than at non-repeats (Table 1). More repeat premises had security patrols—likely a response to repeat burglary incidence. The most important aspect of guardianship concerns visibility of the target to neighbours (Coupe and Fox 2015), and in this respect, repeat premises were markedly safer for burglars. The variables measuring numbers of neighbouring properties with different sorts of views of the target are good candidate indicators for prediction, because they can be easily counted from various points at the burglary scene. The same is true of numbers of roads and paths close to the target.

Certain exposure and access measures also proved distinctive (Table 1). Almost twice as many repeat burglary sites, for instance, did not have a road, open ground or a wood at the side, features that increase offender exposure to neighbours when used to access sites (Coupe and Fox 2015). There was a counter-tendency for repeat burglary sites to back on to a road affording easy site access, which tends to depress visibility (Coupe and Fox 2015). They were also situated farther away from road junctions, suggesting quieter locations. All these are straightforward to observe and record and are also candidate indicators for repeat incidence.

Security was better at repeat burglary sites (Table 1), probably in response to earlier burglaries. As well as more sophisticated delayed audible alarms at repeat premises, there were four times as many hidden CCTV cameras, though only two-thirds more visible cameras, which had filmed twice as many burglars during the previous six months (Table 1). Delayed audible alarms are connected to alarm companies, who covertly alert the police, and hidden CCTV cameras do not signal their presence to offenders, who are likely to respond to visible CCTV cameras with behaviour that hampers their identification.

Evidence of covert security devices like these is important in two ways for using repeat burglary indicators. It suggests that premises owners are aware that it is difficult to deter burglars just through target hardening and recognise the importance of arresting offenders. The second reason is that it indicates that repeat victims are willing to invest in and adopt innovative devices and strategies. This is an essential component of successfully arresting offenders by installing entrapment devices. Many alarmed alerts can be false or involve offenders testing systems or police responses, and as many as 28 out of 29 patrol responses to alarmed alerts at commercial premises may not involve genuine break-ins (Cahalane 2001). However, when responding to an alarmed alert at premises with predicted 'repeat burglary risk' flags, officers would have far greater confidence that a genuine offence is in progress.

Repeat burglaries occurred at distinctive sorts of organisations. There was a marked emphasis on repeat targeting of schools, hotels, leisure and sports centres, community service centres, warehouses, hospitals, health centres, entertainment venues and manufacturing premises (Table 1). Fewer offices, restaurants and churches were affected by repeat burglary, while shops, pubs and service stations

Table 1 Non-residential burglary: differences in target characteristics between repeat and non-repeat incidents

Routine activity concept	Variable	Repeats: mean or %	Non-repeats: mean or %	t	p	Effect size (d)
Guardianship	Number of neighbours with upstairs target view	3.53	4.82	$F = 5.54$	0.0 19	0.28
	Number of neighbours with downstairs target view	3.28	4.73	$F = 7.40$	0.007	0.32
	Non-residential premises with rear of target view	1.32	0.8	$F = 6.69$	0.010	0.31
	Security patrols at premises	26%	12%	$\chi^2 = 8.12$	0.017	0.34
	Five or more roads or paths in vicinity of target	35%	23%	$\chi^2 = 4.86$	0.027	0.26
	No side road	34%	16%	$\chi^2 = 17.46$	0.002	0.51
	No open ground at side of target	57%	30%	$\chi^2 = 21.66$	0.001	0.58
Access	No woods at side of target	55%	31%	$\chi^2 = 21.70$	0.001	0.58
	Road at rear of premises	42.1%	35.1%	$\chi^2 = 5.81$	0.055	0.29
	Distance from nearest road junction (yards)	51	39	$F = 2.95$	0.087	0.20

(continued)

Table 1 (continued)

Routine activity concept	Variable	Repeats: mean or %	Non-repeats: mean or %	*t*	*p*	Effect size (*d*)
Exposure	Brighter street lighting	20.6	24.3	$F = 12.69$	<0.001	
	Security index	1.41	1.35	$F = 6.15$	0.014	0.30
	Alarms fitted (*Y/N*)	32%	16%	$\chi^2 = 9.52$	0.01	0.37
	Delayed audible alarms fitted (*Y/N*)	48%	32%	$\chi^2 = 12.81$	0.005	0.44
	Number of alarms fitted	1.38	1.05	$F = 6.01$	0.015	0.29
	CCTV installed	54%	32%	$\chi^2 = 14.09$	<0.01	0.46
Guardianship objects	Number of CCTV cameras	1.26	0.74	$F = 8.88$	0.003	0.35
	Number of visible CCTV cameras	1.07	0.66	$F = 6.61$	0.011	0.31
	Number of hidden CCTV cameras	0.68	0.19	$F = 8.23$	0.004	0.34
	Number of burglars CCTV filmed in prior six months	4.54	6.79	$F = 15.1$	0.000	0.46
	Reinforced doors fitted at target	63%	45%	$\chi^2 = 9.41$	0.009	0.37
	Extra locks fitted at target	82%	65%	$\chi^2 = 11.31$	0.004	0.41
	Bars, grills and shutters fitted at target	62%	48%	$\chi^2 = 5.82$	0.055	0.29

(continued)

Table 1 (continued)

Routine activity concept	Variable	Repeats: mean or %	Non-repeats: mean or %	t	p	Effect size (d)
	Toughened glass fitted at target	43%	31%	$\chi^2 = 7.26$	0.026	0.32
	Security lighting fitted at target	5%	1%	$\chi^2 = 4.9$	0.086	0.27
Attractiveness	Types of goods stolen	51%	16%	$\chi^2 = 34.53$	<0.001	0.75
Organisation type	Types of premises targeted	43%	21%	$\chi^2 = 15.42$	0.000	0.48
	Organisation employee numbers	19	76	$F = 4.67$	0.032	0.26

were equally liable to be repeat burgled or not. In terms of the goods stolen, repeat burglaries were particularly likely to have had computers, clothes, mobile phones, tools, builders' materials and multiple types of goods taken, together accounting for over three times the losses at premises not repeat burglarised. Less food and fewer consumables and 'other' goods were taken, but there was no difference between repeats and non-repeats with respect to thefts of car parts, petrol, alcohol, personal items, vehicles, industrial equipment, raw materials and electrical goods. Repeat targets were also smaller organisations with fewer employees (Table 1). Poor neighbour guardianship plus an enterprise scale insufficient to justify continuous on-site security personnel out of working hours highlight the vulnerability of these sorts of premises. Organisation type, type of goods stolen and the number of employees are therefore valuable potential indicators.

The variables identified as distinctively characterising repeat burglaries provide indicator markers for repeat burglary incidence. These can be used to score one-off burglaries to identify the subset liable to suffer another break-in.

Predicting Repeat Non-residential Burglaries

Variables that significantly differed between non-repeat and repeat incidents (Table 1) were iteratively tested using binary logistic regression analysis to produce a best-fit model (Table 2) that incorporated measures that could be used by police officers, either through direct observation or from information provided by premises occupants. This model explained 30% of variation in whether or not a premises would be burgled again (Nagelkerke's $R^2 = 0.302$).

A summary score for predicting repeat burglary was derived by multiplying the values (0, 1 according to whether the characteristic is present or absent) of each of the seven variables by the associated odds ratio for each burglary case. This score produces a weighted sum of the six input variables according to effect sizes based on the odds ratios for each case. A score of 0 equates to a very low risk of a repeat

Table 2 Binary logistic regression with non-repeat/repeat burglary the dependent variable

Solvability factor	*B*	S.E.	Wald	*df*	*Sig.*	Exp(*B*)
No open ground at side of target	0.968	0.280	11.951	1	0.001	2.632
Number of visible CCTV cameras	0.176	0.066	7.010	1	0.008	1.192
Type of premises targeted	0.945	0.302	9.759	1	0.002	2.572
Type of goods stolen	1.064	0.298	12.717	1	0.000	2.899
Extra mortise locks fitted	−0.851	0.342	6.181	1	0.013	0.427
Sensor alarm/other alarm type	0.573	0.279	4.212	1	0.040	1.773
Constant	−5.140	1.136	20.484	1	0.000	0.006

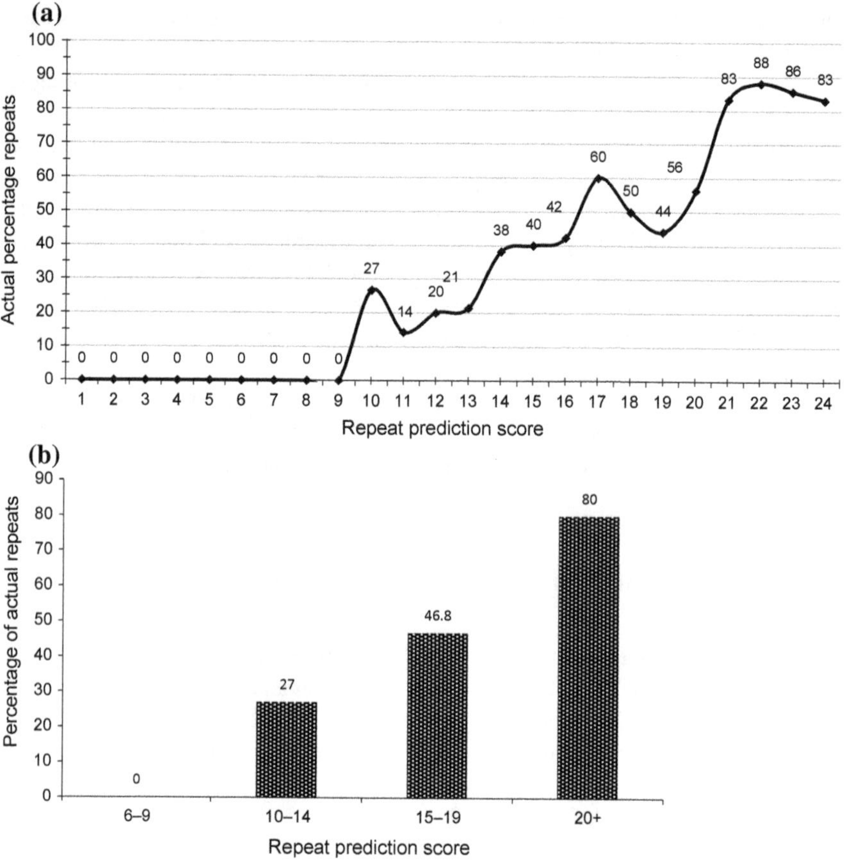

Fig. 2 Repeat prediction score by actual repeat non-residential burglaries: for **a** individual scores, **b** grouped scores

burglary, whereas a high score (>20), indicates an exceptionally high risk of 80% or more.

Repeat predictive score is strongly correlated with the actual incidence of repeat burglary ($r = 0.96, p < 0.001$; Fig. 2). Scores of 20 and above predict a repeat burglary rate of 80%, which is far above the 54% mean for non-residential burglaries. A little more than a fifth of burglaries had predictive scores of 20 or more and consequently an 80% chance of being re-victimised (Fig. 3). These include 38% of all repeat burglaries (Fig. 3). Installing entrapment devices in these premises or using this predictor to inform patrols of a high risk of repeat incidence that justifies an immediate response would be far more cost-effective and operationally feasible than having to consider all burglary premises, which, collectively, have a 54% chance of being re-victimised.

A calculator or an app into which a police officer, informed after responding or by telephone or email, is able to input Yes/No responses to the seven indicator variables

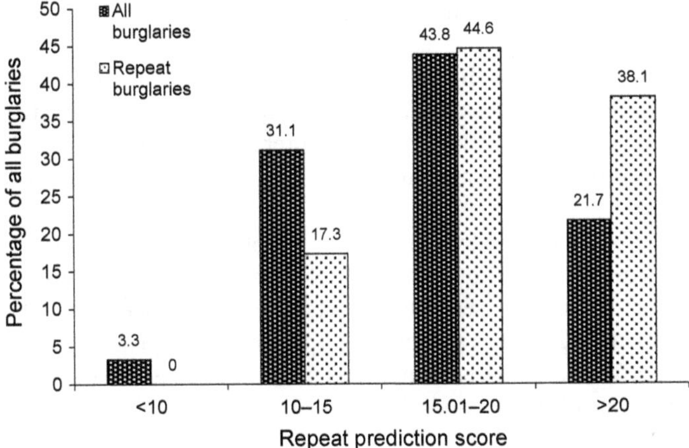

Fig. 3 Repeat prediction score by percentage of repeat non-residential burglaries and all non-residential burglaries

and which then produces a predictive score indicating the probability of a repeat burglary occurring could inform police patrols and premises occupants. This advice can support the installation of devices designed to entrap and provide an early alert for police patrols, aware that such an alert is highly likely to be a genuine burglary in progress. The installation of delayed audible and silent alarms sited deeper inside premises should enable such incidents to be distinguished from other alarmed alerts (Coupe and Kaur 2005), many of which turn out to be false alarms (Cahalane 2001) or offenders testing premises to see whether an alarm will be triggered and, if so, whether that will elicit a patrol response (Coupe 2017).

Non-residential Burglaries: Characteristics of Single Repeat Versus Multiple Repeat Burglaries

If a repeat burglary has already occurred, the probability of additional repeat incidences may be forecasted. The aim of this section is to identify the characteristics that distinguish single repeats from multiple repeats of between two and twelve incidents with a view to identifying the characteristics of the single repeats most at risk of repeat victimisation.

The most striking feature of multiple repeats compared with single repeats was far weaker neighbour guardianship, with strikingly poorer line of sight from neighbouring premises (Table 3). It is due to this, and even lower exposure, that fewer burglars—only two-thirds as many—were sighted at multiple compared with single repeats ($\chi^2 = 7.033, p = 0.008$). Premises subject to multiple repeats were situated farther away from all intervisible neighbours and facing properties and were twice as far away from the closest neighbouring property. They were also overlooked by far fewer non-residential properties with a rear view of premises and there were markedly fewer properties with a facing or side view of the target.

In terms of cover and exposure (Table 3), multiple repeats were situated in streets that were safer for night-time burglary, with poorer street lighting and also had higher front cover from foliage, walling and fencing. Target access via side roads was also easier.

Raw materials, tools, builders' materials, petrol, vehicles, electrical goods and money were stolen twice as often at multiple repeats, and warehouses, factories, service stations, community services, hospitals, health services and entertainment venues accounted for 2.7 times as many multiple as single repeat targets. There were no significant differences between single and multiple repeats in terms of the number of employees, value of stolen goods, incident costs, occupancy or daylight–darkness incidence.

Non-residential Burglary: Predicting Multiple Repeats from Single Repeat Non-residential Burglaries

Variables that significantly differed between single repeat and multiple repeat incidents (Table 3) were iteratively tested using binary logistic regression analysis to produce a best-fit model (Table 4) that incorporated measures that would be feasible to use in the field. This model explained a third of variation in whether or not a premises would be burgled on a third occasion or more (Nagelkerke's $R^2 = 0.332$).

This regression model accounts for 36% of the incidence of multiple repeats compared with single repeats (Nagelkerke's $R^2 = 0.358$; Cox and Snell $R^2 = 0.264$; -2 log likelihood = 157.247). Since it is likely that about half of all burglary risk is due to randomly occurring factors (Coupe and Fox 2015), this best-fit model probably 'captures' about 70% of the target characteristics that systematically affect multiple repeat burglary.

A prediction score with values between 1 (low repeat incidence risk) and 45 (high repeat incidence risk) was derived by summing the products of the odds ratio value of each variable from the best-fit logistic regression. It is possible to eliminate with confidence existing repeat premises that have prediction scores of less than 13.5 with a lower risk—only a one-in-five chance—of further victimisation (Fig. 4). These account for 44% of single repeat targets (Fig. 5). The remainder, which constitute 56% of single repeat incidents, has high odds (at least 53%) of being re-victimised, though prediction scores of over 27 delineate targets with the highest (68%) risk of multiple repeat incidence (Fig. 5).

The smaller numbers of multiple repeat burglaries in the sample mean that there are instances of low numbers of multiple repeats interspersed with high numbers, as seen in Fig. 5. This may also reflect burglars returning to re-victimise premises who,

Table 3 Non-residential burglaries: differences in target characteristics between single and multiple repeats

Routine activity concept	Variable	Single repeats: Mean or %	Multiple repeats: Mean or %	t	p	Effect size (d)
Guardianship	Number of neighbours with upstairs target view	3.70	1.95	$F = 3.30$	0.071	0.30
	Number of neighbours with downstairs target view	3.21	1.17	$F = 6.61$	0.010	0.43
	Non-residential premises with rear of target view	1.59	0.92	$F = 4.61$	0.033	0.36
	Numbers of neighbours with an opposite view	2.75	1.73	$F = 4.07$	0.045	0.33
	Number of neighbours with a side view of rear	1.57	0.93	$F = 3.43$	0.066	0.30
	Distance from closest neighbour (yards)	20.7	10.4	$F = 4.91$	0.028	0.36
	Mean distance from intervisible neighbours (yards)	16	25	$F = 4.10$	0.045	0.33
	Distance from facing neighbouring properties (yards)	15	17	$F = 5.68$	0.018	0.40

(continued)

Table 3 (continued)

Routine activity concept	Variable	Single repeats: Mean or %	Multiple repeats: Mean or %	t	p	Effect size (d)
	Number of roads or paths in vicinity of target	4.43	3.55	$F = 3.36$	0.069	0.30
	Road at side of target	41%	22%	$\chi^2 = 5.43$	<0.05	0.39
Access	Open ground at side of target	10%	28%	$\chi^2 = 3.95$	<0.05	0.33
	Road at rear of premises	49%	67%	$\chi^2 = 3.95$	<0.05	0.33
Exposure	Distance between streetlights	22.6	19.3	$F = 5.05$	0.026	0.37
	Distance of target from nearest streetlight	12.9	42.9	$F = 8.96$	0.003	0.50
	Height of front cover	0.71	1.02	$F = 3.23$	0.074	0.30
Guardianship objects	*No significant variables*					
Attractiveness	Types of goods stolen	17%	32%	$\chi^2 = 4.18$	0.014	0.34
Organisation type	Types of premises targeted	38%	57%	$\chi^2 = 7.08$	0.008	0.44

Table 4 Binary logistic regression with single repeat/multiple repeat the dependent variable

Solvability factor	*B*	S.E.	Wald	*df*	*Sig.*	Exp(*B*)
Number of visible CCTV cameras	0.221	0.095	5.418	1	0.020	1.247
Distance of target from nearest street light	0.019	0.009	4.384	1	0.036	1.019
Number of properties with view of target from downstairs	−0.169	0.079	4.605	1	0.032	0.844
Road at rear of target No/Yes	−0.866	0.413	4.392	1	0.036	0.421
Road at side of target No/Yes	0.853	0.446	3.660	1	0.056	2.347
Height of cover at front of target	0.400	0.192	4.337	1	0.037	1.492
Type of premises	−1.147	0.441	6.775	1	0.009	0.317
Constant	0.068	1.369	0.002	1	0.960	1.070

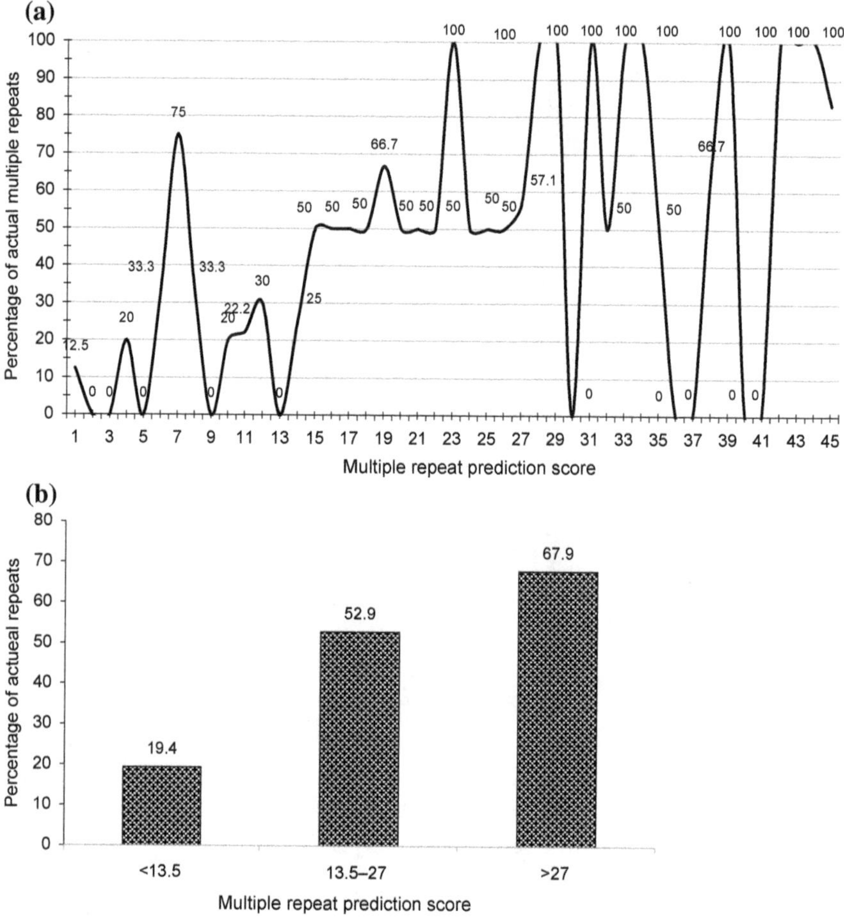

Fig. 4 Multiple repeat prediction score by actual repeat non-residential burglaries: **a** for individual scores, **b** for grouped scores

deterred from breaking in again due to on-the-spot appraisals, are displaced to other targets.

Prediction Scores and Detections

The overall detection rate for the non-residential burglary sample was 6.3%. Neither prediction score was related to whether or not cases were detected (non-repeat vs. single repeat: $F(1, 194) = 0.54, p = 0.46$; single versus multiple repeat: $F(1, 180) =$

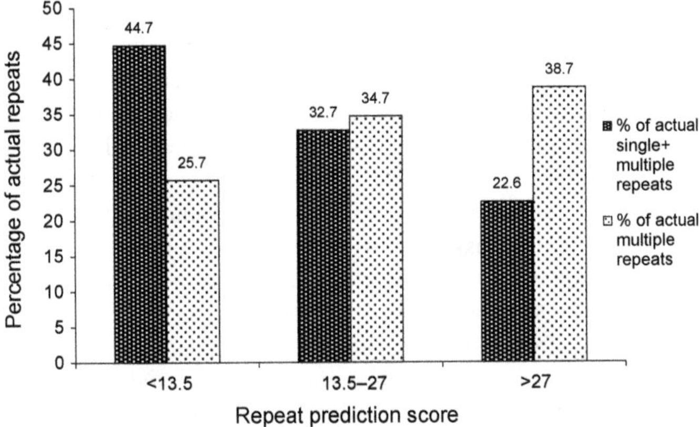

Fig. 5 Repeat prediction score by percentage of repeat non-residential burglaries and by multiple repeat non-residential burglaries

0.63, $p = 0.43$), nor were there any differences in detection rates between non-repeats, single repeats and multiple repeats.

By targeting the quarter of all burglaries with higher repeat prediction scores, there is potential to detect half of repeat burglaries, which constitute 8% of sample burglaries, so that up to an additional 8% of cases might be detected. There is, equally, opportunity to elevate sample detection rates by up to 6.2% by targeting the 61% of repeats with high prediction scores that account for 74% of multiple repeats. Since 23% of the sample burglaries must be targeted to achieve the potential detections based on repeat burglary predictions, but only a tenth to achieve those based on multiple repeat predictions, it is evident that the latter will be 1.7 times more cost-effective.

Potential to Improve Solvability and Detection

The findings suggest that repeat non-residential burglaries may be predicted using burglary characteristics with a degree of confidence sufficient to isolate relatively small sample subsets at a far higher risk that may be targeted cost-effectively. The 22% of non-residential burglaries with prediction scores of 20 have a four-in-five chance of being re-victimised and constitute 38% of all repeat burglaries. By targeting this subset of properties, it is likely that 38% of all repeat burglaries can be cost-effectively targeted and solvability of the sample improved. An additional 44% of burglaries with prediction scores of between 15 and 20 have a 47% probability of re-victimisation and include 45% of all repeat incidents. Including this group with only a 47% chance of re-victimisation widens the target group so that it is not narrowed down sufficiently to be cost-effective.

A likely operational scenario for using these predictions would be to focus on the subset of premises at greatest risk of being re-victimised as first-time repeats, plus those single repeats with the highest risks of being further re-victimised as multiple repeats. None of the burglaries with the highest predicted risk of being repeat burgled was detected, and only 5.6% of those single repeats with the highest risk of further repeat burglary were detected. These burglaries present untapped potential for increasing detections through the use of entrapment intervention devices, which could, for the highest risk category alone, boost detection rates by approximately 2%—improving existing sample detection rates by a third—while requiring intervention in only 3.3% of all burgled premises. Some of the first-time repeats are likely to be successfully detected using the entrapment interventions suggested in this chapter. Entrapment devices can usefully be left installed in the remaining premises at high risk of further, multiple repeat burglaries so that the potential may be as fully realised as possible.

A scenario that also considers premises with the second-highest risk of repeat burglary has, taking into account the risks identified, potential for detecting up to an additional 5.9% of sample burglaries that are currently not solved. Targeting the two highest risk repeat burglary groups and the highest risk multiple repeat burglaries would together offer scope to increase detections by 7.9%, from 6.3 to 14.2%. Together, these two groups constitute 23% of sample properties, so that this intervention could be cost-effective.

Since initial repeats with high prediction scores (an 80% risk of being re-victimised) constitute 22% of sample burglaries, taking account of cases that were in any case solved, 15.6% is the maximum achievable increase in detections, though full realisation of this is highly unlikely. Even so, since a quarter of these high-risk first-repeat premises were re-victimised as multiple repeats, there should be additional opportunities for arrest, unless entrapment circumstances connected to the first repeat, such as a 'near-miss' by a patrol responding to a silent alarm alert, frighten offenders and deter further victimisation. The approach elevates solvability, but its true potential for improving detections will need to be tried out through practical implementation.

Conclusions

Predicting and targeting repeat non-residential burglary incidence present the police with potential to cost-effectively improve clearance. It appears, on the basis of the retrospective approach used in this chapter, that it is possible to predict repeat burglaries using burglary characteristics with a degree of confidence sufficient to isolate relatively small sample subsets at a far higher risk. By these means, it appears possible to identify the 22% of sample burglaries with an 80% risk of being repeat burgled that suffer 38% of all first-time repeat victimisation. Similarly, it is possible to discriminate between the 23% of single repeats, constituting 38% of all multiple repeats, that have a 68% risk of being re-victimised. The ability to predict those incidents that are highly likely to suffer single and multiple repeat victimisation will mean that additional detections may be achieved far more cost-effectively by limiting the proportion of targets in which entrapment devices are installed, instead of using them in every burgled property—the approach taken in research in Huddersfield (Chenery et al. 1997).

The ability to predict the incidents most likely to suffer further victimisation at these two stages in the repeat burglary chain would present potential for selective and prioritised targeting by police agencies. Entrapment devices that either covertly photograph the offender or trigger a covert alarm connected to either an alarm company or directly to police services offer scope to boost solvability and detect more burglary cases. Installing tracking devices inside goods that match those previously stolen can enable known offenders to be pinpointed more easily following the incident and may even indicate where goods are being 'fenced', depending on tracking range. Given the high risks of non-residential premises being re-victimised, retaining entrapment–arrest devices at premises rather than removing them if an offender has been caught within three to six months of the first burglary incident may prove worthwhile.

The true potential for enhanced solvability of such an 'entrapment and arrest' approach can be more appropriately assessed with data collected prospectively so that there is greater certainty about the accuracy of variables. This would be likely to alter the odds ratios, while keeping a similar set of independent variables as predictors. There have been few, if any, studies of repeat burglary—not even retrospective, let alone prospective—that use victim and site surveys to measure burglary site characteristics, despite research into repeat burglary stretching back for over 30 years. The predictive outputs of prospective data collection need ideally to be experimentally tested to determine the probable benefits of an entrapment approach for solvability and detection.

The effectiveness of entrapment will also depend on offender response. Offenders may suspect or realise that these interventions are being employed and take evasive action, such as covering their faces to avoid recognition on CCTV recordings or remaining on premises for shorter periods than it takes for a police patrol to respond. Installing delayed audible or silent alarms well inside premises rather than at entrances or windows helps entrap offenders (Coupe and Kaur 2005). It might be expected that some will cease to re-burgle premises if they realize that what they had viewed as a safe target has become very unsafe. The random use of this entrapment and arrest approach in different parts of large police jurisdictions in order to catch unsuspecting burglars would appear appropriate. The approach may be expected to be of particular value in rural areas, where non-residential burglary incidence exceeds residential burglary and where burglary detection rates are far lower, partly as a result of older offenders travelling longer distances and weaker patrol cover (Wright 2013).

This study extends existing studies of repeat non-residential and near-repeat burglary incidence based on only spatio-temporal measures to include environmental and site variables. It appears likely that the external validity of the findings will be limited to comparable commercial and other non-residential environments. Spatio-temporal variations in solvability and detections due to environmental and premises differences are likely to affect the use of this approach and compound other differences in solvability and detection attributable to variances in investigative techniques and resourcing.

References

Ahlberg, J., & Knutsson, J. (1990). The risk of detection. *Journal of Quantitative Criminology, 6*(1), 117–130.

Ashton, J., Brown, I., Senior, B., & Pease, K. (1998). Repeat victimisation: Offender accounts. *International Journal of Risk, Security and Crime Prevention, 3*(4), 269–279.

Bernasco, W. (2008). Them again? Same-offender involvement in repeat and near repeat burglaries. *European Journal of Criminology, 5*(4), 411–431.

Blumstein, A., Cohen, J., Das, S., & Miotra, D. (1988). Specialization and seriousness during adult criminal careers. *Journal of Quantitative Criminology, 4*(4), 303–345.

Bowers, K., Hirschfield, A., & Johnson, S. (1998). Victimisation revisited: A case study of non-residential repeat burglary on Merseyside. *The British Journal of Criminology, 38*(3), 429–452.

Bowers, K., & Johnson, S. (2005). Domestic burglary repeats and space-time clusters: The dimensions of risk. *European Journal of Criminology, 2*(1), 67–92.

Budd, T. (1999). *Burglary of domestic dwellings: Findings from the British Crime Survey (Home Office Statistical Bulletin 4/99)*. London: Home Office.

Cahalane, M. (2001). Reducing false alarms has a price—so does response: Is the real price worth paying? *Security Journal, 14*(1), 31–53.

Chenery, S., Holt, J., & Pease, K. (1997). *Biting back II: Reducing repeat victimisation in Huddersfield (Crime Detection and Prevention Series, Paper 82)*. London: Home Office.

Coupe, R. T., & Kaur, S. (2005). The role of alarms and CCTV in detecting non-residential burglary. *Security Journal, 18*(2), 53–72.

Coupe, R. T., & Onodu, N. M. (1997). Evaluating the impact of CASE: An empirical comparison of retrospective and cross-sectional survey approaches. *European Journal of Information Systems, 6*(1), 15–24.

Coupe, T. (2017). Burglary decisions. In W. Bernasco, H. Elffers, & J.-L. van Gelder (Eds.), *The Oxford handbook on offender decision making*. Oxford: Oxford University Press.

Coupe, T., & Fox, B. H. (2015). A risky business: How do access, exposure and guardians affect the chances of non-residential burglars being seen? *Security Journal, 28*(1), 71–92.

Coupe, T., & Griffiths, M. (1996). *Solving residential burglary (Police Research Group Crime Detection and Prevention Services, Paper 77)*. London: Home Office.

Eck, J. E. (1979). *Managing case assignments: The burglary investigation decision model replication*. Washington, DC: Police Executive Research Forum.

Ericsson, U. (1995). Straight from the horse's mouth. *Forensic Update, 43*, 23–25.

Farrell, G., & Pease, K. (1993). *Once bitten, twice bitten: Repeat victimisation and its implications for crime prevention (Crime Prevention Unit Series, Paper 46)*. London: Home Office.

Farrell, G., Phillips, C., & Ken Pease, K. (1995). Like taking candy. Why does repeat victimisation occur? *The British Journal of Criminology, 35*(3), 384–399.

Hakim, S., & Shachmurove, Y. (1996). Spatial and temporal patterns of commercial burglaries. *American Journal of Economics and Sociology, 55*(4), 443–456.

Johnson, D. (2008). The near-repeat burglary phenomenon. In S. Chainey & J. Ratcliffe (Eds.), *Crime mapping case studies: Practice and research*. Chichester: Wiley.

Johnson, S. D., & Bowers, K. J. (2004). The burglary as clue to the future: The beginnings of prospective hot-spotting. *European Journal of Criminology, 1*(2), 237–255.

Johnson, S. D., Bowers, K. J., & Hirschfield, A. (1997). New insights into the spatial and temporal distribution of repeat victimisation. *The British Journal of Criminology, 37*(2), 224–241.

Johnson, S. D., Summers, L., & Pease, K. (2009). Offender as forager? A direct test of the boost account of victimisation. *Journal of Quantitative Criminology, 25*(2), 181–200.

Mirrlees-Black, C., & Ross, A. (1996). *Crime against retail and manufacturing premises: Findings from the 1994 Commercial Victimisation Survey*. London: Home Office.

Palmer, E. J., Holmes, A., & Hollin, C. R. (2002). Investigating burglars' decisions: Factors influencing target choice, method of entry, reasons for offending, repeat victimisation of a property and victim awareness. *Security Journal, 15*(1), 7–18.

Pease, K. (1998). *Repeat victimisation: Taking stock (Crime Detection and Prevention Series, Paper 90)*. London: Home Office.

Polvi, N., Looman, T., Humphries, C., & Pease, K. (1991). The time course of repeat burglary victimisation. *The British Journal of Criminology, 31*(4), 411–414.

Shover, N. (1991). Burglary. In M. Tonry & N. Morris (Eds.), *Crime and justice: An annual review of research* (pp. 73–113). Chicago: University of Chicago Press.

Smit, P., Meijer, R. F., & Groen, P.-P. J. (2004). Detection rates, an international comparison. *European Journal on Criminal Policy and Research, 10*(2–3), 225–253.

Spelman, W. (1995). Once bitten, then what? Cross-sectional and time-course explanations of repeat victimisation. *The British Journal of Criminology, 35*(3), 366–383.

Taylor, P., & Bond, S. (2012). *Crimes detected in England and Wales 2011/12 (Home Office Statistical Bulletin 08/12)*. London: Home Office.

Thanassoulis, E. (1995). Assessing police forces in England and Wales using data envelopment analysis. *European Journal of Operational Research, 87*(3), 641–657.

Townsley, M., Homel, R., & Chaseling, J. (2003). Infectious burglaries: A test of the near repeat hypothesis. *The British Journal of Criminology, 43*(3), 615–633.

Tseloni, A., & Pease, K. (2003). Repeat personal victimisation. 'Boosts' or 'flags'? *The British Journal of Criminology, 43*(1), 196–212.

Tseloni, A., & Pease, K. (2004). Repeat personal victimisation: Random effects, event dependence and unexplained heterogeneity. *The British Journal of Criminology, 44*(6), 931–945.

Wright, O. (2013). Urban to rural: An exploratory analysis of burglary and vehicle crime with a rural context (unpublished MSt thesis). University of Cambridge.

Homicide Resources, Solvability and Detection

Rebecca Riggs, Richard Timothy Coupe and Denis O'Connor

Introduction

As the least common and most serious offence (HMIC 2000), UK police services give homicide the highest priority, allocating considerable resources to its investigation and detection. Partly as a result of this, the majority of cases, over 90% (Taylor and Bond 2012), are solved. Those that remain unsolved, therefore, are cases that, despite considerable effort, it is not possible to detect. As such, homicide cases serve to illustrate the limits of incident solvability under conditions where resources are supplied to meet virtually every investigative need. For many other offences, in contrast, there is a risk that insufficient resources result in some solvable cases remaining undetected (see this chapter and Chapter "Investigative Activities, Resources and Burglary Detection"). This chapter has three principal aims. One is to understand homicide solvability by comparing the small subset of homicides that remain undetected with those that were detected in order to identify the ways, if any, in which their characteristics differ. In addition, however, given high detection levels, a second objective is to examine ways of measuring the solvability differences within the detected cases. It is likely that measures of evidence items that result from investigative actions and the numbers of actions needed and time taken to charge suspects will provide viable surrogate indicators of solvability differences, since it is to be expected that less solvable cases will require more investigative actions to be explored, actions will produce fewer evidence items and cases will take longer to solve. Output per unit of investigative effort needed to detect less solvable cases, therefore, can be expected to be lower even if this is offset by the larger number of actions undertaken as detectives explore all possible investigative avenues. A third

R. Riggs (✉)
Metropolitan Police, London, UK
e-mail: rriggs142@aol.com

R. T. Coupe · D. O'Connor
Cambridge University, Cambridge, UK

R. T. Coupe et al. (eds.), *Crime Solvability Factors*,
https://doi.org/10.1007/978-3-030-17160-5_15

objective is to assess the accuracy of pre-investigation, police grading of homicides in terms of their investigative costs. In England and Wales, using experience and knowledge of prior homicides, police forces grade cases in terms of the likely investigative resources needed to detect them and bring the culprits to justice. The accuracy of these grades will be critically evaluated to determine how well investigating officers' predictions about the investigative costs of homicides are borne out in practice.

The study also draws on data on the resourcing of homicide cases to assess the ways in which the investigative needs of different sorts of homicide vary. By examining investigative actions and the numbers of items of evidence or 'exhibits' they produce, the cost-effectiveness of investigating different types of homicide can be established. This can inform ways of improving the match of resources to homicide incidents as part of the planning of investigative strategies. It also offers potential for improved estimation of resource needs at the outset of homicide investigations and for planning the probable annual homicide resourcing requirements in different police jurisdictions. Finally, the study considers geographical contrasts in the ways homicides are investigated between the two jurisdictions.

The study is based on a population of homicides that took place in the English shire counties covered by the Thames Valley and Hampshire Police Forces during a six-year period. It, therefore, provides insight into the balance of different types of homicide, their investigation and outcomes. It is likely that homicide characteristics will differ from those of major cities in the UK and particularly London, where there may be more 'stranger' homicides and gang-related killings. The contrasts are likely to be even greater if the homicide population in this study were compared with North American cities or Caribbean islands, such as Trinidad and Tobago, where homicide rates are higher, gang-related homicide is more prevalent and detection rates for such homicides are far lower than for 'non-stranger' incidents (Richardson 2011).

Existing Studies of Homicide Investigation and Detection

Homicide Solvability and Detection

The characteristics of the offence, victim and temporo-spatial incidence can all have a bearing on whether incidents are solved. Homicide cases differ from other violent offences where victims can often provide the police with suspect descriptions or help identify assailants. Eyewitnesses, however, predictably boost detection rates (Welford and Cronin 1999). Good weather also improves detection rates (Welford and Cronin 1999), presumably reducing the loss of forensic samples as a result of, for instance heavy rain, particularly when offences take place out of doors.

Victim characteristics affect detection outcomes. Detection rates where there are younger victims tend to be lower (Addington 2006; Litwin 2004), while female or child victims, many of which are intra-family offences, were associated with better solvability and detection outcomes (Roberts 2007). Victim–offender relationships are an important solvability factor (Brown and Keppel 2012; Roberts 2014), and incidents where perpetrators and victims are strangers depress them (Innes 2002; Lee 2005; Ousey and Lee 2010; Roberts 2007). This is reflected in better detection rates when homicides occur at private locations (Welford and Cronin 1999). While more cases were solved if knives were used as the murder weapon (Roberts 2007), but homicides where handguns (Welford and Cronin 1999) and firearms (Litwin 2004; Ousey and Lee 2010; Roberts 2007) are used, however, have lower clearance rates, indicating an association with stranger homicide committed in non-private places. Regarding motivation, homicides where drugs were involved may either depress homicide detection (Welford and Cronin 1999) or boost it (Ousey and Lee 2010).

Particular geographical areas (Miethe and Regoeczi 2004) and groups are more likely to be involved in lethal violence as either offenders or victims. Homicide is the most important cause of death of young black men in US black communities characterised by deprivation and joblessness (Sampson and Wilson 2005) while young black men in London are also at high risk of involvement either as victims or offenders (Jackson 2010). While less important for detecting homicide than offence characteristics, both temporal and geographical circumstances had an important bearing on investigative outcomes (Trussler 2010). There is little research on geographical variation in arrests though gang-related murders in Trinidad particularly occur in the capital, Port o' Spain, whereas other types of murder which have higher detection rates are more widespread (Richardson 2011).

The circumstances, offence and victim characteristics of homicides have an important bearing on how easily the police are able to solve them. More of those occurring in private places are intra-familial, are indicative of circumstances where victims know perpetrators and tend to be more solvable. In the UK, 'self-solving' murders predominate and are easier to solve than 'hybrid' or 'who-done-it' cases (Innes 2002, 2007) but this is not the case in other jurisdictions, particularly those with higher homicide rates.

Serial homicides committed by the same offender and homicides with multiple offenders may not always be easier to solve. In the case of the latter, the joint charging of all those present in the UK, albeit controversial, can counter mutual offender blaming which hampers conviction. For the former, UK cases like those of Shipman, a medical doctor who was convicted of murdering 15 patients after a collation of statistics, indicating up to a possible 250 murders (Smith 2003), pointed towards wrongdoing and led to his arrest, and others like Sutcliffe, who murdered 13 prostitutes before being apprehended, demonstrate the challenges faced in detecting some serial offenders as well as sometimes exposing failings in investigative procedures.

This study aims to consider many of the offence and victim characteristics identified by earlier work in order to assess whether any of them affects detection outcomes under circumstances where almost every case is detected. The focus of the chapter, however, is on resourcing homicide investigations and evaluating police effort and cost-effectiveness in order to better appreciate the ways that homicide characteristics shape the length and funding of police actions, to assess the feasibility of measuring solvability using measures of resources when almost every case is detected, and determining the accuracy of police gradings of likely homicide costs at the start of the investigative process.

Homicide Investigations and Resourcing

A majority—70%—of UK homicides are 'self-solvers' where perpetrators are often self-evident and are identified within the first 24–48 h (Innes 2003). The others have no obvious suspects and Innes (2003) terms them 'who-dun-its'. They are far less solvable and their detection is heavily reliant on the senior investigating officer's inferences, hypotheses and intuition (Stelfox 2006; Wright 2008). This chapter aims to assess whether there are, in fact, solvability factors that characterise solved homicides, including these 'who-dun-it' cases, compared with unsolved ones.

Homicide investigations with successful outcomes are characterised by the application of 'Golden hour' principles which describe the early 'fast-track' actions to secure and preserve significant material at crime scenes and to pursue every avenue for collecting evidence. These include early arrests for forensic examinations of suspects, recording the testimony of dying persons or the seizure of CCTV footage, which may be lost or deleted if delayed (Riggs 2017). These actions help to meet the five principles for guiding investigations outlined in the Murder Investigation Manual (National Centre for Policing Excellence 2006), namely to preserve life, preserve the crime scene, secure evidence, identify the victim and to identify the suspect (Riggs 2017). Innes (2003) demonstrates the ways that evidence from forensic samples and victim, witness and suspect interviews is used by detectives to solve murders, given the problems encountered and solutions that are developed to arrive at successful outcomes. This chapter examines these solvability factors to determine the extent to which they reliably predict whether or not cases are solved. As well as the Murder Investigation Manual (National Centre for Policing Excellence 2006), murder investigators rely heavily on the 'Major Incident Room Standardised Administrative Procedures' (National Centre for Policing Excellence 2005) in undertaking homicide investigations (Riggs 2017).

Homicide is one of the most costly offences to investigate and the likely complexity of the investigation and probable scale of resources needed are estimated by the senior investigating officer managing the 'Major Crime Team' allocated to a murder case in the UK by grading them into one of four categories: A+, A, B, C. These reflect a hierarchy of complexity and resource demands from the least complex and lowest resources needed (C) to the greatest complexity and largest resources at A and A+. The A+ category was added following a murder case involving the kidnap and murder of a schoolgirl in 2011 in the jurisdiction commanded at that time by the third author of this chapter. This attracted intense media interest, some of it questionable in that it interfered with the investigation. Following an enquiry (Leveson 2012), the additional costs of murder cases of considerable interest to the media were recognised in the extra murder category. The homicide classification used in the USA—of first, second and third degree homicide—aids prosecutions and sentencing rather than investigative resource and command needs.

There has been no published study of murder investigation costs and how these vary by different types of case. This chapter uses data on investigative costs spent on homicide investigation and relates these to offence characteristics. It also considers the volume of investigative actions and evidence item outputs or 'exhibits' and relates these to resources used in order to determine which types of homicide cases require more and less resource and which are more and less cost-effectively investigated. The chapter will consider whether more complex cases with higher categorisations consume more resources so that the accuracy of detectives' initial estimates of case complexity and investigative effort can be assessed. Resource data can also be compared with solvability factors to enable an understanding—under conditions of what are, in effect, unlimited resources—of the extent to which the level of resources input to investigations improves the odds of detecting cases, when controlling for significant solvability factors.

Methodology

The study is based on a population of 290 homicides committed in the areas policed by Hampshire and Thames Valley Police Forces during April 2006–March 2016. Homicide data were drawn from the forces' joint Record Management System and the Home Office Large Major Enquiry System (HOLMES). The former was the source of homicide data. It receives updates from HOLMES, which is an investigative tool for senior investigating officers to record decisions, actions, murder categories and spending on each case. Data collection involved manual collation undertaken by the first author. A fuller set of variables is available for the 166 Thames Valley Police homicides and these are used to assess in greater detail how homicide characteristics affect detections, how well homicide grades predict costs compared with other homicide characteristics, and the effort, costs and cost-effectiveness of solving homicides.

Definitions

Homicides include murder, manslaughter, infanticide and corporate manslaughter. The definition of a detected case is an offender being charged. In certain cases, the UK Crown Prosecution Service (CPS) may not charge a suspect if there is insufficient evidence for a successful prosecution or because it is not in the public interest. The CPS may decide there should be no further action both before and after charge.

An action is an investigative activity undertaken by the murder investigation detectives to establish significant facts, preserve material or lead to the resolution of an investigation (NCPE 2005). Fast-track actions are similar but involve immediate execution, important facts, evidence preservation and early resolution (NCPE 2006). An exhibit is an item that is presented at court as evidence. Items are recorded on HOLMES and can be used to monitor case evidence. It could, for example, be CCTV footage, a murder weapon or a voice recording of a 999 emergency telephone call made at the time of a murder. Cost and certain other data were not available for every homicide case. There were 186 cases with every variable. The measure of costs used in this study involves only those connected with investigating cases, including staffing and forensic costs.

It is likely that more complex homicide cases will involve more actions and greater effort to achieve a positive outcome. More solvable cases, in contrast, should be detected more quickly using fewer resources, and more cost-effectively, using fewer resources and producing more evidence items per action and per unit cost.

Structure of the Analysis

The analysis is in five parts. There is a description of the characteristics of the homicide population; an examination of the ways in which detected and undetected cases differ in order to identify solvability factors and assess their relative importance compared with investigative effort in explaining detection outcomes; examination of measures of surrogate indicators of solvability and an assessment of the extent to which these depend on different solvability factors and investigative resources; an assessment of how well police homicide grades predict investigative costs; and a comparison of the two forces' homicide investigations.

Findings

Characteristics of Homicides

Most of this section is based on Thames Valley Police data. Most homicides—80% of them—were murders and almost all the others were manslaughters. A negligible proportion (0.6%) involved infanticide. Only 15% of suspects were strangers to victims and the other suspects were equally divided into those who were either friends or from the victim's family or a relative, including spouses or ex-partners (Fig. 1). Homicides with suspects who were strangers or acquaintances especially occurred in public whereas family, spouses or ex-family suspects committed the offences in private places (χ^2 (2, 152) = 31.43, $p = 0.000$, Cramer's $v = 0.45$): 61% of 'stranger' homicides took place in public compared with only 36% where suspects were acquaintances and 5% if from suspects' own families.

Not only do male suspects, as with most other crimes, dominate homicides, they also numerically outweigh male victims: 78% of suspects were male but only 59%

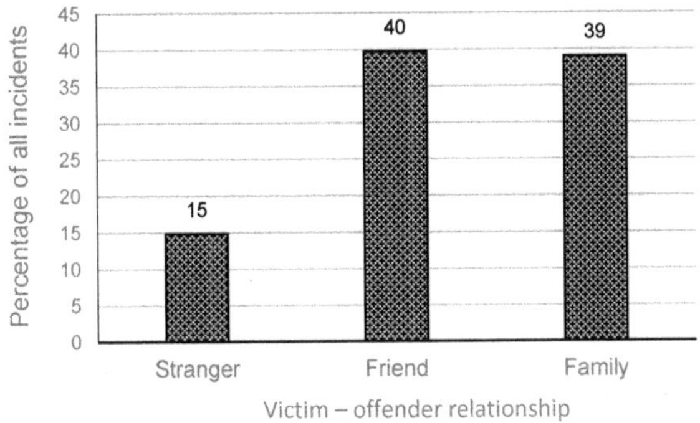

Fig. 1 Importance of homicides with different suspect–victim relationship

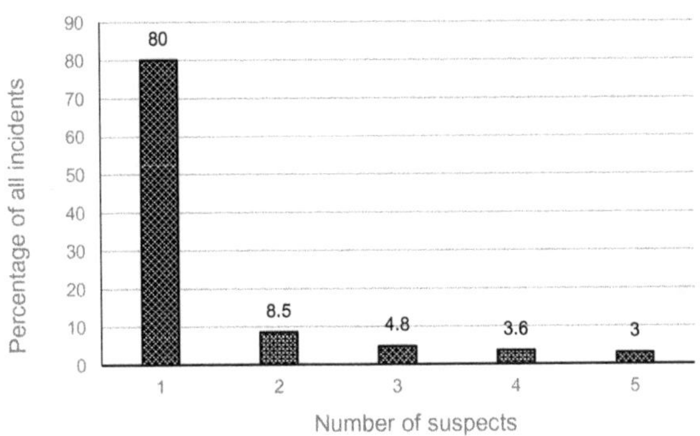

Fig. 2 Percentage of incidents with different numbers of suspects

of victims. 74% of suspects were already known to the police, particularly males, 78% compared with only 44% of females (χ^2 (1, 153) = 8.51, $p = 0.004$, Cramer's $v = 0.24$). More females than males, however, were suspected of manslaughter (χ^2 (1, 153) = 4.2, $p = 0.041$, Cramer's $v = 0.17$), 31% compared with 12% of males. As expected, more female suspects belonged to the same family as the victim as a partner, ex-partner or other relative (χ^2 (1, 153) = 3.9, $p = 0.048$, Cramer's $v = 16$), 63% compared with only 37% of male suspects.

8.5% of cases involved domestic violence (with only 46% male suspects cf. 81% of other homicides (χ^2 (1, 152) = 8.2, $p = 0.004$), 3% mental health (also especially affecting female suspects, (χ^2 (1, 145) = 4.39, $p = 0.036$)), 33% alcohol, and 23% involved drugs. Female suspects were also particularly involved in cases where mental health was an issue: 8% of such cases had female but only 1% male suspects (χ^2 (1, 152) = 4.96, $p = 0.026$, Cramer = 0.18).

Four-fifths of homicides involved a single suspect (Fig. 2) who tended to be older (37 years, sd = 15.1) than cases with two (33 years, sd = 13.6) or three or more suspects (26 years, sd = 6.6) (F (2, 151) = 4.3, $p = 0.015$). Female suspects were older (42 years cf. 34 years for males) (F (1, 152) = 5.2, $p = 0.024$).

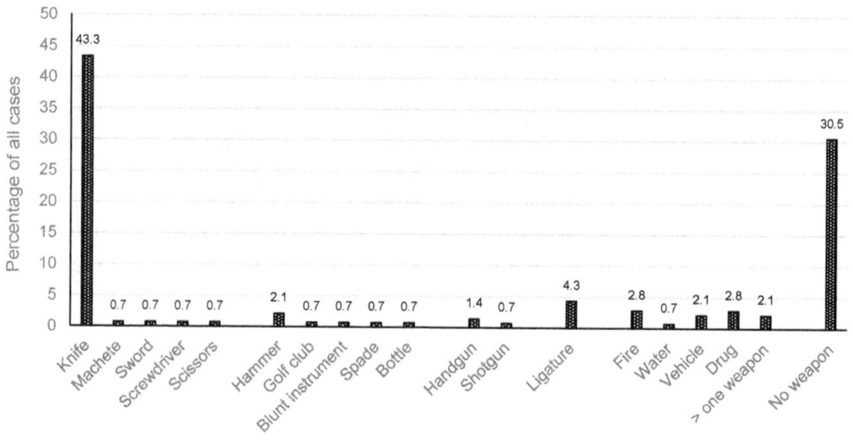

*n=141 (25 cases unknown)

Fig. 3 Weapons used in homicide for Thames Valley data*

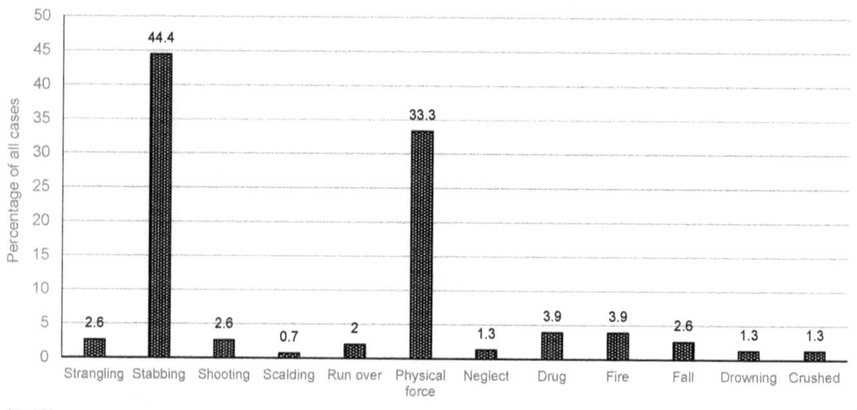

*n=153

Fig. 4 Homicide method for Thames Valley data*

A variety of weapons (Fig. 3) was used in the homicides and these are linked to homicide methods (Fig. 4). The largest group of weapons was used for stabbing, the method used the most, and these include knives, machete, sword, screwdriver and scissors. Physical force was the next most commonly used method (Fig. 4), accounting for a third of all offences, and this includes striking victims with blunt instruments, spade, golf club, bottle and hammers, and where weapons were not used. It is notable that shooting with firearms was less important than strangling using ligaments, as well as other means such as fire and drugs, which like falls and crushing, can be linked with manslaughter.

Suspect gender also differed in terms of weapons used. Men especially dispensed with their victims using bladed weapons, particularly knives. Far fewer female suspects stabbed victims, only 19% compared with 47% of males (χ^2 (1, 154) = 4.7, p = 0.031, Cramer's v = 0.17), and, as expected, fewer used a bladed weapon (χ^2 (1, 154) = 4.5, p = 0.035, Cramer's v = 0.17), 19% compared with 46% of males, or a knife, machete or sword (χ^2 (1, 154) = 3.6, p = 0.057, Cramer's v = 0.15), 19% compared with 44% of male suspects. Women suspects were, however, far more prone to be associated with homicides where victims were killed due to neglect, drugs, a fall, drowning, crushing, electrocution, scalding or from fire (χ^2 (1, 154) = 17.3, p = 0.000, Cramer's v = 0.34), many of which relate to manslaughter, with which more females were involved. Four and half times as many females, 50% compared with only 11% of males were suspected of killing by these means. It is notable that 12.5% of females but only 1.4% of males killed victims by administering drugs (χ^2 (1, 154) = 6.9, p = 0.009, Cramer's v = 0.21).

Resources, Investigations and Detections

The mean cost of homicide investigation was £27,960, but this was very varied indeed (sd = £38,720, n = 228). There was no significant difference between the amount spent on the seven per cent of offences that were not detected and the bulk that were detected (F = 2.10, p = 0.15, df = 1, 226). Investigative effort spent on cases similarly did not differ. On average, there were 262 investigative actions (sd = 483, n = 215) and 541 exhibits (sd = 582, n = 215) output per case and these did not differ between detected and undetected cases either (actions: F = 1.50, p = 0.22; exhibits: F = 0.16, p = 0.69; df = 1, 213). However, less money was spent per action (£183 cf. £44; F = 4.69, p = 0.032, df = 1, 191) and actions resulted in half as many exhibits (exhibits per action: 3.1 cf. 1.5; F = 4.26, p = 0.04, df = 1, 213) for undetected homicides, indicating that, as expected, investigative effort was far less fruitful for undetected than detected cases. So, no less was spent on undetected cases but actions were less costly and each action resulted in fewer exhibits. Detected cases involved more costly actions, each of which resulted in more evidence items or exhibits. It is likely that detected case exhibits were of better quality, something for which this study has no data. With homicides, every investigative activity with any potential for producing evidence must be carried out, and it is not surprising that fewer exhibits per action result for homicides which remain undetected. This helps accounts for the failure to solve these offences and is a reflection of their lower solvability. Sufficient investigative effort to ensure that no stone is left unturned must be and normally is input to every homicide case in England and Wales. Exhaustive investigations into every possible avenue of enquiry are likely to have pushed up the costs of dealing with undetected cases.

More costly cases predictably involved more investigative actions (Pearson's r = 0.50, p = 0.000, n = 193) and more exhibits (Pearson's r = 0.67, p = 0.000, n = 193). The larger the number of actions implemented, predictably, the greater the number of exhibits per case (Pearson's r = 0.82, p = 0.000, n = 193). More expensive investigations also involved more costly investigative actions (Pearson's r

$= 0.51, p = 0.000, n = 215$) and these resulted in more exhibits per action (Pearson's $r = 0.49$, $p = 0.000$, $n = 191$), which were more characteristic of detected rather than undetected cases ($F = 4.69, p = 0.032$, df $= 1, 191$), a mean of 3.1 for detected compared with 1.5 for undetected cases. Spending resources on more costly actions appears to have been productive as well as worthwhile in terms of detection outcomes. No evidence on the quality of different exhibits was collected.

Factors Affecting Detection Outcomes

Binary logistic regression analyses indicate that policing and incident variables both help explain detection outcomes. Number of investigative actions and the type of case in terms of whether the victim and offender/s were strangers, friends or family together account for a third of the variation in detection outcomes (Nagelkerke $R^2 = 0.333$; Table 1B). Each additional investigative action lowers the odds of a detection by 0.003% so that a homicide case at the top decile with 583 actions has 61% poorer odds of being solved (1:1.61) than one at the top of the lowest decile with 46 actions. Between 1000 and 2000 investigative actions more than halved the odds of a positive outcome but such large numbers of actions were carried out only on 2% of cases. Since there is little or no shortage of investigative funding, a larger number of investigative actions indicates that detectives explored a larger number of investigative avenues to attempt to solve cases which, in the event, remained undetected. Homicide type had a negative effect on solving cases. When police jurisdiction (Hampshire/Thames Valley) is included in the regression, costs are no longer significantly related to detection outcomes (Table 1A), given Thames Valley investigative costs are higher per case. Costs, in any case, have little or any effect in the light of funding levels which mean that many detected cases have high amounts of funding in order to accumulate sufficient evidence to charge a suspect. Under these circumstances, costs hinge on solvability and reflect the costs of producing the evidence needed to unlock case solvability.

Incidents where the murderer was a stranger to the victim perhaps surprisingly elevated the detection odds by twice as much as where the suspect and victim were family members or were friends and acquaintances. Homicide detections involving strangers where these do not involve gangs appear to be more solvable than expected. Whether Hampshire or TVP police jurisdiction had no bearing on detection outcomes, and excluding this from the model increased the significance of other factors, such as numbers of actions although exhibit numbers (items of evidence) still did not differ between detected and undetected incidents (Table 1B). Hence, both resources and case characteristics help account for whether cases were or were not detected.

Number of investigative actions and number of exhibits per action were significantly related ($r = -0.45$, $p = 0.000$, $n = 213$). A logistic regression which incorporates exhibits per action rather than actions (Table 2A) shows that this factor is also a strong indicator of solvability, negatively related to investigative actions, with

Table 1 Binary logistic regression with homicide detected /undetected the dependent variable (TVP and Hampshire data)

	(A) Dependent variable: homicide						(B) Dependent variable: homicide					
	Undetected/Detected						Undetected/Detected					
Variable	*B*	S.E.	Wald	df	Sig.	Exp (*B*)	*B*	S.E.	Wald	df	Sig.	Exp (*B*)
Investigative costs	0.000	0.000	2.2	1	0.137	1.000	0.000	0.000	3.64	1	0.056	1.000
Number of actions	−0.003	0.001	4.34	1	0.037	0.997	−0.003	0.001	5.88	1	0.015	0.997
Number of exhibits	0.002	0.001	1.15	1	0.284	1.002	0.002	0.001	1.23	1	0.267	1.002
Stranger offence N/Y	3.72	1.520	5.99	1	0.014	41.289	4.03	1.546	6.78	1	0.009	56.019
Friend N/Y	2.94	0.946	9.68	1	0.002	18.970	2.84	0.921	9.53	1	0.002	17.182
Family N/Y	3.30	0.954	11.94	1	0.001	27.049	3.23	0.933	11.98	1	0.001	25.237
Hampshire/TVP	1.07	0.707	2.28	1	0.131	2.906						
Constant	12.466	3.687	11.43	1	0.001	259,333.95	11.100	3.482	10.17	1	0.001	0.000
BLR model summary	Nagelkerke's $R^2 = 0.33$ Model: $\chi^2 = 29.11, p < 0.000$, 7 df; $n = 193$ 92% predicted correct						Nagelkerke's $R^2 = 0.31$ Model: $\chi^2 = 26.64, p < 0.000$, 6 df; $n = 193$ 93% predicted correct					

each unit increase in exhibits per action resulting in improved odds of detecting a homicide of 2.87:1.

Costs per investigative action were also significantly related to detection outcomes, with the cost per action higher for undetected cases (BLR with undetected/detected the dependent variable: $p = 0.034$; model: $\chi^2\,(1) = 9.08, p = 0.003$), accounting for 11% of variation in detection outcomes (Nagelkerke's $R^2 = 0.011$), with each additional cost per action of £1 boosting detections by 1% (Exp $(B) = 1.01$). When 'stranger/friend/family' variables are included, cost per action is not significant. Cost per action is a weaker solvability measure because of this and also because it explains less variation in detection outcomes than actions or exhibits per action.

Hence, exhibits produced per investigative action, numbers of actions and costs per action are indicators of the effort needed to 'unlock' homicide solvability and may be expected to be related to homicide solvability factors. As such, they may be viewed as the outcome variables for measuring solvability differences for the bulk of cases that were, in fact, detected. The more solvable the case, the more exhibits result from each investigative action and the more efficiently it can be detected. More solvable cases may be more efficiently investigated to produce sufficient evidence to charge suspects. Exhibits per action variable indicate how effectively exhibits may be generated by investigative actions while the number of actions that are undertaken reflects detectives' persistence in investigating less solvable incidents by undertaking actions which might result in useful evidence. For more solvable incidents, initial actions are more likely to provide the necessary evidence for a conviction. Undertaking more and more actions in order to attempt to solve cases remaining undetected appears to lower the costs per action as well as being less productive of exhibits. Costs are relatively high for undetected cases because many investigative but lower cost actions are undertaken, whereas a mixture of cases make up detected cases, ranging from the more easily detected which involve fewer actions and far less solvable ones which require many investigative actions that can elevate costs, particularly when these involve electronic and forensic evidence. Whether a Hampshire or Thames Valley Police investigation did not affect detection outcomes and importance of exhibits per action persisted (Table 2B).

Other Solvability Factors and Detection Outcomes

A fuller set of incident data and, hence, a wider range of solvability factors were available only for Thames Valley Police homicides (Table 3). While neither suspect or victim characteristics differed between undetected and detected incidents, there were significant differences in homicide type, the weapons used, the method of killing and in whether the case was linked to suspect's mental illness (Table 3).

A large number of different categorisations of these variables were tested in binary logistic regressions with detected/undetected as the dependent variable. Types of homicide other than murder boosted the odds of detection by 7.5:1 and cases where the suspect was from the same family as the victim improved detection odds by

Table 2 Binary logistic regression with homicide undetected/detected the dependent variable

	(A) Dependent variable: homicide Undetected/Detected						(B) Dependent variable: homicide Undetected/Detected					
Variable	*B*	S.E.	Wald	df	Sig.	Exp (*B*)	*B*	S.E.	Wald	df	Sig.	Exp (*B*)
Investigative costs	0.000	0.000	1.88	1	0.170	1.000	0.000	0.000	1.17	1	0.279	1.000
Exhibits per action	1.05	0.394	7.15	1	0.008	2.87	0.959	0.393	5.97	1	0.015	2.61
Number of exhibits	−0.001	0.001	1.20	1	0.273	0.999	−0.001	0.001	0.633	1	0.426	0.999
Stranger offence N/Y	3.07	1.34	5.22	1	0.022	21.54	2.89	1.35	4.61	1	0.032	18.07
Friend N/Y	2.34	0.90	6.81	1	0.009	10.35	2.43	0.92	7.04	1	0.008	11.42
Family N/Y	2.13	0.94	5.20	1	0.023	8.42	2.22	0.94	5.60	1	0.018	9.27
Hampshire /TVP							1.19	0.735	2.62	1	0.105	3.28
Constant	−9.15	3.33	7.53	1	0.006	2.000	−10.68	3.57	8.953	1	0.003	0.000
BLR model summary	Nagelkerke's $R^2 = 0.28$ Model: $\chi^2 = 24.64, p < 0.000$, 6 df 95% predicted correct						Nagelkerke's $R^2 = 0.32$ Model: $\chi^2 = 27.6, p < 0.000$, 7 df; 94% predicted correct					

Table 3 Differences in characteristics of undetected and detected homicides (Thames Valley data: $n = 166$)

	Variable	Test value	Cramer's v	p value	df (N)	Not detected: mean or %	Detected: mean or %
	Suspect known to police v. unknown	$\chi^2 = 0.01$	0.01	0.93	1 (162)	9%	91%
Suspect characteristics	Mean suspect age	$F = 0.04$		0.84	1, 153	36	35
	Suspect gender male v. female or male and female	$\chi^2 = 1.87$	0.11	0.17	(155)	9%	91%
	Suspect female v. male or male and female	$\chi^2 = 2.3$	0.12	0.13	(155)	4%	96%
	Suspect male + female v. male or female	$\chi^2 = 0.08$	0.02	0.77	1 (155)	4%	96%
	Number of suspects	$F = 1.86$		0.18	1, 164	1.1	1.5
Victim characteristics	Victim male v. female	$\chi^2 = 0.2.0$	0.11	0.16	(166)	13%	97%
	Victim age	$F = 1.35$		0.25	1, 164	42	36
Homicide type	Murder v. other types	$\chi^2 = 21.6$		0.000	1 (166)	33%	67%
	Manslaughter v. others	$\chi^2 = 23.9$	0.38	0.000	1 (166)	5%	95%
	Family, spouse, ex-partner v. others	$\chi^2 = 3.7$		0.055	1 (166)	14%	86%
	Stranger v. others	$\chi^2 = 0.13$	0.03	0.72	1 (166)	10%	90%
	Acquaintance v. others	$\chi^2 = 1.6$	0.10	0.21	1 (166)	13%	87%
Weapon	Shooting and stabbing v. others	$\chi^2 = 8.6$	0.23	0.003	1 (166)	13%	87%
	Handgun, shotgun, knife, machete, sword v. others	$\chi^2 = 7.7$	0.22	0.005	1 (166)	17%	83%
	Bladed weapon v. others	$\chi^2 = 7.2$	0.21	0.007	1 (166)	16%	84%

(continued)

Table 3 (continued)

	Variable	Test value	Cramer's v	p value	df (N)	Not detected: mean or %	Detected: mean or %
	Machete, sword v. others	$\chi^2 = 6.18$	0.19	0.013	1 (166)	16%	84%
	Handgun or shotgun v. others	$\chi^2 = 0.37$	0.05	0.540	1 (166)	11%	89%
	Hammer, golf club, spade, axe, blunt instrument v. other weapons	$\chi^2 = 1.27$	0.09	0.260	1 (166)	10%	90%
	Bottle v. other weapons	$\chi^2 = 0.12$	0.03	0.730	1 (166)	11%	89%
	Drug v. other	$\chi^2 = 4.53$	0.17	0.033	1 (166)	10%	90%
Homicide method	Shooting and stabbing v. others	$\chi^2 = 8.6$	0.23	0.003	1 (166)	13%	87%
	Shooting v. others	$\chi^2 = 0.49$	0.06	0.500	1 (155)	11%	89%
	Stabbing v. others	$\chi^2 = 7.4$	0.21	0.006	1 (166)	16%	84%
	Strangling v. others	$\chi^2 = 0.49$	0.06	0.480	1 (166)	11%	89%
	Neglect, drugs, fall, drown, crushing, electrocution, scalding and fire v. others	$\chi^2 = 14.82$	0.30	0.000	1 (166)	7%	93%
Other homicide characteristics	Public v. private scene	$\chi^2 = 0.14$	0.03	0.710	1 (166)	12%	88%
	Domestic violence v. other	$\chi^2 = 0.08$	0.02	0.78	1 (162)	8%	92%
	Mental health involved v. not	$\chi^2 = 7.28$	0.22	0.007	1 (166)	33%	67%
	Alcohol involved v. not	$\chi^2 = 0.11$	0.03	0.74	(111)	11%	89%
	Drugs involved v. not	$\chi^2 = 0.09$	0.03	0.76	(111)	11%	89%

4.73 times (Table 4A). Where the method of killing involved neglect, drugs, a fall, drowning, electrocution, scalding or fire, it depressed the odds of a detection by odds of almost 4:1.

There was a tendency for cases with larger numbers of suspects to improve the detection odds. Together, these factors explained 36% of the variation in detection outcomes (Table 4A).

As expected, adding investigative costs into the regression adds little in terms of explanation of detection outcomes (Table 4B), since all investigations are fully funded and investigative actions continue on undetected cases until all avenues have been exhausted. Hence resources do not help account for whether or not homicide cases are detected.

With the very high detection rates of 89.2%, the five solvability factors identified help explain why a small number of residual cases are not solved. Given the high priority placed on solving homicide cases, whatever the greater challenges and resource demands of less solvable cases, most of them were solved. It seems likely that variation in solvability factors ceases to be as discriminating under conditions of near-to-full resourcing of case investigation.

Summary Solvability Score and Detected/Undetected Cases

A summary solvability score value for each case was calculated by summing the product of each of the five significant variables' case values and the odds-ratios shown in Table 4. 89.2% of cases in the Thames Valley Police jurisdiction were detected (93% detected overall for both jurisdictions combined) and, as expected, detected cases had a far higher mean score than undetected cases (2.8 cf. 1.8, F (1, 164) = 50.8, $p = 0.000$). Three quarters of incidents had scores greater than 7.5 and there was a 97% probability of detecting cases in excess of this score (Fig. 5). The solvability score also provides a discriminating indicator for the more difficult 18% and the most difficult to detect 7% of cases with only a 42% chance of being detected (Fig. 5).

Investigative costs are not significantly related to detection outcomes (BLR: p = 0.25), whereas solvability score is (BLR: p = 0.000, Exp (B) = 1.33), with each additional unit increment in solvability boosting the detection odds by 33%. Given virtually unlimited funding to ensure cases are solved, if at all possible, investigative costs tend to respond to solvability demands.

The more solvable the case (with higher solvability scores), the shorter the time taken to charge a suspect (Fig. 6a; F (2, 157) = 16.54, $p = 0.000$), and the fewer investigative actions undertaken per case (Fig. 6d; F (2, 160) = 36.76, $p = 0.000$). The relationships between higher solvability scores and higher costs of an investigative action (Fig. 6b; F (2, 74) = 0.58, $p = 0.56$) and more exhibits per action (Fig. 6c; F (2, 121) = 0.75, $p = 0.48$) were not significant, a probable reflection of missing cases.

Time to charge and number of investigative actions per case, therefore, show the strongest relationship and largest differences with different levels of case solvability.

Table 4 Binary logistic regression with homicide undetected/detected the dependent variable (TVP data only)

	(A) Dependent variable: homicide Undetected/Detected						(B) Dependent variable: homicide Undetected/Detected					
Variable	*B*	S.E.	Wald	df	Sig.	Exp (*B*)	*B*	S.E.	Wald	df	Sig.	Exp (*B*)
Murder v. other types	2.02	0.65	9.60	1	0.002	7.50	1.87	0.66	7.98	1	0.005	6.50
Others v. family, spouse, ex-partner	1.55	0.73	4.49	1	0.034	4.73	1.54	0.73	4.45	1	0.035	4.68
Other methods v. neglect, drugs, fall, drown, crushing, electrocution, scalding and fire	−1.35	0.65	4.38	1	0.036	0.258	−1.20	0.67	3.25	1	0.072	0.30
Other weapons v. hammer, golf club, spade, axe, blunt instrument	−2.22	1.05	4.49	1	0.034	0.109	−2.13	1.05	4.15	1	0.042	0.12
Number of suspects	1.23	0.66	3.45	1	0.063	3.433	1.14	0.67	2.86	1	0.091	3.12
Investigative costs							0.00	0.00	0.55	1	0.459	1.00
Constant	−0.523	1.98	0.07	1	0.791	0.59	−63	1.98	0.10	1	0.751	0.53
BLR model summary	Nagelkerke's $R^2 = 0.36$ Model: $\chi^2 = 32.31, p < 0.000$, 5 df, $n = 167$ 90% predicted correct						Nagelkerke's $R^2 = .37$ Model: $\chi^2 = 33.56, p < 0.000$, 6 df; $n = 165$ 90% predicted correct					

Table 5 Linear regression with investigative actions the dependent variable (Thames Valley Police data only)

	(A) Dependent variable: investigative actions					(B) Dependent variable: investigative actions				
Variable	*B*	S.E.	Beta	*t*	Sig.	*B*	S.E.	Beta	*t*	Sig.
Constant	−240.49	200.66		−1.20	0.233	51.82	207.03		0.25	0.803
Detected/Undetected						−256.45	70.03	−0.29	−3.66	0.000
Other methods v. shooting	316.45	94.39	0.26	3.35	0.001	340.49	90.09	0.28	3.78	0.000
Blunt instrument, hammer, golf club, spade and axe v. others	246.59	63.38	0.30	3.89	0.000	201.03	61.60	0.24	3.26	0.001
Other types v. murder	117.49	58.80	0.16	2.00	0.048	169.55	57.76	0.23	2.94	0.004
Other types v. family-partner-ex-partner	−180.65	47.51	−0.42	−3.80	0.000	−135.17	46.90	−0.31	−2.88	0.005
Others v. acquaintance	−91.39	47.32	−0.21	−1.93	0.056	−45.73	46.74	−0.11	−0.98	0.330
Model summary	$R = 0.55$ adjusted $R^2 = 0.28$ Model: F (5, 120) = 10.52 $p < 0.000$					$R = 0.61$ adjusted $R^2 = 0.34$ Model: F (6, 119) = 11.90 $p < 0.000$				
	(C) Dependent variable: investigative actions					(D) Dependent variable: investigative actions				
Variable	*B*	S.E.	Beta	*t*	Sig.	*B*	S.E.	Beta	*t*	Sig.
Constant	−224.66	202.26		−1.11	0.269	81.98	208.8		0.39	0.695
Detected/Undetected						−263.06	70.25	−0.30	−3.75	0.000
Other methods v. shooting	300.12	97.24	0.25	3.09	0.003	317.76	92.44	0.26	3.44	0.001
Blunt instrument, hammer, golf club, spade and axe v. others	250.44	63.72	0.30	3.93	0.000	205.36	61.69	0.25	3.33	0.001
Other types v. murder	113.65	59.16	0.15	1.92	0.057	165.39	57.84	0.22	2.86	0.005
Other types v. family-partner-ex-partner	−179.19	47.64	−0.41	−3.76	0.000	−131.90	46.96	−0.30	−2.81	0.006
Others v. acquaintance	−95.77	47.80	−0.22	−2.00	0.047	−50.81	46.94	−0.12	−1.08	0.281
Investigative costs	0.000	0.001	0.06	0.72	0.472	0.001	0.001	0.084	1.08	0.281
Model summary	$R = 0.55$ adjusted $R^2 = 0.27$ Model: F (6, 119) = 8.82 $p < 0.000$					$R = 0.62$ adjusted $R^2 = 0.35$ Model: F (7, 118) = 10.39 $p < 0.000$				

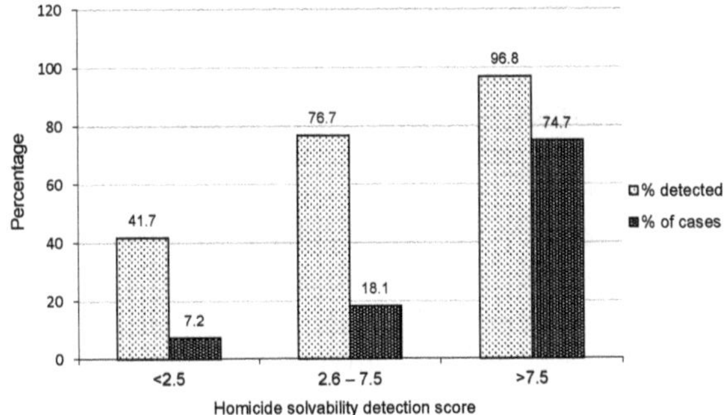

Fig. 5 Homicide summary solvability score by % of cases detected and by % of study cases

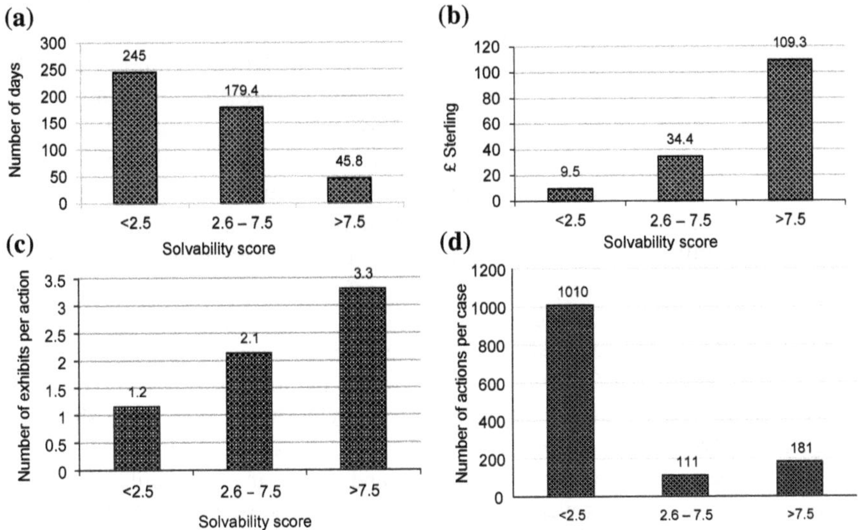

Fig. 6 Summary solvability score by **a** time to charge a suspect, **b** costs per investigative action, **c** exhibits per action, **d** number of investigative actions per case (TVP data only)

Unlike costs per action and exhibits per action, they also differed between undetected and detected cases. As such, they may offer the best prospects as surrogate measures of solvability differences between the 89% of detected cases.

The following sections, therefore, evaluate how well these solvability indicators explain differences in solvability among the 89.2% of detected cases as well as between detected and undetected cases. The sections examine which homicide characteristics best explain variations in these solvability indicators.

Investigative Outputs and Solvability

The analyses above confirmed that *number of investigative actions* and *cost per action* help differentiate between undetected and detected cases and appear to be viable indicators of solvability differences between detected cases, which constitute the majority of the homicides in the study population. *Time taken to detect* cases appears to be a supplementary solvability measure, since it seems reasonable that more solvable cases would be detected more quickly and this did differ between undetected and detected cases and was strongly associated with solvability score. For analysis using both jurisdictions' data, *number of exhibits per action* was also significantly lower for undetected cases and this is also a viable candidate indicator of solvability differences among detected cases.

In this section, these four candidate solvability indicators are examined to determine which may be most easily predicted from solvability factors, by applying best-fit linear regressions to Thames Valley Police data, for which there is a fuller variable set. Unlike the solvability factors considered above, which are based on a comparison between detected and undetected cases, the basis for these solvability factors will be the ability to identify solvability differences across all cases, within the subset of detected cases as well as between them and undetected incidents. In this way, the indicators enable differences in case solvability to be predicted under circumstances where there is full or near-to-full investigative funding and nine-tenths of cases are detected.

Investigative actions. On the basis of applying a best-fit linear regression that excludes whether or not detected, four variables explain 28% (Table 5A: $R^2 = 0.28$; $F\ (5,\ 120) = 10.52$, $p = 0.000$) of the variation in numbers of actions, with cases involving murder (as opposed to manslaughters and a few infanticide cases), shooting and cases involving neglect, drugs, falling, drowning, crushing, electrocution, scalding and fire increasing the number of actions and depressing solvability. Incidents where suspects and victims were acquaintances or members or former members of the same families were more solvable and were associated with fewer investigative actions. When detected/undetected is included in the regression model, it increased the amount of explained variation in detection outcomes by 6%, so that 34% (adjusted $R^2 = 0.344$) in total was accounted for (Table 5B). The other factors retained their significant association with action numbers apart from whether or not victims and offenders were acquaintances (Table 5B). Hence, investigative actions not only help explain which cases are detected and undetected but are likely to be viable indicators of solvability differences between detected cases as well, since the 'number of actions' variable is linked with factors that have been shown in this and other studies to help explain which homicides are detected.

The inclusion of investigative costs in the regression equations indicates that these have no effect on actions as a measure of solvability across cases, whether or not the variable 'case detected/undetected' is taken into account (Table 5C, D). Nor do investigative costs help explain variation in actions for the major subset of detected cases alone. This is hardly to be expected since fewer, more expensive actions were undertaken for the more solvable cases and more, less expensive ones were carried out for the less solvable ones, indicating a tendency for costs to be levelled whatever the differences in solvability.

Exhibits per action. On the basis of applying a best-fit linear regression, three variables predict 9% (Table 6A, $R = 0.34$; adjusted $R^2 = 0.09$; F (3, 120) = 5.24, $p = 0.002$) of the variation in numbers of exhibits per action, with additional suspect numbers boosting them (resulting in higher solvability) and a murder (rather than manslaughter or infanticide) and cases with stranger suspects tending to depress solvability. While each additional exhibit per action triples the odds of detection for data for both forces together (Exp (B) = 3.06, $p = 0.000$) and explains 17% of the variation in detection outcomes (Nagelkerke's $R^2 = 0.173$), exhibits per action are not significantly related to detections for the TVP data alone. When detected/not detected is included in a regression, it therefore fails to increase the statistical explanation of variation in numbers of exhibits per action (Table 6B).

As for investigative actions, the inclusion of investigative costs in the regressions had no effect on exhibits per action, whether or not the variable 'case detected/undetected' is included in the equations (Table 6C, D). Nor do investigative costs help explain variation in actions for the major subset of detected cases alone. As for actions, this would not be expected since cases' solvability differences tend to iron out the resources needed with greater solvability linked with fewer, targeted but expensive actions and lower solvability demanding the investigation of more less promising avenues of enquiry using less costly 'exploratory' actions.

Costs per action. Using data for both forces, the costs per investigative action are higher for detected than undetected cases (F (1, 211) = 3.71, $p = 0.055$), averaging £165 compared with only £44 for undetected cases. Trying various alternative investigative actions which produce insufficient evidence or evidence of too poor quality to enable detection evidently costs less per action than collecting evidence that contributes to cases that are detected. Applying binary logistic regression, costs per action explain 11% of the variation in detection outcomes (Nagelkerke's $R^2 = 0.109$, $n = 213$) and each £1 of additional cost per action boosts the odds of detection by 1% ($p = 0.034$, Exp (B) = 1.01; model: Chi-square (1) = 9.08, $p = 0.003$).

Similarly, linear regression applied to both forces' data confirms the importance of this indicator. For TVP data, only a single variable, number of suspects, helps explain 7% of the variation in costs per action ($R^2 = 0.066$, $t = 2.53$, $p = 0.014$; model: F (1, 75) = 6.38, $p = 0.014$). When detected/undetected is included in the linear regression equation, it shows no significant relationship with costs per action ($t = -94$, $p = 0.35$) although the importance of suspect numbers persists ($t = 2.44$, $p = 0.017$) as does the proportion of variation in costs per action it explains ($R^2 = 0.065$).

Time taken to detect cases. The speed with which homicides were detected averaged 98 days but varied considerably, ranging between zero and 1131 days (Fig. 7). Half were solved within 4 days, 60% within 10 days and 80% within 150 days. Only 5% took over a year to detect. The other 7% of undetected homicides continued to remain open until solved.

Table 6 Linear regression with number of exhibits per action the dependent variable (TVP data only)

	(A) Dependent variable: exhibits per action					(B) Dependent variable: exhibits per action				
Variable	*B*	S.E.	Beta	*t*	Sig.	*B*	S.E.	Beta	*t*	Sig.
Constant	9.29	2.47		3.76	0.000	10.84	3.03		3.58	0.000
Detected/Undetected						−1.16	1.30	−0.08	−0.89	0.375
Number of suspects	0.74	0.28	0.24	2.68	0.009	0.70	0.28	0.22	2.49	0.014
Murder v. other types	−2.64	1.09	−2.21	−2.44	0.016	−2.83	1.11	−0.23	−2.56	0.012
Strangers v. others	−1.55	0.87	−0.16	−1.79	0.076	−1.47	0.87	−0.15	−1.68	0.095
Model summary	$R = 0.34$ adjusted $R^2 = 0.09$ Model: F (3, 120) = 5.24 $p < 0.002$					$R = 0.35$ adjusted $R^2 = 0.09$ Model: F (4, 119) = 4.12 $p < 0.004$				
	(C) Dependent variable: exhibits per action					(D) Dependent variable: exhibits per action				
Variable	*B*	S.E.	Beta	*t*	Sig.	*B*	S.E.	Beta	*t*	Sig.
Constant	9.29	2.47		3.76	0.000	7.35	3.32		2.22	0.029
Detected/Undetected						1.16	1.32	−0.08	−0.88	0.379
Number of suspects	0.74	0.28	0.23	2.60	0.010	0.70	0.29	0.22	2.45	0.016
Murder v. other types	−2.65	1.10	−0.21	−2.41	0.017	−2.83	1.12	−0.23	−2.53	0.013
Strangers v. others	−1.55	0.87	−0.16	−1.78	0.078	−1.47	0.88	−0.15	−1.68	0.097
Investigative costs	0.00	0.00	0.01	0.08	0.936	0.00	0.00	0.00	−0.001	0.999
Model summary	$R = 0.34$ adjusted $R^2 = 0.09$ Model: F (4, 119) = 3.90 $p < 0.005$					$R = 0.35$ adjusted $R^2 = 0.09$ Model: F (5, 118) = 3.27 $p < 0.008$				

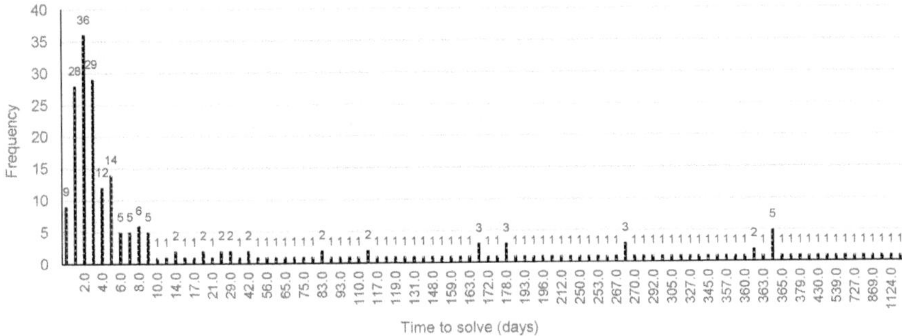

Fig. 7 Frequency chart of number of days taken to charge a suspect

Numbers of actions and exhibits increased markedly the longer cases took to solve (time to detect v. actions: Pearson's $r = 0.46$, $p = 0.000$, $n = 186$; time to detect v. exhibits: Pearson's $r = 0.38$, $p = 0.000$, $n = 186$). The most marked differences, however, are between cases that take over a year to detect (Actions: F (1, 184) = 25.73, p = 0.000; Exhibits: F (1, 184) = 12.66, p = 0.000): number of actions for cases taking longer than a year to detect averaged 971 compared with 211 for less than a year; the equivalent numbers of exhibits were 1183 and 526. Cases that took longer to solve also involved more actions, on average to produce an exhibit (Pearson's $r = 0.20$, $p = 0.006$, $n = 186$). Hence cases that took longer to solve required more investigative effort and this indicates that they were less easily solved. This tends to reinforce the inference that investigative action numbers and number of exhibits per action are useful indicators of solvability differences among all homicides, including those that are detected. The findings are also in line with historic triage findings (Eck 1983). There is no significant relationship between days taken to charge suspects and investigative costs (Pearson's $r = -0.16$, $p = 0.15$, $n = 86$), nor between time to charge and forensic costs (Pearson's $r = -0.14$, $p = 0.17$, $n = 98$ for TVP data only; Pearson's $r = -0.12$, $p = 0.11$, $n = 182$ for TVP and Hampshire data); forensic and total investigative costs are positively related (Pearson's $r = -0.58$ $p = 0.000$, $n = 66$).

Pearson multiple regression indicates that the only variable that helps explain number of days that detected cases were investigated prior to clearance was number of investigative actions ($B = 0.156$, $t = 3.21$, $p = 0.002$). Although number of exhibits was correlated with time taken to solve cases with a medium effect size (Pearson $r = 0.40$, $p = 0.000$, $n = 193$), this is strongly related to numbers of actions (Pearson $r = 0.82$, $p = 0.000$, $n = 193$). The relationship between actions and investigative time persisted when controlling for exhibits (Pearson partial $r = 0.27$, $p = 0.000$, $n = 162$) whereas that between exhibits and investigative time disappears when controlling for actions (Pearson partial $r = 0.03$, $p = 0.742$, $n = 162$), indicating that actions influence time to detect and exhibits are correlated with investigative time only because of their correlation with actions.

The application of a best-fit linear regression to detected cases indicates that five variables explain 26% ($R = 0.53$; adjusted $R^2 = 0.26$; F (5, 138) = 10.87,

$p = 0.000$) of the variation in the time taken to detect cases, measured in terms of charging a suspect. Cases other than murder (i.e. manslaughter cases and those involving family and spouses) took longer to detect, as did cases involving older and female suspects, those involving younger victims and cases not involving domestic violence (Table 7A). Time taken to charge a suspect appears, therefore, to be a viable solvability measure for detected cases. When investigative costs were included in the regression model, the importance of these solvability factors persisted. Investigative costs were not significantly related to time taken to charge, a finding which is in line with the results for regression models with investigative actions and exhibits per action as the dependent variables.

The tendency for continuing investigations of difficult-to-solve cases to push overall costs up with increasing numbers of actions, albeit lower cost actions, has been noted above and contrasted with the higher costs of actions associated with more solvable cases.

Summary for Indicators of Solvability for Detected Cases

Number of actions, number of exhibits per action, costs per action and time to charge a suspect may all be viable indicators of solvability, since all help discriminate between undetected and detected homicide cases and a plausible argument exists for their effects on how easily detected cases are solved. In terms of using solvability factors to predict the solvability of all cases, rather than just to predict the ones which remain undetected due to insufficient inherent solvability, number of investigative actions and time to charge are the most promising. One reason for this is that the proportion of variation in these indicators that can be explained by homicide characteristics is far higher for number of actions (28%) and for time to charge (26%) than for exhibits per action (9%) or costs per action (7%). Of these, time to charge is an indicator only for detected cases. Investigative actions per case are the best alternative (to the solvability measure based on the solvability factors that explain undetected/detected case outcomes) solvability indicator for the full range of cases: more actions must be undertaken for less solvable cases and those that it is not possible to solve. Exhibits per action and cost per action may be viable indicators of solvability, since less solvable cases might also be expected to be less productive in terms of exhibits produced per investigative action so that costs per action will tend to be lower, the less solvable the case. However, these two indicators cannot be as easily predicted as can number of actions (or time to charge), since identifiable homicide characteristics explained so little of their variation.

The only common solvability factor between 'number of actions' and 'time to charge' was whether or not the offence was a murder. The significant factors for action numbers were whether the homicide involved family or partners, whether it involved acquaintances, which made incidents more solvable, and whether the method was shooting or involved either a blunt instrument, hammer, golf club, spade or axe, which depressed solvability. In contrast, younger victims, older suspects and

Table 7 Linear regression with time to charge a suspect the dependent variable (TVP data only)

	(A) Dependent variable: time to charge					(B) Dependent variable: time to charge				
Variable	*B*	S.E.	Beta	*t*	Sig.	*B*	S.E.	Beta	*t*	Sig.
Constant	60.55	102.39		0.59	0.555	37.87	148.25		0.26	0.799
Victim age	−1.45	0.59	−0.21	−2.43	0.016	−2.51	0.89	−0.31	−2.84	0.006
Mean suspect age	2.10	0.78	0.23	2.70	0.008	2.56	1.14	0.25	2.25	0.027
Suspect gender: other v. female	76.41	32.62	0.18	2.34	0.021	207.87	50.33	0.40	4.13	0.000
Murder v. other types	−139.32	26.95	−0.38	−5.17	0.000	−231.11	44.54	−0.47	−5.19	0.000
Domestic violence link Y/N	80.50	35.31	0.17	2.28	0.024	120.54	48.76	0.23	2.47	0.016
Investigative costs						0.00	0.00	0.04	0.43	0.667
Model summary	$R = 0.53$ adjusted $R^2 = 0.26$ Model: F (5, 138) = 10.87 $p = 0.000$					$R = 0.69$ adjusted $R^2 = 0.43$ Model: F (6, 74) = 10.88 $p = 0.000$				

female suspects were associated with longer, less solvable cases, while a domestic violence element in a case made it more easily solved.

The number of investigative actions needed to solve cases is a key indicator of the effort required to 'unlock' homicide solvability: less solvable cases need more actions to bring a suspect to charge. Less solvable cases also involve less productive actions that result in fewer exhibits per action; because these actions are cheaper but there are more of them, investigative costs may be a poorer indicator of solvability differences. However, less solvable incidents which involve more but less productive actions take longer to detect and some remain undetected, so that time to charge suspects is also an indicator that relates to solvability factors.

Therefore, differences in solvability of the nine-tenths of cases that were detected may be better understood by measuring the resources (in terms of costs, investigative actions) needed to unlock the solvability and by relating these measures to homicide characteristics. Hence, the varied solvability of different homicide incidents influences the amount of effort required to unlock individual case solvability, so that the factors which are significantly related to investigative effort indicate solvability differences.

Summary solvability measures for each of 'investigative action' solvability and 'time to charge suspect' solvability were calculated by summing the product of each solvability indicator's significant solvability factor's odds ratio [as shown in Tables 5 (actions) and 7 (time to charge)] and individual data case values, as for the detection solvability index above.

'Action solvability' is unrelated to detection outcome (F (1, 124) = 0.61, p = 0.44) but is correlated with detection solvability variations (Spearman's rho (126) = −0.28, p = 0.001). Time to charge solvability is also related to detection solvability (detected cases only) (Spearman's rho (146) = 0.25, p = 0.002). 'Investigative action solvability' predicts investigative costs (Spearman's = 0.50, p = 0.000, n = 79) but 'time to charge solvability' does not (Spearman's = −0.11, p = 0.33, n = 81). Action solvability and time to charge solvability are not related (Spearman's rho = 0.003, p = 0.98, n = 116).

Resources and Detectives' Homicide Categories

Homicide cases in England and Wales are provided with an initial grade of A, B or C to reflect the expected investigative costs. Grading cases enables the estimation of the resources needed to investigate and solve cases at the outset in terms of personnel and expertise. As indicated above, grade A covers cases likely to be more expensive, B notably less, whereas C includes cases which, on the basis of experience, are viewed as being easier to solve and, therefore, less costly. The latter would typically include incidents involving spouses, family members, including infanticide, the former, stranger and other homicides.

Over three quarters of cases were graded as C and two-thirds of the rest were graded as B (Fig. 8). Only 14% received an A grade. A grade of A+ is allocated to cases likely to generate media interest but none of the cases in this study was allocated this grade. The objective in this section is to determine how accurately the grades predict the actual investigative costs and, using Thames Valley Police data, forensic costs. TVP data will be used to establish what factors influence investigative costs in order to assess whether the bases for allocating grades based on experience can be improved by supplementing this with statistical evidence.

How Well Do Homicide Grades Predict Investigative Costs?

Average costs of investigating cases were £27,960 but differed considerably (Fig. 9) with the lowest £224 and the highest £256,300. For Thames Valley data (the regressions of cost on homicide variables are based on TVP data only), the mean was £28,970, with the lowest £153, and the second highest £145,300 with a single outlier at £200,300. More resources (total investigative costs) were used ($F = 45.96$, $p = 0.000$, $\text{df} = 2, 191$), more actions carried out ($F = 29.92$ $p = 0.000$, $\text{df} = 2, 212$) and more exhibits produced ($F = 43.62, p = 0.000$, $\text{df} = 2, 212$), the higher the homicide category (Fig. 10a, b). Senior investigating officers' initial assessments of homicide complexity and likely investigative demands are generally sound, given that similar, very high proportions of every category of homicide are detected.

Time spent investigating did not differ between category B and C homicides, with both averaging 85 days, but category A cases took markedly longer with a mean of 232 days ($F = 4.76$, $p = 0.01$, $\text{df} = 2, 191$). There is no significant relationship between investigative costs and time taken to charge suspects (measured in days; Pearson's $r = -0.16, p = 0.15, n = 86$ for TVP data; Pearson's $r = -0.12, p = 0.11$, $n = 182$ for TVP and Hampshire data). Total costs were predictably also strongly related to forensic costs ($r = 0.58, p = 0.000$; data for TVP only), which account for an average of 57% of all investigative costs. Forensic costs also differed markedly between homicide grades (Fig. 10a, $F\ (2, 99) = 17.93, p = 0.000$), though like overall

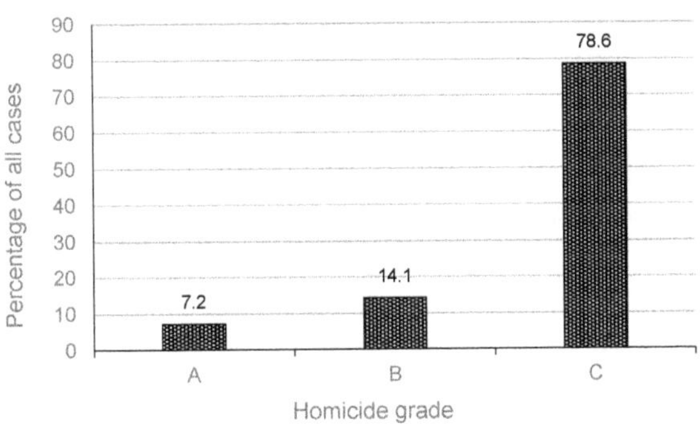

Fig. 8 Proportion of homicides with different grades

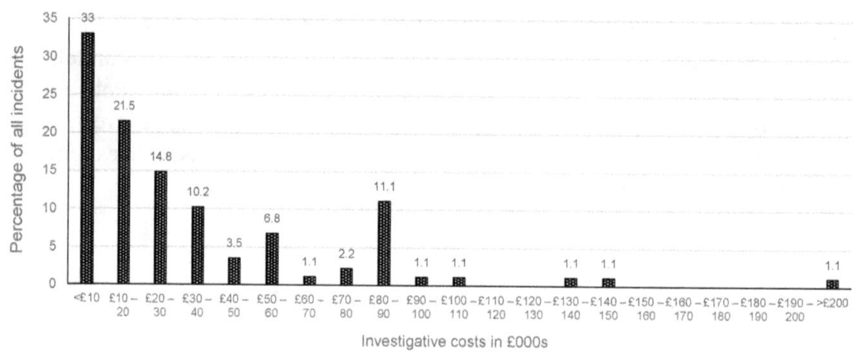

Fig. 9 Investigative costs by percentage of all homicide incidents (TVP and Hampshire data)

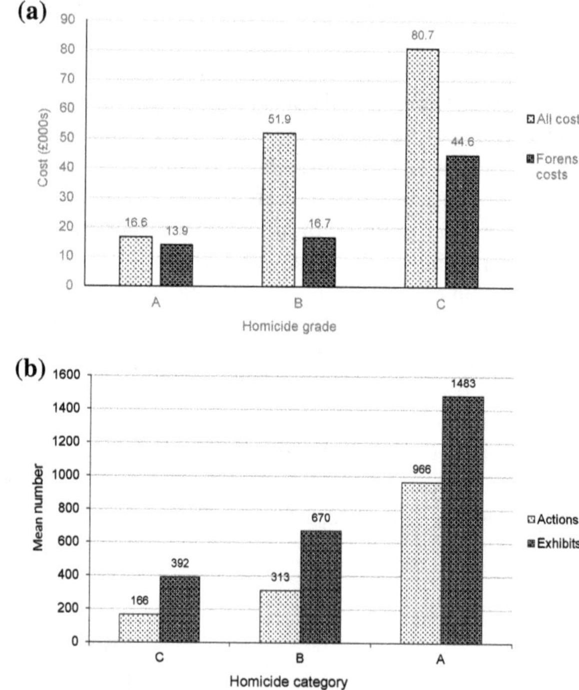

Fig. 10 Homicide grade by **a** mean cost of investigation (all costs for both forces; forensic costs for TVP data) **b** mean number of actions and exhibits (both forces' data)

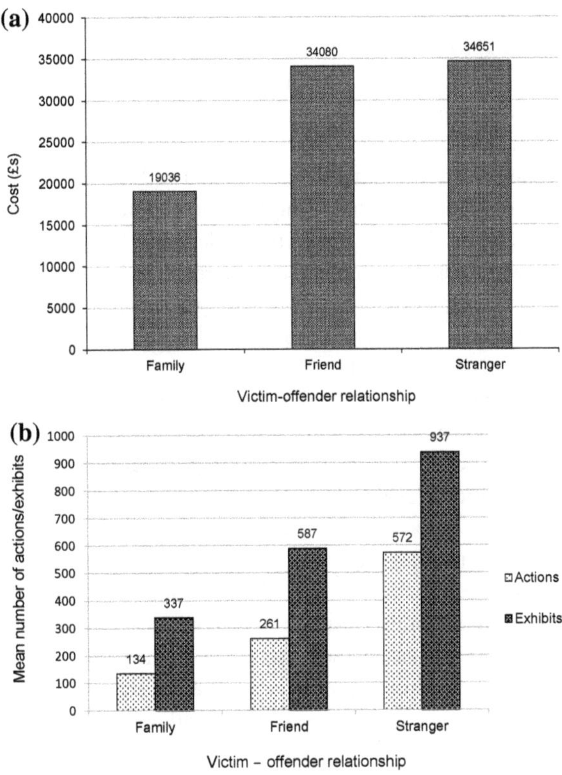

Fig. 11 Victim–offender relationship by **a** investigative costs **b** numbers of actions and exhibits per investigation

costs, they did not differ between detected and undetected cases. Grade A incidents, however, stood out as having very high costs (£44,643, sd = 20.466) compared with B and C homicides which were more similar (B: £16,661, sd = 12,300; C: £13,904, sd = 12,363).

Investigative costs, actions and exhibits also differed markedly by the relationship between the homicide offender and victim (Fig. 11a, b). There were more actions ($F = 9.95$, $p = 0.000$, df = 2, 201) and exhibits ($F = 13.93$, $p = 0.000$, df = 2, 201) the more distant the relationship (Fig. 11b). Although there were significant differences in investigative costs ($F = 4.03$, $p = 0.019$, df = 2, 213), these were the same for homicides involving strangers and friends or acquaintances, but far cheaper for family murders, only 55% of the cost (Fig. 11a).

Although the number of exhibits per action did not differ between homicide grades, suggesting that they may be an imperfect indicators of solvability, the cost of an action ($F = 3.88$, $p = 0.02$, df = 2, 190) and the cost of producing an exhibit did. Category B homicide actions (£271 mean) cost over twice grade A homicides

(£129) and were 1.75 times as costly as C (£155) homicides. The costs of actions are not consistently related to grades.

Overall, differences in homicide grades (between A + B cf. C and A cf. B + C) explained 28% of the variation in investigative costs ($R = 0.54$, $R^2 = 0.28$, $n =$ 227) for the homicides in the two police forces. Grade differences do not explain cases which were and were not detected (Chi-square (2 df) = 0.14, $p = 0.93$) and, as shown above, investigative costs are higher for undetected than detected cases, since additional but less productive actions are undertaken for difficult-to-solve cases, particularly those which remain undetected. Whereas grades account for none of the variation in detection outcomes, whether a stranger, an acquaintance or a family-related homicide explains 13% of this variation (BLR regression, Nagelkerke's R^2 = 0.13).

Analysis of TVP data alone shows that for that force, homicide grades explain 37% of the variation in investigative costs, whereas homicide characteristics account for only 18% (Table 8A–C). Including additional significant homicide characteristics into the regression equation elevates the amount of variation in investigative costs that is explained to 44%. Incorporating supplementary variables—suspect gender, suspect numbers, whether a murder—therefore, improves the prediction of investigative costs based on experience and this indicates that also drawing on statistical prediction is likely to enable more accurate estimate of investigative costs (Table 8B). A linear regression incorporating 'action solvability' variable with detectives' homicide grades also elevated the level of explained explanation by only 4%, from 37–41%, given the association between 'action solvability' and homicide grade (F (2, 123) = 9.62, $p = 0.000$). Despite this, officers' estimates of cost based on experience explain a higher proportion of variation in costs than analysis based on solvability factors alone (Table 8C).

An ordinal regression analysis using TVP data indicates that categories reflect differences in investigative costs, number of actions, and whether or not murderers are strangers to victims. These variables explain 40% of the differences between homicide categories (Nagelkerke's $R^2 = 0.404$). These findings show a substantial level of predictive accuracy and are in line with detectives' assessment of case costs as reflected in their grading of homicide cases.

Geographical Differences in Investigative Resources

Although an average of £27,960 was spent investigating each case, there was striking difference between the two police forces with Hampshire spending only 67% as much as TVP per case, £22,160 cf. £32,260 (sds = 37,700, 39,050, $n = 228$; $F = 3.84$, $p = 0.05$, df = 1, 227, Fig. 12). However, Hampshire cases took 55% longer to investigate (129 cf. 83 days, $F = 3.75$, $p = 0.05$, df = 1, 247) and there were more actions per case (379 cf. 197, $F = 6.4$, $p = 0.014$, df = 1, 191) but no larger number of exhibits per case in Hampshire, so that the cost per exhibit did not differ between forces, even though the costs per action (£224 cf. £103, $F = 13.58$, $p = 0.000$, df =

Table 8 Regressions with investigative costs the dependent variable; independent variables described in A, B, C

	A Independent variables: homicide grades					B: IVs: Homicide grades + characteristics					C IVs: Homicide characteristics				
Variable	B	S.E.	Beta	t	Sig.	B	S.E.	Beta	t	Sig	B	S.E.	Beta	t	Sig
Constant	−49118.2	12777.8		−3.84	0.000	−85907.9	19769.3		−4.35	0.000	−37729.1	20896.7		−1.81	0.075
Grade A v. B + C	29735.4	12273.9	0.226	2.42	0.018	27207.4	11711.0	.207	2.32	0.023					
Grade A + B v. C	35447.9	6708.4	0.492	5.28	0.000	30842.5	6528.0	.428	4.73	0.000					
Number of suspects						4243.4	3211.8	0.117	1.32	0.190	8799.1	3778.8	0.242	2.33	0.022
Male/female suspect						9762.3	3720.4	0.224	2.62	0.010	8705.32	4497.0	0.199	1.94	0.056
Victim age						−160.0	157.9	−0.086	−1.02	0.314	−330.0	188.18	−0.177	−1.75	0.083
Murder v. other types						16949.8	8463.1	0.168	1.99	0.050	28680.6	10004.3	0.286	2.87	0.005
Model summary	R = 0.62 Adjusted $R^2 = 0.37$ Model: F (2, 85) = 26.48 $p < 0.000$					R = 0.70 Adjusted $R^2 = 0.44$ Model: F (6, 81) = 12.58 $p< 0.000$					R = 0.47 Adjusted $R^2 = 0.18$ Model: F (4, 83) = 5.85 $p < 0.000$				

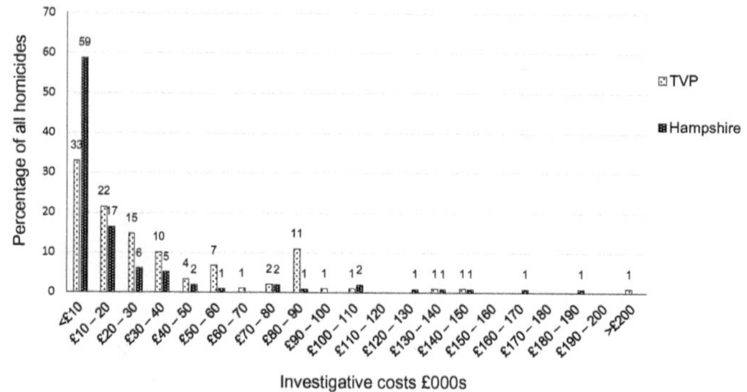

Fig. 12 Investigative costs by percentage of homicides for TVP and Hampshire Police Forces

1, 191) and the exhibits per action (3.6 cf. 2.3, $F = 9.18$, $p = 0.003$, df $= 1, 189$) were far lower in Hampshire. Hampshire carried out nearly twice as many actions at less than half the cost of TVP but only produced 64% as many exhibits per action per case so that there were no more total exhibits per case in Hampshire and the £67 cost of producing an exhibit was identical between the forces ($F = 0.000$, $p = 0.988$, df $= 1, 193$). Hampshire resourced cheaper and larger numbers of actions per case, producing similar numbers of exhibits per case. Investigations were cheaper in Hampshire, took longer to investigate but resulted in the similar number of exhibits per case at a similar cost per exhibit. TVP's quicker investigations appear to reflect larger spending and spending on fewer but more productive actions. Although this may partly reflect homicide differences, it appears that higher spending results in speedier charges and detections.

Discussion and Conclusions

Homicide investigation was expensive, averaging £28,000 a case, and often involved a large number of investigative actions to produce sufficient exhibits (or evidence items) to detect cases. Nine-tenths of all homicides were detected in this 6 year population of homicides committed in two shire counties in England and Wales. Solvability factors explained over a third of detection outcomes. In contrast, investigative costs did not differ between detected and undetected cases, a probable reflection of that fact that less solvable cases demanded almost as much effort since the importance of homicides means the police explore every investigative avenue to ensure no opportunity to solve cases was missed. As a consequence, detected cases were characterised by having more exhibits (or items of evidence output from actions) per action and more costly investigative actions than undetected cases. Although the investigative actions relating to undetected incidents were less costly, because they were more numerous, undetected cases were hardly less expensive to investigate.

The principal solvability factors that affected detection outcomes were suspect–victim stranger relationship, murders compared with other types of homicide and where either a hammer, golf club, spade, axe or blunt instrument was used as a weapon, which depressed the odds of a detection, while more suspects, a suspect with family connections to the victim and homicide methods that included neglect, drugs, a fall, drowning, crushing, electrocution, scalding and fire (often flagging manslaughter), boosted the odds of a detection. For the combined population for the two forces, effort, measured in terms of action numbers and costs and the number of exhibits produced per action, was shown to help explain detection outcomes, reflecting the differences in incident solvability. There were fewer actions, more exhibits per action and higher costs per action when cases were more solvable.

These three measures of investigative effort plus 'time to charge a suspect' were viewed as supplementary solvability indicators across the homicide population, most of which for this study consists of detected cases. Detected cases (as well as undetected ones) require differing amounts of investigative effort to produce sufficient evidence to charge a suspect, so that variables that measure effort are indicators of differences in case solvability. Investigative effort unlocks the solvability, producing the evidence needed to detect cases. Relating these measures of investigative effort to incident characteristics provides alternative insights into the factors that are responsible for variations in homicide case solvability. This measure of case solvability supplements the one based on whether or not cases were detected or remained undetected.

Investigative actions provide the best alternative solvability indicator to the one based on detection/non-detection solvability factors. Higher number of actions indicate lower solvability and characterise difficult-to-solve cases for which additional, often unproductive, investigative activities are undertaken in exhausting all possible investigative avenues. Equally, it appears reasonable that less solvable cases take longer to bring a suspect to charge so that time to charge is a supplementary measure of solvability. Solvability factors were identified that explained a substantial proportion of variation in these two indicators.

Solvability factors predicted 28% of the variation in investigative actions. Cases involving murder (as opposed to manslaughters and a few infanticide cases), shooting and cases involving neglect, drugs, falling, drowning, crushing, electrocution, scalding and fire increased the number of actions and depressed solvability. More solvable incidents where suspects and victims were acquaintances or members or former members of the same families were related to fewer investigative actions.

Some of these findings are in line with prior research, while others are at odds with it. In contrast to existing studies, whether the homicide occurred in a private or public place whether knives or firearms were used had no effect on detections. Stranger homicides were linked with higher not lower odds of detection, in contrast to other studies (cf. Innes 2002; Lee 2005; Ousey and Lee 2010; Roberts 2007) while offences involving drugs tended to improve detection odds, supporting Ousey and Lee's (2010) rather than Welford and Cronin's (1999) findings. Murders were less solvable than other types of homicide, while incidents where the assailants used hammers, golf clubs, spades, axes and blunt instruments as weapons reduced the prospects of a detected outcome.

Further research based on larger data sets with more detailed measures of eyewitness, forensic and electronic evidence is needed to identify a fuller set of solvability factors that help explain more of the variation in detection outcomes. Unlike other offences examined in this volume, given the fact that the police in England and Wales estimate and allocate the resources needed to detect homicides, improved understanding of solvability factors may serve to improve investigative efficiency as much as to improve detection rates. Identifying homicide solvability factors may be of greater value where investigative resources are not available to investigate every homicide, particularly in jurisdictions where stranger, gang-related homicides are more prevalent. More detailed research into which investigative actions are most likely to produce evidence items that will most help solve cases would be especially pertinent for such jurisdictions.

The grades that the police in England and Wales give to homicide cases in order to allocate costs at the start of investigations are based on experience and, for the population studied, provided a sound indication of the eventual costs of investigating and detecting incidents, explaining 37% of the variation in investigative costs. There are other variables that could be taken account of that would improve these cost estimates and grades by c. 7%, but detectives' grades separately explain more variation in costs than the variables available for analysis in this data set. Despite the accuracy of grades in predicting costs, investigative costs varied markedly between the two forces. Investigations were cheaper in Hampshire, took longer to investigate but resulted in the similar number of exhibits per case at a similar cost per exhibit. Thames Valley Police's quicker investigations appear to reflect higher spending and spending on fewer but more productive actions. Speedier detections appear to reflect higher spending but this had no effect on detection rates which did not differ between the two jurisdictions.

It is clear that the considerable experience of specialist homicide teams in investigating crimes under conditions of virtually full investigative funding enables good predictions of investigative costs. It appears feasible to use alternative indicators of solvability where detection rates are very high and to identify supplementary solvability factors that help explain solvability variation. It appears that the only impediments to detecting homicides under these circumstances are deficiencies in witness or forensic evidence. Larger data sets are needed to identify fuller sets of solvability factors. Studies of homicides in other jurisdictions where detection rates are lower—such as where stranger and gang-related homicides are more prevalent—would provide data that enables further insight into solvability factors that discriminate between detected and undetected incidents. Evaluating the cost-effectiveness of individual investigative actions for different sorts of homicide, by relating the quality of evidence items produced in different types of homicide, would help inform ways of reducing investigative costs without loss of the evidence needed to solve cases in all jurisdictions, irrespective of detection rates.

References

Addington, L. (2006). Using national incident-based reporting system murder data to evaluate detection predictors. *Homicide Studies, 10*, 140–152.

Adhami, E., & Browne, D. P. (1996). *Major crime enquiries: Improving expert support for detectives*. Police Research Group Special Interest Series, Paper 9. London: Home Office.

Brown, K. M., & Keppel, R. D. (2012). Child abduction murder: The impact of forensic evidence on solvability. *Journal of Forensic Sciences, 57*, 353–363.

Eck, J. E. (1983). *Solving crimes: The investigation of burglary and robbery*. Washington, DC: Police Executive Research Forum.

Her Majesty's Inspectorate of Constabulary. (2000). *Policing London, winning consent*. London: HMSO.

Innes, M. R. (2002). The 'Process Structures' of police homicide investigations. *British Journal of Criminology, 42*(4), 669–688.

Innes, M. (2003). *Investigating murder: Detective work and the police response to criminal homicide*. Oxford: Oxford University Press.

Innes, M. (2007). Investigation order and major crime inquiries. In T. Newburn, T. Williamson, & A. Wright (Eds.), *Handbook of Criminal Investigation* (Chapter 10). Cullompton: Willan.

Jackson, M. (2010). *Murder concentration and distribution patters in London: An exploratory analysis of ten years of data* (Unpublished M.St. paper). University of Cambridge.

Lee, C. (2005). The value of life in death: Multiple regression and event history analyses of homicide clearance in Los Angeles County. *Journal of Criminal Justice, 33*, 527–534.

Leveson, B. H. (2012). *An inquiry into the culture, practices and ethics of the press*. London: The Stationery Office.

Litwin, K. J. (2004). A multilevel multivariate analysis of factors affecting homicide clearance. *Journal of Research in Crime and Delinquency, 41*, 327–351.

Miethe, T. D., & Regoeczi, W. C. (2004). *Rethinking homicide*. Cambridge: Cambridge University Press.

National Centre for Policing Excellence. (2005). *Guidance on major incident room standardised administrative procedures (MIRSAP)*. Wyboston: ACPO Centrex.

National Centre for Policing Excellence. (2006). *Murder investigation manual*. Wyboston: ACPO Centrex.

Ousey, G. C., & Lee, M. R. (2010). To know the unknown: The decline in homicide clearance rates, 1980–2000. *Criminal Justice Review, 35*, 141–158.

Richardson, M. (2011). *A descriptive analysis of gang homicides in Trinidad and Tobago* (Unpublished M.St. thesis). University of Cambridge.

Riggs, R. (2017). *An assessment of the utility of the categorisation framework of homicide investigations in British policing* (Unpublished M.St. thesis). University of Cambridge.

Roberts, A. (2007). Predictors of homicide clearance by arrest: An event history analysis of NIBRS incidents. *Homicide Studies, 11*, 82–93.

Roberts, A. (2014). Adjusting rates of homicide clearance by arrest for investigation difficulty: Modelling incident- and jurisdiction-level obstacles. *Homicide Studies*, 1–28.

Sampson, R. J., & Wilson, W. J. (2005). Toward a theory of race, crime, and urban inequality. In S. L. Gabbidon & H. Taylor Greene (Eds.), *Race, crime, and justice*. Abingdon: Routledge.

Smith, D. J. (2003). *The Shipman inquiry second report: The police investigation of March 1998*. London: The Stationary Office.

Stelfox, P. (2006). *Factors that determine outcomes in the police investigation of homicide* (Unpublished doctoral thesis). Open University.

Taylor, P., Bond, S. (2012). *Crimes detected in England and Wales 2011/12*. Statistical Bulletin, 08/12. London: Home Office.

Trussler, T. (2010). Explaining the changing nature of homicide clearance in Canada. *International Criminal Justice Review, 20*(4), 366–386.

Wright, M. (2008). *Detective intuition: The role of homicide schemas* (Unpublished Ph.D. thesis). University of Liverpool.

Investigative Activities, Resources and Burglary Detection

Richard Timothy Coupe

Introduction

The objectives of this chapter are to examine, given differences in case solvability, the role that officer resources play in solving residential burglaries and to assess how resources may be more cost-effectively allocated to different investigative activities so as to maximize detections. Solvability depends on incident characteristics, and these affect whether or not it is possible to solve cases. Solving cases, however, also depends on investigative effort, so that realizing the full potential for cost-effective domestic burglary detection depends on the appropriate resourcing of the investigation of solvable incidents and not wasting resources on unsolvable cases. This requires the correct identification of those investigative activities that will result in evidence and, in turn, detection. Different burglaries are solved in different ways. The circumstances of some incidents offer potential for catching offenders red-handed, whereas others may be solved by undertaking other investigations, such as questioning neighbours about possible suspects or collecting and matching forensic samples. Often, a combination of investigative activities that produce a number of evidence items enables case detection. Chapter "The Organisation and Deployment of Patrol Resources: Cost-Effective On-Scene Arrest at Burglaries" considers how patrol resources are best allocated, and Chapter "Solvability Indicators for 'First Officers': Targeting Eyewitness Questioning at Non-residential Burglaries" helps identify those incidents with potential for gaining suspect descriptions from occupants of premises neighbouring burglary scenes. This chapter examines the entire investigative process and considers other investigative activities undertaken by police and the resources needed to 'unlock' evidence from those activities. There is little published material on establishing thresholds for screening cases for investigation, and this chapter provides insights into which incidents resources may be directed

R. T. Coupe (✉)
Institute of Criminology, University of Cambridge, Cambridge, UK
e-mail: rtc23@cam.ac.uk

R. T. Coupe et al. (eds.), *Crime Solvability Factors*,
https://doi.org/10.1007/978-3-030-17160-5_16

at in order to cost-effectively solve cases, and, given variations in solvability, the effectiveness of resource use for different investigative activities and stages.

While resources include buildings, forensic materials, vehicles and technical and electronic devices, labour costs predominate. Staffing accounts for over 80% of policing costs in developed countries, and officer time resources are used to measure policing effort in this study. Police activities are defined as the actions or events that use resources to produce evidence that leads to detection outcomes. This chapter examines the ways in which incident solvability and resources combine to influence evidence outputs and detection outcomes. It also compares the cost-effectiveness of various investigative activities by relating evidence outputs to officer time inputs. The chapter draws on data on the actions of first officers and detectives' further investigations for a sample of residential burglaries from first response by patrol units until incidents are detected or filed as undetected. A central aim of assessing how well resources are matched with the solvability of different offences in terms of cost-effective burglary investigation and detection is to further the understanding of theory and to improve policing practice.

Research Methodology

Research Design and Instruments

The sampling frame covers two divisions of a police jurisdiction in a large UK city, for which data on burglary incidents, investigative activities, evidence, officer time and detections were collected in 1994. Research instruments were questionnaire surveys completed by first response officers attending individual incidents during the shift on which the burglaries occurred and by detectives at the point in investigations when suspects were charged or cases were filed 'undetected'. There were also data from computerized incident logs on the reporting of incidents, patrol response times and the ways that first officers dealt with activities at burglary scenes.

A sample of 695 incidents was selected randomly from 5768 burglaries that occurred over six months. Police officer questionnaire response rates exceeded 80%, and the final sample comprised 573 cases. The arrest and charge of an offender defined a detected case.[1]

There are a variety of residential environments from inner cities to suburbs bordering rural areas in the two divisions with 750,000 residents selected for study. These afford burglars residential targets with varying levels of opportunity and risk. This chapter's findings, therefore, should be generalizable to burglaries in similar urban districts, if not to similar offences that occur in less built-up locations, given the similarities in solvability factors in rural UK environments (Paine and Ariel, Chapter "Population-Level Analysis of Residential Burglaries").

[1]The mean time SOCOs spent at burglary scenes was calculated with data from an additional survey involving 200 interviews with victims, selected randomly from the complete sample of incidents.

Data

Data were collected about individual incidents on the property its occupants and site circumstances, the incident characteristics affecting the solvability of cases, and time spent by police officers on different activities. Police incident records covered the burglary event, offence reporting, premises occupancy and burglar sightings. There were also data on patrol response times and numbers of officers, first officer time spent questioning victims and the occupants of neighbouring premises, and forensic officers' activities at the scene. First response officers' self-completed questionnaires covered dwelling exit and entry, rooms visited by offenders, stolen property, neighbour questioning, suspect vehicle and suspect evidence, forensic officer visits, dwelling occupancy when the offence occurred and whether burglars had been spotted.

Questionnaires completed by detectives provided data on further investigative activities. These included visiting crime scenes, tracing stolen property, analysing crime patterns, sourcing suspect details from informants, forensic matching, and, rarely, surveillance. Detectives also estimated the time spent on each investigative activity for individual cases. Outlying time estimates were checked with officers and, if necessary, adjusted.

Defining and Measuring Resource Use

Police officer time is used to measure resources. These cover the total amount of time used for dealing with the burglaries and include patrol officer numbers and response times, the time spent by first officers at burglary scenes and by detectives. The periods of low capacity utilization when patrols are 'idle' or when dealing with other patrol tasks have not been taken account of in the response time measure in the analysis so that it may be underestimated. Non-warranted support staff time is not measured; it is taken as being proportionate to police officer time. There is no measure of the time 'scenes of crime' or forensic officers spent at individual incidents.

Strengths and Limitations of Data

The data are distinctive. There is a substantial sample, officer questionnaire response rates are high, and there are data from surveys of the burglary sites and victims tied to the same set of individual incidents. Unusually, if not uniquely, there are time records for each distinct police activity from initial patrol responses and patrol officers' activities at crime scenes to further investigative activities. There is no published research measuring staff resources used for every investigative activity linked to individual offence data. Brandl and Frank (1994) measured labour resource input into detectives' investigations using officer time, but did not consider either patrol response or the actions of first officers at crime scenes.

There have been few changes in the investigation and detection of burglaries over the last two decades, and officers face similar incident demand pressures to those encountered in the mid-1990s. When UK crime peaked in 1994, the police service on which this chapter's analysis is based had too few resources to meet demand, so that it was as unlikely then, as now, that the police could properly resource all solvable crime investigation. Case screening, now as then, relies on procedures without statistical solvability estimates (Robinson and Tilley 2009), and catching burglars red-handed and eyewitness descriptions of suspects remain the principal means of solving cases (Tilley et al. 2007; Robinson and Tilley 2009; cf. Coupe and Griffiths 1996). Few arrests, then as now, are solved by using informants, tracing stolen property or from vehicle registrations.

Forensic evidence, however, is responsible for an increasing minority of detected cases (Paine and Ariel, Chapter "Population-Level Analysis of Residential Burglaries"; Donnellan and Ariel, Chapter "Assessing Solvability Factors in Greater Manchester, England: The Case of Residential Burglaries"), rather than only supporting evidence, as previously (e.g. Coupe and Griffiths 1996). Research from Brisbane indicates that there is potential to increase the numbers of solvable cases by improving the fingerprinting skills of forensic specialists (Antrobus and Pilotto 2016), even if the scope for the increased use of DNA appears more limited. Another change has been increasing numbers of 'car-key' burglaries, representing 6% of burglary-dwelling incidents in England and Wales in 2008. Most arrests at these burglaries result from witness evidence or arrest due to rapid patrol responses, with vehicle registrations providing supporting evidence (Carden 2012). Car key burglary incidence has been offset by hacking into owners' electronic key fobs without the need to break into their dwellings.

The objective is to determine the relative importance of incident solvability and resources in explaining variation in detections. The chapter's principal focus, therefore, is not on identifying solvability factors that can be used to improve case screening. Rather, the aim is to understand how resources may be matched to cases of varying solvability at different investigative stages so that evidence and detection outcomes may be cost-effectively maximized. The 1994 data meet this need.

Findings

Investigation Inputs, Intermediate Outputs and Investigative Outcomes

In dealing with burglary, police activities occur in two stages (Fig. 1). During the first, incident characteristics influence both solvability and resource inputs into activities. These comprise response by patrols and activities at burglary scenes, which involve

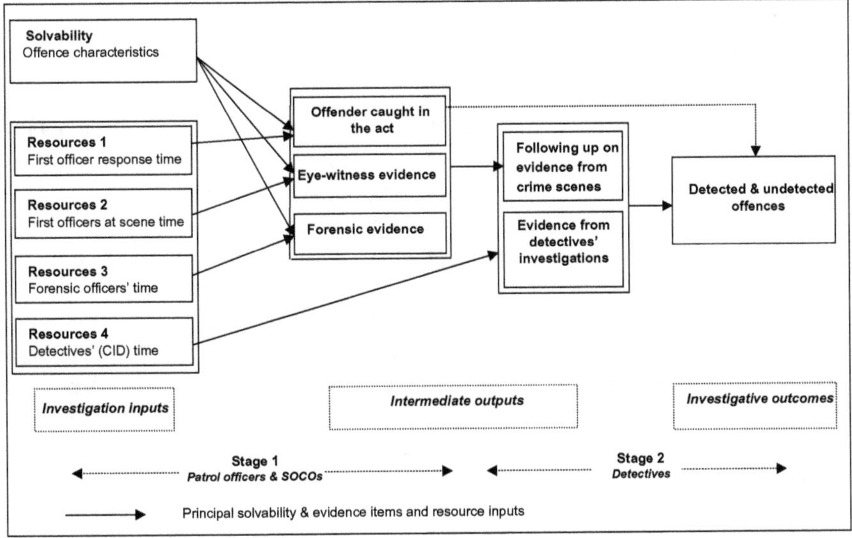

Fig. 1 Role of resources and solvability in reactive investigations of high-volume crime (from Coupe 2016)

witness questioning and the collection of forensic evidence by scenes of crime officers. These may result in 'intermediate outputs' consisting of arrests at the scene, and forensic and suspect evidence from eyewitnesses (Fig. 1).

The second stage involves detectives undertaking further investigative activities. By drawing on outputs for selected cases from first-stage activities, they produce further evidence that results in investigative outcomes: undetected or detected cases. Further investigations include matching suspect evidence to known offender descriptions, checking vehicle registrations, evaluating the results of forensic testing, tracing stolen property, visiting crime scenes, surveillance and using intelligence from informants. Only 19% of incidents where burglars were intercepted at or near burglary scenes were detected as a result of first-stage activities alone. These were principally where offenders were intercepted while still at the scene. The other four-fifths, often involving burglars stopped in nearby streets who had already discarded stolen property, required further investigative activities and additional evidence to produce detected outcomes.

The analysis is in four sections, examining:

- the effects of resource inputs and incident solvability in stage 1 on different intermediate outputs—offenders caught at or near the scene, witness evidence and forensic evidence;
- how these outputs plus any additional evidence arising from further investigations by detectives in stage 2 result in detected cases;
- the overall effects of solvability and resources on burglary detections;
- a comparative evaluation of cost-effectiveness across investigative stages.

Catching Burglars Near or at the Scene and Resource-Solvability

Controlling for patrol response time, incidents with younger victims and where burglars were seen, especially by neighbours and while the burglary was in progress, boosted capture at or near the scene (Table 1). The odds of capture were also increased when there were more patrol officers responding and the by the total time taken in responding to each 'in progress' incident. It is common for more patrol units to respond immediately and more quickly to 'in progress' incidents, since most available units and those dealing with 'routine' incidents who can disengage will respond. This means resources will frequently match the key solvability factor, unless high demand for patrols to attend many incidents exceeds supply of units and depresses their availability (Coupe and Blake 2005). Suspect vehicle sightings, more frequent at incidents carried out by older and experienced burglars, tended to depress the odds of an arrest.

Response time resources and incident solvability characteristics explained 36% of the differences between capture and non-capture (Nagelkerke's $R^2 = .357$). Solvability factors accounted for twice as much of this variation as resources.

A summary solvability index relating to capture ('on-scene arrest solvability'), weighted according to the solvability factors shown in Table 1, was calculated by summing the product of each significant solvability factor's binary value (e.g. burglary occurred in daylight = 1; darkness = 0) and its odds ratio (Exp (B)). The index is an accurate measure of 'on-scene arrest solvability' (Nagelkerke's $R^2 = .966$, 'on-scene arrest solvability' index regressed on significant solvability variables), which is independent of time resources.

Response time was weakly associated with the capture solvability index ($\tau_b = .086, p = .022, n = 481$), indicating that resource allocation is not well aligned with differences in how easily offenders may be caught at different incidents. This is perhaps not unexpected, since there is frequently an insufficient supply of patrols when there is high demand from many 'in progress' incidents, so that it is only during times of weaker demand that the strongest responses can be made. In addition, patrol responses are not graded and prioritized, with the result that burglaries where there are better prospects for on-or-near-scene arrest often do not receive patrol responses in line with their higher solvability.

Resources in terms of patrol officer response time and 'on-scene arrest solvability' are both associated with of on-scene arrest, with large effect sizes (Table 2). The interaction between capture-solvability and resources does not affect on-scene arrest and including it in the regression boosts the independent effects of capture-solvability variables and response time resources (Table 2). This, along with the weak correlation between response time resources and the 'on-scene arrest solvability' index ($\tau_b = .086, p = .02, n = 481$), suggests that resource allocation is not closely aligned with the most solvable cases for successful on-and-near-scene arrest. The non-alignment of patrol response resources with on-or-near-scene arrest potential reflects

Table 1 Binary logistic regression: dependent variable: burglar caught/not caught at or near the scene (from Coupe 2016)

	Variable	*B*	SE	Wald	*p*	Exp (*B*)
Solvability factors	Property stolen	.098	.355	.077	.782	1.103
	Suspect seen while burglary in progress	1.692	.361	22.002	.000	5.430
	Suspect seen when leaving incident	.360	.502	.514	.473	1.434
	Suspect seen/not seen by neighbour	.839	.405	4.284	.038	2.314
	Burglar disturbed at the scene	.410	.402	1.036	.309	1.506
	Smashed entry into premises	−.297	.289	1.063	.303	.743
	Suspect seen	.816	.350	5.435	.020	2.262
	Exited from front versus rear or side	−.285	.284	1.011	.315	.752
	Younger victim (<65 years)	1.137	.417	7.448	.006	3.118
	Burglary occurred in darkness	−.231	.271	.725	.394	.794
	Victim at home when burgled	.279	.348	.643	.422	1.322
	Number of rooms visited	−.039	.280	.020	.888	.961
	Vehicle seen	−1.48	.582	6.479	.011	.227
	Entry by rear versus front or side	−.110	.365	.092	.762	.896
Resources	Travel time resources	.592	.155	14.558	.000	1.808
Constant		−6.47	2.023	10.230	.001	.002

Note: $n = 468$ (cases omitted where daylight/darkness unknown)

patrol shortages when workloads are high and surfeits when demand is low, resulting in patrols often attending in-progress burglaries with poor prospects of arrest.

The 'on-scene arrest solvability' index and resources were categorized into groups of low, medium and high solvability which comprised equal numbers of incidents. Extra resources improved arrest rates for low- and medium-solvability burglaries, and medium-high resources were essential for on-or-near-scene arrest except if offences were highly solvable (Fig. 2a). For incidents with similar levels of response time resources, arrest rates were higher for more solvable incidents (Fig. 2b). The striking group of low-resourced but highly solvable cases with high arrest rates were incidents where offenders were unaware of having been seen entering premises, which allowed time for single patrols to intercept them at the scene.

Table 2 Effects of arrest-solvability and response time resources on on/near-scene capture (from Coupe 2016)

	B	SE	Wald	*p*	Exp (*B*)	*B*	SE	Wald	*p*	Exp (*B*)
Arrest-solvability index	.225	.030	55.83	.000	1.253	.284	.067	18.03	.000	1.329
Response resources index	.355	.075	22.10	.000	1.426	.836	.489	2.93	.087	2.307
Capture-solvability versus response resource						−.019	.019	1.011	.315	.981
Constant	−7.34	.751	95.49	.000	.001	−8.84		27.162	.000	.000

Note: $n = 481$

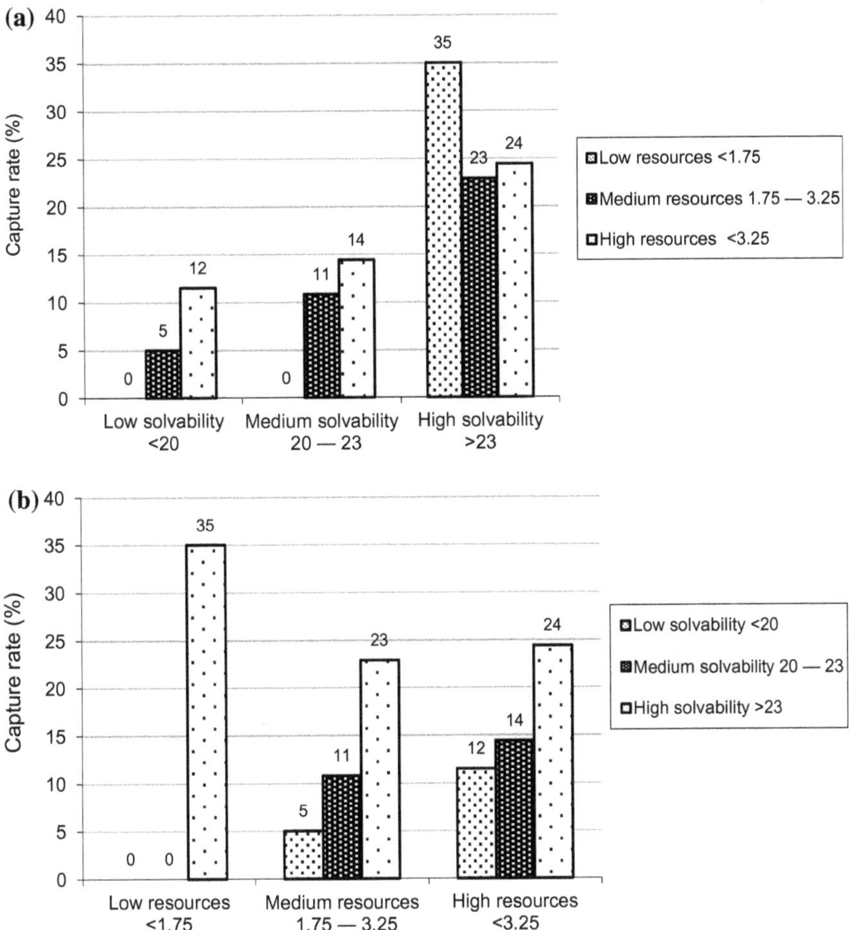

Fig. 2 Caught at/near scene rates for **a** incident solvability groups for different patrol resource inputs, **b** patrol resource groups by different solvability inputs (from Coupe 2016)

On-or-near-scene arrest, therefore, depends on incident solvability, but is increased the more response time resources are allocated. Response time resources markedly affect the relationship between solvability and arrest (Coupe and Blake 2005): larger resource inputs raise arrest rates at incidents of all degrees of solvability, though the effects were larger, the more solvable the incident. That larger resource inputs increase arrests even at highly solvable incidents seems to be at odds with research findings that less effort is needed to detect more solvable incidents (e.g. Eck 1983). However, comparable arrest rates for high solvability incidents, whatever the resources, suggest that high-solvability cases can be detected with fewer resources.

Resources, Solvability and Suspect Evidence from Eyewitnesses

First-responding officers questioned occupants of neighbouring premises and victims who might have seen burglars about suspect descriptions or names. There was a three-category classification of suspect evidence: good quality descriptions, which consisted principally of named suspects and others who had been positively identified; medium quality evidence, comprising 'possible suspect' descriptions; and poor quality evidence, with less specific descriptions, including gender and estimated ages. Suspect vehicle information was also collected.

First officers' time at the scene—a measure of resources—and solvability characteristics together explained a very high proportion—85%—of the variation in the quality of suspect evidence (Nagelkerke's $R^2 = .845$), with solvability characteristics almost three times as important as resources. Suspect evidence was of better quality at burglaries with younger victims (<65 years) and during daylight, when suspects could be more clearly seen. Suspect evidence was poorer when burglars were seen or heard by victims only when leaving the scene (Table 3), often after dark.

Resources, Solvability and Forensic Evidence from Crime Scenes

It was difficult, if not impossible, to find any burglary characteristics that were significantly related to useful (i.e. with the potential to make a match) forensic samples recovered from the crime scene. Whether a burglary was reported 'in progress' was significant ($p = .019$), but explained less than 1% of forensic outcomes (Nagelkerke's $R^2 = .007$). SOCOs visited 90% of burglary scenes for an average of 20 min. The times spent at individual burglaries are unknown so that the effects of resources on useful forensic evidence collection cannot be measured.

Resources, Evidence and Detection: Further Investigations

This section examines the relative importance of detectives' time inputs on detections compared with evidence from their further investigations and the evidence collected earlier at the scene by first officers. Most witness and forensic evidence resulted from resource inputs by first officers and required little of detectives' investigative time per case. Cases where detectives aimed to collect additional evidence needed more time.

Together, evidence quality and resources account for 54% of explained variation in detection outcomes (Nagelkerke's $R^2 = .539$). Detectives' time had a smaller effect—a fifth of the importance of evidence quality—since most witness and forensic evidence resulted from resource inputs by first officers, and detectives' efforts at col-

Table 3 Ordinal regression with suspect evidence collected at the scene the dependent variable (from Coupe 2016)

						95% CI	
	Variable	*B*	SE	Wald	*p*	Lower	Upper
Solvability factors	Burglary occurred in darkness	.595	.302	3.873	.049	.002	1.188
	Suspect seen	8.93	.918	94.629	.000	7.130	10.728
	Suspect seen by neighbour	−.009	.368	.001	.981	−.731	.713
	Suspect seen leaving scene	−.965	.477	4.102	.043	−1.900	−.031
	Dwelling occupied when burgled	.877	.405	4.683	.030	.083	1.672
	Suspect seen at in-progress burglary	.561	.349	2.582	.108	−.123	1.245
	Exited from front versus rear or side	.086	.325	.070	.791	−.551	.723
	Property stolen	.448	.326	1.885	.170	−.191	1.087
	Older victim (>65 years)	−1.18	.382	9.487	.002	−1.927	−.428
	Entry by rear versus front or side	.159	.379	.176	.675	−.584	.903
	Vehicle seen	−.381	.441	.748	.387	−1.246	.483
Resources	First officer time spent at scene	1.223	.322	14.377	.000	.591	1.855

Note: $n = 468$ (cases omitted where daylight/darkness unknown)

lecting fresh evidence were as likely as not to be unproductive. Better-quality suspect descriptions, forensic evidence that enabled suspect identification, and on-or-near-scene arrests were significantly related to burglary detection outcomes, with good-quality suspect descriptions indicating high solvability effects (Table 4). Detectives' activities in collecting additional evidence did not significantly improve detection outcomes, and returning to the scene to question eyewitnesses particularly appears to have been of little value.

Undertaking surveillance, distinctive stolen property and vehicle registration plates were each strongly related to detected/undetected outcomes (surveillance: $\chi^2 = 10.05$, $p = .002$; distinct property: $\chi^2 = 6.98$, $p = .008$; vehicle registrations: $\chi^2 = 11.75$, $p = .001$) but had no significant independent effect on detection outcomes in the logistic regression model. Their low incidence (e.g. distinctive stolen property at only 2% of cases) makes them statistically inconsequential, though it is worthwhile for detectives to pursue them.

Table 4 Binary logistic regression relating evidence, on/near-scene capture and detectives' time to detected/undetected, the dependent variable (from Coupe 2016)

	Variable	*B*	SE	Wald	*p*	Exp (*B*)
Solvability factors	Caught/not caught at/near scene	1.433	.257	31.110	.000	4.192
	Useful forensic evidence/none	1.342	.335	16.021	.000	3.826
	Good suspect evidence versus none (first officer)	3.530	.504	48.976	.000	34.139
	Quite good suspect evidence versus none (first officer)	1.770	.328	29.068	.000	5.871
	Poor suspect evidence versus none (first officer)	.591	.348	2.882	.090	1.807
	Distinctive stolen property/none	1.055	.813	1.683	.194	2.873
	Vehicle registration plate/none	2.014	1327.91	.000	.999	7.490
	Surveillance/no surveillance	1.995	1440.45	.000	.999	7.352
	Information/none from detectives questioning neighbours	.279	.348	.643	.422	1.322
	Information/none from detectives questioning victims	−.693	.988	.493	.483	.500
	Detectives collected/did not collect other sorts of new information (e.g. informants)	2.420	1.688	2.057	.152	11.24
	New information collected/not collected by detectives	−.905	.927	.953	.329	.405
Resources	Detectives' time inputs into further investigations	.063	.021	8.712	.003	1.065
Constant		−26.68	14,404.46	.000	.999	.000

Note: $n = 567$

A summary 'evidence–solvability' index was calculated in the same way as the 'arrest-solvability' index, weighted by regression odds ratios. This index accurately reflects offence solvability in terms of evidence quality (Nagelkerke's $R^2 = .982$, 'evidence-solvability' index regressed on the significant evidence-solvability factors in Table 4).

As expected, the effects of 'evidence-solvability' and detectives' time on detections increased when a variable measuring the interaction between them was added into the regression (Table 5): interaction between them does not help account for variation in detection outcomes. Short amounts of detectives' time were needed for completing the investigation of cases based on evidence due to resource allocation to earlier uniformed officers' activities, particularly fast patrol responses and first officer time at the scene. Detectives' time independently boosted detections, indicating some benefits of spending time on cases involving considerable additional investigation, even if these involved less cost-effective investigative activities.

The 'evidence-solvability' index and further investigative resources were divided into low, medium and high groups, each with equal case numbers. Incidents with higher 'evidence-solvability' scores had superior detection rates (Fig. 3a) for all three resourcing levels. However, cases allocated high and medium levels of detectives' time resources had lower detection rates than cases with low resource inputs (Fig. 3b). Detective resources were particularly input into cases with far better evidence ('intermediate outputs', Fig. 1) from the first officers' activities, and these needed less detectives' time for further investigation.

These tasks included matching forensic and suspect evidence with known offenders' details and arresting burglars using positive identification information. More of the incidents to which low amounts of detectives' times resources were applied had on-or-near-scene arrests ($\chi^2 = 36.45$, 2 df, $p < .001$), good–quality suspect evidence ($\chi^2 = 98.84$, 6 df, $p < .001$) and useful forensic evidence ($\chi^2 = 32.92$, 2 df, $p < .001$). One or more of these features were present in 62% of cases to which low amounts of detective time resources were applied, and 47% of cases to which high amounts of detectives' time were applied. However, they were present in only 22% of cases to which medium amounts of detectives' time were allocated, the category with the lowest detection rates. Evidence collected by first officers during the first stage had a strong effect on successful further investigations. Greater time spent on investigations by detectives, nevertheless, elevated detections for every level of solvability (Fig. 3b), even benefiting high-solvability cases, which seems inconsistent with such cases requiring fewer resources.

Therefore, a large proportion of cases allocated smaller amounts of investigative resources were detected, because, with prior evidence, little extra investigation was required. Many of these cases involved burglars being caught near the scene and in nearby streets, which required some further investigative actions, particularly if stolen goods had been jettisoned. These circumstances lowered the solvability of cases featuring on-or-near-scene arrests. Medium or high detective time resources were used on cases that were less solvable, and these often remained undetected. Not all of the resources used in detectives' investigations were applied cost-effectively.

Table 5 Effects of evidence solvability and detectives' time resources on detections (from Coupe 2016)

	B	SE	Wald	*p*	Exp (*B*)	*B*	SE	Wald	*p*	Exp (*B*)
Evidence-solvability index	.120	.011	110.23	.000	1.128	.126	.013	100.90	.000	1.134
Detective resources index	.064	.020	9.99	.002	1.066	.099	.036	7.48	.006	1.104
Evidence-solvability versus Detective resource						−.002	.002	1.667	.197	.998
Constant	−2.711	.220	151.89	.000	.066	−2.809	.238	139.31	.000	.060

Note: $n = 567$

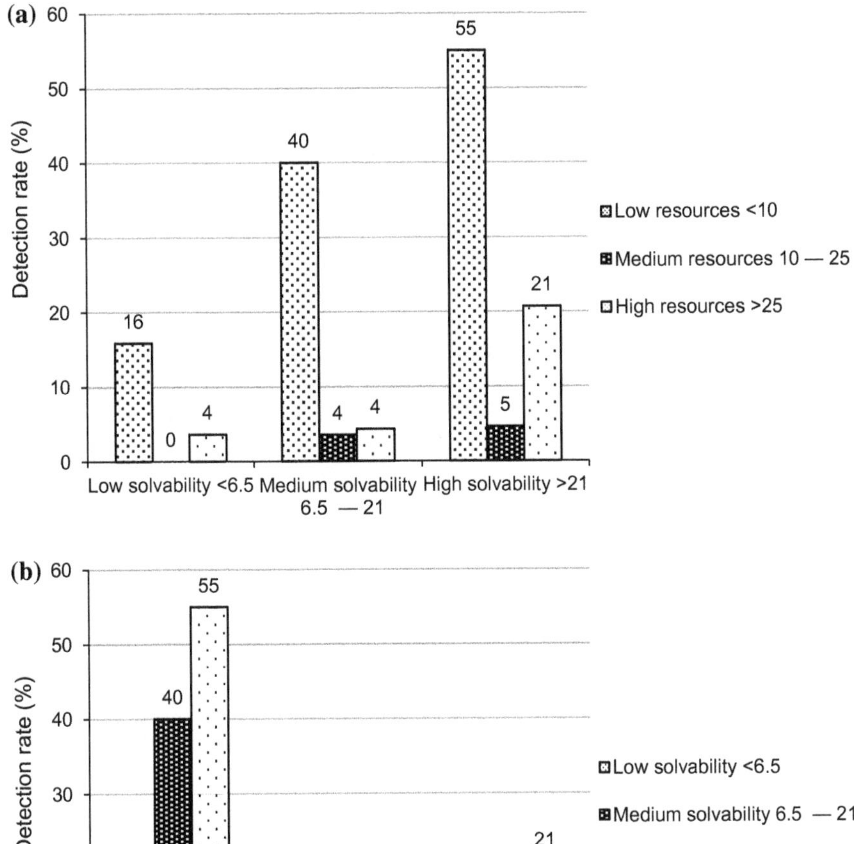

Fig. 3 Detection rates for **a** evidence–solvability groups by different detective resource inputs, **b** different detective resource groups by different evidence–solvability inputs (from Coupe 2016)

Solvability Characteristic, Resource Inputs and Detections

This section examines the comparative effects of all resource inputs in each stage of the investigative process, and incident solvability characteristics overall, on detection outcomes.

A combination of burglary characteristics and resource inputs helps explain whether or not incidents are detected (Table 6). Resources and solvability, together, were responsible for 52% of variation in detection outcomes (Nagelkerke's $R^2 = .517$). With each set of variables entered first, solvability characteristics accounted for 40% of explained variation (Nagelkerke's $R^2 = .402$) and resources 32% (Nagelkerke's $R^2 = .318$). While both have an important part to play, offence solvability is statistically more important than resources. While time resources at every investigative stage helped raise the odds of detection, detectives' investigation time appears to have been the least, and first officers' time at the scene the most, cost-effective (Table 6).

A summary index of the 'overall solvability' of incidents was calculated by summing for each case, the product of each significant solvability factor's binary value and its logistic regression odds ratio (Table 6). A 'resources' index, based on odds ratios for response time, first officers' time at scenes and detectives' time, was derived using the same approach. These indices are precise measures of overall solvability (Nagelkerke's $R^2 = .991$, 'overall solvability' index regressed on significant solvability factors) and overall resource use ($R^2 = .997$, 'resources' index regressed on response time, first officer time at burglary scenes and time used for further investigation by detectives).

Both the 'overall solvability' index and 'overall resources' index independently explain detection outcomes, and incident solvability has a stronger effect (Table 7). In general, the more solvable the incident, the greater the time resource input ($\tau_b = .266, p < .001$), though the effect size is low. The interaction between resources and solvability has a significant relationship with detection outcomes, confirming that the resourcing of solvable cases results in detections. Independently thereof, only solvability retains effects on explained variation (Table 7); resources are no longer related to detection outcomes, and lower the odds of cases being detected. This is due to allocating resources to less solvable cases, which officers do not manage to solve. The persistence of the strong effects of solvability on detection independently of its interaction with resources suggests that higher offence solvability leads to more cases being detected, whatever the resources applied. Certain high-solvability incidents, for instance, were solved with fewer resources, such as with some on-scene arrests. Equally, there are incidents where resources are overinvested in low-solvability cases, such as pointlessly strong patrol responses where on-scene arrest is unlikely, questioning of neighbours who can provide no useful information, or costly further investigations that do not lead to detections.

The 'overall solvability' and 'overall resources' indices were categorized into low, medium and high groups with equal incident numbers. Extra resource inputs raised detections for every solvability level (Fig. 4a), and better case solvability increased

Table 6 Binary Logistic Regression Relating Solvability Factors and Officer Time Resources to Detected/Undetected, the Dependent Variable (from Coupe 2016)

	Variable	*B*	SE	Wald	*p*	Exp (*B*)
Solvability factors	Number of rooms visited	.256	.292	.767	.381	1.292
	Victim at home when burgled	.319	.367	.757	.384	1.376
	Burglary occurred in darkness	.583	.274	4.526	.033	1.791
	Suspect seen when leaving incident	1.646	.592	7.725	.005	5.184
	Suspect seen/not seen by neighbour	.668	.449	2.213	.137	1.949
	Smashed entry into premises	−.106	.289	.134	.714	.900
	Suspect seen	1.276	.382	11.136	.001	3.582
	Suspect seen while burglary in progress	1.624	.425	14.585	.000	5.074
	Younger victim (<65 years)	2.153	.458	22.102	.006	8.609
	Property stolen	.243	.391	.387	.534	1.275
	Exited from front versus rear or side	−.285	.284	1.011	.315	.752
	Entry by rear versus front or side	.514	.408	1.592	.207	1.672
	Burglar disturbed at the scene	.035	.471	.005	.941	1.035
	Vehicle seen	.498	.593	.707	.401	1.646
Resources	Travel time resources	.291	.152	3.678	.056	1.338
	Time spent at scene by first officers	.528	.174	9.235	.002	1.695
	Detectives' investigation time	.068	.019	12.803	.000	1.071
Constant		−17.16	2.536	45.803	.000	.000

Note: $n = 468$ (cases omitted where daylight/darkness unknown)

detections whatever the level of resources (Fig. 4b). The alignment of high resources with high-solvability incidents resulted in the best detection rates, while allocating the least amount of resource to low-solvability cases resulted in the worst detection rates. The fact that detections are elevated by allocating high resources to high-solvability cases is at odds with findings that such cases are solved with the least effort (Eck 1983). Equally, the recommendation that 'triage' assessment be used to screen out less solvable cases (Eck 1983) is not in line with low- and medium-solvability cases

Table 7 Effects of overall solvability and overall time resources on detections (from Coupe 2016)

	B	SE	Wald	*p*	Exp (*B*)	*B*	SE	Wald	*p*	Exp (*B*)
Overall solvability index	.341	.040	72.32	.000	1.407	.236	.058	16.88	.000	1.267
Resources index	.116	.020	32.92	.000	1.123	−.300	.168	3.19	.074	.741
Overall solvability index versus resources index						.011	.005	5.71	.017	1.011
Constant	−15.271	1.650	85.69	.000	.000	−11.229	2.225	24.795	.000	.000

Note: $n = 468$

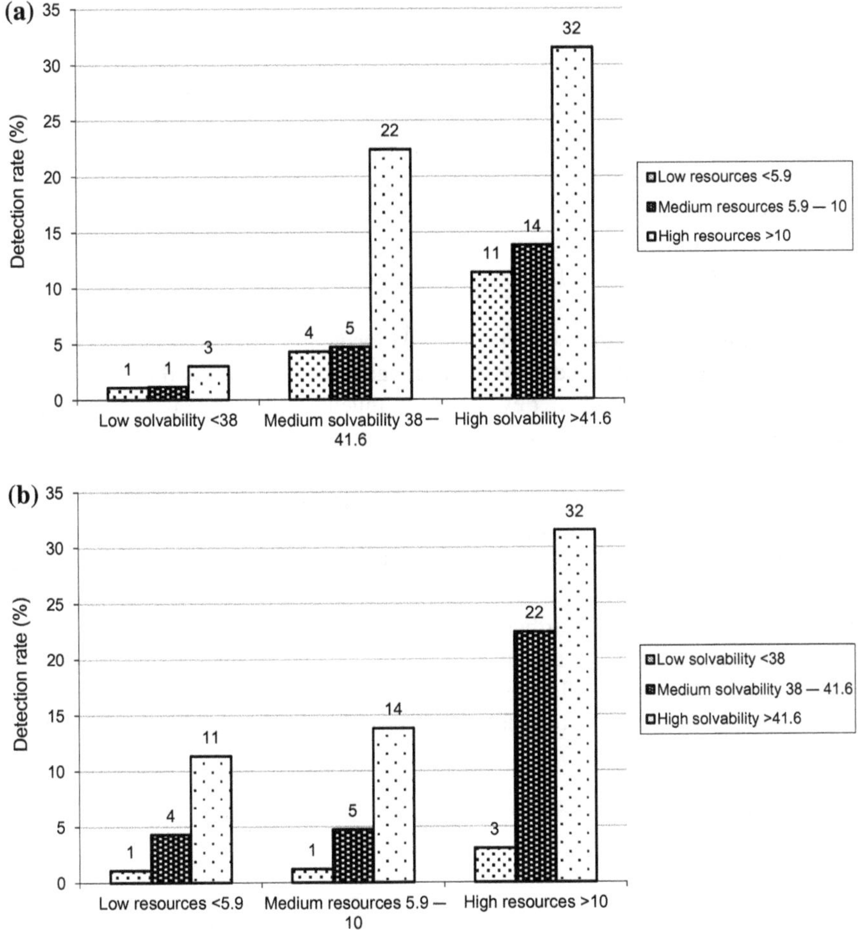

Fig. 4 Detection rates for **a** solvability groups by different resource inputs, **b** resource groups by different solvability inputs (from Coupe 2016)

being solved, especially when high resources were allocated to medium-solvability incidents.

The detection rates achieved from high resource allocations indicate potential to increase detections with high resources, particularly at medium- and high-solvability incidents. Even though there are some low-solvability incidents for which high resource inputs result in detection, it seems that many such incidents will be difficult and some impossible to detect. Even for the best resourced ninth of incidents with the highest solvability, hardly more than a third of investigations produced sufficient evidence to solve cases.

Resource Use and Investigative Activities

Resource allocation decisions not only affect burglary detection outcomes, they also determine how cost-effectively these are achieved.

Detectives spent the most time overall, and the highest amount of time per incident, on both detected and undetected cases (Figs. 5 and 6). First officers used the second highest amounts of overall time and time per incident while at burglary scenes (Figs. 4 and 5). These findings point to the investigative stages that present the largest potential to improve cost-effectiveness by more closely matching officers' activities to the most solvable incidents.

The findings suggest that some resources allocated to detectives' further investigations might be better applied to first officers' activities, especially if it is possible to identify the incidents with better evidence. As much as improving understanding of the solvability factors that predict detection outcomes, improved cost-effectiveness and higher capacity utilization depends on identifying solvability characteristics that enable the prediction of intermediate outputs associated with witness and forensic evidence—the equivalent of those already identified for on-or-near-scene arrest (Coupe and Blake 2005), which can then guide the application of resources. This, above all else, will improve detection outcomes. Superior predictors of case solvability are also needed for further investigations, the more so in the light of the substantial resources used in this investigative stage and because they are used less cost-effectively than when allocated to officers' earlier activities. On this basis, the investigative system may be re-balanced by re-allocating resources between inves-

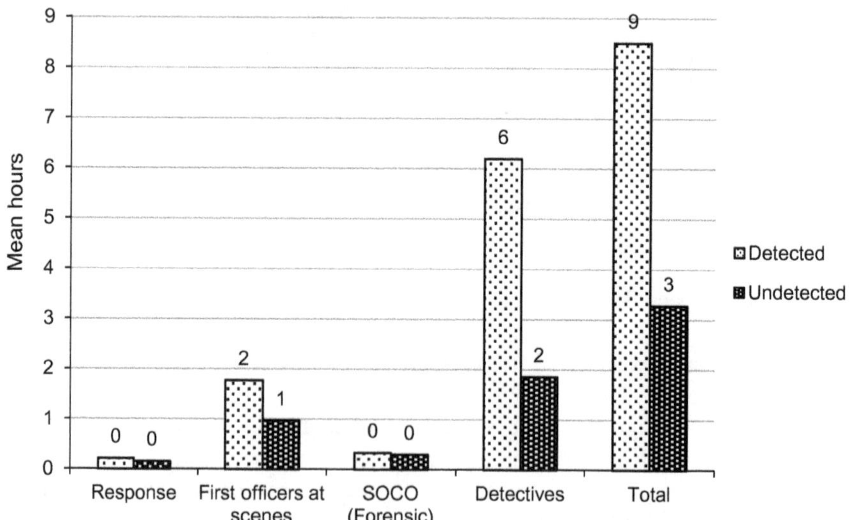

Fig. 5 Average resource time inputs per offence by investigative stage (from Coupe 2016)

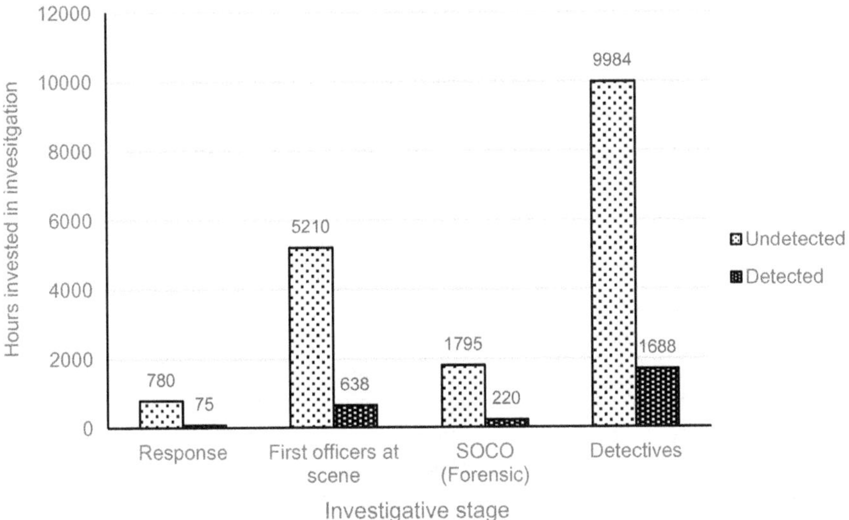

Fig. 6 Total resource time inputs for the burglary population by investigative stage (from Coupe 2016)

tigative stages and address what appears to be the relative overfunding of detectives' time compared with underfunding of earlier police work.

Profiling the resources input into investigative activities and the evidence outputs and detection outcomes for different investigative stages helps understand variations in cost-effectiveness, and where resources and solvability are well aligned or more poorly aligned and therefore, which resource allocation decisions improve or worsen the prospects of detection. It appears that patrol responses are the most efficient activity. The patrol resources used at each incident took account of the sum of response times of every officer who responded to it but, however, did not factor in any other patrol time.[2]

Conclusions

Both solvability and resources affect detection levels, with incident solvability more important. Together, they account for half the variation in detection outcomes—a substantial level, particularly since the use of non-statistical case screening makes it unlikely that investigative resources were in alignment with solvability. This means

[2]Detectives investigations seem to use most resources per detected case. However, the full costs of supporting patrols have not been taken into account. In this study, patrols attended 6.9 incidents per officer day. Taking account of these would make patrol response resource costs higher per case than the further investigations carried out by detectives. Patrols have other functions, such as visual deterrent effects, which would need to also be factored in.

officer effort was probably misspent on unsolvable incidents and that some solvable ones were underfunded, a risk heightened by funding shortfalls being likely due to the study being conducted when UK crime peaked.

The findings confirm that solvability characteristics determine which incidents may be detected, but resource inputs are also needed for successful burglary detection. Resources enable the potential for detection due to solvability to be realized. Applied to cases through investigative activities, they unlock the evidence from cases that enables detection. Solvability characteristics, therefore, control whether it is possible to detect cases and determine the types of investigation and amount of resources needed for detection.

Detection rates were superior for highly solvable and highly resourced incidents, and lower if the converse. Many cases, particularly low-solvability ones, look difficult or impossible to detect irrespective of resource inputs. Nevertheless, even the least solvable third of cases included some that could be detected, particularly with sufficient resource inputs. Additional resources raised detection rates for incidents of every level of solvability, but especially the high-solvability incidents. First officers collect most evidence and do so the most cost-effectively. This is not unexpected, since most evidence derives from crimes scenes for violent, sexual and most property offences, with the exception of cyber offences. For the whole investigative process, this confirms findings that additional patrol inputs can be strikingly successful in boosting on-or-near-scene capture at highly solvable emergencies but have negligible effects at those with low-solvability characteristics (Coupe and Mueller-Johnson, Chapter "Improving Offence Solvability and Detection Rates at Non-residential Burglary: Predicting Single and Multiple Repeat Incidence"; Coupe and Blake 2005). This hardly matches the view, expressed by Eck (1983) and Brandl and Frank (1994), that solvable cases require fewer resources to detect; instead, it appears that more solvable cases consume less detectives' time as a result of better quality evidence from earlier resource inputs at burglary scenes by first officers. Equally, some of this study's least solvable third of cases were detected, even though earlier work had concluded this was not possible (Eck 1983; Brandl and Frank 1994). It appears that rigid adherence to triaging based on solvability may lead to some missed detections, so that officers need also to 'follow the evidence'. Many cases without good quality evidence collected by first officers, which detectives regarded as potentially solvable, however, were medium-solvability incidents that required more resources per case. They subsequently demanded substantial further investigative inputs from detectives and were less cost-effectively detected. On-scene arrest was often achieved with fewer resources per case. Checking suspect vehicle registrations, even if not a statistically significant solvability factor, might be worth pursuing despite the poor odds of producing successful evidence, since it requires little resource.

Examining the links between offence solvability, resources and detections enables investigations to be monitored, cost-effectiveness to be improved and the matching of resources to solvability to be monitored in each investigative stage. This should enhance detection rates and increase the statistical explanation of detection outcomes by solvability and resources. It can also inform screening decisions and their prioritization.

Viewing burglary investigation in two principal stages linked by intermediate outputs may also help screening by, not only viewing incident characteristics as direct predictors of detections, but also as predictors of the evidence items that result in positive detection outcomes. Better solvability predictors, for different subsets of cases, of the activities at the scene that provide the intermediate evidence outputs that result in detection, and of the cases where different further investigations will produce fresh evidence that helps detect cases, would lead to a better match of resources to incident solvability, improved capacity utilization and cost-effective increases in successful detections. Which 'in-progress' burglaries will result in on-or-near-scene arrests and which neighbouring premises are likely to provide suspect descriptions are known (Chapters. "Pickpocketing on Railways" and "The Organisation and Deployment of Patrol Resources: Cost-Effective On-Scene Arrest at Burglaries"). Equivalent indictors for the burglary scenes that are likely to offer useful forensic samples and the incidents at which further investigations by detectives will be profitable are also required so that the cases with evidence to be 'unlocked' may be targeted.

Burglaries of quite different solvability levels are solved, so that estimates of the proportion of solvable cases are likely to be conservative. Research is required to identify the incidents with evidence that can be 'unlocked' in different investigative stages with different activities. Accuracy in terms of cost-effectiveness may be improved by incorporating measures of civilian support staffing, forensic, estate and equipment costs, since they may feature differently in offences with varying types of solvability. It appears likely that statistical crime screening will mean resources are better matched to offence solvability, with more cases detected more cost-effectively. It will also improve the part solvability and resources play in explaining detections.

Acknowledgements The author acknowledges the use in this chapter of 1586 words from Coupe (2016).

References

Antrobus, E., & Pilotto, A. (2016). Improving forensic responses to residential burglaries: Results of a randomized controlled field trial. *Journal of Experimental Criminology, 12*(3), 319–345.

Brandl, S. G., & Frank, J. (1994). The relationship between evidence, detective effort, and the disposition of burglary and robbery investigations. *American Journal of Police, 13*(3), 149–168.

Carden, R. (2012, July, 9–11). *Car key burglaries: An exploratory analysis*. Paper presented at the 5th International Evidence-Based Policing Conference, Cambridge.

Coupe, R. T., & Blake, L. (2005). The effects of patrol workloads and response strength on burglary emergencies. *Journal of Criminal Justice, 33*(3), 239–255.

Coupe, T., & Griffiths, M. (1996). *Solving residential burglary* (Police Research Group Crime Detection and Prevention Services, Paper 77). London: Home Office.

Eck, J. E. (1983). *Solving crimes: The investigation of burglary and robbery*. Washington, DC: Police Executive Research Forum.

Robinson, A., & Tilley, N. (2009). Factors influencing police performance in the investigation of volume crimes in England and Wales. *Police Practice and Research: An International Journal, 10*(3), 209–223.

Tilley, N., Robinson, A., & Burrows, J. (2007). The investigation of high volume crime. In T. Newburn, T. Williamson, & A. Wright (Eds.), *Handbook of criminal investigation* (pp. 226–254). London: Willan Publishing.

The Organisation and Deployment of Patrol Resources: Cost-Effective On-Scene Arrest at Burglaries

Richard Timothy Coupe

Introduction

Successful arrest at or near the crime scene demands the timely allocation of patrol resources to solvable incidents. This partly depends on patrol deployment to beats, since the level of patrol cover governs the likely distances of patrols from incidents and, hence, the time it takes to respond. Double crewing rather than single crewing will reduce these distances markedly and improve response capacity, whereas rapid responses by more units will be easier when demand to respond to incidents is low and more difficult when it is high. The spatio-temporal relationship between patrol supply and incident demand therefore dictates response capacity. Patrol supply might be varied to match demand variations if these appear sufficiently stable. The volume of incidents needing a rapid patrol presence per square mile, however, also plays a key role in providing cost-effective emergency patrol cover. If demand for an immediate response is low, then the deployment of more units per unit area is cost-ineffective, and low-density patrol cover extends the distances over which patrols must respond. This affects most jurisdictions during the small hours but also makes it difficult to provide adequate patrol cover to thinly peopled rural areas at all times.

Equally, the time that offenders will be at or close to burgled premises following the alert has an important bearing on capture probabilities (Blake and Coupe 2001). If officers have longer in which to intercept burglars, then these offences will be more solvable. Incident prioritisation at the time of the alert that takes account of incident solvability should enable rapid response patrol resources to be directed only towards solvable cases and maximise arrests. Burglaries are distinctive offences, as they present reasonable prospects of an arrest if the offenders do not realise they have been seen or heard (Bieck and Kessler 1977), and in-progress burglary circum-

R. T. Coupe (✉)
Institute of Criminology, University of Cambridge, Cambridge, UK
e-mail: rtc23@cam.ac.uk

R. T. Coupe et al. (eds.), *Crime Solvability Factors*,
https://doi.org/10.1007/978-3-030-17160-5_17

stances provide important clues for identifying the subset of incidents that should be prioritised.

Therefore, the objectives of this chapter are to understand the ways in which police resources allocated to patrol areas shape patrol responses, the ways in which the characteristics of in-progress burglaries make incidents more and less solvable, and how the matching of the best-resourced patrol responses with the most solvable cases can improve on-scene arrest. Patrol response includes how many units should respond to burglaries, the types of units to respond, including the use of dogs, and how patrol resources ought to be deployed, including an assessment of the advantages of single crewing or double crewing for arrests. Solvability characteristics include the stage in the burglary at which the offender is seen or heard—whether approaching, breaking in, inside or leaving the target—and who spots the offender and reports the offence: a victim, neighbour or passer-by. Whether it is daylight or darkness at the time of the offence and the number of offenders involved can also change capture probabilities. It is only in the context of solvability characteristics that the varying effects of resources can be properly understood.

Methodology

Research Design and Instruments

The evidence presented in this chapter is based on a study of 'in-progress' residential burglaries carried out in 1996. The use of historic data is justified by their unique type and quality. The research instruments were officer surveys, incident logs and site surveys. All data were linked to individual burglary incidents, permitting arrests and case detection to be linked with police actions, resources and burglary characteristics. It is unusual, if not unique, to be able to link burglary event characteristics to police officer time data for each investigative activity and case outcome. Significantly, therefore, this chapter enables incident characteristics at the time burglaries were reported as being in progress and deployed patrol resources to be related to on-scene arrest. It is the incident characteristics collected in officer questionnaires and site surveys that enable the identification and prioritisation of more solvable cases where arrests are more likely, given a sufficiently rapid response. The collection of data on the time spent by first officers and other officers involved in responding to 'in-progress' incidents permits the cost-effectiveness of police actions to be understood. The sample consists of 454 cases, of which 165 were detected and 289 undetected.

Sampling Frames

The sample was drawn from all 32 basic command units (BCUs) of a large UK conurbation police force. The police force jurisdiction has a population of three million people and is policed by 3000 officers. It includes a variety of residential environments, from inner city to outer suburban, that provide residential properties of varied types and levels of risk to burglars. This suggests that findings should be generalisable to burglaries in other large urban areas, if not, in some ways, to those in villages and market towns, since similar solvability factors feature in burglaries in rural Oxfordshire (Paine and Ariel, Chapter "Population-Level Analysis of Residential Burglaries"). An exception is that forensic evidence plays a rather greater role in Oxfordshire and Manchester (Paine and Ariel, Chapter "Population-Level Analysis of Residential Burglaries"; Donnellan and Ariel, Chapter "Assessing Solvability Factors in Greater Manchester, England: The Case of Residential Burglaries") than elsewhere (e.g. Robinson and Tilley 2009; Tilley et al. 2007), a probable reflection of when and where studies were conducted.

This chapter's findings have a contemporary value owing to the relatively few changes affecting successful responses to burglary emergencies during the last 20 years and the not-dissimilar pressures placed on staffing resources. UK forces are currently absorbing large funding reductions, while 1996 shortly followed the period in which UK crime peaked and when the force providing the data for this study had barely sufficient resources to meet demand, making it unlikely that all solvable incident responses, then as now, could be adequately resourced. Cases are still screened using procedures not grounded in statistical measurement (Robinson and Tilley 2009), and the principal ways of solving them have altered little, with catching burglars red-handed or on the basis of eyewitness evidence about suspects still dominant (Tilley et al. 2007; Robinson and Tilley 2009; cf. Coupe and Griffiths 1996). Few are solved now, as previously, by tracing stolen property or vehicle registrations or by using informants.

Furthermore, despite increases in the use of proactive policing approaches (Newburn 2007), these appear to be more effective for crime prevention (Tilley et al. 2007). They play little role in the investigation of burglary and other high-volume crime, most of which is still dealt with reactively (Jansson 2005; Tilley et al. 2007; Robinson and Tilley 2009; Donnellan and Ariel 2012, Chapter "Assessing Solvability Factors in Greater Manchester, England: The Case of Residential Burglaries"; Paine and Ariel 2013, Chapter "Population-Level Analysis of Residential Burglaries"). Examples of proactive policing of burglary include using informants for crimes to be subsequently committed, using undercover officers to open a false stolen property 'fence' to intercept offenders or installing silent and delayed audible alarms (e.g. Pease 1998) at premises in order to catch repeat offenders. Now, as in 1994, these appear to be of little importance in solving burglary (Coupe and Kaur 2005).

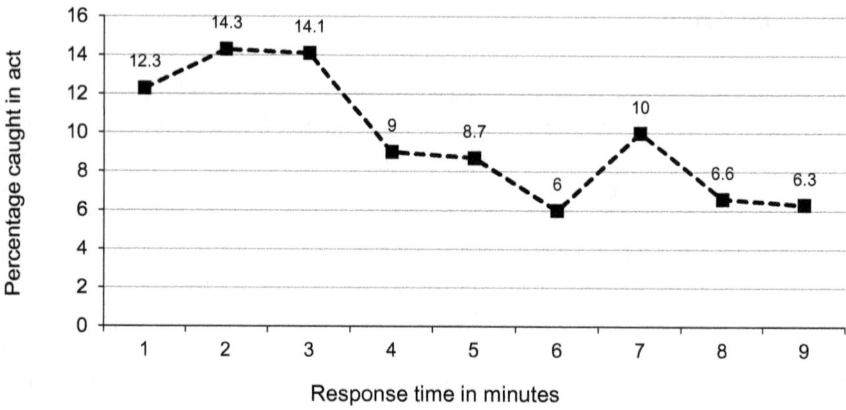

Fig. 1 Time to first patrol arrival at scene and arrest rates for domestic 'in-progress' burglary (Data from Blake 2006)

In-Progress Alerts and Rapid Patrol Response: Existing Evidence

There is mixed evidence about the benefits of rapid patrol response and the effects of additional patrol resources thereon. Studies of police patrols in the 1980s indicated that rapid patrol response was ineffective (e.g. Kelling et al. 1974; Spelman and Brown 1981), but these suffered from methodological shortcomings (Coupe and Blake 2005; Larson 1975) and underestimated patrol benefits. In Kelling et al.'s (1974) study of patrols in Kansas City, for example, patrol units on the beats with high and medium patrol 'treatment doses' assisted patrols in the low-'dose' beats in responding to emergencies, so that the implementation of the experiment was at odds with its design (Larson 1975). Spelman and Brown's (1981) study, which sought to replicate elements of the Kansas City study, furthermore assumed that no offenders would be caught at or near crime scenes if patrols took longer than 5 min to respond, but UK data confound this by showing many burglars captured on or near the scene by patrols after 5 min and as late as 10 min after the alert (Blake 2006; Fig. 1).

Later evidence is more positive about the effectiveness of rapid patrol responses in catching burglars red-handed (Coupe and Griffiths 1996; Coupe and Blake 2005; Robinson and Tilley 2009; Paine and Ariel 2013), confirming Bieck and Kessler's (1977) findings with respect to on-scene capture at burglaries. Mean response time in the study reported here, from the crime being reported until the first units reached the scene, was 4.7 min. This was similar to response times in Seattle (Clawson and Chang 1977) but, notably, substantially quicker than in Kansas City (Bieck and Kessler 1977), one of the most territorially diffuse US cities with the lowest population densities. Moreover, the now-widespread ownership of mobile phones, particularly by poorer people who tend to suffer more burglary and who previously had poor access to fixed-line telephones, is likely to increase the timely reporting of in-progress burglaries, making more of them solvable. This would increase the volume of solvable in-progress burglaries per unit area and help make higher-density patrol deployment cost-effective.

The objective of this chapter is, therefore, to examine evidence on the ways in which patrol resources relate to the on-scene and near-scene capture of burglars. It considers the density of patrol cover in relation to incident demand, response strength and speed, single and double crewing, and the effects of patrol type, including dog vans and vehicle type. The interaction between the provision of resources and the key incident characteristics that shape solvability—where burglars are seen and by whom, the presence of daylight or darkness and offender numbers—is also critically examined.

Findings

Patrol Supply, Incident Demand and On-Scene Capture

There is a clear link between patrol cover, workloads, and response capacity and time. Heavier patrol cover relative to incident numbers enables more rapid responses, which is indispensable for burglary detection (Coupe and Blake 2005). The provision of patrol cover will be more cost-effective when burglaries account for a large proportion of all crimes, as is currently the case in the USA, where almost a quarter of all offences are burglaries and where there are other offences that require the rapid attendance of police officers, such as domestic violence incidents or other sorts of assaults (Olphin and Mueller-Johnson, Chapter "Targeting Factors that Predict Clearance of Non-domestic Assaults"). It will also be more cost-effective to provide denser patrol cover in higher-density population areas in cities rather than in rural areas with diffuse and low-density populations, where patrol cover is commonly lighter, responses lengthier and the prospects for on-scene capture of burglars poorer: it is likely that fewer rapid response patrols will arrive at burglary scenes within 10 min, after which burglars are only rarely caught in the act.

Patrol Deployment and Workloads

Two factors control the number of patrols available to respond. The first is the number of patrol units allocated to patrol areas. The other is the number of incidents, particularly incidents requiring an 'immediate response' in each patrol area during each and every hour. Heavier workloads per patrol mean that responses to burglary emergencies are slower and involve fewer patrol units. The balance between patrol allocation and demand to attend 'routine' and 'immediate response' (i.e. emergency) incidents influences response strength and time.

In the jurisdictions in this study, patrols were allocated across the force so that they matched the overall 'long-run' average number of incidents occurring in each of the 32 BCUs during the six-month study period, with allowance for longer distances

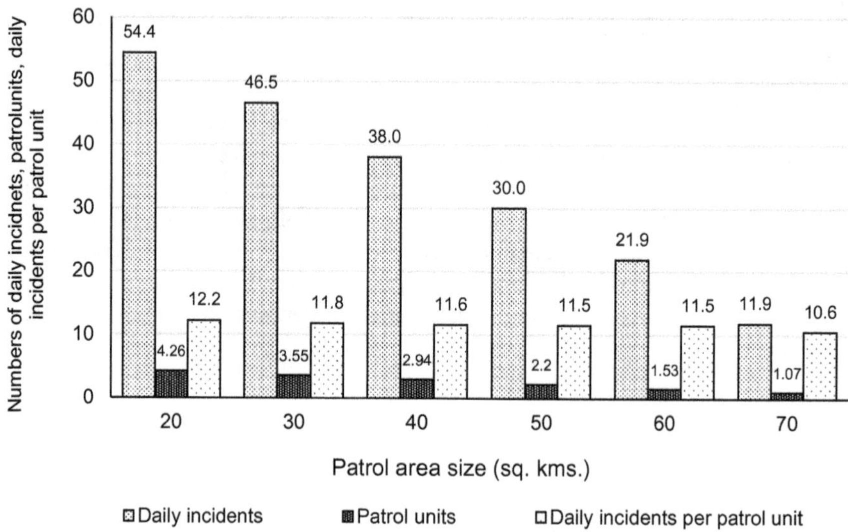

Fig. 2 Patrol deployment and workloads—allocation of patrol units to BCUs by incident number and area size (Coupe and Blake 2005)

for responses in larger areas with fewer offences (Fig. 2). In smaller areas (those close to CBDs), there were more daily incidents and more patrol units allocated per unit area, and in larger areas (those in outer suburbs) fewer incidents and patrols per unit area, so that, despite considerable variation in crime incidence between areas, the mean patrol cover in relation to crime numbers per unit area was very similar. This averaged daily 11.6 incidents per patrol in the larger areas and 12 in smaller areas (Fig. 2).

Despite a similar match of patrols to average workloads across the BCUs, there was considerable short-term fluctuation in the incidence of standard and emergency incidents, so that the workload demands imposed on patrols varied substantially throughout both the day and the week. There was an average of eight incidents per BCU during the hour in which the in-progress burglary incidents occurred, but this varied between nineteen and zero. Short-term fluctuations in workloads determined the numbers of patrols committed to the existing 'immediate response' incidents and to routine incidents, from which it is normally possible to disengage to attend other emergencies, such as the in-progress burglaries studied here. Short-term demand fluctuations in relation to patrol supply, therefore, determine the number of units available hour by hour to deal with burglary emergencies. Figure 3 shows the mismatch between the incidence of all 'immediate alerts' (emergencies) and the sample's in-progress burglaries.

Given a constant patrol supply, it is evident that there is greater demand for immediate police assistance during the evenings, when more in-progress burglary offences are reported. Consequently, fewer patrols responded to in-progress burglary emergencies when workloads were heavier (Fig. 4). When a single unit responded, there were

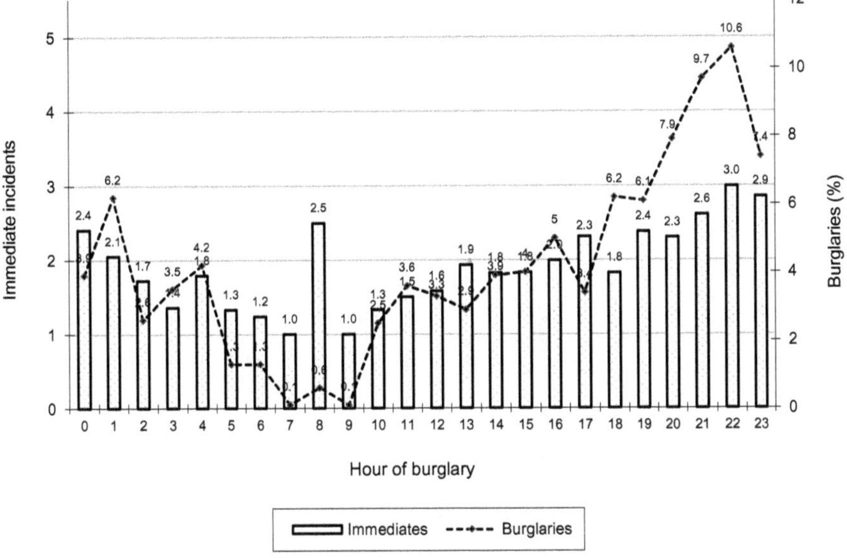

Fig. 3 Incident demand: hourly average number of immediate alerts for all crimes and immediate response burglaries (Blake 2006)

44% more incidents of all types and 82% more 'immediates' (emergencies) to deal with than when six patrol units attended. When a single unit responded, there were an additional 10% of other incidents and 54% more 'immediate' incidents compared to when three units attended. The greater the number of 'routine' (i.e. no urgent need to respond) and other 'immediate' incidents of all types per patrol during the same hour as the sample in-progress burglaries, the fewer units responded to them (other 'immediates' per patrol: $r_s = -.22, p < .001$; 'routines', $r_s = -.17, p = .001$). Other 'immediate' and 'routine' incidents occurring during the hour *prior to* the sample burglaries had a similar effect, since some emergencies keep officers off patrol, for instance, to collect witness statements, deal with an arrestee or stay at hospital with a victim. The occurrence of other 'immediate' incidents had a particularly strong effect in limiting attendance at in-progress burglaries, since it is easier for patrols to disengage from 'routine' incidents while at the scene or while making a response to a 'routine' incident. It is normally not possible to disengage from attendance at other emergencies, and when patrols were busy with these, there were weaker patrol responses to the sample 'in-progress' incidents.

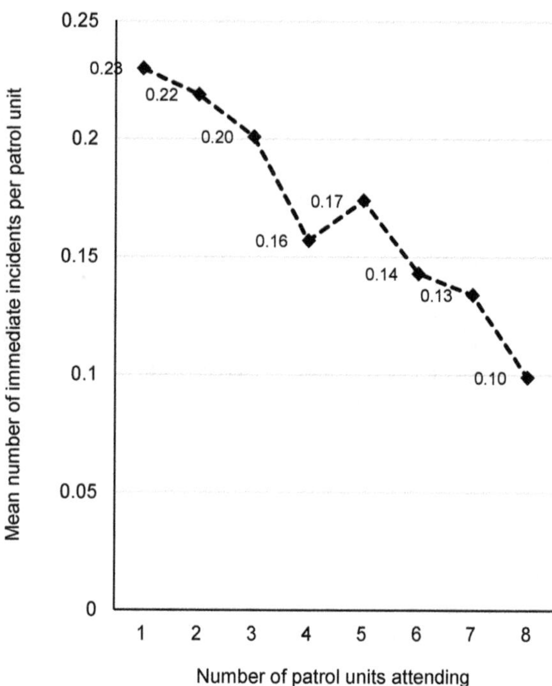

Fig. 4 Effects of workload during the hour the burglary emergency occurred on units attending (Coupe and Blake 2005)

Effects of Workloads and Jurisdiction Size on Travel Distances and Response Times

Workloads affected response distances via the numbers of patrols ready and able to respond. When more units were available, the first unit to arrive at the scene was closer prior to responding and arrived more quickly (Fig. 5). Response distance and the numbers of patrol units responding were negatively related ($\tau_b = -.14, p = .005$). Workload differences across the day affected response times more than the size of the built-up area patrolled, though both played a role (Pearson partial correlations: response time by workloads, controlling for built-up area size, $r = .114$, $p = .015$; response times by built-up area size, controlling for workloads, $r = .10$, $p = .028$). It is clear that the effects of patrol area size and density of cover by patrol units will be more important in rural areas, of which there were only a few enclaves in the jurisdictions covered by this study. Familiarity with the area patrolled (χ^2, $p < .05$) and shift changeovers (χ^2, $p < .05$) also affected quickness of response.

Patrol workloads modified the pre-travel component of patrol response times. Pre-travel time represented a third of the time between officers being alerted and their arrival at the burglary scene. It varied depending on the activity patrol officers were engaged in just prior to setting off ($F, p = .006$): uncommitted patrols had shorter pre-travel times, averaging 1.3 min, than patrols that had to disengage from an existing routine incident, which averaged 1.8 min. Patrols responding from police stations took 1.65 min to start their journey. These were more common during periods when workloads were lighter, indicating a tendency for patrol officers to return to stations

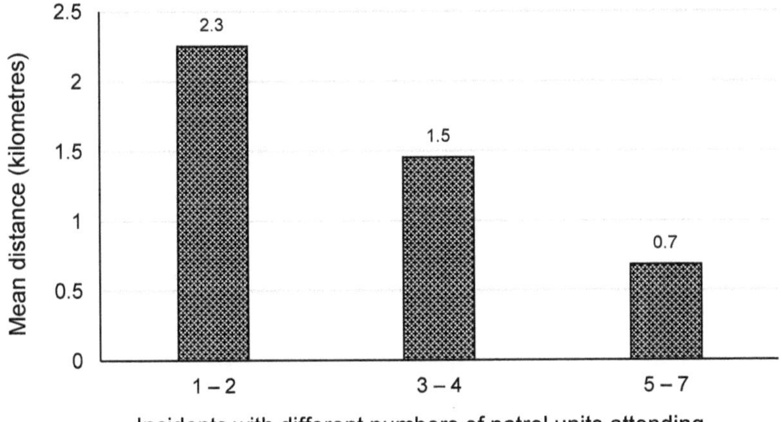

Fig. 5 Average distance from the scene of the closest unit prior to responding by incidents with different numbers of patrols attending (Coupe and Blake 2005)

at quieter times. This offsets the advantages of lighter workload periods when more patrols are available to respond.

Effects of Patrol Numbers and Workloads on On-Scene Arrest

The relationship between patrol numbers and workloads shaped patrol responses and successful on-scene arrest. When patrols failed to make on- or near-scene arrests at burglary emergencies, workloads during the same and prior hours (a weighted measure averaging immediate incidents during the prior and same hour per patrol unit per unit area) were notably heavier ($F = 8.27$, $p = .004$). Logistic regressions that took account of burglary characteristics, such as where the burglar was spotted and who reported the alert, confirm that patrol workloads influenced on-scene arrest independently of key burglary characteristics, with lighter patrol workloads improving arrest probabilities (Tables 1(*A*) and (*B*)). There was an average of 11.8 units patrolling the BCUs in this study, and each additional unit on patrol increased the probability of on-scene arrest at in-progress residential burglaries by 2.4%.

The inclusion of the daylight/darkness variable in the regression resulted in only small changes to significance and odds ratios, indicating that the effects of workloads on arrests operated in both darkness and daylight.

Effects of Patrol Numbers and Response Time on On-Scene Arrest

Quicker responses enabled burglars to be arrested more often (F, $p < .025$), with twice as many caught in the act on arrival at the scene within 4 min of the alert when patrols arrived after 6 min: 15.3% compared with 8.2% (Fig. 6). Response times in part reflected how many patrols responded, so that the response times of the first patrols to reach the scene were shorter when more units responded ($\tau_b = -.15$, $p < .001$). Larger numbers of patrols attending particularly improved the interception

Table 1 Logistic regressions with arrest at or near the scene as dependent variable (Coupe and Blake 2005)

	B	SE	Wald	*p*	Exp (*B*)
(A) Variable					
Call origin (neighbour/victim)	−1.17	.40	8.77	.003	.310
Burglary stage (entering)	2.28	.45	25.49	.000	9.744
Burglary stage (inside)	1.71	.45	14.66	.000	5.548
Daylight/darkness	−.69	.28	6.21	.013	.502
Workload/area/patrol	−.80	.33	5.80	.016	.451
Constant	−1.58	.44	12.99	.000	.206
(B) Variable					
Call origin (neighbour/victim)	−1.28	.39	10.64	.001	.279
Burglary stage (entering)	2.21	.45	24.61	.000	9.124
Burglary stage (inside)	1.62	.44	13.47	.000	5.057
Workload/area/patrol	−.86	.34	6.45	.011	.421
Constant	−1.58	.44	12.99	.000	.206

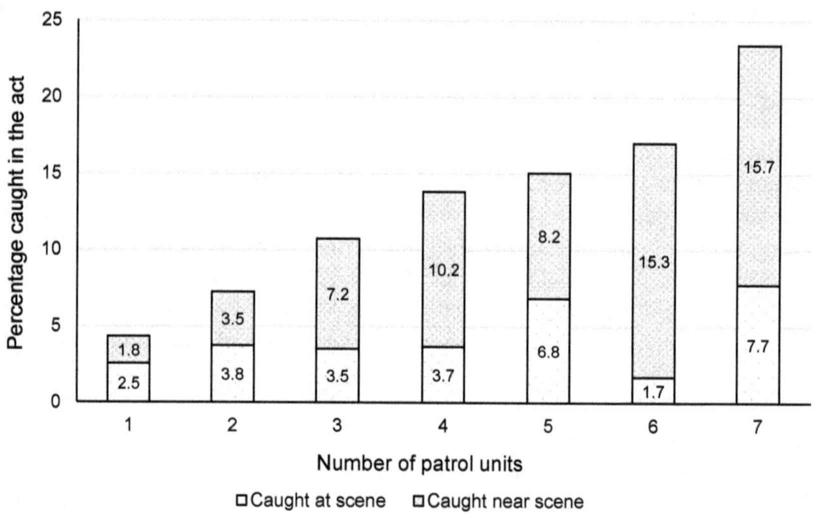

Fig. 6 Number of patrols responding by burglars arrested at or near the scene (Coupe and Blake 2005)

of burglars who had left burglary scenes, with twelve times as many being caught in neighbouring streets when six or seven units responded as when a single unit attended.

Logistic regression analysis confirms that the numbers of patrol units and response times are associated with arrest when controlling for key burglary characteristics

Table 2 Logistic regression with on-scene and near-scene arrest the dependent variable (Coupe and Blake 2005)

Variable	*B*	SE	Wald	*p*	Exp (*B*)
Number of units	.29	.09	9.97	.002	1.33
Response time of first patrol	−.11	.06	3.77	.051	.89
Victim reported/other	−1.14	.34	11.03	.001	.32
Burglary stage (entering)	2.11	.39	29.07	.000	8.27
Burglary stage (inside)	1.57	.39	16.35	.000	4.81
Daylight/darkness	−.57	.26	4.68	.030	.57
Constant	−2.05	.57	13.17	.000	.13

relating to solvability (Table 2). Each additional patrol unit available to respond boosts the odds of an arrest by 33%, while each minute shaved off response time increases the odds by 12% (Table 2).

It is important to keep in mind that the increase in successful arrests when more units respond is due to the first unit to arrive being closer to the scene prior to responding, reflecting conditions of lighter workloads, with more units uncommitted or committed only at routine incidents from which they can disengage. It is consistent with this that arrests are made only by the first few patrols to arrive at burglary scenes with the first units responsible for the lion's share (Figs. 7 and 8). The first units to arrive have by far the greatest success in arresting burglars, particularly at domestic burglaries, where they accounted for 80% of arrests; at non-residential burglaries, they accounted for only 69% (Coupe et al. 2002). This difference may reflect the numbers of offenders involved as well as the environments surrounding burglary sites.

It is evident that only two or three, or four patrols in the case of non-residential burglaries, at most, if available, need to attend burglaries. GPS location systems can inform a directed patrol response by only the two, three or four patrols identified as being the closest to incidents.

Indicators of Solvable In-Progress Residential Burglaries

As well as a sufficiently quick response by a proximate patrol unit, the successful arrest of offenders at or near burglary scenes also hinges on burglary characteristics. An effective response will be of little avail if the circumstances at burglaries make an arrest at the scene difficult or impossible. It is also important to identify the solvable 'in-progress' incidents at which it is possible to catch offenders red-handed and to which the closest patrols, if available and sufficiently proximate, should immediately be dispatched. Certain incident characteristics distinguish those burglaries at which rapidly responding patrols are likely to catch offenders and those at which, on the other hand, this is likely to prove very difficult, if not impossible.

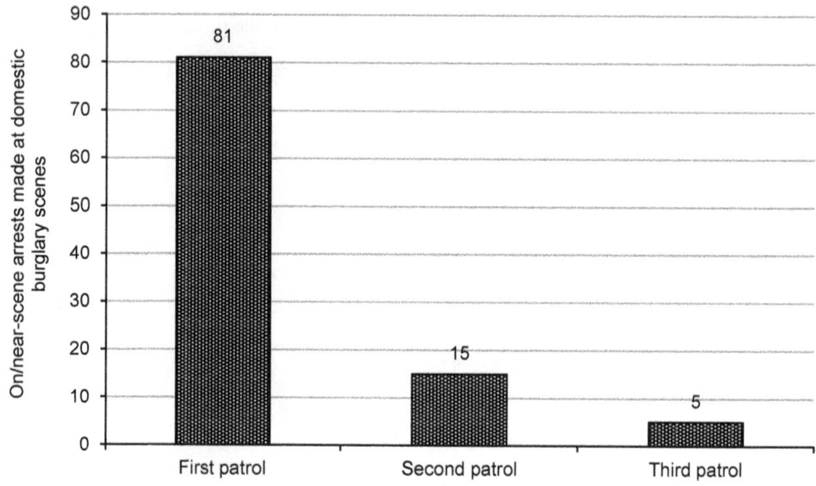

Fig. 7 Percentage of on-/near-scene arrests made by units arriving in order at domestic burglary scenes

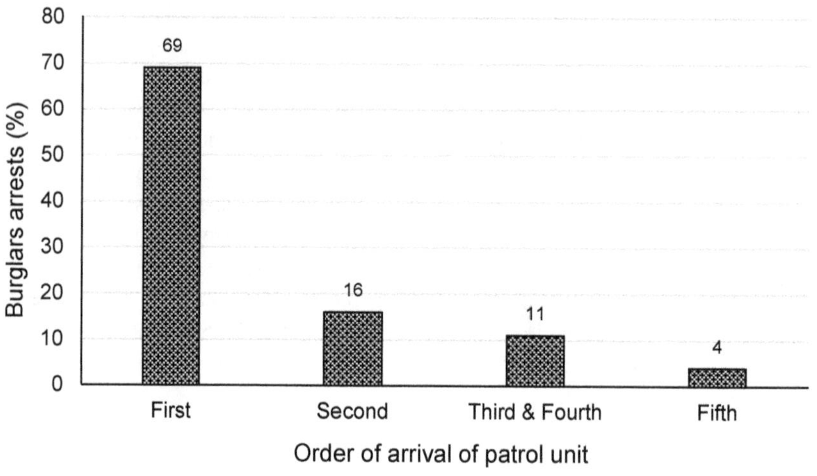

Fig. 8 Percentage of burglars arrested by units arriving at the scene in order at non-residential burglary scenes

Who Reported the Burglary, When the Burglar Was Spotted and Daylight/Darkness

The principal solvability factors for in-progress residential burglaries are who reported the burglary, when the burglar was spotted (i.e. entering, inside or leaving premises) and whether daylight or darkness prevailed (Table 3). If sighted while entering the property, the odds of arrest are 8.27 times higher than if seen only when leaving. Similarly, the odds of capture are 4.81 times higher if the burglar is seen while inside the premises, while a victim reporting an incident reported by a neigh-

Table 3 Solvability factors and on-scene and near-scene capture (Coupe and Blake 2005)

Variable	*B*	SE	Wald	Sig	Exp (*B*)
Number of units	.29	.09	9.97	.002	1.33
Response time of first patrol	−.11	.06	3.77	.051	.89
Victim reported/other	−1.14	.34	11.03	.001	.32
Burglary stage (entering)	2.11	.39	29.07	.000	8.27
Burglary stage (inside)	1.57	.39	16.35	.000	4.81
Daylight/darkness	−.57	.26	4.68	.030	.57
Constant	−2.05	.57	13.17	.000	.13

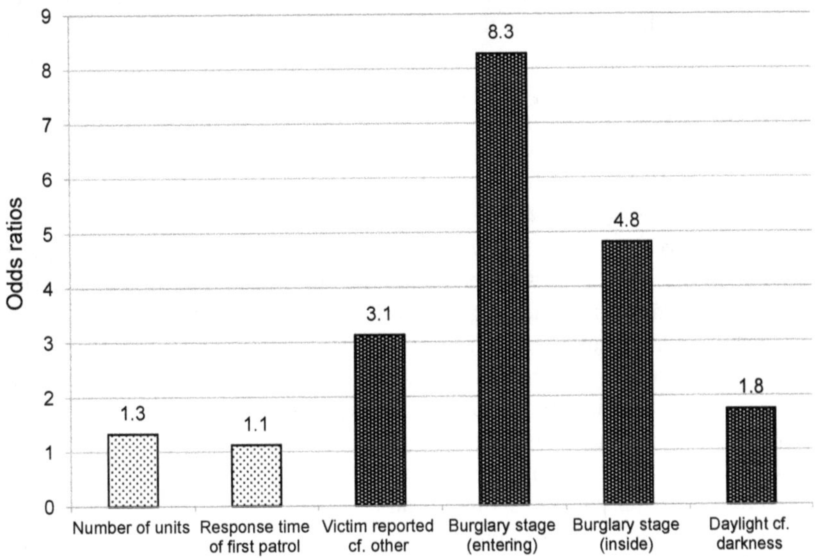

Fig. 9 Importance of solvability factors (dark grey) and resources (light stipple), measured in terms of binary logistic regression odds ratios, for 'in-progress' domestic burglaries

bour means a burglary is three times as likely to be solved as if a victim reported it. The odds of on- or near-scene arrest are 75% higher in daylight compared with darkness (Table 3). The influence of these solvability factors on arrests persists when controlling for the key police response effects on catching burglars red-handed and vice versa (Table 3; Fig. 9).

Targeted Patrol Informed by Incident Characteristics

Findings on the probability of catching offenders in the act at different sorts of incidents indicate which in-progress burglary incidents are more solvable and should be allocated a speedier and 'stronger' patrol response. The answers provided by people who call in alerts to questions about who they are (victim, neighbour or passer-by) and where the burglar was sighted (breaking into, inside or leaving the target)

Table 4 Probability of arresting burglars at or near the scene (Coupe and Blake 2005)

Incident reported by	Burglar's location	When alert received	
	Breaking into dwelling (%)	Inside dwelling (%)	Leaving dwelling (%)
Neighbour or passer-by	21	12	3
Victim	6	6	1

indicate the different prospects of an on-scene or near-scene arrest (Table 4). It is important to allocate the highest response priority to incidents where a burglar is reported by a neighbour entering the premises, at which the probability of an arrest is 21 times higher than when reported by a victim once the burglar is leaving the property (Table 4). Victim-reported incidents most often involve burglars realising the dwelling is occupied and fleeing the scene. Such incidents especially occur in darkness, though the poorer odds of capture when victims report in-progress burglaries—a third of those when neighbours report it—persist when controlling for daylight and darkness (Table 4, Fig. 9).

Stronger patrol responses by two or three units can be allocated to those in-progress domestic burglaries with the highest probabilities of catching the offender red-handed. Information on the burglar's location and the person calling in the alert forms the basis for allocating patrol resources. The most solvable 'in-progress' incidents, where neighbours spot burglars entering, result in far higher arrest returns per patrol resource input (Fig. 10), rising sharply with additional resources. At the least solvable 'in-progress' incidents, where victims report burglars leaving, there are poor arrest outcomes that hardly improve with additional patrol resources.

Therefore, stronger patrol responses lead to more on-scene burglary arrests, but this differs according to incident characteristics, which indicate incident solvability (Fig. 9). A matching of strong patrol responses with solvable offences is needed for successful arrest.

Suspect Numbers

The number of reported suspects is a weaker solvability indicator at in-progress residential burglaries and does not show an independent significant effect in multivariate tests. Suspect numbers were known for 69% of the residential burglaries in the sample, of which 40% were single-offender, 41% two-offender, 15% three-offender and 3% four-offender incidents.

Although more offenders are caught at incidents with more suspects (Fig. 11), this partly reflects stronger responses by more patrol units and the fact that burglaries with more co-offenders tend to occur during daylight (Coupe and Blake 2005), when the chances of on-scene capture are far better.

Nevertheless, it appears sensible to prioritise incidents where more suspects are seen, as indeed happens, given the additional opportunities for arrest that they offer.

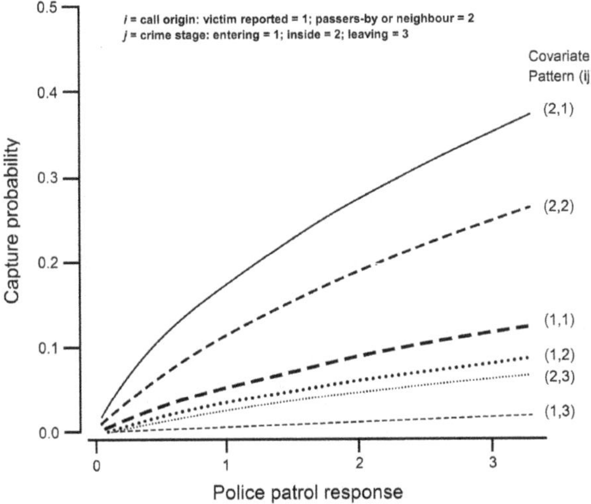

Fig. 10 Effects of patrol response on capture probabilities for non-evening burglaries (the police response variable incorporates response time and number of patrol units: units arriving at burglary scenes sooner are weighted more strongly; Coupe and Blake 2005)

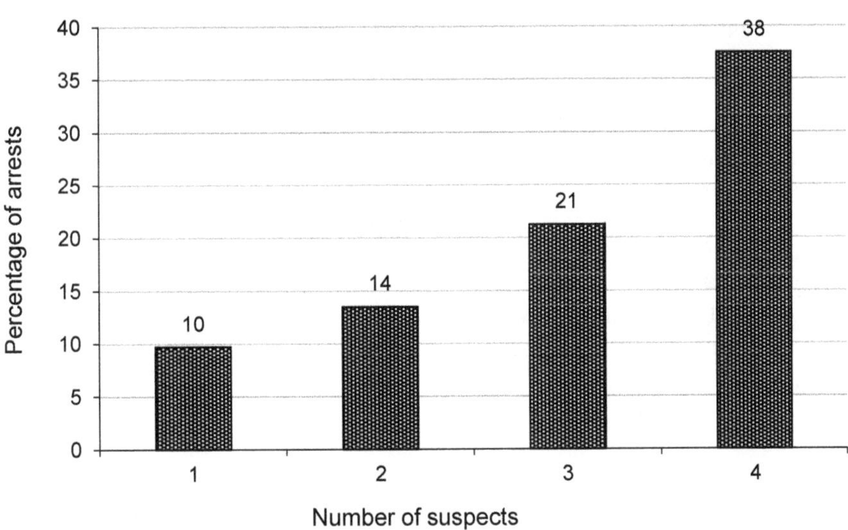

Fig. 11 Suspect numbers and on-/near-scene arrests at 'immediate response' residential burglary incidents (Coupe and Blake 2005)

Not to do so would be a failure to exploit the opportunities afforded by 'in-progress' incidents occurring during daylight hours.

Other Aspects of Patrol Provision

Deploying officers in single- rather than double-crewed units is likely to enable areas to be patrolled more economically or, if similar officer numbers are allocated, enable units to reach crime scenes more quickly and intercept more offenders. Dog vans are also sent to half of domestic burglaries, and the effects of this on arrests are also evaluated. Finally, the use of more powerful patrol vehicles capable of quicker acceleration and higher speeds is compared with the deployment of less powerful vehicles in order to determine whether the need for rapid response justifies larger, more expensive cars.

Dog Vans

Dog vans attended 42% of in-progress burglaries. They were more likely to be called in to deal with victim than neighbour alerts ($\chi^2, p = .04$) and were therefore present at the scene of 47% of night-time, but only 29% of daylight, incidents. Their attendance at victim alerts dropped from 55% in darkness to 22% in daylight.

On-scene or near-scene arrest rates differed little whether or not dog vans attended after dark, being 7% rather than 8% at incidents where no dogs attended. Capture rates, however, were higher when dogs were used in daylight, with arrests at 21% of incidents with dogs compared with 12% without them. For daylight incidents where victims did not call in the alert, arrests were made at 24% of incidents with dog attendance, nearly double the 14% without dogs' help.

It appears reasonable to conclude that dogs are used at the least solvable 'in-progress' incidents—those called in by victims when offenders are commonly fleeing the scene in darkness. Their use at more solvable offences called in by neighbours during daylight hours proved far more successful. This is additional evidence that priority should be placed on the most solvable offences. Even so, arrest rates of 7% after dark where dog vans attended might not have been achieved without the help of dogs.

Single/Double Crewing

Catching burglars red-handed depends on a rapid response by the first three patrols to reach the scene. Deploying more single-officer patrols should enable fewer officers to cover the same area or increase the number of units available to respond (Kaplan 1979). If all double-crewed patrols were, theoretically, to be switched to single crewing, it might be expected that the distances of the closest unit and the two next closest units to an emergency incident would be halved, enabling quicker responses and higher arrest rates at solvable incidents. For equivalent functions, therefore, cost-effectiveness in terms of labour and vehicle costs is approximately twice that of double-crewed patrols (Boydstun et al. 1977).

Although the single-crewed patrol is viewed as being more vulnerable, this is at odds with the evidence (Wilson and Brewer 1992), which indicates that lone officers tend to be safer (Boydstun et al. 1977), less confrontational and no more likely to be injured, irrespective of precinct or shift type, this may reflect their greater prudence and restraint as a result of working alone (Decker and Wagner 1982).

Sixty-one per cent of the units operating over the six months throughout the force in this study were double-crewed. If all of these had been deployed as single-crewed patrols, unit numbers would have increased by 62%, reducing by 39% the area covered per patrol and incident numbers, and contracting by 22% the distance of the nearest unit from the burglary scene. An additional 60% of patrols would increase uncommitted units or those able to easily disengage from existing routine incidents so that a closer patrol could attend. The first patrol would reach the scene an average of one minute sooner, and mean response times would be reduced by over 20% to less than 4 min. If other demands did not make it impracticable, it can be estimated that deploying all 61% of double-crewed officers in single units would improve on-scene arrests by between 44 (estimate based on shorter response time) and 60% (estimate based on extra available patrols). While a randomly controlled trial would resolve the effects of single crewing on catching burglars in the act, a single-to-double-crewing switch implemented in an inner city BCU within the study area indicated a potential for arrests at or near the scene to exceed these theoretical estimates.[1]

Although the double-crewed patrols in this study made quicker responses and were more often the first units to arrive and caught more burglars red-handed, this reflected the fact that more of them were deployed in units that dealt with alerts across the whole of the Operational Command Units (OCUs)[2] ($\chi^2, p < .05$), rather than individual beats like many single-crewed units, and had shorter pre-travel times ($z, p < .001$), since they were more often uncommitted, setting off while patrolling rather than from police stations or by having to disengage from dealing with routine incidents like more of the single-crewed units (Blake and Coupe 2001). As there were more double-crewed units, they were, on average, closer to 'in-progress' scenes, while the double-crewed patrols providing OCU-level cover were particularly directed to attend the more solvable incidents where neighbours reported burglars entering premises (U, $p =$ .02). More double-crewed patrols operated at night (23.00–07.30; $\chi^2, p < .05$) when traffic is lighter and mean travel speeds higher (29 mph vs. 25 mph during daytime; z, $p = .001$). Speed differences between single- and double-crewed units disappeared when controlling for night-time/daytime and activities prior to attending (Blake and Coupe 2001). This underlines the importance of understanding patrol deployment in the context of incident solvability in order to draw lessons about how officers should be best deployed. Though double-crewed units make more arrests, this reflects their volume, deployment, function and availability to respond. Single crewing helps boost arrests.

---

[1]Sheldon, Birmingham, UK, switched to single-crewed deployment in the late 1990s; on- and near-scene arrests doubled.

[2]There were 32 operational command units in this large urban police force, whose jurisdiction had a population of 3 million.

Table 5 Mean travel speeds for vehicle type by response distance

Unit type	All distances	<2.5 miles	>2.5 miles
Less powerful	27.7	25.7	36.6
More powerful	30.0	24.4	41.2

Deployment of officers in single-crewed patrols, as far as is feasible, appears to have considerable benefits[3] for on-scene arrest at burglary that are likely to be true also of other incidents requiring immediate police officer presence, such as non-domestic and domestic assaults. The first officer will arrive more quickly, but, if the circumstances demand it, he or she can await the arrival of the second unit, who would often arrive after a similar response time as if there had been double-crewed deployment. In addition, single crewing may enable smoother shift changes, a source of weaker responses and poorer on-scene arrest rates.

Patrol Vehicle Type

More powerful patrol cars offer little advantage in terms of responding to burglary emergencies in urban areas. All response journeys involve a final leg where units slow as the specific premises are located, even with GPS aids, and the distances of units from incidents in built-up areas mean that only a small part of the response journey is on main roads where the benefit of faster acceleration would be notable. The superiority of more powerful units is evident only over larger distances where patrols are 2–2.5 miles from the burglary scene. Beyond 2.5 miles from the scene, for double-crewed units, more powerful vehicles had a 15.5% speed advantage (41.2 vs. 36.6 mph, $z, p = .05$), whereas, at less than 2.5 miles away, speeds for more and less powerful vehicles did not markedly differ (24.4 for more vs. 25.7 for less powerful vehicles). All vehicles, whatever their power, achieved quicker speeds over longer distances, but powerful vehicles made an average 69% gain in speed, whereas the less powerful fared less well, achieving a gain of only 42% (Table 5).

It is evident that, in rural areas and areas at the fringes of built-up areas, where patrol cover is thinner and response distances longer, more powerful vehicles should be deployed as standard so that, when an emergency response is required, they can reach crime scenes sooner.

Conclusions

Evidence from this study points to important lessons about resourcing patrols so that they are able to make on-scene arrests. It also specifies the solvability factors for in-progress residential burglaries so that the more solvable incidents may be prioritised.

[3]Findings from Blake and Coupe (2001) were used as the basis for a recommendation to deploy officers as single-crewed patrol units in the Police Reform Act 2002. [Editorial note: did you mean the Police Reform Act 2002 (Commencement No. 8) Order 2004? See https://www.legislation.gov.uk/uksi/2004/913/contents/made]

Patrol deployment ideally needs to be at a level that enables the closest patrol to reach the scene in time to catch burglars reported by neighbours while either entering or inside premises, before they leave the scene, or, if three patrols are able to attend, to enable capture in neighbouring streets. This may be enhanced by deploying officers in single-crewed units as far as is feasible. Patrol numbers need to take account of demand and demand fluctuations and of the size of the built-up area to be patrolled so that units sufficiently close to scenes are uncommitted or can disengage if already attending routine incidents. Daily levels of, and fluctuations in, 'immediate response' incidents of all types and of solvable in-progress burglaries are key to determining the patrol unit numbers to be deployed per unit area. In rural areas, especially those more remote and with diffuse settlement, patrol provision at levels enabling units to be sufficiently close to scenes to intercept burglars at solvable incidents will be difficult, if not impossible, to deploy. This will be mitigated in more urbanised rural areas and rural–urban fringes by the use of more powerful vehicles that, at patrol deployment levels in this study, would be of little additional value in built-up areas.

Effective in-progress burglary responses must take account of differences in incident solvability. The more solvable cases involve burglars who are unaware of having been spotted at an early stage in the burglary by neighbours, particularly when these occur in daylight and when more than one suspect is present. Stronger responses to the more solvable burglaries will markedly increase the prospects of an arrest at or near the scene, whereas, at the least solvable incidents, where victims report burglars as they are leaving, extra patrol inputs will result in little or no improvement in the odds of an arrest. The use of dog vans will be likely to bear greater fruit if they are also allocated to the more solvable incidents that occur in daylight as well as to challenging incidents that take place in darkness, where most dogs in this study helped out.

The study illustrates the principle that successful detection hinges on the application of appropriate resources to the more solvable cases. The findings also counter earlier, classic research indicating that patrol resources have no effect on rates of arrest at or near the scene, that reporting times are so long as to preclude timely patrol responses and that no offenders can be caught in the act after the lapse of 5 minutes from the time of the alert.

References

Bieck, W., & Kessler, D. A. (1977). *Response time analysis*. Kansas City: Missouri Board of Police Commissioners.

Blake, L. (2006). *Catching residential burglars in the act* (Ph.D. thesis). University of Birmingham, UK.

Blake, L., & Coupe, R. T. (2001). The impact of single and two-officer patrols on catching burglars in the act. *The British Journal of Criminology, 41*(2), 381–396.

Boydstun, J. E., Sherry, M. E., & Moelter, N. P. (1977). *Patrol staffing in San Diego: One- or two-officer units*. Washington: Police Foundation.

Clawson, C., & Chang, S. K. (1977). Relationship of response delays and arrest rates. *Journal of Police Science and Administration, 5*(1), 53–68.
Coupe, R. T., & Blake, L. (2005). The effects of patrol workloads and response strength on burglary emergencies. *Journal of Criminal Justice, 33*(3), 239–255.
Coupe, R. T., & Kaur, S. (2005). The role of alarms and CCTV in detecting non-residential burglary. *Security Journal, 18*(2), 53–72.
Coupe, T., & Griffiths, M. (1996). *Solving residential burglary* (Police Research Group Crime Detection and Prevention Services, Paper 77). London: Home Office.
Coupe, R. T., Erwood, N., & Kaur, S. (2002). *Solving non-residential burglary* (Unpublished Home Office Report). London: Home Office.
Decker, S. H., & Wagner, A. E. (1982). The impact of police patrol staffing on police–citizen injuries and dispositions. *Journal of Criminal Justice, 10*(5), 375–382.
Donnellan, G. and Ariel, B. (2012, July, 4–6). *Burglary solvability factors*. Paper presented at 4th International Evidence-Based Policing Conference, Cambridge.
Jansson, K. (2005). *Volume crime investigations—A review of the research literature* (Home Office Online Report OLR 44/05). London: Home Office.
Kaplan, E. H. (1979). Evaluating the effectiveness of one-officer versus two-officer patrol units. *Journal of Criminal Justice, 7*(4), 325–355.
Kelling, G., Pate, T., Dieckman, D., & Brown, C. (1974). *The Kansas City preventive patrol experiment*. Washington DC: Police Foundation.
Larson, R. (1975). What happened to patrol operations in Kansas City? A review of the Kansas City preventive patrol experiment. *Journal of Criminal Justice, 3*(4), 267–297.
Newburn, T. (2007). Understanding investigation. In T. Newburn, T. Williamson, & A. Wright (Eds.), *Handbook of criminal investigation*. Cullompton: Willan Publishing.
Paine, C., & Ariel, B. (2013, July, 8–10). *Solvability analysis: Increasing the likelihood of detection in completed, attempted and in-progress burglaries*. Paper presented at the 6th International Evidence-Based Policing Conference, Cambridge.
Pease, K. (1998). *Repeat victimisation: Taking stock* (Crime Detection and Prevention Series, Paper 90). London: Home Office.
Robinson, A., & Tilley, N. (2009). Factors influencing police performance in the investigation of volume crimes in England and Wales. *Police Practice and Research: An International Journal, 10*(3), 209–223.
Spelman, W., & Brown, D. K. (1981). *Calling the police: Citizen reporting of serious crime*. Washington, DC: Police Research Executive Forum.
Tilley, N., Robinson, A., & Burrows, J. (2007). The investigation of high volume crime. In T. Newburn, T. Williamson, & A. Wright (Eds.), *Handbook of criminal investigation* (pp. 226–254). London: Willan Publishing.
Wilson, C., & Brewer, N. (1992). One- and two-person patrols: A review. *Journal of Criminal Justice, 20*(5), 443–454.

Resources, Solvability and Detection: A Theoretical Model

Richard Timothy Coupe

Introduction

The objective in this chapter is to draw on the findings from the solvability research presented in this volume and to explore and consolidate an understanding of what incident solvability consists of, its origins in jurisdictional offender profiles and environmental variation, and the extent to which it can be modified. The ways in which detection outcomes reflect the interaction between case solvability and police resources will also be critically reviewed in order to appreciate how best to inform case-screening decisions and the allocation of officer time to investigative activities. Solving crimes depends on incident solvability but is conditional on the resourcing of investigations. To realise the potential to detect crimes, resources should meet the investigative demands of solvable offences or the ones it is possible to solve. The appropriate allocation of resources to various investigative activities enables the 'unlocking' of the evidence that results in case clearance. A coherent theoretical model is described that provides a guide to case screening and insight for scholarship.

Incident Solvability: Characteristics and Origins

Offence solvability varies between different crime types and within crime types. It also varies geographically owing to spatial differences in offenders and the varying opportunities for crime presented by different environmental circumstances. There are also differences in officer resources and decisions about the allocation of resources to different investigative activities between jurisdictions, which, together with solv-

R. T. Coupe (✉)
Institute of Criminology, University of Cambridge, Cambridge, England, UK
e-mail: rtc23@cam.ac.uk

R. T. Coupe et al. (eds.), *Crime Solvability Factors*,
https://doi.org/10.1007/978-3-030-17160-5_18

ability variations, help account for differences in jurisdictional detection rates. The following sections extend and develop these points.

Offence Solvability and Different Crime Types

Detection rates vary considerably between different sorts of incidents of the same crime type. They also differ markedly between types of crime (Burrows and Tarling 1982). As the research in this volume shows, this reflects contrasts in their inherent solvability as well as investigative resources.

Violent crimes are more solvable and far more are detected than property crimes: 44% of violent crimes are detected in England and Wales compared with 13% of burglaries, 11% of thefts of or from vehicles, and 22% of frauds and forgeries (Taylor and Bond 2012). This is partly because all violent crimes are 'contact crimes', so that, with the exception of homicide, victims are frequently able to identify assailants or provide suspect descriptions. This has been borne out by the role played by eyewitnesses in non-domestic assault solvability and detection (Olphin and Mueller-Johnson, Chapter "Targeting Factors that Predict Clearance of Non-domestic Assaults") and by the higher solvability and detection rates of faith hate assaults compared with criminal damage offences, fewer of which are witnessed (Rose et al., Chapter "Solvability Factors and Investigative Strategy for Faith Hate Crime: Anti-Semitic and Islamophobic Assault, Criminal Damage and Public Order Offences in London").

The differences in detection rates of violent and sexual compared with property offences may also reflect higher resources being allocated to more serious or harmful offences. That 95% of homicides in England and Wales are detected undoubtedly reflects this as well as a predominance of 'acquaintance homicide' (Innes 2002; Riggs et al., Chapter "Homicide Resources, Solvability and Detection"). Reported sex offences also have relatively high clearance rates of 30% in England and Wales (Taylor and Bond 2012), since, for instance, many rapes involve previously acquainted victims and perpetrators (Curtis 1974). Differences in detection rates between violent, sexual and property offences are mirrored in this volume's findings. Non-domestic assault detection rates (55%) are higher than those for sex offences on railways (31%), which, in turn, are far higher than those for residential burglary (13%) or rail metal theft (11%) (respectively, Olphin and Mueller-Johnson, Chapter "Targeting Factors that Predict Clearance of Non-domestic Assaults"; Jones et al., Chapter "Reporting, Detection and Solvability of Sex Offences on Railways"; Paine and Ariel, Chapter "Population-Level Analysis of Residential Burglaries"; Robb et al., Chapter "Metal Theft Solvability and Detection"). That detection rates for faith hate assaults are higher than for faith hate public order offences may also in part reflect differences in seriousness and funding.

Cybercrimes that involve sexual and hate offences as well as fraud have variable—though generally very low—detection rates. Detection rates as low as 0.6% are estimated for cyber property offences, attributable partly to the separation between offender and victim, who may be located not only in different jurisdictions but also very often in other countries and beyond the easy reach of the force within whose jurisdiction the victim lives. Low solvability has particular origins for this offence type with the lowest of detection rates.

It is clear that varied detection rates between crime types, as well as the variations within crime types identified in this volume, reflect solvability differences. However, it is evident from the empirical studies of resources covered in Chapters "Homicide Resources, Solvability and Detection" and "Investigative Activities, Resources and Burglary Detection" that these also play an important role. Officers' assessments of solvability determine case-screening and resourcing decisions, and it is funded investigations of solvable incidents that enable case detection.

Geographical Variation in Crime Solvability, Resources and Detection

Offence solvability and detection vary according to when and where different types of crimes occur and who commits them. The proportion of residential burglaries with at least one solvability factor, for instance, varies by up to a third between local police areas in England's Thames Valley Police jurisdiction (Paine and Ariel, Chapter "Population-Level Analysis of Residential Burglaries"), indicating that the characteristics of burglary incidents substantially differ geographically. The solvability of anti-Semitic and Islamophobic offences similarly varies across London's 32 boroughs and are also spatially uncorrelated with each other.

Metal theft solvability and detection rates also vary markedly between different rail regions in England and Wales (Robb et al., Chapter "Metal Theft Solvability and Detection"). This reflects spatial differences in the metal theft crime types and differences in the sorts of offences prioritised and resourced for investigation. Even though checking scrap metal dealers with criminal records is a promising source of evidence for solving railway metal theft, dealers were visited in connection with 32% of copper cable thefts in what used to be known as the North Western British Transport Police Area, but only 4% in the London South Police Area, where only half as many cases were solved (Robb et al., Chapter "Metal Theft Solvability and Detection"). There are also differences in weather that can shorten the survival of forensic evidence in the open air where there is heavy rainfall, such as the north-west railway region. The solvability and detection rates of sexual offences on railway property varied geographically to at least as great an extent. They were markedly lower in London and the south-east areas where most of the high-volume, low-solvability offences occur on trains and, in particular, on the London Underground (Jones et al., Chapter "Reporting, Detection and Solvability of Sex Offences on Railways").

There can also be equally striking temporal variations in solvability, which can reflect the volumes of different offences occurring at various times of the day, week and month, as well as solvability differences due to these timing contrasts (Tompson and Coupe 2017). Burglars are at almost double the risk of being caught red-handed at in-progress domestic burglaries that occur in daylight as at night, given improved guardianship due to superior daytime visibility (Coupe, Chapter "Investigative Activities, Resources and Burglary Detection"). Overstretched resources can also affect temporal variations in burglars caught at or near the scene. Given a constant supply of patrol units across the day for different police areas, fluctuations in offences requiring an immediate response over the course of the day lead to notable temporal variations in demand for patrol officers. This results in strong, quicker responses and high arrest rates when demand is low and weaker responses and poor arrest rates when it is high (Coupe, Chapter "The Organisation and Deployment of Patrol Resources: Cost-Effective On-Scene Arrest at Burglaries"). Varying resource inputs into investigative activities for cases of similar solvability at different times or in different areas will cause detection outcomes to vary, because under-resourcing of cases capable of being solved means evidence is not unlocked and opportunities for detection are not exploited.

Causes of Geographical Variation in Solvability

Solvability differs spatially irrespective of resources. This concerns differences in crime types that reflect differing offender populations and contrasting offending environments. Spatial variations in crime solvability (measured in terms of identified solvability factors) also have origins in resources that do not match the investigative demands of solvable offences in different jurisdictions, so that the potential to solve solvable crimes is left unrealised.

Geographical Variation in Resources

Police resources vary spatially. In English police services, resources have been poorly aligned with crime levels, and officers per 1000 crimes a year range from only 14 to as high as 37 (Audit Commission 1993). Resources are positively related to investigative outcomes and account for 36% of the variation in detections (Audit Commission 1993). Such large cross-jurisdictional variations in resources and poor matching of resources to offence numbers and solvable incidents across forces, at basic command unit (BCU) level (Burrows et al. 2005) and across the day within BCUs (Coupe and Blake 2005) means that both the capacity to solve crime and detection rates will vary substantially between jurisdictions.

Spatial Variation in Offenders, Environments and Crime Incidence

Offending behaviour reflects the offender populations and the opportunities for crime presented by different environments. Environments and offender populations vary temporally and spatially, and the interactions between them give rise to jurisdictional differences in the mix of different crime types and the characteristics of offences within them. This results in spatial and temporal variation in solvable incidents and, hence, jurisdictional differences in the amounts of officer resources needed to detect all solvable crimes.

The socio-demographic, economic and behavioural characteristics of jurisdictions' workday and resident populations help shape their routine activities (Cohen and Felson 1979). These activities and the features of the built environment present opportunities for offenders with different expertise and offending propensities to commit different crimes (Brantingham and Brantingham 1998) while exposing them to varying risks of being arrested and having their crimes solved (Coupe and Blake 2006). Offender characteristics and environments frame offending and target selection (Wright and Logie 1988; Nee and Taylor 2000; Bernasco 2010) so that the incidence of crime reflects the interaction between crime opportunities and offenders' activity space (Brantingham and Brantingham 1984) and criminal intentions. The environment influences solvability through its effects on target exposure and guardianship, which affect eyewitness evidence (Coupe and Fox 2015) and the ease with which officers can catch criminals (Coupe and Blake 2010).

The mobility, geographical distribution and characteristics of offender populations also vary geographically. This also modifies the spatial incidence of different types of offences and their solvability. The risk of offenders being caught depends on their prolificacy (Ahlberg and Knutsson 1990), but arrest also hinges on offenders' risk-averseness and expertise in offence and targeting decisions, since it is these, together with chance events (Rengert et al. 1999; Tseloni 2000), that make offences more or less solvable. By planning more (van Koppen and Jansen 1998), operating singly or with co-offenders (Bernasco 2006), and targeting property or people in different areas at different times of day (Coupe and Blake 2005) or in different seasons (Tompson and Coupe 2017), incident solvability changes, and criminals are exposed to varying risks of being seen or caught in different ways (Coupe and Blake 2010). More experienced, older criminals travel farther (van Koppen and Jansen 1998) and are caught less often and less easily (Lamme and Bernasco 2013), with some committing more than 50 offences before being arrested (Ahlberg and Knutsson 1990).

Investigative Activities, Evidence and Detections

To appreciate the ways in which resources and incident solvability interact to produce detection outcomes, it is useful to consider individual investigative activities. Most crime consists of less serious violent and high-volume property offences, most of which are necessarily dealt with reactively (Tilley et al. 2007) in response to calls for assistance from the public. A small minority is cleared using proactive approaches.

Reactive crime investigation has two stages (Fig. 1). First-stage activities are influenced by offence characteristics, which determine case solvability and resource inputs, as shown in Chapter "Investigative Activities, Resources and Burglary Detection" (Coupe). It involves the initial response to and investigations at the crime scene, including first officers questioning eyewitnesses and forensic officers collecting samples. These activities can result in 'intermediate outputs', such as offenders caught red-handed, and suspect, vehicle and forensic evidence that often leads to further investigations (Fig. 1). Unsolvable cases with no useful evidence may be filed 'undetected' if they are not serious offences.

In the second stage, detectives undertake further investigation of selected cases with outputs from first-stage activities to produce investigative outcomes in the form of detected or undetected cases. Activities include checking vehicles, tracing stolen property, collating forensic evidence, matching suspect descriptions with known offenders, visiting crime scenes to question potential witnesses, consulting registered informants, and carrying out suspect surveillance. Without strong first-stage evidence, further investigation is often carried out only for very serious offences, although evidence from crime scenes plays a key role in solving these offences as well. Even most on- or near-scene arrests are 'intermediate outputs' that need further investigative work to achieve detected outcomes (Coupe, Chapter "Investigative Activities, Resources and Burglary Detection").

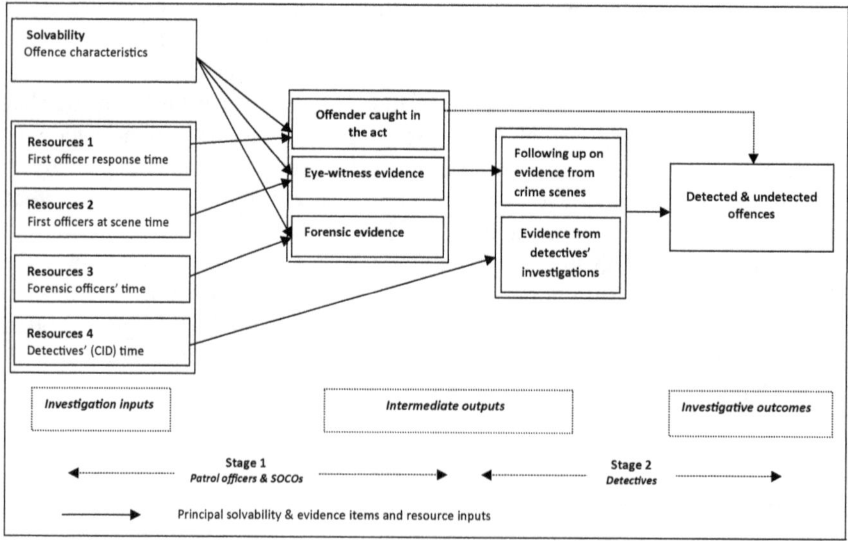

Fig. 1 Role of resources and solvability in reactive investigations of high-volume crime (Diagram 1 from Coupe 2016)

Resource Input–Evidence Output Activities

Policing actions, such as patrol response, questioning neighbours or passersby or collecting forensic evidence, are 'resource input–evidence output' activities that should be undertaken according to the solvability characteristics of incidents. Rather than allocating the same resource to provide a uniform response to 'in-progress' incidents such as burglaries by using the alert call from the public as a solvability factor, it would be more cost-effective to ensure a 'strong' and fast patrol response only at the subset of 'in-progress' incidents shown by an analysis of incident characteristics to be likely to result in on- or near-scene arrest. For burglaries, these characteristics or 'solvability indicators' would include by whom the incident is reported and when the burglar is spotted (Coupe, Chapter "The Organisation and Deployment of Patrol Resources: Cost-Effective On-Scene Arrest at Burglaries").

Patrol Resource Inputs–Arrest Outputs

The on- or near-scene capture of offenders at residential burglaries may be used to illustrate the ways in which patrol resource inputs to 'in-progress' incidents of varying solvability relate to arrest outputs. Stronger patrol responses result in more on-scene arrests, but this is contingent on burglary characteristics. The most solvable cases—where burglars are seen entering premises by neighbours—result in far higher arrest outputs per unit of patrol resource input, which rise steeply with additional resources (Fig. 2). The least solvable ones—where victims report burglars as they leave premises—have very low arrest outputs, which barely improve with additional patrol resources. At the most solvable incidents, even weak patrol responses result in considerable success. At the least solvable, even strong patrol responses meet with little success, confirming that successful detection depends on the resourcing of solvable cases for particular activities. In the case of patrol strength at in-progress burglaries, key indicators of solvability are call origin (who reported the offence) and burglary stage (when the burglar was seen), while other characteristics, such as whether the offence occurred in daylight or darkness, are also important (Coupe, Chapter "The Organisation and Deployment of Patrol Resources: Cost-Effective On-Scene Arrest at Burglaries").

Arrest rate does not decline with increasing resource inputs, indicating that patrol response capacity is underfunded compared with offence solvability, with extra solvability potential to be realised by selectively allocating more resources to those incidents with promising solvability indicators.

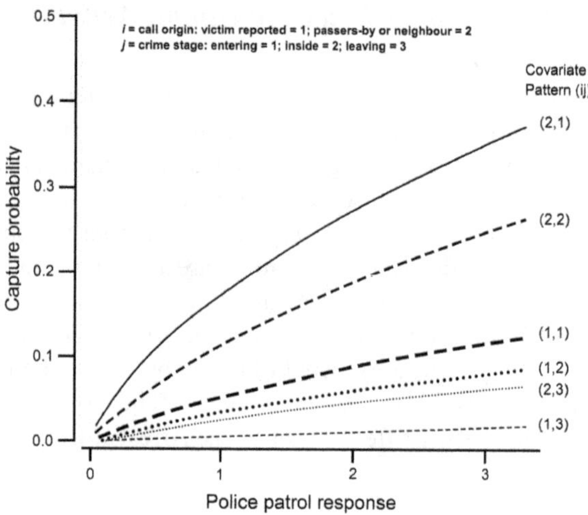

Fig. 2 Effects of police response on capture probabilities for non-evening burglaries—The police response variable incorporates response time and number of patrol units: units arriving at burglary scenes sooner are weighted more strongly (Fig. 6 from Coupe and Blake 2005)

Solvability Indicators for Other Offences

Different crimes have different detection potential, and the activities that produce the evidence that helps solve them also vary. Equivalent solvability indicators are needed to identify which incidents for each investigative activity are likely to produce the additional evidence that will contribute to successful suspect identification and arrest. This volume helps to meet this need. A related question is how much effort is to be input into each activity per case and whether there are points at which declining returns in terms of evidence outputs make resourcing an investigative activity markedly less cost-effective.

Chapter "Solvability Indicators for 'First Officers': Targeting Eyewitness Questioning at Non-residential Burglaries" (Coupe) illustrates the intervisibility characteristics at targets that may be used to inform first-responding officers about those non-residential burglaries at which they ought to question occupants of neighbouring premises in order to collect named suspect or detailed suspect evidence. Eyewitness information and on-scene arrest are important to most types of violent or faith hate assaults and criminal damage and public order offences (e.g. Olphin and Mueller-Johnson, Chapter "Targeting Factors that Predict Clearance of Non-domestic Assaults"; Rose et al., Chapter "Solvability Factors and Investigative Strategy for Faith Hate Crime: Anti-Semitic and Islamophobic Assault, Criminal Damage and Public Order Offences in London") as well as property crimes, while forensic evidence is of growing significance for the detection of high-volume crimes such as burglary (Paine and Ariel, Chapter "Population-Level Analysis of Residential Burglaries"; Donnellan and Ariel, Chapter "Assessing Solvability Factors in Greater Manchester, England: The Case of Residential Burglaries"). Tracing stolen goods, though generally less important, is effective for detecting vehicle theft and metal theft, for which scrap metal dealer checks are one of the strongest solvability factors (Robb et al., Chapter "Metal Theft Solvability and Detection").

For many crimes, there are investigative activities for which solvability indicators are unknown, and more research needs to be carried out to identify these. Without them, or where they are not used, case selection is likely to be haphazard, and solvable cases may be missed while unsolvable ones are investigated. Alternatively, every case can be investigated to uncover the solvable ones with evidence, but this would be cost-ineffective. Some investigative activities without accurate solvability indicators are, therefore, liable to consume heavy resource inputs—some necessarily so, like certain homicides, rapes and serious assaults that result in permanent injury, offences which most police forces make strenuous efforts to solve. Even if used sparingly, some activities such as surveillance are costly and rarely applied to high-volume crimes (Tilley et al. 2007).

Existing research into solvability factors has principally examined the incident characteristics that predict detected compared with undetected cases, such as suspect identity information or useful forensic samples. However, environmental or offence solvability indicators are also needed for each investigative activity so that cases may be screened and resources targeted at cases that are solvable in terms of the use of particular investigative activities. Extending the application of solvability factors or indicators to each investigative activity promises to improve detection rates cost-effectively. The more different items of evidence that result from the application of different investigative activities, the more solvable a case will be.

Strength and Numbers of Evidence Items

Given sufficient investigative resources, the more solvable the case, the greater the number of items of evidence, the stronger the evidence items in terms of effect size, and the more cases are detected. For rail metal theft, the number of evidence items accurately reflects variations in significant solvability factors, accounting for almost two-thirds of differences in detection outcomes (Fig. 3; Robb et al., Chapter "Metal Theft Solvability and Detection"). The strongest three factors with very high odds ratios in the range of 26:1–32:1 occur in 93% of solved cases. These are patrol interception, the event being witnessed, and scrap metal dealer checks. With further investigation, additional items of medium strength (covert activities, forensic evidence) with a third of the effect size of the strongest factors, and weaker evidence items (CCTV, vehicle registration details, alarmed incident) with a tenth of the effect size, combine to raise the odds of detection. Detection odds reflect incident solvability, which depends on the aggregated effect sizes of evidence items of different strengths present in each case.

Understanding how strong and weaker evidence items combine in solved cases indicates which investigative activities are most important for different types of crime. Activities that provide the strongest evidence items should be accorded the highest investigative priority. For such cases, investigative activities that are likely to pro-

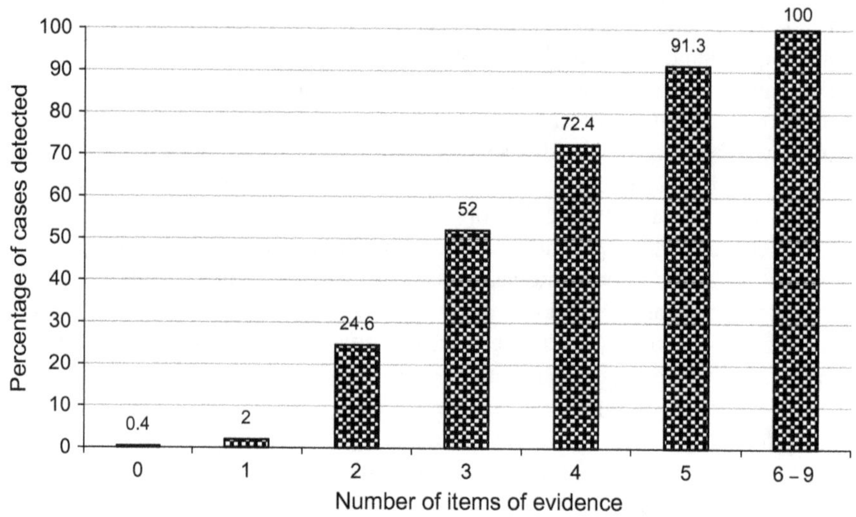

Fig. 3 Number of items of evidence and detection rates for railway metal theft (Fig. 5 from Robb et al. 2015)

duce additional evidence items should also be resourced in the light of findings that adding items of medium or weaker effect size notably boosts the odds of detecting cases (Robb et al., Chapter "Metal Theft Solvability and Detection"). Establishing priorities between different types of crime may also take account of other issues such as the effects on victims, including physical harm and financial loss. Subsets of different crime types should similarly be prioritised. These include more serious sexual offences such as rape and penetrative assault compared with non-penetrative assault or indecent exposure (Jones et al., Chapter "Reporting, Detection and Solvability of Sex Offences on Railways"), assaults that result in life-changing injury for victims compared with those that do not (Olphin and Mueller-Johnson, Chapter "Targeting Factors that Predict Clearance of Non-domestic Assaults"), and faith hate assaults compared with most faith hate criminal damage and public order offences (Rose, Coupe and Ariel, Chapter "Solvability Factors and Investigative Strategy for Faith Hate Crime: Anti-Semitic and Islamophobic Assault, Criminal Damage and Public Order Offences in London").

The investigative activities needed to unlock each case's solvability differ in terms of cost-effectiveness, with evidence outputs of varying strength for each unit of input resource. If there are precise solvability indicators, investigative activities can be resourced frugally for only those cases likely to result in evidence. Activities for which there are less specific solvability indicators require more resources, and evidence is likely to be output less cost-effectively. If there are less specific solvability indicators or no solvability indicators, or if indicators exist but are not used and every case is examined, this will raise the costs of resourcing each item of evidence output. No research study has yet identified those characteristics of residential burglaries that flag the subset most likely to provide useful forensic samples (Coupe, Chapter "Investigative Activities, Resources and Burglary Detection"). The costs of certain policing activities may also depend on circumstances. If officers are able to question neighbours when they first respond, this may demand only marginal additional resources; if, however, questioning neighbours requires a separate trip, as with certain non-residential burglaries where crime scene visits do not always occur, this will cost far more, unless there are solvability indicators for targeting the subset of cases most likely to provide useful information (Coupe, Chapter "Solvability Indicators for 'First Officers': Targeting Eyewitness Questioning at Non-residential Burglaries").

Summary

More solvable incidents possess a greater combined strength of evidence items that can be 'unlocked'. Case detection will depend on applying sufficient resources to those investigative activities that will unlock the evidence. Identifying the solvable subsets of cases for which different resource input–evidence output activities are to be undertaken enables more cost-effective detection, with larger outputs of evidence or arrests per unit of input resource. Incident characteristics determine whether there are more and stronger evidence items or fewer and weaker ones and, hence, control the potential for successful detection. They influence the proportions of more and less solvable cases for each type of crime and the distribution of solvable cases within the same sort of crime for a given jurisdiction. Solvability profiles define the limits on possible detection outcomes for a set of offences and the resources and activities needed to detect all solvable cases.

Cost-Effective Strategies and Solvability Characteristics

The combined solvability characteristics of different crimes in jurisdictions will affect the cost-effectiveness of investigations and detection outcomes. Three solvability levels are important for case-screening decisions and resource allocation.

Lower, Middle and Upper Resource Thresholds

There is a lower solvability threshold below which there is no realistic prospect of solving a case, and above which the prospects for detection progressively improve until the middle threshold at which they start to decline. There is also an upper threshold where committing more resources would not help improve the prospects of detecting a case as sufficient resources have been allocated to 'unlock' all solvability potential.

In terms of rapid patrol response to burglaries, incidents reported long after offenders have left the scene would fall below the lower threshold, as would those occurring in remote rural areas with low population densities where patrol cover that would enable offenders to be intercepted at or near the scene would be prohibitively costly. For in-progress burglaries, detection probabilities improve with faster and stronger patrol responses (Fig. 2). The middle threshold, marking the point at which declining arrest returns are evident, will be reached when more easily solvable incidents have been detected and additional resources are increasingly being directed at incidents of progressively worsening solvability, such as those at which burglars are seen and reported while leaving the scene and there are lower prospects for an arrest in nearby streets. The relationship between patrol resources and the odds of capturing burglars indicates that the middle threshold has not yet been reached for the sample depicted in Fig. 2, so that additional patrols would be expected to yield extra arrest increments.

At the upper threshold, where all solvable in-progress burglaries at which an arrest is possible have been fully resourced, patrol activities may be viewed as fully funded. Improving patrol cover reduces response times and distances, but at the point at which there is sufficient patrol capacity to deal with all solvable offences, extra patrol resources would be redundant. Any additional resources would represent overfunding, since they could be directed only at unsolvable 'in-progress' incidents or those not reported while in progress. Incident characteristics, therefore, limit solvability, and this determines when additional resources cease to improve detection rates and patrol activities are 'overfunded'. Thus, incident solvability places a ceiling on productive investigation, evidence outputs and the resources needed to realise arrests.

For the patrol illustration, each combination of burglary characteristics has a distinctive resource–solvability–arrest relationship (Fig. 2), and the aggregate of these determines the overall maximum arrest outputs from patrol resource inputs, assuming sufficient patrol resources. The jurisdictional potential for solving burglaries by arrest therefore depends on the numbers and geographical distribution of 'in-progress' incidents with combinations of burglary characteristics of varying solvability. This determines the overall patrol resources required to arrest burglars at all solvable burglary emergencies.

Hence, offence characteristics control solvability, potential detection rates and the resources needed for each type of investigative activity to fully exploit the potential for evidence outputs.

Cost-Effective Investigative Strategies

Maximum cost-effectiveness will be attained if investigative activities applied to solvable offences are funded at the minimum levels that enable detection. Funding investigations beyond the middle threshold involves declining returns, as more officers improve detection rates by declining marginal increments. Detections cannot be improved beyond the fully funded upper threshold, so that additional officers or working overtime will further depress cost-effectiveness. Proportions of solvable offences determine the maximum amount of resources needed to solve all offences in a jurisdiction at the 'solvability ceiling'.

Different offences will vary in terms of how cost-effectively they can be solved, since some investigative activities are more expensive than others, and some crimes may be cleared using cheaper activities. Offences that are cheaper to solve are likely to continue to be more cost-effectively detected even if funding per crime rises, as they show declining returns. Unless different offences require markedly different investigative activities and activities differ notably in terms of cost-effectiveness or are overfunded, shifting resource inputs may only redistribute failure and success, leaving overall detection outcomes little altered. Hence, decisions about resourcing successful activities and offences may be self-determining: resources switched between two underfunded activities will inevitably improve detection rates in one at the expense of the other.

The number of solvable offences—not the numbers of all offences—controls detection rates. Despite additional resources per offence, falling crime rates might even lower detection rates, let alone raise them. A drop in less experienced, lifestyle-limited offenders (Smith 2007), but not older, more experienced ones, may mean that the quantities of unsolvable offences remain unchanged despite falling crime numbers. Similarly, the impact of additional resources on clearance rates could be offset by rising quantities of unsolvable incidents. Crime circumstances and offender populations limit the quantities of solvable cases, potentially disrupting the expected relationships between officer workloads and detection rates.

Upper Resource Threshold, Full Funding of Solvable Cases and Jurisdictional Detections

The potential for detecting crimes in any area will depend, therefore, on the numbers of different types of crimes of differing solvability and the realisation of potential detection rates on matching resources to solvable incidents. If there are more violent crimes, solvability will be higher and there will be potential to achieve more detections, often more cost-effectively. By carrying out investigative activities on appropriate subsets of cases identified using solvability indicators, the greatest number of—and the strongest—evidence items and detected outcomes may be produced as cost-effectively as possible.

Better-resourced police services possess a better capacity to investigate and detect crime. However, if this capacity exceeds the combined investigative resource demands of all solvable offences in a jurisdiction, additional resources will not increase detection rates. The resources needed to fund the investigation, and detection of all solvable offences defines the upper resource threshold at which jurisdictional investigation is fully funded. With additional resources above this threshold, crime investigation would be overfunded; below it, the shortfall in resources means it is underfunded. The different mixture of crimes committed in different jurisdictions means the quantities of solvable offences vary, so that the resources needed to meet the fully funded upper threshold and bring all solvable offences to detection will also differ.

As resources drop progressively farther below the full-funding threshold, detection levels can be expected to fall. If resources meet the investigative demands of all solvable offences in a jurisdiction, additional resources will not improve detection rates. The proportion of solvable offences will determine detection rates if jurisdictional resources exceed the full-funding threshold, assuming investigative activities are carried out optimally. Resources will only be correlated with detection rates only across jurisdictions with resource shortages. The 'system overload' model (Geerken and Gove 1977; Pontell 1978), which describes the way in which rising crime increases police workloads, depresses arrests and weakens deterrence, therefore, can only apply if there is underfunding relative to solvable case resource demands, with resource inputs below the 'solvability ceiling' at which the investigations of all solvable offences can be fully funded. The measurement of crime solvability, therefore, must be included in tests of theoretical models linking investigative resources and workloads with jurisdictional detection rates.

It appears unlikely that many police forces in Western countries have excess resources to deal with crime investigation and detection, given the scale and changing nature of offending. The chapters in this volume illustrate the solvability challenges of 'new' offences created through the criminalisation of behaviours such as hate offences (Rose et al., Chapter "Solvability Factors and Investigative Strategy for Faith Hate Crime: Anti-Semitic and Islamophobic Assault, Criminal Damage and Public Order Offences in London"), more determined policing of offences such as domestic violence and sexual offences (Jones et al., Chapter "Reporting, Detection and Solvability of Sex Offences on Railways"), the need to combat terrorism, and the vast increase in cyber-offending (Duffy and Coupe, Chapter "Detecting and Combating Internet Telephony Fraud"). Underfunding is likely to be exacerbated by unequal resource allocation among jurisdictions, as in England and Wales, where resources have varied by as much as 164% (Audit Commission 1993).

Proactive Investigative Activities

The prior discussion has been framed in terms of reactive policing. Proactive activities appear more effective for crime prevention (Tilley et al. 2007). They are used for detecting crime and include using informants before crimes are committed or using a false stolen property 'fence' set up by undercover officers to entrap offenders. Other undercover operations are used to investigate organised crime. These include cross-border weapons smuggling, people or drug trafficking, and illegal political activities, such as animal rights terrorism (Donovan and Coupe 2013). Indicator variables that help predict dwellings and commercial premises at high risk of repeat burglary make such burglaries solvable. This may be achieved with a rapid patrol response and on-scene arrest following the triggering of a delayed audible or silent alarm or by the subsequent identification of offenders using covert CCTV or by installing tracking devices in goods likely to be stolen and catching offenders with these in their possession (Coupe and Mueller-Johnson, Chapters "Boosting Offence Solvability and Detections: Solving Residential Burglaries by Predicting Single and Multiple Repeats", "Improving Offence Solvability and Detection Rates at Non-residential Burglary: Predicting Single and Multiple Repeat Incidence"). Though initially cost-effective, these activities appear liable to declining rates of arrest if burglars realise how they are being caught.

Hence, proactive activities can also use indicators to enhance output evidence or arrests per resource input. While initially high, cost-effectiveness may decline, so that intermittent and random use may be appropriate. Proactive activities promise to intermittently improve solvable offence numbers, elevate full-funding thresholds and raise detection rates.

Effects of Policing Strategies on Offences, Solvability and Resource Supply

Policy and strategy decisions control resource allocations to forces' patrol and investigative activities. These are informed by longer-run crime profiles and spatio-temporal incidence. It is to be expected that existing resource allocations will persist while accommodating short-term adjustments and longer-term shifts to contain and combat offences of continuing public concern. Supply shortages of various officer resources—uniformed officers and detectives—mean that not every investigative demand due to case solvability and screening decisions can be satisfied, necessitating prioritisation. Cost-effectiveness and the harmfulness of offences will be screening criteria. It is, however, important that a proportion of even the least serious offences are investigated and solved if deterrence is to be maintained. Public knowledge of the fact that, as for jurisdictions in England and Wales, cyber-offences resulting in the loss of property or shoplifting thefts below a certain value will not be investigated is likely to encourage offences below these thresholds. UK Ministry of Justice figures indicate that fixed penalty notices for shoplifting items of less than £100 have more than halved between 2015 and 2017, from 12,063 to 5651 (Ford 2018). If minor offences are not investigated and solved, the opportunity for rehabilitative intervention is missed, and there is a risk that those committing minor offences will subsequently progress to more serious crimes. If police are pressed for resources, then at least selecting a proportion of these less serious yet solvable offences for investigation will highlight the the risks of arrest and may help contain the scale of these offences, in addition to disrupting other offending, since offenders tend to be versatile (Blumstein et al. 1988). The harm caused by different offences may be the basis for setting different lower solvability thresholds, so that fewer pickpocketing offences on railways (Sharp and Coupe, Chapter "Pickpocketing on Railways"), which are at the lower margins of solvability, might be screened in for continued investigation than assaults (Olphin and Mueller-Johnson, Chapter "Targeting Factors that Predict Clearance of Non-domestic Assaults")—particularly serious assaults—even if this elevates the 'false positive' investigated cases more for the latter.

Police activities and strategies can modify the mix of jurisdictional offences and their solvability (Weisburd and Eck 2004). For forces whose investigative activities are underfunded relative to offence solvability, additional resources can be expected to drive an iterative process of raised detections, convictions and, despite attrition (Robinson and Tilley 2009), higher incarceration. This will tend to remove prolific and more serious offenders from criminal populations, enhance deterrence (Geerken and Gove 1977; Pontell 1978) and depress police workloads. More cost-effective strategies have a similar impact. Imprisonment can reduces offending (Levitt 2004; Spelman 2006) and may especially lower the incidence of violent crime, which, given its higher solvability and detection rate, may depress overall detection rates.

The preventive effects of strategies such as hot-spot patrols (Sherman and Strang 1995) can also change jurisdictional crime profiles, their solvability and spatio-temporal incidence. Neighbourhood policing may improve the public's perceptions of police legitimacy (Tyler 2004) as well as improve willingness to provide eye-witness evidence and, hence, boost solvability, although there is little published evidence to demonstrate this. While preventive strategies may depress offending, increased patrolling may also raise detection rates as officers spot and make arrests for 'in-progress' public order offences and visible street crimes, such as pickpocketing, street robbery and sexual offences, which might otherwise remain unreported (Ahlberg and Knutsson 1990).

Therefore, while certain policing strategies can affect crime levels (Levitt 2004), they may alter the numbers of solvable offences. Some strategies deter crime, which may depress solvable offences, while others may displace crime (Guerette and Bowers 2009) or proactively boost detection rates, partly by changing incident solvability. Extra patrols may raise the number of solved visible street offences while depressing incidence through targeted prevention. Since these strategies are likely to be carried out selectively in different jurisdictions, they will be an additional source of geographical variation in offence profiles and solvable incidents. Funding preventive policing may be more cost-effective in reducing overall crime than allocating resources to the investigation of the additional crimes that would otherwise take place. However, the effects of offending environments and offender populations on solvable and unsolvable crime profiles appear to far exceed that of preventive policing and other strategies.

As well as driving investigative resourcing, incident solvability, therefore, is itself modified by policing policies and strategies. The police resourcing–solvability relationship is, therefore, reciprocal. Policy and strategy, however, reflect jurisdictional offence characteristics to an important extent and control the resources available to satisfy the investigative needs of solvable offences.

Resourcing–Solvability Theoretical Model

In the light of the previous discussion, a theoretical model of detection can be presented which incorporates solvability, resources, and the origins of solvability in environmental circumstances and offender populations, and considers geographical variations in solvable and unsolvable cases and funded capacity to investigate offences and detections (Fig. 4).

The allocation of resources to the investigation of solvable offences explains crime detection (Fig. 4): more resources improve detection rates if these are allocated to effective investigative activities applied to cases that they can help to solve. While proactive activities may boost incident solvability and be the means by which cases are detected, most investigation of reported crime is necessarily reactive, with the characteristics of incidents determining the investigative activities that must be undertaken, resource needs and detection outcomes (Fig. 4). The assessment of solvability, or how easily and whether an incident may be solved, informs case-screening decisions. Environmental and crime event characteristics determine the evidence that can be unlocked and the activities required to achieve this. Case solvability enables and limits detection, which is conditional on the allocation of sufficient resources to conduct appropriate investigative activities. Incident solvability thus controls the resources needed to solve cases.

If, for some investigative activities, there are only poor or no solvability indicators, cases from which no evidence can be unlocked will also have to be investigated. This will lessen cost-effectiveness, weaken the match of resources to solvable cases and reduce the model's explanatory power. Successfully outputting evidence from investigative activities requires matching the resourcing of activities to the cases that are solvable in terms of those specific activities. Investigations consist of 'resource input–evidence output' activities applied to subsets of cases.

Detecting cases depends on the strength and numbers of items of evidence. Investigative activities often provide a few strong items of evidence and a larger number of less-strong evidence items, which accrue in individual cases to improve the odds of detection. The greater the combined strength of evidence items, the better the odds of solving a case. The presence of strong evidence items in a case often encourages supplementary investigative activities to strengthen evidence to a point that enables detection.

Solvability inherently varies both within the same type of offence and between different types of crime (Fig. 4). Offending environments show spatio-temporal variation, providing different offending opportunities to different sorts of offenders, so that crime profiles, characteristics and solvability also vary geographically and over time. Resources are unequally allocated to different forces and within forces to combat crime, more on the basis of numbers of crimes than numbers of solvable offences. Fluctuations in crime, some seasonal but also diurnal (Tompson and Coupe 2017), tend to exacerbate any mismatch of resource supply to investigative demand. Mismatches between resources and the investigative demands of offences of varying solvability are responsible for differences in jurisdictional detection rates, but only if there are shortfalls in resources to meet the investigative needs of all solvable incidents.

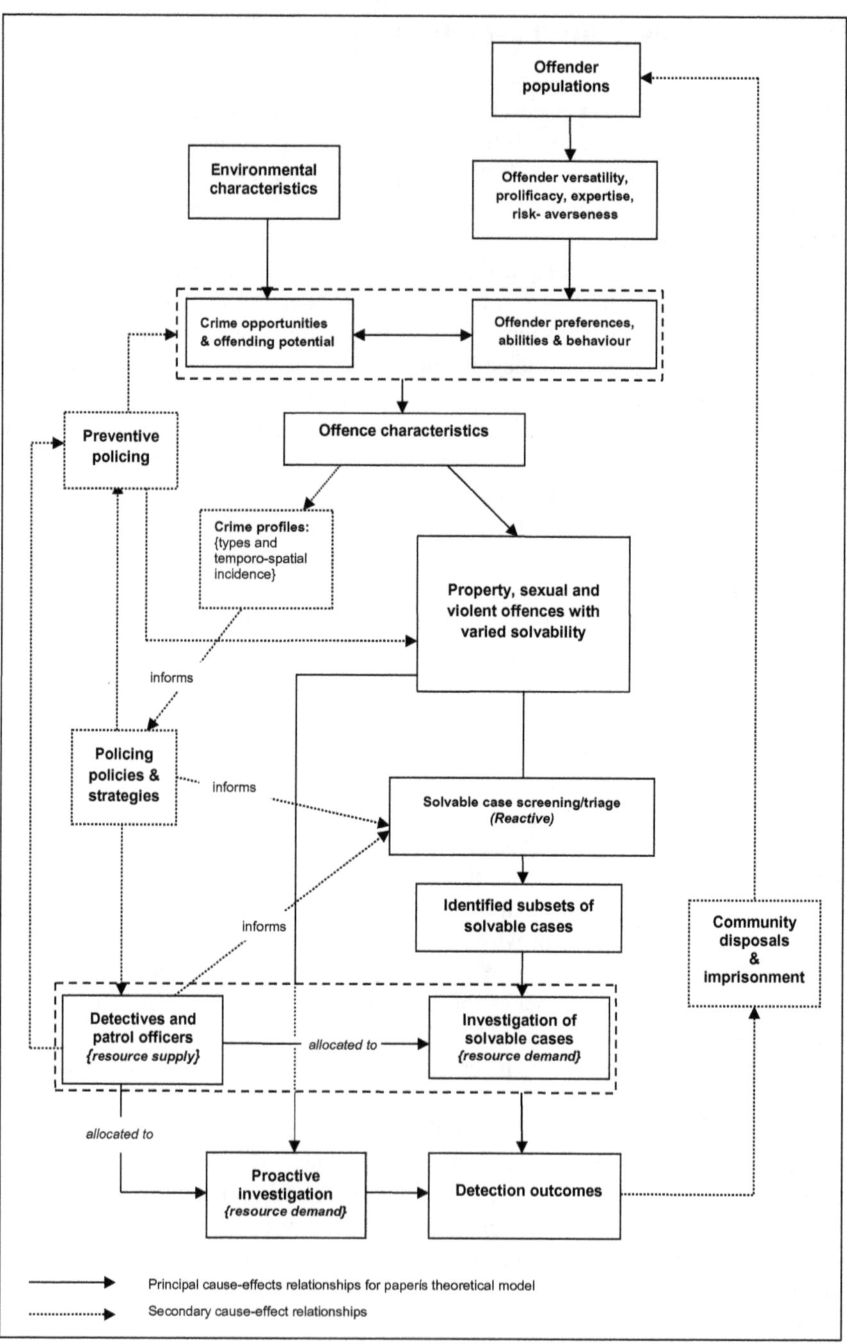

Fig. 4 Relationships between offending environments, resources, offence solvability and detections

Resource–solvability–detection relationships involve lower thresholds below which no cases may be detected, middle thresholds up to which extra increments of resources increase detections and beyond which they enhance performance less and cost-effectiveness falls, and upper thresholds, which demarcate over- and underfunding, and above which no additional offences may be detected, irrespective of resource inputs. The upper threshold is a 'solvability ceiling' at which the investigative resource demands of all solvable crimes are fully met. In police jurisdictions funded beyond this upper threshold, extra resources will not and cannot produce any additional detections, so that any correlation between detection rates and resources can be expected to weaken the more resources are allocated above the upper solvability threshold. If, in contrast, forces are underfunded, they will have insufficient capacity to clear all solvable offences, depressing detection rates. However, police forces need spare capacity to deal with resource shortages due to short-term fluctuations in crime, such as covering varying demand for time-critical patrol responses across the day.

Middle thresholds—at which the resources needed to produce an evidence item increase and cost-effectiveness falls—affect most investigative activities given inherent declines in solvability for most types of crime. For some activities, such as 'in-progress' patrol responses, declining returns reflect solvability characteristics, so that the odds of unlocking evidence deteriorate. In other cases, such as entrapment using silent alarms, it is the offenders' probable behavioural responses, in taking account of the new risks they face, that are likely to result in declining arrest or evidence returns as offenders exercise greater caution.

In practice, policing activities and resources may not be well aligned with solvable crimes. Both the capacity to fund investigations and crime-screening procedures vary. Hence, resources may be directed at difficult-to-solve cases, and some solvable cases may not receive sufficient resources. This will depress cost-effective investigation, and potential detections will be only partially achieved. In the absence of reliable solvability indicators, the misallocation of resources is unavoidable. It is, for instance, difficult to predict at which crime scenes forensic examination will be beneficial. Resource–solvability misalignment diminishes the explanatory strength of the resourcing–solvability model. Optimal alignment between resources and case solvability will only rarely be achieved, since this would require knowledge of solvability indicators for the application of every investigative activity and an understanding of the resource input levels at which declining returns and full funding occur for every type of offence.

References

Ahlberg, J., & Knutsson, J. (1990). The risk of detection. *Journal of Quantitative Criminology, 6*(1), 117–130.

Audit Commission. (1993). *Helping with enquiries: Tackling crime effectively*. London: HMSO.

Bernasco, W. (2006). Co-offending and the choice of target areas in burglary. *Journal of Investigative Psychology and Offender Profiling, 3*(3), 139–155.

Bernasco, W. (2010). A sentimental journey to crime: Effects of residential history on crime location choice. *Criminology, 48*(2), 389–416.
Blumstein, A., Cohen, J., Das, S., & Miotra, D. (1988). Specialization and seriousness during adult criminal careers. *Journal of Quantitative Criminology, 4*(4), 303–345.
Brantingham, P. J., & Brantingham, P. L. (1984). *Patterns in crime*. New York: Macmillan Publishing Company.
Brantingham, P. J., & Brantingham, P. L. (1998). Crime pattern theory. In R. Wortley, L. Mazerolle, & S. Rombouts (Eds.), *Environmental criminology and crime analysis* (pp. 78–93). Cullompton, Devon: Willan.
Burrows, J., Hopkins, M., Hubbard, R., Robinson, A., Speed, M., & Tilley, N. (2005). *Understanding the attrition process in volume crime investigations* (Home Office Research Study 295). London: Home Office.
Burrows, J., & Tarling, R. (1982). *Clearing up crime*. London: HMSO.
Cohen, L. E., & Felson, M. (1979). Social change and crime rate trends: A routine activity approach. *American Sociological Review, 44*(4), 588–608.
Coupe, R. T. (2016). Evaluating the effects of resources and solvability on burglary detection. *Policing and Society: An International Journal of Research and Policy, 5*, 563–587.
Coupe, R. T., & Blake, L. (2005). The effects of patrol workloads and response strength on burglary emergencies. *Journal of Criminal Justice, 33*(3), 239–255.
Coupe, R. T., & Blake, L. (2006). Daylight and darkness targeting strategies and the risks of being seen at residential burglaries. *Criminology, 44,* 431–464.
Coupe, R. T., & Blake, L. (2010). The effects of target characteristics on the sighting and arrest of offenders at burglary emergencies. *Security Journal, 24*(2), 157–178.
Coupe, T., & Fox, B. H. (2015). A risky business: How do access, exposure and guardians affect the chances of non-residential burglars being seen? *Security Journal, 28*(1), 71–92.
Curtis, L. A. (1974). *Criminal violence: National patterns and behavior*. Lexington, MA: Lexington Books.
Donovan, J., & Coupe, R. T. (2013). Animal rights extremism: Victimization, investigation and detection of a campaign of criminal intimidation. *European Journal of Criminology, 10*(1), 113–132.
Ford, R. (2018, March 21). Shoplifting doubles as thefts under £200 go unpunished. *The Times*.
Geerken, M., & Gove, W. R. (1977). Deterrence, overload and incapacitation: An empirical evaluation. *Social Forces, 56*(2), 424–427.
Guerette, R. T., & Bowers, K. J. (2009). Assessing the extent of crime displacement and diffusion of benefits: A review of situational crime prevention evaluations. *Criminology, 47*(4), 1331–1368.
Innes, M. (2002). The 'process structures' of police homicide investigations. *The British Journal of Criminology, 42*(4), 669–688.
Lamme, M., & Bernasco, W. (2013). Are mobile offenders less likely to be caught? The influence of the geographical dispersion of serial offenders' crime locations on their probability of arrest. *European Journal of Criminology, 10*(2), 168–186.
Levitt, S. D. (2004). Understanding why crime fell in the 1990s: Four factors that explain the decline and six that do not. *Journal of Economic Perspectives, 18*(1), 163–190.
Nee, C., & Taylor, M. (2000). Examining burglars' target selection: Interview, experiment or ethnomethodology? *Psychology, Crime & Law, 6*(1), 45–59.
Pontell, H. (1978). Deterrence: Theory versus practice. *Criminology, 16*(1), 3–22.
Rengert, G., Piquero, A., & Jones, P. (1999). Distance decay re-examined. *Criminology, 37*(2), 427–445.
Robb, P., Coupe, T., & Ariel, B. (2015). 'Solvability' and detection of metal theft on railway property. *European Journal on Criminal Policy and Research, 21*(4), 463–484.
Robinson, A., & Tilley, N. (2009). Factors influencing police performance in the investigation of volume crimes in England and Wales. *Police Practice and Research: An International Journal, 10*(3), 209–223.

Sherman, L. W., & Strang, H. (1995). General deterrent effects of police patrol in crime 'hotspots': A randomised, controlled trial. *Justice Quarterly, 12*(4), 625–648.

Smith, D. J. (2007). Crime and the life course. In M. Maguire, R. Morgan, & R. Reiner (Eds.), *The Oxford handbook of criminology* (4th ed.). Oxford: Oxford University Press.

Spelman, W. (2006). The limited importance of prison expansion. In A. Blumstein & J. Wallman (Eds.), *The crime drop in America*. Cambridge: Cambridge University Press.

Taylor, P., & Bond, S. (2012). *Crimes detected in England and Wales 2011/12* (Home Office Statistical Bulletin 08/12). London: Home Office.

Tilley, N., Robinson, A., & Burrows, J. (2007). The investigation of high volume crime. In T. Newburn, T. Williamson, & A. Wright (Eds.), *Handbook of criminal investigation* (pp. 226–254). London: Willan Publishing.

Tompson, L., & Coupe, R. T. (2017). Time and criminal opportunity. In G. J. N. Bruinsma & S. D. Johnson (Eds.), *The Oxford handbook of environmental criminology*. Oxford: Oxford University Press.

Tseloni, A. (2000). Personal criminal victimisation in the United States: Fixed and random effects of individual and household characteristics. *Journal of Quantitative Criminology, 16*(4), 415–442.

Tyler, T. R. (2004). Enhancing police legitimacy. *Annals of American Academy of Political and Social Science, 593*(1), 84–99.

van Koppen, P. J., & Jansen, R. W. J. (1998). The road to the robbery: Travel patterns in commercial robberies. *The British Journal of Criminology, 38*(2), 230–246.

Weisburd, D., & Eck, J. E. (2004). What can the police do to reduce crime, disorder and fear? *The Annals of the American Academy of Political and Social Science, 593*(1), 42–65.

Wright, R., & Logie, R. H. (1988). How young house burglars choose targets. *Howard Journal of Criminal Justice, 27*(2), 92–104.

Conclusions

Richard Timothy Coupe and Barak Ariel

Introduction

The case studies presented in this volume show how to develop investigative strategies based on predicting the solvability and detection odds of different types of crime. Incident solvability is indispensable for understanding the investigation of crime and provides insights into how detection rates may be cost-effectively improved. The solvability of an offence is its potential to provide evidence, which controls whether or not crimes may be detected, the ease with which detection can be achieved and the investigative resources needed to realise this. Solvability derives from incident characteristics, and these limit the number of offences that may be solved and control the amount of funding needed to investigate and solve crimes.

Solvability differs between different crime types and within offences of the same crime type. It has origins in environmental circumstances and the characteristics of offender populations, which vary across jurisdictions. As a consequence, the mix of crimes, their solvability and the amount of resource needed to detect all solvable offences vary geographically. An ability to predict solvability and detection odds also makes possible a more accurate estimate of the costs of investigating all the crimes in a given police jurisdiction. While resources include police support staff, buildings, equipment and technical knowledge, the focus in this volume has been on police officer resources, since these are the most important measure of policing capacity to meet the objectives of maintaining public order and combating crime.

The evidence in this volume indicates that incident solvability determines whether or not offences can be solved but that successful detection is contingent on resources. Allocating resources to investigative activities enables the potential for detection due

R. T. Coupe (✉) · B. Ariel
Institute of Criminology, University of Cambridge, Cambridge, England, UK
e-mail: rtc23@cam.ac.uk

B. Ariel
e-mail: ba285@cam.ac.uk

R. T. Coupe et al. (eds.), *Crime Solvability Factors*,
https://doi.org/10.1007/978-3-030-17160-5_19

to solvability to be realised by 'unlocking' evidence. The detection of solvable cases, therefore, may be limited by insufficient or misapplied investigative resources.

The overall strength of evidence in a case enables it to be solved. Solvability factors possess varying strengths and most cases that are solved have at least one strong evidence item combined with one or more weaker items of evidence. Stronger evidence items commonly constitute the bases for detection to which additional evidence items are added in order to produce detected cases. Railway metal thefts, for instance, are solved by combinations of solvability factors and the odds of detection rise fivefold for every additional factor present in a case. This is mirrored by improvements in the accurate prediction of residential burglary investigation outcomes: with one factor, predictive accuracy is 62% with a single factor present in a case but with four or more factors, it rises to 89% (Chapter "Population-Level Analysis of Residential Burglaries"). More generally, the larger the number of stronger solvability factors (BLR odds ratios > 10.0), the better the predictive accuracy for different types of offence (Spearman's rho = .68, $p = .03$, $n = 8$; Fig. 1). This points to differences in the potential for cost-effectiveness investigation between crimes and between different offences within customary crime groupings: railway metal theft, faith hate and sex offences are groups of crimes that contain distinctive offences of varied solvability and detection potential.

The potential for detecting crime is often not being met with existing resources, either because investigations of some solvable offences are wrongly discontinued, or because investigative resources are allocated to less solvable offences which, in the event, remain undetected. However, it is also apparent that, even if resources matched case solvability well, the potential for achieving detections would not be fully realised, given overall shortages in investigative resources. There are substantial proportions of cases with solvability factors whose combined strength in terms of effect size indicates a high probability of detection which are not, in the event, solved,

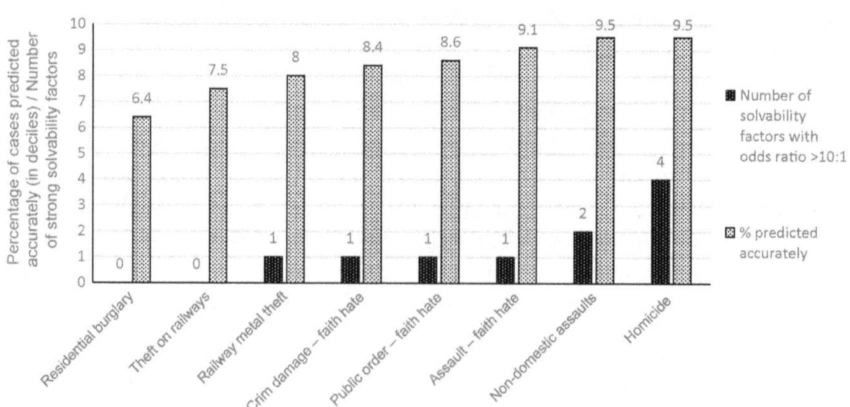

Fig. 1 For different offences: the percentage of cases* with detection outcomes accurately predicted and number of solvability factors present with BLR odds ratios greater than 10:1 [* divided by 10, e.g. 90% = 9.0]

while some cases of 'medium' and even 'low' solvability are, in practice, detected. This points to a potential for more detections that are currently limited by investigative resource shortages. The availability of these resources will partly depend on how they are divided between uniformed patrol officers and detectives and on their priorities, which, for patrol officers, include costly searches for missing persons, dealing with non-crime domestic incidents, crime related incidents involving mental health issues and growing numbers of racially motivated public order incidents or assaults that do not incur injuries.

Importance of Solvability Factors for Different Crimes

Figure 2 shows the importance of different categories of solvability factors for the crimes examined in this volume.

For many, but not all, offences—most cybercrimes are obvious exceptions—most solvability factors and evidence items derive from police activities at the scene, where offenders can be arrested and eyewitnesses, including the crime victims themselves, provide named suspect evidence or suspect descriptions that enable subsequent arrest. Hence, factors relating to characteristics of the place, time and environment and witnessing offences are most numerous, and there are few offences for which eyewitnesses are not significant (Fig. 3). These solvability factors were important, combined with factors relating to police patrol for rail metal theft, pickpocketing on railways, non-domestic assault and burglary. Solvability measures relating to timely, direct

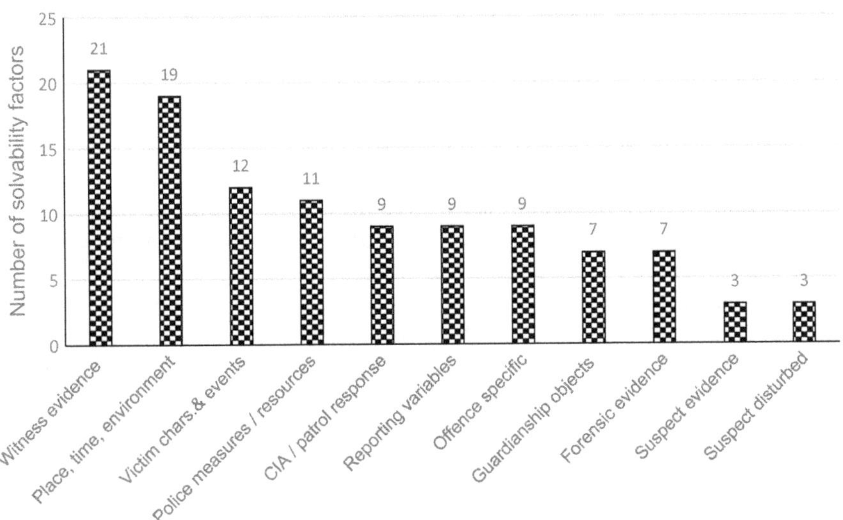

Fig. 2 Importance of different types of solvability factor

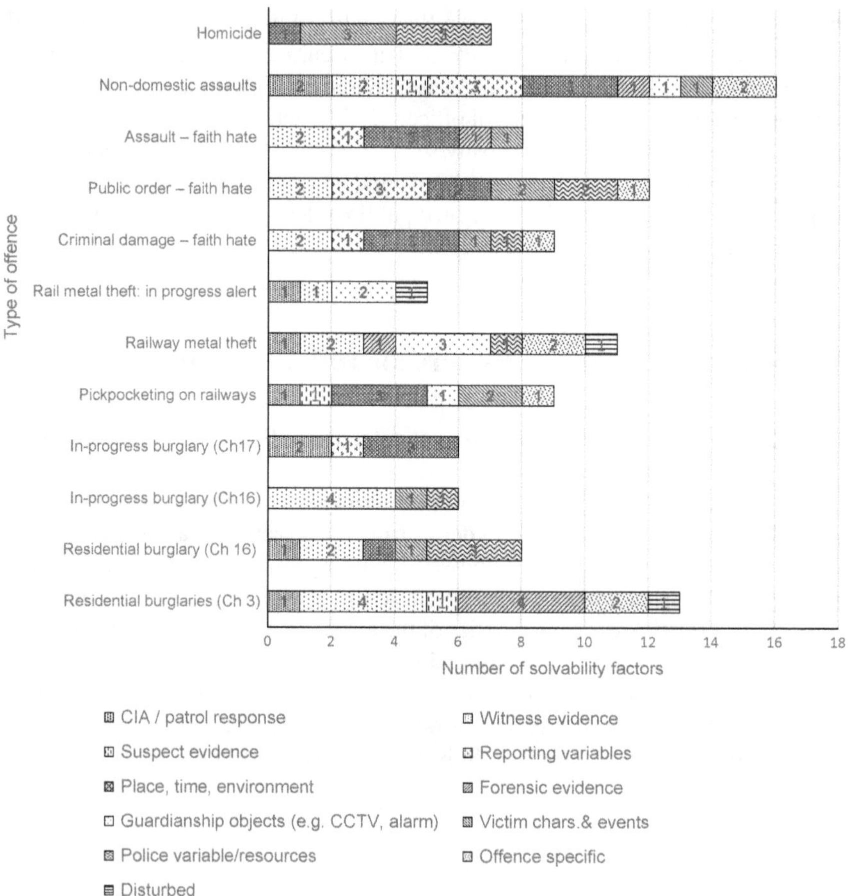

Fig. 3 Importance of different groups of solvability factors for different offence types

reporting and how and to whom offences are reported affected the investigation and detection of assaults, criminal damage, public order offences and 'in-progress' burglary (Fig. 3), types of crimes also affected by solvability factors involving victim characteristics (Fig. 3).

Crime scenes are also the source of useful forensic evidence that can be collected and matched with known offenders or used to reconstruct crimes and provide insight into likely perpetrators or their behaviour. Both this and suspect evidence were associated with fewer but frequently 'stronger' factors, while disturbing suspects lowered case solvability and detections, characterising metal theft and burglary investigations. Guardianship object factors elevated the solvability and detection of assaults, railway metal theft and pickpocketing, while offence specific factors proved to be significant, often as strong factors, for metal theft (detectives visiting scrap-metal dealers),

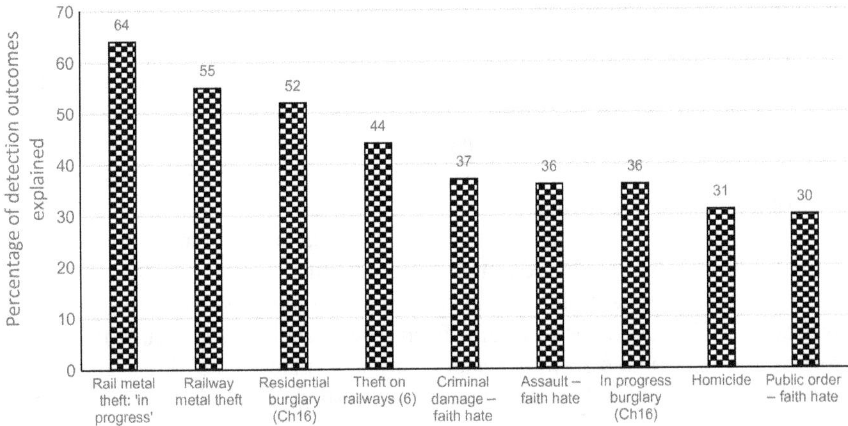

Fig. 4 Percentage of detection outcomes explained by significant solvability factors, using Nagelkerke's R^2 values for different types of crime

for faith hate offences (victims who were drivers, in the security industry; whether Muslim or Jewish victim).

Further investigations by detectives realise the potential of evidence and information collected at the scene, for instance, by collating forensic evidence, matching suspect information with police records or tracing stolen property. Fewer lines of enquiry initiated later by detectives themselves resulted in detected cases, and such investigations may be less cost-effective and can be more difficult to justify for high-volume, low-harm offences unless they lead to the arrest of previously unknown offenders. There are exceptions to this where detectives' actions match or even outweigh first officers' in terms of securing arrests. These include rail metal theft, for which subsequent visits to scrap-metal dealers by detectives prove valuable, or cyber-fraud, at which the need for rapid intervention at the offender's bank location from where fraudulently transferred funds are finally withdrawn is likely to be impossible for first response officers to meet. They also include serious offences that justify undercover police work.

Differences in the proportions of detection outcomes explained by significant solvability factors, as measured by Nagelkerke's R^2 are shown in Fig. 4; values tend to be higher for offences with stronger odds ratios and this enables a clearer boundary to be delineated between detected and undetected cases.

'Lean Policing' and a Scientific Approach to Solving Crime

Scientific analysis of the solvability factors that lead to cases being detected offers the potential to improve the cost-effectiveness of investigations. Statistical techniques enable the prediction of low-solvability cases—those with exceptionally low chances of being detected—and cases where solvability factors indicate higher odds of detection and which ought to be prioritised if resources are scarce. In doing so, solvability factor analysis complements existing practice by systematising and informing decisions. Scientific analysis, therefore, supports rather than replaces police officers' case-screening and prioritisation decisions based on experience. Its use promises better quality utilization of investigative capacity and greater cost-effectiveness, the principal aims of 'lean policing'.

Statistical case screening, however, can involve the loss of a small proportion of detections attributable to what, on the basis of identified solvability factors, appear to be low-solvability cases but which officers, in practice, solve. However, these losses are notably outweighed by gains from solving incidents which, with existing informal non-statistical screening systems, officers currently neglect to investigate and remain unsolved. By discriminating more clearly and reliably between solvable and unsolvable cases, overall detection rates can be raised, and the cost-effectiveness of detecting crime can be improved by better understanding where the line is to be drawn so that neither are achievable detection opportunities missed nor are resources wasted on exceptionally difficult to solve crimes.

Scientific solvability analysis, therefore, has the potential to improve and support crime investigation and detection. It does not radically alter current approaches to crime screening and investigative practices. Rather, it provides greater accuracy to and control over existing decision-making procedures. Decisions about which cases to investigate can take explicit and measured account of the case characteristics that determine solvability factors, the strength of the evidence items and the statistical odds of case clearance. Hence, statistical evidence aids rational decision-making and enables prioritisation on the basis of solvability, given differences in crime seriousness. The approach lends itself to minimising resource wastage and maximising cost-effectiveness. If there are small streams of detected offences that derive from distinctive or atypical investigative procedures, these can be built in side by side with the mainstream of offences to which statistical screening is applied.

It appears that statistically based screening and prioritisation will improve the alignment of resources with incident solvability and boost detection rates compared with assessments based on experience alone. It also promises superior demand management and more effective investigative capacity utilisation. Gains should be higher for crimes with lower solvability and detection rates since greater numbers of low-solvability incidents may provide more scope for the misapplication of investigative effort to cases with little or no chance of being detected.

Since there have been no crime-screening systems that draw on statistical analyses of solvability factors, however, the solvability studies in this volume are necessarily based on experience-based investigative systems, where the quality of officers' assessments may affect which solvable cases are investigated. This presents a risk that potential to detect offences has been missed or undervalued. Even if officers are currently able to accurately identify solvable cases on the basis of experience, resource shortages may mean that many of them remain uninvestigated. However, evidence from this volume, such as that relating to assaults and theft, indicates this to be imperfectly carried out. Research is, therefore, needed in which police officers are able to explore all possible investigative avenues that hold any promise of detection, in order to provide, for different crime types, insights into the full sets of solvability characteristics that predispose cases to detection, as well as the resource thresholds at which cost-effectiveness declines and there is full funding of all solvable offences. Randomised control trials would then be required to test the benefits of statistical screening and prioritisation using these solvability factors compared with experience-based approaches.

Crime Seriousness, Resources and Continuing/Discontinuing Investigations

Investigative strategies involving crime screening or prioritisation can be steered using scientific knowledge of the solvability factors for each principal type of crime. It is clear that the most serious offences, such as homicide, rape, aggravated assault that result in permanent disablement, and crimes involving substantial financial thefts must not only receive greater investigative priority but must be pursued even in cases of very low solvability.

A crime harm scale, such as the one devised by the UK Home Office (Ashby 2017), could provide guidance in grading cases in a way that is comparable with the aim of this volume's study of solvability factors in so far that it offers a measured approach to investigative prioritisation and detection maximisation. As with solvability factors, so with the measurement of the harm that victims suffer, there must be exceptions so that these statistical measures are not applied slavishly. Just as there are serious low-solvability offences which police officers must investigate and be seen to investigate, reliance purely on harm to determine case prioritisation would be impracticable and imprudent. Even relatively small financial losses may have serious consequences for low-income victims (Barnard 2015) and crime harm grades reliant on measures such as different sentence lengths may not match citizens' views about the relative seriousness of violent and property crimes. In order to maintain public confidence in the police, it is important that any use of 'victim harm' measures for prioritisation should be evaluated to ensure they reflect the views of ordinary people and crime victims. Though the US Federal Sentencing Guidelines have been evaluated in this way (Jacoby and Cullen 1999), UK Sentencing Guidelines have not, so that doubts remain about using harm scales not validated by the public for prioritising cases and allocating investigative effort.

Neglecting to investigate and detect solvable low-harm offences risks missing opportunities for offender rehabilitation and damaging the public confidence that sustains police services. Arrest is likely to help sustain normative compliance and deters some offenders (Von Hirsch et al. 1999), and the sooner after the offence that arrest occurs, the greater any deterrent effect that may occur is likely to be. Preventive 'hot-spot patrol', for example, relies on an assumption of the effects of visible deterrence from the guardianship provided by police officers on offenders contemplating street crimes. It is, similarly, apparent that the incidence of high-volume, lower-harm offences generally is likely to be affected by the perceived risks of arrest, which often depend on the visual deterrence of informal guardians, including victims, alerting police officers. Evidence from burglary 'super cocooning' studies indicates that foot patrol can significantly reduce repeat and near-repeat incidence following dwelling burglaries (Rowley 2013; Weems 2014), evidently as a result of visible formal guardianship. This suggests that perceived risk of being caught deters many burglars and assists enforcement. High risks of interception by police patrols also can deter more serious offences involving firearms, resulting in declines in homicide incidence (Blakely 2018).

Offences accorded a low policing priority, such as shoplifting (Hamilton 2018), or where the risks of being arrested are very low are likely to find favour among criminals and flourish. Recent rises in shop theft, motor scooter robbery and knife crime in England and Wales are thought to reflect this process, though few, if any, scientific studies have yet been conducted that measure this. The cybercrime 'pandemic' may do so less, despite exceptionally low arrest rates and the belief that offences involving smaller losses of less than £600 may be rarely investigated. Since it involves many 'economic criminals', fewer perpetrators of online fraud may be deterred by the risk of formal sanctions such as arrest (Paternoster and Tibbetts 2016). White-collar criminals appear to be resilient and better able to shrug off the negative effects of sanctions (Payne 2016). It, nevertheless, seems prudent that a proportion of these offences that is sufficiently large to present a perception of risk of arrest to offenders is investigated and detected since there may be subsets of white-collar criminals who fear custodial sentences. The arrest of offenders also may serve to meet victims' needs to see justice served and, if possible, the return of their property, to enable offender rehabilitation and halt their criminal actions.

Studies of burglary, theft on railways and non-domestic assault (Chapters "Population-Level Analysis of Residential Burglaries", "Pickpocketing on Railways", "Targeting Factors that Predict Clearance of Non-domestic Assaults", respectively) show how declining case solvability, and detections could be traded against the waste of investigative resources: as incident solvability declines, the lower the proportions of investigated cases that are detected, so that increasing increments of investigative resource are expended to achieve each detection. This decline may be more rapid for some offences than others so that decisions to prioritise detections over resource wastage may be tipped towards the former. If the loss in incident solvability is more gradual so that more investigative resources must be spent to achieve additional detected cases, criteria such as crime seriousness or harm to victims may inform where the threshold for screening in cases for continuing investigation is drawn. For the most serious or harmful offences, the offence solvability threshold for investigation might be set very low, at a level at which a very small proportion of offences can be detected. For less serious offences, the threshold might be set at higher probabilities to minimise wasted investigative effort on offences with very poor prospects for detection. In this way, investigative decisions based on specific solvability characteristics and the harm the crime causes to victims can inform decisions about where to draw the investigative line between missed detections and resource waste, rather akin to setting the dial on a toaster. Decisions about where to set the line between continuing/discontinuing investigation of cases also affect the selection of burglaries at which to install 'entrapment' devices (Chapters "Boosting Offence Solvability and Detections: Solving Residential Burglaries by Predicting Single and Multiple Repeats" and "Improving Offence Solvability and Detection Rates at Non-residential Burglary: Predicting Single and Multiple Repeat Incidence"), where the probability of a repeat burglary may influence the costs of devices and their installation and monitoring per burglar arrest.

Offender Prolificacy and Versatility

An assumption in focusing on more solvable offences and inputting less effort into cases that are predicted to defy detection, provided these are not serious offences, is that offenders are both prolific and versatile, so that there will be further opportunities for arrest at subsequent and varying types of incidents, some of which may be more solvable. In one sense, this approach has parallels in other domains, such as medicine. Less serious conditions, such as varicose veins or certain toe and foot problems associated with ageing, receive a lower priority as medical procedures are evaluated for cost-effectiveness in terms of additional months of benefit per unit cost. Correcting these conditions may, nevertheless, enable patients to improve their health by exercising more and lessen other future medical needs.

Offending shares some similarities with medicine since it also involves external costs and opportunity costs. Offences are also linked both in terms of the offender–offence series and co-offenders and across crimes due to individual offender versatility. These linkages can confer unintended but valuable beneficial effects since arrest at a burglary may help prevent a continuing series of future burglaries, robberies and other offences, including serious assault, as well as disrupt co-offending endeavours, particularly if an older 'organiser' is removed by incarceration or monitored more closely.

For a large part, the studies in this volume have focused on data linked to individual offences. However, offences involving co-offenders have been considered, such as in the study of the offender–offence profiling (Chapter "Offender–Offence Profiling: Improving Burglary Solvability and Detection"). Some crimes, like the less serious sexual offences—including indecent exposure or touching or rubbing victims through clothing—which dominate sexual crime, involve less co-offending, but in others, such as burglary, it is common. Equally, there are many crimes committed by versatile offenders who do not focus exclusively on that particular offence, as well as others for whom circumstances affect offending, such as an offender who, if faced by a dwelling occupant, will commit aggravated burglary. There is a large overlap between violent and property crimes (Blumstein et al. 1988), and between sexual, property and violent offending (Jackman 2016), particularly among younger male adults and male youths, who constitute the majority of offenders, so that an arrest and intervention for any category of crime will help curtail future offending in a variety of other crimes. As well as inhibiting the progression of criminal careers, this is an important reason for investigating and detecting less serious, solvable crimes.

Cyberoffending

Few cybercrimes are solved. The few that are—estimated at between 1 and 4% of cases—likely to be positively skewed towards incidents where offenders and victims are in the same national jurisdiction. International cybercrime detection rates are almost certainly even lower than this. Although prevention may be the most promising strategy to combat cyber-fraud, it is manifestly failing. Existing UK investigative practice that screens out cyber-fraud cases with losses below a given threshold, for instance, £600, is likely to encourage the proliferation of thefts of a lower value. Selecting even 3% of the more solvable lower-value cases for investigation and publicising subsequent arrests well may serve to raise the levels of risk perceived by potential offenders and possibly deter some.

That very large proportions of cyber offences, such as internet telephone theft (Chapter "Detecting and Combating Internet Telephony Fraud"), are perpetrated from different national jurisdictions presents a far greater obstacle to arrest or preventing such offences through the rehabilitation of arrested offenders. Global police forces with cross-national jurisdictional powers—if they existed—would be better placed to deal with global offending. In practice, cross-national policing often depends on ad hoc cooperation for individual cases, which is often far too slow to intercept offenders in other national jurisdictions, even if an electronic audit trail is available to help investigators pin down the final parking place for stolen funds. Unless it is to mutual advantage, the arrest of cyber-offenders can also hinge on the determination and relative power positions of a victim country compared with an offender country, with some nations, such as the USA, having the ability to apply 'outreach' arrest powers over citizens in other countries who commit offences on their territory. For some countries, gains from cybercrime and other offences can make notable contributions to national income, and this hampers cooperation. Anticipating further cyber-offences and, electronically and with police officers, tracking funds funnelled abroad in near to 'real time' with the objective of targeting banks in 'offender' countries to which stolen funds have been previously frequently been passed is an approach that promises to be worthwhile, given extradition agreements and cooperating police agencies.

Rapid Response and Directed Patrol

The findings from Chapters "Assessing Solvability Factors in Greater Manchester, England: The Case of Residential Burglaries", "Targeting Factors that Predict Clearance of Non-domestic Assaults" and "The Organisation and Deployment of Patrol

Resources: Cost-Effective On-Scene Arrest at Burglaries" underline the importance of supporting rapid patrol response capability. This particularly affects the on-scene arrest of burglars but also enables early intervention at a variety of crimes, including assaults, faith hate public order offences, railway metal theft and theft and sexual offences committed in public, such as on railway property. For these offences, solvability factors connected to rapid response and patrol officer attendance at the scene played a significant role. A rapid patrol response is also likely to have benefits for offences not examined in this volume, such as robbery and domestic assault, and is reportedly affecting the homicide decline in US cities like New York and Chicago, where the real-time reporting of firearm discharges threatens offenders involved with interception by immediate rapid patrol responses, which help deter shootings (Blakely 2018).

Unfortunately, the costs of maintaining an effective rapid patrol response capability can be high, even allowing for lighter patrol deployment at times, such as the small hours, when few crimes are reported (Tompson and Coupe 2018). This issue is highlighted by the challenges of providing patrol cover in rural areas, even those near larger urban areas, which are vulnerable to burglary, particularly of commercial and agricultural premises, and vehicle theft often perpetrated by mobile older urban offenders (Wright 2013). There is likely to be a critical mass in terms of the numbers of crimes for which a rapid patrol response is an important solvability factor so that the quantities of 'in-progress' offences that can benefit from rapid interception of offenders at or near the scene will determine the cost-effectiveness of providing the necessary patrol deployment across jurisdictions. The quantities of 'in-progress' offences per unit area are likely to have been boosted by the ownership of mobile telephones on the one hand and the use of 'real-time' algorithmic reporting systems on the other. These appear to be set to increase the potential benefits of rapid reactive patrol and lower the threshold of total crime quantities needed to make it cost-effective by elevating the numbers of more solvable incidents at which the odds of on-scene or near-scene arrest are high.

Despite the costs of maintaining the capacity to provide fast patrol responses, its benefits include enabling the interception of unknown offenders. This may be contrasted with approaches that rely on the targeting of known offenders, such as offender–offence profiling, described in Chapter "Offender–Offence Profiling: Improving Burglary Solvability and Detection". Approximately 40% of detected burglary cases, for instance, reflect interception by patrol officers at or near crime scenes (Coupe 2016). While environmental circumstances shape the solvability factors that result in half of these arrests, the other half reflect chance factors (Coupe and Fox 2015). This means that some more skilful, experienced and rarely or never caught offenders, including those starting criminal careers and those who have switched 'activity space' (Coupe 2017) as a result of greater mobility due to vehicle ownership, are also likely to be intercepted. Rapid patrol, therefore, helps expand the 'pool' of known offenders.

Geographical Variation in Solvability, Resources and Detections

Most of the crimes evaluated in this volume varied geographically, not only with regard to incidence, but also in terms of solvability factors and detection outcomes. Since solvability controls the resources needed to combat crime through investigation and detection, the funding needed to fully resource solvable crime investigation will vary between jurisdictions. The incidence, solvability and detection of anti-Semitic hate offences, for instance, were unevenly distributed across London's 32 boroughs; types of railway metal theft, their solvability and detections varied markedly across the UK's regions; and sex offences on railways disproportionately affected London and the South-East, where detection rates were notably lower.

In part, these differences reflect investigative resources and decisions. A mismatch between resources and the high volume of sexual offences on railway property, particularly trains, in London was a factor that depressed detections there, while fewer visits made by detectives to scrap-metal dealers in the South-East Rail Region undoubtedly lowered railway metal theft detection rates.

Geographical variation in the solvability of offences also reflected environmental differences. The proportion of residential burglaries with at least one solvability factor varied by 50% across the police areas in the Thames Valley Police jurisdiction (Chapter "Population-Level Analysis of Residential Burglaries"), partly a reflection of environmental differences between these areas, which include varying proportions of villages, small towns and larger urban settlements. Similarly, a large volume of the UK's sexual offences on railway property, such as indecent exposure, non-penetrative touching and offending public decency were committed on London underground trains, which, unlike most other trains, stop very frequently, enabling offenders to flee the scene. Geographical variations in crimes mean that the crime type profiles vary from one jurisdiction to another so that different resources are needed to match the investigative demands of varying quantities of different types of solvable offences. This means that jurisdictions face different investigative challenges and, given solvability differences, detection rates are unlikely to be the same.

The alignment of resources with incident solvability across jurisdictions, therefore, would be improved if the funding of police services, the districts within them and detection targets were tailored to the quantities of different types of solvable crimes. Without this, investigation must be carried out with different funding per offence in different places. As it is, there is very unequal funding and marked contrasts in crime solvability and detection outcomes across jurisdictions, as in England and Wales. This is compounded by differences in the prioritisation of crime detection and in case-screening practices, circumstances unlikely to either equalise or optimise the match of resources to solvability or maximise cost-effective investigation or detection. It indicates a need for further research to understand and improve the soundness and cost-effectiveness of incident prioritisation decision in jurisdictions with different crime solvability profiles.

Investigative Capacity, Policing Demand and Changing Detection Levels

Detection rates in England and Wales have halved since 2013 from 19% to little more than 9% of all offences in 2017, in part reflecting a 16.6% fall in officer numbers between 2010 and 2018 (Ungoed-Thomas et al. 2018).[1] The measure of 'detected' used is an offender caught and punished, but even a measure based on arrest and charge places detection rates at no more than 14%. However, there were c. 22 officers per thousand crimes in 2017–18, and in 1993, forces with this level of officer resource per crime achieved primary detection rates of the order of 21% (Audit Commission 1993). Taken at face value, it might appear that performance and the effective utilisation of capacity were poorer in recent years. Part of the difference in detection outcomes between recent years and the 1990s might be attributable to managerialist targets in the 1990s fostering a culture reflecting Goodhart's Law: with detection measures used as targets, they ceased to be good measures (Strathern 1997). This could involve measurement issues attributable to attempting to meet detection targets by any means (Smith and Goddard 2002), including prioritising less serious but easily solved offences.

It appears more likely, however, that the changing profile of offending, particularly the striking escalation of low solvability cybercrimes of which few are ever detected, has contributed to lower detection rates. In part, this may also reflect the increased allocation of officer resources to non-crimes, often involving vulnerable persons, such as recovering missing persons, which can consume a fifth of patrol resources (Doyle 2018), and dealing with 'new' offences such as hate crimes has also switched effort away, not only from crimes like shoplifting, but also from high-volume property offences like burglary and vehicle theft, since the detection rates for these have halved, respectively, to 3% (6.3% in 2013) and 1.6% (4.4% in 2013) (Ungoed-Thomas et al. 2018). Detection rates for sexual and violent offences have also plummeted by a third to 8.3% in 2017 (Ungoed-Thomas et al. 2018) suggesting that recent drops in investigative funding as well as increasing incidence may both play a role, one not necessarily independent of the other. It is clear that some restoration of funding and elevating investigative capacity and using it in the ways suggested in this volume will be needed to reverse falling detection rates. It is important that all solvable offences within these crime groups are investigated and detected if deterrence is to be maintained and criminals rehabilitated and public confidence in police services sustained.

As well as contributing to more efficient investigation and detection, the scientific approach advocated here to help improve cost-effectiveness and the way capacity is used may also help limit the resources used to deal with non-crime events, which now consume so much police resource, some used formerly for dealing with crime. Algorithmic approaches to prediction can help, for instance, with the identification

[1]Using data from the data.police.uk database, for which data are sourced from a private server managed by the UK Home Office, to which police forces upload their monthly records which the MoJ verifies.

of the very few missing persons at risk of any harm. In practice, very few persons—about 0.5%—come to any harm while missing but these people can be predicted (Vo and Coupe 2017). These are not especially persons graded by the police as being at high risk of harm and there are no differences in harm suffered for those regarded as high risk, irrespective of whether the police recovered them or whether they returned of their own accord. Given risk management grounded in evidence, the use of this algorithm for dealing with missing persons, and developing equivalent predictors for other non-crime police tasks, promises to provide the means for releasing scarce resources for crime investigation, thereby improving the effective use of investigative capacity and furthering 'lean policing' objectives.

Crime Solvability and Detection Potential

The estimates of detection potential in this volume draw on data from investigative systems that rely on non-statistical screening, often with resources that are insufficient to match solvability needs, and where solvability indicators for targeting investigations and resources sometimes are used inconsistently. It appears likely, therefore, that the potential to solve cases will be far higher than the research presented here suggests. It is striking that, where resources are available to match the investigative needs of cases, detection rates can be exceptionally high, as is the case for homicides in England and Wales. Unusually high detection rates tend to also confirm this potential, such as with burglary detection rates of 23% for Bournemouth, UK (Johnson 2008).

It seems likely that the detection of many types of offences is limited by insufficient resources which prevent the 'unlocking' of evidence. Improved funding and the tailoring of the investigative effort to the specific activities in different stages that are most productive of more and stronger evidence items for different offences promise to raise detection rates and to do so cost-effectively. Equally, developments in electronic technologies, real-time algorithmic assessment and forensic analyses promise to raise potential solvability, the realisation of which, in the form of additional detections, will require matching investigative resources.

There is a dearth of knowledge on the links between resources on the one hand and solvability and detection on the other and the origins of solvability in environmental characteristics and offender populations. Although this volume provides insight into how 'in-progress' burglaries ought to be prioritised for rapid patrol response and which neighbours of commercial burglary victims should be questioned in order to collect suspect evidence, solvability indicators are needed for other investigative activities and for other crimes so that which investigative activities should be applied to which subsets of cases in different investigative stages may be better understood. By these means, our understanding of the process of unlocking and accumulating evidence items will be made more complete, enabling police forces to undertake these actions more efficiently.

Measuring estate, back-office labour, equipment and forensic collection and analysis costs may improve accuracy in so far as these differentially affect the investigation of different types of offences. Including them may, therefore, improve the ability to match resources to solvability so that more cases can be detected more cost-effectively and the way capacity is used improved.

Evidence presented in Chapter "Investigative Activities, Resources and Burglary Detection" is somewhat at odds with earlier solvability studies. Surprisingly, perhaps, not all low-solvability offences are unsolvable, while additional resources may, in fact, boost detection rates of highly solvable offences, which still benefit from higher resource inputs. Since many more solvable cases are not detected, and some medium- and even some low-solvability cases are, it is evident that the detection outcomes achieved in practice do not perfectly match the outcomes predicted by the analysis of solvability factors. They are also at odds with the potential for detection predicted by earlier studies of case solvability and triaging, which regarded fewer cases to be solvable (Eck 1983). This may partly reflect differences in investigative effort as well as, to some extent, improvements in case solvability.

Although statistical analysis of offence solvability provides an important guide to screening and investigative prioritisation, solvability needs to be better understood beyond indicating the most promising solvability factors for each crime. Identifying solvability indicators for targeting resources at different activities and cases in different investigative stages is crucial to solving more offences cost-effectively. This is particularly the case for undertaking the investigative activities that 'unlock' the two or three strongest evidence items that enable detection. Equally, collecting weaker items of evidence that improve detection odds can also consume disproportionate amounts of resource, unless investigative activities are directed at the appropriate subsets of solvable cases. Thus, identifying solvability indicators for targeting those investigative activities most likely to provide the evidence items most helpful in identifying perpetrators and resulting in arrest and charge will help cost-effectively boost detection levels.

Cost-effectiveness gains are likely to be greater for property offences, such as burglary, where solvability is poorer: with fewer offences easily solved and with screening decisions based on experience alone, there may be greater risks of allocating resources to investigating cases that are difficult, if not impossible, to solve, and neglecting to fully investigate some of the cases that can be solved. This may be illustrated by the greater gains in predictive accuracy from applying solvability factor algorithms to pickpocketing offences on railways with low detection rates than to non-domestic assaults with far higher ones. Even if informal and experiential crime-screening procedures dominate and there is uneven resourcing of police forces, it is evident that a better understanding of resources and incident solvability is indispensable to ensuring that resourcing of police forces matches their investigative needs and achieving more cost-effective crime investigation and higher detection rates.

Conclusion

Incident solvability frames detection potential that may be realised through well-allocated investigative funding. Resources need to be well matched with appropriate investigative activities that reflect case solvability, but, in general, are not. This is partly due to insufficient resources, but also reflects the investigation of some incidents with poor prospects of being solved, which, in the event, are not solved and missed opportunities to investigate some solvable offences. Poor matching of resources to incidents with varied solvability also reflects a dearth of studies that measure not only incident solvability, but more especially resources, with the consequence that it is difficult to establish cost-effectiveness of investigating different types of crimes. There is, in particular, insufficient knowledge for different crimes on the subsets of cases with different solvability characteristics for which various investigative activities should be undertaken in different investigative stages. Immediate response patrol studies and first officer questioning of neighbours at burglary scenes examined in this volume are exceptions. Research involving individual crime data is needed to fill these knowledge gaps, some of which require environmental or crime event data to inform solvability indicators.

Crime detection and arrest play an important part in enabling offender rehabilitation, help identify unknown offenders and combat serious crimes and high crime incidence through the incarceration of dangerous and prolific criminals. Arrest also enables the possibility of redress to victims, reducing fear and sustaining public confidence in police services and, hence, helping cement normative compliance with regard to offending behaviour.

While escalating cybercrimes involving fraud may be more effectively dealt with via preventive approaches, it nevertheless makes sense, if possible, to complement this with detections and arrests in order to provide the possibility of victim redress, offender rehabilitation and to stop serious offending involving large sums of money and smaller sums that have considerable impact on the well-being of the less well off. As with other crimes viewed as less serious, a proportion of cybercrimes where losses are counted in terms of a few hundred pounds ought to be investigated through to arrest since there may be offenders who may be deterred by timely and well-publicised detections that increase the perceived risks of arrest, even if research indicates that rational white-collar criminals, in general, are less deterred by these risks (Paternoster and Tibbetts 2016; Payne 2016). There is little, if any, evidence on the deterrent effects of arrest on the offending behaviour of cybercriminals, but current risks in the UK are exceptionally low, especially if operating from a different national jurisdiction and if small sums per victim are stolen.

Solvability factor analysis confirms that evidence and information from crime scenes remain the bedrock of investigative success. Effective patrol response, evidence from co-operative eyewitnesses able to provide high-quality suspect descriptions and suspect evidence and the speed and mode of reporting and to whom crimes are first reported to emerge as important factors in predicting detection outcomes of many, if not most, types of offences. Environmental factors and victim and event characteristics also account for important solvability factors, and this confirms their influence in shaping case solvability. Forensic evidence recovered from crime scenes, with the exception of most cybercrimes relating to fraud, also features as solvability factors.

There is potential to detect more crimes if incident solvability is itself improved through improvements to forensic techniques and by predicting repeat incidence and entrapping criminals, some of whom may be unknown to the police, while innovative approaches like offender–offence classifications, described in Chapter "Offender–Offence Profiling: Improving Burglary Solvability and Detection", promise to be of value in matching known offenders to unsolved offences, following further research and development. Equally, research into matching effort in terms of particular investigative activities to the appropriate subsets of solvable cases will require the identification of solvability 'indicators'. By using large individual incident populations of data from police services across different offence types, those incidents with evidence that can be 'unlocked' in various stages using different activities may be identified. This provides good prospects for improving cost-effectiveness, thereby maximising the successful detection outcomes from given resource inputs. A central message of this volume is to promote a scientific approach to solving crimes that complements and enhances decisions based on experience. Through more accurate prediction of solvability at each investigative stage, investigative capacity can be better utilised and further progress towards 'lean policing' achieved.

References

Ashby, M. P. J. (2017). Comparing methods for measuring crime harm severity. *Policing: A Journal of Policy and Practice, 12*(4), 439–454.

Audit Commission. (1993). *Helping with enquiries: Tackling crime effectively*. London: HMSO.

Barnard, P. (2015). *Online vehicle sales fraud: Can police target prevention messages more efficiently and effectively*? (M.St. thesis). University of Cambridge.

Blakely, R. (2018, January 08). US murder rate plunges after police algorithm predicts crime. *The Times*.

Blumstein, A., Cohen, D., Das, S., & Miotra, D. (1988). Specialization and seriousness during adult criminal careers. *Journal of Quantitative Criminology, 4*(4), 303–345.

Coupe, T. (2017). Burglary decisions (Chapter 31). In W. Bernasco, H. Ellfers, & J.-L. van Gelder (Eds.), *Oxford handbook on offender decision making* (pp. 655–683). Oxford: OUP.

Coupe, R. T. (2016). Evaluating the effects of resources and solvability on burglary detection. *Policing & Society: An International Journal of Research and Policy, 26*(5), 563–587.

Coupe, T., & Fox, B. H. (2015). A risky business: How do access, exposure and guardians affect the chances of non-residential burglars being seen? *Security Journal, 28*(1), 71–92.

Doyle, R. (2018). Personal communication regarding use of patrol resources in Devon and Cornwall Police Service, U.K.

Eck, J. E. (1983). *Solving crimes: The investigation of burglary and robbery*. Washington, D.C: Police Executive Research Forum.

Hamilton, F. (2018). Shoplifters can get away with taking less than £50. *The Times*, 29/11/18.

Von Hirsch, A., Bottoms, A. E., Burney, E., & Wikstrom, P. O. (1999). *Criminal deterrence and sentence severity: An analysis of recent research*. Oxford: Hart Publishing.

Jackman, R. (2016). *Profiling sex offending in Norfolk* (M.St. thesis). University of Cambridge.

Jacoby, J. E., & Cullen, F. T. (1999). The structure of punishment norms: Applying the Rossi-Berk model. *Journal of Criminal Law and Criminology, 89*(1), 245–312.

Johnson, D. (2008). The near-repeat burglary phenomenon. In S. Chainey & J. Radcliffe (Eds.), *Crime mapping cases studies: Practice and research*. Chichester: Wiley.

Paternoster, R., & Tibbetts, S. G. (2016). White-collar crime and perceptual deterrence. In S. R. Van Slyke, M. L. Benson, & F. Cullen (Eds.), *The Oxford handbook of white-collar crime*. Oxford: OUP.

Payne, B. K. (2016). Effects on white-collar defendants of criminal justice attention and sanctions. In S. R. Van Slyke, M. L. Benson, & F. Cullen (Eds.), *The Oxford handbook of white-collar crime*. Oxford: OUP.

Rowley, C. (2013). *A level 2 outcome evaluation of a police intervention aimed at reducing future burglary dwellings in the immediate vicinity of a burglary dwelling* (Unpublished M.St. thesis). University of Cambridge, Institute of Criminology.

Smith, P., & Goddard, M. (2002). Performance management and operational research: A marriage made in heaven? *Journal of the Operational Research Society, 53*(3), 247–255.

Strathern, M. (1997). Improving ratings: Audit of the British university system. *European Review, 5*, 305–321.

Tompson, L., & Coupe, R. T. (2018). Time and criminal opportunity (Chapter 29). In W. Bernasco & S. Johnson (Eds.), *Oxford handbook of environmental criminology*. Oxford: OUP.

Ungoed-Thomas, J., Clark, R., & Henry, R. (2018, June 17). Where's the justice? Struggling police solve only 9% of all crime. *The Sunday Times*, p. 4.

Vo, Q., & Coupe, R. T. (2017). Tracking the outcomes of 6,000 missing persons. In *National Missing Persons Conference*, Sydney, Australia, November, 2017.

Weems, J. (2014). *Testing PCSO cocooning of near repeat burglary locations* (Unpublished M.St. thesis). University of Cambridge, Institute of Criminology.

Wright, O. (2013). *Urban to rural: An exploratory analysis of burglary and vehicle crime within a rural context* (M.St. thesis). Cambridge University.

Index

R. T. Coupe et al. (eds.), *Crime Solvability Factors*,
https://doi.org/10.1007/978-3-030-17160-5